Handbook of Research on Intelligent Techniques and Modeling Applications in Marketing Analytics

Anil Kumar
BML Munjal University, India

Manoj Kumar Dash
ABV-Indian Institute of Information Technology and Management, India

Shrawan Kumar Trivedi
BML Munjal University, India

Tapan Kumar Panda
BML Munjal University, India

A volume in the Advances in Business Information Systems and Analytics (ABISA) Book Series

IGI GLOBAL
DISSEMINATOR OF KNOWLEDGE

www.igi-global.com

Published in the United States of America by
IGI Global
Business Science Reference (an imprint of IGI Global)
701 E. Chocolate Avenue
Hershey PA, USA 17033
Tel: 717-533-8845
Fax: 717-533-8661
E-mail: cust@igi-global.com
Web site: http://www.igi-global.com

Library of Congress Cataloging-in-Publication Data

Names: Kumar, Anil, 1980- editor. | Dash, Manoj Kumar, editor. | Trivedi, Shrawan Kumar, 1985- editor.
Title: Handbook of research on intelligent techniques and modeling applications in marketing analytics / Anil Kumar, Manoj Kumar Dash, Shrawan Kumar Trivedi, and Tapan Kumar Panda, editors.
Description: Hershey : Business Science Reference, [2017] | Series: Advances in business information systems and analytics | Includes bibliographical references and index.
Identifiers: LCCN 2016028045| ISBN 9781522509974 (hardcover) | ISBN 9781522509981 (ebook)
Subjects: LCSH: Marketing research. | Marketing research--Data processing.
Classification: LCC HF5415.2 .H2886 2017 | DDC 658.8/3--dc23 LC record available at https://lccn.loc.gov/2016028045

This book is published in the IGI Global book series Advances in Business Information Systems and Analytics (ABISA) (ISSN: 2327-3275; eISSN: 2327-3283)

British Cataloguing in Publication Data
A Cataloguing in Publication record for this book is available from the British Library.

Advances in Business Information Systems and Analytics (ABISA) Book Series

Madjid Tavana
La Salle University, USA

ISSN:2327-3275
EISSN:2327-3283

Mission

The successful development and management of information systems and business analytics is crucial to the success of an organization. New technological developments and methods for data analysis have allowed organizations to not only improve their processes and allow for greater productivity, but have also provided businesses with a venue through which to cut costs, plan for the future, and maintain competitive advantage in the information age.

The **Advances in Business Information Systems and Analytics (ABISA)** Book Series aims to present diverse and timely research in the development, deployment, and management of business information systems and business analytics for continued organizational development and improved business value.

Coverage

- Business Models
- Business Decision Making
- Data Governance
- Decision Support Systems
- Business Process Management
- Legal information systems
- Business Intelligence
- Information Logistics
- Forecasting
- Business Information Security

IGI Global is currently accepting manuscripts for publication within this series. To submit a proposal for a volume in this series, please contact our Acquisition Editors at Acquisitions@igi-global.com or visit: http://www.igi-global.com/publish/.

The Advances in Business Information Systems and Analytics (ABISA) Book Series (ISSN 2327-3275) is published by IGI Global, 701 E. Chocolate Avenue, Hershey, PA 17033-1240, USA, www.igi-global.com. This series is composed of titles available for purchase individually; each title is edited to be contextually exclusive from any other title within the series. For pricing and ordering information please visit http://www.igi-global.com/book-series/advances-business-information-systems-analytics/37155. Postmaster: Send all address changes to above address.

Editorial Advisory Board

List of Contributors

Table of Contents

Detailed Table of Contents

The aim of this chapter is proposing a novel integrated Fuzzy Group Multiple Attribute Decision Making (FGMADM) and Fuzzy C-Means Clustering (FCM) as a DM tool for segmentation of customers (retailers), based on an updated RFM model. For this purpose, the most important criteria to evaluate retailers from the in depth literature survey and experts' opinion are added to the traditional RFM model. In addition, in order to make the model more efficient, FGMADM approach, in this paper, Fuzzy Group Step-wise Weight Assessment Ratio Analysis (FGSWARA) is used to weight KPIs. Then, FCM is applied to segment customers, based on their purchase behavior (RFM scores). A case study in one of the most famous Fast Moving Consumer Goods (FMCG) companies in Iran illustrated the applicability of the proposed model.

Customer segmentation has been one of hottest topics of marketing efforts. The traditional sources of data used for segmentation are demographics, monetary value of transactions, types of product/service selected. Today, data gathered by location based services can also be used for customer segmentation. In this chapter a real world case study is summarized and the initial segmentation results are presented. As the application, data gathered from beacons sited in 4000 locations and Fuzzy c-means clustering algorithm are used. The steps of the application are as follows: (1) Categorization of the shops, (2) Summarization of the location data, (3) Applying fuzzy clustering technique, (4) Analyzing the results and profiling. Results show that customers' location data can provide a new perspective to customer segmentation.

classification and bank datasets using 10 fold cross validation. The results, in terms of Mean Absolute Percentage Error (MAPE,) are compared with that of K-Means+Multilayer perceptron (MLP) imputation, K-Medoids+MLP, K-Means+GRNN, K-Medoids+GRNN, PSO_Covariance imputation, and ECM-Imputation. It is concluded that the proposed methods achieved better imputation in most of the datasets as evidenced by the Wilcoxon signed rank test.

Most of the marketing problems are complex and unstructured due to the business dynamics and considerable uncertainty involved in the operating environments. Hence decision making in marketing involves evaluation of several parameters and thus multi criteria decision makings are a good choice in most of the decision-making tasks like supplier selection; market places selection; target marketing; etc. This chapter begins with a brief introduction of the theory of rough set which is an intelligent technique for handling uncertainty aspect in the data. However, the notions of fuzzy rough set and intuitionistic fuzzy rough (IFR) sets are defined, and its properties are studied. Thereafter rough set on two universal sets has been studied. In addition, intuitionistic fuzzy rough set on two universal sets has been extensively studied. Furthermore, this chapter shows that intuitionistic fuzzy rough set can be successfully practiced in decision making problems.

In this chapter, we model association rule mining as a Fuzzy multi-objective global optimization problem by considering several measures of strength such as support, confidence, coverage, comprehensibility, leverage, interestingness, lift and conviction by utilizing various fuzzy aggregator operators. In this, pdel, each measure has its own level of significance. Three fuzzy multi-objective association rule mining techniques viz., Fuzzy Multi-objective Binary Particle Swarm Optimization based association rule miner (FMO-BPSO), a hybridized Fuzzy Multi-objective Binary Firefly Optimization and Threshold Accepting based association rule miner (FMO-BFFOTA), hybridized Fuzzy Multi-objective Binary Particle Swarm Optimization and Threshold Accepting based association rule miner (FMO-BPSOTA) have been proposed. These three algorithms have been tested on various datasets such as book, food, bank, grocery, click stream and bakery datasets along with three fuzzy aggregate operators. From these experiments, we can conclude that Fuzzy-And outperforms all the other operators.

Bollywood is not only one of the biggest film producers in India but also one of the largest centers of film production in the world. Seat occupancy rate and pricing of each seat are important parameters that determines the revenue of a cinema business. The objective of the chapter is to enable theater managers to determine the prices at the time of booking according to the occupancy rate so that the revenue is improved based on preferred demand for the respective seats. A multi criteria analysis is applied with seat occupancy rate as dependent variable and other factors as independent variables like Show time, Poster Size, Day of week and Timing of Release. Further, a predictive analysis can be carried out to determine the occupancy rate for the upcoming movies. Based on the occupancy rate, the managers at theater can adopt variable pricing concept to improve the revenue. This work shows an integrated method to develop a seating plan based on occupancy rate to improve the revenue using EMSR-b heuristic with an illustrated example for a theater.

Section 3
Consumer Analytics: Multi-Criteria (MCDM) Applications and Sentiment Analysis

Introducing a new product to the market is a complex, costly and time-consuming process which requires research on consumer preferences. On the basis of information on the characteristics of the new product and its competitors, as well as on the competitors and their market shares, the company has to estimate future market shares and to determine the profile of potential consumers inclined to purchase the new product. The purpose of our paper is to present a method of consumer preference research when introducing a new product, using a multiple criteria method called Stochastic Multicriteria Acceptability Analysis (SMAA). To apply this method, no information requiring tedious research is needed. SMAA allows to obtain essential information on the potential market power of the new product already at an early stage of its preparation. Furthermore, the flexibility of the SMAA method allows to easily expand the scope of the analysis by including additional information and various techniques of the modeling of the consumer selection process.

In order to understand consumers, researchers are forced to gather primary data on Likert scale. Such data is usually considered as ordinal or at best interval scaled data. One key requirement in research is to identify components which have high individual contribution to understanding the research problem. Hence the concept of ranking of the components comes under consideration. Most of the ranking techniques are based on simplistic mean ranks or overtly complicated methods. In this chapter the authors highlight two techniques - Grey Relational Analysis (GRA) and RIDIT - for the purpose. In this chapter the authors explain the techniques of the two methods and then try to show the simplicity and efficiency of GRA and RIDIT algorithms in analyzing a commonly available dataset. The outcome of the GRA and RIDIT analysis is also compared with the commonly used techniques and the authors would examine if GRA and RIDIT does a better job at ranking data than the commonly used techniques.

landscape of competition among SMEs in a global market economy prompts the necessity of adopting online marketing. With these, the decision-making process of SMEs in this area becomes complex and the decisions must integrate complex and interrelating criteria and constructs in order to provide a more holistic solution. Thus, this work adopts a multi-criteria decision-making (MCDM) method particularly the analytic network process (ANP) in order to evaluate the practicability of using online marketing for service SMEs. It becomes highly relevant as it provides significant insights to decision-makers in SMEs regarding the use of online marketing strategy. The contribution of this chapter lies in the application of MCDM in evaluating viability of online marketing in service SMEs.

In this chapter, first, the definition, the advantages and disadvantages of e-retailing are given and the related literature about e-retailing is briefly explained in order to give a background to unfamiliar readers. Then, the qualitative and quantitative criteria which affect the e-retailer selection are determined and some e-retailers are evaluated by using a multi-phase, integrated Multi Criteria Decision Making (MCDM) approach. In first phase of proposed MCDM approach, the weight of each criterion is determined. In second phase, a pre-evaluation is made and some of the e-retailers are eliminated. In last phase, the remaining retailers are evaluated and the best one is determined. Finally, the study is concluded by discussions, inferences and recommendations for future work.

In this chapter, we are planning to make a comparison between conventional Time Series Models and Fuzzy Time Series Models by an application in an e-commerce company. Future sales of furniture will be predicted. The performance of different models and forecasting periods are going to be analyzed to discuss advantages and disadvantages of each method. MAE is chosen as performance indicators of each model and forecasting period combination. As a conclusion to this chapter, generic strategies for prediction in an e-commerce company will be formulated in consideration of these indicators.

Smartphone users download the apps after the enormous popularity in this mobile world and then eventually delete those apps. There are various factors like frequency, relevance and space it consumes in the phone, which decide a user's preference for an app. All the app provider companies are trying hard

Derivatives play an important role in social and economic studies. They describe the behavior of conditional expectations. Once a phenomena is characterized by parametric specifications, the conditional expectation m(x) may be modeled by a regression function. Then, derivatives may be computed by fitting the regression function. In applications, parametric estimators are commonly used, because of the unknowledge of other more effective methods. The validity of a regression fitting approach depends on the knowledge of certain aspects related with the true functional form. In this paper, we develop a study on the usage of soft computing methods for providing an alternative to the use of non-parametric regression. We develop our modeling including neural networks and rough sets approaches. The studied problem is the eutrophication due to the growth of the population of algae. Real life data is provided by a study on a fresh water basin. They are used for developing a comparison of different approaches. A methodology is recommended for implementing a monitoring system of the water quality.

This is an introductory work to the field of automatizing futures markets, related to commodities, so far operated by human traders. First, we build a mathematical framework for a futures market with many producers and consumers represented by automated traders in the market platform. Then we suggest an automatic trading strategy for the automatons. This strategy takes into account the forecasts of supply and demand streams as well as the evolution of nominal price. Later, we recall a set of analytical criteria used to measure the performance of a trading strategy. Next, we illustrate our approach by showing a price pattern generated by the automatic strategy and calculate its performances. Finally, we exhibit a heuristic based on simulation allowing to compute a quasi-optimal parameters matrix for this automatic trading system.

Preface

The complete work of this book is divided into five sections. In the first section titled "Consumer Analytics: Fuzzy Applications" which includes all the chapters related to consumer analytics with fuzzy applications. In the second section titled "Computational Intelligence: Business Analytics" contains all the chapters related to computational intelligent techniques and their applications in business analytics. In the third section titled "Consumer Analytics: Multi-Criteria (MCDM) Applications and Sentiment Analysis" contains all the chapters related to applications of multi-criteria decision making and sentiment analysis for consumer analytics. All chapters related to applications of marketing analytics in digital marketplace are in the fourth section titled "Marketing Analytics: Digital Market Place". In the last section includes some authors' chapters whose applied advanced modelling application in business analytics and titled "Advanced Modelling Applications: Business Analytics". The brief description of each section as follows:

Consumer analytics using fuzzy applications, to facilitate this objective of the book, in Chapter 1, Mohammad Hasan Aghdaie and Parham Fami Tafreshi explain that nowadays, marketing becomes overly customer-oriented as customers are playing more and more critical role in strategic decisions of all companies. Furthermore, with the fast changing environment and fierce market competition, every organization needs to create a strong relationship with its own customers. As the customers are not equal and there are not unlimited resources to satisfy them, customer lifetime value (CLV) becomes a debatable topic for a host of companies. They propose a new RFM based model to CLV analysis, using fuzzy group step-wise weight assessment ratio analysis (FGSWARA) as a fuzzy group multiple attribute decision making (FGMADM), and fuzzy c-means clustering, as a data mining (DM) tool, to evaluate and segment customers. A case study in one of the most famous fast moving consumer goods (FMCG) companies in Iran is illustrated to show the applicability of the model.

To contribute the same section objective, in Chapter 2, Başar Öztayşi, Ugur Gokdere, Esra Nur Simsek, and Ceren Salkin Oner discuss customer segmentation and say that the traditional sources of data used for segmentation are demographics, the monetary value of transactions, types of product/service selected. Today, data gathered by location-based services can also be used for customer segmentation. In this chapter with the help of a real-world case study, they summarized that customers' location data can provide a new perspective to customer segmentation.

In Chapter 3, Mashhour Baeshen, Malcolm J. Beynon, and Kate L. Daunt explain the importance of fuzzy clustering in mobile phone industry related to their service quality. They present a study of the development of the clustering methodology to data analysis, with particular attention to the analysis of a crisp environment to a fuzzy environment. An applied problem concerning service quality (using SERVQUAL) of mobile phone users, and subsequent loyalty and satisfaction forms the data set to demonstrate the clustering issue. Following details on both the crisp k-means and fuzzy c-means clustering techniques, comparable results from their analysis are shown, on a subset of data, to enable both graphical and statistical elucidation. Fuzzy c-means is then employed on the full SERVQUAL dimensions, and the established results interpreted before tested on external variables, namely the level of loyalty and satisfaction across the different clusters established.

In Chapter 4, Gaurav Kabra and A Ramesh, analyze of the interactions among the enablers of information communication technology in humanitarian supply chain management using fuzzy based relationship modelling approach. They say that the rise in the occurrence of disasters has hampered the development of many countries. Practitioners and academicians are making continuous demands to enhance the utilization of information communication technologies (ICTs) in humanitarian supply chain management (HSCM) in order to continue or enhance the pace of economic growth and development of countries, as well as to reduce the impact of disaster on society. Identifying and analysing key decision variables improving the utilization of ICT in HSCM is essential in trying to improve overall performance. Therefore, to assist the organizations involved in HSCM, their study explores eleven enablers to enhancing the utilization of ICTs, with a focus on the mutual relationship among them using an integrated interpretive structural modeling (ISM) and fuzzy cross-impact matrix multiplication applied to classification (F-MICMAC) analysis. This study seeks to advance the understanding on enablers of ICTs in HSCM and to classify them, on the basis of driving and dependence power.

Section 2 contains all the chapters related to applications of computational intelligent in business analytics and entitled "*Computational Intelligent: Business Analytics*". To follow this, in Chapter 5, Chandan Gautam and Vadlamani Ravi examine auto associative extreme learning machine based hybrids for data imputation. They presents three novel hybrid techniques for data imputation viz., (1) Auto-associative Extreme Learning Machine (AAELM) with Principal Component Analysis (PCA) (PCA-AAELM), (2) Gray system theory (GST) + AAELM with PCA (Gray+PCA-AAELM), (3) AAELM with Evolving Clustering Method (ECM) (ECM-AAELM). Our prime concern is to remove the randomness in AAELM caused by the random weights with the help of ECM and PCA. This chapter also proposes local learning by invoking ECM as a pre-processor for AAELM. The proposed methods are tested on several regression, classification and bank datasets using 10 fold cross validation. The results, in terms of Mean Absolute Percentage Error (MAPE,) are compared with that of K-Means+Multilayer perceptron (MLP) imputation, K-Medoids+MLP, K-Means+GRNN, K-Medoids+GRNN, PSO-Covariance imputation, and ECM-Imputation. It is concluded that the proposed methods achieved better imputation in most of the datasets as evidenced by the Wilcoxon signed rank test.

To follow the same objective, in Chapter 6, Tapan Kumar Das says that most of the marketing problems are complex and unstructured due to the business dynamics and considerable uncertainty involved in the operating environments. Hence, decision making in marketing involves evaluation of several parameters and thus multi-criteria decision makings are a good choice in most of the decision-making tasks like supplier selection; market-places selection; target marketing etc... In his chapter, he begins with a brief introduction of the theory of rough set which is an intelligent technique for handling uncertainty aspect in the data. However, the notions of fuzzy rough set and intuitionistic fuzzy rough (IFR) sets are defined, and its properties are studied. Thereafter rough set on two universal sets has been studied. In addition, intuitionistic fuzzy rough set on two universal sets has been extensively studied. Furthermore, this chapter shows that intuitionistic fuzzy rough set can be successfully practiced in decision-making problems.

Contribute to the same section objective, in Chapter 7, Ganghishetti Pradeep and Vadlamani Ravi use evolutionary computation for fuzzy multi-objective association rule mining using and model association rule mining as a Fuzzy multi-objective global optimization problem by considering several measures of strength such as support, confidence, coverage, comprehensibility, leverage, interestingness, lift and conviction by utilizing various fuzzy aggregator operators. In this model, each measure has its own level of significance. Three fuzzy multi-objective association rule mining techniques viz., Fuzzy Multi-objective Binary Particle Swarm Optimization based association rule miner (FMO-BPSO), a hybridized Fuzzy Multi-objective Binary Firefly Optimization and Threshold Accepting based association rule miner (FMO-BFFOTA), hybridized Fuzzy Multi-objective Binary Particle Swarm Optimization and Threshold Accepting based association rule miner (FMO-BPSOTA) have been proposed. These three algorithms have been tested on various datasets such as book, food, bank, grocery, click stream and bakery datasets along with three fuzzy aggregate operators. From these experiments, we can conclude that Fuzzy-And outperforms all the other operators.

In Chapter 8, Kedar Pandurang Joshi and Nikhil Lohiya discuss about improved seating plans for movie theatre to improve revenue and used an integrated best worst method with EMSR-B. They say that Bollywood is not only one of the biggest film producers in India but also one of the largest centers of film production in the world. Seat occupancy rate and pricing of each seat are important parameters that determines the revenue of a cinema business. The objective of the chapter is to enable theater managers to determine the prices at the time of booking according to the occupancy rate so that the revenue is improved based on preferred demand for the respective seats. A multi criteria analysis is applied with seat occupancy rate as dependent variable and other factors as independent variables like Show time, Poster Size, Day of week and Timing of Release. Further, a predictive analysis can be carried out to determine the occupancy rate for the upcoming movies. Based on the occupancy rate, the managers at theatre can adopt variable pricing concept to improve the revenue. This work shows an integrated method to develop a seating plan based on occupancy rate to improve the revenue using EMSR-b heuristic with an illustrated example for a theatre.

Section 3 entitled "Consumer Analytics: Multi-Criteria (MCDM) Applications and Sentiment Analysis" contains all the chapters related to applications of multi-criteria decision making and sentiment analysis for consumer analytics. To support this in Chapter 9, Tadeusz Trzaskalik, Piotr Namieciński, Andrzej Bajdak, and Slawomir Jarek contribute to section objective about applications of the stochastic multi-criteria acceptability analysis method for consumer preference study. They explain that introducing a new product to the market is a complex, costly and time-consuming process which requires research on consumer preferences. On the basis of information on the characteristics of the new product and its competitors, as well as on the competitors and their market shares, the company has to estimate future market shares and to determine the profile of potential consumers inclined to purchase the new product. The purpose of their stydy is to present a method of consumer preference research when introducing a new product, using a multiple criteria method called Stochastic Multi-criteria Acceptability Analysis (SMAA). To apply this method, no information requiring tedious research is needed. SMAA allows to obtain essential information on the potential market power of the new product already at an early stage of its preparation. Furthermore, the flexibility of the SMAA method allows to easily expand the scope of the analysis by including additional information and various techniques of the modeling of the consumer selection process.

Contribute to the same section objective, in Chapter 10, Rohit Vishal Kumar discuss about modeling consumer opinion using ridit and grey relational analysis. They explain that in order to understand consumers, researchers are forced to gather primary data on Likert scale. Such data is usually considered as ordinal or at best interval scaled data. One key requirement in research is to identify components which have high individual contribution to understanding the research problem. Hence the concept of ranking of the components comes under consideration. Most of the ranking techniques are based on simplistic mean ranks or overtly complicated methods. In this chapter the authors highlight two techniques - Grey Relational Analysis (GRA) and RIDIT - for the purpose. In this chapter the authors explain the techniques of the two methods and then try to show the simplicity and efficiency of GRA and RIDIT algorithms in analyzing a commonly available dataset. The outcome of the GRA and RIDIT analysis is also compared with the commonly used techniques and the authors would examine if GRA and RIDIT does a better job at ranking data than the commonly used techniques.

Chapter 11 and 12, contribute to sentiment analysis part of the section, in Chapter 11, Nicola Capolupo, Gianpaolo Basile, and Giancarlo Scozzese examine that sentiment analysis as a tool to understand the cultural relationship between consumer and brand and said that One of the most relevant issues that companies, offices and marketing experts, sociologists and scholars must address studying a new brand or product launch is without any doubt the impact - in terms of feedback - on the consumer sentiment. The study of users opinion on a specific product or brand has changed with the advent of Web 2.0, which has overcome the old surveys model leading consumers in a too complex and not genuine area, reaching more sophisticated research or even better tracking their opinions directly “on the field”, i.e. in the community where this exchange of views and information happens naturally and not artificially. The analysis of consumers’ opinion on social media provides enormous opportunities for the public and the private spheres. Concerning the last on the reputation of a certain product/brand or firm is strongly influenced by the voices and negative opinions published and shared by users on social networks. Indeed, companies need to adapt their behaviour monitoring public opinion.

In Chapter 12, Vinay Kumar Jain and Shishir Kumar contribute about improving customer experience using sentiment analysis in e-commerce and said that in today’s world, millions of online users post their opinions on product features, services, quality, benefits and other values of the products. These opinions or sentiment data generated via different communication mediums often include vital data points that can be fruitful for businesses in understanding customer experiences, products quality and services. The E-commerce companies considered social media platform for new product launch, promotion of products and features or establishing a successful business to customer relationship which produces great results. Analytics on this Social media data helps in identifying the customers in the right demographic, psychographic and lifestyle group. This chapter identifying important characteristics of customer reviews which help businesses houses to improve their marketing strategies.

Section 4 contains all chapters related to application of marketing analytics techniques in digital platform entitled “Marketing Analytics: Digital Market Place”. The first chapter includes in section is “adoption of online marketing for service SMEs with multi-criteria decision-making approach” and position as Chapter 13. In this chapter, Lanndon Ocampo, Rosalin Merry Berdin Alarde, Dennis Anthony Kilongkilong, and Antonio Esmero attempts to fill in the gap of evaluating the viability of adopting online marketing for small and medium enterprises (SMEs) in service industries. As SMEs are generally characterized by shortage of resources, the use of online marketing strategies is apparently difficult. However, the current landscape of competition among SMEs in a global market economy prompts the necessity of adopting online marketing. With these, the decision-making process of SMEs in this area becomes complex and the decisions must integrate complex and interrelating criteria and constructs in order to provide a more holistic solution. Thus, this work adopts a multi-criteria decision-making (MCDM) method particularly the analytic network process (ANP) in order to evaluate the practicability of using online marketing for service SMEs. It becomes highly relevant as it provides significant insights to decision-makers in SMEs regarding the use of online marketing strategy. The contribution of this chapter lies in the application of MCDM in evaluating viability of online marketing in service SMEs.

In Chapter 14, Zehra Kamisli Ozturk and Mehmet Alegoz explain concept of E-retailing from past to future definitions, analysis, problems and perspectives. Firstly, they provide some definitions and the advantages and disadvantages of e-retailing are given and the related literature about e-retailing is briefly explained in order to give a background to unfamiliar readers. Then, the qualitative and quantitative criteria which affect the e-retailer selection are determined and some e-retailers are evaluated by using a multi-phase, integrated Multi Criteria Decision Making (MCDM) approach. In first phase of proposed MCDM approach the weight of each criterion is determined. In second phase, a pre-evaluation is made and some of the e-retailers are eliminated. In last phase, the remaining retailers are evaluated and the best one is determined. Finally, the study is concluded by discussions, inferences and recommendations for future work.

To contribute the same section objective, in Chapter 15, Ali Karasan, İsmail Sevim, and Melih ÇINAR discuss about fuzzy time series-an application in e-commerce and firstly they do comparison between conventional Time Series Models and Fuzzy Time Series Models by an application in an e-commerce company. Future sales of furniture will be predicted. The performance of different models and forecasting periods are going to be analyzed to discuss advantages and disadvantages of each method. MAE is chosen as performance indicators of each model and forecasting period combination. As a conclusion to this chapter, generic strategies for prediction in an e-commerce company will be formulated in consideration of these indicators.

In Chapter 16, Geetika Jain and Sapna Rakesh contribute about understand the frequency of application usage by smartphone users -Door is open, but closes quickly. The authors say that smartphone users download the apps after the enormous popularity in this mobile world and then eventually delete those apps. There are various factors like frequency, relevance and space it consumes in the phone, which decide a user's preference for an app. All the app provider companies are trying hard to fit into right place, so that they can increase the engagement with the users. Companies are upgrading their technology to make an app convenient and relevant based on user's requirement. This study is trying to understand the frequency of application usage and the importance of various factors like time to complete transaction, relevance, space it consumes, features, User Index, and ease of use for a user which leads to purchase intention. The study has found that UX/UI is the most important factor followed by other factors. The output of the study has the practical implication for online retailer.

Section 5 includes some authors' chapters those applied Advance modeling applications in business analytics and entitled "Advanced Modelling Applications: Business Analytics" In Chapter 17, António Carrizo Moreira, Monica Gouveia, and Pedro Macedo discuss about Car Safety: A Statistical Analysis for Marketing Management. They said that Car safety is an essential feature of marketing strategies for automobile companies. In this work, a statistical analysis on crash tests is conducted based on data available from European New Car Assessment Programme (Euro NCAP). The Euro NCAP carries safety tests to automobiles in order to support those who want to buy a car and encourage manufacturers to invest in safety and equipment that reduce the likelihood of driver error, so that damage caused by a road accident can be avoided -or at least reduced. The research work developed in this chapter presents a statistical analysis of the information produced by Euro NCAP, using the SPSS and MATLAB software, and seeks to answer the following research questions: 1) are there statistically significant differences on adult occupant safety in the six years under study?, 2) are there statistically significant differences among the best-selling car classes regarding safety in frontal collisions?, 3) are electric and hybrid automobiles less secure than their traditional counterparts with respect to frontal collisions?. It is worth to mention that due to the increasing number of hybrid and electric vehicles on the roads and its expected growth in the next years, given the economic and environmental aspects of its use, the study on the safety of these vehicles is an important tool for marketers. In order to answer to these questions data were collected resulting from safety tests for the years 2010, 2011, 2012, 2013, 2014, and 2015 from the Euro NCAP site (www.euroncap.com). The sample consists of 236 vehicles from several brands, types of fuel and classes such as small family cars, small MPVs, small off-road 4x4, and hybrid and electric vehicles, among others. For each question, beyond the methodological details-such as, descriptive statistics, t-tests, analysis of variance, normality tests, among others-, a thorough discussion of the results is carried out.

In Chapter 18, Saroj Kant Jena, Anil Kumar, and Maheshwar Dwivedy talk about banking credit scoring assessment using predictive k-nearest neighbour (PKNN) classifier and said that Credit scoring models is a scientific methodology adopted by credit providers to assess the credit worthiness of applicants. The primary objective of such models has been to predict the potentiality of the loan applicant. A proper evaluation of the credit can help the service provider to determine whether to grant or to reject credit. Therefore, the objective of the study is to predict banking credit scoring assessment using Predictive K-Nearest Neighbour (PKNN) classifier. For the purpose of analysis two different credit approval datasets: Australian credit and German credit have been used. The results from the study show that the proposed model used for classification works better on credit dataset. Here, the study firstly attempted to find the optimal 'K' value of the neighbourhood so that the classifier is tuned to forecast the credit worthiness and secondly, validated our proposed model on two credit approval datasets by checking the performance of the proposed models on the basis of classification accuracy.

In Chapter 19, Carlos N. Bouza-Herrera, Sira M. Allende Alonso, Daniel C. Chen, Agustin Santiago-Moreno, and Jose M. Sautto-Vallejo contribute about prediction of the quality of fresh water in a basin. Derivatives play an important role in social and economic studies. They describe the behavior of conditional expectations. Once a phenomena is characterized by parametric specifications, the conditional expectation may be modeled by a regression function. Then, derivatives may be computed by fitting the regression function. In applications, parametric estimators are commonly used, because of the unknowledge of other more effective methods. The validity of a regression fitting approach depends on the knowledge of certain aspects related with the true functional form. In this paper, we develop a study on the usage of soft computing methods for providing an alternative to the use of non-parametric regression. We develop our modeling including neural networks and rough sets approaches. The studied problem is the eutrophication due to the growth of the population of algae. Real life data is provided by a study on a fresh water basin. They are used for developing a comparison of different approaches. A methodology is recommended for implementing a monitoring system of the water quality.

Chapter 20 is all about operating commodities market by automated traders, in this chapter, Fodil Laib, Mohammed Said Radjef, build a mathematical framework for a futures market with many producers and consumers represented by automated traders in the market platform. Then we suggest an automatic trading strategy for the automatons. This strategy takes into account the forecasts of supply and demand streams as well as the evolution of nominal price. Later, we recall a set of analytical criteria used to measure the performance of a trading strategy. Next, we illustrate our approach by showing a price pattern generated by the automatic strategy and calculate its performances. Finally, we exhibit a heuristic based on simulation allowing to compute a quasi-optimal parameters matrix for this automatic trading system.

Acknowledgment

The editors would like to acknowledge the help of all the people involved in this project and, more specifically, to the authors and reviewers that took part in the review process. Without their support, this book would not have become a reality.

We would like to thank each one of the authors for their contributions. The editors wish to acknowledge the valuable contributions of the reviewers regarding the improvement of quality, coherence, and content presentation of chapters. Most of the authors also served as referees; we highly appreciate their double task.

We are grateful to all members of IGI publishing house for their assistance and timely motivation in producing this volume.

We hope the readers will share our excitement with this important scientific contribution the body of knowledge about various applications of Intelligent Techniques and Modeling in Marketing Analytics.

Anil Kumar
BML Munjal University, India

Manoj Kumar Dash
ABV-Indian Institute of Information Technology and Management, India

Shrawan Kumar Trivedi
BML Munjal University, India

Tapan Kumar Panda
BML Munjal University, India

Section 1

Consumer Analytics:
Fuzzy Applications

Chapter 1
A New Perspective on RFM Analysis

Mohammad Hasan Aghdaie
Shomal University, Iran

Parham Fami Tafreshi
Shomal University, Iran

ABSTRACT

The aim of this chapter is proposing a novel integrated Fuzzy Group Multiple Attribute Decision Making (FGMADM) and Fuzzy C-Means Clustering (FCM) as a DM tool for segmentation of customers (retailers), based on an updated RFM model. For this purpose, the most important criteria to evaluate retailers from the in depth literature survey and experts' opinion are added to the traditional RFM model. In addition, in order to make the model more efficient, FGMADM approach, in this paper, Fuzzy Group Step-wise Weight Assessment Ratio Analysis (FGSWARA) is used to weight KPIs. Then, FCM is applied to segment customers, based on their purchase behavior (RFM scores). A case study in one of the most famous Fast Moving Consumer Goods (FMCG) companies in Iran illustrated the applicability of the proposed model.

INTRODUCTION

Customers are one of the significant assets of every organization and without satisfied and loyal customers there is no chance of success. In addition, due to the rapid altering environment and facing with fierce market competition, creating a strong relationship with customers is an obligatory task. Furthermore, a limited number of resources makes impossible to satisfy all customers. To wrestle with the above mentioned issues, market segmentation is one of the best suggested approaches. The term was introduced by Wendell R. Smith, an American marketing researcher in the late 1950s (Smith, 1956). Dividing a market into different sections in order to select some of which as target markets and provide the most appropriate production mix, is the whole aim of market segmentation.

A company should think strategically about its relationship with consumers, and perhaps they had better not to have "one fixed strategy". Retailers are one of the most important parts of channel manage-

DOI: 10.4018/978-1-5225-0997-4.ch001

ment. Furthermore, an appropriate retailer segmentation strategy can increase competitive advantage and customer satisfaction, decrees distribution cost and it can accelerate the purchasing process. Retailer segmentation is the process of dividing a set of retailers into distinct subset of retailers, where any subset can be considered as a target group or be treated differently.

One important question in marketing is that whether customers are equal or not. The answer to this question is obvious: "No". Thus, how much is a customer worth? In order to answer this question, a concept, namely Customer Lifetime Value (CLV) in marketing was proposed. According to Jain and sing (2002) CLV for a firm is the net profit or loss to the firm from a customer over the entire life of transactions of that customer with the firm. In addition, CLV can be used in designing marketing programs (Reinartz & Kumar 2003; Rust et al., 2004). RFM models, probability models, econometric models, persistence models, computer science models, and diffusion/growth models are some of CLV models. Amongst different ones, RFM analysis is one of the famous and traditional customer evaluation metrics. It is a common approach for understanding consumer's purchase behaviour. As the name explains, RFM stands for three KPIs, includes Recency, Frequency and Monetary or Money. It is quite desirable, especially in the retail industry (Tsiptsis & Chorianopoulos, 2011). Furthermore, RFM segmentation has been applied for more than thirty years by direct marketers to target a subgroup of customers, decrease mailing costs and improve profit. Also, RFM is suitable to target marketing program at specific customers with the objective to improve response rates. Traditional RFM model cannot satisfy all needs of every industry and every business ought to use its own model. To deal with this, a firm can increase number of KPIs according to its needs and circumstances.

Recently, managers need to use more complicated tools applying huge amount of data to make more accurate decisions. A discipline which can extract the hidden and unknown information from abundance of data is Data Mining (DM). Amongst DM techniques, cluster analysis is widely used as a segmentation technique in many real problems. This is a convenient method to identify and define segments.

Decision making process frequently deals with discrete alternatives in the presence of different and often conflict criteria. This kind of decision making in Operations Research (OR)/Management Science (MS) literature is named Multiple Attribute Decision Making (MADM). Moreover, decision makers have widely recognized that most decisions made in the real world situations, because of their complexity, have vague and unclear constrains, and thus, the problem cannot be exactly defined or precisely represented in a crisp value (Bellman & Zadeh, 1970). To solve this kind of problems, Zadeh (1965) suggested employing the fuzzy set theory as a modelling tool for complex systems that can be controlled by humans but are hard to define literally. What is more, many recent decisions need to be made by a group of experts as they are inherently group decision making. The combination of fuzzy sets, MADM, and group decision making has led to a sub-discipline, namely, Fuzzy Group Multiple Attribute Decision Making (FGMADM). The present study aims to contribute to these subjects:

1. Creating an improved RFM model (based on traditional RFM);
2. Combining DM and FGMADM as a new hybrid model;
3. Using Fuzzy Group Step-wise Weight Assessment Ratio Analysis (FGSWARA) method to identify experts' preferences in a group decision making environment with vague information;
4. Applying Fuzzy C-Means (FCM) clustering method to segment retailers;
5. The case study in Fast Moving Consumer Goods (FMCG) manifests the applicability of the suggested model.

The outline of the chapter is as follows. Section 2 reviews the background information. Section 3 presents the proposed methodology combining FGSWARA and FCM. Section 4 comprises a case study to show the applicability of the proposed model and obtained results. Finally, conclusion and future researches directions are provided in Section 5.

BACKGROUND INFORMATION

To follow the purpose of this chapter, this section will review the related work in three parts: market segmentation, RFM analysis, and FGMADM.

Market Segmentation

The term market segmentation was initially coined by an American marketing researcher, in the late 1950s (Smith, 1956). He constructed his idea based on an economic theory of imperfect competition which was introduced by Robinson (1938). Smith viewed a market as a composition of heterogeneous consumers with their multitude of needs and wants and in order to deal with this diversity a firm had to divide a marketplace into segments. Furthermore, market segmentation stands on the fact that different customers require different products, and therefore, the market is inherently heterogeneous. In other words, to satisfy the whole consumers, a company should have infinite resources. Thus, it is much more practical to divide a market into different parts and select one or more as a target market or target markets. This concept invariably plays a principal role in a battery of marketing plans. McDonald and Dunbar (2004) defines market segmentation as "the process of splitting customers, or potential customers, in a market into different groups, or segments, within which customers share a similar level of interest in the same, or comparable, set of needs satisfied by a distinct marketing proposition" (p. 37). Some of the beneficial outcomes of using this approach are as: it provides a better understanding of customers' requirements (Aghdaie et al., 2013) it is a key decision to undertake marketing and strategic planning (McDonald & Wilson, 2011) it can be considered as a product differentiation strategy to tackle diversity in the marketplace (Geraghty & Torres, 2009) and it is a base for other marketing decisions (Weinstein, 1994). Moreover, it enhances efficacy and effectiveness of business (Chiu et al., 2009).

RFM Analysis

The lifetime value of a customer is an integral and useful concept in interactive marketing (Pfeifer, & Carraway, 2000). Additionally, according to shin and Sohen (2004) 20% of customers provide 80% percent of income. CLV is one of the key metrics in marketing and it is considered as a cardinal segmentation base (Donkers et al., 2007). As a result, it is absolutely imperative that a company has a periodic CLV evaluation plan.

RFM stands for three attributes, namely, recency, frequency, and monetary or money. It creates cells or group of customers based on three measures. This behaviour-based model, applies data to predict customers' future behaviour according to their past ones. Purchase behaviour models are one of the most powerful ways to segment customers by historic value. RFM criteria are best predictors for distinction of behaviourally loyal customers from non/less-loyal clients (Bucknix & Van den Poel, 2005). It is a very efficient to segment consumers (Newell, 1997). Virtually all companies struggle to maximize this backward looking metric (Kumar & Rajan, 2009). What is more, it is one of the famous metrics, since, it is quick, easy and descriptive, with only three-variable formula, which can aid monitoring early chain signals and grade your customers. Moreover, it is still handy when models are not practical depending on industry and customer lifecycle. It is also good for future personalization service and how likely to respond a firm's marketing plans. It can be used to test the short and long-term effect of the segmentation program as well (Miglautsch, 2000).

The original idea was developed by Arthur Hughes (1994) and from that moment on, this method has been applied in both academic and practical environments to evaluate CLV. He defined three attributes and used five equal frequency spectrums to range every factor. The result was a three dimensional cube with 125 cells and each cell can be used as a target market. For example, a score of one indicated that the most recent transaction was a long time ago. With the ordering customers based on the model, one could have a very useful view of the consumers. Bult and Wansbeek (1995) used RFM model for direct mail campaign target selection. R is defined as the difference between now and the last purchase, how many times did the buyer purchase is definition of F, and M defined as how much money was spent, all in a certain time period (Bult & Wansbeek, 1995). One of the first ideas that mentioned different weights ought to be assigned to RFM measures depending on industry characteristics, was suggested by Stone (1995). He concluded that frequency should have the highest and monetary should have the lowest value, however, his weighting systems was subjectively, without using a systematic approach. Marcus (1998) applied Boston Consulting Group (BCG) matrix to segment consumers based on average purchase and purchase frequency. Kahan (1998) used the mathematical computation RFM to enhance marketing initiatives. One year later, a simple stochastic RFM model to rank customers regarding their expected contribution was developed by Colombo and Jiang (Colombo & Jiang, 1999). Jonker et al. (2004) illustrated the application of RFM framework in direct-mailing, using stochastic dynamic programming to developing an optimized strategy for customer segmentation. A heuristic Genetic Algorithm (GA) was embedded in clustering by Tsai and Chiu (2004) to guarantee that the same consumers in a segment, have the same purchase pattern according to RFM analysis. Ten years after idea of weighting attributes by Stone (1995), Liu and Shih (2005b) applied the Analytical Hierarchy Process (AHP) to calculate the relative importance of the RFM measures. Liu and Shih (2005a) proposed a Weighted-RFM (WRFM) method combined with K-means clustering, preference-based Collaborative Filtering (CF) and association rule mining to recommend the products as well. In the same year, it is proved by Buckinx and Van den Poel (2005) and Fader et al. (2005) that RFM variables can predict precisely the CLV and the indicators are functional predictors for CLV. Chan (2008) presented a novel approach to mix market segmentation and market targeting using GA and RFM for campaign strategies. Shih and Liu (2008) used CF, K-means clustering and WRFM in order to create a system that could provide different recommendations and ranked them. Yeh et al. (2009) expands RFM into RFMTC by encompassing two factors (Time since first purchase and Churn probability), using Bernoulli sequence. Chen et al. (2009) created RFM-Apriori algorithm to find all RFM sequential patterns from customers' data-sequences. Cheng and Chen (2009) joined quantitative value of RFM attributes and K-means algorithm into Rough Set theory (RS theory) to extract meaning rules for achieving an excellent Customer Relationship Management (CRM) for enterprises. Chang and Tsai (2011) proposed a new framework named Group RFM (GRFM) which applied constrained-based clustering and the characteristic of purchase behaviours. Khajvand et al. (2011) applied AHP to weight RFM attributes and used K-means to segment consumers. ARIMA model was applied to predict the future of each segment based on WRFM obtained results (Khajvand & Traokh, 2011). Chiang (2011) added Discount and Return Cost in traditional RFM model and made

RFMDR. He employed supervised Apriori algorithm, Ward's method and discrimination analysis to RFMDR in an online shopping market. Li et al. (2011) used LRFM (L for length) model with two-stage cluster analysis in textile manufacturing business. A case study in children's dental clinic based on Self-Organizing Maps (SOM) dental and LRFM was conducted by Wei et al. (2012). A year later, Wei et al. (2013) applied SOM and K-means methods to apply in RFM and they found four categories of consumer. Dhandayudam and Krishnamurthi (2014) developed RFMP (P for payment details) and proposed a new clustering algorithm MADO (Minimum Average Dissimilarity between Objects) for categorical data based on elements of (Rough Set Theory) RST. Hu and Yeh (2014) developed RFM-pattern-tree and RFMP-growth algorithm for mining a complete set of RFM-patterns.

FGMADM

OR/MS is the discipline that deals with using advanced analytical methods to aid decision makers in order to make better decisions. Complex decision making problems are frequently consisted of a legions of elements such as criteria and alternatives (Tafreshi et al., 2016). In many real-life problems, it is not possible to model a system with only one fixed objective function. In addition, multiple criteria should be considered in many decision making environments and they are often in conflict. Thus, Multiple Criteria Decision Making (MCDM) becomes very useful approach to deal with these situations. Two classes of MCDM are Multi Objective Decision Making (MODM) and Multiple Attribute Decision Making (MADM). MADM methods invariably deal with problems with discrete alternatives in the presence of different and often conflict criteria.

A bunch of decision makers need to be taken in a group due to the fact that group decision making outcomes are more effective and accurate. On the top of that, in MADM problems, decision makers need to reach consensus for weighting criteria, evaluating alternatives or interact to make a choice and reach a final decision. As a result, MADM under group decision making situations attracted great attention. The combination of group decision making approach in MADM has led scholars to create new GMADM methods.

Vagueness, uncertainty, and unclear information can be found in a battery of complex systems. In addition, these problems cannot be exactly defined or precisely represented in a crisp value (Bellman & Zadeh, 1970). To tackle with them, Zadeh (1965) suggested employing fuzzy set theory as a new perspective to model complex systems that can be controlled by humans but are hard to define exactly. His idea was used in FGMADM problems in practical problems.

METHODOLOGY

This section presents a novel hybrid model, including FGSWARA, FCM algorithm, and modified RFM for segmentation and framework. The first part of proposed methodology describes FGSWARA as a group decision making tool for evaluation process. The second part describes FCM to segment retailers. The third part explains modified RFM method for scoring retailers. Finally, the last part explains the proposed framework for retailers' evaluation and segmentation process.

Fuzzy Group Step-Wise Weight Assessment Ratio Analysis (FGSWARA)

Decision making problems need a mechanism to calculate the weight of all criteria to rank alternatives. Moreover, it is an integral part of the multitude of MADM problems. Step-wise Weight Assessment Ratio Analysis (SWARA), first introduced by Keršuliene et al. in 2010 in order to assess dispute resolution methods from economic and social perspectives. A year later, Kersuliene and Turskis (2011), applied SWARA in architect selection problem. Similar to many MADM methods, an expert has a tremendous role on the SWARA output. The SWARA procedure is as follows:

Step 1: Sort all criteria in descending order based on their importance.
Step 2: Calculate the relative importance of criterion j in relation to the previous $(j-1)$ criterion, till reach the last criterion (see Table 1). The ratio is called Comparative importance of average value, S_j (Keršuliene et al., 2010).
Step 3: Calculate the coefficient of k_j with the following formula:

$$k_j = \begin{cases} 1 & j = 1 \\ s_j + 1 & j \succ 1 \end{cases} \quad (1)$$

Step 4: The recalculated weight of q_j as follows:

$$q_j = \begin{cases} 1 & j = 1 \\ \dfrac{k_j - 1}{k_j} & j \succ 1 \end{cases} \quad (2)$$

Steps 5: Finally, the relative weights of the all evaluation criteria are determined as follows:

$$w_j = \frac{q_j}{\sum_{k=1}^{n} q_k}, \quad (3)$$

where w_j denotes the relative weight of criterion j.

As mentioned earlier, there is a fuzzy concept in dozens of comparisons due the fact that real world is full of ambiguity and vagueness. In addition, orthodox MADM cannot be applied in all complex problems owing to have imprecise information. For instance, in Saaty's traditional AHP scale (Saaty, 1997), importance is measured on an integer-valued 1-9 scale (Kahraman, 2008). Ergo, incorporation of imprecise information and vagueness is an unavoidable requirement of fine decision making models. For pairwise comparisons' scale, we applied Triangular Fuzzy Numbers (TFNs). A TFN can be denoted by a triplet (l, m, u) where $l \le m \le u$ .The fuzzy pairwise scale (linguistic variables for evaluation process) is defined in Table 1. The proposed scale is simple and needs lower pairwise comparisons comparing the AHP.

Table 1. Linguistic variables for fuzzy pairwise scale

Linguistic Scale	Triangular Fuzzy Scale	Triangular Fuzzy Reciprocal Scale
Extremely more important (EM)	$\tilde{1}=(1,1,1)$	$\tilde{1}^{-1}=(1,1,1)$
Judgment values between very strongly and extremely (JS)	$\tilde{2}=(1,2,3)$	$\tilde{2}^{-1}=\left(\frac{1}{3},\frac{1}{2},1\right)$
Very strongly more important (VS)	$\tilde{3}=(2,3,4)$	$\tilde{3}^{-1}=\left(\frac{1}{4},\frac{1}{3},\frac{1}{2}\right)$
Judgment values between strongly and very strongly (JV)	$\tilde{4}=(3,4,5)$	$\tilde{4}^{-1}=\left(\frac{1}{5},\frac{1}{4},\frac{1}{3}\right)$
Strongly more important (SI)	$\tilde{5}=(4,5,6)$	$\tilde{5}^{-1}=\left(\frac{1}{6},\frac{1}{5},\frac{1}{4}\right)$
Judgment values between moderately and strongly (JB)	$\tilde{6}=(5,6,7)$	$\tilde{6}^{-1}=\left(\frac{1}{7},\frac{1}{6},\frac{1}{5}\right)$
Moderately more important (M)	$\tilde{7}=(6,7,8)$	$\tilde{7}^{-1}=\left(\frac{1}{8},\frac{1}{7},\frac{1}{6}\right)$
Judgment values between equally and moderately (J)	$\tilde{8}=(7,8,9)$	$\tilde{8}^{-1}=\left(\frac{1}{9},\frac{1}{8},\frac{1}{7}\right)$
Equally important (EI)	$\tilde{9}=(8,9,9)$	$\tilde{9}^{-1}=\left(\frac{1}{9},\frac{1}{9},\frac{1}{8}\right)$
If factor i has one of the above numbers assigned to it when compared to factor j, then j has the reciprocal value when compared with i		Reciprocals of above $M_1^{-1}\approx\left(1/u_1,1/m_1,1/l_1\right)$

For aggregation of group decisions, geometric mean operations were used. Geometric mean operations were applied in many studies for group decision making by Equation (4), for more information, see Davies (1994) and Buckley (1985).

$$l_{ij}=\left(\prod_{k=1}^{k} l_{ijk}\right)^{1/k}, m_{ij}=\left(\prod_{k=1}^{k} m_{ijk}\right)^{1/k}, u_{ij}=\left(\prod_{k=1}^{k} u_{ijk}\right)^{1/k} \tag{4}$$

In our study, for evaluation of the qualitative criteria TFNs scale (see Table 1) were used. For aggregation of group decisions, geometric mean operations of TFNs were applied. Fuzzy mean approach as a defuzzification method was used to make crisp numbers.

Fuzzy-C-Means (FCM)

Clustering or cluster analysis is one of the significant categories of DM in marketing, however, other methods of DM such as association, classification, forecasting, regression, sequence discovery, and visualization have important roles in solving management problems. Due to the nature of market segmentation problem which is dividing customers into different segments, it is widely used in segmentation studies. This is an unsupervised learning method with the object of assigning a set of items into different clusters or groups based on identified similarity index. In other words, every cluster should have the same objects and different clusters should have different objects. Distance measures are very common to calculate similarity and dissimilarity of groups. Hard cluster analysis uses the crisp values to assign. Ergo, each item either belongs to a cluster or not (one or zero). This approach provides sharp classification results (Sahu et al., 2012). The problem is frequently happen when the distance between two cluster centers is the equal and one of which has to be selected by force. To tackle this, fuzzy clustering methods by membership functions were proposed. In this approach, an item can belong to more than one cluster with different membership functions.

FCM algorithm, which is very similar to K-means algorithm, was developed by Dunn in 1973, and then improved by Bezdek in 1981. Furthermore, it is one of the widely used fuzzy clustering methods in pattern recognition. The procedure is based on dividing n-dimensional data into C fuzzy clusters, via minimizing an objective function, in an iterative process.

$$J_m = \sum_{i=1}^{C}\sum_{j=1}^{n} u_{ij}^{m} \left\| x_j - c_i \right\|^2 , 1 \le m \le \infty \tag{5}$$

where m is any genuine number bigger than 1, the degree of membership of x_j in the cluster i is u_{ij}, the j-th element of d-dimensional measured data, c_i is the center of the cluster i, ||*|| is any norm expressing the similarity between any measured data and the center (Keskin, 2015).

$$\sum_{i=1}^{c} u_{ij} = 1, \forall j = 1,\dots,n \tag{6}$$

$U = \left(u_{ij}\right)_{cxn}$ is the membership function, u_{ij}^{m} is degree of membership of individual k in cluster i, and the meaning of condition (6) is that, for a given individual, the degrees of membership across the clusters sum to one.

Fuzzy clustering starts by minimization of the objective function presented in Equation (5) in an iterative process by updating fuzzy membership function and centers of the clusters shown in Equations (7) and (8).

$$c_i = \frac{\sum_{j=1}^{n} u_{ij}^m x_j}{\sum_{j=1}^{n} u_{ij}^m}, \forall i = 1,...,C \tag{7}$$

$$u_{ij} = \frac{1}{\sum_{k=1}^{C} \left(\|x_j - c_i\| / \|x_j - c_k\| \right)^{-2/(m-1)}} \forall i = 1,...,C; \forall j = 1,...,n \tag{8}$$

The condition to stop the iteration is according to the following rule:

$$\left\| u_{ij}^{k+1} - u_{ij}^{k} \right\| \prec \zeta \tag{9}$$

Modified RFM

In traditional RFM model, R stands for recency, F indicates frequency and M indicates monetary. One of the aims of this chapter is modifying traditional RFM approach by increasing the number of factors to make the evaluations more accurate and suitable. Thus, the numbers of factors are expanded as: T indicates Time since first purchase (days), D indicates Discounts, promotions, product samples, etc. dividing by M (Percent), C stands for cost of distribution divides by M (Percent), A shows an average number of items in every invoice (Number), V stands for variety of all purchased items in the certain period (Number), G stands for cost of returned Goods divides by M (Percent), and P indicates the average time interval between Payment and purchase date (Days). F, M, T, A, and V are benefit criterion (The maximum of this criterion is desirable) whereas R, D, C, G, and P are all cost criterion (The minimum of this criterion is desirable). For normalization of benefit criterion, each factor is divided by the maximum of all factors of the same category, and for cost criterion, the minimum of the all factors should be divided by each factor. These factors are taken from the review of the related literature and experts' idea which are relevant to business-to-business (B2B) retailers' analysis. The RFM traditional score is calculated as follows:

RFM score = (Recency score × Recency weight) + (Frequency score × Frequency weight) + (Monetary score × Monetary weight)

The Framework

The proposed procedure is depicted in Figure 1. In the first phase, the most important criteria for retailers' lifetime value were identified based on in-depth literature review. Then, a group of experts evaluated the criteria and the improved RFM model was constructed. In the second phase, FGSWARA method was used as a group decision making tool by experts to weight different criteria. Next, the retailers' scores from the data base and according to the new model were calculated. Finally, customers were grouped into different segments by FCM algorithm and cluster validity was checked. Interpretation of segments was explained in order to provide useful information about retailers in the third phase as well.

Figure 1. The proposed procedure

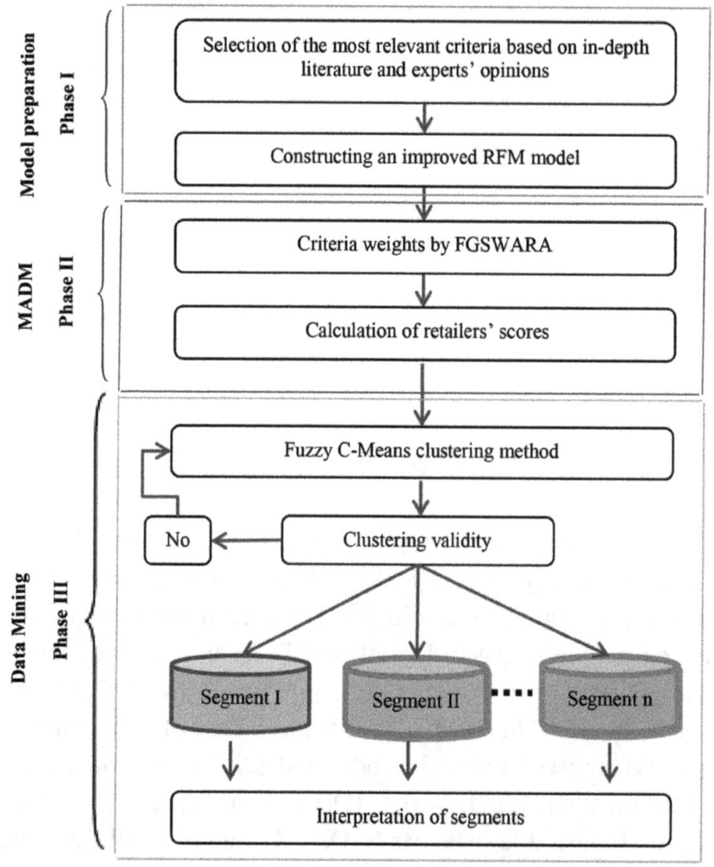

ILLUSTRATIVE CASE STUDY

Company Profile

In order to show the applicability of the proposed model, a case study in one of the biggest and most reputable companies in Iran is illustrated. XYZ Company produces, trades, distributes and sells in more than ten countries. Processed food, dairy products, ice cream, and non-alcoholic beverages are offered by the XYZ Company. The company has virtually fifteen thousand employees, forty-four branches in Iran, more than one thousand different products in 54 groups, with annually one billion dollars turn over. XYZ products are daily distributed to more than 140,000 supermarkets, 20,000 restaurants and fast-foods, 1,000 hotels and 600 chain stores, in Iran. XYZ uses direct-store delivery approach and eighty percent portion of the company's income receives via supermarkets (retailers) and retailers play a critical role in channel management of the XYZ Company.

Results and Discussion

This section concentrates on obtained numerical results. In this study, we use retailers' data from a large manufacturer and distributor to illustrate the proposed framework empirically. Retailers are located in widespread areas, with diverse potentials and behaviours. Furthermore, Iran dairy and food market is demanding high quality with low price products and the market size has multiplied recently in terms of customers. In this dynamic environment, managing retailers is a critical task. To deal with this issue, FMCG companies should segment their retailers fruitfully.

After realizing the criticality of defining the project in the company, a project team with seven experts, including sales manager, CEO, supply chain manager, marketing manager, sales and operations planning manager, advertising manager, and brand manager, were selected for carrying out the project. As a pilot study, Alborz province was chosen with 8570 supermarkets. In this study, 8570 customers' (supermarkets) transactions are extracted from the database in summer and fall 2015. Despite the fact that six-month period might not be long, we believe that it is suitable since we are dealing with an FMCG retailer with an average visit time of four times a week by a salesperson, which led to an average visit rate of 208 times a year.

First, the most important criteria list was created based on literature survey. Second, by experts' opinions, and using Delphi method, the final list was made. Delphi method was used to achieve unanimity to create an improved RFM model (see Table 2). Table 3 shows the descriptions of factors.

In the second phase, criteria weights were calculated through FGSWARA. Delphi method was applied to reach the same ranking of the criteria by the group of experts (first step of FGSWARA). Then, via TFNs, every expert scored the distance between pair criterion (see Table 4) by pursuing the second step of FGSWARA. The last column of Table 4 is the result of the fuzzy geometric mean of seven experts' evaluations using Equation (4). After that, by following the steps 3 to 5 the final weights of all factors were calculated (Table 5).

After calculation of the importance of factors, the initial decision matrix was made (see Table 6). Considering the fact that the weight of each factor and being the benefit or cost criterion, the weighted normalized decision matrix was calculated (see Table 7). Next, the final score of every consumer was calculated by sum of the scores of each factor.

Table 2. The definitions of RFM model factors

Variables	Definitions
Recency (R)	It refers to the number of days since last purchase (Days)
Frequency (F)	It means that how many times the retailer have purchased (Numbers)
Monetary (M)	It refers to the sum of the retailer's payment (Rials)
Time since first purchase (T)	It means duration relationship time (Days)
Discount (D)	It indicates all the cost of discounts, promotions, product samples, etc. dividing by M (Percent)
Cost of distribution (C)	It refers to the cost of distribution dividing by M (Percent)
Average number of items in every invoice (A)	It refers to the average purchase amount per transaction (Numbers)
Variety of all purchased items (V)	It means all the variety of purchased items in a certain period (Numbers)
Cost of returned Goods (G)	It stands for cost of returned goods divides by M (Percent)
Payment on time (P)	It is the difference between the purchase time and the payment time (Days)

Table 3. The descriptions of RFM model factors

	Maximum	Minimum	Average	Standard Deviation
R	163	1	13	33.92
F	101	1	35	26.16
M	2,035,027,599	1,149,100	348,966,696	85,730,846
T	1800	5	720	50.02
D	22%	2%	7%	3.31%
C	20%	8%	14%	2.68%
A	21	3	10	8.42
V	47	7	16	4.16
G	9%	0.4%	4%	1.76%
P	30	1	8	2.74

Table 4. Fuzzy comparative importance of average value s_j by seven experts

Criterion	E1	E2	E3	E4	E5	E6	E7	Fuzzy Geometric Mean of Seven Experts for Each Criterion
R	$\tilde{1}$	$\tilde{1}$	$\tilde{1}$	$\tilde{1}$	$\tilde{1}$	$\tilde{1}$	$\tilde{1}$	(1,1,1)
M	$\tilde{4}^{-1}$	$\tilde{1}^{-1}$	$\tilde{3}^{-1}$	$\tilde{2}^{-1}$	$\tilde{3}^{-1}$	$\tilde{2}^{-1}$	$\tilde{2}^{-1}$	(0.33,0.45,0.7)
P	$\tilde{2}^{-1}$	$\tilde{3}^{-1}$	$\tilde{3}^{-1}$	$\tilde{3}^{-1}$	$\tilde{6}^{-1}$	$\tilde{3}^{-1}$	$\tilde{4}^{-1}$	(0.23,0.31,0.46)
G	$\tilde{5}^{-1}$	$\tilde{2}^{-1}$	$\tilde{4}^{-1}$	$\tilde{2}^{-1}$	$\tilde{2}^{-1}$	$\tilde{2}^{-1}$	$\tilde{3}^{-1}$	(0.28,0.4,0.64)
D	$\tilde{3}^{-1}$	$\tilde{3}^{-1}$	$\tilde{7}^{-1}$	$\tilde{3}^{-1}$	$\tilde{3}^{-1}$	$\tilde{3}^{-1}$	$\tilde{3}^{-1}$	(0.23,0.3,0.43)
F	$\tilde{3}^{-1}$	$\tilde{2}^{-1}$	$\tilde{3}^{-1}$	$\tilde{3}^{-1}$	$\tilde{4}^{-1}$	$\tilde{3}^{-1}$	$\tilde{2}^{-1}$	(0.26,0.36,0.58)
C	$\tilde{5}^{-1}$	$\tilde{3}^{-1}$	$\tilde{3}^{-1}$	$\tilde{7}^{-1}$	$\tilde{3}^{-1}$	$\tilde{4}^{-1}$	$\tilde{9}^{-1}$	(0.18,0.23,0.3)
A	$\tilde{3}^{-1}$	$\tilde{2}^{-1}$	$\tilde{7}^{-1}$	$\tilde{4}^{-1}$	$\tilde{3}^{-1}$	$\tilde{3}^{-1}$	$\tilde{3}^{-1}$	(0.23,0.3,0.45)
V	$\tilde{2}^{-1}$	$\tilde{3}^{-1}$	$\tilde{2}^{-1}$	$\tilde{2}^{-1}$	$\tilde{4}^{-1}$	$\tilde{2}^{-1}$	$\tilde{6}^{-1}$	(0.26,0.37,0.62)
T	$\tilde{6}^{-1}$	$\tilde{6}^{-1}$	$\tilde{7}^{-1}$	$\tilde{6}^{-1}$	$\tilde{5}^{-1}$	$\tilde{7}^{-1}$	$\tilde{5}^{-1}$	(0.14,0.17,0.20)

The goal of clustering is to group customers into different partitions and deal with them suitably. Therefore, the modified RFM score (see last column of Table 7) was used as an input for FCM algorithm to build clusters by attributes. Ward's method (1967) is one of the most famous hierarchical clustering methods to find the optimum number of clusters. In addition, Ward's minimum variance was worked well in earlier studies (Hair et al., 1995). Thus, it was applied to find the optimal number of clusters. Schwarz's

Table 5. Final results of FGSWARA results method in weighting modified RFM

Criterion	Comparative Importance of Average Value s_j (Defuzzification by Fuzzy Mean)	Coefficient $k_j = s_j + 1$	Recalculated Weight $w_j = \frac{x_{j-1}}{k_j}$	Weight $q_j = \frac{w_j}{\sum w_j}$
R		1.0	1.0	0.293
M	0.49	1.49	0.67	0.196
P	0.33	1.33	0.50	0.147
G	0.43	1.43	0.35	0.103
D	0.32	1.32	0.27	0.079
F	0.40	1.40	0.19	0.056
C	0.24	1.24	0.15	0.045
A	0.32	1.32	0.12	0.034
V	0.41	1.41	0.08	0.024
T	0.17	1.17	0.07	0.021

Table 6. The initial decision making matrix

	Customer ID	R	F	M	T	A	V	D	C	G	P
1	1456960	41	20	9,084,100	197	10	28	5%	8%	5%	6
2	1900004	5	31	1,625,657,934	89	13	19	8%	10%	4%	11
3	1900012	72	16	49,785,921	281	7	11	7%	10%	6%	4
…	…	…	…	…	…	…	…	…	…	…	…
8569	1911416	1	99	1,850,321,760	1245	17	35	11%	9%	7%	3
8570	1911452	21	14	33,125,671	362	6	10	6%	13%	1%	21

Table 7. The weighted normalized decision making matrix

	Customer ID	R	F	M	T	A	V	D	C	G	P	Modified RFM Score
1	1456960	0.007	0.039	0.001	0.011	0.037	0.033	0.018	0.034	0.002	0.003	0.187
2	1900004	0.059	0.113	0.118	0.005	0.049	0.023	0.011	0.027	0.002	0.002	0.409
3	1900012	0.004	0.031	0.004	0.016	0.026	0.013	0.013	0.027	0.002	0.005	0.141
…	…		…	…	…	…	…					
8569	1911416	0.293	0.193	0.134	0.072	0.064	0.042	0.008	0.030	0.001	0.007	0.844
8570	1911452	0.014	0.027	0.002	0.021	0.022	0.012	0.015	0.021	0.010	0.001	0.146

Bayesian criterion and the total average coefficient were used to assess partitioning. The quality of the clustering is good with an average silhouette coefficient 0.7 greater than 0.50. If an average silhouette coefficient is greater than 0.5 then, this indicates reasonable clustering, whereas a coefficient less than 0.2 denotes a problematic solution (Tsiptsis & Chorianopoulos, 2011). In addition, analysis of variance was conducted to test whether RFM variables could discriminate 5 clusters. The analysis result would reject H0, because the p-values are significant ($p < 0.05$). Having rejected the H0, the result confirmed that 5 clusters would be discriminated based on ten factors significantly. Most computations were done by Microsoft Excel 2010 while MATLAB was applied for FCM cluster analysis. Graphical representation of cluster sizes is depicted in Figure 2. The smallest cluster size is 909 and the largest one is 2596, and the ration size is 2.86. The averages of scores of the segments are presented in Table 8.

In order to facilitate the explanations, the sign ↑ denotes that the value is greater than an average and sign ↓ denotes that the value is smaller than an average. Interpretations based on clustering results and marketing strategies are as follows:

Cluster 1: This segment consists of everyday shoppers. They have the second smallest basket size and monetary value. The mean RFM score of this segment is 0.35. Furthermore, the mean scores of all factors are below averages. In addition, they have the highest cost of distribution. Only T factor is above an average amongst all factors and it might be used as a potential. Considering the T,

Figure 2. Cluster sizes

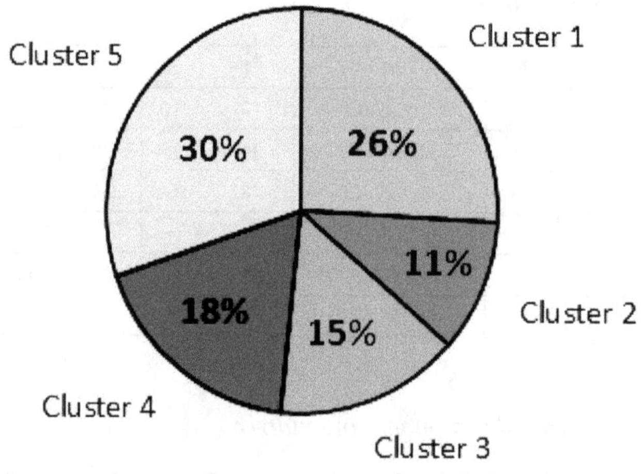

Table 8. The average scores of the segments

Cluster Number	R	F	M	T	D	C	A	V	G	P	Modified RFM Score
Cluster 1	10	29	94,751,234	1050	9%	18%	10	12	4%	11	0.35
Cluster 2	5	73	1,453,145,635	1077	13%	16%	18	35	5%	7	0.81
Cluster 3	8	49	765,123,543	750	5%	14%	15	21	3%	9	0.72
Cluster 4	15	39	294,956,214	650	4%	12%	11	19	6%	5	0.53
Cluster 5	21	19	3,584,513	340	7%	10%	5	9	2%	6	0.19

the company can take advantage of their length of relationship and set some marketing plans to increase their purchasing rate.

Cluster 2: These retailers are superstars with the top RFM value. They are the most loyal consumers, with the best recency score, and the highest monetary value and frequency. With the factors above averages, for instance, A↑ and V↑, their tendency is to buy variety of company's products. Despite the fact that they are supertasters, some factors such as D↓, C↓, G↓ and P↓ show that there are still possibilities to enhance their potentials. The highest score of G shows that they are high respond promotion customers. Thus, the company's strategy can be concentration on decreasing the cost related factors and improve the payment index in order to profit as much as possible from working with them. It is small but strategic segment and in expert's opinions, another option can be trying to keep this long relation and use their perspectives to aid in designing new marketing plans. Furthermore, keeping sustainable relationship with them is obligatory.

Cluster 3: The third cluster consists of retailers with the second highest RFM score. These golden customers have the factors with scores above averages, for instance, F↑, M↑, T↑, A↑, and G↑. These golden customers have the lowest discount rate and they tend to pay on time. Comparing with others, D and G criteria are very good and the only P index should be decreased as a short term plan. According to experts' point of view, it has the second highest potential and they are ready to opt new strategies to reach superstars' level. Therefore, it can be a good idea to spend some budget of supertasters to increase willingness of this segment in order to cooperate as in this segment, cost related factors are by far less than cluster 2. Maybe after some time these consumers can improve their monetary value as well.

Cluster 4: This segment consists of mediocre customers with RFM score of 0.53 which is more than of total average of all segments (an average of all consumers RFM score is 0.44). These typical customers have the lowest discount rate. By considering this positive aspect, it is advisable to focus on them to increase their monetary value. They do not have very low RFM score, but one possible approach is to boost their RFM score by focusing on monetary value and push them toward the golden customers' level.

Cluster 5: The worst customers are located in this segment. These dormant customers have the lowest RFM score (0.19). They are dormant customers. All factors are the worst ones, however, the returned factor is very good. It seems that they buy only when they need. Strategically, it is advisable to eliminate at least some of them. Replacing them can be a favorable strategy and the company can expand its buying-interactions with other clusters.

CONCLUSION AND DIRECTIONS FOR FUTURE RESEARCH

In an era of CRM emphasis and requiring swimming in a sea of customer data, owing to fierce competitive market, quickly changing environment and inconstant consumer needs, creating a long term relationship with customers is critical for survival of a business. Moreover, consumers are invariably the core of long term growth plans of many companies. In addition, the market is bursting with demanding customers and there are limited resources to satisfy them. With above mentioned factors, firm should ponder about the value of customers and evaluate their lifetime value.

The aim of this chapter is using FGSWARA as a new FGMADM, and FCM, as a DM tool, to evaluate and segment customers based on their CLV. To our best knowledge, this chapter constitutes the first application of FGSWARA. Second, a new fuzzy scale for pairwise comparisons in SWARA was introduced. Third, a modified RFM based model is applied for CLV analysis. Forth, a recent synergy between DM and MADM which was proposed by Aghdaie et al. (2014) was applied in this study.

This study has several limitations and drawback. Firstly, when RFM analysis was not mixed with other significant product attributes, such as lifecycle stage of the customers or product and product preferences, fails to provide a full understanding of a customer behaviour. Secondly, the RFM based factors are not only powerful predictors but also convenient to use. But they omit the fact that the organizations past marketing activities may cause the recent consumers' behaviours. Thus, past marketing plans might divert the results. Thirdly, there might be relationships between factors that it was not considered in this study.

Future works will address these themes. It is possible to use other clustering methods for segmentation and compare the results. In addition, it is highly recommended to add or delete some criteria in modified RFM model and compare the ranks. Grey relation analysis or Z-number can be used instead of fuzzy logic for evaluation process. Using other MADM methods to calculate weights are also advisable. The model was applied for retailers but it can be used for wholesalers or in other industries.

ACKNOWLEDGMENT

The authors express their gratitude to the Solico Group (Food industries) for the financial support of this project. We also thank the respectful editors for their constructive comments.

REFERENCES

Aghdaie, M. H., Zolfani, S. H., & Zavadskas, E. K. (2013). Market segment evaluation and selection based on application of fuzzy AHP and COPRAS-G methods. *Journal of Business Economics and Management*, *14*(1), 213–233. doi:10.3846/16111699.2012.721392

Aghdaie, M. H., Zolfani, S. H., & Zavadskas, E. K. (2014). Synergies of data mining and multiple attribute decision making. *Procedia: Social and Behavioral Sciences*, *110*, 767–776. doi:10.1016/j.sbspro.2013.12.921

Bellman, R. E., & Zadeh, L. A. (1970). Decision-making in a fuzzy environment. *Management Science*, *17*(4), B-141–B-164. doi:10.1287/mnsc.17.4.B141

Bezdek, J. C. (1981). *Pattern Recognition with Fuzzy Objective Function Algorithms*. Kluwer Academic Publishers. doi:10.1007/978-1-4757-0450-1

Buckinx, W., & Van den Poel, D. (2005). Customer base analysis: Partial defection of behaviourally loyal clients in a non-contractual FMCG retail setting. *European Journal of Operational Research*, *164*(1), 252–268. doi:10.1016/j.ejor.2003.12.010

Buckley, J. J. (1985). Fuzzy hierarchical analysis. *Fuzzy Sets and Systems*, *17*(3), 233–247. doi:10.1016/0165-0114(85)90090-9

Bult, J. R., & Wansbeek, T. (1995). Optimal selection for direct mail. *Marketing Science*, *14*(4), 378–394. doi:10.1287/mksc.14.4.378

Chan, C. C. H. (2008). Intelligent value-based customer segmentation method for campaign management: A case study of automobile retailer. *Expert Systems with Applications*, *34*(4), 2754–2762. doi:10.1016/j.eswa.2007.05.043

Chang, H. C., & Tsai, H. P. (2011). Group RFM analysis as a novel framework to discover better customer consumption behavior. *Expert Systems with Applications*, *38*(12), 14499–14513. doi:10.1016/j.eswa.2011.05.034

Chen, Y. L., Kuo, M. H., Wu, S. Y., & Tang, K. (2009). Discovering recency, frequency, and monetary (RFM) sequential patterns from customers' purchasing data. *Electronic Commerce Research and Applications*, *8*(5), 241–251. doi:10.1016/j.elerap.2009.03.002

Cheng, C. H., & Chen, Y. S. (2009). Classifying the segmentation of customer value via RFM model and RS theory. *Expert Systems with Applications*, *36*(3), 4176–4184. doi:10.1016/j.eswa.2008.04.003

Chiang, W. Y. (2011). To mine association rules of customer values via a data mining procedure with improved model: An empirical case study. *Expert Systems with Applications*, *38*(3), 1716–1722. doi:10.1016/j.eswa.2010.07.097

Chiu, C. Y., Chen, Y. F., Kuo, I. T., & Ku, H. C. (2009). An intelligent market segmentation system using k-means and particle swarm optimization. *Expert Systems with Applications*, *36*(3), 4558–4565. doi:10.1016/j.eswa.2008.05.029

Colombo, R., & Jiang, W. (1999). A stochastic RFM model. *Journal of Interactive Marketing*, *13*(3), 2–12. doi:10.1002/(SICI)1520-6653(199922)13:3<2::AID-DIR1>3.0.CO;2-H

Davies, M. A. P. (1994). A Multicriteria Decision Model Application for Managing Group Decisions. *The Journal of the Operational Research Society*, *45*(1), 47–58. doi:10.1057/jors.1994.6

Dhandayudam, P., & Krishnamurthi, I. (2014). A rough set approach for customer segmentation. *Data Science Journal*, *13*(0), 1–11. doi:10.2481/dsj.13-019

Donkers, B., Verhoef, P. C., & de Jong, M. G. (2007). Modeling CLV: A test of competing models in the insurance industry. *Quantitative Marketing and Economics*, *5*(2), 163–190. doi:10.1007/s11129-006-9016-y

Dunn, J. C. (1973). A Fuzzy Relative of the ISODATA Process and Its Use in Detecting Compact Well-Separated Clusters. *Journal of Cybernetics*, *3*(3), 32–57. doi:10.1080/01969727308546046

Fader, P. S., Hardie, B. G., & Lee, K. L. (2005). RFM and CLV: Using iso-value curves for customer base analysis. *JMR, Journal of Marketing Research*, *42*(4), 415–430. doi:10.1509/jmkr.2005.42.4.415

Geraghty, S., & Torres, A. M. (2009). The Irish wine market: A market segmentation study. *International Journal of Wine Business Research*, *21*(2), 143–154. doi:10.1108/17511060910967980

Hair, J. F., Anderson, R. E., Tatham, R. L., & Black, W. C. (1995). *Multivariate data analysis*. Upper Saddle River, NJ: Prentice Hall.

Hu, Y. H., & Yeh, T. W. (2014). Discovering valuable frequent patterns based on RFM analysis without customer identification information. *Knowledge-Based Systems*, *61*, 76–88. doi:10.1016/j.knosys.2014.02.009

Hughes, A. M. (1994). *Strategic database marketing*. Chicago, IL: Probus Publishing.

Jain, D., & Singh, S. S. (2002). Customer lifetime value research in marketing: A review and future directions. *Journal of Interactive Marketing*, *16*(2), 34–46. doi:10.1002/dir.10032

Jonker, J. J., Piersma, N., & Van den Poel, D. (2004). Joint optimization of customer segmentation and marketing policy to maximize long-term profitability. *Expert Systems with Applications*, *27*(2), 159–168. doi:10.1016/j.eswa.2004.01.010

Kahan, R. (1998). Using database marketing techniques to enhance your one-to-one marketing initiatives. *Journal of Consumer Marketing*, *15*(5), 491–493. doi:10.1108/07363769810235965

Kahraman, C. (2008). *Fuzzy multi-criteria decision making: theory and applications with recent developments*. New York: Springer. doi:10.1007/978-0-387-76813-7

Kersuliene, V., & Turskis, Z. (2011). Integrated fuzzy multiple criteria decision making model for architect selection. *Technological and Economic Development of Economy*, *17*(4), 645–666. doi:10.3846/20294913.2011.635718

Kersuliene, V., Zavadskas, E. K., & Turskis, Z. (2010). Selection of Rational Dispute Resolution Method by Applying New Step-Wise Weight Assessment Ratio Analysis (SWARA). *Journal of Business Economics and Management*, *11*(2), 243–258. doi:10.3846/jbem.2010.12

Keskin, G. A. (2015). Using integrated fuzzy DEMATEL and fuzzy C: Means algorithm for supplier evaluation and selection. *International Journal of Production Research*, *53*(12), 3586–3602. doi:10.1080/00207543.2014.980461

Khajvand, M., & Tarokh, M. J. (2011). Estimating customer future value of different customer segments based on adapted RFM model in retail banking context. *Procedia Computer Science*, *3*, 1327–1332. doi:10.1016/j.procs.2011.01.011

Khajvand, M., Zolfaghar, K., Ashoori, S., & Alizadeh, S. (2011). Estimating customer lifetime value based on RFM analysis of customer purchase behavior: Case study. *Procedia Computer Science*, *3*, 57–63. doi:10.1016/j.procs.2010.12.011

Kumar, V., & Rajan, B. (2009). Profitable customer management: Measuring and maximizing customer lifetime value. *Management Accounting Quarterly*, *10*(3), 1.

Li, D. C., Dai, W. L., & Tseng, W. T. (2011). A two-stage clustering method to analyze customer characteristics to build discriminative customer management: A case of textile manufacturing business. *Expert Systems with Applications*, *38*(6), 7186–7191. doi:10.1016/j.eswa.2010.12.041

Liu, D. R., & Shih, Y. Y. (2005a). Hybrid approaches to product recommendation based on customer lifetime value and purchase preferences. *Journal of Systems and Software*, *77*(2), 181–191. doi:10.1016/j.jss.2004.08.031

Liu, D. R., & Shih, Y. Y. (2005b). Integrating AHP and data mining for product recommendation based on customer lifetime value. *Information & Management*, *42*(3), 387–400. doi:10.1016/j.im.2004.01.008

Marcus, C. (1998). A practical yet meaningful approach to customer segmentation. *Journal of Consumer Marketing*, *15*(5), 494–504. doi:10.1108/07363769810235974

McDonald, M., & Dunbar, I. (2004). *Market segmentation: How to do it, how to profit from it*. Butterworth-Heinemann.

McDonald, M., & Wilson, H. (2011). *Marketing plans: How to prepare them, how to use them*. John Wiley & Sons.

Miglautsch, J. R. (2000). Thoughts on RFM scoring. *The Journal of Database Marketing*, *8*(1), 67–72.

Newell, F. (1997). *The new rules of marketing: How to use one-to-one relationship marketing to be the leader in your industry*. New York: McGraw-Hills Companies Inc.

Pfeifer, P. E., & Carraway, R. L. (2000). Modeling Customer Relationships as Markov Chains. *Journal of Interactive Marketing*, *14*(2), 43–55. doi:10.1002/(SICI)1520-6653(200021)14:2<43::AID-DIR4>3.0.CO;2-H

Reinartz, W. J., & Kumar, V. (2003). The impact of customer relationship characteristics on profitable lifetime duration. *Journal of Marketing*, *67*(1), 77–99. doi:10.1509/jmkg.67.1.77.18589

Robinson, J. (1938). *The Economics of Imperfect Competition*. London: McMillan.

Rust, R. T., Lemon, K. N., & Zeithaml, V. A. (2004). Return on marketing: Using customer equity to focus marketing strategy. *Journal of Marketing*, *68*(1), 109–127. doi:10.1509/jmkg.68.1.109.24030

Saaty, T. L. (1977). A scaling method for priorities in hierarchical structures. *Journal of Mathematical Psychology*, *15*(3), 234–281. doi:10.1016/0022-2496(77)90033-5

Sahu, H. B., Mahapatra, S. S., & Panigrahi, D. C. (2012). Fuzzy C-means Clustering Approach for Classification of Indian Coal Seams with Respect to Their Spontaneous Combustion Susceptibility. *Fuel Processing Technology*, *104*, 115–120. doi:10.1016/j.fuproc.2012.03.017

Shih, Y. Y., & Liu, D. R. (2008). Product recommendation approaches: Collaborative filtering via customer lifetime value and customer demands. *Expert Systems with Applications*, *35*(1), 350–360. doi:10.1016/j.eswa.2007.07.055

Shin, H. W., & Sohn, S. Y. (2004). Segmentation of stock trading customers according to potential value. *Expert Systems with Applications*, *27*(1), 27–33. doi:10.1016/j.eswa.2003.12.002

Smith, W. R. (1956). Product differentiation and market segmentation as alternative marketing strategies. *Journal of Marketing*, *21*(1), 3–8. doi:10.2307/1247695

Stone, B. (1995). *Successful direct marketing methods*. Lincolnwood, IL: NTC Business Books.

Tafreshi, P. F., Aghdaie, M. H., Behzadian, M., & Abadi, M. G. (2016). Developing a Group Decision Support System for Advertising Media Evaluation:A Case in the Middle East. *Group Decision and Negotiation*, *25*(1), 1021–1048. doi:10.1007/s10726-015-9464-4

Tsai, C. Y., & Chiu, C. C. (2004). A purchase-based market segmentation methodology. *Expert Systems with Applications*, *27*(2), 265–276. doi:10.1016/j.eswa.2004.02.005

Tsiptsis, K. K., & Chorianopoulos, A. (2011). *Data mining techniques in CRM: inside customer segmentation*. John Wiley & Sons.

Ward, J. Jr. (1963). Hierachical Grouping to Optimize an Objective Function. *Journal of the American Statistical Association, 58*(301), 236–244. doi:10.1080/01621459.1963.10500845

Wei, J. T., Lee, M. C., Chen, H. K., & Wu, H. H. (2013). Customer relationship management in the hairdressing industry: An application of data mining techniques. *Expert Systems with Applications, 40*(18), 7513–7518. doi:10.1016/j.eswa.2013.07.053

Wei, J. T., Lin, S. Y., Weng, C. C., & Wu, H. H. (2012). A case study of applying LRFM model in market segmentation of a children's dental clinic. *Expert Systems with Applications, 39*(5), 5529–5533. doi:10.1016/j.eswa.2011.11.066

Weinstein, A. (1994). *Market segmentation: Using demographics, psychographics, and other niche marketing techniques to predict and model customer behavior*. Probus Publishing Company.

Yeh, I. C., Yang, K. J., & Ting, T. M. (2009). Knowledge discovery on RFM model using Bernoulli sequence. *Expert Systems with Applications, 36*(3), 5866–5871. doi:10.1016/j.eswa.2008.07.018

Zadeh, L. A. (1965). Fuzzy sets. *Information and Control, 8*(3), 338–353. doi:10.1016/S0019-9958(65)90241-X

Chapter 2
A Novel Approach to Segmentation Using Customer Locations Data and Intelligent Techniques

Başar Öztayşi
Istanbul Technical University, Turkey

Esra Nur Simsek
Blesh Incorporated, Turkey

Ugur Gokdere
Blesh Incorporated, Turkey

Ceren Salkin Oner
Istanbul Technical University, Turkey

ABSTRACT

Customer segmentation has been one of hottest topics of marketing efforts. The traditional sources of data used for segmentation are demographics, monetary value of transactions, types of product/service selected. Today, data gathered by location based services can also be used for customer segmentation. In this chapter a real world case study is summarized and the initial segmentation results are presented. As the application, data gathered from beacons sited in 4000 locations and Fuzzy c-means clustering algorithm are used. The steps of the application are as follows: (1) Categorization of the shops, (2) Summarization of the location data, (3) Applying fuzzy clustering technique, (4) Analyzing the results and profiling. Results show that customers' location data can provide a new perspective to customer segmentation.

INTRODUCTION

Customer segmentation could be explained as the process of distinguishing customers into diversified, meaningful, and homogeneous subgroups according to various properties. In marketing domain, it is basically utilized for understanding the customers and build differentiated strategies, services, and products customized to their characteristics. Wind and Bell (2007), state that effective marketing and business strategy necessitate a disintegration of the market into corresponding segments, a comprehension of the needs and desires of these segments, the design and implementation of products and services that

DOI: 10.4018/978-1-5225-0997-4.ch002

satisfy those needs and enhancement of marketing directions to effectively reach the target segments. Different segmentation types are appeared according to the segmentation criteria used but conventionally the organizations generally use demographics based segmentation and value based segmentation. In particular, customers can be divided into subgroups according to their sociodemographic and personal information, and their behavioral wishes and loyalty specialties (Tsiptsis & Chorianopoulos, 2009).

Cravens and Piercy (2012) investigate segmentation as operating at three decision-making levels. At the strategic level, strategic segmentation is used to associate the administrative vision and strategic plans and emphasize product yields according to diversified rangers of buyers. At the managerial level, segmentation is dealing with assigning resources with respect to segment targets, involving them in marketing provisions, and composing organizational processes considering them. And finally at the operational level, segmentation problems that are related with the marketing provisions are necessitated to have available segment goals with advertising and promotions, and evaluated with delivery systems.

As one of the basic field of marketing activities, customer segmentation has taken a great attention due to the fierce global competition and rapid changes in information and mobile technologies. Appropriately constructed customer segmentation ensures companies to capture individual customers' special requests and preferences which could enlarge customer faith and attraction and gain invaluable advantages related to competiveness in the market. At this point, data analysis for customer segmentation requires well-organized information system infrastructure for handling updated customer needs and enable superiority on providing these needs in a rapid way. In this regard, customer segmentation based on the preferences of customers in terms of grouping these customers considering similarities has become vital.

Tsiptsis and Chorianopoulos (2009) explain various usage fields of segmentation in marketing; one could be the better realization of customers that provide the specification of latest marketing opportunities. Secondly, the process of new product or services design, development and product ranges formed to each segment's properties instead of the mass market are the other inferences of segmentation. For this purpose, customized product design suggests strategies related to available customers with respect to each segment's identified wants and needs should be clearly understood. Offering tailored rewards and incentives is another aspect for the purpose of segmentation. Evaluating and choosing the proper advertising and communication message and channels and electing the appropriate sales and service channel could be the other aim for clustering customers. Note that designating the brand image and the critical product yields to be touched with the specific properties of each segment and fractionations in customer service considering each segment's significant are essential issues for selecting appropriate resource allocation according to the potential value gathered from each division. Finally, prioritization of the marketing interferences which intend customer dependence and improvement according to each segment's significance and value, is invaluable aspect for grouping customers.

In marketing domain, segmentation can be accomplished either by simple categorizations or by using analytical techniques. The main analytical tool used for segmentation is cluster analysis. Clustering analysis is a data mining technique that correlates data elements to mystery groups with considering high similarity (Han et al. 2011). The clustering techniques in the literature can be grouped as partitional or hierarchical algorithms. The partitional clustering is distinguishing of the data elements to non-conflicting groups which implies that each item pertains to definitely one cluster. Partitional methods involve the determination of clusters' number primarily. On the other hand, partitional methods take the advantage of enabling the optimization of a criterion considering the compatibilities of objects within clusters or incompatibilities between clusters. In addition to that, hierarchical algorithms can be grouped as agglomerative or divisive. The agglomerative hierarchical clustering initiates with the clusters obtaining single elements and then aggregates them until all elements are taken in identical cluster. Each iteration, two indistinguishable clusters are aggregated and after that, divisive hierarchical clustering initiates with one cluster and repetitively divided clusters into minor clusters. Additionally, both agglomerative and divisive hierarchical algorithms generate a nested alignment of clusters as a unique all-inclusive cluster at the top, and single-element clusters at the bottom. The final structure of the sequenced clusters provides a simple representation of the considerable number of clusters via dendrogram which could be expressed the form of a graphical representation of the explained variance at related clustering level On the other hand, hierarchical methods do not ensure the assignment of correct groups of objects that may have been "erroneously" classified or divided in an early stage (Migueis et al. 2012). Another classification can be done according to the formation of clusters; the clusters can be fuzzy or crisp. In crisp clustering, the data is divided into a pre-determined number of mutually exclusive subsets which implies the singular elements either does or does not pertain to a cluster. However, in fuzzy clustering, the objects can pertain to various clusters concurrently, with respect to considering particular degrees of membership. In this study, fuzzy c-means algorithm, which is a fuzzy partitional algorithm, is applied in order to better represent the customer behaviors.

In real world organizations, clustering analysis is done using customer information which is stating in the companies' data marts and data warehouse. For some additional segmentation studies, a market survey is necessary to save up the essential segmentation information, such as needs/attitudes, loyalty information, since the concerning properties are unachievable or outdated in the company's information and data processing systems. The aim of this chapter a novel criterion is used for segmentation and initial results are presented. With the emergence of new technologies location based services have become popular. Beacons are one of the key technologies used for indoor positioning, in this study the data used for the segmentation is collected from a beacon network company, Blesh.com in Turkey. The signals from more than 200,000 users have been collected from the network for more than four months. The location signals are then preprocessed in order to prepare the data for segmentation process. Best to our knowledge customers' physical location data has not been used for segmentation purposes and the results show that there is a huge potential for using location data for segmentation purposes.

The rest of the paper is organized as follows: a literature review of location based systems are presented in background part. After that, location based segmentation application is explained in with respect to business need and methodology step by step. Additionally, results are interpreted for the extraction of valuable solutions. Finally, conclusions and future research directions are provided.

BACKGROUND

'Mobility is a fundamental and irreplaceable human movement that ensures to be capable to support independent lives with a daily tempo' (Kayama et al. 2003). In business aspect, the action of location based monitoring and recommendation that could be precisely explained as the consideration of location data to support people or systems to determine progression towards expected outcomes with respect to mobile devices. A characteristic motivation of location-based monitoring, segmentation and recommendation would be able to take into account for the effective utilization of sources in order to cope with delivery results and fast turnings by detecting location (Michael & Michael, 2011). Since the rapid growth and new regulations in trade, companies are forced to make changes in their business stages for facilitating their marketing activities. This provides many advantages for coping with the relentless competition in terms of fast reactions and attractive sales activities. Gathering customer comments and reflections that the essential clue of customer disposition with traditional methods requires huge amount of data that means a vast of time, money and manpower in the process of making strategic offerings. Thus, right segmentation of users is invaluable tools for making special offerings to the customers (Suh et al., 2004).

As the consequence of mobile technologies having been widely used and improved, mobile-wireless technologies are getting popular day by day (Kuo et al., 2009). Therefore, location based applications via mobile devices have been progressively utilized in order to make suitable and special offerings according to the customers' location data which was extracted from wireless indoor positioning systems in which one could easily detect the position of an item or person utilizing Wi-Fi and Bluetooth infrastructure based on GPS-like signals (Liu, 2007). As a result of increasing demand on mobile technologies on smartphones, the automatic object location based applications have been used widespread that ease traceability of individuals' physical moving and purchasing tendency of the customers in different indoor shopping fields. For this reason, especially personal positioning techniques and algorithms acquire a critical role on detecting individuals' positions and locations in shopping mall which enable making practical analysis for the determination of group of customers, indoor shopping tendencies etc. In other words, location-aware systems that satisfies customer's shopping requests with location based suggestions and promotions, play an important role for coping with competition. In addition to that, great attention on location based systems appeared in academic journals and books as seen from Figure 1.

Basically, indoor positioning systems are one of the location based systems that could be operated in closed areas. There are mainly some indoor positioning system technologies such as Wi-Fi based Positioning Systems (WPS), Radio Frequency Identification (RFID) and Bluetooth Technology. First of all, Wi-Fi technology is widely applied in closed area in daily life. Nearly all of the houses, offices, schools, shopping centers –all of the buildings could be adopted to this technology. Cell ID, reference nodes and RSSI could be mentioned as Wi-Fi technologies. RFID is another indoor positioning technology that reader receives signals from the active or passive tags by using antenna and results are then transferred to the computer (EPC RFID, 2013). Finally, Bluetooth technology which switched on its location that precised up to 5 m to the beacon in closed areas enables electronic devices to communicate with each other by using radio waves (Thompson, 2013). On the other hand, RFID based technologies integration are not suitable due to the compatibility issues appeared in some of the mobile phones and inadequate

Figure 1. Number of publications related to location based systems from 2006 to 2015

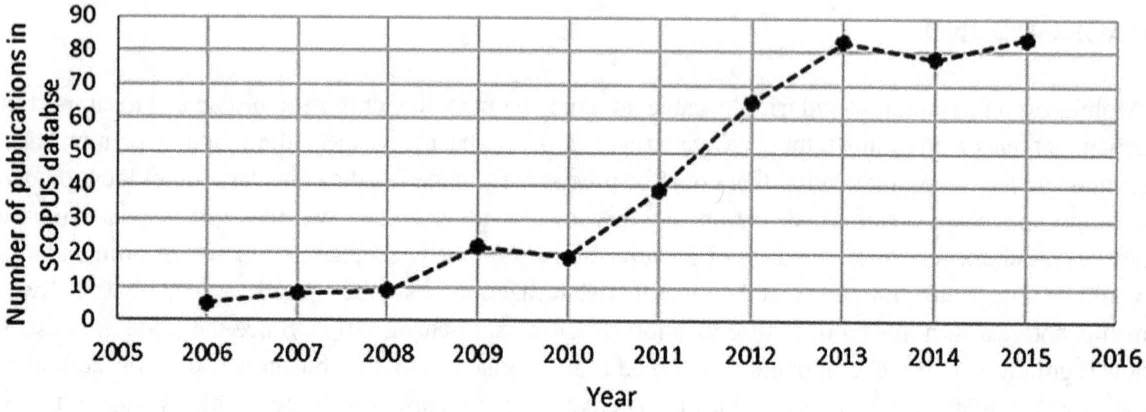

gravitational field. Additionally, all cases that are actualized by RFID technologies are also implemented with Bluetooth Smart technology is the other aspect for the developments and applications of Beacons.

Another critical aspect is the selection of appropriate position prediction. The prediction of the user or mobile station position is conducted with some techniques. These techniques can be gathered under three topics: (1) Closest Access Point, (2) Distance/Angle Measurement, (3) Fingerprinting. Closest Access Point is based on the idea of the determination of the mobile station's location according to the nearest access point. Sometimes access point might be far away from the mobile station and that decreases the accuracy of the prediction system. Besides that, the main approach under Distance/Angle Measurement technique is the measurement of time difference of arrival and departure with respect to the angles of the multiple signals. Additionally, fingerprinting techniques are the most complicated and most accurate indoor positioning technique that data mining approaches are used in the calculation processes. In this technique, RSS database in which measurements at several locations are collected and this database formation phase is called as off-line phase. In online phase, received signal is evaluated to predict the position of the mobile station. This evaluation process uses data mining techniques such as k-nearest neighbor, artificial neural networks, fuzzy logic, Bayesian classification methods (Yim, 2008).

Since Bluetooth 4.0 standards are introduced in 2013, Beacon based technologies and projects are used especially for making recommendations in retailer side. The main idea of using Beacons is the determination of users' location and grouping the users with respect to location similarity, demographic properties and habits etc. (URL1). Other applications with the same idea could be realized in tourism sector such as offering work of arts in museums (Louvre Museum in France, Bristol Museum in UK, Philips Museum in Nederland and Brooklyn Museum in USA), making suggestions related with attractive activities to tourists (Ghent, Belgium case) etc. (URL2). Different from these areas, location based systems are also applied in music, movie, e- learning tools, news, website and entertainment offerings in order to satisfy customer needs and draw interest of potential customers to the services (Narayanan & Cherukuri, 2016). In recent years, user segmentation is also adopted with the utilization of social network activities and profiles by gathering essential information which was declared by the users as seen from Tussyadiah (2012) and Liu et al. (2014)'s study. In addition to that, motion analysis is included in order to the investigation of users' movements and indirectly, users' routine (Millonig & Gartner, 2011). According to the critical points mentioned above, recent academic studies are classified in terms of location based systems both in different fields in order to capture important points for future improvements that could be applied in indoor location based systems. Most recent studies could be seen in the following table. Papers are grouped according to the problem domain and additionally, methodology and specific points of the studies are given for understanding the originality of the research paper. As seen from the table, one could easily observe the location based applications especially in advertising and shopping using social networks and relations. The main trend turns to make specific suggestions to the users considering location situation, consumer characteristics, and social network structure as mentioned in previous paragraph. Concordantly to this situation, location based applications in academic case studies are mostly practiced in advertising, e-commerce and e-business cases in order to understand users' behavior from visiting to buying actions.

Most of the location based applications are constructed on database management and information retrieval, artificial intelligence and information systems and applications. Furthermore, marketing, social network analysis and technology management areas are other critical areas for improving location based systems.

Table 1. Comparisons of related works selected from literature

Problem Domain	Author(s)	Study	Methodology	Specific Point of the Study
Shopping with social networks	Tussyadiah (2012)	A Concept of Location-Based Social Network Marketing	Stimulus-response model	Integrated approach based on location, consumption issues with consumer properties and social network links
Group buying	Li and Li (2014)	A social recommender mechanism for location-based group commerce	Social network analysis	Considering user preference, geographic convenience, and friends' influence, a group-coupon recommender system is proposed for promoting location-sensitive products
Mobile applications for shopping	Yang et al. (2008)	A location-aware recommender system for mobile shopping environments	Information retrieval	A recommender system for vendors' webpages – include suggestions and promotions
Motion analyze for determining shopping behavior	Millonig & Gartner (2011)	Identifying motion and interest patterns of shoppers for developing personalized way finding tools	Clustering	Shoppers' stopping behavior, subgroups of visited facilities and personal priorities are analyzed for customized navigational and environmental information
Advertising	Dao et al. (2012)	A novel recommendation model of location-based advertising: Context-Aware Collaborative Filtering using GA approach	Genetic algorithm, collaborative filtering	Context aware recommendation system based on GA and collaborative filtering of mobile device data.
	Mahmoud and Yu (2006)	Havana agents for comparison shopping and location-aware advertising in wireless mobile environments	Agent based modeling	Mobile agent platform for benchmarking of shopping activities in a wireless environment
	Li and Du (2012)	Building a targeted mobile advertising system for location-based services	Intelligent searching	A platform to support both commercialists and consumers with context-aware advertisements
Marketing	Tang et al. (2013)	A prediction framework based on contextual data to support Mobile Personalized Marketing	Multi-dimensional and sequential rule	Correlation between user preferences and mobility of the users

As realized from the literature, the most significant aim for location based systems is building up the essential infrastructure for making proper recommendations at the right time in the right location. For this purpose, user profile should be specified accurately and this profile should be matched with the appropriate choice in advance. In order to make correct suggestions, a great variety of methodologies are developed. For instance, over the last twenty years, researchers have investigated user segmentation in recommender systems in terms of two basic methodologies: content based filtering which implies grouping related to similar items for offering new items in accordance with past preferences and collaborative filtering which infers finding the most convenient option depending on users' preferences in order to predict new users' preferences (Zhang et al., 2007). In addition to that, applying data mining techniques to location based systems was the most popular approach while determining user preferences and similarities such as, heuristic methods, regression, neural network, kNN, link analysis, decision tree, clustering, association rule mining (Park et al., 2012).

Specifically, as Park et al. (2012) mentioned in their research paper, collaborative filtering which utilizes historical data has two important issues in practice: data sparsity, cold start issues and scalability problems. Besides that, content based filtering which utilizes user rates for identifying user preferences causes overspecialized recommendations that provoke similar-neighborhood recommendations. On the other hand, the most emphasized point in literature is the cold start problem and data sparsity which reduces segmentation and recommendation accuracy. In order to solve these problems, hybrid models are preferred with the assistance of cloud computing and machine learning algorithms in order to inhibit negative aspects. In addition to that, runtime of the qualitative and quantitative techniques is playing a key role for establishing proposed location based systems.

LOCATION BASED SEGMENTATION APPLICATION

Context and Business Need

The iBeacon devices (hereafter Beacons) broadcast low energy radio signals, interact with the smart devices in their coverage zone, and exchange information with them. The coverage zone of a Beacon device is 50 meters, and their interaction distance can be fine-tuned within this range. This interaction, which is extremely power-efficient, is based on Bluetooth's innovative network technology Bluetooth Low Energy (BLE), or the trademarked name, Bluetooth® Smart. When a mobile device encounters an Beacon device in a venue, the mobile device automatically refers to a software program (SDK) embedded into an application. Consequently, it consults to the Beacon's server. According to the command from the server, the mobile device performs any action, such as displaying a message or serving as a micro-location sensor.

The beacon device, the embedded SDK in the application, and the server, together consist the sensor-management platform of Blesh that realizes the Beacon communication. Blesh offers enterprises the whole platform along with the assisting service to manage, focusing on refining the opportunities that come along with this platform, and how this new communication method can produce business solutions. As Blesh beacon, mobile application and enterprise network grows, the beacon management platform turns gradually into an advertising platform for marketing agencies to get involved in. Exceeding 12.000 beacons in over 50 cities in Turkey, amounting to roughly 4.000 points of interest, Blesh beacons are placed in more than 100 shopping malls, prominent airports, leading banks, top retail shops, subway stations, cafés and restaurants and among many other venues.

As mobile advertising projects grew in number, an increasing demand followed from interested parties, in order to use this new channel to get in touch with customers. While these communications took place, the requirement for classification and segmentation of customers similar to other conventional channels, presented itself. A study conducted by Network Advertising Initiative (NAI) with more than 10 advertising networks, proves that conversion rates for the targeted ads are %142 higher compared to the non-targeted ones. (Beales, 2010). This study confirms the value of behavioral targeted advertising to advertisers, publishers and customers. The expectancy of higher sensitivity, better precision and conversion quickly followed (URL-3).

In order to enable a more accurate customer targeting for mobile advertising platform, developments were initiated to meet this requirement. The focus on relevancy and behavioral targeting in other media, bore the need for even higher sensitivity in mobile advertising, considering the platform in use was the screens of personal phones subject to an increasing attention to maintaining privacy. The raw data gathered by beacon sensors meant locations visited by smart phone owners. Although the data was anonymous, the ability to distinguish unique users meant a possible thread was available for segmentation. Tagging the beacon devices as shopping malls, differing types of restaurants, cafes, banks, airports, etc. and taking the frequency of customers visiting these tagged locations in consideration, a location type-based classification could be possible.

A thorough analysis was conducted for the available locations. The category for each point was determined and they were tagged accordingly. The location visit data for approximately 290.000 customers was cross-referenced with the already tagged locations. A separation of passer-by customers from the ones who actually spent time at the locations supported the segmentation process. Filtering passer-by customers out varied based on the characteristics of the location. For example, a visit span of 30 minutes was required for shopping malls, in comparison to a 15 minute period which was deemed sufficient for cafes. Another layer of filtering was determined to be necessary, in order to render the processed data as statistically meaningful as possible: the frequent activity. The segmentation studies were narrowed down to frequently active users, in such a way that new-comers were left out of analyses until they contributed to a certain amount of input and were qualified to be included.

In the following subsections, first fuzzy clustering method is introduced, then application steps are explained and results are presented.

Fuzzy C-Means Clustering

Clustering is defined as the process of dividing a set of observations into subgroups which are entitled clusters. Various techniques can be used for clustering and the aim of these techniques is to organize input data so as to make similar objects in a cluster, and dissimilar objects in different clusters (Han et al. 2011). Clustering techniques are based on similarity term which is calculated by mathematical distance (Babuska, 2009). Clustering is an unsupervised learning technique, in other words there are no predefined groups and a single correct solution. Instead, cluster validity term is generally used for quantitative evaluation of the results of a clustering algorithm (Theodoridis & Koutroumbas,2008).

The literature provides various algorithms for clustering and these algorithms categorized according to the formation of clusters. In this perspective, the clusters can be formed using fuzzy data or crisp data (Oztaysi & Cevik Onar, 2014). Crisp clustering is based on classical sets theory and as a result of the process the input data is grouped into mutually exclusive subsets. The reader may recall that in classical set theory an element is either in a set or out of a set. Based on this fact, in crisp clustering algorithms each input data belongs to one of the clusters. In the second group, fuzzy clustering algorithms, fuzzy sets theory is used and in this approach an element can take place in several clusters simultaneously with different degrees of membership. This membership degree ranges between 0 and 1 and the result of fuzzy clustering provides membership degrees of each input data to all clusters which is more natural when compared to crisp clustering (Oztaysi & Isik, 2014). For a better understanding of the difference, an example can be given about the objects near to the boundaries of a cluster. In this case crisp clustering does not provide any information that can be used to differentiate these objects. If the objects are in the cluster then they get the membership value of 1. However in fuzzy clustering the objects get different membership values and one can differentiate the objects with higher membership values form others.

In clustering problem the input is a set of observations or objects each of which consists of different attributes.

The data used in cluster analysis are gathered from observations each of which consists of n measured variables. Each individual observation (O_k) forms an n-dimensional column vector $O_k = [o_{1k},..., o_{nk}]^T$, and the dataset that consists of N observations is represented as an n x n matrix. Fuzzy clustering aims to partition the data set O into a specific number of clusters "c" which is defined before the based on prior knowledge,

$$O = \begin{bmatrix} o_{11} & o_{12} & \cdots & o_{1N} \\ o_{21} & o_{22} & \cdots & o_{2N} \\ \vdots & \vdots & \vdots & \vdots \\ o_{n1} & o_{n2} & \cdots & o_{nN} \end{bmatrix} \tag{1}$$

The result of cluster analysis produces the clusters and membership of each data point to these clusters. These outputs are represented by the partition matrix R. In this matrix, each element r_{ij} shows the degree to which element o_j belongs to cluster cls_i. The difference between fuzzy and crisp clustering methods can be easily seen from this resulting matrix. While the membership function r_{ij} gets the value 0 or 1 in crisp methods, fuzzy clustering methods produce any real value in [0, 1] as membership function.

$$R = \begin{bmatrix} r_{11} & r & \cdots & r_{1N} \\ r_{21} & r_{22} & \cdots & r_{2N} \\ \vdots & \vdots & \vdots & \vdots \\ r_{c1} & r_{c2} & \cdots & r_{cN} \end{bmatrix} \tag{2}$$

Ruspini (1970) defines the conditions for a fuzzy partition matrix as follows:

$$\mu_{ik} \in [0,1], 1 \le i \le c, 1 \le k \le N \tag{3a}$$

$$\sum_{i=1}^{c} \mu_{ik} = 1, 1 \le k \le N \tag{3b}$$

$$0 < \sum_{k=1}^{N} \mu_{ik} < N, 1 \le i \le c \tag{3c}$$

Equation (3b) constrains the sum of each column to 1, and thus the total membership of each o_k in *O* equals one.

One of the most popular fuzzy clustering methods is fuzzy c-means (FCM) which is based on minimization of the following objective function:

$$J(Z,U,V) = \sum_{i=1}^{c} \sum_{j=1}^{N} (\mu_{ij})^m \left\| z_j - v_i \right\|^2 \tag{4}$$

where Z is the data set to be partitioned, U is the fuzzy partition matrix, V is the vector of cluster centers. In the formula, N represents the number of observations, c is the number of clusters and μ shows the membership value, m is the parameter called fuzzifier which determines the fuzziness of the resulting clusters. The fuzzifier parameter can get values 1 and more. When the fuzzifier parameter equals to one, then the clusters are formed in crisp format. In the formula, $z_k - v_i$ shows the distance between observation k and the center of cluster i.

The minimization of the mention objective function represents a nonlinear optimization problem that can be solved by using a variety of methods such as iterative minimization, simulated annealing or genetic algorithms. Babuska (2009) gives the steps of fuzzy c-means (FCM) algorithm as follows:

1. Initialize $U=[u_{ij}]$ matrix, $U^{(0)}$
2. At *k*-step: calculate the centers vectors $V^{(k)}=[v_i]$ with $U^{(k)}$

$$v_i = \frac{\sum_{i=1}^{N} \mu_{ij}^m \cdot z_j}{\sum_{i=1}^{N} \mu_{ij}^m}$$

3. Update $U^{(k)}$, $U^{(k+1)}$

$$\mu_{ij} = \frac{1}{\sum_{k=1}^{c} \left(\frac{\left\| z_j - v_i \right\|}{\left\| z_j - v_k \right\|} \right)^{\frac{2}{m-1}}}$$

If $\left\| U^{(k+1)} - U^{(k)} \right\| < \delta$ then STOP; otherwise return to step 2.

In order to get beneficial results, the analyzer should set some parameters before the analysis. When clustering, the analyzer has to set some important parameters for getting beneficial results from the analysis. The most important parameters that must be set are; number of clusters, fuzzifier and termination criteria.

The number of clusters is represented with the character "c" and is the parameter that influences the clustering results most. Before the clustering study, if the analyzer does not have any priori information about the structure of the data, (s)he has to make assumptions about how many clusters can exist within the data. The FCM algorithm then searches for chosen number of clusters. It is expected that when the number of clusters parameter is equal to the number of groups that actually exist in the data, the FCM will identify them correctly. But if this is not the case, misclassifications appear, and the clusters are not correctly separated. Put in another way, the algorithm finds the expected number of clusters regardless of whether they are really thus the validity of the results has to be checked. In the literature, validity measures are proposed to assess the goodness of the obtained partition (Bezdek, 1981; Gath & Geva, 1989; Pal & Bezdek, 1995).

In the literature, there are some validity measures that help analyzers to identify the right c value. One of them is the Xie-Beni index (Xie & Beni, 1991) has been found to perform well in practice (Han et al. 2011).

$$X\left(Z;U,V\right)=\frac{\sum_{i=1}^{c}\sum_{j=1}^{N}(\mu_{ij})^{m}\left\|z_{j}-v_{i}\right\|^{2}}{c\cdot\min_{i\neq j}\left\|v_{i}-v_{j}\right\|^{2}} \tag{5}$$

This index shows the ratio of the total within-group variance and the separation of the cluster centers. For different number of cluster, the best is the one that minimizes the Xie-Beni index.

Fuzziness parameter, fuzzifier, is the weighting exponent m at the objective function. As m approaches one from above, the partition becomes crisp and the membership values get values 0 or 1. As m gets higher values, the partition becomes completely fuzzy and the membership values goes to the limit 1/c. These limit properties of are independent of the optimization method used in (Pal and Bezdek, 1995). Generally, the value of the fuzzifier is set to two initially.

The FCM algorithm does not stop unless the difference between "U" in two consequent iterations is smaller than the termination parameter. The general choice for the criterion is 0.001, however the value 0.01 works well in most cases, while drastically reducing the computing times.

Steps of the Application

The real world application is done using data collected from a Beacon Network established by Blesh, a company working on beacons and sensor technologies. The basic data that can be collected from such an infrastructure contains a user stamp, time stamp, and beacon signal stamp. The beacon signal is associated with a specific location, such as a cinema, shopping mall or a shop it can be used to represent the specific location.

The application can be analyzed in four steps:

1. **Categorization of the Locations:** There are 12000 beacons which have been located in over 4000 locations. In order to maintain a sound customer behavior, the locations are first categorized. The categorization is done based on the value proposition of the business that is run on that location. As a result, 23 categories are identified which are: shopping malls, clothing, café, women, bank, restaurant, home decoration, airport, shoes & bags, accessories, super market, men, youngster, street shop, wagering, technology, cinema, metro, sweetshop, bake house, fast food, university, hotel.
2. **Summarization of the Location Data:** When a mobile device and a Beacon device interact, a transaction data is generated and stored in a database. Since Beacon devices periodically send signals, transaction data can be also generated periodically. In order to summarize this transaction data, different approaches can be used. In this study, we call a *session* if there is at least 30 minutes between signals. So if there are ten transaction data with-in the same 30 minutes, it is handled as the same session. Using this approach, the total sessions in a location type (listed in the first step)

are counted and monthly average values are used. A summarized version of the matrix determined is given in Figure 2. In this matrix, the first column shows the user identifiers and other columns represent the monthly average sessions in related location type. For example, the first row in Figure 2 shows that the user, id =1336803, has a monthly average of 4 sessions in cafes, 6.6 sessions in clothing shops and zero sessions in banks, women, and restaurant locations.

3. **Applying Fuzzy Clustering Technique:** As mentioned in the earlier sections in the application phase, fuzzy clustering approach is used, which gives membership degree of each customer to all segments. By this way, users who are close more than one cluster can be determined, in other words, a customer can take place in more than one segment. Fuzzy clustering is applied using the R 3.2.1 version and e1071 package. In order to determine the number clusters, Xie-Beni index is used. The algorithm is run with different values for c parameter. The results of these runs are given in Table 2.
4. **Analyzing the Results and Profiling:** In order to understand the formed groups, the best way is to analyze the centroid table. Centroid table shows the typical characteristic of each cluster by calculating the cluster centers. Table 3 shows the resulting centroid table for the study when c is equal to eight.

The centroid table shows that Cluster 6 is the most active cluster when compared with others. For nearly every location Cluster 6 has the highest values. Cluster 5 has the highest values for home decoration shops, Cluster 1 has the highest value in Airport locations, Cluster 8, on the other hand, has nearly the second highest values for each locations. Cluster 2 is shows the lowest values nearly in all location types.

Results

The most important result from this study is to identify the characteristics of the segments. Based on the centroid table given in Table 3, the segments are entitled as listed in Table 4. The customers in cluster one are using airports dramatically higher than the remaining customers. These customers also use banks and cafes frequently. In order to represent this characteristic this group is entitle *Professional Flyers.*

Figure 2. Preprocessed data used in the study

SUBSCR	s. mall	clothng	cafe	woman	bank	restrnt
1336803	7.8	6.6	4	0	0	0
1353917	10.25	21	31.38	0	0	0
1674348	0	0	2	0	0	0
2021074	91.75	94.25	19.25	1.25	0	0
2172158	21.21	1.55	3.29	1.45	0	0.13
2177753	8	0	8	0	0	0
2180314	0	0	0	0	0	0
2186217	23.91	4.09	2	3	0	0
2191085	2.75	0.25	1	0	0	1
2193228	5.33	3.89	2.44	0	0	0.22
2196099	23.75	0	0.25	0	0	0.5

Table 2. Xie-Beni index values for different values of c parameter

C	Xie - Beni
2	1.63×10^{-06}
3	1.13×10^{-06}
4	1.09×10^{-05}
5	4.45×10^{-05}
6	3.29×10^{-05}
7	2.68×10^{-06}
8	9.28×10^{-07}
9	10.2×10^{-05}
10	4.92×10^{-05}
11	9.31×10^{-05}
12	6.89×10^{-05}
13	6.51×10^{-05}

The lower values of Xie-Beni index refers to better clustering results, thus for this study c value is selected as eight, which means in the study eight clusters are formed.

Table 3. Centroid table of fuzzy c-means algorithm (c=8)

Locations	Clstr1	Clstr2	Clstr3	Clstr4	Clstr5	Clstr6	Clstr7	Clstr8
Shopping malls	21.22	2.19	67.23	9.75	40.13	916.42	11.63	304.22
Clothing	2.43	0.1	10.5	1.04	4.2	244.1	1.4	68.6
Café	29.19	1.92	15.01	6.63	38.8	83.56	11.01	27.2
Women	0.57	0.03	2.87	0.28	1	66.76	0.35	19
Bank	30.63	1.27	5.54	5	53.26	61.08	11.51	16.53
Restaurant	4.42	0.57	6.77	2.37	7.9	40.09	2.48	16.16
Home decoration	12.97	0.55	9.01	6.4	845.13	35.48	7.22	14.49
Airport	882.1	0.86	6.39	64.33	18.93	20.06	289.17	11.68
Shoes & bags	2.69	0.14	1.7	0.47	4.77	35.71	1.01	9.25
Accessories	0.23	0.01	0.99	0.1	0.39	20.27	0.12	5.92
Supermarket	3.67	0.7	6.39	4.7	7.7	9.64	3.04	5.87
Men	0.35	0.01	0.83	0.1	0.6	21.22	0.16	5.58
Youngster	1.67	0.14	1.21	0.53	2.84	11.54	0.69	3.04
Street shop	4.58	0.37	1.21	1.02	7.84	9.78	1.94	2.91
Wagering	4.04	0.39	1.25	0.93	7.02	10.13	1.71	2.77
Technology	2.48	0.11	1.13	0.69	4.11	8.86	1.13	2.7
Cinema	0.12	0.03	0.48	0.08	0.24	6.83	0.09	2.11
Metro	2.22	0.16	0.75	0.53	3.46	4.88	0.95	1.63
Sweetshop	0.5	0.13	0.98	0.31	1.6	3.12	0.29	1.36
Bake house	0.44	0.18	1.04	0.33	0.72	1.72	0.24	1.21
Fast food	1.58	0.14	0.92	0.5	2.67	4.36	0.65	1.21
University	0.66	0.04	0.28	0.17	1.24	2.13	0.27	0.57
Hotel	0.32	0.02	0.15	0.12	0.61	0.64	0.15	0.24

Table 4. Segment titles

Cluster No.	Titles
1	Professional Flyers
2	Low Socials
3	Shopping Women
4	Passive Flyers
5	Hedonics
6	Active Ones
7	Frequent Flyers
8	Shoppers

Second cluster has the lowest visibility in all kinds of locations, thus they are entitled *Low Socials*. The customers in this segment have mostly been detected in shopping malls, cafes and banks and the locations that they rarely use are hotels, men and women shops.

The third cluster is entitled as *Shopping Women* since they spend post of their time in shopping malls, clothing related shops and women shops. Their visibility in bake houses and super markets is also above average. The customers in this group rarely go to cinemas, universities and hotels.

The characteristic that differs cluster four from other clusters is their high visibility in airports. But since cluster one and cluster seven have higher values, this segment entitled *Passive Flyers*. The customer in this segment also has high visibility in shopping malls and cafes. Cinemas, accessories and men shops are the locations that this segment rarely visits.

The most important property of cluster five is in most of the locations they have the above average visibility. But especially they have the highest visibility in home decoration shops. Banks, cafes and shops are the other locations that this segment frequently goes. The customers in this segment rarely go to cinemas and accessory shops.

Cluster six is entitled *Active Ones* and the customers in this segment have the highest visibility nearly in all segments. Only in airports and home decoration locations they do not have the highest values.

The customers in cluster seven have a very high visibility in airports the other locations they are detected are shopping malls, cafes and banks. Accessories, men and women shops are the locations that this segment shows minimal visibility.

Cluster eight is entitled "Shoppers" since they show a very high visibility in shopping malls. Another important characteristic of the segment is that the show above average visibility in most of the location types.

SOLUTIONS AND RECOMMENDATIONS

The emerging technologies enable new business processes and new business models. One of the technologies is called Beacon technology, which is based on communication and used for indoor positioning systems. The technology is based on Bluetooth Low Energy, which is a wireless network technology used for transmitting data over short distances. As the name indicates, the devices are designed for low energy consumption and cost, while maintaining a communication range.

Beacons can be used for detecting users' location in an indoor location such as a shopping mall, a retail store etc. To detect users' location, various services can be maintained such as an advertisement or navigation to a specific location. In this chapter, a novel use of this data is proposed and initial result from a real world case study is given. To this end data from a beacon network is collected, preprocessed and clustered.

The initial results show that there are eight customer segments in the considered customer base. Results indicate that such a location data from various locations has the potential to show customers' life style and interests. In traditional marketing segmentation, segmentation is generally based on demographics or customer value. Surveys are rarely used to identify customers' needs and lifestyle but the proposed segmentation approach is more accurate since it is based on real location data. As a result, market segmentation based on customer location data propose a high potential for segmentation and get insight about each individual customer.

FUTURE RESEARCH DIRECTIONS

Customer segmentation based on location data, which is presented in this chapter, can lead to various future research. First of all, the different preprocessing activities can be employed when the transaction data is prepared for the study. In this study, occurrence of a customer in a location is used as the main data unit, in further studies the duration that a customer spends in a location can be calculated and used as the main data unit. This may change the clustering results because in the current study, we do not distinguish a person that just stopped by a location for a while with another person who stayed at the same location for an hour. In this study, the locations are classified based on the service they provide, another perspective can be about classifying them based on their target customer class such as economy, business and luxury. Tough it can be hard to determine base classes; the results can be very beneficial since such a study can enable us to segment customers from a different perspective. Further research can be done by using other clustering methods and the results can be compared with the results of this study.

The results show that there are strong differences between the number of customers in clusters. In order to overcome this, a hierarchical clustering approach can be applied. For example, in the first level segmentation is done using the total signal levels (without location detail) and define main segments such as highly, moderate and low active customers, and then use location details to make micro segmentations.

For further studies, a research direction can be defined as repeating similar studies periodically and observing customers' segment change within time. Doing such research can also lead to observe seasonality in customer behaviors.

Integrating the current location data with campaign management can also be a novel marketing research. By doing so, the effects of campaigns on customers can be observed from two different perspectives. In campaign management, conversion rate is a success indicator and it is calculated by closed sales or read messages. Using location based data, bringing customer to a physical store can also be used as a conversion rate parameter. In the second perspective, location data can be used as a trigger to special offers or campaigns. When a person is observed in a specific location than a campaign message can directly be sent to him/her.

A final research direction can focus on analyzing the location data with customers' buying behavior. This analysis can provide companies new insights about their customers in which products/services they are interested in and which ones they are buying. The results of this analysis have the potential of showing which potential products/services can be sold to the customers.

CONCLUSION

In this study, a novel segmentation approach which is based on location-based services is presented. The data used for the application is collected from a beacon network company, Blesh. The signals from more than 200,000 users have been collected from the network for more than four months. The location signals are then preprocessed in order to prepare the data for segmentation process.

Fuzzy c-means algorithm is used for clustering the customers. Different parameters are tested and the best clustering is determined when c= 8 according to Xie – Beni Index. The results show that one of the clusters, which is entitled as *Active Youngster* have the highest activities in nearly all location types. On the opposite side, Cluster 2, *Low Socials* have appeared as the group of customers who shows lowest amount of signals from all location types. The main reason for this result can be about the acceptance level of the technology. Since the technology is relatively new, users who are relatively innovative and young prefer to use it. As the technology matures, different groups may occur and change this structure.

Since the traditional segmentation methods depend on demographics, lifetime status or buying behavior of the customer, the proposed approach form a totally new dimension to segmentation. Capturing location data from a Beacon network and using this for segmentation gives insight about customers' preferences and interests which can directly be used for further marketing purposes. The results of this study can be used for campaign management, customer targeting, and product/service recommendation. Further analysis can be done if the location data can be integrated with customers' spending behaviors.

ACKNOWLEDGMENT

This work is supported by Scientific and Technological Research Council of Turkey (TÜBİTAK), TEYDEB 1507, Grant No: 7141304.

REFERENCES

Babuska, R. (2009). *Fuzzy And Neural Control Disc Course Lecture Notes*. Retrieved 5 October 2012 from http://www.dcsc.tudelft.nl/~disc_fnc/transp/fncontrol.pdf

Beales, H. (2010). *The Value of Behavioral Targeting*. Retrieved from www.networkadvertising.org/pdfs/Beales_NAI_Study.pdf

Behavioral Ads Offer a Windfall for Marketers, Publishers. (n.d.). Retrieved from http://www.forbes.com/2010/03/24/behavioral-targeted-ads-advertising-ftc-privacy-cmo-network-ads.html

Bezdek, J. C. (1981). *Pattern Recognition with Fuzzy Objective Function Algorithms*. Plenum press. doi:10.1007/978-1-4757-0450-1

Cravens, W. D., & Piercy, N. F. (2012). *Strategic Marketing*. McGraw-Hill Higher Education.

Dao, T. H., Jeong, S. R., & Ahn, H. (2012). A novel recommendation model of location-based advertising: Context-Aware Collaborative Filtering using GA approach. *Expert Systems with Applications*, *39*(3), 3731–3739. doi:10.1016/j.eswa.2011.09.070

Data Mining in Dynamic Social Networks and Fuzzy Systems. (2014). User Segmentation Based on Twitter Data Using Fuzzy Clustering: the Case of Sports News. IGI Global.

EPC RFID. (2013). *What is RFID?* Retrieved March 24, 2015, from http://www.epc-rfid.info/rfid

Gath, I., & Geva, A. B. (1989). Unsupervised optimal fuzzy clustering. *IEEE Transactions on Pattern Analysis and Machine Intelligence*, *11*(7), 773–781. doi:10.1109/34.192473

iBeacon - Creative iBeacon Solutions. (n.d.). Available from: http://www.ibeacon.com.tr/#news

iBeacon Wars- A guide to the major iBeacon solutions, iBeacon.com Insider. (n.d.). Available from: http://www.ibeacon.com/ibeacon-wars-a-guide-to-the-major-ibeacon-companies/

Li, J., & Li, L. (2014). A Location Recommender Based on a Hidden Markov Model: Mobile Social Networks. *Journal of Organizational Computing and Electronic Commerce*, *24*(2-3), 2–3, 257–270. doi:10.1080/10919392.2014.896730

Li, K., & Du, T. C. (2012). Building a targeted mobile advertising system for location-based services. *Decision Support Systems*, *54*(1), 1–8. doi:10.1016/j.dss.2012.02.002

Liu, H., Darabi, H., Banerjee, P., & Liu, J. (2007). Survey of Wireless Indoor Positioning Techniques and Systems. *IEEE Transactions on Systems, Man and Cybernetics. Part C, Applications and Reviews*, *37*(6), 1067–1080. doi:10.1109/TSMCC.2007.905750

Mahmoud, Q. H., & Yu, L. (2006). Havana agents for comparison shopping and location-aware advertising in wireless mobile environments. *Electronic Commerce Research and Applications*, *5*(3), 220–228. doi:10.1016/j.elerap.2005.09.005

Michael, K., & Michael, M. G. (2011). The social and behavioral implications of location-based services. *Journal of Location Based Services*, *5*(3-4), 3–4, 121–137. doi:10.1080/17489725.2011.642820

Miguéis, V. L., Camanho, A. S., & Cunha, J. F. (2012, August). Customer data mining for lifestyle segmentation. *Expert Systems with Applications*, *39*(10), 9359–9366. doi:10.1016/j.eswa.2012.02.133

Millonig, A., & Gartner, G. (2011). Identifying motion and interest patterns of shoppers for developing personalised way finding tools. *Journal of Location Based Services*, *5*(1), 1, 3–21. doi:10.1080/17489725.2010.535029

Narayanan, M., & Cherukuri, A. K. (2016). A study and analysis of recommendation systems for location-based social network (LBSN) with big data. *IIMB Management Review*, 1–6.

Oztaysi, B., & Isik, M. (2014). Supplier Evaluation Using Fuzzy clustering. In *Supply Chain Management Under Fuzziness: Recent Developments and Techniques*. Springer.

Pal, N. R., & Bezdek, J. C. (1995). On cluster validity for the fuzzy c-means model. *IEEE Transactions on Fuzzy Systems*, *3*(3), 370–379. doi:10.1109/91.413225

Park, D. H., Kim, H. K., Choi, Y., & Kim, J. K. (2012). A literature review and classification of recommender systems research. *Expert Systems with Applications*, *39*(11), 10059–10072. doi:10.1016/j.eswa.2012.02.038

Ruspini, E. H. (1970). Numerical methods for fuzzy clustering. *Information Sciences*, *2*(3), 319–350. doi:10.1016/S0020-0255(70)80056-1

Shiou Yang, W., Chi Cheng, H., & Ben Dia, J. (2008). A location-aware recommender system for mobile shopping environments. *Expert Systems with Applications*, *34*(1), 437–445. doi:10.1016/j.eswa.2006.09.033

Suh, E., Lim, S., Hwang, H., & Kim, S. (2004). A prediction model for the purchase probability of anonymous customers to support real time web marketing: A case study. *Expert Systems with Applications*, *27*(2), 245–255. doi:10.1016/j.eswa.2004.01.008

Tang, H., Liao, S. S., & Sun, S. X. (2013). A prediction framework based on contextual data to support Mobile Personalized Marketing. *Decision Support Systems*, *56*, 234–246. doi:10.1016/j.dss.2013.06.004

Theodoridis, S., & Koutroumbas, K. (2008). *Pattern Recognition* (4th ed.). Elsevier.

Thompson, D. (2013). *Introduction To Ibeacon: Taking Bluetooth Le For A Test Drive*. Retrieved March 27, 2015 from http://nerdery.com/mentions/346

Tsiptsis, K., & Chorianopoulos, A. (2009). *Data Mining Techniques in CRM: Inside customer segmentation*. John Wiley and Sons, Ltd.

Tussyadiah, I. P. (2012). A Concept of Location-Based Social Network Marketing. *Journal of Travel & Tourism Marketing*, *29*(3), 205–220. doi:10.1080/10548408.2012.666168

Wind, Y. J., & Bell, D. R. (2007). Market segmentation. In M. Baker & S. Hart (Eds.), *The Marketing Book*. Butterworth Heinemann.

Xie, X. L., & Beni, G. (1991). A validity measure for fuzzy clustering. *IEEE Transactions on Pattern Analysis and Machine Intelligence, Volume*, *13*(8), 841–847. doi:10.1109/34.85677

Yim, J. (2008). Introducing a decision tree-based indoor positioning technique. *Expert Systems with Applications*, *34*(1), 1296–1302. doi:10.1016/j.eswa.2006.12.028

Zhang, X., Edwards, J., & Harding, J. (2007). Personalized online sales using web usage data mining. *Computers in Industry*, *58*(8-9), 772–782. doi:10.1016/j.compind.2007.02.004

KEY TERMS AND DEFINITIONS

Beacon: A technology that assists indoor location based system using Bluetooth Low Energy.

Bluetooth: A technology that connects mobile devices via wireless connection infrastructure.

Campaign Management: Supporting marketing activities using convenient data for offering appropriate choices to right customer.

Clustering: An allocation or mapping of data according to the various criterion.

Customer Relationship Management: Coping with customer interaction including complaints, problems and notices in order to get positive feedbacks by improving valuable processes.

Data Mining: Methodologies that contribute the extraction of information among large scale data.

Fuzzy Clustering: Decomposition of data elements with respect to each element could be belong to one or more classes via a set of membership functions.

Fuzzy Logic: A form of explanations of crisp values to 0-1 values in order to represent the "truth" via determining membership function.

Hierarchical Clustering: A data mining method for gathering hierarchical structure when grouping related data via top down or bottom up approach.

Indoor Positioning: Determination of position of an item or person utilizing Wi-Fi and Bluetooth infrastructure based on GPS-like signals.

Location Based Services: Consideration of location and movement data to support people or systems with respect to mobile devices.

Partitional Clustering: Dissociating a data set into a set of disjoint clusters.

Segmentation: Grouping individuals according to the similar properties.

Chapter 3
Fuzzy Clustering:
An Analysis of Service Quality in the Mobile Phone Industry

Mashhour H. Baeshen
Cardiff University, UK

Malcolm J. Beynon
Cardiff University, UK

Kate L. Daunt
Cardiff University, UK

ABSTRACT

This chapter presents a study of the development of the clustering methodology to data analysis, with particular attention to the analysis from a crisp environment to a fuzzy environment. An applied problem concerning service quality (using SERVQUAL) of mobile phone users, and subsequent loyalty and satisfaction forms the data set to demonstrate the clustering issue. Following details on both the crisp k-means and fuzzy c-means clustering techniques, comparable results from their analysis are shown, on a subset of data, to enable both graphical and statistical elucidation. Fuzzy c-means is then employed on the full SERVQUAL dimensions, and the established results interpreted before tested on external variables, namely the level of loyalty and satisfaction across the different clusters established.

INTRODUCTION

This chapter presents a study of the development of the clustering methodology to data analysis (Punj and Stewart, 1983). In particular, the development of a clustering technique from its original crisp environment to working within a fuzzy environment is described. From the introduction of fuzzy set theory in Zadeh (1965), as an extension of the classical notion of a set, it has grown and itself advanced to offer novel dimensions to traditional (crisp) analysis approaches (see for example, Bonarini *et al.*, 2000; Estrada *et al.*, 2008; Gader, 1995; Zarandi *et al.*, 2002). Related to the context of this chapter,

DOI: 10.4018/978-1-5225-0997-4.ch003

Tokushige *et al.* (2007) undertook the consideration of multivariate functional data, using clustering, in crisp and fuzzy environments.

Pertinent to the analysis reported in this chapter, Beynon *et al.* (2012) consider clustering, importantly moving from the consideration of data within a crisp environment to an ambiguous (fuzzy) environment. In their discussing of this crisp to fuzzy understanding, and important for the type of data considered in this chapter, they state (p. 7):

... it is important to acknowledge that there may not be distinct clusters of objects ... Instead, objects may be ambiguously associated with established clusters ... This may be particularly evident in the analysis of perceptual data, which is inherently ambiguous. As a result, technical developments which acknowledge the ambiguous association of objects to clusters may be particularly valuable ...

This statement acknowledges the practicalities of the data being considered, namely that it is, or may be, perceptual (fuzzy), and it cannot simply be argued as simply black or white (Cheng et al., 1998).

The applied problem considered in this chapter is in respect to the consumer-based issue of service quality (Powell, 1995). Underpinned by consumers' evaluations of expectations and/or performance, service quality is demonstrated to be a powerful predictor of consumers' positive and negative evaluations of service. Service quality is also shown to drive customer loyalty and thus ultimately impacts the firm's bottom line and the development and expansion of business (Parasuraman *et al.*, 1985; 1988; Cronin and Taylor, 1992). Typically, in this area of research, emphasis is on both technical and applied understanding. Zeithaml (1987) states (in Najjar & Bishu, 2006, p. 36):

... service quality is a consumer judgment about an entity's overall excellence or superiority. It is a form of attitude, and results from a comparison and expectations to perceptions of performance received.

In technical terms, two clustering techniques will be exposited. These techniques demonstrate the development of clustering across the traditional crisp environment, with the employment of crisp *k*-means clustering (MacQueen, 1967; Johnson and Wichern, 2002), through to the more nascent fuzzy environment, with the employment of fuzzy *c*-means clustering (Bezdek, 1980, 1981). The fuzzy *c*-means technique becomes the main focus of the technical analysis, after its comparison with the more traditional *k*-means approach.

In applied terms, the main consideration is the elucidation of SERVQUAL (Parasuraman *et al.*, 1985; 1988), a scale which assesses the expectations-performance gap to measure customers' perceptions of service quality with service provider firms. The five SERVQUAL based dimensions, Tangibles, Reliability, Responsiveness, Assurance and Empathy will be considered in depth. Using survey data, the variables will be clustered using fuzzy *c*-means clustering (and compared with crisp *k*-means clustering on a smaller subset of these). The combination of the consideration of SERVQUAL and fuzzy *c*-means clustering places this chapter directly in the area of marketing analytics (Hauser, 2007).

This chapter will consider consumers' perceived quality of service with their mobile phone provider, and how the SERVQUAL dimensions may link with consumer loyalty and satisfaction (Gaudet, 2004). Previous findings in this area have suggested that there is a positive relationship between high levels of perceived service quality and consumer satisfaction and loyalty (Fournier & Mick, 1999; Keiningham et al., 1999). These constructs will be tested here (bringing also the inclusion of graphical and statistical analysis with the fuzzy *c*-means clustering undertaken).

CLUSTERING

Clustering (in Marketing)

Cluster analysis was developed due to the demand for exploratory data analysis techniques. According to Van Dongen (2000, p. 1) cluster analysis is "*the mathematical study of methods for recognizing natural groups within a class of entities*". Cluster analysis has been employed across multiple areas within management (Anderberg, 2014). For example, clustering been applied in accounting, finance, public sector management, marketing, strategic management, and human resource management studies (Beynon et al., 2012). Therefore, cluster analysis is a unique and a smart approach, for marketing and consumer behaviour researchers, since it helps to explore various relationships among groups of objects (respondents/consumers) in a specific context (e.g., service quality).

There are many techniques to apply clustering. Traditional approaches include, the hierarchical Ward's method (Ward, 1963) and the non-hierarchical crisp *k*-means (CKM - MacQueen, 1967; Johnson & Wichern, 2002). According to Frayley and Raftery (1998), hierarchical clustering takes a tree shape form built from the progressive agglomeration of objects, by contrast, the non-hierarchical approach divides objects based on a pre-specified number of clusters by the establishment of cluster centroids. In other words, objects are assigned to the cluster when reaching the closest centre point over attribute domains (Andrews & Beynon, 2010).

Fuzzy *c*-means (FCM), however, is a developed approach of CKM that enable objects to be assigned degrees of association (membership) to single clusters. Fuzzy set theory was introduced by Zadeh (1965) and is used to treat problems that involve uncertainty answers. Fuzzy clustering is an appropriate technique for dealing with unclear data that usually exist because of incomplete answers or information that consists of informants' biases (Andrews & Beynon, 2010). As a result, FCM provides a way to consider the objects' ambiguous cluster membership.

Ketchen and Shook (1996) provide three major issues in the appropriate implementation of clustering technique:

1. The choice of the clustering constructs to uphold the segmentation of objects.
2. The decision in regards of number of clusters to create.
3. The interpretation of findings from each cluster analysis.

However, the authors note two main advantages of employing a non-hierarchical method over a hierarchical one. First, non-hierarchical is not strongly affected by outlier objects. Second, the repetition of the process of comparing all the *n* objects with each random seed through the data makes the final solution optimizes within cluster homogeneity and between cluster heterogeneity. In other words, non-hierarchical helps to reduce the researcher biases when interpreting cluster results. Within a marketing context, lack of understanding in the clustering methodology, especially regarding what and how many clusters should be considered, is perhaps, the main reason behind the failure of the employment cluster analysis techniques by many researchers (Punj & Stewart, 1983).

Cluster analysis has been primarily employed in the process of marketing segmentation. According to Mooi and Sarstedt (2011, p. 238) "*The segmentation of customers is a standard application of cluster analysis*". Also, clustering has been used to: study consumer purchasing behaviours by classifying homogeneous groups of buyers, develop new products by clustering existing brands and products, test market selection, and develop aggregates of data that are more generic and easier to manage compared with personal observation (Punj & Stewart, 1983). Romesburg (2004, p. 69) adds that marketing and advertising professionals have also employed cluster techniques to subset groups of similar objects. Hence, owing to the above documented benefits and applications, cluster analysis has become a common tool for marketing researchers.

Technical details on the two clustering techniques considered here, CKM and FCM, are next presented (which further contributes to the elucidation of the development of clustering from a crisp to a fuzzy environment).

Crisp K-Means

The crisp *k*-means (CKM) clustering non-hierarchical technique (MacQueen, 1967; Johnson & Wichern, 2002) starts with *c* initial cluster centroids $C^{(0)} = \left\{c_1^{(0)}, c_2^{(0)}, \ldots, c_c^{(0)}\right\}$ (seeds), one for each cluster to be established. All the *n* objects are then compared with each seed by means of the Euclidean distance and assigned to the closest cluster seed, generally given by the objective function (for the tth iteration):

$$J_{CKM}\left(U, C\right) = \sum_{i=1}^{n} \sum_{j=1}^{c} \left\| x_i - c_j^{(t)} \right\|,$$

The procedure is then repeated over and over again. In each stage the seed of each cluster is recalculated by using the average vector of the objects assigned to the cluster. The algorithm stops when the changes in the cluster seeds from one stage to the next are close to zero or smaller than a pre-specified value ε, namely if $\left\| c_j^{(t)} - c_j^{(t-1)} \right\| < \varepsilon$, for $j = 1, \ldots, c$.

The accuracy of the CKM procedure is very dependent upon the choice of the initial random seeds (Milligan & Cooper, 1980). To obtain better performance the initial seeds should be very different among themselves. One of the advantages of this method is that we do not have to calculate the distance measures between all pairs of subjects (such as in Ward's method), therefore seems much more efficient or practical when you have very large datasets.

Fuzzy C-Means

The fuzzy *c*-means (FCM) algorithm (Bezdek, 1980, 1981), is described by Belacel *et al.*, (2002) as follows. The fundamental development on the *crisp* *k*-means technique is to assign (allocate) the set of objects to a given number of clusters such that each of them may belong to more than one cluster with different degrees of membership. An $n \times c$ matrix $U = [u_{ij}]$, denotes unknown cluster membership degrees for object *i* with respect to cluster *j*, with $0 \leq u_{ij} \leq 1$ and $\sum_{j=1}^{c} u_{ij} = 1$, for $i = 1, \ldots, n, j = 1, \ldots, c$. The fuzzy clustering problem may then be formulated as a heuristic, summarized in two steps:

Step 1 (Initialization): Let $C^{(0)} = \{ c_1^{(0)}, c_2^{(0)}, \ldots, c_c^{(0)} \}$ be an initial given set of *c* centroids (the centres of the clusters); fix values for *m* (> 0) and for *ε* (a small positive constant); set iteration counter $t = 1$.

Step 2 (Iterations):

- **Membership:** Given set of centroids $c_j^{(t-1)}$, $j = 1, \ldots, c$, calculated in iteration $t - 1$, compute the optimal $u_{ij}^{(t)}$, for $i = 1, \ldots, n$ and $j = 1, \ldots, c$, using the following formula:

$$u_{ij}^{(t)} = \begin{cases} \dfrac{1}{\sum_{q=1}^{c} \left(\dfrac{\left\| x_i - c_j^{(t-1)} \right\|}{\left\| x_i - c_q^{(t-1)} \right\|} \right)^{2/(m-1)}}, & c_j^{(t-1)} \neq x_i, j = 1, \ldots, c \\ 1, & c_j^{(t-1)} = x_i \\ 0, & c_j^{(t-1)} = x_k, k \neq i \end{cases}$$

- **Centroids:** Compute the centroid vectors $c_j^{(t)}$, for $j = 1, \ldots, c$, with $u_{ij}^{(t)}$ fixed, using the formula:

$$c_j^{(t)} = \frac{\sum_{i=1}^{n} \left(u_{ij}^{(t)} \right)^m x_i}{\sum_{i=1}^{n} \left(u_{ij}^{(t)} \right)^m}.$$

- **Test:** If $\left\| c_j^{(t)} - c_j^{(t-1)} \right\| < \varepsilon$, for $j = 1, \ldots, c$, calculate the objective function:

$$J_{FCM}(U, C) = \sum_{i=1}^{n} \sum_{j=1}^{c} (u_{ij}^{(t)})^m \left\| x_i - c_j^{(t)} \right\|,$$

and stop, otherwise set $t = t + 1$ and go to Step 2(a).

Convergence of the fuzzy *c*-means algorithm to a local optimum has been proved in Bezdek (1980). However, finding a global optimum of J_{FCM} appears to be very difficult. When both U and C are unknown, which is the general case, the objective function J_{FCM} is neither convex nor concave and usually has many local optima.

SERVICE QUALITY (INCLUDING LOYALTY AND SATISFACTION)

Marketing scholars widely accept that customer's expectation plays a significant role in evaluating the level of service performance of any given company (see for example, Oliver, 1980; Parasurman et al., 1991; Parasuraman et al., 1985; 1988; 1994; Brown & Swartz, 1989). Yet, debate exists as to theoretical and practical sufficiency of expectations in underpinning the conceptualisation and measurement of service quality. These discussions have led to the development of two distinct paradigms (Robledo, 2001, p. 23):

1. **The Disconfirmation Paradigm:** This approach claims that customers evaluate the quality of service provision based on a comparison between their pre-existing expectations (what they think

they will receive) and perceptions of the service received (what they perceived they actually received). The most important conceptualisation and measure developed from this position is termed SERVQUAL (Parasuraman et al., 1985).

2. **The Performance Paradigm:** By contrast to the disconfirmation paradigm, the performance approach queries the utility of customers' expectations in conceptualising and measuring consumers' evaluations of service quality. In particular, the service performance approach highlights the inherent biases associated with measuring customers' expectations and notes that expectations may lead to delusive information. To remedy these concerns Cronin and Taylor (1992) developed the SERVPERF conceptualisation and measurement of service quality which assesses only consumers' evaluations of service performance and does not capture consumers' expectations.

Accordingly, the service quality literature reveals that there are two popular methods with which to measure service quality, SERVQUAL and SERVPERF. While both measures essentially use the same bank of items across different service quality dimensions, in their original formats each approach is distinguished by the way in which service quality is gauged and captured. (Parasuraman et al., 1994). To detail, SERVPERF measures the actual level of service received. By contrast, SERVQUAL measures the discrepancy between perceived service and expected service. Here, the SERVQUAL approach is considered throughout.

When the SERVQUAL scale was developed by Parasuraman *et al.* (1985, 1988), they aimed to provide a substantial instrument for measuring service quality over a wide range of service industries. Parasuraman *et al.* (1985) concluded that consumer evaluation are based on comparing expectations with perceptions across ten dimensions: tangibles, reliability, responsiveness, communication, credibility, security, competence, understanding/knowing customers, courtesy, and access. However, after further work (Parasuraman *et al.*, 1988), the authors reduced the original ten dimensions to five. Tangibles, refers to physical facilities, equipment, and appearance of employees. Reliability reflects the ability to deliver the promised service dependably and accurately by the service provider. Responsiveness denotes the service firm's willingness to help customers and offer prompt service. Assurance evaluates the knowledge and courtesy of employees and their ability to build trust and confidence. Finally, Empathy refers to caring and individualized attention provided to customers by the firm and its employees.

Each dimension consists of a number of questions (items) that equate 22 items for the entire measure (see Table 6 in Appendix). In completing the SERVQUAL survey, respondents use a seven-point Likert-type scale to rate their level of agreement (where 1 "strongly disagree" to 7 "strongly agree") with questions which correspond to each of the SERVQUAL dimensions. The five dimensions of service quality were introduced empirically by employing factor analysis and are considered as independent attributes, contributing separately to customers' evaluation of overall service performance (Johns et al., 2004).

Customer Loyalty

Dick and Basu (1994) define customer loyalty as the relationship between relative attitude and repeat patronage. Zeithaml et al. (1996) add that loyalty is an attribution of measuring behavioural intentions and it consists of five dimensions, which are: repurchase intentions, word of mouth, loyalty, complaining behaviour, and price sensitivity. Differentiating between purchase, attitude and cognition in a service context, Caruana (2002, p.813) define service loyalty as "the degree to which a customer exhibits repeat purchasing behavior from a service provider, possesses a positive attitudinal disposition toward the provider, and considers using only this provider when a need for this service exists". Multiple studies have examined the drivers and consequences of customer loyalty across diverse online and offline organisational contexts (Gwo-Guang & Lin, 2005; Ramanathan & Ramanathan, 2013; Blut et al., 2014).

Specifically, loyalty is shown to be the corner-stone of marketing where profits and market share gains are driven through repeat consumer patronage. Such ongoing relationships and dialogue with customers enable organisations to gain valuable insight into the development of consumers' lives, wants, preferences and resulting trends and thus develop new products and services accordingly (Olsen, 2002; Nelson, 2007). From the customer's perspective loyalty can result in emotional benefits and reduce the uncertainty and time associated with making purchases (Dick & Basu, 1994). Focusing on research that links service quality and customer loyalty, Olorunniwo *et al.* (2006) revealed that service quality is important in understanding customer loyalty dynamics, while Kim and Yoon (2004) found that service quality, product quality and features, and brand image all positively impact customer loyalty judgements. Interrogating the relationship between service quality and customer loyalty, Caruana (2002) forwards evidence to suggest that the relationship is mediated by customer satisfaction.

In this study five items derived from Zeithaml et al. (1996) were utilised to gauge service loyalty, see Table 7 in the Appendix.

Customer Satisfaction

Market-orientated organizations strive to provide excellent service quality to enhance customer satisfaction (Iacobucci et al., 1995). According to Kotler and Armstrong (2012),, satisfaction is a post-purchase evaluation of products or services taking into consideration customers; expectations. Also viewing expectations as key, Iacobucci et al. (1995 p.278) define customer satisfaction as a "function of the discrepancy between consumer's prior expectations and his or her perception regarding the purchase".

Since expectations and the perceived level of disconfirmation have a direct impact on satisfaction, it can be argued that the degree of perceived quality may play a role in determining the degree of customer satisfaction. Understanding consumer needs and wants, and taking into account the type of product or service offered, is important to understanding the level of consumer satisfaction experienced (Ramachandran and Chidambaram 2012, p. 71). Lee *et al.* (2000) argue that customer satisfaction is based on the level of service quality offered by the service provider. Moreover, some researchers believe that overall assessment of service experience accumulates customer satisfaction (Jones and Suh 2000). Parasuraman *et al.,* (1985) suggest that customer satisfaction increases as long as perceived service quality is high. These claims reinforce the argument that high levels service quality is strongly associated with high levels of customer satisfaction.

In this study four items derived from Oliver (1980) were considered to describe customer satisfaction, see Table 7 in the Appendix.

Loyalty and Satisfaction

While this chapter examines both customers' evaluations of satisfaction and loyalty it is noted that the two constructs are associated. Fornell *et al.* (1996) offer evidence of a statistically significant relationship between customer satisfaction and customer loyalty, while Anderson *et al.* (1994) state that customer satisfaction is key to building strong customer loyalty. In addition, Thomas (2013) contends that customer satisfaction is a major driver of loyalty, while Yi-Ting and Dean (2001) led a study to explore the role of emotions in satisfaction on consumer loyalty.

DESCRIPTION OF DATA

This section briefly describes the data considered here. A total of 344 survey responses were collected over a five week period, in regard to the service from the respondents' phone providers. However, it is important to ensure that data are clean from missing values in order to reach valid results. It is recommended before conducting a cluster analysis to clean data for excessive missing values, inconsistent responses, and outliers (Sharma and Kumar, 2006, p.381). In respect to this, missing values were removed and actual means only were available and used to compare the two applied methods of cluster analysis. In addition, refined data were used to draw figures that describe the clusters results. As a result, 184 out of 344 under SERVQUAL dimensions and 172 out of 184 under loyalty and satisfaction dimensions were valid to conduct, reliability tests, and the subsequent two forms of cluster analysis.

According to Saunders et al. (2012, p. 192) reliability is important to assess "whether your data collection techniques and analytic procedures would produce consistent findings if they were repeated on another occasion or if they were replicated by a different researcher". A measure of construct reliability (Cronbach's alpha) was performed to examine the reliability of the set of items of each variable. Nunnally (1967) provides the guideline for basic research (Cronbach's alpha coefficient $\geq$ 0.707). As a rule, alphas.70 or greater reflect excellent reliability of the items measuring the variable. Based on the items reflecting each SERVQUAL dimension, the Cronbach scores were; Tangibles (0.765), Reliability (0.851), Responsiveness (0.779), Assurance (0.826) and Empathy (0.88). Acceptable Cronbach alpha scores were also revealed for Loyalty (0.889) and Satisfaction (0.830).

TECHNICAL EXPOSITION/COMPARISON OF CLUSTERING

In this section, a technical emphasis is given on the exposition of clustering in regard to the phone-provider-service data set described previously. Here both the crisp *k*-means (CKM) and fuzzy *c*-means (FCM) clustering techniques will be employed/compared. To enable a helpful graphical elucidation of the clustering undertaken (in this technical exposition), a subset of the SERVQUAL factors (variables) presented in the previous section are considered. Moreover, only two dimensions (factors) of SERVQUAL are considered namely Tangibles and Reliability, thus allowing scatter-plot visualisation of all the respondents considered, and the subsequent partitioning of them across different numbers of clusters (importantly enabling elucidation of the variations in the clustering solutions from the different clustering techniques).

Two Cluster Solution (CKM and FCM)

In this section the two cluster solutions from the separate employment of CKM and FCM are exposited.

The first results shown, see Figure 1, are scatter-plots of the 184 respondents across the two SERVQUAL dimensions, Tangibles and Reliability.

Figure 1. Scatter-plot representation of clustering based on tangible and reliability dimensions of SERVQUAL, for 184 respondents, using a) crisp k-means and b) fuzzy c-means, over the two two-cluster solutions

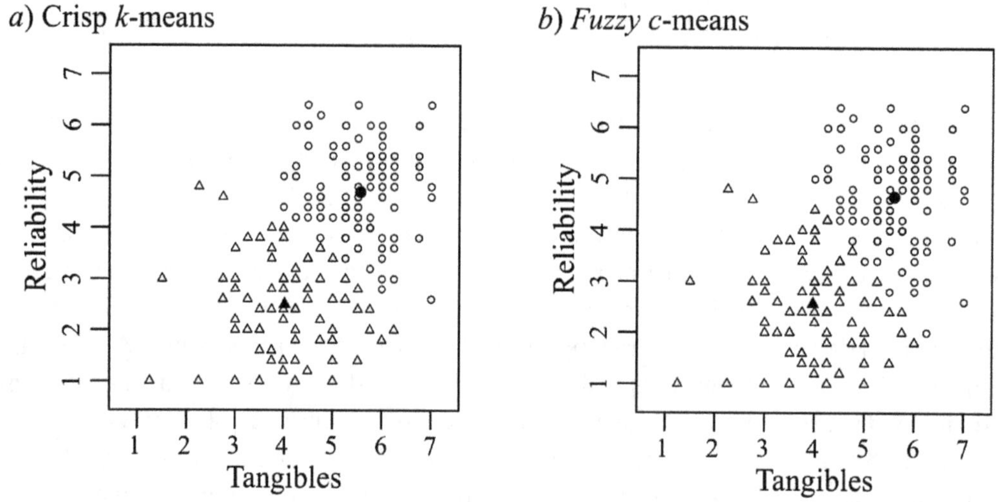

In each scatter-plot in Figure 1, the association of the 184 respondents across the two clusters is discerned using the two symbols, circle and triangle. Also shown with dark circles and triangles are the mean positions of the groups of respondents associated with each cluster. A further breakdown of this representation is given in Figure 2, where the means, termed dimension cluster means, of each dimension are shown on each dimension domain, themselves shown using notched box-plots (McGill et al., 1978).

A comparison of these results, in terms of the cluster solutions found using CKM and FCM, indicate very little difference across the two two-cluster solutions. While each solution appears to have the same number of respondents in the two established clusters, the respective cluster means across the Tangibles and Reliability dimensions are different. The reason for this discrepancy is evidenced in Table 1.

Figure 2. Constituent dimension cluster means (tangible and reliability dimensions of SERVQUAL), using a) crisp k-means and b) fuzzy c-means, over the two two-cluster solutions

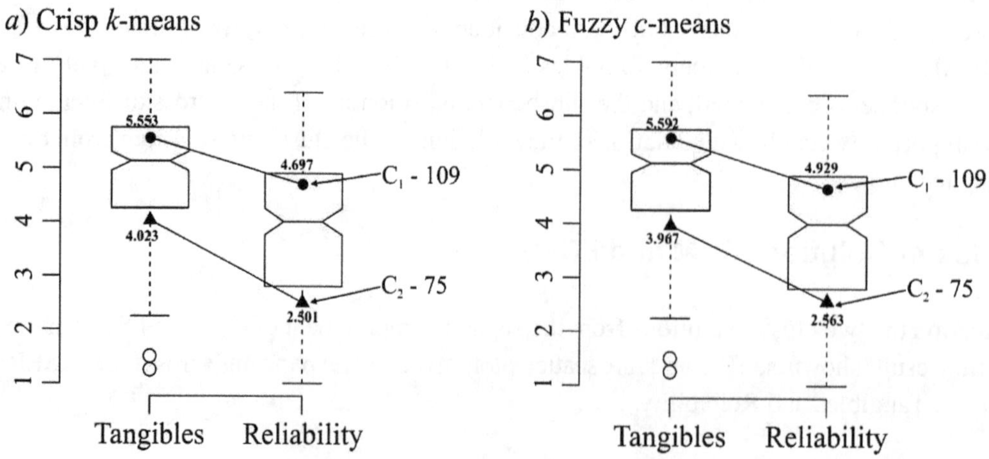

Table 1. Breakdown of frequency overlap of two two-cluster solutions

		FCM		Total
		C_1	C_2	
CKM	C_1	106	3	109
	C_2	3	72	75
Total		109	75	184

Table 1 shows the level of consistency in the respondents being in the nearest equivalent 'same' clusters across the two cluster solutions, using CKM and FCM. Indeed, the table shows movements of three respondents from each 'same' cluster to the other across the two two-cluster solutions (hence the same number of respondents in each cluster in the two cluster solutions – but some different respondents having swapped between them). Close inspection of the labelling of the respondents in the scatter-plots shown in Figure 1 shows a small number of respondents differently labelled across the two scatter-plots.

Within a cluster solution the statistical significance of the differences between the dimension values of respondents in each cluster can be exposited. For a two cluster solution the associated ANOVA results will demonstrate this statistical significance. For the CKM and FCM cluster solutions the associated ANOVA results are (in form F-score (significance)), CKM: Tangibles 147.302 (0.000) and Reliability 278.931 (0.000), and FCM: Tangibles 185.692 (0.000) and Reliability 221.921 (0.000). For each of the clustering solutions shown, the descriptive statistics and ANOVA results show the clusters are statistically different from each other across the two cluster solutions (based on the SERVQUAL dimensions, Tangibles and Reliability, considered here).

Three-Cluster Solution (CKM and FCM)

In this section the three cluster solutions from the separate employment of CKM and FCM are exposited.

The first results shown, see Figure 3, are scatter-plots of the 184 respondents across the two SERVQUAL dimensions, Tangibles and Reliability.

In each scatter-plot in Figure 3, the association of the 184 respondents across the three clusters is discerned using the three symbols, circle, triangle and square. Also shown with dark circles, triangles and squares are the mean positions of the groups of respondents associated with each cluster. A further breakdown of this representation is given in Figure 4, where the means, termed dimension cluster means, of Tangibles and Reliability are shown on each dimension domain, themselves shown using notched box plots.

A comparison of these results, in terms of the cluster solutions found using CKM and FCM, indicate some difference across the two cluster solutions. There is difference across both the numbers of respondents in each cluster as well as the dimension cluster means. To further elucidate on this difference, a breakdown on the membership of respondents across the three clusters on each three-cluster solution is given in Table 2.

Table 2 shows the level of consistency in the respondents being in the nearest equivalent 'same' clusters across the two three-cluster solutions, using CKM and FCM. Indeed, the table shows movements of noticeable numbers of respondents from each 'same' cluster to the other across the three-cluster solutions. Inspection of the labelling of the respondents in the scatter-plots shown in Figure 3 shows these numbers

Figure 3. Scatter-plot representation of clustering based on tangible and reliability dimensions of SERVQUAL, for 184 respondents, using a) k-means and b) fuzzy c-means, over the two three-cluster solutions

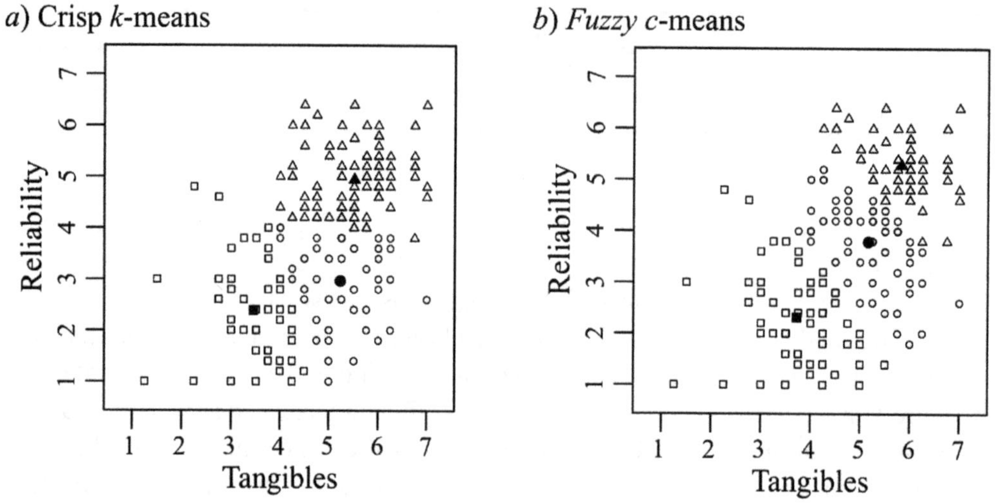

Figure 4. Constituent dimension cluster means (tangible and reliability dimensions of SERVQUAL), using a) crisp k-means and b) fuzzy c-means, over the two three-cluster solutions

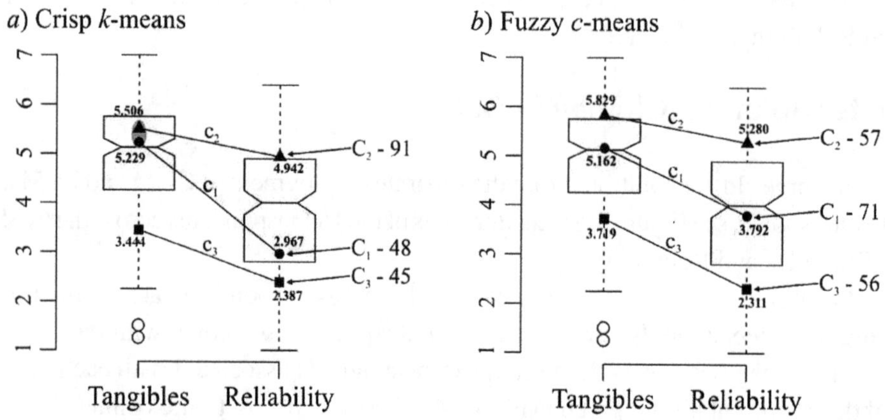

Table 2. Breakdown of frequency overlap of over the two three-cluster solutions

		FCM			Total
		C_1	C_2	C_3	
CKM	C_1	35	1	12	48
	C_2	35	56	0	91
	C_3	1	0	44	45
Total		71	57	56	184

of respondents differently labelled across the two scatter-plots. The case of FCM cluster C_1 (circle in Figure 3) is of interest since the respondent members of that cluster are split almost equally across the membership of C_1 and C_2 in the CKM three-cluster solution, the inference being that the cluster solution established are not suggesting the same typologies of clusters from the different cluster techniques employed (some of which the two-cluster solutions were predominantly doing).

Within a cluster solution the statistical significance of the differences between the dimension values of respondents in each cluster can be exposited. For a three cluster solution the associated ANOVA and pot-hoc results (see Hair et al., 2006) will demonstrate this statistical significance, see Table 3.

For each of the clustering solutions shown, the descriptive statistics and ANOVA results show the clusters are statistically different from each other across the two cluster solutions (based on the SERVQUAL dimensions, Tangibles and Reliability, considered here).

Variations between CKM and FCM

With two different techniques to clustering employed, a discussion is next briefly be given on the variations in results, again demonstrating the underlying crisp to fuzzy environment shift from the use of these two clustering techniques, CKM and FCM, respectively.

When looking across both the two-cluster and three-cluster solutions, the evidenced similarities and differences that it is not assured that variations in the results will come from the employment of FCM over CKM. When differences were identified, in the three-cluster solutions, the FCM results did exhibit better discernment across the two SERVQUAL dimensions (in terms of post-hoc results - in terms of between C_1 and C_2 - see Table 3).

FCM ANALYSIS OF PHONE-PROVIDER-SERVICE DATA SET

Following the comparison of FCM with CKM in terms of the demonstrated acknowledgement in variations in their operation (using two dimensions of SERVQUAL), this section considers the full phone-provider-service data set, with all five dimensions of SERVQUAL now considered, namely, Tangibles, Reliability, Responsiveness, Assurance and Empathy. Further, beyond the clustering process, consideration of the clusters of respondents established is made with the inclusion of external variables, looking beyond SERVQUAL, and now to customers' evaluations of loyalty and satisfaction, to consider outside of those variables used in the clustering process.

Table 3. Statistical results describing the differences between clusters in the three-cluster solution, from CKM and FCM (ANOVA and post-hoc results presented)

		CKM		FCM	
		Tangibles	**Reliability**	**Tangibles**	**Reliability**
ANOVA		122.8 (0.00)	195.7 (0.00)	119. 2 (0.00)	215.0 (0.00)
Post-hoc Bonferroni	C_1 and C_2	0.28 (0.11)	1.98 (0.00)	0.67 (0.00)	1.49 (0.00)
	C_1 and C_3	1.78 (0.00)	0.58 (0.00)	1.44 (0.00)	1.48 (0.00)
	C_2 and C_3	2.06 (0.00)	2.56 (0.00)	2.11 (0.00)	2.97 (0.00)

Four Cluster Solution

This subsection presents information on the clustering of the respondents across all five SERVQUAL dimensions, using the graphical option of the cluster mean graph (sadly now unable to use the scatter-plot approach previously employed since more than two dimensions now considered). Different numbers of clusters (cluster solutions) were considered, based on clarity of understanding (McDermot et al., 2013), the established four cluster solution was decided to be reported. Based on the clustering of the respondents interpretation to the formed clusters is given. ANOVA and post-hoc results add statistical significance to the differences across the established clusters.

The results in Figure 5 shows the dimension cluster means for the five dimensions of SERVQUAL (Tangibles, Reliability, Responsiveness, Assurance and Empathy), overlaid on the spread of the respondent values across these dimensions (again using the notched box plot form of data representation). The values of each dimension cluster mean are shown, and to the right the frequency of membership of the respondents in each established cluster. The statistical significance of the differences between the dimension cluster means across each cluster is reported in Table 4.

The statistical results presented in Table 4, both ANOVA and post hoc values, indicate that there is predominant significant difference between the dimension cluster means (the exception being between

Figure 5. Constituent dimension cluster means (tangibles, reliability, responsiveness, assurance and empathy dimensions of SERVQUAL), using fuzzy c-means, over the four-cluster solution

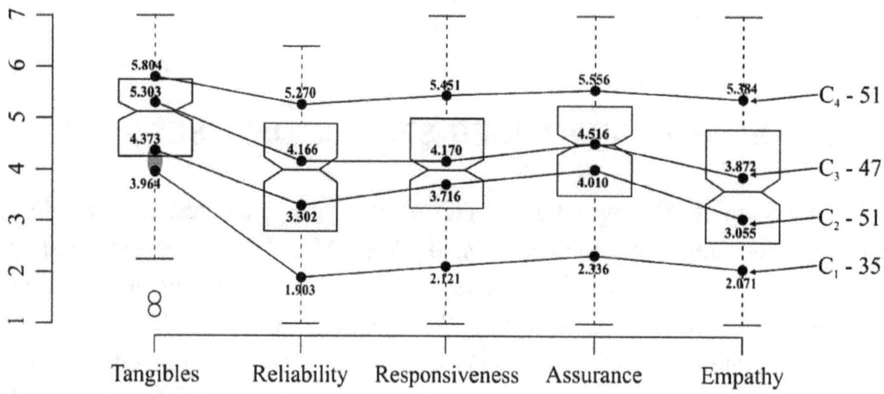

Table 4. Statistical results describing the differences between clusters in the four cluster solution, from FCM (ANOVA and post-hoc results presented)

		Tangibles	Reliability	Responsiveness	Assurance	Empathy
ANOVA		40.8 (0.00)	154.9 (0.00)	166.0 (0.00)	137.1 (0.00)	152.3(0.00)
Post-hoc Bonferroni	C_1 and C_2	0.41 (0.21)	1.40 (0.00)	1.59 (0.00)	1.67 (0.00)	0.98 (0.24)
	C_1 and C_3	1.34 (0.00)	2.26 (0.00)	2.04 (0.00)	2.18 (0.00)	1.80 (0.00)
	C_1 and C_4	1.84 (0.00)	3.37 (0.00)	3.33 (0.00)	3.22 (0.00)	3.31 (0.00)
	C_2 and C_3	.93 (0.00)	0.86 (0.00)	0.45 (0.01)	0.51 (0.01)	0.82 (0.00)
	C_2 and C_4	1.43 (0.00)	1.97 (0.00)	1.74 (0.00)	1.54 (0.00)	2.33 (0.00)
	C_3 and C_4	.50 (0.03)	1.10 (0.00)	1.28 (0.00)	1.04 (0.00)	1.34 (0.00)

the C_1 and C_2 clusters on the Tangibles and Empathy dimensions). With the statistical evidence supporting the clustering undertaken, inference on the established clusters can be gauged.

The clusters, from C_1 up to C_4, have increasing values across each of the dimensions, hence, when recalling the scales used in the questions from which the dimensions were found, means the clusters C_1 to C_4 include respondents with increasing agreement in the items making up the respective dimensions. This allows the clusters to be qualitatively interpreted;

C_1: Low perceived service quality.
C_2: Low medium perceived service quality.
C_3: High medium perceived service quality.
C_4: High perceived service quality.

External Variables

Beyond the clustering of the respondents, further consideration will be given in terms of how the clusters of respondents identified compare against other variables not used in the clustering process, termed external variables (Ketchen & Shook, 1996). Cluster mean graphs again form the graphical elucidation undertaken on the external variables, see Figure 6). Statistical significance is tested again using ANOVA and post-hoc tests, see Table 5.

The results in Figure 6 and Table 5 shows there is graphical and statistical discernment amongst the respondents across most of the clusters in regards to Loyalty and Satisfaction (noticeable exceptions across both variables is between the clusters C_2 and C_3, and between C_1 and C_2 specifically for loyalty).

Figure 6. Constituent dimension cluster means (loyalty and satisfaction), using fuzzy c-means, over the four-cluster solution

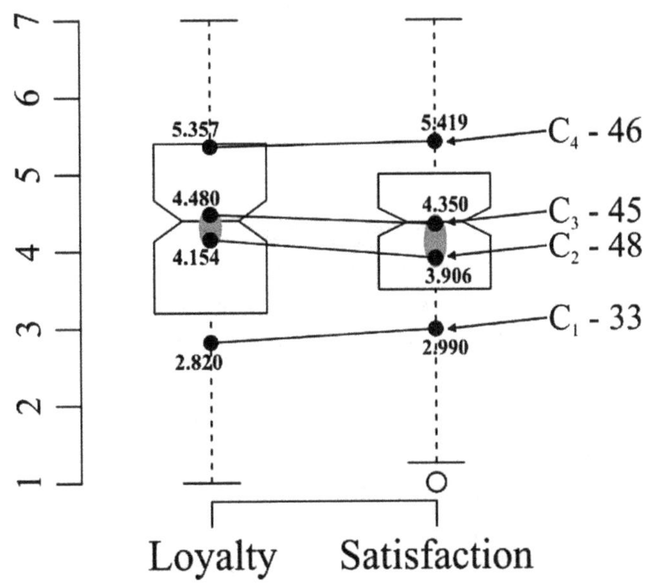

Table 5. Statistical results describing the differences between clusters in the four-cluster solution, from FCM (ANOVA and post-hoc results presented)

		Loyalty	Satisfaction
ANOVA		33.4 (0.00)	33.9 (0.00)
Post-hoc Bonferroni	C_1 and C_2	1.33 (0.21)	0.92 (0.00)
	C_1 and C_3	1.66 (0.00)	1.36 (0.00)
	C_1 and C_4	2.54 (0.00)	2.43 (0.00)
	C_2 and C_3	0.33 (0.98)	0.44 (0.31)
	C_2 and C_4	1.20 (0.00)	1.51 (0.00)
	C_3 and C_4	.88 (0.00)	1.07 (0.00)

When compared against the earlier qualitative descriptions of the clusters from low (C_1) to high (C_4) perceived service quality, the ordering of evaluations is similarly from low to high loyalty and satisfaction.

FUTURE RESEARCH DIRECTIONS

Cluster analysis has been employed frequently in management studies and has gained more popularity (Beynon et al., 2012). Since cluster analysis provides numbers of groups of objects that share similar characteristics, it can be considered as one of the most productive methods for management and business studies because of its capability of examining relationships between groups of objects. In this chapter, the cluster analysis has provided evidence that it can contribute in addressing an applied marketing problem. According to Beynon et al. (2012, p. 22) "Cluster analysis is based on finding groups in data, rather than associational or causation analysis". Future research should take advantage of the ability of clustering techniques to conduct more studies that explore relationships from different point of view rather than causal relationships.

CONCLUSION

This chapter has presented an example driven exposition of the development of the clustering approach to data analysis from its traditional crisp environment to its operations within a fuzzy environment. The two clustering techniques exposited, crisp *k*-means and fuzzy *c*-means, are a clear demonstration of the ability of a well-known analysis technique to be able to be developed to enable its operation within an uncertain environment.

The applied problem of considering the clustering of users of mobile phones based on service quality and subsequent loyalty and satisfaction to the respective company is a good example of the potential of clustering as a pertinent tool in marketing analytics.

REFERENCES

Anderberg, M. (2014). *Cluster analysis for applications: Probability and Mathematical Statistics: A Series of Monographs and Textbooks. 19*. London: Academic press.

Anderson, E., Fornell, C., & Lehmann, D. (1994). Customer satisfaction, market share, and profitability: Findings from Sweden. *Journal of Marketing*, *58*(3), 53–66. doi:10.2307/1252310

Andrews, R., & Beynon, M. (2010). Organizational form and strategic alignment in a local authority: A preliminary exploration using fuzzy clustering. *Public Organization Review*, *11*(3), 201–218. doi:10.1007/s11115-010-0117-4

Belacel, N., Hansen, P., & Mladenovic, N. (2002). Fuzzy J-means: A new heuristic for fuzzy clustering. *Pattern Recognition*, *35*(10), 2193–2200. doi:10.1016/S0031-3203(01)00193-5

Beynon, M., McDermott, A., & Heffernan, M. (2012). Psychological Contracts and Job Satisfaction: Clustering Analysis using Evidential C-Means and Comparison with other Techniques. *Intelligent Systems in Accounting, Finance & Management*, *19*(4), 247–273. doi:10.1002/isaf.1334

Bezdek, C. (1980). A convergence theorem for the fuzzy ISODATA clustering algorithms. *IEEE Transactions on Pattern Analysis and Machine Intelligence*, *2*(1), 1–8. doi:10.1109/TPAMI.1980.4766964 PMID:22499617

Bezdek, J. C. (1981). *Pattern Recognition with Fuzzy Objective Function Algorithms*. New York, NY: Plenum Press. doi:10.1007/978-1-4757-0450-1

Blut, M., Beatty, S. E., Evanschitzky, H., & Brock, C. (2014). The impact of service characteristics on the switching costs-customer loyalty link. *Journal of Retailing*, *90*(2), 275–290. doi:10.1016/j.jretai.2014.04.003

Bonarini, A., Bonacina, C., & Matteucci, M. (2000). Fuzzy and crisp representations of real-valued input for learning classifier systems. In Learning Classifier Systems (pp. 107-124). Springer Berlin Heidelberg. doi:10.1007/3-540-45027-0_5

Brown, S., & Swartz, T. (1989). A gap analysis of professional service quality. *Journal of Marketing*, *53*(2), 92–98. doi:10.2307/1251416

Caruana, A. (2002). Service loyalty: The effects of service quality and the mediating role of customer satisfaction. *European Journal of Marketing*, *36*(7/8), 811–828. doi:10.1108/03090560210430818

Cheng, H. D., Chen, J. R., & Li, J. (1998). Threshold selection based on fuzzy c-partition entropy approach. *Pattern Recognition*, *31*(7), 857–870. doi:10.1016/S0031-3203(97)00113-1

Cronin, J., & Taylor, S. (1992). Measuring service quality: A re-examination and extension. *Journal of Marketing*, *56*(3), 55–68. doi:10.2307/1252296

Duncan, E., & Elliott, G. (2002). Customer service quality and financial performance among Australian retail financial institutions. *Journal of Financial Services Marketing*, *7*(1), 25–41. doi:10.1057/palgrave.fsm.4770070

Estrada, A., Real, R., & Vargas, J. (2008). Using crisp and fuzzy modelling to identify favourability hotspots useful to perform gap analysis. *Biodiversity and Conservation, 17*(4), 857–871. doi:10.1007/s10531-008-9328-1

Fornell, C., Johnson, M., Anderson, E., Cha, J., & Bryant, B. (1996). The American customer satisfaction index: Nature, purpose, and findings. *Journal of Marketing, 60*(4), 7–18. doi:10.2307/1251898

Fournier, S., & Mick, D. (1999). Rediscovering satisfaction. *Journal of Marketing, 63*(4), 5–23. doi:10.2307/1251971

Frayley, C., & Raftery, E. (1998). How many clusters? Which clustering method? Answers via model-based cluster analysis. *The Computer Journal, 41*(8), 578–588. doi:10.1093/comjnl/41.8.578

Gader, P., Mohamed, M., & Chiang, J. (1995). Comparison of crisp and fuzzy character neural networks in handwritten word recognition. *Fuzzy Systems. IEEE Transactions on, 3*(3), 357–363.

Gaudet, A. (2004). *Customer relationship marketing and effects of demographics and technology on customer satisfaction and loyalty in financial services*. Old Dominion University.

Gremler, D., & Brown, S. (1996). Service loyalty: its nature, importance and implications. In Caruana, A. (2002). Service loyalty: the effects of service quality and the mediating role of customer satisfaction. *European Journal of Marketing, 36*(7/8), 811–828.

Gwo-Guang, L., & Lin, H.-F. (2005). Customer perceptions of e-service quality in online shopping. *International Journal of Retail & Distribution Management, 33*(2), 161–176. doi:10.1108/09590550510581485

Hair, J. F., Black, W. C., Babin, B. J., Anderson, R. E., & Tatham, R. L. (2006). *Multivariate data analysis* (Vol. 6). Upper Saddle River, NJ: Pearson Prentice Hall.

Hauser, W. J. (2007). Marketing analytics: The evolution of marketing research in the twenty-first century. *Direct Marketing: An International Journal, 1*(1), 38–54. doi:10.1108/17505930710734125

Iacobucci, D., Ostrom, A., & Grayson, K. (1995). Distinguishing service quality and customer satisfaction: The voice of the consumer. *Journal of Consumer Psychology, 4*(3), 277–303. doi:10.1207/s15327663jcp0403_04

Johns, N., Avci, T., & Karatepe, O. (2004). Measuring service quality of travel agents: Evidence from Northern Cyprus. *Service Industries Journal, 24*(3), 82–100. doi:10.1080/0264206042000247777

Johnson, R., & Wichern, D. (2002). *Applied Multivariate Statistical Analysis* (5th ed.). Upper Saddle River, NJ: Prentice Hall.

Jones, M., & Suh, J. (2000). Transaction-specific satisfaction and overall satisfaction: An empirical analysis. *Journal of Services Marketing, 14*(2), 147–159. doi:10.1108/08876040010371555

Keiningham, T., Goddard, M., Vavra, T., & Source, A. (1999). Customer delight and the bottom line. *Marketing Management, 8*(3), 57–63.

Ketchen, D. Jr, & Shook, C. (1996). The application of cluster analysis in strategic management research: An analysis and critique. *Strategic Management Journal, 17*(6), 441–458. doi:10.1002/(SICI)1097-0266(199606)17:6<441::AID-SMJ819>3.0.CO;2-G

Kim, H., & Yoon, C. (2004). Determinants of subscriber churn and customer loyalty in the Korean mobile telephony market. *Telecommunications Policy*, *28*(9), 751–765. doi:10.1016/j.telpol.2004.05.013

Kotler, P., & Armstrong, G. (2012). Principles of Marketing. Studia Universitatis Babes-Bolyai, 58(3), 3-19.

Lee, H., Lee, Y., & Yoo, D. (2000). The determinants of perceived service quality and its relationship with satisfaction. *Journal of Services Marketing*, *14*(3), 217–231. doi:10.1108/08876040010327220

MacQueen, J. (1967). Some methods for classification and analysis of multivariate observations. In *Proceedings of the 5th Berkeley Symposium on Mathematical Statistics and Probability*. University of California Press.

McDermott, A. M., Heffernan, M., & Beynon, M. J. (2012). When the nature of employment matters in the employment relationship: A cluster analysis of psychological contracts and organizational commitment in the non-profit sector. *International Journal of Human Resource Management*, *24*(7), 1490–1518. doi:10.1080/09585192.2012.723635

McGill, R., Tukey, J. W., & Larsen, W. A. (1978). Variations of box plots. *The American Statistician*, *32*(1), 12–16.

Milligan, G., & Cooper, M. (1980). An examination of the effect of six types of error perturbation on fifteen clustering algorithms. *Psychometrika*, *45*(3), 159–179. doi:10.1007/BF02293907

Mooi, E., & Sarstedt, M. (2011). *Cluster analysis*. Heidelberg, Germany: Springer Berlin.

Najjar, L., & Bishu, R. (2006). Service quality: A case study of a bank. *The Quality Management Journal*, *13*(3), 35–44.

Nelson, O. N. (2007). Relationship marketing and customer loyalty. *Marketing Intelligence & Planning*, *25*(1), 98–105. doi:10.1108/02634500710722425

Oliver, R. (1980). A cognitive model of the antecedents and consequences of satisfaction decisions. *JMR, Journal of Marketing Research*, *17*(4), 460–469. doi:10.2307/3150499

Oliver, R. (1997). Satisfaction: A behavioral perspective on the customer. New York: Academic Press.

Oliver, R. (1999). Whence consumer loyalty? *Journal of Marketing*, *63*, 33–44. doi:10.2307/1252099

Olorunniwo, F., Hsu, M., & Udo, G. (2006). Service quality, customer satisfaction, and behavioral intentions in the service factory. *Journal of Services Marketing*, *20*(1), 59–72. doi:10.1108/08876040610646581

Olsen, S. (2002). Comparative evaluation and the relationship between quality, satisfaction, and repurchase loyalty. *Journal of the Academy of Marketing Science*, *30*(3), 240–249. doi:10.1177/0092070302303005

Parasuraman, A., Zeithaml, V., & Berry, L. (1985). A conceptual model of service quality and its implications for future research. *Journal of Marketing*, *49*(4), 41–50. doi:10.2307/1251430

Parasuraman, A., Zeithaml, V., & Berry, L. (1988). SERQUAL. *Journal of Retailing*, *64*(1), 12–40.

Parasuraman, A., Zeithaml, V., & Berry, L. (1991). Refinement and reassessment of the SERVQUAL scale. *Journal of Retailing*, *67*(4), 420–450.

Parasuraman, A., Zeithaml, V., & Berry, L. (1994). Alternative scales for measuring service quality: A comparative assessment based on psychometric and diagnostic criteria. *Journal of Retailing*, *70*(3), 201–230. doi:10.1016/0022-4359(94)90033-7

Powell, T. (1995). Total quality management as competitive advantage: A review and empirical study. *Strategic Management Journal*, *16*(1), 15–37. doi:10.1002/smj.4250160105

Punj, G., & Stewart, D. (1983). Cluster analysis in marketing research: Review and suggestions for application. *JMR, Journal of Marketing Research*, *20*(2), 134–148. doi:10.2307/3151680

Ramachandran, A., & Chidambaram, V. (2012). A review of customer satisfaction towards service quality of banking sector. *Periodica Polytechnica Social and Management Sciences*, *20*(2), 71–79. doi:10.3311/pp.so.2012-2.02

Ramanathan, U., & Ramanathan, R. (2013). Investigating the impact of resource capabilities on customer loyalty: A structural equation approach for the UK hotels using online ratings. *Journal of Services Marketing*, *27*(5), 404–415. doi:10.1108/JSM-12-2011-0186

Robledo, M. (2001). Measuring and managing service quality: Integrating customer expectations. Managing Service Quality. *International Journal (Toronto, Ont.)*, *11*(1), 22–31.

Romesburg, C. (2004). *Cluster Analysis for Researchers*. Lulu Press.

Saunders, M., Lewis, P., & Thornhill, A. (2012). *Research Methods for Business Students* (6th ed.). Harlow: Person.

Sharma, S., & Kumar, A. (2006). Cluster Analysis and Factor Analysis. In *Grover, R., and Vriens, M. (2006). The handbook of marketing research: uses, misuses, and future advances* (pp. 365–393). Sage Publications. doi:10.4135/9781412973380.n18

Thomas, S. (2013). Linking customer loyalty to customer satisfaction and store image: A structural model for retail stores. *Indian Institute of Management Calcutta*, *40*(1), 15–25.

Tokushige, S., Yadohisa, H., & Inada, K. (2007). Crisp and fuzzy k-means clustering algorithms for multivariate functional data. *Computational Statistics*, *22*(1), 1–16. doi:10.1007/s00180-006-0013-0

Van Dongen, S. (2000). *Graph clustering by flow simulation.* (Unpublished PhD Thesis). Centre for Mathematics and Computer Science (CWI) in Amsterdam. Available at: http://dspace.library.uu.nl/bitstream/handle/1874/848/full.pdf?sequence=1

Ward, J. H. Jr. (1963). Hierarchical grouping to optimize an objective function. *Journal of the American Statistical Association*, *58*(301), 236–244. doi:10.1080/01621459.1963.10500845

Yi-Ting, Y., & Dean, A. (2001). The contribution of emotional satisfaction to consumer loyalty. *International Journal of Service Industry Management*, *12*(3), 234–250. doi:10.1108/09564230110393239

Zadeh, L. (1965). Fuzzy Sets. *Information and Control*, *8*(3), 338–353. doi:10.1016/S0019-9958(65)90241-X

Zarandi, M., Turksen, I., & Saghiri, S. (2002). Supply chain: Crisp and fuzzy aspects. *International Journal of Applied Mathematics and Computer Science*, *12*(3), 423–435.

Zeithaml, V. (2000). Service quality, profitability, and the economic worth of customers: What we know and what we need to learn. *Journal of the Academy of Marketing Science*, *28*(1), 67–85. doi:10.1177/0092070300281007

Zeithaml, V., Berry, L., & Parasuraman, A. (1996). The behavioural consequences of service quality. *Journal of Marketing*, *60*(2), 31–46. doi:10.2307/1251929

KEY TERMS AND DEFINITIONS

Assurance: A dimension of SERVQUAL, evaluates the knowledge and courtesy of employees and their ability to build trust and confidence.

Crisp Clustering: Clustering undertaken where there is discrete 0 or 1 membership of objects to a cluster.

Empathy: A dimension of SERVQUAL, refers to caring and individualized attention provided to customers by the firm and its employees.

Fuzzy Clustering: Clustering undertaken where there are grades of membership of between 0 to 1 objects to each cluster.

Loyalty: The degree to which a customer is willing to repeat patronage.

Responsiveness: A dimension of SERVQUAL, denotes the service firm's willingness to help customers and offer prompt service.

Satisfaction: A post-purchase evaluation of products or services taking into consideration customers; expectations.

SERVQUAL: A scale which assesses the expectations-performance gap to measure customers' perceptions of service quality with service provider firms.

Tangibles: A dimension of SERVQUAL, refers to physical facilities, equipment, and appearance of employees.

APPENDIX

This Appendix contains the questions employed to gather the opinions of SERVQUAL across the phone industry problem considered. See Tables 6 and 7.

Table 6. Description of questions associated with SERVQUAL dimensions, tangibles, reliability, responsiveness, assurance and empathy*

Dimension	Questions
Tangibles	A1) The company has modern-looking equipment.
	A2) The company's physical facilities (such as desks) are visually appealing.
	A3) The company's employees are neat in appearance.
	A4) Materials associated with the service (such as promotional screens, self-service machines) are visually appealing
Reliability	A5) When the company promises to do something, it does so.
	A6) When I have a problem, the company shows a sincere interest in solving it.
	A7) The company performs the service right the first time.
	A8) The company provides its services at the time its promises to do so.
	A9) The company always delivers error free billing.
Responsiveness	A10) Employees of the company tell me exactly when services will be performed.
	A11) Employees of the company provide prompt service.
	A12) Employees of the company are always willing to help me.
	A13) Employees of the company are never too busy to respond to my requests.
Assurance	A14) I trust company employees.
	A15) Employees of the company make me feel safe during my transactions.
	A16) Employees of the company are consistently courteous towards me.
	A17) Employees of the company have the knowledge to answer my questions.
Empathy	A18) The company gives me individual attention.
	A19) The company has convenient operating hours.
	A20) The company has employees who give me personal attention.
	A21) The company has my best interests at heart.
	A22) Employees of the company understand my specific needs.

* SERVQUAL items adopted from Parasuraman et al. (1988).

Table 7. Description of questions associated with external variable dimensions, loyalty and satisfaction

Dimension	Questions
Loyalty*	B1) I intend to use this company more in the future.
	B2) I am very likely to encourage my friends to use this mobile phone company.
	B3) As long as the present standard of service continues, I would use this company again.
	B4) I intend to use this company less in the future.
	B5) I consider this company to be my first choice.
Satisfaction**	B6) I am satisfied with my decision to use this company.
	B7) My choice to use this company was a wise one.
	B8) I think I did the right thing when I chose this company.
	B9) I feel dissatisfied with my company services.

* Loyalty items adopted from Zeithaml et al. (1996).

** Satisfaction items adopted from Oliver (1980).

Chapter 4
An Analysis of the Interactions among the Enablers of Information Communication Technology in Humanitarian Supply Chain Management:
A Fuzzy-Based Relationship Modelling Approach

Gaurav Kabra
Indian Institute of Technology Roorkee, India

A Ramesh
Indian Institute of Technology Roorkee, India

ABSTRACT

The rise in the occurrence of disasters has hampered the development of many countries. Practitioners and academicians are making continuous demands to enhance the utilization of information communication technologies (ICTs) in humanitarian supply chain management (HSCM) in order to continue or enhance the pace of economic growth and development of countries, as well as to reduce the impact of disaster on society. Identifying and analysing key decision variables improving the utilization of ICT in HSCM is essential in trying to improve overall performance. Therefore, to assist the organizations involved in HSCM, this study explores eleven enablers to enhancing the utilization of ICTs, with a focus on the mutual relationship among them using an integrated interpretive structural modeling (ISM) and fuzzy cross-impact matrix multiplication applied to classification (F-MICMAC) analysis. This study seeks to advance the understanding on enablers of ICTs in HSCM and to classify them, on the basis of driving and dependence power.

DOI: 10.4018/978-1-5225-0997-4.ch004

1. INTRODUCTION

The application of information technology has been widely recognized in the area of humanitarian supply chain management (HSCM). The information is the key and foremost important resource for any successful relief operations. The application of IT such as information systems has been acknowledge in several disasters such as 9/11 and the London 7/7 bombing as cited by (Prasanna & Huggins, 2016). To effectively manage the relief operations, the end users' should have the prior knowledge of the ways to manage different disasters. "Access to information is critical to successful disaster risk management. You cannot manage what you cannot measure." Thus, the relief activities are mainly guided by the information coming from the disaster site, clarity of the situation and the management of information (Long & Wood, 1995; Perry, 2007; Simchi-Levi, Kaminsky, & Simchi-Levi, 2003). Thus, it is vital to develop such information technology based systems which provide the critical information rapidly to the decision makers' so they can make decisions quickly and accurately.

There has been substantive research that examine the factors affecting the information technology acceptance and utilization among end- users in commercial context. For example, online purchasing tickets (Rodríguez, Busco, & Flores, 2014), mobile-RFID services (Jeong, Yoo, & Heo, 2009). Many researchers have highlighted the potential of IT in emergency management (Rao, 2007; Marcus Vogt, Hertweck, & Hales, 2011). These research have resulted in several barriers and enablers to improve the performance of HSCM. Several studies have explored the technologies for first line responder to the disasters. For example, knowledge management system (KMS) to support disaster response (Dorasamy, Raman, & Kaliannan, 2013), information management system such as IMASH (Iakovou & Douligeris, 2001); and PeopleFinder (Murphy & Jennex, 2006). In addition, many studies focuses on the design and development aspects of emergency management information system. However, there has been comparatively limited research that examines the enablers of information technology in humanitarian supply chain management in Indian context. Therefore, this study is an attempt to address the critical research gap. In nutshell, the objectives of this paper are as follows:

- Identifying and ranking the enablers to the IT enablement of HSCM;
- Establishing the relationships between the enablers to the IT enablement of HSCM; and
- Classification of the identified enablers into various categories; and to derive key managerial insights.

The rest of the paper is organized as follows: Section 2 discusses the enablers to the IT enablement of HSCM. Section 3 explains the methodology adopted for this study. Section 4 explain the results and findings of this study. Finally, Section 6 presents the conclusion of the study.

2. LITERATURE REVIEW

During the 1990s, organizations tended to implement IT in their internal SC processes. However, numerous studies suggest that since the year 2000, many organizations have shifted towards the implementation of IT in their SC (Chou, Tan, & Yen, 2004). Beynon-Davis (2009) defined IT as "any technology used to support information gathering, processing, distribution and use and is composed of hardware, software, data and communication technology." The use of IT in HSC has become fundamental to enhancing performance as it offers a platform to facilitate information sharing among the actors in HSCM (Chan, Killeen, Griswold, & Lenert, 2004; Jefferson, 2006; National Research Council, 1999; Overstreet, Hall, Hanna, & Kelly Rainer, 2011; Stephenson & Anderson, 1997; Telleen & Martin, 2002). The utilization of IT is found to be beneficial for organizations to improve the HSC performance.

Various information communication technologies (ICTs) such as geographic information systems (GIS), global positioning systems (GPS), etc. have been extensively utilized in the past disaster relief operations. This will help the stakeholders in sharing and process real-time information, in order to establish diverse communication channels for working for the betterment of the society (Jaeger et al., 2007; Kapucu, 2006; Shneiderman & Preece, 2007). Tomasini & Van Wassenhove (2009) also supported that ICTs act as a dominant lubricant for enabling the disaster response to be more agile. Several enablers to IT enablement of HSCM are discueed in the subsequent section.

2.1 Identification of Enablers for IT Enablement in HSCM

Based on the available literature and discussion with domain experts, eleven enablers to IT enablement of HSCM are identified within the context of India. These enablers are presented in Table 1.

3. RESEARCH METHODOLOGY

The overall approach has mainly included interactions with several experts from industry and academics, as well as from newspaper articles and informal discussions with local residents. As a result, eleven enablers were identified in the process of IT enablement of HSCM. The interrelationships among these enablers are obtained using an integrated ISM and Fuzzy MICMAC analysis.

Table 1. Enablers for IT enablement in HSCM

S. No.	Factors	References
F1	Top management commitment	(Christopher & Peck, 2004; Gustavsson, 2003)
F2	Information sharing	(Cozzolino, 2012; Fugate, Sahin, & Mentzer, 2006; Maiers, Reynolds, & Haselkorn, 2005)
F3	Automated supply chain processes	(Agostinho, 2013; Kabra & Ramesh, 2015b; Maiers et al., 2005)
F4	IT awareness	(Agostinho, 2013; Kabra & Ramesh, 2015b; Maiers et al., 2005; Yadav & Barve, 2015)
F5	Investment for utilization of ICT	(Agostinho, 2013; Gustavsson, 2003; Kabra & Ramesh, 2015a)
F6	Long term commitment from donors	(Balcik, Beamon, Krejci, Muramatsu, & Ramirez, 2010; Gustavsson, 2003; Whiting & Ayala-Öström, 2009)
F7	Proactive behavior	(Agostinho, 2013; Pettit & Beresford, 2009; Van Wassenhove, 2006)
F8	Strategic planning	(Balcik et al., 2010; Kovacs & Spens, 2007; McEntire, 2002; Van Wassenhove, 2006)
F9	IT infrastructure	(Kabra & Ramesh, 2015b; Maiers et al., 2005)
F10	Trust among actors	(Kabra, Ramesh, & Arshinder, 2015; Kehler, 2004; Pasupuleti, 2013; Sheffi & Rice, 2005)
F11	Improved performance	(Davidson, 2006; der Laan, De Brito, & Vergunst, 2009; Klumpp, Abidi, de Leeuw, & Klumpp, 2014)

3.1 ISM Methodology

J. Warfield has proposed ISM in 1973 to analyse the complex systems. It is an interactive learning process in which various directly or indirectly interrelated variables are combined into a multilevel structural model. ISM model is based on the expert's experience and its opinions. ISM refer to "the systematic application of some elementary notions of graph theory in such a way that theoretical, conceptual, and computational leverage is exploited to efficiently construct a directed graph, or network representation, of the complex pattern of a contextual relationship among a set of elements" (Malone, 1975). The various steps to develop ISM model are given below (source: Thakkar, Kanda, & Deshmukh, 2008):

Step I - Development of Self-Structural Interaction Matrix (SSIM): In this step, a contextual relationship of "guide the occurrence" between the enablers to the IT enablement of HSCM is established. The following four symbols are used for the above relation between two enablers:

- **V:** Enabler i guide the occurrence of j;
- **A:** Enabler j guide the occurrence of i;
- **X:** Element i and j both guide the occurrence of each other;
- **0:** Element i and j are not related.

Step II - Development of Reachability Matrix: In this step, Initial reachability matrix (IRM) is developed from SSIM by substituting X, A, V, and O by 1 and 0 as per the rule shown in Box 1.

- The transitivity relation i.e. element A is related to element B and element B is further related to element C, then element A will be necessarily related to element C. These relations are checked to develop final reachability matrix (FRM).

Step III - Level Partition: In this step, the reachability, antecedent and intersection set for each enabler is established. The reachability set consists of itself and other enablers, whose occurrence guided by it, whereas the antecedent set consists of itself and the other enablers, which guided its occurrence. Thereafter, intersection of reachability and antecedent set is derived for each enabler's. The enabler for which reachability and intersection sets are similar, will be placed at the top level of ISM model. The whole process is repeated until each enabler will be placed at some level.

Step IV - Classification of Enablers: The enablers have been classified into four groups, namely autonomous, dependent, linkage, and driver variables, based on their driving power and dependence power.

Step V - Development of Digraph: From the canonical matrix form obtained in step III, the directed graph or digraph is drawn by means of vertices or nodes and lines of edges. Further, digraph is converted into the structural model known as ISM model.

Box 1.

Entry in SSIM (i, j)	V	A	X	O
Entry in reachability matrix (i, j)	1	0	1	0
Entry in reachability matrix (j, i)	0	1	1	0

3.2 ISM Fuzzy MICMAC Analysis

To overcome the drawback of ISM MICMAC analysis model, i.e. the relationship between two enablers cannot be always binary (0 or 1). Fuzzy MICMAC analysis has been used in this study to overcome the limitation of binary relationship as some relations may be very low, some may be low, some may be medium, some may be strong, some may be especially strong and some relations may be better. The steps for fuzzy MICMAC analysis as suggested by (S J Gorane & Kant, 2013) are explain as follows

Step 1 - Binary Direct Relationship Matrix (BDRM): BDRM is obtained by examining the direct relationship between the factors in the ISM and the diagonal entries are converted to zero.

Step 2 - Development of Fuzzy Direct Relationship Matrix (FDRM): Again the opinion of same experts have been utilized to reconsider the relationship between the factors on the basis of Table 2. The values for the relationship between factors are then superimposed on the BDRM (table without transitivity) to obtain a FDRM.

Step 3 - Fuzzy MICMAC Stabilized Matrix: The FDRM matrix is multiplied repeatedly until the hierarchies of the driver and dependence power stabilize using the following rule (Kandasamy, Smarandache, & Ilanthenral, 2007) as given below:

$$C= A,B = \max k \, [(\min (a_{ik}, b_{kj})]$$

where $A = [a_{ik}]$ and $B= [b_{kj}]$.

The driving and dependence power in fuzzy MICMAC is derived by summing the entries of possibilities of interactions in the rows and columns respectively.

4. RESULTS AND DISCUSSION

The enablers to IT enablement of HSCM (as listed Table 1) are modelled using ISM. For the purpose, opinions of experts were used to fill an initial matrix SSIM [step I, Section 3.1] by denoting "influences" relationships to the chosen enablers. This is followed by the other steps (step II to step IV) as given in Section 3.1. Based on the conditions in the (Section 3.1, step II) reachability matrix is formed.

In this paper eleven variables were explored using an extensive literature review and discussion with the domain experts. The interrelation between variables is obtained with the opinion of experts (see Figure 1). Figure 1 depicts that top management support, IT awareness, proactive behaviour are at level 1. Strategic planning and long term commitment from donors are at level 2 and level 3 respectively. Investment in IT is at level 4 while automated supply chain and improved IT infrastructure are at level 5. The level 6 constitutes trust and information sharing among actors. All the levels collectively lead to improved HSCM performance. If all the levels of ISM model are implemented then effective and efficient delivery of relief materials can be done.

Table 2. Possibility of numerical value of the reachability

Possibility of Reachability	No	Very Low	Low	Medium	High	Very High	Complete
Value	0	0.1	0.3	0.5	0.7	0.9	1

Table 3. Step I: formation of SSIM

	Factors	F1	F4	F5	F6	F7	F8	F9	F10	F11	F13	F14
F1	Top management commitment		V	V	X	V	V	X	V	V	V	V
F2	Information sharing			A	A	A	O	A	A	A	X	V
F3	Automated supply chain processes				A	A	A	A	A	X	V	V
F4	IT awareness					V	V	V	V	V	V	V
F5	Investment for utilization of ICT						A	A	A	V	V	V
F6	Long term commitment from donors							A	A	V	V	V
F7	Proactive behavior								V	V	V	V
F8	Strategic planning									V	V	V
F9	IT infrastructure										V	V
F10	Trust among actors											V
F11	Improved performance											

Table 4. Step II: reachability matrix

	Factors	F1	F4	F5	F6	F7	F8	F9	F10	F11	F13	F14
F1	Top management commitment	1	1	1	1	1	1	1	1	1	1	1
F2	Information sharing	0	1	0	0	0	0	0	0	1	1	1
F3	Automated supply chain processes	0	1	1	0	0	0	0	0	1	1	1
F4	IT awareness	1	1	1	1	1	1	1	1	1	1	1
F5	Investment for utilization of ICT	0	1	1	0	1	0	0	0	1	1	1
F6	Long term commitment from donors	0	1	1	0	1	1	0	0	1	1	1
F7	Proactive behavior	1	1	1	1	1	1	1	1	1	1	1
F8	Strategic planning	0	1	1	0	1	1	0	1	1	1	1
F9	IT infrastructure	0	1	1	0	0	0	0	0	1	1	1
F10	Trust among actors	0	1	0	0	0	0	0	0	0	1	1
F11	Improved performance	0	0	0	0	0	0	0	0	0	0	1

To fulfil other objective of this paper, F-MICMAC analysis was used (see Figure 2). All 11 variables are divided into 4 clusters. For the purpose, opinions of same expert's used in developing ISM model, were used to develop Fuzzy Direct Relationship Matrix" (Table 5) and "F-MICMAC stabilized matrix" (Table 6) by following procedural steps (step 5 to step 7). Finally, enablers are classified on the basis of driving and dependence power into 4 categories as shown in Figure 2.

- **Autonomous Variables:** These variables have weak dependent powers and weak driver powers. There is no autonomous variable as an enabler to IT enablement of HSC. Therefore, management of the organisations involved in HSC should pay attention to all the enablers.
- **Driver Variables:** Driver variables are those variables that required attention on priority basis because there are other factors which are affected by them. F1 (Top management commitment),

Figure 1.

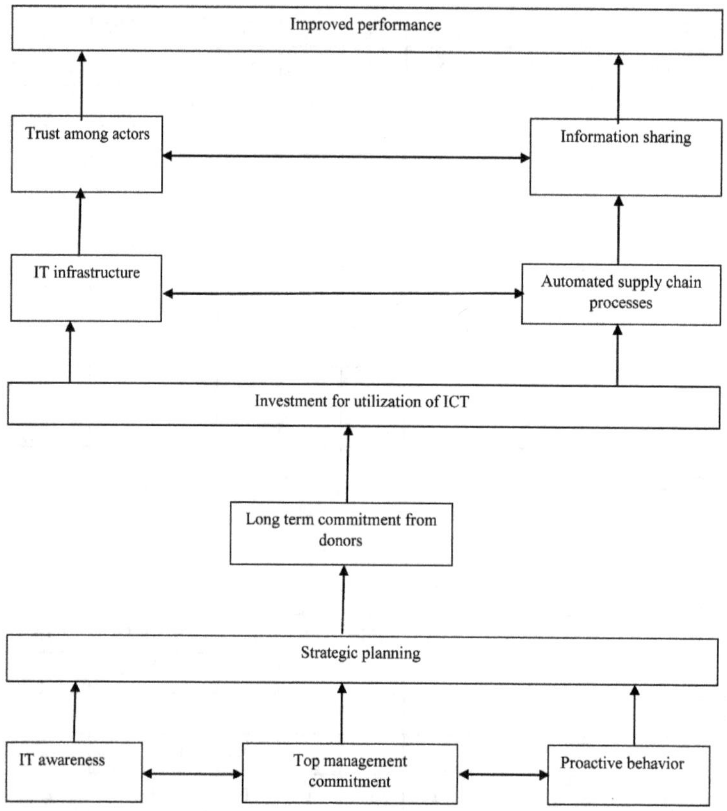

Figure 2. MICMAC analysis

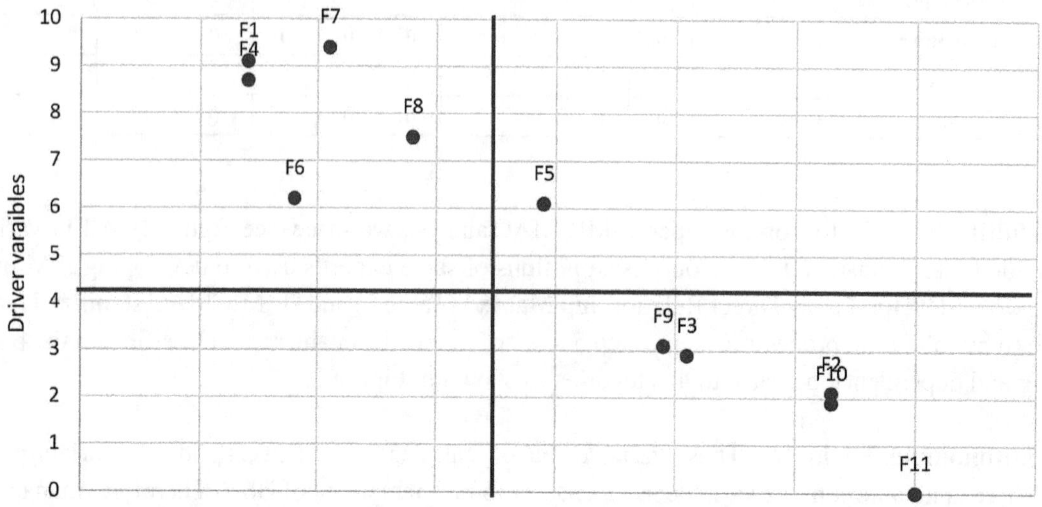

Table 5. Fuzzy direct relationship matrix

	Factors	F1	F4	F5	F6	F7	F8	F9	F10	F11	F13	F14
F1	Top management commitment	0	0.3	0.3	0.7	0.9	0.3	0.7	0.7	0.5	0.7	0.7
F2	Information sharing	0	0	0	0	0	0	0	0	0	0.7	0.5
F3	Automated supply chain processes	0	0.7	0	0	0	0	0	0	0.3	0.5	0.5
F4	IT awareness	0.7	0.3	0.3	0	0.7	0.3	0.7	0.7	0.5	0.7	0.7
F5	Investment for utilization of ICT	0	0.7	0.9	0	0	0	0	0	0.9	0.7	0.9
F6	Long term commitment from donors	0	0	0.5	0	0.7	0	0	0	0.5	0.3	0.3
F7	Proactive behavior	0.7	0.3	0.3	0.7	0.7	0.3	0	0.7	0.5	0.7	0.5
F8	Strategic planning	0	0.5	0.5	0	0.9	0.5	0	0	0.7	0.5	0.7
F9	IT infrastructure	0	0.7	0.9	0	0	0	0	0	0	0.5	0.7
F10	Trust among actors	0	0.7	0	0	0	0	0	0	0	0	0.9
F11	Improved performance	0	0	0	0	0	0	0	0	0	0	0

Table 6. Fuzzy MICMAC stabilized matrix

	Factors	F1	F4	F5	F6	F7	F8	F9	F10	F11	F13	F14	Sum
F1	Top management commitment	0	0.7	0.9	0.7	0.9	0.3	0.7	0.7	0.9	0.7	0.9	7.4
F2	Information sharing	0	0	0	0	0	0	0	0	0	0.7	0.7	1.4
F3	Automated supply chain processes	0	0.7	0	0	0	0	0	0	0.3	0.5	0.7	2.2
F4	IT awareness	0.7	0.7	0.7	0	0.7	0.5	0.7	0.7	0.7	0.7	0.7	6.8
F5	Investment for utilization of ICT	0	0.7	0.9	0	0	0	0	0	0.9	0.9	0.9	4.3
F6	Long term commitment from donors	0	0.7	0.9	0	0.9	0	0	0	0.7	0.7	0.7	4.6
F7	Proactive behavior	0.7	0.7	0.7	0.7	0.7	0.5	0.7	0.7	0.7	0.7	0.5	7.3
F8	Strategic planning	0	0.7	0.7	0	0.7	0.5	0	0.7	0.7	0.7	0.7	5.4
F9	IT infrastructure	0	0.7	0.3	0	0	0	0	0	0	0.7	0.7	2.4
F10	Trust among actors	0	0.7	0	0	0	0	0	0	0	0	0.5	1.2
F11	Improved performance	0	0	0	0	0	0	0	0	0	0	0	0
Sum		1.4	6.3	5.1	1.4	3.9	1.8	2.1	2.8	4.9	6.3	7	

F4 (IT awareness), F6 (Long term commitment from donors), F7 (Proactive behavior) and F8 (Strategic planning) are driver variables.

- **Linkage Variables:** Linkage variables are those variables that any change occurred to these variables will have an effect on others and also a feedback on themselves. F5 (Investment for utilization of ICT) is linkage variable which are interconnected with each other in two ways.
- **Dependent Variables:** Finally, F2 (Information sharing), F3 (Automated supply chain processes), F9 (IT infrastructure), F10 (Trust among actors) and F11 (Improved performance) are dependent on many other factors. Therefore, these are strong driving variables and may be treated as the root causes for all other enablers, so supply chain managers need to address these enablers as apriority to improve the utilization of IT in HSCM.

5. CONCLUSION

This study is an attempt to ascertain and examine the interrelationship among the enablers to enhance the utilization of ICT in HSCM. Initially, eleven enabler's to IT enablement of HSCM have been identified through an extensive literature review allied with the discussion with experts. Thereafter, an integrated ISM and fuzzy MICMAC analysis on the set of identified enablers was used to develop an ISM model for enhancing the utilization of ICT in HSCM. Finally, these enablers are classified into four categories based on the driving and dependence power, namely autonomous, driver, dependent and linkage variables using fuzzy MICMAC analysis. This considers the relationship between two variables as strong, especially strong, medium, weak or very weak instead of a binary relationship as in the ISM model. This is the first kind of study to consider the enablers to improve the utilization of ICT in HSCM and also extends the relatively limited literature in this field. Despite the contributions in the present body of literature in the area of HSCM, the current study is also not free from limitations. One of the most complex issues in this research is the weightage of ISM model; it is based on expert's opinion. A questionnaire survey could be conducted in future on these enablers as the developed model has not been statistically validated.

REFERENCES

Agostinho, F. (2013). *Humanitarian Logistics: How to Help Even More?*. doi:10.3182/20130911-3-BR-3021.00075

Balcik, B., Beamon, B. M., Krejci, C. C., Muramatsu, K. M., & Ramirez, M. (2010). Coordination in humanitarian relief chains: Practices, challenges and opportunities. *International Journal of Production Economics, 126*(1), 22–34. doi:10.1016/j.ijpe.2009.09.008

Beynon-Davis, P. (2009). *Business Information Systems*. Palgrave Macmillan.

Chan, T. C., Killeen, J., Griswold, W., & Lenert, L. (2004). Information technology and emergency medical care during disasters. *Academic Emergency Medicine : Official Journal of the Society for Academic Emergency Medicine, 11*(11), 1229–1236. doi:10.1111/j.1553-2712.2004.tb00709.x PMID:15528589

Chou, D. C., Tan, X., & Yen, D. C. (2004). Web technology and supply chain management. *Information Management & Computer Security, 12*(4), 338–349. doi:10.1108/09685220410553550

Christopher, M., & Peck, H. (2004). Building the resilient supply chain. *The International Journal of Logistics Management, 15*(2), 1–14. doi:10.1108/09574090410700275

Cozzolino, A. (2012). *Humanitarian {Logistics}: {Cross}-{Sector} {Cooperation} in {Disaster} {Relief} {Management}*. Springer Science & Business Media. doi:10.1007/978-3-642-30186-5

Davidson, A. L. (2006). *Key performance indicators in humanitarian logistics* (Thesis). Massachusetts Institute of Technology.

der Laan, E. A., De Brito, M. P., & Vergunst, D. A. (2009). Performance measurement in humanitarian supply chains. *International Journal of Risk Assessment and Management, 13*(1), 22–45. doi:10.1504/IJRAM.2009.026388

Dorasamy, M., Raman, M., & Kaliannan, M. (2013). Knowledge management systems in support of disasters management: A two decade review. *Technological Forecasting and Social Change*, *80*(9), 1834–1853. doi:10.1016/j.techfore.2012.12.008

Fugate, B., Sahin, F., & Mentzer, J. T. (2006). Supply Chain Management Coordination Mechanisms. *Journal of Business Logistics*, *27*(2), 129–161. doi:10.1002/j.2158-1592.2006.tb00220.x

Gorane, S. J., & Kant, R. (2013). Modelling the SCM enablers: An integrated ISM-fuzzy MICMAC approach. *Asia Pacific Journal of Marketing and Logistics*, *25*(2), 263–286. doi:10.1108/13555851311314059

Gorane, S. J., & Kant, R. (2013). Supply chain management: Modelling the enablers using {ISM} and fuzzy {MICMAC} approach. *International Journal of Logistics Systems and Management*, *16*(2), 147–166. doi:10.1504/IJLSM.2013.056158

Gustavsson, L. (2003). *Humanitarian logistics: Context and challenges*. Academic Press.

Iakovou, E., & Douligeris, C. (2001). An information management system for the emergency management of hurricane disasters. *International Journal of Risk Assessment and Management*. Retrieved from http://www.inderscienceonline.com/doi/abs/10.1504/IJRAM.2001.001508

Jaeger, P. T., Shneiderman, B., Fleischmann, K. R., Preece, J., Qu, Y., & Fei Wu, P. (2007). Community response grids: E-government, social networks, and effective emergency management. *Telecommunications Policy*, *31*(10–11), 592–604. doi:10.1016/j.telpol.2007.07.008

Jefferson, T. L. (2006). Evaluating the role of information technology in crisis and emergency management. *Vine*, *36*(3), 261–264. doi:10.1108/03055720610703542

Jeong, N., Yoo, Y., & Heo, T.-Y. (2009). Moderating effect of personal innovativeness on mobile-RFID services: Based on Warshaw's purchase intention model. *Technological Forecasting and Social Change*, *76*(1), 154–164. doi:10.1016/j.techfore.2008.08.007

Kabra, G., & Ramesh, A. (2015a). An emprical investigation of enablers in {Humanitarain} {Supply} {Chain} {Management} in {India}: {A} {Case} {Study}. *Journal of Advances Research in Management*, *11*(1).

Kabra, G., & Ramesh, A. (2015b). Analyzing ICT Issues in Humanitarian Supply Chain Management: A SAP-LAP Linkages Framework. *Global Journal of Flexible Systems Management*, 1–15. doi:10.1007/s40171-014-0088-3

Kabra, G., Ramesh, A., & Arshinder, K. (2015). Identification and prioritization of coordination barriers in humanitarian supply chain management. *International Journal of Disaster Risk Reduction*.

Kandasamy, W. B. V., Smarandache, F., & Ilanthenral, K. (2007). *Elementary fuzzy matrix theory and fuzzy models for social scientists*. Academic Press.

Kapucu, N. (2006). Interagency Communication Networks During Emergencies Boundary Spanners in Multiagency Coordination. *American Review of Public Administration*, *36*(2), 207–225. doi:10.1177/0275074005280605

Kehler, N. (2004). *Coordinating Humanitarian Assistance: A Comparative Analysis of Three Cases*. Virginia Polytechnic Institute and State University.

Klumpp, M., Abidi, H., de Leeuw, S., & Klumpp, M. (2014). Humanitarian supply chain performance management: A systematic literature review. *Supply Chain Management: An International Journal*, *19*(5/6), 592–608. doi:10.1108/SCM-09-2013-0349

Kovacs, G., & Spens, K. M. (2007). Humanitarian logistics in disaster relief operations. *International Journal of Physical Distribution & Logistics Management*, *37*(2), 99–114. doi:10.1108/09600030710734820

Long, D. C., & Wood, D. F. (1995). The logistics of famine relief. *Journal of Business Logistics*, *16*, 213–213.

Maiers, C., Reynolds, M., & Haselkorn, M. (2005). Challenges to effective information and communication systems in humanitarian relief organizations. *IEEE Proceedings*.

Malone, D. W. (1975). An introduction to the application of interpretive structural modeling. *Proceedings of the IEEE*, *63*(3), 397–404. doi:10.1109/PROC.1975.9765

McEntire, D. A. (2002). Coordinating multiorganisational responses to disaster: Lessons from the {March} 28, 2000, {Fort} {Worth} tornado. *Disaster Prevention and Management: An International Journal*, *11*(5), 369–379. doi:10.1108/09653560210453416

Murphy, T., & Jennex, M. E. (2006). Knowledge Management and Hurricane Katrina Response. *International Journal of Knowledge Management*, *2*(4), 52–66. doi:10.4018/jkm.2006100104

National Research Council. (1999). *Reducing Disaster Losses Through Better Information*. Washington, DC: National Academy Press.

Overstreet, R. E., Hall, D., Hanna, J. B., & Kelly Rainer, R. Jr. (2011). Research in humanitarian logistics. *Journal of Humanitarian Logistics and Supply Chain Management*, *1*(2), 114–131. doi:10.1108/20426741111158421

Pasupuleti, R. S. (2013). Designing culturally responsive built environments in post disaster contexts: Tsunami affected fishing settlements in Tamilnadu, India. *International Journal of Disaster Risk Reduction*, *6*, 28–39. doi:10.1016/j.ijdrr.2013.03.008

Perry, M. (2007). Natural disaster management planning. *International Journal of Physical Distribution & Logistics Management*, *37*(5), 409–433. doi:10.1108/09600030710758455

Pettit, S., & Beresford, A. (2009). Critical success factors in the context of humanitarian aid supply chains. *International Journal of Physical Distribution & Logistics Management*, *39*(6), 450–468. doi:10.1108/09600030910985811

Prasanna, R., & Huggins, T. J. (2016). Factors affecting the acceptance of information systems supporting emergency operations centres. *Computers in Human Behavior*, *57*, 168–181. doi:10.1016/j.chb.2015.12.013

Rao, X. R. (2007). *Issues and Challenges of Humanitarian Logistics in china*. University of Nottingham.

Rodríguez, D., Busco, C., & Flores, R. (2014). Technology in Society Information technology within society ' s evolution. *Technology in Society*, 1–9. doi:10.1016/j.techsoc.2014.08.006

Sheffi, Y., & Rice, J. B. (2005). A Supply Chain View of the Resilient Enterprise. *MIT Sloan Management Review, 47*(1).

Shneiderman, B., & Preece, J. (2007). *911.Gov: Community Response Grids*. Academic Press.

Simchi-Levi, D., Kaminsky, P., & Simchi-Levi, E. (2003). *Designing and Managing the Supply Chain: Concepts, Strategies, and Case Studies*. McGraw Hill Professional.

Stephenson, R., & Anderson, P. S. (1997). Disasters and the information technology revolution. *Disasters, 21*(4), 305–334. doi:10.1111/1467-7717.00065 PMID:9455005

Telleen, S., & Martin, E. (2002). Improving information access for public health professionals. *Journal of Medical Systems, 26*(6), 529–543. doi:10.1023/A:1020244726109 PMID:12385535

Thakkar, J., Kanda, A., & Deshmukh, S. G. (2008). Interpretive structural modeling (ISM) of IT-enablers for Indian manufacturing SMEs. *Information Management & Computer Security, 16*(2), 113–136. doi:10.1108/09685220810879609

Tomasini, R. M., & Van Wassenhove, L. N. (2009). From preparedness to partnerships: Case study research on humanitarian logistics. *International Transactions in Operational Research, 16*(5), 549–559. doi:10.1111/j.1475-3995.2009.00697.x

Van Wassenhove, L. N. (2006). Humanitarian aid logistics: Supply chain management in high gear†. *The Journal of the Operational Research Society, 57*(5), 475–489. doi:10.1057/palgrave.jors.2602125

Vogt, M., Hertweck, D., & Hales, K. (2011). Strategic ICT Alignment in Uncertain Environments: An Empirical Study in Emergency Management Organizations. *2011 44th Hawaii International Conference on System Sciences*. doi:10.1109/HICSS.2011.387

Whiting, M. C., & Ayala-Öström, B. E. (2009). Advocacy to promote logistics in humanitarian aid. *Management Research News, 32*(11), 1081–1089. doi:10.1108/01409170910998309

Yadav, D. K., & Barve, A. (2015). Analysis of critical success factors of humanitarian supply chain: An application of Interpretive Structural Modeling. *International Journal of Disaster Risk Reduction*, 1–13. doi:10.1016/j.ijdrr.2015.01.008

Section 2
Computational Intelligence:
Business Analytics

Chapter 5
Auto Associative Extreme Learning Machine Based Hybrids for Data Imputation

Chandan Gautam
Institute for Development and Research in Banking Technology, India

Vadlamani Ravi
Institute for Development and Research in Banking Technology, India

ABSTRACT

This chapter presents three novel hybrid techniques for data imputation viz., (1) Auto-associative Extreme Learning Machine (AAELM) with Principal Component Analysis (PCA) (PCA-AAELM), (2) Gray system theory (GST) + AAELM with PCA (Gray+PCA-AAELM), (3) AAELM with Evolving Clustering Method (ECM) (ECM-AAELM). Our prime concern is to remove the randomness in AAELM caused by the random weights with the help of ECM and PCA. This chapter also proposes local learning by invoking ECM as a preprocessor for AAELM. The proposed methods are tested on several regression, classification and bank datasets using 10 fold cross validation. The results, in terms of Mean Absolute Percentage Error (MAPE,) are compared with that of K-Means+Multilayer perceptron (MLP) imputation (Ankaiah & Ravi, 2011), K-Medoids+MLP, K-Means+GRNN, K-Medoids+GRNN (Nishanth & Ravi, 2013) PSO_Covariance imputation (Krishna & Ravi, 2013) and ECM-Imputation (Gautam & Ravi, 2014). It is concluded that the proposed methods achieved better imputation in most of the datasets as evidenced by the Wilcoxon signed rank test.

INTRODUCTION

Missing data can be observed in many datasets, which have been collected in real time. It can occur due to many reasons like sometimes people don't answers all query during surveydue to privacy or sometimes data entry operator leave blank space due to lack of concentration or some other reasons etc. Failure of any system or snsor nodes in wireless sensor network can also lead to missing data. Missing data is a very challenging issue in the field of analytics because the completeness and quality of the data always

DOI: 10.4018/978-1-5225-0997-4.ch005

plays a crucial role in analyzing the available data. Replace the missing value by an appropriate value is called imputation. In general, data mining algorithms are not capable of handling data incompleteness on its own. So, it is necessary to impute those missing value by some appropriate vaue using some suitable data imputation algorithm (Ankaiah & Ravi, 2011; Abdella & Marwala, 2005; García & Kalenatic, 2011; Nishanth, Ravi, Ankaiah & Bose, 2012).

Kline (1988) proposed following procedure to handle missing data:

1. Deletion procedure viz., Listwise deletion and Pairwise deletion (Song & Shepperd, 2007),
2. Imputation procedure (Schafer, 1997),
3. Model based procedure, and
4. Machine learning methods.

The remainder of this chapter is organized as follows: first, a brief review of literature on imputation of missing data is presented. Further, proposed method is explained. Then, description of the dataset and Experimental design is described in next section. Results and discussions are presented in second last section and last section states about conclusion.

BACKGROUND

In case of numerical attributes, missing data can be handled in various ways. Numerous type of imputation is possible like: machine learning (ML) based, deletion of missing values, model based approaches etc. There are various ML based approaches like auto-associative neural network imputation with genetic algorithms (Abdella & Marwala, 2005), SOM (Merlin, Sorjamaa, Maillet & Lendasse, 2010), multi-layer perceptron (Gupta & Lam, 1996), K-Nearest Neighbor (Batista & Monard, 2002), fuzzy-neural network (Gabrys, 2002) etc. Batista and Monard (2002, 2003) and Jerez, Molina, Subirates and Franco (2006) employed K-nearest neighbour (K-NN) for handling missing data. Mutual K-NN method proposed by Liu and Zhang (2012) to classify noisy and incomplete data. For handling missing data, Samad and Harp (1992) employed SOM based approach, Austin and Escobar (2005) employed Monte Carlo simulations. Several studies employed Multi-layer perceptron (MLP) for imputation, we train MLP using data without missing attribute as autoassociative model and furthet pass data with missing attribute to trained model for imputation Sharpe and Solly (1995), Nordbotten (1996), Gupta and Lam (1996), Yoon and Lee (1999), Silva-Ramírez, Pino-Mejías, López-Coello and Cubiles-de-la-Vega (2011) and Nkuna and Odiyo (2011). The authors used MLP for data imputation. Auto-associative neural network (AANN) has also been employed for this task by keeping input and output variable identical (Marseguerra & Zoia, 2002; Marwala & Chakraverty, 2006). Ragel and Cremilleux (1999) employed Robust Association Rules Algorithm (RAR) to address multiple missing values in database. Chen, Huang, F. Tian and S. Tian (2008) proposed selective Bayes classifier to handle missing data. Fuzzy c-means algorithm has been employed by Nouvo (2011) to handle incomplete data. Principles of chaos theory has been employed by Elshorbagy, Simonovic and Panu (2002) to handle missing data in stream flow data. Expectation maximization (EM) algorithm has been employed by Dempster, Laird and Rubin (1977) to handle missing values in multivariate data. García and Kalenatic (2011) also proposed Genetic algorithm (GA) based approach to handle missing attribute in multivariate data. Ankaiah and Ravi (2011) handled missing data using hybrid method in two stages. In first stage, K-means has been employed and in second stage, MLP has been employed.

Nishanth, Ravi, Ankaiah and Bose (2012) have also deployed K-means and MLP in 2-stages to handle missing value for assessing the severity of phishing attacks. Doove, Buuren and Dusseldorp (2013) used recursive partitioning; Kang (2013) proposed locally linear construction; Garcia-Laencina, multi-task learning with MLP based approache has been employed by Sancho-gomez and Figueiras-vidal (2013) for the same purpose; multi-layered artificial immune system and genetic algorithm based approach has been proposed by Duma, Marwala, Twala and Nelwamondo (2013); a hybrid of dynamic programming, neural networks and GA is proposed by Nelwamondo, Golding and Marala (2013); Rahman and Islam (2013) deployed decision trees and forests for handling missing data, it can handle both type of missing attributes viz., categorical and numerical; Aydilek and Arslan (2013) hybridized fuzzy c-means support vector regression and GA for imputation. Zhang (2012) employed GST based imputation by using K-NN algorithm and Tian, B. Yu, D. Yu and Ma (2013) proposed hybrid imputation technique by hybridization of GST and entropy based clustering. Recently, Nishanth and Ravi (2013) proposed four hybrid methods, one online and 3 offline methods, to resolve imputation problem. They employed ECM with General regression neural network (GRNN) for online imputation, K-Means and K-Medoids with GRNN and K-Medoids with MLP for offline imputation. Krishna and Ravi (2013) proposed a new imputation technique PSO_Covariance and later, Ravi and Krishna (2014) proposed general regression autoassociative neural network based imputation, Gautam and Ravi (2014) proposed ECM based imputation. Most recently, Gautam and Ravi (2015a, 2015b) proposed Extreme Learning Machine and Counter propagation based autoassociative neural network for imputation.

In this chapter, we proposed three novel hybrid techniques for data imputation by different combinations of Autoassociative neural network, ELM, PCA, GST and ECM. Many researchers have previously employed hybridization with ELM to resolve classification or regression problem. Like, Castaño, Fernåndez-Navarro and Hervás-Martínez (2013) proposed PCA-ELM and Han, Yao and Ling (2012) proposed Particle Swarm optimization (PSO)+Improved ELM (I-ELM) for classification task.

PROPOSED METHODOLOGY

We proposed three imputation methods based on various existing methods viz., extreme learning machine (ELM), evolving clustering method (ECM), principal component analysis (PCA) and gray system theory (GST). Extreme Learning Machine (Huang, Zhu & Siew, 2004, 2006) is a simple and tuning free algorithm. Simple math is sufficient for implementing ELM. Ensemble of various AAELMs is termed as Autoassociative Extreme Learning Factory (AAELF). Ballings and Poel (2013) proposed Kernel Factory and based on this above name AAELF has been coined.

Architecture of Autoassociative Extreme Learning Factory (AAELF)

Until now ELM has been used extensively in two fields, classification and regression problems. This chapter will show the extension of ELM as an Autoassociative ELM (AAELM) and use it in data imputation. An AAELF is constructed by ensemble of several AAELMs. Architecture is shown in Figure 1. Out of three layers of traditional ELM, first two layer of AAELM (Figure. 1) is similar to traditional ELM but third layer is different from traditional ELM and it will be identical to first layer. Number of

Figure 1. Architecture of AAELM

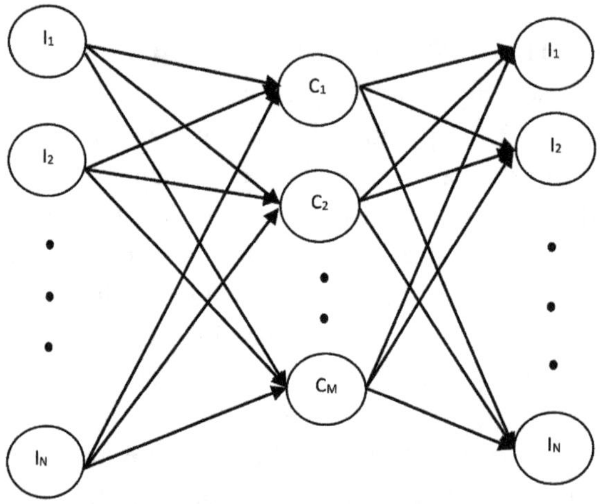

hidden nodes is decided by the user. The value of input weights and hidden biases is selected randomly in AAELM like traditional ELM, but different type of random distribution like Uniform, Normal and Logistic distributions has been employed by us and two different activation functions viz., Sigmoid and Gaussian are used in the implementation of AAELM.

Algorithm for Autoassociative Extreme Learning Factory

The training procedure is stated in following steps:

1. Data is normalized between 0 and 1.
2. After computing the hidden layer output matrix H, calculate the output weight β. using following equation:

$$\beta = H^{\dagger}T \tag{1}$$

3. Compute mean absolute percentage error (MAPE) value to measure the quality of the imputation (Flores, 1986):

$$MAPE = \frac{100}{n}\sum_{i=1}^{n}\left|\frac{\hat{x}_i - x_i}{x_i}\right| \tag{2}$$

where, n is the number of missing values in a given dataset, $\widehat{x_i}$ is predicted by the proposed AAELF for the missing values and x_i is the actual value.

4. Repeat above procedure 10 times and take the average as an outcome.

Since the predicted value at output layer deviate too much due to random parameter of AAELM. So, in order to overcome random behavior of Ensembled AAELM, following methods have been proposed:

- PCA-AAELM,
- Gray+PCA-AAELM,
- ECM-AAELM.

Algorithm for the Proposed Method PCA-AAELM

A new technique is proposed by hybridization of autoassociative neural network, ELM and Principal Component Analysis (PCA). PCA performs dimensionality reduction, which transforms set of correlated variable to set of uncorrelated variable but still possesses most of the information. It generates new set of variables, called principal component. Each principal component is a linear combination of the original variables. All the principal components are orthogonal to each other, so there is no redundant information (MathWorks Inc., 2010). The full set of principal components is as large as the original set of variables (Figure 2).

1. Input data is normalized between 0 and 1.
2. Mn Imputation has been applied on incomplete dataset.
3. Perform PCA with the complete set of records.
4. Number hidden node is decided based on number of principal components selected for explaining the variance in the data.
5. Newly generated matrix by dimensionality reduction in previous steps is passed to some activation function for non-linear transformation and generate hidden layer matrix.

Figure 2. Architecture of PCA-AAELM

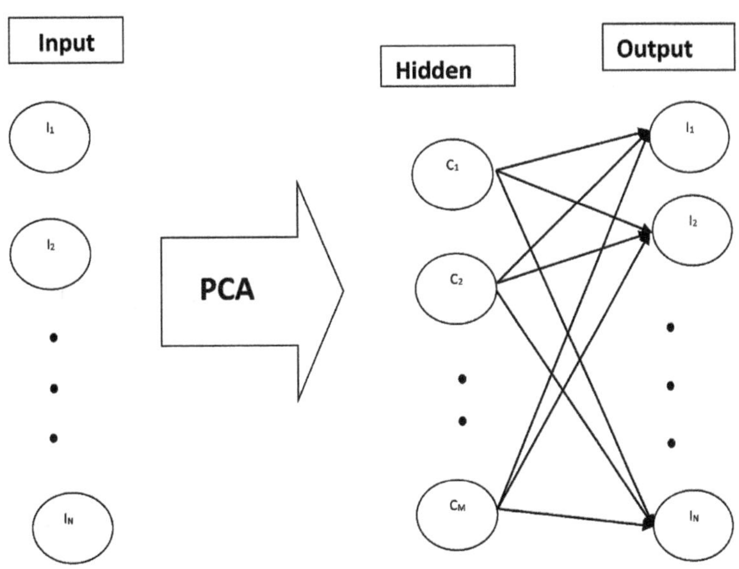

6. Afterwards, apply Moore-Penrose generalized inverse on hidden layer matrix to calculate output layer weights similar to traditional ELM (Huang, Zhu & Siew, 2004, 2006).
7. Compute the mean absolute percentage error (MAPE) value.

Algorithm for the Proposed Gray Distance + PCA-AAELM Method

To select nearest neighbour for imputation, we used Gray Relational Analysis (GRA) (Figure 3). GRA is a method of Gray System Theory (GST) which is proposed by Deng (1982). GRA is based on gray relational model measures the relationship between two systems or two elements of a system (Zhang, 2012). Three steps are required for distance calculation in case of missing data:

1. Normalize the data in the range of [0, 1].
2. Compute GRC by using following formula:

$$GRC(x_{kp}^{mis}, x_i) = \frac{\min_{\forall i} \min_{\forall p} | x_{kp}^{mis} - x_{ip} | + \zeta \max_{\forall i} \max_{\forall p} | x_{kp}^{mis} - x_{ip} |}{| x_{kp}^{mis} - x_{ip} | + \zeta \max_{\forall i} \max_{\forall p} | x_{kp}^{mis} - x_{ip} |}$$

$$\begin{aligned} &p = 1,2,3,......,m. \\ &k = 1,2,3,......,n. \\ &i = 1,2,3,.......,o. \\ &0 \leq \zeta \leq 1 \end{aligned} \tag{3}$$

In above equation, x_{kp}^{mis} is the kth incomplete record and p is the pth attribute with non-missing values. x_i is the ith complete record of the dataset. The calculation only happens when p[th] attribute of x_k^{mis} exists. Another crucial parameter is $\zeta \in [0,1]$. $\zeta = 0$ shows that there is no comparison environment.

Figure 3. Architecture of Gray+PCA-AAELM

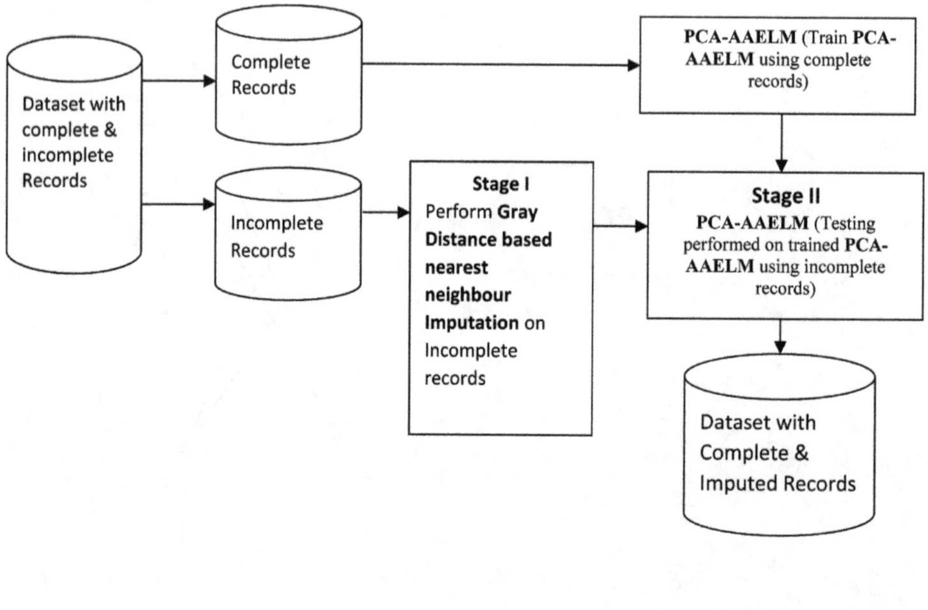

Nevertheless, no methods have been proposed to select optimum value of ζ. Instead, researchers usually select 0.5 for calculation of GRC. The value of $GRC\left(x_{kp}^{mis}, x_i\right)$ is in the range of [0, 1] (Tian, B. Yu, D. Yu & Ma, 2013).

If $GRC\left(x_{kp}^{mis}, x_1\right) > GRC\left(x_{kp}^{mis}, x_2\right)$ then the similarity between x_k and x_1 is larger than that between x_k and x_2; otherwise former is smaller than the latter.

If x_k and x_1 have same value for the attribute p then $GRC(x_{kp}^{mis}, x_1) = 1$ i.e. similarity is maximal.

3. Compute Gray Relational Grade (GRG) according to following formula:

$$GRG\left(x_k^{mis}, x_i\right) = \frac{1}{m}\sum_{p=1}^{m} GRC\left(x_{kp}^{mis}, x_i\right)$$
$$i = 1,2,\ldots\ldots,o. \qquad (4)$$
$$k = 1,2,\ldots\ldots,n.$$

If $GRG\left(x_k^{mis}, x_1\right) > GRG\left(x_k^{mis}, x_2\right)$ then the similarity between x_k and x_1 is larger than that between x_k and x_2; otherwise former is smaller than the latter (Zhang, 2012).

So, missing attribute in an incomplete record is imputed by the corresponding attribute of most similar record among complete set of records and similarity is measured by above 3-steps procedure.

In PCA-AAELM, missing records is imputed based on mean-imputation then pass those records for approximation by PCA-AAELM but in Gray+PCA-AAELM method (Figure. 3), all missing records are imputed based on Gray distance and then pass those records for global approximation by PCA-AAELM algorithm as we discussed in previous section.

Proposed ECM-AAELM Method

Earlier, we hybridized an unsupervised learning technique, PCA, with AAELM. Now, we will use a clustering algorithm, Evolving Clustering Method (ECM), instead of PCA. Since, PCA only performs linear transformation; it doesn't have any local learning capability. So, it didn't perform well compared to other existing methods (Ankaiah & Ravi, 2011; Nishanth & Ravi, 2013; Krishna & Ravi, 2013; Gautam & Ravi, 2014). Therefore, we employed ECM with AAELM. ECM is a one-pass, fast clustering method based on normalized Euclidean distances.

1. **Overview of Online Evolving Clustering Method:** ECM is proposed by Song and Kasabov (2000, 2001), which is a distance based clustering method. In this clustering algorithm, radius of clustering is *Dthr*, which is used as deciding criteria of number of clusters and maximum size of cluster (Song and Kasabov, 2000, 2001). So, if radius of any cluster is going beyond threshold then expansion of that cluster needs to be stopped. We will see further that how selection of proper *Dthr* is very important for our proposed methods.
2. **Algorithm for Proposed ECM-AAELM Method (Figure 4):**
    a. Input data is normalized between 0 and 1.
    b. Dataset is separated into two sets: one set consists of all complete records and other set consists of incomplete records.

c. ECM is employed on complete records and ECM will yield cluster centers based on complete records.
d. Perform ECM based imputation on the set of incomplete records. Attribute value, say x_k, in an incomplete record is imputed by the corresponding value of the attribute in the center of the nearest cluster by measuring the Euclidean distance between the incomplete record excluding the missing value and the cluster centers excluding the value in the same position. The Euclidean distance is measured by using the following formula:

$$D_j = \sum_{i=1;i\neq k}^{n} \left|x_i - c_j\right|^2 \tag{5}$$

where,

j – Number of cluster centers.
n – Number of complete components in each record.

e. Use these cluster centers as hidden nodes in AAELM architecture.
f. Normalized Euclidean distance is computed between cluster centers and input data.
g. Obtained value in previous step is passed to some activation function for non-linear transformation and generate hidden layer matrix.
h. Afterwards, apply Moore-Penrose generalized inverse on hidden layer matrix to calculate output layer weights similar to traditional ELM (Huang, Zhu & Siew, 2004, 2006).
i. Compute the mean absolute percentage error (MAPE).

EXPERIMENTAL DESIGN

Our proposed algorithms have been tested on various types of dataset as listed in Table 1. These datasets are generated by different-different researchers as listed in the last column of the Table 1. First, we removed the class columns from the datasets and then delete some value randomly from the datasets

Figure 4. Architecture of ECM-AAELM

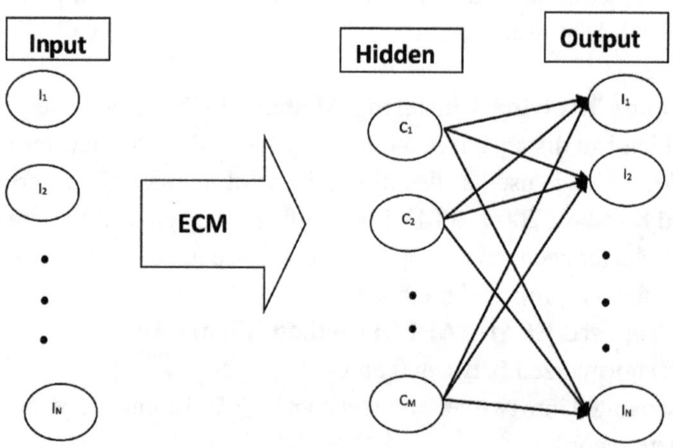

Table 1. Description of datasets

Dataset	Number of Records	Number of Attributes	Reference to Obtain the Dataset
Auto mpg	392	7	Ramos and Donoho (Last accessed by 6 Dec 2015)
Body fat	252	14	Johnson (Last accessed by 6 Dec 2015)
Boston Housing	506	13	Harrison and Rubinfeld (Last accessed by 6 Dec 2015)
Forest fires	516	10	Cortez and Morais (Last accessed by 6 Dec 2015)
Iris	150	4	Fisher (Last accessed by 6 Dec 2015)
Prima Indian	768	8	Sigillito (Last accessed by 6 Dec 2015)
Spanish	66	9	Olmeda and Fernandez (1997)
Spectf	267	44	Cios, Kurgan and Goodenday (Last accessed by 6 Dec 2015)
Turkish	40	12	Canbas and Kilic, Canbas (Last accessed by 6 Dec 2015), Caubak and Kilic (2005)
UK bankruptcy	60	10	Beynon and Peel (2001)
UK Credit	1225	12	Thomas, Edelman and Crook (2002)
Wine	178	13	Forina (Last accessed by 6 Dec 2015)

for creating missing value as initially datasets had no any missing value. Approximately 10% value is deleted from the data. Further, we performed 10-fold cross validation. 9 folds are used for training and remaining one fold is used for testing. But we kept always complete records in training fold and missing records in testing fold.

Afterwards, mean imputation has been performed at initial stage for missing data as we cannot pass blank cell to any machine learning methods directly. Performance measurement has been done by calculation of MAPE. As we are performing 10-fold cross validation here, so 10 MAPE values has been computed for each fold and then take average of MAPE value of all 10 folds as final evaluation criteria. MAPE value computed by our proposed methods is compared with the methods proposed by Ankaiah and Ravi (2011), Nishanth and Ravi (2013), Krishna and Ravi (2013), Gautam and Ravi (2014).

We performed Wilcoxon signed rank test to test the statistical significance between the results of these two models (Lowry, 2008; Wilcoxon, 1945; Siegel, 1956). Varieties of activation functions have been proposed till date to improve the performance of artificial neural network. 8 activation functions are used in this chapter to show the fact that how it affects the output of neural network if activation function is altered (see in Table 2).

RESULTS AND DISCUSSIONS

We applied the proposed methods viz., PCA-AAELM, Gray+PCA-AAELM, ECM-AAELM on several datasets and compared our outcomes from various methods viz., K-Means+MLP, K-Medoids+MLP, K-Means+GRNN, K-Medoids+GRNN and PSO_COV. The average MAPE values obtained over 10-fold cross validation for the proposed method is presented in the Table 6. For online data imputation, the number of clusters obtained by ECM is dictated by a parameter known as the distance threshold *Dthr*. The *Dthr* value that yielded the best reduction in MAPE is obtained by varying the large range of *Dthr* value from 0.001 to 0.999, in steps of 0.001 and the least MAPE value thus obtained is tabulated. We

Table 2. List of activation functions with their formula

Activation Function Names	Formula for Activation Function
Sigmoid	H = 1. / (1 + exp (-x))
Sinh	H = sinh (x)
Cloglogm (Gomes, Ludermir & Lima, 2011)	H=1-2*exp (-0.7*exp (x))
Bipolar Sigmoid (Bsigmoid) (Karlik & Olgac, 2011)	H= (1 - exp (-x)). / (1 + exp (-x))
Sin	H = sin (x)
Tribas	H = Tribas (x) = 1 - abs(x), if -1 <= x <= 1 = 0, Otherwise
Radbas	H = Radbas (x) = exp (-x^2)
Softplus (soft) (Glorot, Bordes & Bengio, 2011)	H=log (1+exp (x))

kept same *Dthr* value for all folds. Similarly, PCA, which was employed in PCA-AAELM, has a parameter known as variance, which is accountable for the selection of necessary principal components for the dataset. The value of variance that yields the least MAPE is selected by varying this parameter and the corresponding MAPE value is tabulated. In Gray+PCA-AAELM, a crucial parameter is $\zeta \in [0,1]$, we kept its value as 0.5 for all the datasets.

Performance Analysis of Various Activation Functions on Our Proposed Methods

In all proposed methods viz., ECM-AAELM, Gray+PCA-AAELM, PCA-AAELM, activation function played crucial role to minimize the MAPE value.

In case of ECM-AAELM, it can be observed by the Table 3 and Figure 5 that there is no substantial influence of activation functions on this proposed method. Except UK bankruptcy dataset, ECM-AAELM yielded satisfactory results for all activation functions compared to other proposed methods. Tribas activation function yielded best result among all activation functions. It yielded least MAPE value for 6 out of 12 datasets compared to other activation functions. For rest of the 5 datasets, Tribas activation function yielded 1% more MAPE value compared to the other activation function which yielded least MAPE value. For Spanish dataset only, it yielded 2.7% more MAPE value compared to the Softplus activation function.

In case of PCA-AAELM (Table 4 and Figure 6), Softplus activation function yielded least MAPE value among all activation functions and its MAPE value is nearly 1% more than the least MAPE value obtained by all activation functions for 5 datasets. For UK Credit only, Softplus activation function yielded 1.83% more MAPE value compared to the Sin activation function. Sigmoid, Sinh, Bsigmoid, Sin, Radbas and Softplus activation function yielded least MAPE value for 2 datasets, 1 dataset, 2 datasets, 1 dataset, 2 datasets and 4 datasets respectively. Rest of the 2 activation functions viz., Cloglogm and Tribas were not be able to obtain least MAPE value for any of the 12 datasets.

In case of Gray+PCA-AAELM (Table 5 and Figure 7), both Softplus and sigmoid activation function yielded least MAPE value for 4 datasets, 4 datasets respectively compared to other activation functions. A variation of Sigmoid activation function viz., Bsigmoid activation function achieved least MAPE value

Table 3. Average MAPE value over 10 folds ECM-AAELM

	Sigmoid	Sinh	Cloglogm	Bsigmoid	Sin	Tribas	Radbas	Softplus
Auto mpg	**17.38**	17.49	17.47	17.44	17.43	17.4	18.07	17.46
Body fat	5.34	5.37	5.38	5.38	5.39	**5.33**	6.25	5.34
Boston Housing	16.79	17.32	17.29	17.28	17.27	**16.48**	17.07	16.9
Forest fires	**21.54**	21.63	21.61	21.58	21.56	21.59	21.93	21.62
Iris	5.13	5.12	5.11	5.11	**5.1**	5.17	5.28	5.14
Prima Indian	**23.95**	27.5	27.49	27.48	27.47	24.56	24.05	23.99
Spanish	22.41	23.67	23.38	23.43	23.37	24.79	25.12	**22.09**
Spectf	8.07	8.17	8.18	8.19	8.2	8.08	8.2	**8.05**
Turkish	22.22	22.16	22.15	22.18	22.20	**21.49**	24.85	22.20
UK bankruptcy	40.63	44.47	44.26	44.28	44.21	**40.06**	41.51	40.77
UK Credit	27.09	27.1	27.09	27.08	27.07	**26.85**	27.33	27.13
Wine	14.88	14.95	14.93	14.91	14.9	**14.88**	15.54	14.94

Figure 5. Behavior of ECM-AAELM on different activation functions

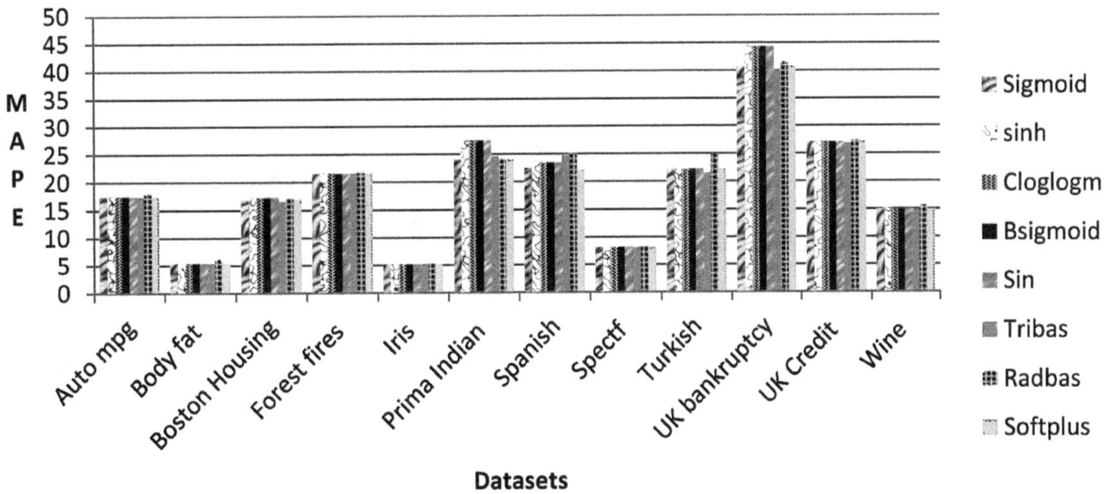

for 3 datasets and Radbas yielded least MAPE value for 1 dataset. Rest of the 4 activation functions viz., Sinh, Cloglogm, Sin and Tribas, were not be able to obtain least MAPE value for any of the 12 datasets.

Performance Analysis of Our Proposed Methods vs. Hybrid Methods in Literature

Following are the comparative discussion between our proposed methods vs. hybrid methods presented by Ankaiah and Ravi (2011), Nishanth and Ravi (2013), Krishna and Ravi (2013), Gautam and Ravi (2014):

As regards the Auto MPG dataset, Gray+PCA-AAELM yielded best outcomes among all the three proposed methods and all methods proposed by Ankaiah and Ravi (2011), Nishanth and Ravi (2013),

Table 4. Average MAPE value over 10 folds PCA-AAELM

	Sigmoid	Sinh	Cloglogm	Bsigmoid	Sin	Tribas	Radbas	Softplus
Auto mpg	30.41	31.07	28.67	29.18	28.9	47.45	43.28	**28.63**
Body fat	6.06	8.24	6.92	6.75	7.67	8.65	6.69	**6.01**
Boston Housing	22.17	22.96	23.64	23.41	24.78	26.86	23.92	**20.9**
Forest fires	**19.41**	21.89	21.03	21.03	20.82	21.74	20.22	19.45
Iris	14.48	12.53	11.34	11.49	12.1	14.01	**10.23**	13.17
Prima Indian	22.62	22.48	22.08	**22.06**	22.15	23.68	22.10	22.07
Spanish	46.81	31.27	30.4	**30.09**	35.19	70.3	60.38	37.27
Spectf	11.7	9.73	13.61	12.48	10.81	13.72	12.75	**9.11**
Turkish	**30.18**	39.03	39.67	39.22	41.25	49.43	36.29	31.56
UK bankruptcy	38.54	**37.7**	39.32	39.18	41.14	44.27	42.02	38.92
UK Credit	27.12	29.93	27.4	27.44	**26.53**	28.47	28.86	28.36
Wine	17.97	17.8	17.87	18.04	18.23	17.88	**16.6**	17.38

Figure 6. Behavior of PCA-AAELM on different activation functions

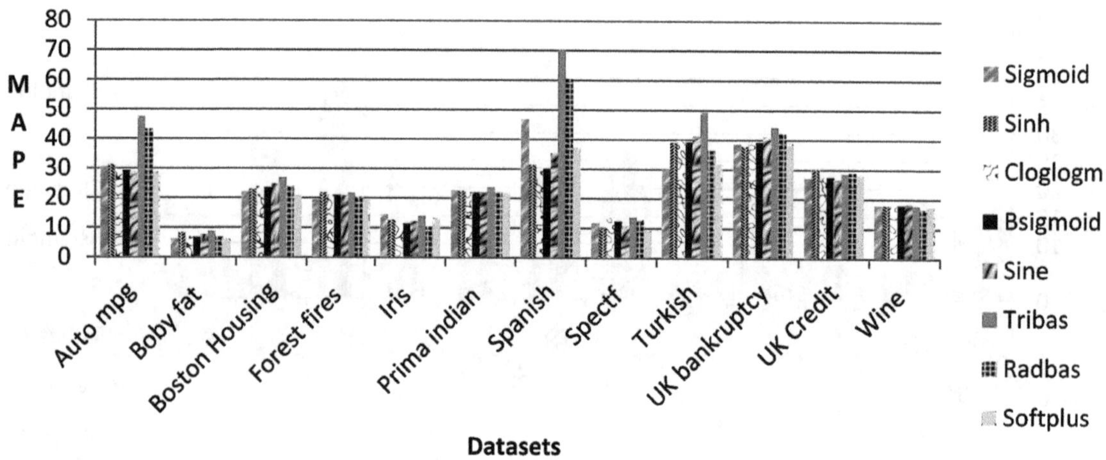

Krishna and Ravi (2013), Gautam and Ravi (2014) except K-Medoids+GRNN. However, the difference of MAPE value between Gray+PCA-AAELM and K- Medoids+GRNN is 0.26 only. A drastic reduction of 11.71% in MAPE value is observed by employing Gray distance based imputation at first stage and PCA-AAELM at second stage. The MAPE is reduced from 28.63% to 16.92% when we employed Gray+PCA-AAELM instead of PCA-AAELM. PCA-AAELM is worst performer among all the proposed methods for this dataset.

As regards the Body fat dataset, the MAPE value is observed less than 6.1% for all the proposed imputation techniques. PCA- AAELM outperformed 5 out of 7 methods employed by Ankaiah and Ravi (2011), Nishanth and Ravi (2013), Krishna and Ravi (2013), Gautam and Ravi (2014) viz., K-Means+MLP, K-Means+GRNN, K-Medoids+MLP, PSO_COV and ECM-Imputation. The MAPE is reduced from 6.01% to 5.41% by employing Gray Distance based imputation at first stage and PCA-AAELM at sec-

Table 5. Average MAPE value over 10 folds Gray+PCA-AAELM

	Sigmoid	Sinh	Cloglogm	Bsigmoid	Sin	Tribas	Radbas	Softplus
Auto mpg	20.37	17.92	17.44	**16.92**	17.99	44.05	41.55	19.13
Body fat	5.43	7.18	6.64	6.34	7.42	7.80	6.42	**5.41**
Boston Housing	18.22	18.82	19.55	19.16	20.34	22.82	21.42	**17.46**
Forest fires	**20.89**	23.92	23.70	23.68	23.38	24.19	23.44	21.30
Iris	7.27	6.50	5.87	**5.79**	6.47	8.98	6.13	6.58
Prima Indian	22.43	25.92	24.04	24.02	23.51	24.89	23.05	**22.03**
Spanish	39.12	30.49	28.26	**28.06**	32.18	57.31	44.26	29.44
Spectf	10.05	9.75	12.75	11.12	10.71	12.82	11.15	**8.38**
Turkish	**27.38**	36.29	30.67	30.33	29.98	43.55	37.88	28.27
UK bankruptcy	**37.95**	38.71	38.97	39.21	39.82	43.18	41.78	38.59
UK Credit	**27.79**	29.52	28.54	28.56	28.68	30.12	28.76	27.86
Wine	15.81	15.54	15.27	15.33	15.47	14.95	**14.78**	15.43

Figure 7. Behavior of Gray+PCA-AAELM on different activation functions

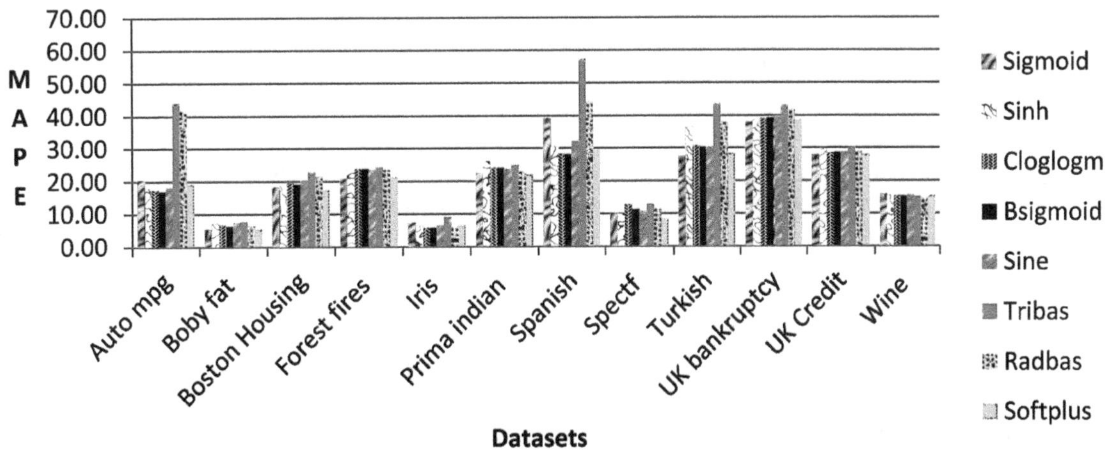

ond stage. The MAPE value is reduced further from 5.41% to 5.33% by ECM-AAELM. ECM-AAELM yielded best outcomes among all the proposed methods and existed methods listed in the Table 6.

As regards the Boston housing dataset, PCA-AAELM yielded less MAPE value compared to K-Means+MLP and PSO_COV but outperformed by rest of the methods. The value of MAPE is reduced from 20.9% to 17.46% by employing Gray distance based imputation in first stage and PCA-AAELM at second stage (Gray+PCA-AAELM). It outperformed all the methods presented by Ankaiah and Ravi (2011), Nishanth and Ravi (2013), Krishna and Ravi (2013), Gautam and Ravi (2014). The MAPE value is further reduced from 17.46% to 16.48% by employing ECM-AAELM instead of Gray+PCA-AAELM and it outperformed all the methods listed in the Table 6. PSO_COV performed worst among all the methods presented in the Table 6.

Figure 8.

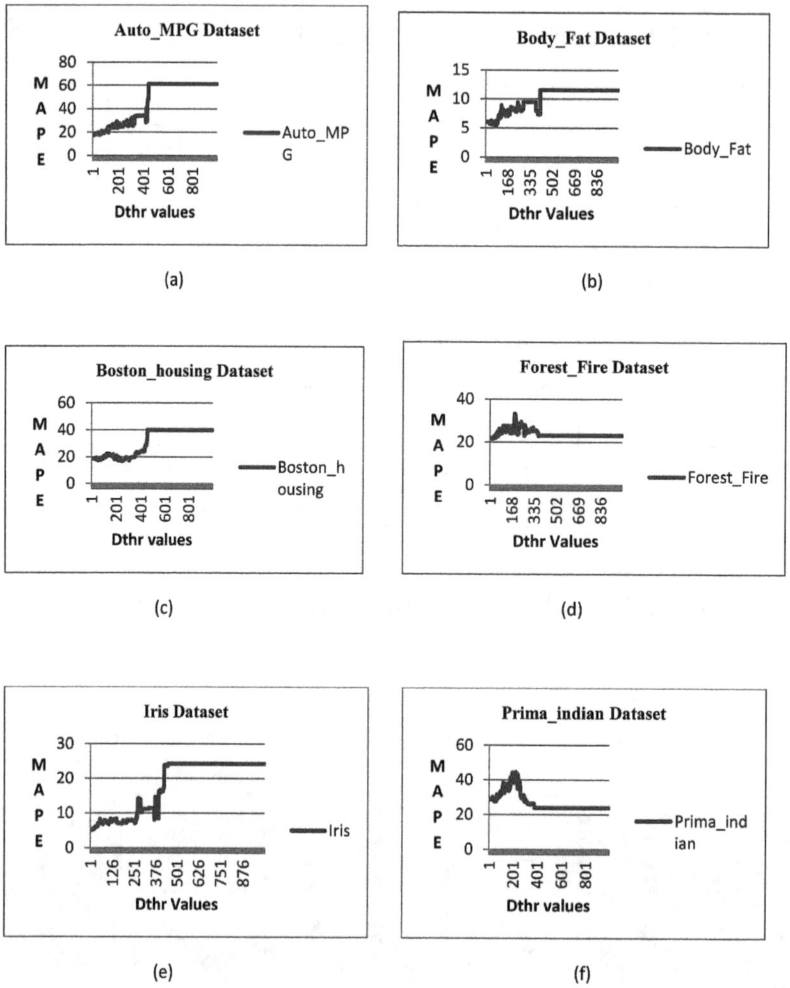

As regards the Forest Fire dataset, all the three proposed methods viz., ECM-AAELM, PCA-AAELM and Gray+PCA-AAELM, outperformed all the methods proposed by Ankaiah and Ravi (2011), Nishanth and Ravi (2013), Krishna and Ravi (2013), Gautam and Ravi (2014). PCA-AAELM yielded least MAPE value among all three proposed methods.

As regards the Iris dataset, ECM-AAELM yielded best outcomes and PCA-AAELM yielded worst outcomes among all the methods listed in the Table 6. The MAPE value is reduced from 10.23% to 5.79% by employing Gray+PCA-AAELM instead of PCA- AAELM. Gray+PCA-AAELM yielded better outcomes compared to all previous methods listed in Table 6 except ECM-Imputation.

As regards the Prima Indian dataset, Gray+PCA-AAELM is the best performer among all the methods listed in the Table 6. The MAPE value is reduced from 23.95% to 22.06% by employing PCA-AAELM instead of ECM- AAELM. The MAPE value is further reduced from 22.06% to 22.03% by employing Gray Distance based imputation at first stage and PCA-AAELM at second stage. So, our proposed methods outperformed all the existing methods listed in Table 6 for this dataset.

Table 6. Average MAPE value over 10 folds of the proposed and existing methods

	Mean	K-Means + MLP	K-Medoids + MLP	K-Means + GRNN	K-Medoids + GRNN	ECM + GRNN	PSO_COV	ECM_ Imputation	ECM-AAELM	PCA-AAELM	Gray + PCA-AAELM	
											Stage 1	**Stage 2**
Auto mpg	59.7	23.75	20.70	20.27	**16.66**	17	24.53	18.03	17.38	28.63	16.73	16.92
Body fat	11.61	7.83	6.46	6.96	5.37	5.56	7.13	6.31	**5.33**	6.01	7.65	5.41
Boston Housing	37.77	21.01	17.69	19.57	17.68	18.08	24.85	17.84	**16.48**	20.9	19.28	17.46
Forest fires	24.72	26.61	24.46	26.21	22.97	24.38	24.85	22.29	21.54	**19.41**	22.89	20.89
Iris	23.57	9.41	9.17	8.79	8.04	6.3	8.71	5.27	**5.1**	10.23	5.34	5.79
Prima Indian	24.02	29.7	26.63	28.3	26.33	26.51	27.57	27.71	23.95	22.06	28.06	**22.03**
Spanish	55.53	39.91	32.45	37.96	26.01	34.11	33.25	31.98	**22.09**	30.09	36.29	28.06
Spectf	14.85	12.14	10.65	10.61	10.22	10.35	10.34	10.21	**8.05**	9.11	11.6	8.38
Turkish	66.00	33.01	26.90	25.9	**19.34**	22.34	30.20	27.90	21.49	30.18	36.63	27.38
UK bankruptcy	37.07	30.96	29.69	29.06	**28.39**	29.07	35.67	46.14	40.06	37.7	39.75	37.95
UK Credit	28.43	32.17	25.42	29.8	24.04	**21.93**	37.94	27.40	26.85	26.53	28.9	27.79
Wine	29.99	21.58	15.73	16.21	**14.75**	15.61	18.98	15.61	14.88	16.6	17.58	14.78

As regards the Spanish dataset, the MAPE value is reduced from 30.09% to 28.06% by employing Gray+PCA-AAELM instead of PCA-AAELM. It outperformed all the methods except K-Medoids+GRNN employed by Ankaiah and Ravi (2011), Nishanth and Ravi (2013). The MAPE value is drastically reduced from 30.09% to 22.09% by employing ECM-AAELM instead of PCA-AAELM. ECM-AAELM performed better compared to all the methods listed in the Table 6.

As regards the Spectf dataset, our all three proposed methods viz., ECM-AAELM, Gray+PCA-AAELM, PCA-AAELM, outperformed all the methods presented by Ankaiah and Ravi (2011), Nishanth and Ravi (2013), Krishna and Ravi (2013), Gautam and Ravi (2014). The MAPE value is reduced from 9.11% to 8.38% by employing Gray+PCA-AAELM instead of PCA-AAELM. ECM performed best among all the proposed and existed methods listed in the Table 6.

As regards the Turkish dataset, the MAPE value is reduced from 30.18% to 27.38% by employing Gray+PCA-AAELM instead of PCA-AAELM. A drastic reduction of 8.69% in MAPE value is observed by employing ECM-AAELM instead of PCA-AAELM. ECM-AAELM outperformed all the methods except K-Medoids+GRNN employed by Ankaiah and Ravi (2011), Nishanth and Ravi (2013), Krishna and Ravi (2013), Gautam and Ravi (2014). However, remaining two proposed methods are outperformed by all the proposed methods presented by Ankaiah and Ravi (2011), Nishanth and Ravi (2013). But PCA-AAELM performed better than only two methods PSO_COV and Gray+PCA-AAELM performed better than PSO_COV and ECM-Imputation.

As regards the UK bankruptcy dataset, there are no proposed methods, which performed well compared to any of the methods employed by Ankaiah and Ravi (2011), Nishanth and Ravi (2013), Krishna and Ravi (2013). Our proposed methods performed better than only one method viz., ECM-Imputation.

As regards the UK Credit dataset, PCA-AAELM yielded least MAPE value among all the proposed methods. PCA-AAELM outperformed 5 out of 7 methods proposed by Ankaiah and Ravi (2011), Nishanth and Ravi (2013), Krishna and Ravi (2013), Gautam and Ravi (2014) viz., K-Means+MLP, K-Means+GRNN, K-Medoids+MLP, PSO_COV and ECM-Imputation. The MAPE value is reduced from 26.85% to 25.53% by employing PCA-AAELM instead of ECM-AAELM.

As regards the Wine dataset, Gray+PCA-AAELM is the best performer among all the proposed methods. The MAPE value is reduced from 16.6% to 14.78% by employing Gray Distance based imputation at first stage and PCA-AAELM at second stage. ECM-AAELM and Gray+PCA-AAELM outperformed all the methods except K-Medoids+GRNN. Nevertheless, difference of MAPE value between K-Medoids+GRNN and both of the proposed methods, ECM-AAELM and Gray+PCA-AAELM, is only 0.13% and 0.03% respectively.

Wilcoxon two-tailed signed rank test has been performed on the proposed methods and existing methods to test the statistical significance of the output of our proposed methods. The Wilcoxon test values for all the proposed methods are presented in Table 7 (a-d). As difference between AAELM and other methods is very large, so, Wilcoxon test has not been performed with AAELM. We need to check the significance of the value obtained by performing Wilcoxon test, it depends upon whether obtained value is lesser or equal to a critical value or not. The critical value is retrieved from the table (Hole, Last accessed by 6 Dec 2015) for N=10, which is 3. This procedure has been employed for all proposed and existing methods over all the datasets mentioned in the Table 1.

The following points are to be noted from the above discussion:

- When we employed Gray distance based imputation with PCA-AAELM then the performance of Gray+PCA-AAELM was degraded for 3 datasets viz., Forest fire, UK bankruptcy and UK Credit. Otherwise, Gray distance aided PCA-AAELM to enhance its performance for rest of the 9 datasets.

Table 7. Wilcoxon signed rank test values of three proposed methods

	PCA-AAELM vs. Gray+PCA-AAELM	PCA-AAELM vs. ECM-AAELM	Gray+PCA-AAELM vs. ECM-AAELM
Auto mpg	2.78	2.78	0.64
Body fat	0.94	0.64	0.03
Boston Housing	2.57	2.78	0.64
Forest fires	1.25	1.66	1.25
Iris	2.68	2.78	1.35
Prima Indian	0.03	2.78	2.06
Spanish	0.23	1.86	2.27
Spectf	1.86	2.37	1.25
Turkish	0.64	1.96	1.25
UK bankruptcy	0.43	0.03	0.13
UK Credit	2.78	2.57	1.96
Wine	1.86	1.25	0.43

Table 8. Wilcoxon signed rank test values of PCA-AAELM

	K-Means + MLP vs. PCA-AAELM	K-Medoids + MLP vs. PCA-AAELM	K-Means + GRNN vs. PCA-AAELM	K-Medoids + GRNN vs. PCA-AAELM	ECM + GRNN vs. PCA-AAELM	ECM_Imputation vs. PCA-AAELM
Auto mpg	1.86	2.17	2.37	2.78	2.78	2.78
Body fat	1.66	0.94	1.66	0.64	0.43	0.23
Boston Housing	0.23	0.94	0.33	1.45	1.45	2.17
Forest fires	2.78	2.06	2.57	2.17	2.06	1.96
Iris	0.33	0.43	0.94	1.55	2.47	2.78
Prima Indian	2.78	2.78	2.68	2.47	1.76	2.78
Spanish	1.96	0.43	0.13	1.04	0.13	0.84
Spectf	2.47	2.06	2.37	1.96	1.45	2.27
Turkish	0.64	0.84	0.84	1.76	1.35	0.43
UK bankruptcy	1.66	2.06	2.06	1.86	1.86	1.66
UK Credit	1.76	0.43	1.15	0.54	0.94	0.84
Wine	2.57	0.54	0.33	1.15	0.54	0.74

Table 9. Wilcoxon signed rank test values of ECM-AAELM

	K-Means + MLP vs. ECM-AAELM	K-Medoids + MLP vs. ECM-AAELM	K-Means + GRNN vs. ECM-AAELM	K-Medoids + GRNN vs. ECM-AAELM	ECM + GRNN vs. ECM-AAELM	ECM_Imputation vs. ECM-AAELM
Auto mpg	2.27	1.55	1.35	0.03	0.03	0.64
Body fat	2.47	1.66	1.35	0.13	0.13	2.78
Boston Housing	2.57	0.84	1.55	0.94	0.84	0.74
Forest fires	2.47	1.25	1.96	0.43	1.45	2.78
Iris	2.37	2.37	2.27	1.66	1.15	2.17
Prima Indian	2.68	2.17	2.37	1.96	1.76	2.57
Spanish	2.68	2.47	1.55	0.33	0.64	2.06
Spectf	2.78	2.78	2.78	2.78	2.37	2.78
Turkish	0.43	0.13	0.84	1.76	0.54	2.47
UK bankruptcy	1.45	2.17	2.27	2.57	2.37	2.57
UK Credit	1.45	1.04	0.43	1.25	1.55	0.84
Wine	2.68	0.94	1.25	0.13	0.74	1.76

Table 10. Wilcoxon signed rank test values of Gray+PCA-AAELM

	K-Means + MLP vs. Gray+PCA-AAELM	K-Medoids + MLP vs. Gray+PCA-AAELM	K-Means + GRNN vs. Gray+PCA-AAELM	K-Medoids + GRNN vs. Gray+PCA-AAELM	ECM + GRNN vs. Gray+PCA-AAELM	ECM_Imputation vs. Gray + PCA-AAELM
Auto mpg	2.27	1.55	1.66	0.33	0.33	0.94
Body fat	2.57	1.86	1.55	0.43	0.23	1.25
Boston Housing	2.17	0.94	1.25	0.13	0.43	0.03
Forest fires	2.47	1.45	2.06	0.74	1.55	1.86
Iris	2.37	2.06	2.06	1.25	0.23	0.94
Prima Indian	2.78	2.47	2.78	2.37	1.76	2.78
Spanish	2.27	1.25	0.74	0.54	0.33	0.13
Spectf	2.78	2.78	2.78	2.78	2.47	2.78
Turkish	0.03	0.54	0.54	1.76	1.55	0.23
UK bankruptcy	1.86	2.27	2.17	2.57	2.57	1.04
UK Credit	1.15	1.25	0.23	1.35	2.17	0.74
Wine	2.78	1.25	1.25	0.23	0.64	0.03

Table 11. Average MAPE value over 10 folds AAELM

	ECM-AAELM	PCA-AAELM	Gray+PCA-AAELM	Uniform-Sigmoid	Uniform -Gaussian	Gaussian-Sigmoid	Gaussian-Gaussian	Logistic-Sigmoid	Logistic-Gaussian
Auto mpg	17.38	28.63	**16.92**	35.11	35.96	33.99	33.99	37.2	47.24
Body fat	**5.33**	6.01	5.41	12.92	25.91	11.68	12.09	13.03	33.66
Boston Housing	**16.48**	20.9	17.46	29.2	35.65	25.42	26.43	29.38	42.2
Forest fires	21.54	**19.41**	20.89	22	31.73	22.33	22.91	22.17	47.74
Iris	**5.1**	10.23	5.79	21.96	19.7	20.81	17.54	21.11	18.95
Prima Indian	23.95	22.06	**22.03**	23.41	26.29	23.03	24.4	22.88	29.34
Spanish	**22.09**	30.09	28.06	43.59	133.23	41.91	60.87	38.56	270.48
Spectf	**8.05**	9.11	8.38	17.05	29.20	22.87	22.89	24.29	36.52
Turkish	**21.49**	30.18	27.38	37.49	98.01	33.52	40.13	37.94	185.77
UK bankruptcy	40.06	**37.7**	37.95	36.05	42.51	38.53	37.7	38.58	49.43
UK Credit	26.85	**26.53**	27.79	30.84	36.04	31.92	32.19	30.83	40.41
Wine	14.88	16.6	**14.78**	22.65	33.27	21.26	21.92	24.07	47.59

- For those datasets, where PCA-AAELM performed better than Gray+PCA-AAELM, the difference of MAPE value of Gray+ PCA-AAELM and PCA-AAELM is very less. However, where Gray+ PCA-AAELM performed better than PCA-AAELM, MAPE value of both the proposed methods is differ by significant amount.
- When we closely observed the MAPE value of ECM-Imputation and ECM-AAELM then we observed that ECM-AAELM always improved the accuracy for all datasets due to hybridization of the concept of global approximation and local learning.
- For UK bankruptcy dataset, even Mean imputation outperformed our all the proposed methods.
- ECM-AAELM and Gray+PCA-AAELM performed best among our four proposed methods.
- It is recommended to use Softplus activation function for PCA-AAELM and Gray+PCA-AAELM.
- ECM-AAELM outperformed PCA-AAELM for 9 out of 12 datasets because ECM-AAELM has strong local learning capability due to ECM and PCA does not perform any local learning task, it simply does linear transformation of the data.
- MAPE values are oscillating wildly from one activation function to other activation function in case of PCA-AAELM and Gray+PCA-AAELM. In contrast, MAPE values of ECM-AAELM are not oscillating wildly by changing activation function.
- We experimented on a large range of threshold values from 0.001 to 0.999, in steps of 0.001 (horizontal axis of Fig. 8 denotes 0.001 as 1 and so on), in order to see which value of *Dthr* perform better compared to other methods. When we observe the graph from Fig. 8(a) to 8(l) (horizontal axis of Fig. 8 denotes 0.001 as 1 and so on), we conclude that approximately after 0.399, MAPE values are constant irrespective of any threshold value which is greater than 0.399. These graphs are depicted for the behavior of the Sigmoid activation function on ECM-AAELM over a large range of *Dthr* values for 12 datasets. We experimented similar for all activation functions over a large range of *Dthr* value from 0.001 to 0.999 and experienced the same result as discussed above.
- We did not discuss the results of AAELM because all 3 proposed methods outperformed it by a large margin. It can be observed in Table 8.

CONCLUSION AND FUTURE WORK

In this chapter, we proposed three new imputation algorithms for data imputation viz., PCA-AAELM, Gray+PCA-AAELM and ECM-AAELM imputation. Based on the results, we conclude that ECM-AAELM should be preferred for imputation out of all methods owing to its consistently the best imputation for most of the datasets. Further, we conclude that ECM-AAELM is not influenced by the choice of the activation function. So, out of 8 mentioned activation functions, any activation function can be employed with ECM-AAELM. In contrast, Softplus activation function is recommended for PCA-AAELM and Gray+PCA-AAELM because it exhibited the best imputation capability compared to other activation functions. The results demonstrate that there is a significant reduction in MAPE after employing gray distance based imputation instead of Mean imputation with PCA-AAELM. The results obtained by our proposed algorithms are statistically significant as evidenced by the Wilcoxon test under the 10-fold cross validation. Our proposed algorithms are fast but user's intervention is required for selection of the both parameters viz., *Dthr* for ECM and ζ for GRC, in order to obtain better performance. Our future work will be focused on the selection of optimal parameters value without altering predictive efficiency of the algorithm.

Figure 9. Influence of Dthr value on MAPE values for all datasets

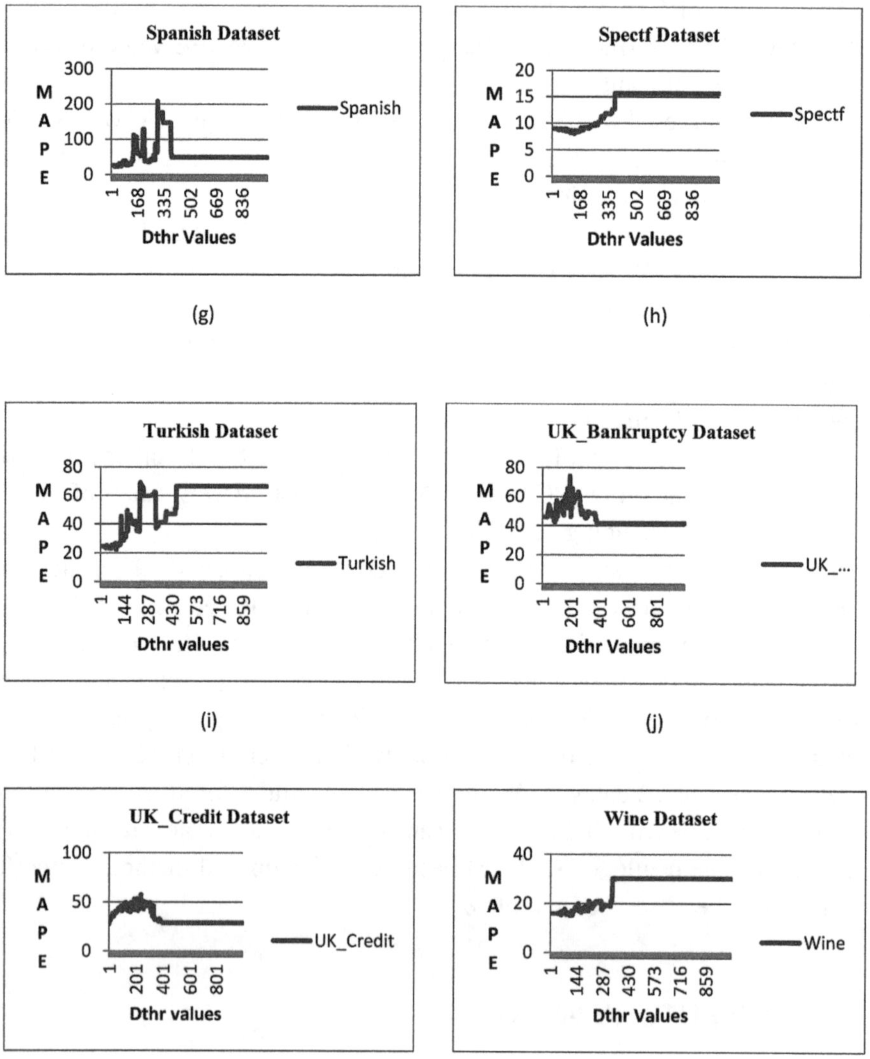

REFERENCES

Abdella, M., & Marwala, T. (2005). The use of genetic algorithms and neural networks to approximate missing data in database. In *Proceedings of the IEEE 3rd international conference on computational cybernetics*. doi:10.1109/ICCCYB.2005.1511574

Ankaiah, N., & Ravi, V. (2011). A novel soft computing hybrid for data imputation. In *Proceedings of the 7th international conference on data mining (DMIN)*.

Austin, P. C., & Escobar, M. D. (2005). Bayesian modeling of missing data in clinical research. *Computational Statistics & Data Analysis*, *49*(3), 821–836. doi:10.1016/j.csda.2004.06.006

Aydilek, I. B., & Arslan, A. (2013). A hybrid method for imputation of missing vlaues using optimized fuzzy c-means with support vector regression and a genetic algorithm. *Information Sciences*, *233*, 25–35. doi:10.1016/j.ins.2013.01.021

Ballings, M., & Poel, D. V. D. (2013). Kernel Factory: An ensemble of kernel machines. *Expert Systems with Applications*, *40*(8), 2904–2913. doi:10.1016/j.eswa.2012.12.007

Batista, G., & Monard, M. C. (2002). A study of K-nearest neighbor as an imputation method. Hybrid intelligent systems, ser front artificial intelligence applications. IOS Press.

Batista, G., & Monard, M. C. (2003). *Experimental comparison of K-nearest neighbor and mean or mode imputation methods with the internal strategies used by C4.5 and CN2 to treat missing data. Technical Report*. University of Sao Paulo.

Beynon, M. J., & Peel, M. J. (2001). Variable precision rough set theory and data discretisation: An application to corporate failure prediction. *Omega*, *29*(6), 561–576. doi:10.1016/S0305-0483(01)00045-7

Canbas, S., Caubak, A., & Kilic, S. B. (2005). Prediction of commercial bank failure via multivariate statistical analysis of financial structures: The Turkish case. *European Journal of Operational Research*, *166*(2), 528–546. doi:10.1016/j.ejor.2004.03.023

Canbas, S. C., & Kilic, S. B. (n.d.). *Spanish dataset*. Retrieved from http://www.tbb.org.tr/english/bulten/yillik/2000/ratios.xls

Castaño, A., Fernández-Navarro, F., & Hervás-Martínez, C. (2013). PCA-ELM -A Robust and Pruned ELM Approach Based on PCA. *Neural Processing Letter*, *37*, 377–392. doi:10.1007/s11063-012-9253-x

Chen, J., Huang, H., Tian, F., & Tian, S. (2008). A selective Bayes Classifier for classifying incomplete data based on gain ratio. *Knowledge-Based Systems*, *21*(7), 530–534. doi:10.1016/j.knosys.2008.03.013

Cios, K. J., Kurgan, L. A., & Goodenday, L. S. (n.d.). *Spectf Heart dataset*. Retrieved from http://archive.ics.uci.edu/ml/machine-learning-databases/spect

Cortez, P., & Morais, A. (n.d.). *Forest Fire dataset*. Retrieved from http://archive.ics.uci.edu/ml/machine-learning-databases/forest-fires/forestfires.csv

Dempster, A. P., Laird, N. M., & Rubin, D. B. (1977). Maximum-likelihood from incomplete data via the EM algorithm. *Journal of the Royal Statistical Society. Series A (General)*, *39*, 1–38.

Deng, J. L. (1982). Control problems of grey system. *Systems & Control Letters*, *1*(5), 288–294. doi:10.1016/S0167-6911(82)80025-X

Doove, L. L., Buuren, S. V., & Dusseldorp, E. (2013). Recursive partitioning for missing data imputation in the presence of interaction effects. *Computational Statistics & Data Analysis*, *27*, 92–104.

Duma, M., Marwala, T., Twala, B., & Nelwamondo, F. (2013). Partial imputation of unseen records to improve classification using a hybrid multi-layered artificial immune system and genetic algorithm. *Applied Soft Computing*, *13*(12), 4461–4480. doi:10.1016/j.asoc.2013.08.005

Elshorbagy, A., Simonovic, S. P., & Panu, U. S. (2002). Estimation of missing stream flow data using the principles of chaos theory. *Journal of Hydrology (Amsterdam)*, *255*(1-4), 123–133. doi:10.1016/S0022-1694(01)00513-3

Fisher, R. A. (n.d.). *Iris dataset.* Retrieved from http://archive.ics.uci.edu/ml/machine-learning-databases/iris/iris.data

Flores, B. E. (1986). A pragmatic view of accuracy measurement in forecasting. *Omega*, *14*(2), 93–98. doi:10.1016/0305-0483(86)90013-7

Forina, M. (n.d.). *Wine dataset.* Retrieved from http://archive.ics.uci.edu/ml/machine-learning-databases/wine/wine.data

Gabrys, B. (2002). Neuro-fuzzy approach to processing inputs with missing values in pattern recognition problems. *International Journal of Approximate Reasoning*, *30*(3), 149–179. doi:10.1016/S0888-613X(02)00070-1

García, J. C. F., Kalenatic, D., & Bello, C. A. L. (2011). Missing data imputation in multivariate data by evolutionary algorithms. *Computers in Human Behavior*, *27*(5), 1468–1474. doi:10.1016/j.chb.2010.06.026

Garcia-Laencina, P. J., Sancho-gomez, J., & Figueiras-vidal, A. R. (2013). Classifying patterns with missing values using Multi-Task Learning perceptrons. *Expert Systems with Applications*, *40*(4), 1333–1341. doi:10.1016/j.eswa.2012.08.057

Gautam, C., & Ravi, V. (2014). Evolving clustering based data imputation. In *Proceedings of the 3rd international conference on Circuits, Power and Computing Technologies (ICCPCT)*, (pp. 1763-1769). doi:10.1109/ICCPCT.2014.7054988

Gautam, C., & Ravi, V. (2015). Counter Propagation Auto Associative Neural Network based Data Imputation.Information Sciences, 325, 288-299.

Gautam, C., & Ravi, V. (2015). Data Imputation via Evolutionary Computation. *Clustering and a Neural Network, Neurocomputing, Elsevier*, *153*, 134–142.

Glorot, X., Bordes, A., & Bengio, Y. (2011). Deep Sparse Rectifier Neural Networks.*International Conference on Artificial Intelligence and Statistics.*

Gomes, G. S. S., Ludermir, T. B., & Lima, L. M. M. R. (2011). Comparison of new activation functions in neural network for forecasting financial time series. *Neural Computing and Applications, Springer*, *20*, 417–439. doi:10.1007/s00521-010-0407-3

Gupta, A., & Lam, M. S. (1996). Estimating missing values using neural networks. *The Journal of the Operational Research Society*, *47*(2), 229–238. doi:10.1057/jors.1996.21

Han, F., Yao, H. F., & Ling, Q. H. (2012). An Improved Extreme Learning Machine Based on Particle Swarm Optimization, Bio-Inspired Computing and Applications.*7th International Conference on Intelligent Computing.*

Harrison, D., & Rubinfeld, D. L. (n.d.). *Boston Housing dataset.* Retrieved from http://archive.ics.uci.edu/ml/machine-learning-databases/housing/housing.data

Hole, G. (n.d.). Retrieved from www.sussex.ac.uk/Users/grahamh/RM1web/WilcoxonTable2005.pdf

Huang, G. B., Zhu, Q., & Siew, C. (2004). Extreme Learning Machine: A New Learning Scheme of Feedforward Neural Networks.*International Joint Conference on Neural Networks*, 2, 985-990.

Huang, G. B., Zhu, Q., & Siew, C. (2006). Extreme Learning Machine: Theory and Applications. *Neurocomputing*, *70*(1-3), 489–501. doi:10.1016/j.neucom.2005.12.126

Jerez, J., Molina, I., Subirates, J., & Franco, L. (2006). Missing data imputation in breast cancer prognosis. In *Proceedings of the 24th IASTED international conference on biomedical engineering (BioMed'06).*

Johnson, R. W. (n.d.). *Bodyfat dataset.* Retrieved from http://lib.stat.cmu.edu/datasets/bodyfat

Kang, P. (2013). Locally linear reconstruction based missing value imputation for supervised learning. *Neurocomputing*, *118*, 65–78. doi:10.1016/j.neucom.2013.02.016

Karlik, B., & Olgac, A. V. (2010). Performance Analysis of Various Activation Functions in Generalized MLP Architectures of Neural Networks. *International Journal of Artificial Intelligence and Expert Systems*, *1*, 111–122.

Kline, R. B. (1998). *Principles and Practice of Structural Equation Modeling*. New York: Guliford Press.

Krishna, M., & Ravi, V. (2013). Particle swarm optimization and covariance matrix based data imputation.*IEEE International Conference on Computational Intelligence and Computing Research (ICCIC).* doi:10.1109/ICCIC.2013.6724232

Liu, H., & Zhang, S. (2012). Noisy data elimination using mutual k-nearest neighbor for classification mining. *Journal of Systems and Software*, *85*(5), 1067–1074. doi:10.1016/j.jss.2011.12.019

Lowry, R. (2008). *Concepts & Applications of Inferential Statistics*. Academic Press.

Marseguerra, M., & Zoia, A. (2002). The auto-associative neural network in signal analysis II. Application to on-line monitoring of a simulated BWR component. *Annals of Nuclear Energy*, *32*(11), 1207–1223. doi:10.1016/j.anucene.2005.03.005

Marwala, T., & Chakraverty, S. (2006). Fault classification in structures with incomplete measured data using auto associative neural networks and genetic algorithm. *Current Science India*, *90*, 542–548.

MATLAB version 7.10.0. (2010). Natick, MA: The MathWorks Inc.

Merlin, P., Sorjamaa, A., Maillet, B., & Lendasse, A. (2010). X-SOM and L-SOM: A double classification approach for missing value imputation. *Neurocomputing*, *73*(7-9), 1103–1108. doi:10.1016/j.neucom.2009.11.019

Nelwamondo, F. V., Golding, D., & Marala, T. (2013). A dynamic programing approach to missing data estimation using Neural Networks. *Information Sciences*, *237*, 49–58. doi:10.1016/j.ins.2009.10.008

Nishanth, K. J., & Ravi, V. (2013). A Computational Intelligence Based Online Data Imputation Method: An Application For Banking. *Journal of Information Processing Systems*, *9*(4), 633–650. doi:10.3745/JIPS.2013.9.4.633

Nishanth, K. J., Ravi, V., Ankaiah, N., & Bose, I. (2012). Soft computing based imputation and hybrid data and text mining: The case of predicting the severity of phishing alerts. *Expert Systems with Applications*, *39*(12), 10583–10589. doi:10.1016/j.eswa.2012.02.138

Nkuna, T. R., & Odiyo, J. O. (2011). Filling of missing rainfall data in Luvuvhu River Catchment using artificial neural networks. *Physics and Chemistry of the Earth Parts A/B/C*, *36*(14-15), 830–835. doi:10.1016/j.pce.2011.07.041

Nordbotten, S. (1996). Neural network imputation applied to the Norwegian 1990 population census data. *Journal of Official Statistics*, *12*, 385–401.

Nuovo, A. G. D. (2011). Missing data analysis with fuzzy C-Means: A study of its application in a psychological scenario. *Expert Systems with Applications*, *38*(6), 6793–6797. doi:10.1016/j.eswa.2010.12.067

Olmeda, I., & Fernandez, E. (1997). Hybrid classifiers for financial multicriteria decision making: The case of bankruptcy prediction. *Computational Economics*, *10*(4), 317–335. doi:10.1023/A:1008668718837

Ragel, A., & Cremilleux, B. (1999). MVC—a preprocessing method to deal with missing values. *Knowledge-Based Systems*, *12*(5-6), 285–291. doi:10.1016/S0950-7051(99)00022-2

Rahman, M., & Islam, M. Z. (2013). Missing value imputation using decision trees and decision forests by splitting and merging records: Two novel techniques. *Knowledge-Based Systems*, *53*, 51–65. doi:10.1016/j.knosys.2013.08.023

Ramos, E., & Donoho, D. (n.d.). *Auto MPG dataset*. Retrieved from http://archive.ics.uci.edu/ml/machine-learning-databases/auto-mpg/auto-mpg.data

Ravi, V., & Krishna, M. (2014). A new online data imputation method based on general re-gression auto associative neural network. *Neurocomputing, Elsevier*, *138*, 207–212.

Samad, T., & Harp, S. A. (1992). Self-organization with partial data network. *Computation in Neural Systems*, *3*(2), 205–212. doi:10.1088/0954-898X_3_2_008

Schafer, J. L. (1997). *Analysis of incomplete multivariate data*. Chapman & Hall. doi:10.1201/9781439821862

Sharpe, P. K., & Solly, R. J. (1995). Dealing with missing values in neural network based diagnostic systems. *Neural Computing & Applications*, *3*(2), 73–77. doi:10.1007/BF01421959

Siegel, S. (1956). *Non-parametric statistics for the behavioral sciences*. New York: McGraw-Hill.

Sigillito, V. (n.d.). *Owner of dataset: National Institute of Diabetes and Digestive and Kidney Diseases, Pima Indian Diabetes dataset*. Retrieved from http://archive.ics.uci.edu/ml/datasets/Pima+Indians+Diabetes

Silva-Ramírez, E. L., Pino-Mejías, R., López-Coello, M., & Cubiles-de-la-Vega, M. D. (2011). Missing value imputation on missing completely at random data using multilayer perceptrons. *Neural Networks*, *24*(1), 121–129. doi:10.1016/j.neunet.2010.09.008 PMID:20875726

Song, Q., & Kasasbov, N. (2000). Dynamic Evolving Neural-Fuzzy Inference System (DENFIS): On-line Learning and Application for Time-series Prediction. In *Proc. 6th International Conference on Soft Computing*.

Song, Q., & Kasasbov, N. (2001). ECM — A Novel On-line, Evolving Clustering Method and Its Applications. In *Proceedings of the Fifth Biannual Conference on Artificial Neural Networks and Expert Systems*.

Song, Q., & Shepperd, M. (2007). A new imputation method for small software project data sets. *Journal of Systems and Software*, *80*(1), 51–62. doi:10.1016/j.jss.2006.05.003

Thomas, L. C., Edelman, D. B., & Crook, J. N. (2002). *Credit scoring and its applications*. Philadelphia: SIAM. doi:10.1137/1.9780898718317

Tian, J., Yu, B., Yu, D., & Ma, S. (2013). Missing data analyses: A hybrid multiple imputation algorithm using Gray System Theory and entropy based on clustering. *Applied Intelligence*, *40*(2), 376–388. doi:10.1007/s10489-013-0469-x

Wilcoxon, F. (1945). *Individual comparisons by ranking methods*. Academic Press.

Yoon, S. Y., & Lee, S. Y. (1999). Training algorithm with incomplete data for feed-forward neural networks. *Neural Processing Letters*, *10*(3), 171–179. doi:10.1023/A:1018772122605

Zhang, S. (2012). Nearest neighbor selection for iteratively kNN imputation. *Journal of Systems and Software*, *85*(11), 2541–2552. doi:10.1016/j.jss.2012.05.073

KEY TERMS AND DEFINITIONS

Activation Function: Provides non-linearity, thereby becoming a necessity of neural network.

Autoassociative Neural Network: Also called as autoencoder. An autoencoder has been generally used to learn representation from a dataset as well as for dimensionality reduction. In Autoassociative neural network, output is identical to input i.e. trying to reconstruct input at output layer.

Data Imputation: The procedure of replacing missing data with some substituted value. Missing data can occur due to many reasons like if some sensor does not respond in wireless sensor network or if people do not reply of some question during survey then that field would be blank in dataset.

Evolving Clustering Method (ECM): A one-pass, fast clustering method based on normalized Euclidean distances. It can be applied in two modes: on-line and off-line mode. It yields results in just one pass only. It processes one data only one time, there is no iteration require to process the one time processed data gain and again.

Gray System Theory (GST): A method of Gray System Theory (GST) which measures the degree of similarity between two systems. Two things are needed to be calculated for GRA: Gray Relational Coefficient (GRC), Gray Relational Grade (GRG). A larger value of GRG indicates two systems or elements are more similar and smaller value indicates less similarity of the systems or elements.

Principal Component Analysis (PCA): A very popular dimensionality reduction technique. It converts correlated variable into linearly uncorrelated variable, which will be orthogonal to each other. Each principal component is a linear combination of the original variables i.e. correlated variables. So, it is not feature selection technique but dimensionality reduction technique.

Chapter 6
Multi-Criteria Decision Making in Marketing by Using Fuzzy Rough Set

Tapan Kumar Das
VIT University, India

ABSTRACT

Most of the marketing problems are complex and unstructured due to the business dynamics and considerable uncertainty involved in the operating environments. Hence decision making in marketing involves evaluation of several parameters and thus multi criteria decision makings are a good choice in most of the decision-making tasks like supplier selection; market places selection; target marketing; etc. This chapter begins with a brief introduction of the theory of rough set which is an intelligent technique for handling uncertainty aspect in the data. However, the notions of fuzzy rough set and intuitionistic fuzzy rough (IFR) sets are defined, and its properties are studied. Thereafter rough set on two universal sets has been studied. In addition, intuitionistic fuzzy rough set on two universal sets has been extensively studied. Furthermore, this chapter shows that intuitionistic fuzzy rough set can be successfully practiced in decision making problems.

1. INTRODUCTION

Multi-Criterion Decision Making (MCDM) is a process in which decision makers critically evaluate each alternate according to multiple criteria. Many typical methods are proposed to solve MCDM problem in business and industry areas (Kahraman, Cebeci & Ulukan, 2003; Büyüközkan, 2004). However, most of these approaches consider the decision making with certain information of the weights and decision values, which does not make any appreciation when managing uncertain, imperfect or fuzzy knowledge. However, in our day to day life, most of the situations and associated data we come across are of not certain due to presence of uncertainties in the physical world. Uncertainty exists almost everywhere, even in the most idealized circumstances. Data set from real-life applications like marketing, medical, economics, etc. is not crisp and has uncertainties. In addition, uncertainty is an attribute of information

DOI: 10.4018/978-1-5225-0997-4.ch006

and usually decision-relevant information is uncertain and imprecise. It is imperative to model these day to day problems involving uncertainties mathematically. To this end theory like probability theory, fuzzy set theory (Zadeh,1965), intuitionistic fuzzy set (Atanasov, 1986), rough set theory (Pawlak, 1982) those deal with problems involving uncertainties are immensely useful. However each theory has their lim itations. In fact, the inadequacy of the parameterization tool in these theories does not allow them to handle vagueness properly. In 1999, Molodtsov (Molodtsov, 1999) introduced the concept of soft sets and established the fundamental results of the new theory. Soft set theory somehow is free from the difficulties present in fuzzy set theory, rough set theory, probability theory, etc. In 2002, P.K. Maji (Maji & Roy, 2002) studied the theory of soft sets and exhibited some results of the soft set in decision making tasks.

In recent past, several attempts have already been made to use the rough sets theory in decision support system (Pawlak & Slowinski, 1994). The rough set approach is intended to deal with inconsistency due to which it is successfully applied to MCDA (Greco, Matarazzo & Slowinski, 2001). Finally, the output of the analysis, i.e. the model of preferences in terms of decision rules seems very convenient for decision support because it is transparent and analogous to data mining technique. The original rough set approach is not able, however, to deal with preference-ordered attribute domains and decision classes. Solving this problem was crucial for application of the rough set approach to multicriteria decision analysis (MCDA). Multi criteria fuzzy decision making has been studied by (Hong & Choi, 2000). Further multi-criteria decision making using intuitionistic fuzzy rough set is being discussed in many literatures (Das, Acharjya & Patra, 2015; Das, Mohapatro & Abburu, 2015).

This chapter begins with a brief introduction of rough set and then describes generalizations of it. This chapter endeavors to forge a connection between fuzzy set and rough set and depicts a new model fuzzy rough set and further intuitionistic fuzzy rough set to address the challenges of vagueness and impreciseness. Furthermore, we attempt to elucidate intuitionistic fuzzy rough set in two universal sets which cuts across some definitions and operations. At the end, we explain the application of intuitionistic fuzzy rough set for a marketing problem where the decision making is of multi criteria.

2. FOUNDATIONS OF ROUGH COMPUTING

At the present age of internet, a huge repository of the data is available across various domains. Therefore, it is very hard to extract useful information from voluminous data available in the universe. So, information retrieval and knowledge representation has become one of the most popular areas of recent research. Information retrieval and acquisition of knowledge is one of the important components of an information system. But, the real challenge lies in converting voluminous data into knowledge and to use this knowledge to make proper decisions. In order to transform the processed data into useful information and knowledge, there is a need of new techniques and tools. Rough set theory developed by Pawlak (1982) used to process uncertain and incomplete information is a tool to the above mentioned problem. One of its strength is the attribute dependencies, their significance among inconsistent data. At the same time, it does not need any preliminary or additional information about the data. Therefore, it classifies imprecise, uncertain or incomplete information expressed in terms of data acquired from experience.

2.1 Rough Sets

In this section we recall the definitions of basic rough set theory developed by Pawlak (1991). Let U be a finite nonempty set called the universe. Suppose $R \subseteq (U \times U)$ is an equivalence relation on U. The equivalence relation R partitions the set U into disjoint subsets. Elements of same equivalence class are said to be indistinguishable. Equivalence classes induced by R are called elementary concepts. Every union of elementary concepts is called a definable set. The empty set is considered to be a definable set, thus all the definable sets form a Boolean algebra and (U, R) is called an approximation space. Given a target set X, we can characterize X by a pair of lower and upper approximations. We associate two subsets $\underline{R}X$ and $\overline{R}X$ called the R-lower and R-upper approximations of X respectively and are given by

$$\underline{R}X = \cup\left\{Y \in U / R : Y \subseteq X\right\}$$

$$\underline{R}X = \cup\left\{Y \in U / R : Y \cap X \neq \phi\right\}$$

The R-boundary of X, $BN_R(X)$ is given by $BN_R(X) = \overline{R}X - \underline{R}X$. We say X is rough with respect to R if and only if $\overline{R}X \neq \underline{R}X$, equivalently $BN_R(X) \neq \phi$. X is said to be R- definable if and only if $\overline{R}X = \underline{R}X$ or $BN_R(X) = \phi$. So, a set is rough with respect to R if and only if it is not R-definable.

2.1.1 An Example

Consider the information system shown in Table 1.

Table 1. A sample information system

Company	Business Domain	Based On	Fortune 500
C1	Healthcare	USA	Yes
C2	IT	India	Yes
C3	IT	USA	Yes
C4	FMCG	India	No
C5	Electric Equipment	Japan	No
C6	Healthcare	USA	Yes
C7	Chemicals	Iran	Yes
C8	FMCG	India	No
C9	IT	India	Yes
C10	Chemicals	Iran	Yes

The information system represented in Table 1. shows 10 companies (c1,c2,….,c10) ; their business domain (Healthcare, IT, FMCG, Electric Equipment, Chemicals) ; based on country(India, China, USA, Iran, Japan) and whether they belongs to Fortune 500 class or not.

By considering business domain only,

$$U / R_1 = \{\{c1, c6\}, \{c2, c3, c9\}, \{c4, c8\}, \{c5\}, \{c7, c10\}\}$$

where $R_1 : c_i R c_j$ if c_i and c_j are same business domain.

It shows that the universe of 10 companies in the information system are partitioned into five classes., c1 and c6 are of same business domain; c2, c3 and c9 are of same business domain and so on. Basing on the business domain only we cannot differentiate c1 and c6, hence they are of the same concept.

By taking into account business domain, based on and Fortune500, we have

$$U / R = \{\{C1, C6\}, \{C2, C9\}, \{C4, C8\}, \{C7,C10\},\{C3\},\{C5\}\}$$

Here R is an equivalence class which partition the universe of 10 companies into six groups.

From above clearly that c1 and c6 are identical in respect to all the attributes, i.e. business domain, based on and Fortune500, so they belong to a concept. Similarly, c2 and c9 are indistinguishable. Furthermore, c4 and c8 are of same concept and so on. This example explains the basis of equivalence class.

2.2 Rough Set on Fuzzy Approximation Space

To unfold the article, we present the definitions, notions and results of rough set on fuzzy approximation spaces as studied by Das and Acharjya (2014). We first define the following concepts leading to the introduction of rough set on fuzzy approximation space. We use the standard notation μ(x) for membership functions associated with fuzzy set.

Let U be universe of discourse. A fuzzy relation on U is a fuzzy subset of $(U \times U)$. A fuzzy relation R on U is said to be a fuzzy proximity relation if $\mu_R(x,x) = 1$ for all x $\in U$ and μ_R (x; y) = μ_R (y; x) for all x; y $\in U$. For a given $\alpha \in [0,1]$, the α-cut of R is given by $R_\alpha = \mu_R(x,y) \geq \alpha$. We say that two elements x and y are α-similar with respect to R if $(x,y) \in R_\alpha$ and we write $xR_\alpha y$. We say that two elements x and y are α-identical with respect to R if either x is α-similar to y or x is transitively α-similar to y with respect to R, i.e., there exists a sequence of elements $(u_1, u_2, u_3, \ldots, u_n)$ in U such that

$$xR_\alpha u_1, u_1 R_\alpha u_2, u_2 R_\alpha u_{3,} \ldots, u_n R_\alpha y.$$

If x and y are α-identical with respect to fuzzy proximity relation R, then we write (x; y) $\in R(\alpha)$. It is easy to see that for any $\alpha \in [0,1]$, $R(\alpha)$ is an equivalence relation on U. We use R_α^* to denote the set of equivalence classes generated by the equivalence relation $R(\alpha)$ for any $\alpha \in [0,1]$. We denote the

$R(\alpha)$-equivalence class of an element x in U by $[x]_\alpha$. The pair (U,R) is called fuzzy approximation space.

Let $X \subseteq U$, the rough set on fuzzy approximation space of X in the generalized approximation space $(U,R(\alpha))$ is denoted by ($\underline{X}_\alpha, \overline{X}_\alpha$) where

$$\underline{X}_\alpha = \cup\{ Y : Y \in R_\alpha^* \text{ and } Y \subseteq X \}$$

$$\overline{X}_\alpha = \cup\{ Y : Y \in R_\alpha^* \text{ and } Y \cap X \neq \phi \}$$

The α boundary of X with respect to R is defined as $BN_{R_\alpha} = \overline{X}_\alpha$ -. $\underline{X}_\alpha$ The set X is said to be α-discernible with respect to R if and only if $\overline{X}_\alpha = \underline{X}_\alpha$ and α-rough set with respect to R if and only if $\overline{X}_\alpha \neq \underline{X}_\alpha$. If $\alpha = 1$ then rough set on fuzzy approximation space reduces to Pawlak's rough sets.

2.2.1 An Example

We discuss how the above concept can be applied to real life problems. We consider an example in which we establish the relation between resource persons working in a project. We consider the number of hours of work over a period of week. We define the relation between any two resources as

$$s(x,y) = 1 - \frac{|x-y|}{40}$$

The information about the small universe

$$U = \{x_1, x_2, x_3, x_4, x_5, x_6, x_7, x_8\}$$

is of the eight resource persons and the number of hours of work over a week in a project is presented in Table 2.

The fuzzy proximity relation R on U is shown below in Table 3.

For $\alpha \geq 0.95$, we get

$$U / R_{0.95} = \{\{x_1, x_2, x_3, x_5, x_6, x_7, x_8\}, \{x_4\}\}.$$

Table 2. Resource persons and number of hours worked

Resource Persons	x_1	x_2	x_3	x_4	x_5	x_6	x_7	x_8
Number of Hours	40	36	40	32	36	38	40	34

Table 3. Fuzzy proximity relation R

R	x_1	x_2	x_3	x_4	x_5	x_6	x_7	x_8
x_1	1	0.9	1	0.8	0.9	0.95	1	0.85
x_2	0.9	1	0.9	0.9	1	0.95	0.9	0.95
x_3	1	0.9	1	0.8	0.9	0.95	1	0.85
x_4	0.8	0.9	0.8	1	0.9	0.85	0.8	0.95
x_5	0.9	1	0.9	0.9	1	0.95	0.9	0.95
x_6	0.95	0.95	0.95	0.85	0.95	1	0.95	0.9
x_7	1	0.9	1	0.8	0.9	0.95	1	0.85
x_8	0.85	0.95	0.85	0.95	0.95	0.9	0.85	1

The above expression represents α-equivalence class obtained from Table. 2. It shows that resource persons $x_1, x_2, x_3, x_5, x_6, x_7, x_8$ belongs to one concept and they are almost similar for $\alpha \geq 0.95$. This is the basis of rough set on fuzzy approximation space.

2.3 Rough Set on Intuitionistic Fuzzy Approximation Space

To unfold the chapter, the definitions, notions and results of rough set on intuitionistic fuzzy approximation spaces discussed in chapter 1 and chapter 2 are presented here. In real time environment we face a lot of problem while studying information retrieval from large databases. This is because of inconsistent and ambiguous dataset that are precise in character. The basic rough set philosophy for information retrieval developed by Pawlak (1991) depends upon equivalence relations. However, such types of relations are rare in practice while studying information system containing numerical values. Therefore, the equivalence relation is generalized to fuzzy proximity relation and it leads to rough sets on fuzzy approximation spaces (De, 1999). The fuzzy proximity relation is further generalized to intuitionistic fuzzy proximity relation (Atanasov, 1986). Thus rough set on fuzzy approximation spaces is generalized to rough set on intuitionistic fuzzy approximation spaces. Further it is observed that, rough set on intuitionistic fuzzy approximation spaces is a better model over rough set and rough set on fuzzy approximation space (Acharjya, 2009). However, for completeness of the chapter we provide the basic notions of rough sets on intuitionistic fuzzy approximation spaces. We use standard notation μ for membership and ν for non-membership functions associated with an intuitionistic fuzzy set.

An intuitionistic fuzzy relation R on a universal set U is an intuitionistic fuzzy set defined on $(U \times U)$. An intuitionistic fuzzy relation R on U is said to be an intuitionistic fuzzy proximity relation if the following properties hold.

$\mu_R(x,x) = 1$ and $\nu_R(x,x) = 0$ for all $x \in U$

$\mu_R(x,y) = \mu_R(y,x)$ and $\nu_R(x,y) = \nu_R(y,x)$ for all $x,\, y \in U$

Then for any $(\alpha,\, \beta) \in J$, where

$$J = \left\{(\alpha,\, \beta) : \alpha,\, \beta \in [0,1] \; and \; 0 \leq (\alpha + \beta) \leq 1\right\}$$

$(\alpha,\, \beta)$-cut, $R_{\alpha,\beta}$, of R is given by

$$R_{\alpha,\beta} = \left\{(x,\, y) : \mu_R(x,y) \geq \alpha \; and \; \nu_R(x,y) \leq \beta\right\}$$

We say that two elements x and y are $(\alpha,\, \beta)$-similar with respect to R if $(x,y) \in R_{\alpha,\beta}$ and we write $x\, R_{\alpha,\beta}\, y$. In addition, we say that two elements x and y are $(\alpha,\, \beta)$-identical with respect to R for $(\alpha,\, \beta) \in J$, written as $x\, R(\alpha,\, \beta)\, y$ if and only if $x\, R_{\alpha,\beta}\, y$ or there exists a sequence of elements $u_1,\, u_2,\, u_3,\, \cdots,\, u_n$ in U such that $x\, R_{\alpha,\beta}\, u_1,\; u_1\, R_{\alpha,\beta}\, u_2,\; u_2\, R_{\alpha,\beta}\, u_3,\; \cdots,\; u_n\, R_{\alpha,\beta}\, y$. In the last case, we say that x is transitively $(\alpha,\, \beta)$-similar to y with respect to R.

It is also easy to see that for any $(\alpha,\, \beta) \in J$, $R(\alpha,\, \beta)$ is an equivalence relation on U. We denote $R^*_{\alpha,\beta}$ the set of equivalence classes generated by the equivalence relation $R(\alpha,\, \beta)$ for each fixed $(\alpha,\, \beta) \in J$. The pair (U, R) generated in this way is an intuitionistic fuzzy approximation space (IF-approximation space). An IF-approximation space (U, R) generates usual approximation space (U, $R(\alpha,\, \beta)$) of Pawlak for every $(\alpha,\, \beta) \in J$. The rough set on X in the generalized approximation space (U, $R(\alpha,\, \beta)$) is denoted by $\left(\underline{X}_{\alpha,\beta},\, \overline{X}_{\alpha,\beta}\right)$ where

$$\underline{X}_{\alpha,\beta} = \cup\left\{Y : Y \in R^*_{\alpha,\beta} \; and \; Y \subseteq X\right\}$$

and

$$\overline{X}_{\alpha,\beta} = \cup\left\{Y : Y \in R^*_{\alpha,\beta} \; and \; Y \cap X \neq \phi\right\}.$$

Let X be a rough set in the generalized approximation space (U, $R(\alpha, \beta)$). Then we define the (α, β)-boundary of X with respect to R denoted by $BNR_{\alpha,\beta}(X)$ as $BNR_{\alpha,\beta}(X) = \overline{X}_{\alpha,\beta} - \underline{X}_{\alpha,\beta}$. The target set X is (α, β)-discernible with respect to R if and only if $\overline{X}_{\alpha,\beta} = \underline{X}_{\alpha,\beta}$ and X is (α, β)-rough with respect to R if and only if $\overline{X}_{\alpha,\beta} \neq \underline{X}_{\alpha,\beta}$.

2.4 Almost Indiscernibility Relation

An information system provides all available information and knowledge about the objects under certain consideration. Objects are only perceived or measured by using a finite number of properties without considering any semantic relationship between attribute values of a particular attribute. Therefore, in general one uses the trivial equality relation on values of an attribute as discussed in Pawlak's rough set theory. However, in many real life applications it is observed that the attribute values are not exactly identical but almost identical. At this point we generalize Pawlak's approach of indiscernibility. Keeping view to this, the almost indiscernibility relation is generated and is the basis of rough set on intuitionistic fuzzy approximation space as discussed in the previous section.

Let U be the universe and A be a set of attributes. With each attribute $a \in A$, we associate a set of its values V_a, called the domain of a. The pair $S = (U, A)$ will be called an information system. Let $B \subseteq A$. For a chosen $(\alpha, \beta) \in [0, 1]$ we denote a binary relation $R_B(\alpha, \beta)$ on U defined by $xR_B(\alpha, \beta)y$ if and only if $x(a)R_B(\alpha, \beta)\ y(a)$ for all $a \in B$, where $x(a) \in V_a$ denotes the value of attribute x in a. Obviously, it can be proved that the relation $R_B(\alpha, \beta)$ is an equivalence relation on U. Also, we notice that $R_B(\alpha, \beta)$ is not exactly the indiscernibility relation defined by Pawlak (1991); rather it can be viewed as an almost indiscernibility relation on U. For $\alpha = 1, \beta = 0$ the almost indiscernibility relation, $R_B(\alpha, \beta)$ reduces to the indiscernibility relation. Thus, it generalizes the Pawlak's indiscernibility relation. The family of all equivalence classes of $R_B(\alpha, \beta)$ i.e., the partition generated by B for $(\alpha, \beta) \in [0, 1]$, will be denoted by $U / R_B(\alpha, \beta)$. If $(x, y) \in R_B(\alpha, \beta)$, then we will say that x and y are (α, β)-indiscernible. Blocks of the partition $U / R_B(\alpha, \beta)$ are referred as $B_{\alpha,\beta}$-elementary concepts. These are the basic concepts of our knowledge in the theory of rough set on intuitionistic fuzzy approximation space.

3. ROUGH SET BASED ON TWO UNIVERSAL SETS

An information system provides a means to describe a finite set of objects called a universe with a finite set of attributes thereby represents all the available information and knowledge. But in many real life situations an information system sets up relation with more than one universe. This extends the concept of rough set on single universal set to rough sets on two universal sets. This eventually extends the scope of rough sets to extract knowledge. Liu (2010) generalized the rough set models using two distinct universal sets. Let U and V be two universal sets and $R \subseteq (U \times V)$ be a binary relation. A relational system (U, V, R) denotes an approximation space. For an element $x \in U$, right neighborhood or the R-relative set of x in U is defined as

$r(x) = \cup\{y \in V : (x, y) \in R\}$.

Similarly, for an element $y \in V$, the left neighborhood or the R-relative set of y in V is defined as

$l(y) = \cup\{x \in U : (x, y) \in R\}$.

For any two elements $x_1, x_2 \in U$, x_1 and x_2 are equivalent if $r(x_1) = r(x_2)$. Thus, $(x_1, x_2) \in E_U$ if and only if $r(x_1) = r(x_2)$, where E_U denotes the equivalence relation on U. Hence, E_U partitions the universal set U into disjoint subsets. Similarly for any two elements $y_1, y_2 \in V$, we say y_1 and y_2 are equivalent if $l(y_1) = l(y_2)$. Thus, $(y_1, y_2) \in E_V$ if and only if $l(y_1) = l(y_2)$, where E_V denotes the equivalence relation on V and partitions the universal set V into disjoint subsets. Therefore for the approximation space (U, V, R), it is clear that $E_V \circ R = R = R \circ E_U$, where $E_V \circ R$ is the composition of R and E_V. For any $Y \subseteq V$ and the binary relation R, we associate two subsets $\underline{R}Y$ and $\overline{R}Y$ called the R-lower and R-upper approximations of Y respectively, which are given by:

$\underline{R}Y = \cup x\{\in U : r(x) \subseteq Y\}$

and

$\bar{R}Y = \cup\{x \in U : r(x) \cap Y \neq \phi\}$

The R-boundary of Y is denoted as $BN_R(Y) = \bar{R}Y - \underline{R}Y$. The pair $(\bar{R}Y, \underline{R}Y)$ is called as the rough set of $Y \subseteq V$ if $\bar{R}Y \neq \underline{R}Y$ or equivalently $BN_R(Y) \neq \phi$. Further, if U and V are finite sets, then the binary relation R from U to V can be represented as $R(x, y)$, where

$$R(x, y) = \begin{cases} 1 & if\ (x, y) \in R \\ 0 & if\ (x, y) \notin R \end{cases}$$

The characteristic function of $X \subseteq U$ is defined for each $x \in U$ as follows:

$$\chi(x) = \begin{cases} 1 & if\ x \in X \\ 0 & if\ x \notin X \end{cases}$$

Therefore, the R - lower and R - upper approximations can also be presented in an equivalent form as shown below. Here $\wedge$ and $\vee$ denote the minimum and the maximum operators respectively.

$$(\underline{R}Y)x = \wedge_{y \in V}\left((1 - R(x, y)) \vee Y(y)\right)$$

and

$$(\bar{R}Y)x = \bigvee_{y \in V} \left(R(x,y) \wedge Y(y) \right)$$

3.1 Topological Characterization of Rough Set on Two Univeral Sets

In this section, we state an interesting topological characterization of rough set on two universal sets employing the notion of the lower and upper approximation. It results four important and different types of rough sets on two universal sets as discussed by Das, Acharjya and Patra (2015).

Type 1: If $\underline{R}Y \neq \phi$ and $\bar{R}Y \neq U$, then we say that Y is roughly R-definable on two universal sets.
Type 2: If $\underline{R}Y = \phi$ and $\bar{R}Y \neq U$, then we say that Y is internally R-undefinable on two universal sets.
Type 3: If $\underline{R}Y \neq \phi$ and $\bar{R}Y = U$, then we say that Y is externally R-undefinable on two universal sets.
Type 4: If $\underline{R}Y = \phi$ and $\bar{R}Y = U$, then we say that Y is totally R-undefinable on two universal sets.

3.3 Intuitionistic Fuzzy Rough Set on Two Universal Sets

A fuzzy relation is an extension of the concept of binary relation on any set U. Therefore, fuzzy rough sets by Dubois and Prade (1990) generalize the concepts of Pawlak rough sets. Further it is generalized to fuzzy rough sets in two universal sets by Liu (2010). In fuzzy set theory it is taken into consideration that there exist a membership value for all the elements of the set and we do not consider non membership values of the elements of the set. However, it is not true in many real life problems due to the presence of hesitation. In fuzzy set theory, if $\mu(x)$ be the degree of membership of an element x, then the degree of non membership of x is calculated using mathematical formula $(1-\mu(x))$ with the assumption that full part of the degree of membership is determinism and in-deterministic part is zero. This is not always applicable in real life and hence intuitionistic fuzzy set theory is better. At the same time, intuitionistic fuzzy set theory reduces to fuzzy set theory if in-deterministic part is zero. It indicates that intuitionistic fuzzy set model is a generalized model over fuzzy set model. Therefore, intuitionistic fuzzy rough set on two universal sets is a better model than fuzzy rough set on two universal sets.

Now, we present the definitions, notations and results of intuitionistic fuzzy rough set on two universal sets as established and introduced by Tripathy and Acharjya (2012). We define the basic concepts leading to intuitionistic fuzzy rough set on two universal sets in which we denote μ for membership and ν for non membership functions that are associated with an intuitionistic fuzzy rough set on two universal sets.

- **Definition (Atanasov, 1986):** Let U be a universe of discourse and x is a particular element of U. An intuitionistic fuzzy set X of U is defined as $\langle x, \mu_X(x), \nu_X(x) \rangle$, where the function $\mu_X(x): U \to [0,1]$ and $\nu_X(x): U \to [0,1]$ define the degree of membership and non membership respectively of the element $x \in U$. For every element $x \in U$, $0 \leq \mu_X(x) + \nu_X(x) \leq 1$. The amount $1-(\mu_X(x)+\nu_X(x))$ is called the hesitation part, which may cater either membership value or non membership value or the both. For simplicity we will use (μ_X, ν_X) to denote the intuitionistic fuzzy set X. The family of all intuitionistic fuzzy subsets of U is denoted by $IF(U)$. The complement of an intuitionistic fuzzy set X is denoted by

$$X' = \left\{\left\langle x, \nu_X(x), \mu_X(x)\right\rangle \mid x \in U\right\}$$

- **Definition (Atanasov, 1986):** Let U and V be two non empty universal sets. An intuitionistic fuzzy relation R_{IF} from $U \to V$ is an intuitionistic fuzzy set of $(U \times V)$ characterized by the membership function $\mu_{R_{IF}}$ and non-membership function $\nu_{R_{IF}}$ where

$$R_{IF} = \left\{\left\langle (x,y), \mu_{R_{IF}}(x,y), \nu_{R_{IF}}(x,y)\right\rangle \mid x \in U, y \in V\right\}$$

with

$$0 \le \mu_{R_{IF}}(x,y) + \nu_{R_{IF}}(x,y) \le 1$$

for every $(x,y) \in U \times V$.

- **Definition (Acharjya & Tripathy, 2012):** Let U and V be two non empty universal sets and R_{IF} is a intuitionistic fuzzy relation from U to V. If for $x \in U$, $\mu_{R_{IF}}(x,y) = 0$ and $\nu_{R_{IF}}(x,y) = 1$ for all $y \in V$, then x is said to be a solitary element with respect to R_{IF}. The set of all solitary elements with respect to the relation R_{IF} is called the solitary set S. That is,

$$S = \left\{x \mid x \in U, \mu_{R_{IF}}(x,y) = 0, \nu_{R_{IF}}(x,y) = 1 \forall y \in V\right\}$$

- **Definition (Acharjya & Tripathy, 2012):** Let U and V be two non empty universal sets and R_{IF} is a intuitionistic fuzzy relation from U to V. Therefore, (U, V, R_{IF}) is called a intuitionistic fuzzy approximation space. For $Y \in IF(V)$, an intuitionistic fuzzy rough set is a pair $\left(\underline{R_{IF}}Y, \overline{R_{IF}}Y\right)$ of intuitionistic fuzzy set on U such that for every $x \in U$

$$\underline{R_{IF}}Y = \left\{\left\langle x, \mu_{\underline{R_{IF}(Y)}}(x), \nu_{\underline{R_{IF}(Y)}}(x)\right\rangle \mid x \in U\right\}$$

$$\overline{R_{IF}}Y = \left\{\left\langle x, \mu_{\overline{R_{IF}(Y)}}(x), \nu_{\overline{R_{IF}(Y)}}(x)\right\rangle \mid x \in U\right\}$$

where

$$\mu_{\underline{R_{IF}}(Y)}(x) = \bigwedge_{y \in V} \left[\nu_{R_{IF}}(x,y) \vee \mu_Y(y) \right]$$

$$\nu_{\underline{R_{IF}}(Y)}(x) = \bigvee_{y \in V} \left[\mu_{R_{IF}}(x,y) \wedge \nu_Y(y) \right]$$

$$\mu_{\overline{R_{IF}}(Y)}(x) = \bigvee_{y \in V} \left[\mu_{R_{IF}}(x,y) \wedge \mu_Y(y) \right]$$

and

$$\nu_{\overline{R_{IF}}(Y)}(x) = \bigwedge_{y \in V} \left[\nu_{R_{IF}}(x,y) \vee \nu_Y(y) \right]$$

The pair $\left(\underline{R_{IF}}Y, \overline{R_{IF}}Y\right)$ is called the intuitionistic fuzzy rough set of Y with respect to (U,V,R_{IF}), where $\underline{R_{IF}}$, $\overline{R_{IF}} : IF(U) \to IF(V)$ are referred as lower and upper intuitionistic fuzzy rough approximation operators on two universal sets.

3.3.1 Algebraic Properties of Intuitionistic Fuzzy Rough Set on Two Universal Sets

This section discusses the algebraic properties of intuitionistic fuzzy rough set on two universal sets through solitary set as established by Tripathy and Acharjya (2012). These are interesting and valuable in the study of intuitionistic fuzzy rough sets on two universal sets and are useful in finding knowledge from the information system that establishes relation between two universes.

Let U and V be two universal sets. Let R_{IF} be an intuitionistic fuzzy relation from U to V and further let S be the solitary set with respect to R_{IF}. Then for $X, Y \in IF(V)$, the following properties holds:

1. $\underline{R_{IF}}(V) = U$ and $\overline{R_{IF}}(\phi) = \phi$
2. If $X \subseteq Y$, then $\underline{R_{IF}}(X) \subseteq \underline{R_{IF}}(Y)$ and $\overline{R_{IF}}(X) \subseteq \overline{R_{IF}}(Y)$
3. $\underline{R_{IF}}(X) = (\overline{R_{IF}}(X'))'$ and $\overline{R_{IF}}(X) = (\underline{R_{IF}}(X'))'$
4. $\underline{R_{IF}}\phi \supseteq S$ and $\overline{R_{IF}}V \subseteq S'$, where S' denotes the complement of S in U.
5. For any given index set J, $X_i \in IF(V)$, $\underline{R_{IF}}\left(\bigcup_{i \in J} X_i\right) \supseteq \bigcup_{i \in J} \underline{R_{IF}}X_i$ and $\overline{R_{IF}}\left(\bigcap_{i \in J} X_i\right) \subseteq \bigcap_{i \in J} \overline{R_{IF}}X_i$.
6. For any given index set J, $X_i \in IF(V)$, $\underline{R_{IF}}\left(\bigcap_{i \in J} X_i\right) = \bigcap_{i \in J} \underline{R_{IF}}X_i$ and $\overline{R_{IF}}\left(\bigcup_{i \in J} X_i\right) = \bigcup_{i \in J} \overline{R_{IF}}X_i$.

4. APPLICATIONS TO MULTI CRITERION DECISION MAKING

This section depicts a real life application of intuitionistic fuzzy rough set on two universal sets to multi criterion decision making. The model application is explained as intuitionistic fuzzy rough set upper approximation. Let us consider the multi criteria decision making in the case of supermarkets in a particular city. However, it is observed that due to several factors such as best possible value for customer's money, quality of the product, style and the behaviour of supporting staff, customers depend on more than one supermarket. Therefore, from customer behaviour it is clear that they are not happy with one supermarket. Hence, intuitionistic fuzzy relation better depicts the relation between the customers and supermarkets.

Let us set the criteria

$$V = \{y_1, y_2, y_3, y_4, y_5, y_6\},$$

in which y_1 denotes best possible value of customer's money; y_2 denotes quality of the product; y_3 denotes the behavior of supporting staff; y_4 denotes the location of supermarket; y_5 denotes availability of items; and y_6 denotes offers. Let us consider the decisions $U = \{d_1, d_2, d_3, d_4, d_5\}$, in which d_1 denotes excellent; d_2 denotes very good; d_3 denotes good; d_4 denotes average; and d_5 denotes poor. Several variety of customers and professionals are invited to the survey that only focuses on the criterion of best possible value of customers money in a supermarket. Therefore, (U, V, R_{IF}) be an intuitionistic fuzzy approximation space, where

$$U = \{d_1, d_2, d_3, d_4, d_5\}$$

and

$$V = \{y_1, y_2, y_3, y_4, y_5, y_6\}.$$

If 15% people select "excellent" and 10% people select "not excellent"; 25% select "very good" and 20% select "not very good"; 35% select "good" and 5% select "not good"; 10% select "average" and 20% select "not average"; and 15% select "poor" and 10% select "not poor", then the vector can be obtained as

$$(0.15, 0.1; 0.25, 0.2; 0.35, 0.05; 0.1, 0.2; 0.15, 0.1)^t,$$

where t represents the transpose. Similarly, the decisions based on other criteria are obtained as follows:

$$(0.1, 0.2; 0.35, 0.21; 0.25, 0.15; 0.1, 0.8; 0.2, 0.7)^t,$$

$\left(0.55, 0.1; 0.15, 0.45; 0.2, 0.15; 0, 0.6; 0.1, 0.3\right)^t,$

$\left(0.1, 0.7; 0.1, 0.4; 0.4, 0.2; 0.2, 0.3; 0.2, 0.1\right)^t,$

$\left(0, 0.6; 0, 0.5; 0.15, 0.3; 0.35, 0.1; 0.5, 0.15\right)^t,$

and

$\left(0.25, 0.1; 0.25, 0.2; 0.2, 0.4; 0.1, 0.4; 0.2, 0.3\right)^t.$

Based on the decision vectors, the intuitionistic fuzzy relation R_{IF} from U to V is presented by the following matrix. We define the intuitionistic fuzzy relation $R_{IF} \in IF(U \times V)$ by the following matrix.

$$R_{IF} = \begin{array}{c} \\ d_1 \\ d_2 \\ d_3 \\ d_4 \\ d_5 \end{array} \begin{array}{cccccc} y_1 & y_2 & y_3 & y_4 & y_5 & y_6 \end{array} \begin{pmatrix} 0.15, 0.1 & 0.1, 0.2 & 0.55, 0.1 & 0.1, 0.7 & 0, 0.6 & 0.25, 0.1 \\ 0.25, 0.2 & 0.35, 0.21 & 0.15, 0.45 & 0.1, 0.4 & 0, 0.5 & 0.25, 0.2 \\ 0.35, 0.05 & 0.25, 0.15 & 0.2, 0.15 & 0.4, 0.2 & 0.15, 0.3 & 0.2, 0.4 \\ 0.1, 0.2 & 0.1, 0.8 & 0, 0.6 & 0.2, 0.3 & 0.35, 0.1 & 0.1, 0.4 \\ 0.15, 0.1 & 0.2, 0.7 & 0.1, 0.3 & 0.2, 0.1 & 0.5, 0.15 & 0.2, 0.3 \end{pmatrix}$$

We assume that there are two categories of customers, where right weights for each criterion in V are

$$Y_1 = \left(\langle d_1, 0.35, 0.15\rangle, \langle d_2, 0.15, 0.3\rangle, \langle d_3, 0.2, 0.3\rangle, \langle d_4, 0.1, 0.5\rangle, \langle d_5, 0.1, 0.4\rangle, \langle d_6, 0.1, 0.2\rangle\right)$$

and

$$Y_2 = \left(\langle d_1, 0.2, 0.3\rangle, \langle d_2, 0.4, 0.1\rangle, \langle d_3, 0.15, 0.4\rangle, \langle d_4, 0.1, 0.3\rangle, \langle d_5, 0.1, 0.3\rangle, \langle d_6, 0.05, 0.5\rangle\right)$$

respectively. Thus, by using upper approximation we have:

$$\begin{aligned} \mu_{\overline{R_{IF}(Y_1)}}(d_1) &= \vee_{y \in V} \left[\mu_{R_{IF}}(d_1, y) \wedge \mu_{Y_1}(y)\right] \\ &= [0.15 \wedge 0.35] \vee [0.1 \wedge 0.15] \vee [0.55 \wedge 0.2] \vee [0.1 \wedge 0.1] \vee [0 \wedge 0.1] \vee [0.25 \wedge 0.1] \\ &= 0.15 \vee 0.1 \vee 0.2 \vee 0.1 \vee 0 \vee 0.1 \\ &= 0.2 \end{aligned}$$

$$\nu_{\overline{R_{IF}(Y_1)}}(d_1) = \bigwedge_{y\in V}\left[\nu_{R_{IF}}(d_1,y) \vee \nu_{Y_1}(y)\right]$$
$$= [0.1 \vee 0.15] \wedge [0.2 \vee 0.3] \wedge [0.1 \vee 0.3] \wedge [0.7 \vee 0.5] \wedge [0.6 \vee 0.4] \wedge [0.1 \vee 0.2]$$
$$= 0.15 \wedge 0.3 \wedge 0.3 \wedge 0.7 \wedge 0.6 \wedge 0.2$$
$$= 0.15$$

$$\mu_{\overline{R_{IF}(Y_1)}}(d_2) = \bigvee_{y\in V}\left[\mu_{R_{IF}}(d_2,y) \wedge \mu_{Y_1}(y)\right]$$
$$= [0.25 \wedge 0.35] \vee [0.35 \wedge 0.15] \vee [0.15 \wedge 0.2] \vee [0.1 \wedge 0.1] \vee [0 \wedge 0.1] \vee [0.25 \wedge 0.1]$$
$$= 0.25 \vee 0.15 \vee 0.15 \vee 0.1 \vee 0 \vee 0.1$$
$$= 0.25$$

$$\nu_{\overline{R_{IF}(Y_1)}}(d_2) = \bigwedge_{y\in V}\left[\nu_{R_{IF}}(d_2,y) \vee \nu_{Y_1}(y)\right]$$
$$= [0.2 \vee 0.15] \wedge [0.21 \vee 0.3] \wedge [0.45 \vee 0.3] \wedge [0.4 \vee 0.5] \wedge [0.5 \vee 0.4] \wedge [0.2 \vee 0.2]$$
$$= 0.2 \wedge 0.3 \wedge 0.45 \wedge 0.5 \wedge 0.5 \wedge 0.2$$
$$= 0.2$$

$$\mu_{\overline{R_{IF}(Y_1)}}(d_3) = \bigvee_{y\in V}\left[\mu_{R_{IF}}(d_3,y) \wedge \mu_{Y_1}(y)\right]$$
$$= [0.35 \wedge 0.35] \vee [0.25 \wedge 0.15] \vee [0.2 \wedge 0.2] \vee [0.4 \wedge 0.1] \vee [0.15 \wedge 0.1] \vee [0.2 \wedge 0.1]$$
$$= 0.35 \vee 0.15 \vee 0.2 \vee 0.1 \vee 0.1 \vee 0.1$$
$$= 0.35$$

$$\nu_{\overline{R_{IF}(Y_1)}}(d_3) = \bigwedge_{y\in V}\left[\nu_{R_{IF}}(d_3,y) \vee \nu_{Y_1}(y)\right]$$
$$= [0.05 \vee 0.15] \wedge [0.15 \vee 0.3] \wedge [0.15 \vee 0.3] \wedge [0.2 \vee 0.5] \wedge [0.3 \vee 0.4] \wedge [0.4 \vee 0.2]$$
$$= 0.15 \wedge 0.3 \wedge 0.3 \wedge 0.5 \wedge 0.4 \wedge 0.4$$
$$= 0.15$$

$$\mu_{\overline{R_{IF}(Y_1)}}(d_4) = \bigvee_{y\in V}\left[\mu_{R_{IF}}(d_4,y) \wedge \mu_{Y_1}(y)\right]$$
$$= [0.1 \wedge 0.35] \vee [0.1 \wedge 0.15] \vee [0 \wedge 0.2] \vee [0.2 \wedge 0.1] \vee [0.35 \wedge 0.1] \vee [0.1 \wedge 0.1]$$
$$= 0.1 \vee 0.1 \vee 0 \vee 0.1 \vee 0.1 \vee 0.1$$
$$= 0.1$$

$$\nu_{\overline{R_{IF}(Y_1)}}(d_4) = \bigwedge_{y\in V}\left[\nu_{R_{IF}}(d_4,y) \vee \nu_{Y_1}(y)\right]$$
$$= [0.2 \vee 0.15] \wedge [0.8 \vee 0.3] \wedge [0.6 \vee 0.3] \wedge [0.3 \vee 0.5] \wedge [0.1 \vee 0.4] \wedge [0.4 \vee 0.2]$$
$$= 0.2 \wedge 0.8 \wedge 0.6 \wedge 0.5 \wedge 0.4 \wedge 0.4$$
$$= 0.2$$

$$\mu_{\overline{R_{IF}(Y_1)}}(d_5) = \bigvee_{y \in V} \left[\mu_{R_{IF}}(d_5, y) \wedge \mu_{Y_1}(y)\right]$$
$$= [0.15 \wedge 0.35] \vee [0.2 \wedge 0.15] \vee [0.1 \wedge 0.2] \vee [0.2 \wedge 0.1] \vee [0.5 \wedge 0.1] \vee [0.2 \wedge 0.1]$$
$$= 0.15 \vee 0.15 \vee 0.1 \vee 0.1 \vee 0.1 \vee 0.1$$
$$= 0.15$$

$$\nu_{\overline{R_{IF}(Y_1)}}(d_5) = \bigwedge_{y \in V} \left[\nu_{R_{IF}}(d_5, y) \vee \nu_{Y_1}(y)\right]$$
$$= [0.1 \vee 0.15] \wedge [0.7 \vee 0.3] \wedge [0.3 \vee 0.3] \wedge [0.1 \vee 0.5] \wedge [0.15 \vee 0.4] \wedge [0.3 \vee 0.2]$$
$$= 0.15 \wedge 0.7 \wedge 0.3 \wedge 0.5 \wedge 0.4 \wedge 0.3$$
$$= 0.15$$

Hence, the upper approximation for Y_1 is given as:

$$\overline{R_{IF}}Y_1 = \left\{\left\langle d_1, 0.2, 0.15\right\rangle, \left\langle d_2, 0.25, 0.2\right\rangle, \left\langle d_3, 0.35, 0.15\right\rangle, \left\langle d_4, 0.1, 0.2\right\rangle, \left\langle d_5, 0.15, 0.15\right\rangle\right\}^t$$

Similarly, for the set Y_2 we get the following:

$$\mu_{\overline{R_{IF}(Y_2)}}(d_1) = \bigvee_{y \in V} \left[\mu_{R_{IF}}(d_1, y) \wedge \mu_{Y_2}(y)\right]$$
$$= [0.15 \wedge 0.2] \vee [0.1 \wedge 0.4] \vee [0.55 \wedge 0.15] \vee [0.1 \wedge 0.1] \vee [0 \wedge 0.1] \vee [0.25 \wedge 0.05]$$
$$= 0.15 \vee 0.1 \vee 0.15 \vee 0.1 \vee 0 \vee 0.05$$
$$= 0.15$$

$$\nu_{\overline{R_{IF}(Y_2)}}(d_1) = \bigwedge_{y \in V} \left[\nu_{R_{IF}}(d_1, y) \vee \nu_{Y_2}(y)\right]$$
$$= [0.1 \vee 0.3] \wedge [0.2 \vee 0.1] \wedge [0.1 \vee 0.4] \wedge [0.7 \vee 0.3] \wedge [0.6 \vee 0.3] \wedge [0.1 \vee 0.5]$$
$$= 0.3 \wedge 0.2 \wedge 0.4 \wedge 0.7 \wedge 0.6 \wedge 0.5$$
$$= 0.2$$

$$\mu_{\overline{R_{IF}(Y_2)}}(d_2) = \bigvee_{y \in V} \left[\mu_{R_{IF}}(d_2, y) \wedge \mu_{Y_2}(y)\right]$$
$$= [0.25 \wedge 0.2] \vee [0.35 \wedge 0.4] \vee [0.15 \wedge 0.15] \vee [0.1 \wedge 0.1] \vee [0 \wedge 0.1] \vee [0.25 \wedge 0.05]$$
$$= 0.2 \vee 0.35 \vee 0.15 \vee 0.1 \vee 0 \vee 0.05$$
$$= 0.35$$

$$\nu_{\overline{R_{IF}(Y_2)}}(d_2) = \bigwedge_{y \in V} \left[\nu_{R_{IF}}(d_2, y) \vee \nu_{Y_2}(y)\right]$$
$$= [0.2 \vee 0.3] \wedge [0.21 \vee 0.1] \wedge [0.45 \vee 0.4] \wedge [0.4 \vee 0.3] \wedge [0.5 \vee 0.3] \wedge [0.2 \vee 0.5]$$
$$= 0.3 \wedge 0.21 \wedge 0.45 \wedge 0.4 \wedge 0.5 \wedge 0.5$$
$$= 0.21$$

$$\mu_{\overline{R_{IF}(Y_2)}}(d_3) = \bigvee_{y\in V}\left[\mu_{R_{IF}}(d_3, y) \wedge \mu_{Y_2}(y)\right]$$
$$= [0.35 \wedge 0.2] \vee [0.25 \wedge 0.4] \vee [0.2 \wedge 0.15] \vee [0.4 \wedge 0.1] \vee [0.15 \wedge 0.1] \vee [0.2 \wedge 0.05]$$
$$= 0.2 \vee 0.25 \vee 0.15 \vee 0.1 \vee 0.1 \vee 0.05$$
$$= 0.25$$

$$\nu_{\overline{R_{IF}(Y_2)}}(d_3) = \bigwedge_{y\in V}\left[\nu_{R_{IF}}(d_3, y) \vee \nu_{Y_2}(y)\right]$$
$$= [0.05 \vee 0.3] \wedge [0.15 \vee 0.1] \wedge [0.15 \vee 0.4] \wedge [0.2 \vee 0.3] \wedge [0.3 \vee 0.3] \wedge [0.4 \vee 0.5]$$
$$= 0.3 \wedge 0.15 \wedge 0.4 \wedge 0.3 \wedge 0.3 \wedge 0.5$$
$$= 0.15$$

$$\mu_{\overline{R_{IF}(Y_2)}}(d_4) = \bigvee_{y\in V}\left[\mu_{R_{IF}}(d_4, y) \wedge \mu_{Y_2}(y)\right]$$
$$= [0.1 \wedge 0.2] \vee [0.1 \wedge 0.4] \vee [0 \wedge 0.15] \vee [0.2 \wedge 0.1] \vee [0.35 \wedge 0.1] \vee [0.1 \wedge 0.05]$$
$$= 0.1 \vee 0.1 \vee 0 \vee 0.1 \vee 0.1 \vee 0.05$$
$$= 0.1$$

$$\nu_{\overline{R_{IF}(Y_2)}}(d_4) = \bigwedge_{y\in V}\left[\nu_{R_{IF}}(d_4, y) \vee \nu_{Y_2}(y)\right]$$
$$= [0.2 \vee 0.3] \wedge [0.8 \vee 0.1] \wedge [0.6 \vee 0.4] \wedge [0.3 \vee 0.3] \wedge [0.1 \vee 0.3] \wedge [0.4 \vee 0.5]$$
$$= 0.3 \wedge 0.8 \wedge 0.6 \wedge 0.3 \wedge 0.3 \wedge 0.5$$
$$= 0.3$$

$$\mu_{\overline{R_{IF}(Y_2)}}(d_5) = \bigvee_{y\in V}\left[\mu_{R_{IF}}(d_5, y) \wedge \mu_{Y_2}(y)\right]$$
$$= [0.15 \wedge 0.2] \vee [0.2 \wedge 0.4] \vee [0.1 \wedge 0.15] \vee [0.2 \wedge 0.1] \vee [0.5 \wedge 0.1] \vee [0.2 \wedge 0.05]$$
$$= 0.15 \vee 0.2 \vee 0.1 \vee 0.1 \vee 0.1 \vee 0.05$$
$$= 0.2$$

$$\nu_{\overline{R_{IF}(Y_2)}}(d_5) = \bigwedge_{y\in V}\left[\nu_{R_{IF}}(d_5, y) \vee \nu_{Y_2}(y)\right]$$
$$= [0.1 \vee 0.3] \wedge [0.7 \vee 0.1] \wedge [0.3 \vee 0.4] \wedge [0.1 \vee 0.3] \wedge [0.15 \vee 0.3] \wedge [0.3 \vee 0.5]$$
$$= 0.3 \wedge 0.7 \wedge 0.4 \wedge 0.3 \wedge 0.3 \wedge 0.5$$
$$= 0.3$$

Hence, the upper approximation for Y_2 is given as:

$$\overline{R_{IF}}Y_2 = \left\{\langle d_1, 0.15, 0.2\rangle, \langle d_2, 0.35, 0.21\rangle, \langle d_3, 0.25, 0.15\rangle, \langle d_4, 0.1, 0.3\rangle, \langle d_5, 0.2, 0.3\rangle\right\}^t$$

From the above analysis, according to the principle of maximum membership, the decision for the first category of customers is "good" whereas the decision for the second category of customers is "very good".

5. CONCLUSION

In this chapter, we have discussed the theory of rough set based on the equivalence relation, but equivalence class is not feasible in most practical scenarios. To handle this, we have defined almost indiscernibility relation. Hence rough set on fuzzy approximation space has been discussed which works as the basis of almost indiscernibility relation. Afterward rough set on intuitionistic fuzzy approximation space has been discussed. Subsequently, we have defined rough set on two universal sets. The concept of intuitionistic fuzzy rough sets has been extended on two universal sets. We have elaborated a real-life application on multi-criterion decision making in marketing by using intuitionistic fuzzy rough set on two universal sets. The main objective is to furnish the application of intuitionistic fuzzy rough set in multi criteria decision making problems.

REFERENCES

Acharjya, D. P. (2009). Comparative study of rough sets on fuzzy approximation spaces and intuitionistic fuzzy approximation spaces. *International Journal of Computational and Applied Mathematics*, *4*(2), 95–106.

Acharjya, D. P. (2013). Rough computing based Information Retrieval in Knowledge Discovery Databases. In Information and Knowledge Management-Tools, Techniques and Practices (pp. 123 - 153). New Delhi: New India Publishing Company.

Acharjya, D. P., & Tripathy, B. K. (2012). Intuitionistic fuzzy rough set on two universal sets and knowledge representation. *Mathematical Sciences International Research Journal*, *1*(2), 584–598.

Atanasov, K. T. (1986). Intuitionistic fuzzy sets. *Fuzzy Sets and Systems*, *20*(1), 87–96. doi:10.1016/S0165-0114(86)80034-3

Büyüközkan, G. (2004). Multi-criteria decision making for e-marketplace selection. *Internet Research*, *14*(2), 139–154. doi:10.1108/10662240410530853

Das, T. K., & Acharjya, D. P. (2014). A decision making model using soft set and rough set on fuzzy approximation spaces, Int. J. *Intelligent Systems Technologies and Applications*, *13*(3), 170–186. doi:10.1504/IJISTA.2014.065172

Das, T. K., Acharjya, D. P., & Patra, M. R. (2015). General Characterization of Classifications in Rough Set on Two Universal Sets. *Information Resources Management Journal*, *28*(2), 1–19. doi:10.4018/IRMJ.2015040101

Das, T. K., Acharjya, D. P., & Patra, M. R. (2015). Multi- Criterion Decision Making using Intuitionistic Fuzzy Rough Set on Two Universal Sets, I.J. *Intelligent Systems and Applications*, *7*(4), 26–33. doi:10.5815/ijisa.2015.04.04

Das, T. K., Mohapatro, A., & Abburu, S. (2015). A Decision Making Mechanism During Disaster Event Monitoring and Control. *Middle-East Journal of Scientific Research*, *23*(9), 2251–2255.

De, S. K. (1999). *Some aspects of fuzzy sets, rough sets and intuitionistic fuzzy sets*. (Ph.D. Thesis). Kharagpur: IIT.

Dubois, D., & Prade, H. (1990). Rough fuzzy sets and fuzzy rough sets. *International Journal of General Systems*, *17*(2-3), 191–208. doi:10.1080/03081079008935107

Greco, S., Matarazzo, B., & Slowinski, R. (2001). Rough sets theory for multicriteria decision analysis. *European Journal of Operational Research*, *129*(1), 129–147. doi:10.1016/S0377-2217(00)00167-3

Hong, D. H., & Choi, C. H. (2000). Multi-criteria fuzzy decision making problems based on vague set theory. *Fuzzy Sets and Systems, Vol*, *114*(1), 103–113. doi:10.1016/S0165-0114(98)00271-1

Kahraman, C., Cebeci, U., & Ulukan, Z. (2003). Multi-criteria supplier selection using fuzzy AHP. *Logistics Information Management*, *16*(6), 382–394. doi:10.1108/09576050310503367

Liu, G. L. (2010). Rough set theory based on two universal sets and its applications. *Knowledge-Based Systems*, *23*(2), 110–115. doi:10.1016/j.knosys.2009.06.011

Maji, P. K., Roy, A. R., & Biswas, R. (2002). An Application of Soft Sets in A Decision Making Problem. *Computers & Mathematics with Applications (Oxford, England)*, *44*(8-9), 1077–1083. doi:10.1016/S0898-1221(02)00216-X

Molodtsov, D. (1999). Soft Set Theory-First Results. *Computers & Mathematics with Applications (Oxford, England)*, *37*(4-5), 19–31. doi:10.1016/S0898-1221(99)00056-5

Pawlak, Z. (1982). Rough Sets. *International Journal of Computer and Information Sciences*, *11*(5), 341–356. doi:10.1007/BF01001956

Pawlak, Z. (1983). Rough Classification. *International Journal of Man-Machine Studies*, *20*(5), 469–483. doi:10.1016/S0020-7373(84)80022-X

Pawlak, Z. (2004). Decision rules and flow networks. *European Journal of Operational Research*, *154*(1), 184–190. doi:10.1016/S0377-2217(03)00004-3

Pawlak, Z., & Sowinski, R. (1991). *Rough Sets, Theoretical aspect of Reasoning about Data*, Kluwer Academic Publishers, Pawlak, Z. and Slowinski, R. (1994). Rough set approach to multi attribute decision analysis. *European Journal of Operational Research*, *72*(3), 443–459. doi:10.1016/0377-2217(94)90415-4

Tripathy, B. K., & Acharjya, D. P. (2012). Approximation of Classification and Measures of Uncertainty in Rough Set on Two Universal Sets. *International Journal of Advanced Science and Technology*, *40*, 77–90.

Zadeh, L. (1965). Fuzzy Sets. *Information and Control*, *8*(3), 338–353. doi:10.1016/S0019-9958(65)90241-X

Chapter 7
Fuzzy Multi-Objective Association Rule Mining Using Evolutionary Computation

Ganghishetti Pradeep
IDRBT, India

Vadlamani Ravi
Institute for Development and Research in Banking Technology, India

ABSTRACT

In this chapter, we model association rule mining as a Fuzzy multi-objective global optimization problem by considering several measures of strength such as support, confidence, coverage, comprehensibility, leverage, interestingness, lift and conviction by utilizing various fuzzy aggregator operators. In this, pdel, each measure has its own level of significance. Three fuzzy multi-objective association rule mining techniques viz., Fuzzy Multi-objective Binary Particle Swarm Optimization based association rule miner (FMO-BPSO), a hybridized Fuzzy Multi-objective Binary Firefly Optimization and Threshold Accepting based association rule miner (FMO-BFFOTA), hybridized Fuzzy Multi-objective Binary Particle Swarm Optimization and Threshold Accepting based association rule miner (FMO-BPSOTA) have been proposed. These three algorithms have been tested on various datasets such as book, food, bank, grocery, click stream and bakery datasets along with three fuzzy aggregate operators. From these experiments, we can conclude that Fuzzy-And outperforms all the other operators.

INTRODUCTION

Association rule mining, an important task in data mining, is used to find the frequent patterns, potential associations, correlations, of objects among huge data. The rules help find unknown relationships that can be the basis of decision making. It is extensively applied in many diverse areas: market basket analysis, graph mining, sequential pattern mining, medical diagnosis, times series pattern mining, text mining, fraud detection in web, churn modeling in credit card business, click stream mining, discovering protein sequences. The ideas of association rules was pioneered by Agrawal et al. (1993). Here, an association

DOI: 10.4018/978-1-5225-0997-4.ch007

rule is an inference as follows: A→B, where A and B represent antecedent and consequent parts which in turn are item sets (I) or a group of features/items. An item set is a subset of all possible items $\{i_1, i_2, \ldots, i_m\}$ in a transactional database They proposed a priori algorithm (Agrawal & Srikant, 1994) for mining association rules from large customer datasets. The algorithm can be divided into two stages: Frequent item set generation stage and Rule generation stage. In the first stage, frequent item-sets are generated level by level from 1 item-sets by using a measure called support count (SUP). In the second stage, various rules are generated using another user-defined parameter called confidence.

The algorithm suffers from a drawback of repeated database scan during every item-set generation. This drawback has been overcome by FP-Growth algorithm, proposed by Han et al. (2000), which is built on the lines of divide and conquer strategy and requires just two database scans. During its first database scan, it generates F-List i.e., it computes a list of frequent items sorted by frequency in descending order. The second database scan is utilized for transformation F-List into a hierarchical structure called FP-tree. Later on, the algorithm begins to extract rules from FP-tree for each item whose support is larger than the minimum support by recursively building its conditional FP-tree.

Other algorithms include the AIS (Agrawal et al, 1993), the set-oriented algorithm (Houtsma & Swami, 1995), DHP algorithm (Part et al, 1995), the DIC (Sergey et al, 1997), the sampling algorithm (Toivonen, 1997), the cluster-based association rule (CBAR) approach (Tsay et al, 2005) which concentrate on improving the efficiency and accuracy. The well-known drawbacks of most of these algorithms include the need to specify minimum support and confidence, finding the right combination of user-defined parameters. The latter is mostly based on either domain knowledge or trial & error approach. Therefore, here we propose the use of MO-BPSO, MO-BFFO-TA and MO-BPSO-TA developed by Pradeep and Ravi (2014) for association rule mining considering several objectives of interest.

The remaining chapter is organized as follows. In section2, we present a review of literature related to association rule mining and the utilization of Metaheuristics to solve rule mining problems. In Section 3, we introduce different optimization algorithms used in this research followed by Section 4 where we briefly present various steps of our devised strategies. In section 5, we present results and discussion related to various datasets followed by Conclusions Section.

BACKGROUND

Evolutionary computational techniques have been widely applied for mining association rule. Saggar et al. (2004) suggested a technique wherein Genetic Algorithm was used to optimize the association rules obtained by the a priori algorithm. Waiswa et al (2008)proposed Pareto-based GA-centered multi objective evolutionary algorithm mining technique to extract the association rules considering several measures like J-measure, interestingness and comprehensibility as changed objectives of association mining problems. Ghosh et al. (2004) proposed multi-objective association rule mining framework using pareto based GA by considering comprehensibility, interestingness, predictive accuracy and found it suitable for large databases. Anandhavalli et al. (2009) used GA centered approach for mining association rules containing negative attributes with more than one attribute in consequent part. Gupta (2012) used weighted particle swarm optimization (WPSO) for association mining to determine appropriate threshold values for minimum confidence and minimum support. Asadi et al (2012)adopted particle swarm optimization (PSO) to find the minimum confidence and minimum support threshold values for the a priori algorithm. Minaei-Bidgoli et al (2013) proposes multi-objective GA for mining numerical association rules considering interestingness, confidence and comprehensibility as various intents to multi objective optimization and the best rules were obtained by using pareto optimality. Nandhini et al.(2012) devised PSO and domain ontology based algorithm for mining association rules where the number of rules generated is reduced without sacrificing quality of rules. Kaya et al. (2004) extracts partial optimized fuzzy association rules using multi objective GA. Here, three measures viz., confidence, support and amplitude of fuzzy sets are used as objectives. Alatas et al. (2008), used pareto-centered multi-objective differential evolution (DE) algorithm for mining precise and comprehensive numeric association rules. These rules are optimal in broader sense so that no other rules are superior to them when all the objectives are considered simultaneously. They formulated the association rule mining as a four-objective optimization problem, where confidence, support and comprehensibility of rules are maximized, while the amplitude of the intervals, which conforms the item set and rule is minimized. Hadian et al (2010) proposed a Cluster-Based Multi-Objective Genetic Algorithm (CBMOGA) which minimizes the support by clustering the database. Clustering is performed on basis of the number of items in each transaction. Kuo et al. (2011) propsoed PSOto determine the user defined parameters quickly and objectively which in turn improves the performance in large databases. Luna et al (2013) proposed grammar guided genetic programming (G3P) models to enable for extracting numerical and nominal association rules in the single objective and multi objective frameworks.. Beiranvand et al (2014) proposed multi-objective particle swarm optimization algorithm-MOPAR for extracting numerical attributes and results show that it extracted rules with higher reliable, comprehensible and interesting rules when compared to confidence, comprehensibility and interestingness. Martínez-Ballesteros et al (2014) developed multi-objective evolutionary algorithm for obtaining quantitative association rules and applied to microarray data of yeast cell cycle and results were in accordance with biological knowledge related to gene association networks. Martínez-Ballesteros et al (2014) applied PCA to obtain condensed subset of measures to be included in fitness function and validated that the new fitness function applied showed significant improvement compared the original fitness function. Minaei-Bidgoli et al (2013) proposed multi-objective genetic algorithm for extracting association rules for numerical data considering confidence, interestingness, comprehensibility. Naveen et al. (2012) proposed firefly optimization to mine classification rules. This paper motivated us to apply Firefly Optimization technique to association rule mining. Further, Maheshkumar et al (2013) proposed PSOTA hybrid for unconstrained continuous optimization. This paper also inspired us in devising the hybrid techniques using Binary Firefly and Threshold accepting algorithms. Most recently, Sarath and Ravi (2013) proposed binary particle swarm optimization (BPSO) based association rule miner for extracting association rules without specifying minimum confidence and support. This paper also forms background to our current work. The motivation for current work is that BPSO (Sarath and Ravi, 2013) has to be run M times to get top M rules. However, running M times is not an attractive proposition in practical applications.

VARIOUS OPTIMIZATION BASED STRATEGIES

Meta-heuristics are very popular and widely used algorithms for optimization since several decades and are widely used in various spheres. These techniques have several advantages over conventional algorithms. In this section, we describe three such strategies:

Firefly Optimization Algorithm (FFO)

Yang (2010) proposed a nature inspired population based optimization viz., Firefly algorithm. This algorithm is built on the natural behavior of fireflies of light emission, light absorption and attraction.

All fireflies are unisex and go towards more good-looking and brighter ones. The algorithm based on the fireflies motion helps in attaining optimal solutions. Every firefly in the population is associated with a corresponding objective function or fitness value. The extent of attractiveness of one firefly towards the other is proportional to its brightness and depends on the distance between them. The attractionveness of a firefly increases as the distance decreases and vice versa. This is due to the very reason of light getting absorbed by air as the distance increases. In case, there is no other firefly in the population which is more attractive than any particular one, then it moves randomly. The degree of intensity of a firefly is attributed to value of an objective function. The attractiveness, β of a firefly is represented by a function that decreases monotonically with the distance between any two fireflies, r and is described as follows:

$$\beta = \beta_0 e^{-\gamma r^2} \tag{1}$$

The movement of ith firefly at position x_i towards other j[th] brighter firefly at position x_j is characterized as:

$$x_i(t+1) = x_i(t) + \beta_0 e^{-\gamma r^2}(x_i - x_j) + \alpha(rand() - 0.5) \tag{2}$$

Here, t indicates the previous iteration of firefly algorithm, rand() is a function which generates random number in between 0 and 1, β0 isthe attractiveness constant, γ is the coefficient of light absorption that controls the degree of the intensity of light, α is the randomization parameter which has value between 0 and 1. The α is the randomness parameter and is proportionately decreases by a constant delta, Δ after each and every iteration for faster convergence of the algorithm.

The distance between one firefly i at position xi with other firefly j at positions xj is determined centered on the following Euclidean distance, r_{ij} is given by:

$$r_{ij} = \left\|x_i - x_j\right\| = \sqrt{\sum_{k=1}^{d}\left(x_{ik} - x_{jk}\right)^2} \tag{3}$$

Here d indicates the dimensions of the position vector.

The various steps in the firefly algorithm are defined as follows:

Step 1: Initialize the algorithm parameters(n, β_0, γ, α,MaxIterations) and define the Objective Function $f(x)$, $x = \left(x_1, \ldots, x_d\right)^T$.

Step 2: Generate initial population of fireflies $X_i(i=1, 2, \ldots, n)$.

Step 3: For each firefly, calculate Light intensity L_i at x_i which is obtained by $f(x_i)$.

Step 4:

```
while(t<MaxIterations)
for i = 1:n all n fireflies
                 for j=1:n all n fireflies
                          if(Lj>Li)
Move ith firefly towards jth one in d-dimensions as per  equation.1 and 2
end if
                          Determine new solutions and update intensities of
light of the fireflies.
                 end of j
end of i
Obtain the current best by ranking the fireflies
end of while
```

Step 5: Finally, identify the firefly one with the highest light intensity as optimal solution.

The steps present inside the while loop are repeated until a predefined termination criteria is met. The termination criteria can be fixed number of iterations or can be a case of failure to make progress for a fixed number of iterations or can be based on any other criteria based on problem necessity.

Threshold Acceptance (TA)

Deuck and Sheuer(1990) proposed Threshold Accepting algorithm, which is a general purpose algorithm for the solution of combinatorial optimization problems and is a simple and, faster variation of simulated annealing. This approach is similar to Monte Carlo method that performs a local search where in a subset of solutions is explored by moving from one solution to another solution in the neighborhood. TA is a point based search technique. Here, a local search starts with a random feasible solution and then examines its neighborhood by moving in the solution space, accepting any new solution produced if and only if it improves the objective function. While using TA, there is no possibility of stopping in local minima as it accepts new solutions which are not much worse than the current solution. In order to avoid premature convergence and getting stuck in local minima the algorithm occasionally accepts an inferior solution. This mechanism allows it to wriggle out of local maximum. The TA algorithm is presented in Figure 1.

Here, we generate new candidate solutions as follows.

Let a rule contain 2n bits(n=number of items/features) in the dataset. Here, Cand_Soln[i][j], indicates the jth bit value of the 2n bits in the ith candidate solution. The candidate solutions in the neighborhood are generated by using the scheme presented in Figure 2.

In this manner, we obtain rules of different lengths (like 2,3,4,...). If there are 25 items in dataset, k is fixed at 0.1. This, we have fixed after many computations. The value of k is to be fixed as inversely proportional to the number of items in dataset.

Binary Firefly Optimization (BFFO)

The firefly optimization algorithm which is applicable for continuous optimization problems is described in Section 3.1. So, we adapted this optimization algorithm to solve our multi-objective combinatorial

Figure 1. TA algorithm

```
▪ Consider the solution of the weakest particle(firefly) of
  BPSO/BFFO as first solution.
▪ Set global iteration counter, inner iteration counter,itr=0,
  old=99999,thresh, thrtol, eps
▪ fi=fitness value of initial solution captured from the BPSO/BFFO
  algorithm
▪ Repeat the following step until termination criteria
  whileitr<gitr // gitr is the maximum no of global iterations
  DO
        itr=itr+1
        ii=0 // ii - inner iteration value
        while ii < limit or del1 > thresh
        DO
              ii=ii+1
              Generate a candidate solution in the neighborhood
              fj=fitness value for the solution
              del1=fi-fj
              If del1 < thresh,
                    set fi = fj
              If thresh <thrtol,
                    set del2 = (new - old) / old
                    Report current solution as the optimal one
                    if abs(del2) <acc and exit if itr<gitr
              Else
                    old=new
                    thresh=thresh*(1-eps)
  END
```

Figure 2. Candidate solutions

```
for(i=0;i<2×n;i++)
{
      if(rand()<k)
      {
            Cand_Soln[i][j]=1;
      }
      else
      {
            Cand_Soln[i][j]=0;
      }
}
```

global optimization problem by formulating the binary version of firefly algorithm. In our binary version, the position vector of each firefly can have only values of 0 or 1 in every dimension. The value of xi is obtained probabilistically based on the rate of change of real value of xi. Here, in our binary version, the movement of one firefly towards the other is defined as follows:

$$x_{i+1} = x_i + \beta_0 e^{-\gamma r^2}\left(x_i - x_j\right) + \alpha(rand - 0.5)$$

```
if (rand () < S (x_{i+1}))
then
```

$x_{i+1}=1$

```
else
```

$x_{i+1}=0$

where S is the Sigmoid function, *rand()* is the uniform random number in between *0 and 1*, β_0, the attractiveness constant, γ, is the coefficient of absorption and r, the Euclidean distance between the two fireflies i and j. The sigmoid function S(x) adopted in our algorithm is given $S(x)=\dfrac{1}{1+e^{-x}}$.

Particle Swarm Optimization (PSO)

Kennedy and Eberhart (1995) introduced PSO algorithm as a population based optimization technique. It belongs to the class of swarm intelligence, inspired by the behavioral models of bird flocking. It is too popular to be described in more details here.

Binary Particle Swarm Optimization (BPSO)

Sarath and Ravi (2013) developed association rule miner based binary particle swarm optimization technique which extracts Top M rules in exactly M runs. The position of each particle can take only binary values. For further details on BPSO based association rule miner, reader is referred to Sarath and Ravi (2013).

Feature Selection

This is a preprocessing step to be followed when the number of features is more than 50. We devised this special mechanism to reduce the number of features to be considered for rule generation. In order to obviate unnecessary computations for the algorithm and to remove extremely rare rules, we discarded all the features with item support < α, where α is a very low pre-specified value. This is found to be extremely useful in reducing the features. The steps involved in feature selection are depicted in Figure 4.

BPSO/BFFO-TA/BPSO-TA FOR ASSOCIATION RULE MINING

The proposed fuzzy based hybrid multi-objective algorithms consist of two stages -data preprocessing stage and rule extraction stage. In the first stage i.e, data preprocessing stage, the transactional data is transformed into a set of binary records for faster scanning of data. In the second stage, our various rule extraction models are applied in order to mine association rules. Each execution/run of the models work in the following manner. The first step involves binary encoding/representation of firefly positions. The second step is generation of population of fireflies whose fitness values are greater than 0.001. If fitness of the initial population is entirely zero, then the algorithm gets stuck up. Hence, this condition is necessary for the algorithm to run smoothly towards global optima. The respective algorithms are applied and discovery of rules is carried on until the termination criteria of maximum number of iterations are reached.

Transformation to Binary Data

Here in order to extract top M rules from the transactional databases, we first transform the data into appropriate binary encoded format in which each record is expressed in terms of 0's and 1's (Wur and Leu, 1998). This transformation facilitates not only faster database scanning operation but also allows easier and faster calculation of various measures of strength discussed in section 4.3.This preprocessing step of transformation is depicted in Figure 1. Let there be five transactions /records, say T1 to T5 in original data. Each of these records is transformed and stored as a binary data type. For example, there are a total of five different products in the database, so five cells exist for each transaction. Take B4 as an example. In this transaction, products I_1 and I_2 are only purchased. Hence, the values of cells I_1 and I_3 are both "1's" whereas cells I_3, I_4 and I_5 are "0's".

Rule Representation

The key aspect in applying optimization techniques in order to mine efficient association rules lies in the strategy followed in representing the association rules in the population of firefly. For representing these rules, there are two popular approaches viz., Pittsburg approach and Michigan approach. In case of Pittsburg method, each chromosome represents a set of rules. However, in Michigan approach, each chromosome can be represented by a separate rule. In this chapter, we followed Michigan approach for rule representation.

The rule representation of a firefly position is shown in Table 2. Suppose there are *N* numbers of items in the dataset. Here, the information about each item is denoted by two bits. Each bit takes only the binary values 1 or 0. In case if the first bit is 1, it indicates that the item is present, else if it is 0, it indicate that it is absent in the rule. The second bit indicates whether the item is present in the antecedent or consequent part. In case, the second bit value is 1, it indicates that the item is present in antecedent part, otherwise the item is present in consequent part of the rule. For instance, if value of I_i is 11, this indicates that the ith item is present and is included in the antecedent part of the rule. Similarly, if the value of I_i is 10, it indicates the item is present in consequent part of the rule. If the value of I_i is 00 or 01 then the ith item is not present in the rule. This same procedure is followed in (Sarath & Ravi, 2013).

Measures of Strength

In order to assess quality of strength of association rules, considering only support and confidence doesn't suffice. There are other measures in order to know how good a rule is. They are given below:

Let the rule be represented as A→B where A is antecedent part and B is called consequent part of the rule. It should be noted that confidence alone is not sufficient owing to its sensitivity to the frequency of the consequent part of the database. The sensitivity is attributed to the way confidence is evaluated because the consequents with higher values of support will automatically have higher values of confidence even though there may be no associations among them.

Apart from support and confidence, another measure is Interestingness, which indicates how interesting a rule is. In other words, sometimes, a rule with low support is also useful, as long as it conveys some important information. For instance, rare rules have low support but they signify anomalous behavior. Such rules are very useful in fraud detection, intruder detection etc. Then there is Comprehensibility. If the number of conditions in the antecedent part of an association rule is less than that of the consequent part then the rule is said be more comprehensible.

Further, Lift is another measure of significance. Confidence alone is not sufficient as it does not consider the consequent part baseline frequency. Hence, the measure lift was introduced. If a rule has a lift of 1, it means that there is no association between antecedent and consequent. If lift is > 1, it indicates that there is association between antecedent and consequent. Therefore, it is potentially a useful rule. If lift is less than 1, then antecedent and consequent are negatively associated.

Then, Leverage indicates how many more items, antecedent and consequent put together are sold than anticipated. Furthermore, Conviction is proposed as an alternative to confidence as it is found not to capture the direction of association sufficiently. It is monotonical function of lift and confidence. Its advantage over confidence is that it considers both the supports of antecedent and consequent parts of the rule. If conviction is between 0 and 1 then the dependence is negative and positive otherwise. Finally, Coverage is defined as antecedent support and indicates how often a rule is valid in a database. For further details on the mathematical definitions of these measure, reader is referred to Paradeep and Ravi (2014).

MODELLING IMPRECISION IN DECISION MAKING USING FUZZY LOGIC

Fuzzy Sets, proposed by Zadeh (1965) are a generalization of classical sets and fuzzy logic made steady inroads into many diverse disciplines owing to their inherent capability to model uncertainty, ambiguity, imprecision, incomplete information, conflicting information, and partial truth in datasets and.

Fuzzy Multi-Objective Optimization

Fuzzy optimization, pioneered by Zimmermann (1991), opened up newer ways of formulating and solving multi objective optimization problems, where objective functions and/or constraints are fuzzy in nature. Normally, multiple and sometimes conflicting objective functions are found in most of the optimization problems. In such situations, an improvement in one objective function does not necessarily improve the other ones. Our goal is to determine a decision making strategy to satisfy all the constraints and optimization of these measures. The appropriate selection of objective function is useful in assessing the priority of every individual firefly in the population.

To extract quality rules, considering single objective is not sufficient. Hence, we need to consider several measures to mine reliable, significant and efficient rules. The challenging issue in this case is that most of these objectives are non-commensurable, conflicting, and competing.

The mainstay of fuzzy multi-objective optimization framework has been modeling various objective functions as fuzzy sets and connecting them through t-norms in order to obtain a final fuzzy set that represents a decision, which takes care of tradeoffs between conflicting objective functions (Zimmermann, 1991; Ravi et al., 2000). Popular t-norms connecting/aggregating fuzzy sets can be found in Zimmermann (1991). In this chapter, all the eight measures of quality of association rule mining are considered as fuzzy sets and because of the conflicting nature of some of them, we formulated the association rule mining problem as a fuzzy multi-objective optimization problem and solved by invoking various hybrid evolutionary techniques such as BPSO, BPSO-TA and BFFO-TA. Some of the aggregators are presented as follows:

1. **Product Operator:**

$$\mu_{product}(x) = \prod_{i=1}^{m} \mu_i$$

where μ_i is the membership function of ith quality measure ranging from support to coverage.

2. **Fuzzy And:**

$$\mu_{and}\left(\mu_1(x), \mu_2(x) \ldots \mu_8(x)\right)$$
$$= \gamma \cdot \min\left(\mu_1(x), \mu_2(x) \ldots \mu_8(x)\right) + \frac{(1-\gamma)\left(\mu_1(x), \mu_2(x) \ldots \mu_8(x)\right)}{2}, x \in X, \gamma \in [0,1]$$

Fuzzy And is an aggregation operator suggested by Werners (1988) that combines minimum and arithmetic mean of membership functions. It permits compensation between the fuzzy sets.

3. **Compensatory And:** Zimmerman &Zysno (1980) proposed a new model for aggregating fuzzy sets for decision-making process viz., the 'compensatory AND'. It is very much required to contemplate a strategy which allows certain degree of compensation as non-verbal aggregation techniques do not agree to either of non-compensatory 'AND' or fully-compensatory 'OR'. This degree takes shape in a parameter,γ, a real number between 0, corresponding to no compensation and 1, corresponding to full compensation. We considered γ value 0.5 in our case.

$$\mu_{A_{i,comp}}(x) = \left(\prod_{i=1}^{m} \mu_i(x)\right)^{(1-\gamma)} \left(1 - \prod_{i=1}^{m} \left(1 - \mu_i(x)\right)\right)^{\gamma}, x \in X, \gamma \in [0,1].$$

where, x ϵ X, γ ϵ [0,1] μ_i is the membership function of ith measures ranging from support to coverage. Compensatory operator is a combination of algebraic product and the algebraic sum of membership functions.

Steps Involved in BPSO

Since, these are described in Pradeep and Ravi (2014). Hence, they are not repeated here for the sake of brevity. Interested reader is referred to Pradeep and Ravi (2014) for further details. We need to run the algorithm M times in order to get all the top M rules in the database. In each run, we store the rules obtained by the population and at the end of all runs, the rules are ranked and duplicate ones are discarded. Then we pick the top M rules according to the objective function.

The main idea behind running this algorithm M times is as follows: By the stochastic nature of the evolutionary algorithms the user obtains different rules in each run. Hence, running the MOF BPSO several times and followed by ranking the rules and picking up the top M rules is akin to ensembling for obtaining rules. All the steps involved in MOF BPSO based association rule miner are depicted in Figure 2. The various parameters used in MOF BPSO are given in Table 4.

Steps Involved in BFFO-TA and BPSO-TA

Interested reader is referred to Pradeep and Ravi (2014) for further details. The steps involved in BFFO-TA based association rule miner are depicted in Figure 3. The parameters of BFFO-TA are presented in Table 3. The parameters of MOF BPSO-TA are presented in Table 5. All the steps involved in MOF BPSO-TA based association rule miner are depicted in Figure 3.

Table 1. Parameters chosen for multi-objective fuzzy based BPSO rule miner on various datasets

Dataset	N	Inertia	C1	C2	Max Iterations
Book	30	0.8	2	2	50
Food	30	0.8	2	2	50
Grocery	30	0.8	2	2	100
Bank	50	0.8	2	2	50
Click stream	30	100.8	2	2	50
Bakery	30	0.8	2	2	50

Table 2. Rule representation

I_1		I_2		I_3		…	I_N	
V_{11}	V_{12}	V_{21}	V_{22}	V_{31}	V_{32}	…	V_{N1}	V_{N2}

Table 3. Parameters chosen for MOF BFFO-TA rule miner

Dataset	n	β_0	Υ	Δ	α	Max Iterations	Prob_TA	eps	acc	Thresh Total	Thresh	Max Inner Iteration	Max Outer Iterations
Book	10	2	2.5	1	0.5	50	0.2	0.01	0.5	0.00018	0.0002	100	25
Food	10	2	2.5	1	0.5	50	0.3	0.01	0.5	0.00018	0.0002	100	25
Grocery													
Bank	10	2	2.5	1	0.5	150	0.2	0.01	0.5	1.8E-07	2E-07	200	25
Click stream	10	2	2.5	1	0.5	50	0.3	0.01	0.5	0.000018	0.00002	200	25
Bakery	10	2	2.5	1	0.5	200	0.8	0.01	0.5	1.8E-06	0.000002	200	25

Table 4. Parameters chosen for MOF BPSO-TA rule miner

Dataset	n	Inertia	C1	C2	Max Iterations	Prob_TA	eps	acc	Thresh Total	Thresh	Max Inner Iterations	Max Outer Iterations
Book	30	0.8	2	2	50	0.1	0.01	0.5	0.000018	0.00002	50	5
Food	30	0.8	2	2	50	0.3	0.01	0.5	0.00018	0.0002	50	5
Grocery	30	0.8	2	2	100	0.1	0.01	0.5	0.00018	0.0002	50	5
Bank	50	0.8	2	2	50	0.7	0.01	0.5	1.8E-06	0.000002	50	5
Click stream	30	100.8	2	2	50	0.1	0.01	0.5	8E-09	1E-08	50	5
Bakery	30	0.8	2	2	50	0.1	0.01	0.5	0.000018	0.00002	300	25

GI-Global Iterations; II-Inner Iterations

Figure 3. Binary transformation of the original dataset

T_1	I_2	I_3		
T_2	I_1	I_2	I_5	
T_3	I_1	I_3	I_4	I_5
T_4	I_1	I_2		
T_5	I_2	I_5		

⇒

	I_1	I_2	I_3	I_4	I_5
B_1	0	1	1	0	0
B_2	1	1	0	0	1
B_3	1	0	1	1	1
B_4	1	1	0	0	0
B_5	0	1	0	0	1

Table 5. Results of books datasets using BPSO

	M_1	M_2	M_3	M_4	M_5	M_6	M_7	M_8	Fitness
Fuzzy-And	1.71	93.79	1.83	66.22	1.65	61.95	43.31	17.88	0.692316
Comp-And	16.44	69.90	24.28	63.08	6.71	27.03	2.91	2.24	0.00105
Product	16.44	71.32	24.20	61.30	6.72	27.94	3.16	2.93	1.23E-05

Advantages of Proposed Approaches

In our current study, we extract rules considering not only support or confidence but in a - framework considering several objectives each having its own significance. Also, there is no burden on the user to specify minimum thresholds for each measure unlike a priori and FP-Growth. BPSO-TA produces rules which are not redundant unlike a priori and FP-Growth strategies. Here, the rules extracted are of varied length and are independent of frequent Item sets as against fixed rule lengths obtained in a priori and FP-Growth. Overall, the MOF BPSO-TA and BFFO-TA consume less computational times to mine association rules compared to these traditional strategies. In case of BPSO-TA, BFFO-TA, it is found to yield top M rules in a single run, where the user has to specify the number M.

Figure 4. Block diagram of our proposed MOF BPSO method

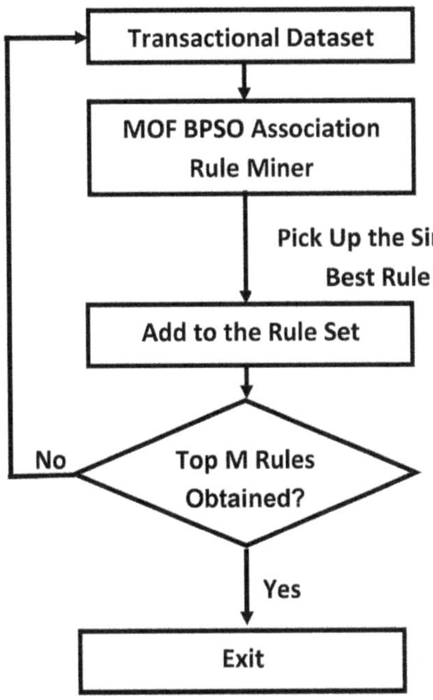

Figure 5. Block diagram of the MOF BFFO-TA/MOF BPSO-TA method

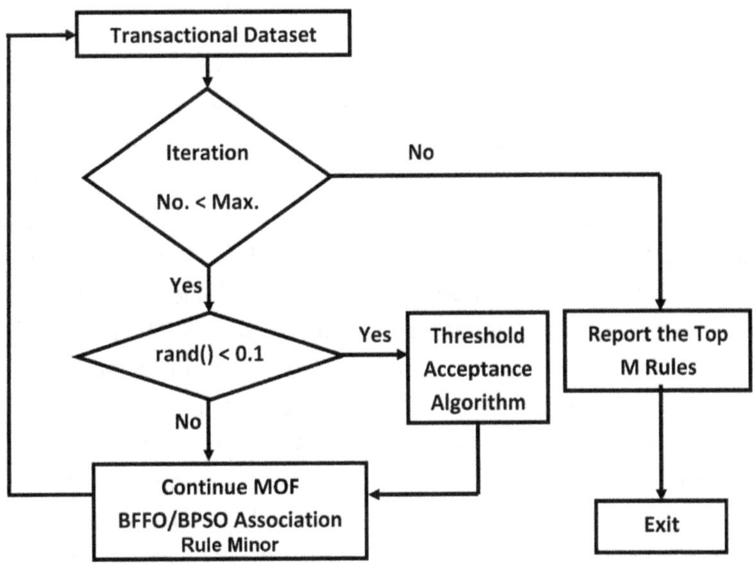

Time Complexity Analysis

The complexity of a priori is O ($d^2 \times n$), *where d is the* total number of transactions and n is the number of items in the dataset. Time complexity of BPSO algorithm for a single run is $O(I \times d \times n \times p)$, where I and p denote respectively the number of iterations and population size of the present BPSO algorithm. Similarly, the time complexity of BFFO-TA is $O(I \times d \times n \times p^2 + pr \times d \times n \times (\text{GI} \times \text{II}))$ where pr is the prob-

Figure 6. Reduction of feature for sparse dataset

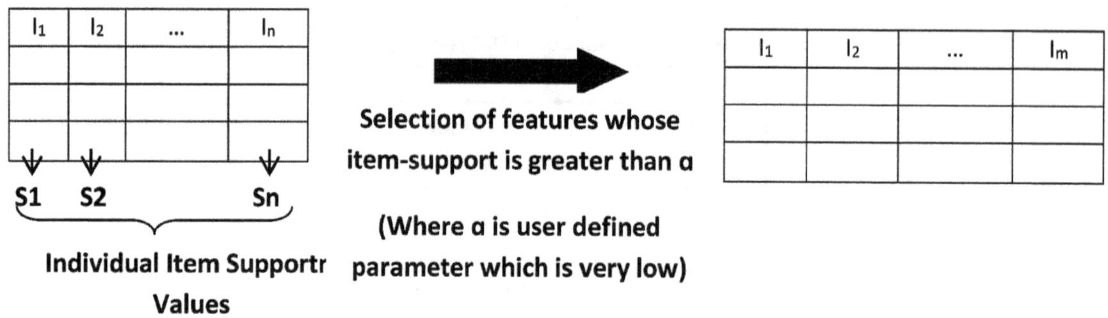

ability of invoking the TA, GI is number of global iterations and II denotes the number of inner iterations. Even though, the time complexity of BFFO-TA is more compared to BFFO, the overall run time is reduced since it requires only one run. Finally, the time complexity in case of BPSO-TA is O($I \times d \times n + pr \times d \times n \times (\mathrm{GI} \times \mathrm{II})$).

RESULTS AND DISCUSSION

In the present study the experiments were conducted on computer with Intel Core i5 processor of clock speed 2.53GHz containing 4 GB RAM. Proposed algorithms were coded using JDK 1.7 Java software with Eclipse IDE. In order to demonstrate effectiveness of the algorithms and to carryout comparative analysis, we analyzed six data sets. These datasets differ in many ways namely, transaction count and sparsity. Books dataset with 10 types of Books and 2000 customer records used in this study is the first one. The source of this data is XLMINER (www.solver.com/xlminer-data-mining) tool. The second one is the Food dataset that has 11 types food items and 1000 records of transaction. The data source for this set is IBM SPSS Modeler tool available at www.ibm.com/software/analytics/spss. The grocery dataset is third one, which has 20 different products of grocery and 1001 transactional records. The data is taken from SAS enterprise tool accessed from http://www.sas.com/technologies/analytics/datamining/miner. The next data set used is a real world sparse dataset taken from a commercial bank, say XYZ Bank. It consists of 12191 customers' records related to their transactions pertaining to 134 various products and services. The Bakery dataset is the fifth one consisting of 10 types coffee drinks, 40 types of pastry items and 1000 records of transactions. The last and sixth one is an Anonymous dataset named as Clickstream dataset taken from the web source http://archive.ics.uci.edu/ml/datasets/Anonymous+Microsoft+Web+Data. The data consists of records of 37711 anonymous, randomly-selected users visited sites in a timeframe of one week listing from all areas (Vroots). The dataset consists of 294 various website links with different features. The results obtained on various datasets are discusses in the following sections. In Tables and figures, the measures support, confidence, Coverage, Comprehensibility, Leverage, Interestingness, Lift and conviction are denoted as M_1, M_2, M_3, M_4, M_5, M_6, M_7 and M_8 respectively.

Books Dataset

We applied Multi-objective based BPSO Association rule miner to the Books dataset by setting values for various parameters. We considered number of particles, n as 30, inertia as 0.8, constants c_1 and c_2 as2 and MaxIterations= 50. With these parameters, we applied the operators Fuzzy-And, Compensatory-And, Fuzzy-Product and for each operator top ten rules are obtained. The measures corresponding to these top ten rules in each case are averaged and presented in Table 5. The result of BPSO rule miner on Books dataset show that the aggregator Fuzzy-And operator produced higher Confidence, Comprehensibility, Interestingness, Lift and Conviction. In case of Compensatory-And, rules produced have higher Support and Coverage values. On the other hand, Product operator produced higher Support, Confidence, and Leverage values.

We also extracted rules using the BPSO-TA algorithmwith the same parameters as BPSO. Here for TA algorithm, we chose inner iterations as 50, outer iterations as 5, accuracy as 0.5, epsilon as 0.1 and TA is invokedis called with a probability of 10% of number of iterations.

With this algorithm, Fuzzy-And extracted rules with higher levels of Confidence, Comprehensibility, Interestingness, Lift, Conviction values. On the other hand, Compensatory-And operator produced rules with higher values of Support, Conviction, Leverage.

Later, we applied BFFO-TA based Association rule miner. We chose the number of fireflies as 10, attractiveness constant (β_0) as 2, gamma (Υ) as 2.5 and alpha (α) as 0.5, and TA algorithm is invoked with a probability of 20% of total number of iterations. With this algorithm, Fuzzy-And produced higher Confidence, Lift, Conviction values; whereas compensatory-And operator produced higher Support, Conviction, Leverage, Interestingness; Product operator produced higher Comprehensibility values.

From the above results, we can conclude that Fuzzy-and outperforms compensatory-and and product operator for all the three algorithms as the fitness values are very high. This can also be attributed to the fact that it extracted rules with higher values for many measures of quality compared to other operators. The fitness value indicates that the overall strength of the rules is very high with respect to all of them.. Out of all the algorithms, it can be observed that BPSO produced better results in terms of fitness values compared to BPSO-TA and BFFO-TA for the three operators. The BPSO-TA produced fitness values nearer to that of BPSO. So, in applications where the time complexity is of prime importance, BPSO-TA can be preferred compared to BPSO. BFFO-TA is found to produce inferior fitness values w.r.t. all operators.

Food Dataset

Here, all the parameters for BPSO, BPSO-TA, and BFFO-TA are kept the same as for books dataset. However, the probability of invoking TAis increased to 30% for BPSO-TA and BFFO-TA for better performance.

As regards BPSO, Fuzzy-And extracted rules having Confidence, Lift, Conviction, while Compensatory-And extracted rules with higher Support, Leverage and Interestingness values; Product operator produced higher Support, Coverage, Comprehensibility, Leverage, Interestingness values.

As regards BPSO-TA, Fuzzy-And produced higher Confidence, Lift, Conviction values, whereas Compensatory-And produced rules with higher Support, Conviction, Comprehensibility, Leverage, Interestingness values. The product operator extracted rules with higher Support, Leverage, Interestingness values.

In the case of BFFO-TA, Fuzzy-And produced rules with higher Confidence, Leverage, Interestingness, Lift, Conviction values. Compensatory-And operator produced rules with higher Comprehensibility. The Product operator extracted rules with higher Support, Conviction values.

Similar to Books dataset, Fuzzy-and outperformed all other operators on food dataset.

Grocery Dataset

Herfe, the parameters for BPSO, BPSO-TA, and BFFO-TA are kept the same as for books dataset except that the maximum iterations for BPSO is increased to 100 for better performance.

In the case of BPSO, Fuzzy-And operator produced rules with higher Confidence, Lift, Conviction values, while compensatory-And operator extracted rules with higher Comprehensibility, Leverage, Interestingness values. Product operator produced rules with higher Support and Coverage.

In case of BPSO-TA, Fuzzy-And extracted rules with higher Confidence, Lift, Conviction values, while compensatory-And operator produced higher Support. But, product operator, it extracted rules with higher Coverage, Comprehensibility, Leverage, Interestingness values.

The parameters for BFFO-TA on Grocery dataset are kept the same as for Books dataset except the number of iterations is increased to 200; probability of invoking TA is increased to 80% of iterations. As regards the performance of BFFO-TA, Compensatory-And operator extracted rules with high Support, Confidence, Coverage, leverage, interestingness, lift, conviction. Product operator extracted rules with Comprehensibility.

Similar to Books dataset, Fuzzy-and outperformed all other operators on grocery dataset.

Bank Dataset

Here, all the parameters for BPSO are kept the same as for books dataset except that the number of particles is increased to 50. Here, we performed feature selection in order reduce unnecessary computations as discussed in section 3.6.

In case of BPSO, Fuzzy-And operator yielded rules with higher Confidence, Lift, Conviction values, while Compensatory-And operator yielded rules with high Support, Leverage, Interestingness values; the product operator extracted rules with higher Support, Coverage, Comprehensibility, Leverage, Interestingness.

In case of BPSO-TA, the number of particles is increased to 50 and the TA is invoked with a probability of 70% of total number of iterations.

Fuzzy-And extracted rules with high Confidence, whereas compensatory-And extracted rules with high Support, Lift, Conviction. The product operator extracted rules with high Comprehensibility, Leverage, and Interestingness.

The parameters for BFFO-TA algorithm on Bank dataset are kept the same as for Books dataset except that the number of iterations are increased to 150. Fuzzy-And operator extracted rules with high Confidence, Comprehensibility, Leverage, Interestingness, Lift, Conviction. Compensatory-And operator extracted rules with high Support, Coverage.

Similar to Books dataset, Fuzzy-and outperformed all other operators on Bank dataset.

Bakery Dataset

Here, the parameters for BPSO are kept the same as for books dataset. As regards BPSO, Fuzzy-And extracted rules with higher Comprehensibility, Interestingness, Lift values while Compensatory-And operator extracted rules with higher Coverage values. The Product operator extracted rules with higher Support, Confidence, Leverage, Conviction values.

The parameters for BPSO-TA are kept the same as for books dataset except the max inner iterations and max outer iterations for TA are fixed at 300 and 25 respectively. Fuzzy-And operator extracted rules with high Confidence and Lift; Compensatory-And extracted rules with higher values of Conviction. The Product operator extracted rules with higher Support, Coverage, Comprehensibility, Leverage, and Interestingness.

Similar to Books dataset, Fuzzy-and outperformed all other operators on Bakery dataset.

Clickstream Dataset

Here, the parameters for BPSO, BPSO-TA are kept the same as for books dataset except that the inertia for BPSO is increased to 100.8 due to nature of the dataset. Here we performed feature selection in order to reduce unnecessary computations as discussed in section 3.6.

In the case of BPSO, Fuzzy-And extracted rules with higher Confidence, Comprehensibility, Interestingness, Lift, while Compensatory-And operator extracted rules with higher Support, Coverage, Leverage. The Product operator extracted rules with high Conviction values.

In the case of BPSO-TA, Fuzzy-And operator extracted rules with higher Confidence, Comprehensibility, Interestingness, Lift, while compensatory-And extracted rules with higher Support, Coverage, Leverage values. The Product operator extracted rules with high Conviction.

Here. the parameters for BFFO-TA are kept the same as for food dataset. In the case of BFFO-TA, Fuzzy-And extracted rules with high Confidence, Lift, and Conviction, whereas compensatory-And extracted rules with higher Support, Coverage, Leverage; Product operator extracted rules with higher Support, Comprehensibility, Leverage. Similar to Books dataset, Fuzzy-and outperformed all other operators on Click Stream dataset.

Table 6. Results of books datasets using BPSOTA

	M_1	M_2	M_3	M_4	M_5	M_6	M_7	M_8	Fitness
Fuzzy-And	2.06	95.40	2.17	61.09	1.94	35.46	19.22	24.32	0.66453
Comp-And	17.46	69.39	25.59	60.78	6.88	24.04	1.71	2.02	0.00101
Product	16.61	71.41	23.93	60.78	6.55	26.58	2.86	2.26	1.06E-05

Table 7. Results of books datasets using BFFOTA

	M_1	M_2	M_3	M_4	M_5	M_6	M_7	M_8	Fitness
Fuzzy-And	0.51	78.89	0.69	63.12	0.47	10.55	20.90	3.46	0.538113
Comp-And	16.75	53.63	32.57	64.71	6.32	22.54	1.67	1.52	0.000784
Product	14.89	53.51	28.45	66.32	6.13	21.73	1.78	1.53	5.75E-06

Table 8. Results of food datasets using BPSO

	M_1	M_2	M_3	M_4	M_5	M_6	M_7	M_8	Fitness
Fuzzy-And	5.52	90.62	6.33	51.83	3.65	15.78	12.87	6.82	0.54982
Comp-And	13.25	71.15	20.64	55.16	7.07	25.57	2.37	3.70	0.001321
Product	13.25	67.69	21.84	58.08	7.07	25.57	2.37	3.41	1.9E-05

Table 9. Results of food datasets using BPSOTA

	M_1	M_2	M_3	M_4	M_5	M_6	M_7	M_8	Fitness
Fuzzy-And	4.76	87.92	5.39	47.18	3.16	13.38	4.46	8.33	0.535073
Comp-And	13.25	67.69	21.84	58.08	7.07	25.57	2.37	3.41	0.001248
Product	13.25	71.15	20.64	55.16	7.07	25.57	2.37	3.70	2.11E-05

Table 10. Results of food datasets using BFFOTA

	M_1	M_2	M_3	M_4	M_5	M_6	M_7	M_8	Fitness
Fuzzy-And	6.61	54.60	12.31	61.91	3.05	11.36	8.00	2.33	0.470274
Comp-And	7.12	33.32	23.08	68.48	2.77	10.56	1.92	1.38	0.000293
Product	8.06	29.23	26.49	64.71	1.89	10.01	1.24	1.14	2.64E-06

Table 11. Results of grocery datasets using BPSO

	M_1	M_2	M_3	M_4	M_5	M_6	M_7	M_8	Fitness
Fuzzy-And	10.31	87.03	12.04	56.78	7.28	39.72	487.15	1313.96	0.608219
Comp-And	14.64	81.35	18.77	69.68	10.35	53.12	472.88	920.46	0.005349
Product	18.46	76.19	25.47	62.56	10.25	38.14	290.04	338.18	6.6E-05

Table 12. Results of grocery datasets using BPSOTA

	M_1	M_2	M_3	M_4	M_5	M_6	M_7	M_8	Fitness
Fuzzy-And	14.47	82.95	18.92	64.89	7.53	29.75	3.38	14.37	0.583074
Comp-And	20.90	74.95	28.42	63.91	8.39	30.84	2.19	5.23	0.002066
Product	19.59	70.78	28.93	65.65	9.45	36.57	2.80	2.94	4.92E-05

Table 13. Results of bank datasets using BPSO

	M_1	M_2	M_3	M_4	M_5	M_6	M_7	M_8	Fitness
Fuzzy-And	0.76	88.18	0.90	56.63	0.71	14.83	122.08	6.53	0.624155
Comp-And	2.16	65.54	3.77	60.78	1.85	19.72	10.92	3.62	0.00012
Product	2.16	48.93	4.91	69.56	1.85	19.72	10.92	2.29	4.73E-07

Table 14. Results of bank datasets using BPSOTA

	M_1	M_2	M_3	M_4	M_5	M_6	M_7	M_8	**Fitness**
Fuzzy-And	0.90	80.06	1.37	58.09	0.82	15.01	268.41	3.23	0.5324
Comp-And	2.17	63.50	3.72	64.71	1.80	16.47	831.41	292.78	0.000108
Product	2.16	48.93	4.91	69.56	1.85	19.72	10.92	2.29	4.73E-07

Table 15. Results of bank datasets using BFFOTA

	M_1	M_2	M_3	M_4	M_5	M_6	M_7	M_8	**Fitness**
Fuzzy-And	0.89	31.85	2.43	66.32	0.74	5.69	8.65	1.70	0.442907
Comp-And	0.97	21.67	5.57	63.40	0.55	3.33	5.32	1.21	3.6E-06
Product	0.80	19.17	3.42	63.09	0.61	4.48	5.60	1.23	7.47E-08

Table 16. Results of bakery datasets using BPSO

	M_1	M_2	M_3	M_4	M_5	M_6	M_7	M_8	**Fitness**
Fuzzy-And	2.84	51.27	6.03	75.22	2.61	39.51	61.57	1.72	0.554776
Comp-And	4.20	50.46	8.26	69.56	3.61	32.50	8.83	1.92	0.000369
Product	4.26	55.91	7.99	69.86	3.73	36.69	9.52	3.17	3.07E-06

Table 17. Results of bakery datasets using BPSOTA

	M_1	M_2	M_3	M_4	M_5	M_6	M_7	M_8	**Fitness**
Fuzzy-And	2.13	66.99	4.47	62.70	1.84	16.57	10.84	1.47	0.511506
Comp-And	4.54	54.96	8.25	63.09	3.81	27.11	6.31	2.04	0.00035
Product	4.56	53.95	8.44	66.32	3.88	30.98	7.31	2.01	2.34E-06

Table 18. Results of grocery datasets using BFFOTA

	M_1	M_2	M_3	M_4	M_5	M_6	M_7	M_8	**Fitness**
Fuzzy-And	12.46	37.32	35.88	67.01	2.36	13.49	1.34	1.15	7.74E-07
Comp-And	21.35	57.20	37.82	65.01	5.65	23.83	1.64	1.49	0.554664
Product	11.52	36.08	33.61	69.62	2.54	12.06	1.36	1.29	0.001337

Table 19. Results of click stream datasets using BPSO

	M_1	M_2	M_3	M_4	M_5	M_6	M_7	M_8	**Fitness**
Fuzzy-And	0.00	100.00	0.00	82.54	0.00	100.00	32711.00	1.00	0.653152
Comp-And	5.61	63.36	9.82	63.40	3.49	19.31	4.72	3.31	0.000299
Product	5.12	63.10	8.95	65.01	3.44	21.37	5.72	3.36	1.75E-06

Table 20. Results of click stream datasets using BPSOTA

	M_1	M_2	M_3	M_4	M_5	M_6	M_7	M_8	Fitness
Fuzzy-And	0.43	98.33	0.47	72.47	0.37	51.28	15811.90	2.91	0.607492
Comp-And	5.70	63.92	9.81	63.09	3.50	18.78	4.52	3.27	0.000295
Product	5.52	65.33	9.62	63.40	3.42	18.98	4.76	3.90	1.68E-06

Table 21. Results of click stream datasets using BFFO

	M_1	M_2	M_3	M_4	M_5	M_6	M_7	M_8	Fitness
Fuzzy-And	0.80	68.61	1.35	64.54	0.69	18.29	4075.25	1.96	0.516699
Comp-And	2.10	19.11	13.90	65.01	0.90	4.65	2.31	1.13	1.58E-05
Product	2.10	20.59	11.61	70.14	0.90	6.61	4.95	1.17	3.38E-08

Table 22. Computational times for various approaches

Data Set	MOF BFFO-TA	MOF BPSO-TA	MOF BPSO
Books	4.2s	2.34s	19.53s
Food	1.77s	3.42s	11.20s
Grocery	26.11s	3.71s	25.34s
XYZ Bank	59.92s	142.13s	893.76s
Clickstream	109.75s	82.65 s	1017.53s
Bakery		39.92 s	371.71 s

Figure 7. Results of book dataset using BPSO

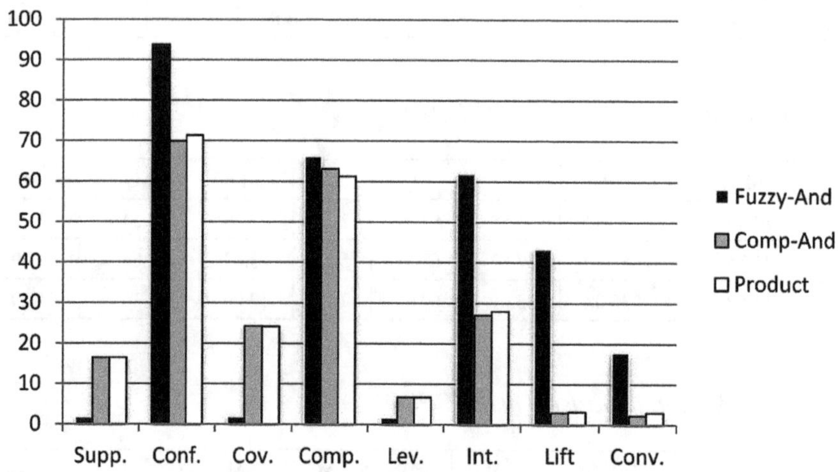

Figure 8. Results of book dataset using BPSOTA

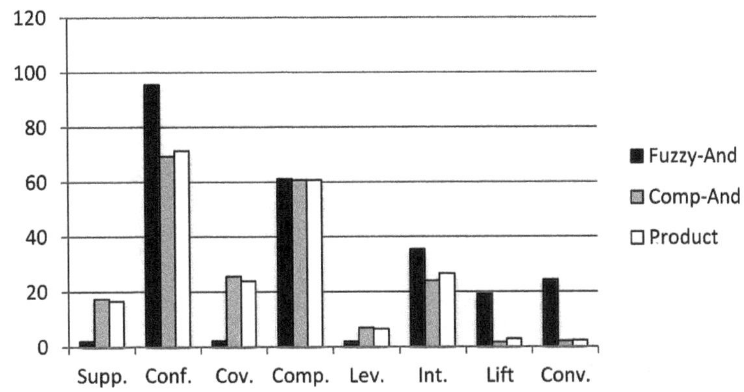

Figure 9. Results of book dataset using BFFOTA

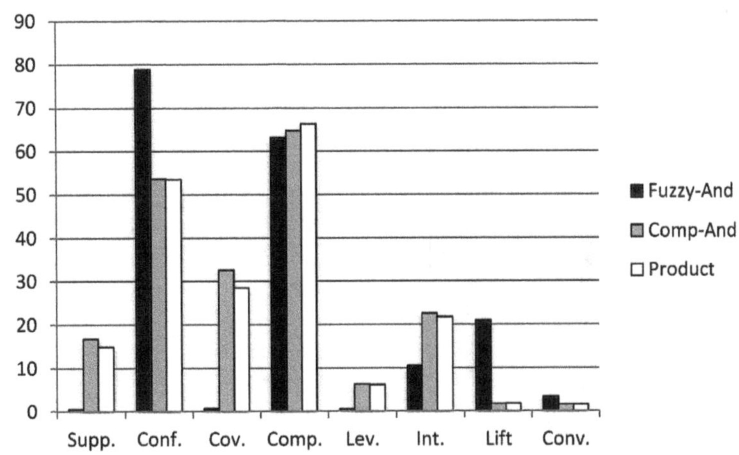

Figure 10. Results of food dataset using BPSO

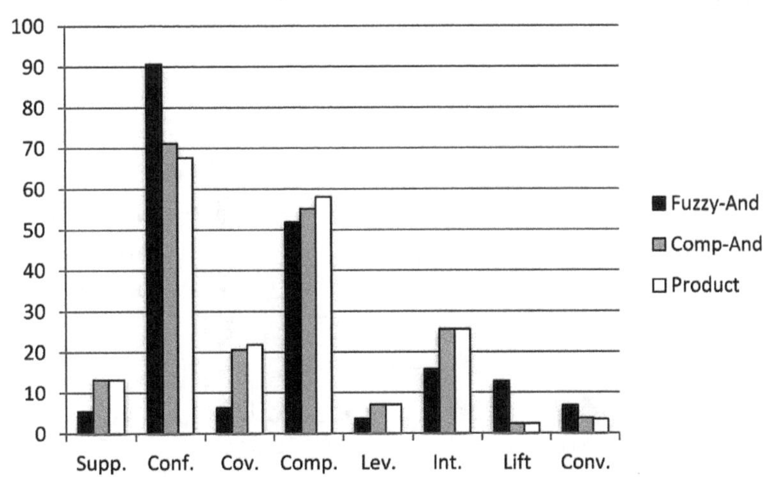

Figure 11. Results of food dataset using BPSOTA

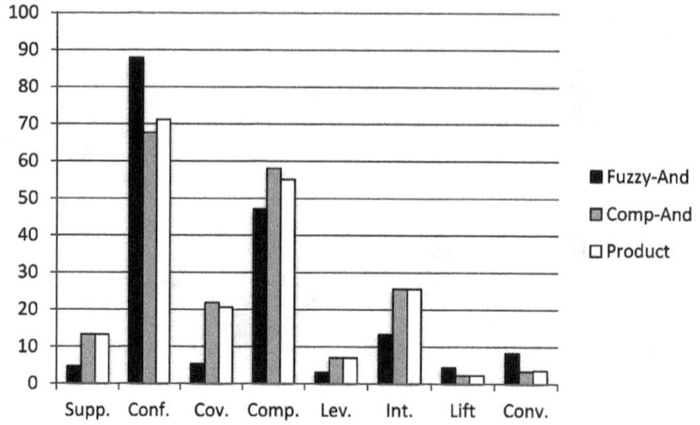

Figure 12. Results of food dataset using BFFOTA

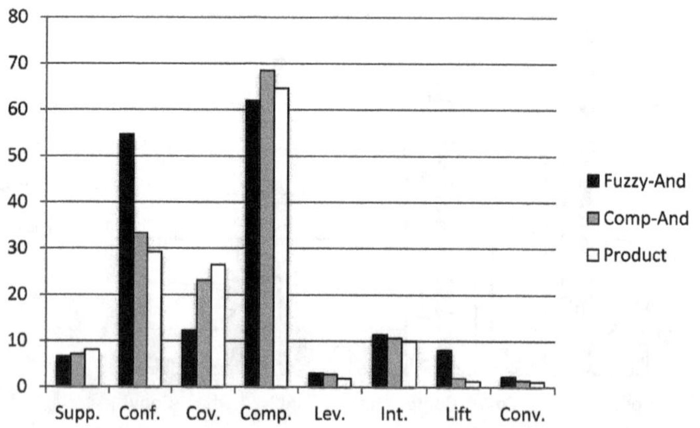

Figure 13. Results of grocery dataset using BPSO

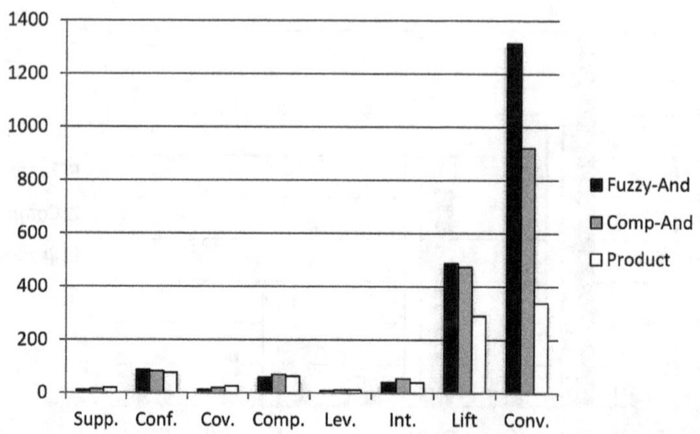

Figure 14. Results of grocery dataset using BPSOTA

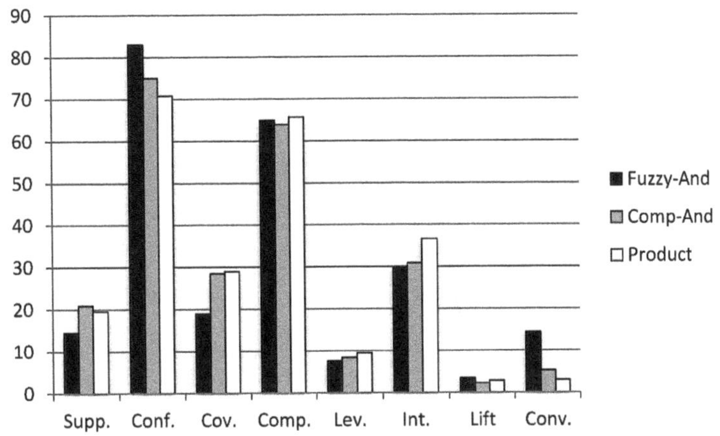

Figure 15. Results of grocery dataset using BFFOTA

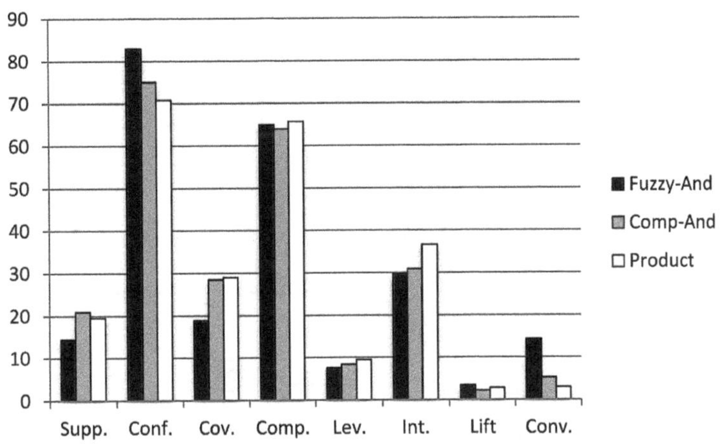

Figure 16. Results of bank dataset using BPSO

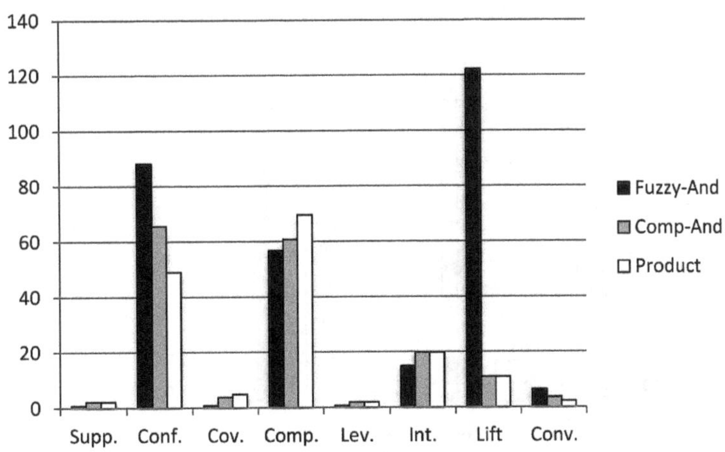

Figure 17. Results of bank dataset using BPSOTA

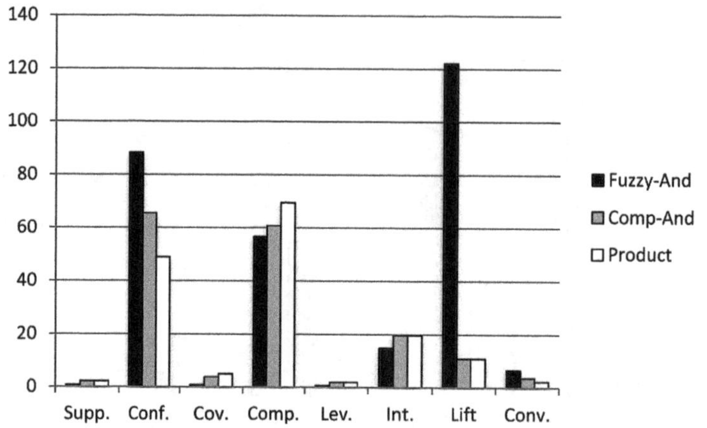

Figure 18. Results of bank dataset using BFFOTA

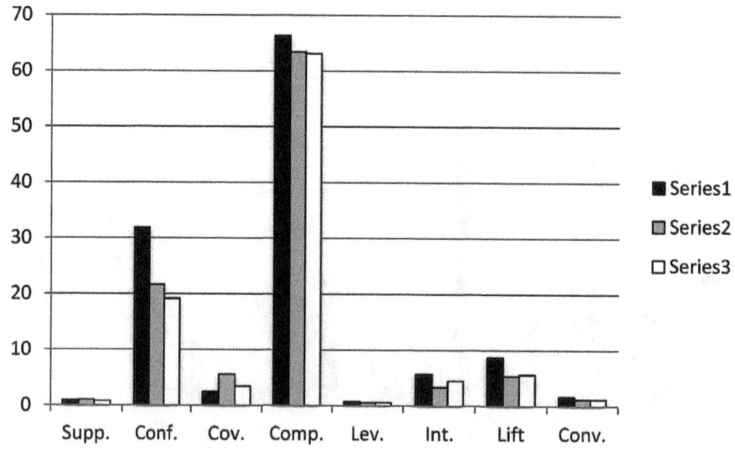

Figure 19. Results of bakery dataset using BPSO

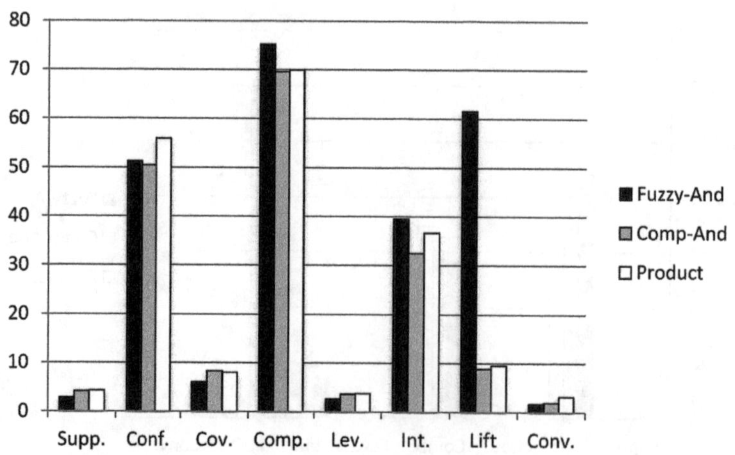

Figure 20. Results of bakery dataset using BPSOTA

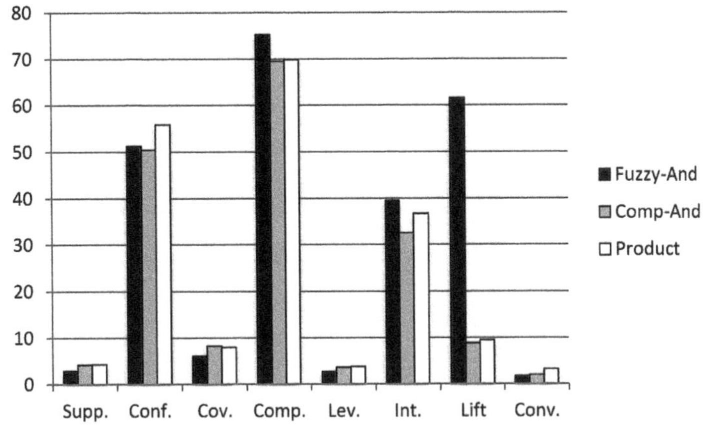

Figure 21. Results of bakery dataset using BFFO-TA via fuzzy fitness function

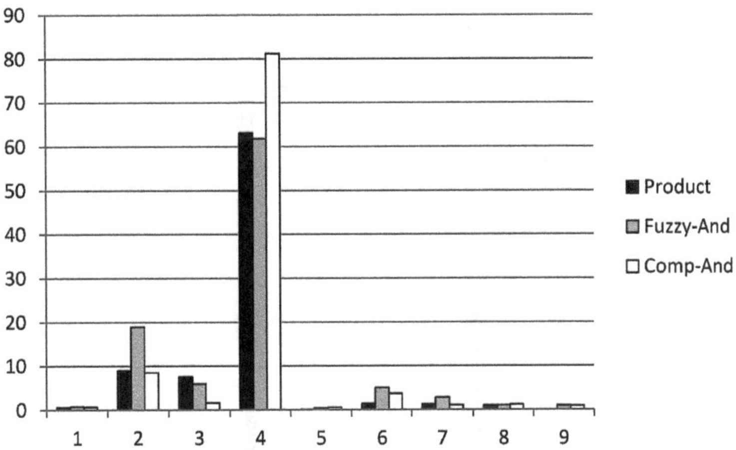

Figure 22. Results of click stream dataset using BPSO

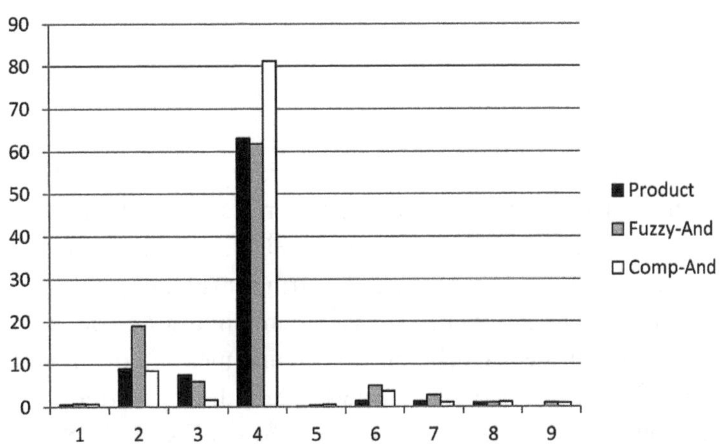

Figure 23. Results of click stream dataset using BPSOTA

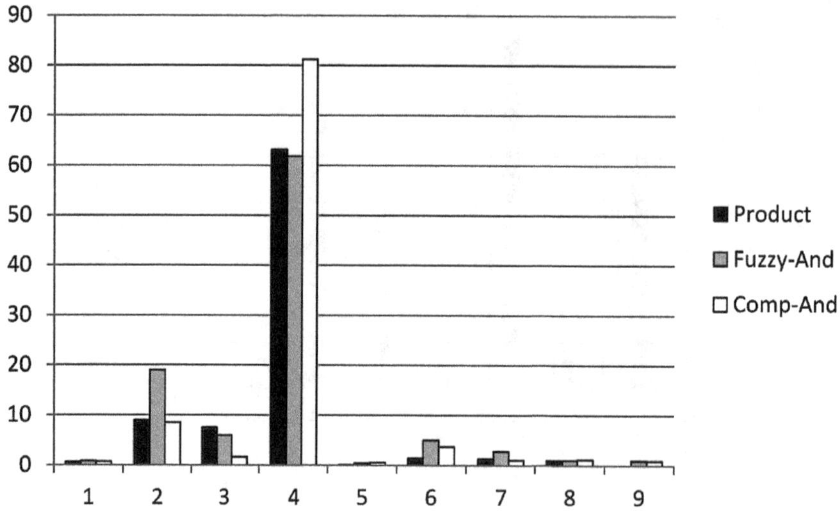

Figure 24. Results of clickstream dataset using BFFOTA

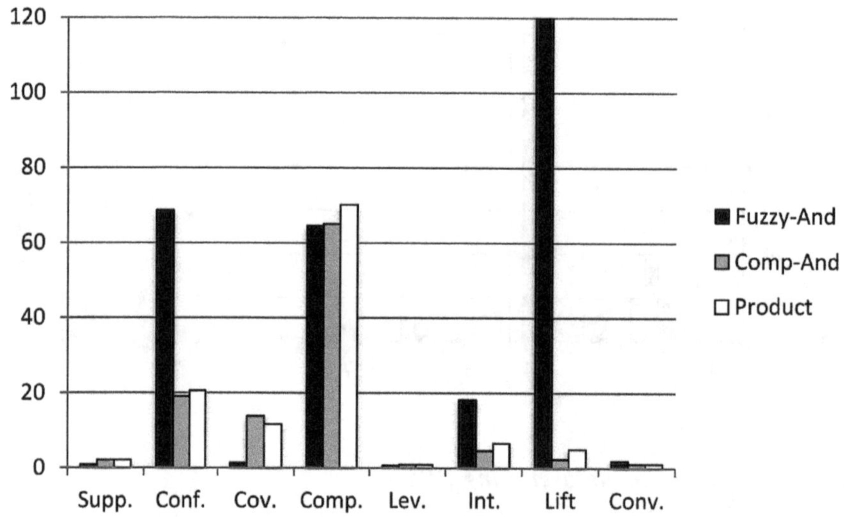

CONCLUSION

In this chapter, we formulated association rule mining as a fuzzy multi-objective optimization problem, where the quality measures of association rules are considered as conflicting fuzzy objective functions. We solved the problem using BPSO, BPSO-TA and BFFO-TA We extracted association rules from transactional databases in 6 different datasets by considering several objectives. The advantages of the proposed approach are (i) the user does not need to specify minimum support and minimum confidence (ii) fuzzy optimization helps considering different conflicting measure of strength simultaneously and (iii) BFFA-TA and BPSO-TA Rule Miners are able generate all the top 10 rules only in a single run. This is a very significant improvement over BPSO. (iv) Overall, BFFO-TA and BPSO-TA also consumed less computational times on all datasets compared to a priori, FP-Growth. This is a noteworthy improvement in today's world where computational time is of major importance. (v) These approaches also overcome the demerits associated with traditional approaches of generating redundant rules. Based on the results, we conclude that the Fuzzy-and operator outperforms other algorithms and that BPSO-TA shows superior performance compared to other strategies.

REFERENCES

Agrawal, R., Imielinski, T., & Swami, A. (1993). Mining association rules between sets of items in large databases. In *Proceedings of the 1993 ACM SIGMOD Conference on Management of Data*(pp. 207-216). Washington, DC:ACM Press. doi:10.1145/170035.170072

Agrawal, R., & Srikant, R. (1994). Fast algorithms for mining association rules. In *Proceedings of the 20th International Conference on VLDB Conference*(pp. 487-499).

Alatas, B., Akim, E., & Akim, E. (2008). MODENAR: Multi-objective differential evolution algorithm for mining numeric association rules. *Applied Soft Computing*, *8*(1), 646–656. doi:10.1016/j.asoc.2007.05.003

Anandhavalli, M., Kumar, S.S., Kumar, A., & Ghose, M. K. (2009). Optimized association rule mining using genetic algorithm. *Advances in Information Mining*, 1-4.

Asadi, A., Afzali, M., Shojaei, A., & Sulaimani, S. (2012). New binary PSO based method for finding best thresholds in association rule mining. *Applied Soft Computing*, 260–264.

Beiranvand, V., Kashani, M. M., & Bakar, A. (2014). Multi-objective PSO algorithm for mining numerical association rules without a priori discretization. *Expert Systems with Applications*, *41*(9), 4259–4273. doi:10.1016/j.eswa.2013.12.043

Breese, J., Hackerman, D., & Kadie, C. (1998). *Anonymous Microsoft Web Dataset*. Retrieved August 13, 2013, from http://archive.ics.uci.edu/ml/datasets/Anonymous+Microsoft+Web+Data

Dekhtyar, A., & Verburg, J. (2009). *Extended Bakery Dataset*. Retrieved August 13, 2013, fromhttps://wiki.csc.calpoly.edu/datasets/wiki/ExtendedBakery

Dueck, G., & Scheuer, T. (1990). Threshold Accepting: A general purpose optimization algorithm appearing superior to simulated annealing. *Journal of Computational Physics*, *90*(1), 161–175. doi:10.1016/0021-9991(90)90201-B

Eberhart, R. C., & Kennedy, J. (1995). A new optimizer using particle swarm theory. In *Proceedings of Sixth International Symposium on Micro Machine and Human Science*(pp. 39-43). Nagoya, Japan: IEEE Press. doi:10.1109/MHS.1995.494215

Eberhart, R. C., & Kennedy, J. (1995). Particle swarm optimization. *Proceedings of Neural Networks*, *4*, 1942–1948.

Eberhart, R. C., & Kennedy, J. (1997). A discrete binary version of the particle swarm algorithm. In *Proceedings of the Conference on Systems, Man, and Cybernetics*(pp. 4104-4109). Orlando, FL: IEEE Press.

Ghosh, A., & Nath, B. (2004). Multi-Objective rule mining using genetic algorithms. *Information Sciences, 163*(1-3), 123–133. doi:10.1016/j.ins.2003.03.021

Gupta, M. (2012). Application of weighted particle swarm optimization in association rule mining. *International Journal of Computer Science and Informatics, 1*, 2231–5292.

Hadian, A., Nasiri, M., & Bidgoli, B. M. (2010). Clustering based multi-objective rule mining using genetic algorithm. *International Journal of Digital Content Technology and its Applications, 4*, 37-42.

Han, J., Pei, H., & Yin, Y. (2000). Mining frequent patterns without candidate generation. In *Proceedings of Conference on the Management of Data, SIGMOD 2000* (pp. 1–12). Dallas, TX: ACM Press. doi:10.1145/342009.335372

Houtsma, M., & Swami, A. (1995). Set-oriented data mining in relational databases. *Data & Knowledge Engineering, 17*(3), 245–263. doi:10.1016/0169-023X(95)00024-M

Kaya, M., & Alhajj, R. (2004). Mining optimized fuzzy association rules using multi-objective genetic algorithm. In *Proceedings of8th IEEE International Conference on Intelligent Engineering Systems* (pp.38-43). Cluj-Napoca, Romania: IEEE Press.

Kuo, R. J., & Tapia, A. (2011). Application of particle swarm optimization to association rule mining. *Applied Soft Computing, 11*(1), 326–336. doi:10.1016/j.asoc.2009.11.023

Li, Y., Ning, P., Wang, X. S., & Jajodia, S. (2003). Discovering calendar-based temporal association rules. *Data & Knowledge Engineering, 44*(2), 193–218. doi:10.1016/S0169-023X(02)00135-0

Luna, J. M., Romero, J. R., & Ventura, S. (2013). Grammar-Based Multi-Objective Algorithms for Mining Association Rules. *Data & Knowledge Engineering, 86*, 19–37. doi:10.1016/j.datak.2013.01.002

Maheshkumar, Y., Ravi, V., & Abraham, A. (2013). A particle swarm optimization-threshold accepting hybrid algorithm for unconstrained optimization. *Neural Network World*, 191-221.

Martínez-Ballesteros, M., Martínez-Álvarez, F., Lora, A. T., & Riquelme, J. C. (2014). Selecting the best measures to discover quantitative association rule. *Neurocomputing, 126*, 3–14. doi:10.1016/j.neucom.2013.01.056

Martínez-Ballesteros, M., Nepomuceno-Chamorro, I. A., & Riquelme, J. C. (2014). Discovering gene association networks by multi-objective evolutionary quantitative association rule. *Journal of Computer and System Sciences, 80*(1), 118–136. doi:10.1016/j.jcss.2013.03.010

Minaei-Bidgoli, B., Barmaki, R., & Nasir, M. (2013). Mining numerical association rules via multi-objective genetic algorithms. *Information Sciences, 233*, 15–24. doi:10.1016/j.ins.2013.01.028

Nandhini, M., Janani, M., & Sivanandham, S. N. (2012).Association rule mining using swarm intelligence and domain ontology. In *Proceedings ofIEEE International Conference on Recent Trends in Information Technology(ICRTIT)* (pp. 537-541). Coimbatore, Tamilnadu: IEEE Press. doi:10.1109/ICRTIT.2012.6206763

Naveen, N., Ravi, V., Rao, C. R., & Sarath, K. N. V. D. (2012). Rule extraction using firefly optimization: application to banking. In *Proceedings of IEEE International Conference on Industrial Engineering and Engineering Management*(vol. 38, pp. 237-288). Hong Kong, China: IEEE Press.

Park, J. S., Chen, M. S., Jeffrey, D., & Yu, P. S. (1995). An Effective Hash Based Algorithm For Mining Association Rules. In *Proceedings of the 1995 ACM SIGMOD International Conference on Management of Data*(pp. 175-186). New York, NY: ACM Press. doi:10.1145/223784.223813

Pradeep, G., & Ravi, V. (2014). *Association Rule Mining via Evolutionary Multi-objective Optimization* (pp. 35–46). Bangalore: MIWAI.

Ravi, V., Reddy, P. J., & Zimmermann, H.-J. (2000). Fuzzy global optimization of complex system reliability. *IEEE Transactions on Fuzzy Systems*, *8*(3), 241–248. doi:10.1109/91.855914

Saggar, M., & Agrawal, A. K. (2004).Optimization of association rule mining using improved genetic algorithms. In *Proceedings of the IEEE International Conference on Systems Man and Cybernetics*(vol. 4, pp. 3725-3729). IEEE Press. doi:10.1109/ICSMC.2004.1400923

Sarath, K. N. V. D., & Ravi, V. (2013). Association rule mining using binary particle swarm optimization. *Engineering Applications of Artificial Intelligence*, *26*(8), 1832–1840. doi:10.1016/j.engappai.2013.06.003

Sergey, B., Rajeev, M., Jeffrey, D., & Shalom, T. (1997). Dynamic itemset counting and implication rules for market basket data. In *Proceedings of the 1997 ACM SIGMOD international conference on Management of data*(vol. 26-2, pp. 255-264). New York, NY: ACM Press.

Toivonen, H. (1996). Sampling Large Databases for Association Rules. In *Proceedings of VLDB '96 Proceedings of the 22th International Conference on Very Large Data Bases*(pp. 134-145). Mumbai, India: Morgan Kaufmann Publishers.

Tsay, Y. J., & Chiang, J. Y. (2005). CBAR: An efficient method for mining association rules. *Knowledge-Based Systems*, *18*(2-3), 99–105. doi:10.1016/j.knosys.2004.04.010

Waiswa, P. P. W., & Baryamureeba, V. (2008). Extraction of interesting association Rules using genetic algorithms. *International Journal of Computing and ICT Research*, *2*(1), 26–33.

Werners, B. (1988). Aggregation models in mathematical programming. In G. Mitra (Ed.), *Mathematical Models for Decision Support* (pp. 295–319). Berlin: Springer. doi:10.1007/978-3-642-83555-1_19

Wur, S. Y., & Leu, Y. (1998).An effective Boolean algorithm for mining association rules in large databases. In *Proceedings of the 6th International Conference on Database Systems for Advanced Applications*(pp. 179-186). Hsinchu, Taiwan: IEEE Press.

Yang, X. S. (2012). Firefly Algorithm, Stochastic test functions and design optimization. *International Journal of Bio-inspired Computation*, *2*(2), 78–84. doi:10.1504/IJBIC.2010.032124

Zadeh, L. (1965). Fuzzy Sets. *Information and Control*, *8*(3), 338–353. doi:10.1016/S0019-9958(65)90241-X

Zimmermann, H.-J. (1991). *Fuzzy Set Theory and Applications* (2nd ed.). Boston, MA: Kluwer. doi:10.1007/978-94-015-7949-0

Zimmermann, H.-J., & Zysno, P. (1980). Latent connectives in human decision making. *Fuzzy Sets and Systems*, *4*(1), 37–51. doi:10.1016/0165-0114(80)90062-7

KEY TERMS AND DEFINITIONS

Association Measures of Strength: The metrics to identify the quality of rules.

Combinatorial Global Optimization: Involves finding optimal object from a finite set of objects and also finding the optima over all input values instead of finding local optima.

Fuzzy Aggregate Operators: These operators provide a way for several fuzzy sets to be combined in a desirable way to produce a single fuzzy set.

Multi-Objective Optimization: A sub area of multiple criteria decision making dealing with mathematical optimization problems involving more than one objective function to be optimized simultaneously.

Chapter 8
Improved Seating Plans for Movie Theatre to Improve Revenue:
An Integrated Best Worst Method with EMSR-B

Kedar Pandurang Joshi
T. A. Pai Management Institute, India

Nikhil Lohiya
T. A. Pai Management Institute, India

ABSTRACT

Bollywood is not only one of the biggest film producers in India but also one of the largest centers of film production in the world. Seat occupancy rate and pricing of each seat are important parameters that determines the revenue of a cinema business. The objective of the chapter is to enable theater managers to determine the prices at the time of booking according to the occupancy rate so that the revenue is improved based on preferred demand for the respective seats. A multi criteria analysis is applied with seat occupancy rate as dependent variable and other factors as independent variables like Show time, Poster Size, Day of week and Timing of Release. Further, a predictive analysis can be carried out to determine the occupancy rate for the upcoming movies. Based on the occupancy rate, the managers at theater can adopt variable pricing concept to improve the revenue. This work shows an integrated method to develop a seating plan based on occupancy rate to improve the revenue using EMSR-b heuristic with an illustrated example for a theater.

DOI: 10.4018/978-1-5225-0997-4.ch008

INTRODUCTION

The Indian film industry is the largest multi-lingual and the largest in the world in terms of buying the highest number of tickets. India is the second largest screen count and number of films produced and 5th largest in terms of revenue according during 2014. The profitability of a cinema business is primarily determined by the revenue generated by the seats sold. So seat occupancy rate and pricing of each seat are important criteria which decides the revenue of a box office. In Indian cinema seat occupancy rate at theaters vary across different days of week, show timings, months of a year and mainly vary across different movies. Box office success or failure affects the seat occupancy rate at the theaters.

The demand for each movie comes from diverse strata of the society. According to such demand pattern, the managers at theaters can utilize the concept of variable pricing including advanced pricing analytics. Usually such demand would be positively dependent on the success of a movie. With this approach, the various factors which may affect the box office success or failure of a movie are explained. This would help to even out the variation in seat occupancy rate and maximize the profitability for theaters.

The study of historical box offices successful movies helps in accessing the various variables that affect the success of movies. Some of the important variables are production cost, releases by major studios, sequel to successful movies, film genre, release date and movie casts, director and rating. One of the major difficulties faced by the owners of multiplex theaters is to maximize their revenue under situation of film getting hit or flop. Revenue management is a science of applied microeconomics with regard to perishable products or services (Phillips, 2005; Talluri and Van Ryzin, 2006). The applications of revenue management practices are spread over many services like airlines, hotels, movies, healthcare etc. (Yeoman and McMahon-Beattie, 2004). This work benefits managers of movie theaters to update seating plans for their customers on tactical basis based on an integrated MCDM method and EMSR-b heuristics.

Following sections describe movie industry and ticket booking scenario in Bollywood and relevant issues raised in the literature, current method, proposed method, an illustration and conclusions.

MOVIE INDUSTRY AND TICKET BOOKING

The Bollywood films are multi-million dollar productions, with the record exclusive productions valuation up to 1 billion rupees. Recently, an increasing trend of making digital movies in India is observed as shown in Figure 1. According to Kimes *et al.* (1998) movie theaters are positioned as fixed duration and fixed pricing. The movie theaters have grater scope to apply variable pricing but they usually limit themselves to apply routines price discrimination schemes like Silver class, Gold class, Platinum class etc.

Kimes and Chase (1998) pointed out the need of adopting variable pricing practices in movie ticket booking based on timing as well as seat allocation (capacity management). Few researcher worked upon forecasting box office revenue of a movie before its theatrical release which is a tough and puzzling problem (Kim *et al,* 2013; Ghiassi *et al.,* 2015; Zhang *et al.*, 2009). Zhang *et al.* (2009) employed a multi-layer BP neural network (MLBP) with multi-input and multi-output to build the model for prediction. Kim *et al.* (2013) applied social network services (SNS) which is influencing the movie industry in South Korea. In their work, the issue of forecasting box-office revenue highlighted and analyzed the data in the Korean movie market. These studies mainly focus on forecasting aspect of market demand rather than dynamic pricing in movie industry. For the success of box office star cast is generally con-

Figure 1. Movies production in India from 2010 to 2014

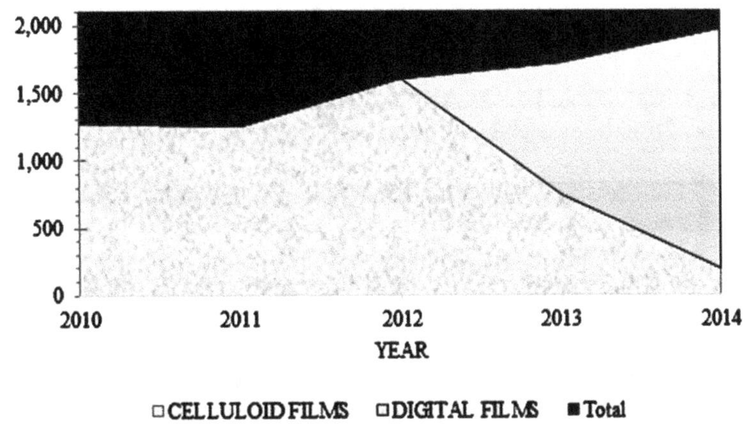

sidered an important factor. Joshi (2015) argues that big star cast may not promise profits because their presence results in minimised weekly revenue volatility. There are few studies about movie analytics like El Assady *et al.* (2013) and Haughton *et al.* (2015).

There is limited work on an independent fencing based pricing in the context of revenue management for movie theaters on tactical basis. Mainly such kind of works are spread over literature with emphasis on fairness related to application of revenue management techniques in that context (Choi *et al.*, 2015). The authors of this chapter have not come across any work where efforts on integrating the multi-criteria decision making technique with a revenue management technique in the movie theaters. This gap in literature on applying such integrated method worth exploring.

AN INTEGRATED MCDM METHOD FOR SEATING PLAN

Any movie lover who intends to purchase a movie ticket online or offline can search various options in terms of timings type of seats and then zero down on their desired choice of class based tickets. Many movie theaters classify their pricing classes like Silver, Gold and Platinum (in ascending order of fare). Based on customer's segment they belong the demand is observed, which in turn provides revenue to the theater. This section details the current and proposed product search process. To maximize the revenue of the movie theater during a particular movie is running, various factors like competitors pricing, price of DVDs play a critical role. To demonstrate applicability with the intention of ease in adoption a new integrated method is proposed to maximize revenue through changing seating plans tactically. Before the new method is described, the current method is explained below.

Current Seat Booking Method

Currently, the movie theatres generally has three different classes. Each classes has fixed number of seats for any type of show. The prices of each seats in a class are fixed for a particular show. The prices vary along shows depending on show timing, movie, day of the week etc. Seats in each class are booked on first come first serve basis. Once all the seats are booked for a particular class, the bookings are closed for that class irrespective of the hierarchy of the class. The method is described in stepwise in Figure 2.

Figure 2. Current seat booking method

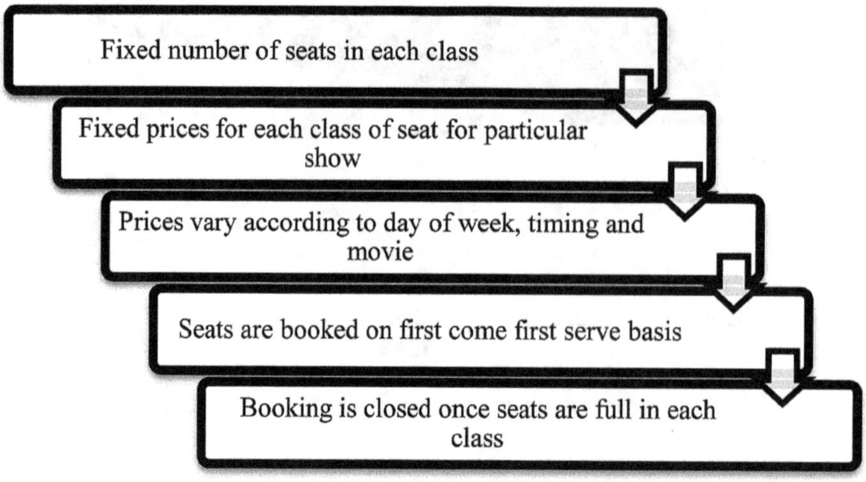

Proposed Seat Booking Method

With the proposed method first the occupancy levels of a movie is predicted based on factors influencing it. The occupancy of seats or seat demand is mainly affected by four factors namely, Show time, Poster Size, Day of the Week and Timing of release. The weightage of each factor and sub factors will be calculated by best and worst method. Each factors has various sub factors as mentioned in the Table 1. The proposed method use EMSR-b to protect the seats for higher class. EMRS-b would be based on historic demand behavior. Each movie is categorized under three occupancy level namely high, medium and low. The occupancy level for a particular movie will be calculated based on Best and Worst method.

Step 1: Calculate weight for each factor and sub factor.

Best and Worst Method (BWM) is used to calculate the weightage for each factor and sub factor to know the relative importance of each factor (Rezaei, 2015). The higher the weightage the higher the importance. Best and worst method assign ranks to each factor based on the reference factor. It ranks factors on best and worst basis. The 1st ranked factor in each basis becomes the reference factor to rank other factors.

Table 1. Factors affecting seat occupancy

Show Time	Poster Size	Day of Week	Timing of Release
Morning	Big	Weekdays	Festive
Noon	Medium	Weekends	Non Festive
Evening	Small		
Late Evening			

For e.g.: The best factor among all 4 factors is classified as Poster size, thus this factor will be assigned rank 1 and then the remaining factors will be assigned ranked according to this factors. Once, the ranks are assigned, the below formula is applied to calculate the weight:

$$MinMax\left\{\frac{w_b}{W} - R_i, \frac{W}{w_w} - R_j\right\}$$

where,

w_b = Weight of Best,
w_w = Weight of Worst,
W = Weight of each factor,
R_i = Rank of each factor under best ranking,
R_j = Rank of each factor under worst ranking.

The same will be explained in Figure 3. Once the weights are determined for the factors, the same procedure will be followed to calculate weight for each sub factor.

Step 2: Calculate the range of scale and divide it into three levels of occupancy.

After the weights are calculated, the highest score that a movie can get can be calculated by choosing the most important sub factor i.e. with highest weightage under each factor and multiplying its weight with the factor weight and summing it all to get the highest score. Similarly the lowest score a movie can get can be calculated by choosing the least important sub factor i.e. with lowest weightage under each factor and multiplying its weight with the factor weight and summing it all to get the lowest score. The difference between the highest score and lowest score will give the range of the scale to measure occupancy level.

Figure 3. Proposed seat booking method with integrated Best-Worst Method and EMSR-b

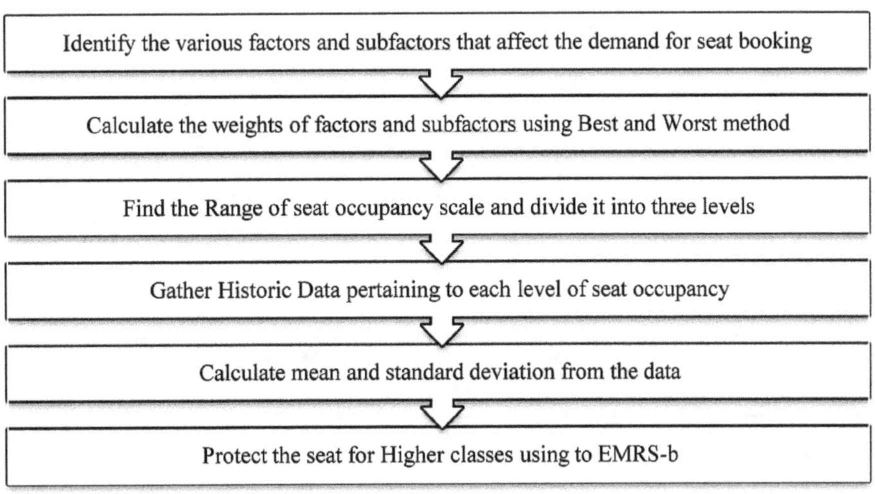

Once the range is found, divide the range into three. This would denote the three different levels of occupancy namely, high medium and low.

Step 3: Calculate occupancy level for a movie show and apply EMSR-b to protect seats.

Calculate the score for a particular movie show based on its show time, poster size, and day of week and timing of release. The score can be calculated by multiplying the weights of the sub factors corresponding to that movie show with their respective factors and summing it all to. Once the score is calculated, assign it to one of the three occupancy levels according to its score.

According to the occupancy level for the movie show, based on the historic data for that occupancy level, apply EMSR-b to protect seats for higher class. For the detailed steps of EMSR-b, kindly refer Bodea and Ferguson (2014).

Gather historic data pertaining to each of the three occupancy level about mean demand and standard deviation. The data would also capture the book seats and booking rejected due to house full to calculate the mean and standard deviation. Such historic data can be updated based on previous box office records for the theatre.

AN ILLUSTRATION

To operationalize the proposed method an illustration is presented here. In the best ranking case, Poster size is given the 1st rank, day of week is given 2nd rank which means that poster size is twice more important than day of the week, then timing of release is given 4th rank and show timing is given 8th rank.

Similarly under worst ranking, Show timing is given the 1st rank and ranks for others are shown in Table 2.

Then according to the Best-Worst method, the weights are calculated for the four factors. Similarly the weights for the sub factors are calculated as shown in Table 3 and Table 4.

Table 2. Factors deciding occupancy rate

	Show Time	Poster Size	Day of Week	Timing of Release
Best	8	1	2	4
Worst	1	8	4	2
Weight	0.05	0.44	0.18	0.33

Table 3. Showtime

	Morning	Noon	Evening	Late Evening
Best	4	6	1	2
Worst	2	1	6	4
Weight	0.23	0.07	0.41	0.30

Table 4. Poster size

	Big	Medium	Small
Best	1	4	6
Worst	6	3	1
Weight	0.75	0.19	0.06

The weights day of week and timing of release is directly calculated as both has just 2 sub factors. The more important factor is given 67% and the other is given 33%. Thus, once the weights are calculated, the highest score is that a show can get is

(0.05*0.41+0.44*0.75+0.18*0.67+0.33*0.67) i.e. 0.690

and the lowest score a show can get is

(0.05*0.07+0.44*0.06+0.18*0.33+0.33*0.33) i.e. 0.198.

Thus the ranges are shown in Table 5.

Now, Consider a Movie show which has a show time in evening and is a Big poster size movie, shown on weekend and timing of release is non festive. Thus, the score for the show is 0.581. Thus, this show falls under high occupancy level. The mean demand for the different classes of seat under high occupancy level is shown in Table 6.

Thus, using EMSR-b as shown in Figure 4, one would get the protected seats for each fare class.

It can be observed that the expected revenue for premium class from seat 38 is less than revenue from gold class. Thus we would protect the 37 seats for premium class. Similarly, this can be done to protect seat for gold class when comparing with silver class.

Thus, the complete details of protected seats for each fare class is given in Table 7.

Table 5. Range for low, medium, and high

Occupancy Level	Low	Medium	High
Range of Score	0.198-0.362	0.362-0.526	0.526-0.690

Table 6. Mean and standard deviation

	Platinum	Gold	Silver
Mean	40.200	210.867	235.800
Standard deviation	6.139	21.531	24.687

Figure 4. Expected fare among different classes Platinum, Gold and Silver based on EMSR-b

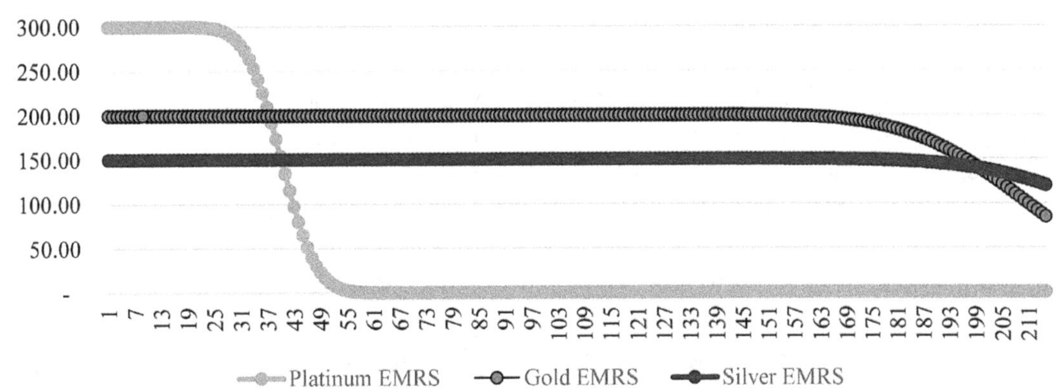

Table 7. Protection intervals for different classes

Fare Class	Fare	Protected Seats	Booking Limit
Platinum	300	37	220
Gold	200	163	
Silver	150	20	

FUTURE RESEARCH DIRECTIONS

A large shift is happening towards M-commerce due to penetration of smart mobile phones across the country. Such trend shows that there is a research potential exists in extracting real-time demand data using M-commerce for updating seat booking plans for theatre managers. In reality, many other factors might influence at seat occupancy for a movie other than the factors considered in this study. With more granularity and contextual factors this study can be extended further.

In current work, authors consider only three levels of fences in seat booking plan. In fact, such limited fences can be extended to multiple fencing based upon demand pattern of each seat in the theater. Now a days a buzz on social media creates a lot of awareness about the movie popularity.

CONCLUSION

In today's era of Mcommerce, companies reach to each individual through their smartphone devices as intermediaries is becoming popular across developing countries like India. Box office success is an important indicator in movie industry. Higher the seat occupancy higher the revenue as this seats acts like a perishable services. Seat occupancy rate at theaters vary across different days of week, show timings, months of a year and mainly vary across different movies. In this integrated approach, the various factors that affect the box office success and failure of a movie and predictions of occupancy rate are described. This is an attempt to match the demand with varying supply through well-known EMSR-b heuristic to maximize the profitability for theaters.

Noticeable features of the proposed method are:

- Simplified method of predicting seat occupancy levels for a movie during a period.
- Incorporation of historical demand behavior to define booking limits.
- An integrated method i.e. Best-Worst Method and EMSR-b.
- Improving the profitability with revenue management and tactical pricing.

This chapter presents an effort to utilize an improved MCDM method namely Best Worst Method. This method uses a well-known EMSR-b heuristic to fix up booking limit for each class. Managers will be aided to incorporate frequent changes in the seats availability to take various decisions in tactical pricing.

REFERENCES

Belobaba, P. (1987). *Air travel demand and airline seat inventory management*. Cambridge, MA: Flight Transportation Laboratory, Massachusetts Institute of Technology.

Belobaba, P. P. (1989). OR Practice-Application of a Probabilistic Decision Model to Airline Seat Inventory Control. *Operations Research*, *37*(2), 183–197. doi:10.1287/opre.37.2.183

Bodea, T., & Ferguson, M. (2014). *Segmentation, Revenue Management and Pricing Analytics*. Routledge.

Choi, C., Jeong, M., & Mattila, A. S. (2015). Revenue management in the context of movie theaters: Is it fair&quest. *Journal of Revenue & Pricing Management*, *14*(2), 72–83. doi:10.1057/rpm.2014.30

El Assady, M., Hafner, D., Hund, M., Jäger, A., Jentner, W., Rohrdantz, C.,... Keim, D. A. (2013). Visual Analytics for the Prediction of Movie Rating and Box Office Performance. *IEEE VAST Challenge USB Proceedings*.

Fetscherin, M. (2010). The main determinants of Bollywood movie box office sales. *Journal of Global Marketing*, *23*(5), 461–476. doi:10.1080/08911762.2010.521117

Ghiassi, M., Lio, D., & Moon, B. (2015). Pre-production forecasting of movie revenues with a dynamic artificial neural network. *Expert Systems with Applications*, *42*(6), 3176–3193. doi:10.1016/j.eswa.2014.11.022

Haughton, D., McLaughlin, M. D., Mentzer, K., & Zhang, C. (2015). *Movie Analytics: A Hollywood Introduction to Big Data*. Academic Press.

Joshi, A. (2015). Movie Stars and the Volatility of Movie Revenues. *Journal of Media Economics*, *28*(4), 246–267. doi:10.1080/08997764.2015.1094079

Kim, T., Hong, J., & Kang, P. (2015). Box office forecasting using machine learning algorithms based on SNS data. *International Journal of Forecasting*, *31*(2), 364–390. doi:10.1016/j.ijforecast.2014.05.006

Kim, T., Hong, J., & Koo, H. (2013). Forecasting box-office revenue by considering social network services in the Korean market. *Sains Humanika*, *64*(2), 97–101.

Kimes, S. E., & Chase, R. B. (1998). The strategic levers of yield management. *Journal of Service Research*, *1*(2), 156–166. doi:10.1177/109467059800100205

Kimes, S. E., Chase, R. B., Choi, S., Lee, P. Y., & Ngonzi, E. N. (1998). Restaurant revenue management applying yield management to the restaurant industry. *The Cornell Hotel and Restaurant Administration Quarterly*, *39*(3), 32–39. doi:10.1177/001088049803900308

Phillips, R. (2005). *Pricing and revenue optimization*. Stanford University Press.

Rezaei, J. (2015). Best-worst multi-criteria decision-making method. *Omega*, *53*, 49–57. doi:10.1016/j.omega.2014.11.009

Talluri, K. T., & Van Ryzin, G. J. (2006). *The theory and practice of revenue management* (Vol. 68). Springer Science & Business Media.

Yeoman, I., & McMahon-Beattie, U. (2004). *Revenue management and pricing: Case studies and applications*. Cengage Learning EMEA.

Zhang, L., Luo, J., & Yang, S. (2009). Forecasting box office revenue of movies with BP neural network. *Expert Systems with Applications*, *36*(3), 6580–6587. doi:10.1016/j.eswa.2008.07.064

Section 3

Consumer Analytics:

Multi-Criteria (MCDM) Applications and Sentiment Analysis

Chapter 9
Applications of the Stochastic Multicriteria Acceptability Analysis Method for Consumer Preference Study

Tadeusz Trzaskalik
University of Economics in Katowice, Poland

Andrzej Bajdak
University of Economics in Katowice, Poland

Piotr Namieciński
University of Lodz, Poland

Slawomir Jarek
University of Economics in Katowice, Poland

ABSTRACT

Introducing a new product to the market is a complex, costly and time-consuming process which requires research on consumer preferences. On the basis of information on the characteristics of the new product and its competitors, as well as on the competitors and their market shares, the company has to estimate future market shares and to determine the profile of potential consumers inclined to purchase the new product. The purpose of our paper is to present a method of consumer preference research when introducing a new product, using a multiple criteria method called Stochastic Multicriteria Acceptability Analysis (SMAA). To apply this method, no information requiring tedious research is needed. SMAA allows to obtain essential information on the potential market power of the new product already at an early stage of its preparation. Furthermore, the flexibility of the SMAA method allows to easily expand the scope of the analysis by including additional information and various techniques of the modeling of the consumer selection process.

INTRODUCTION

Planning to introduce a new product to the market is a complex, costly and time-consuming process. Already at the very beginning it is necessary to determine the appropriate goals and marketing strategies. A company has to answer the following questions: Should we modify an existing product or introduce an entirely new one? What features should the new product have to successfully compete for the market

DOI: 10.4018/978-1-5225-0997-4.ch009

share? What is the profile of the consumer who will be inclined to choose this particular product and what market share can we expect?

To effectively answer these questions, it is necessary to construct an appropriate market model. First, the company has to find out consumer preferences. Unfortunately, the necessary market research is time-consuming and costly.

It turns out, however, that we can approach this issue from a different point of view, using multicriteria Stochastic Multicriteria Acceptability Analysis (SMAA). We will show that on the basis of easily accessible data, related to the technical specifications of the product being introduced and to its potential competitors, as well as to the market shares of the existing products, it is possible to predict the division of the market and to characterize the potential buyers of each new product.

The purpose of the present paper is to present a method for researching consumer preferences when introducing a new product to the market, using a multiple criteria method called Stochastic Multicriteria Acceptability Analysis (SMAA).

The basic assumption of the method proposed is the restriction of the analysis to those goods whose purchase is preceded by a carefully thought-out decision. This means that prior to each purchase, customers gather detailed information on the products available and rationally choose the product which best satisfies their needs, taking into account many different evaluation criteria.

In the case of such goods the basic assumptions of the neoclassical theory of consumer choice remain valid. It is also possible to represent the decision making process using an arbitrary multiple criteria decision analysis (MCDA) method. This is in so far important as the SMAA method is very flexible and capable of being combined with an arbitrary model of consumer choice, provided the model allows to rank the selection alternatives. To facilitate the computations, we have assumed that consumers make their choices according to one of the most popular multiple criteria method, namely PROMETHEE II.

The first section of the paper constitutes an overview of basic issues of the theory of consumer choice and of the preference measuring techniques. Next, we present the theoretical foundations of the SMAA method in its classical approach as an MCDA method as well as those of the PROMEHEE II method. The next section is devoted to the presentation of our new method of researching consumer preferences and to the effects of introducing a new product to the market. Our method applies the approach which is used also in the SMAA and PROMEHEE II methods. Further in our paper we present an illustrative example which shows how our method is applied to a specific situation. Remarks on directions of future research, conclusions, and bibliography conclude the paper.

BACKGROUND

Consumer Preferences

The notion of preference can be represented as a mathematical relation. It has the following properties:

- The preference is transitive, that is, given three goods of which the first is better than the second, and the second better than the third, then it follows that the first good is also better than the third one;
- The preference is reflexive, that is, the same goods are evaluated in the same way;
- The preference is complete, that is, we can compare any two goods.

Using the preference relation we can compare and rank the goods analyzed. Each good has certain attributes or characteristics which can take on certain values. Further in the paper we will use them as decision criteria.

When constructing a consumer preference model we have to consider the approach to the criteria. Two types of models are distinguished: compensational and non-compensational. In compensational models a decrease of the value of one criterion can be compensated by an increase of the value of another one (Lilien, Kotler & Moorthy, 1992). In non-compensational models it is assumed that a decrease of the value of one criterion cannot be compensated by the values of other criteria. Moreover, criteria have certain threshold values, below which the goods are excluded from further analysis. Both types of models are shown in Figure 1.

Methods of Consumer Preference Research

The analysis of the premises underlying customers decisions is based on certain assumptions which follow directly from a certain direction of economic thought. The first concise and consistent system describing the process of economic management originated in the 18th century thanks to Adam Smith. This direction of economic thought is called "classical economics" in the literature. Its essential assumption is the rationality of the decisions of participants in the market. Since the customer decides to purchase a certain good, he/she does it to satisfy certain needs and to achieve personal profit, which is related to the increase of the welfare of the community in which he/she functions. An important role in the decision making process falls to the invisible hand of the market, which guarantees an optimal allocation of goods.

Figure 1. Models of consumer preferences
Source: Bąk (2004, p. 39) based on Zwerina (1997).

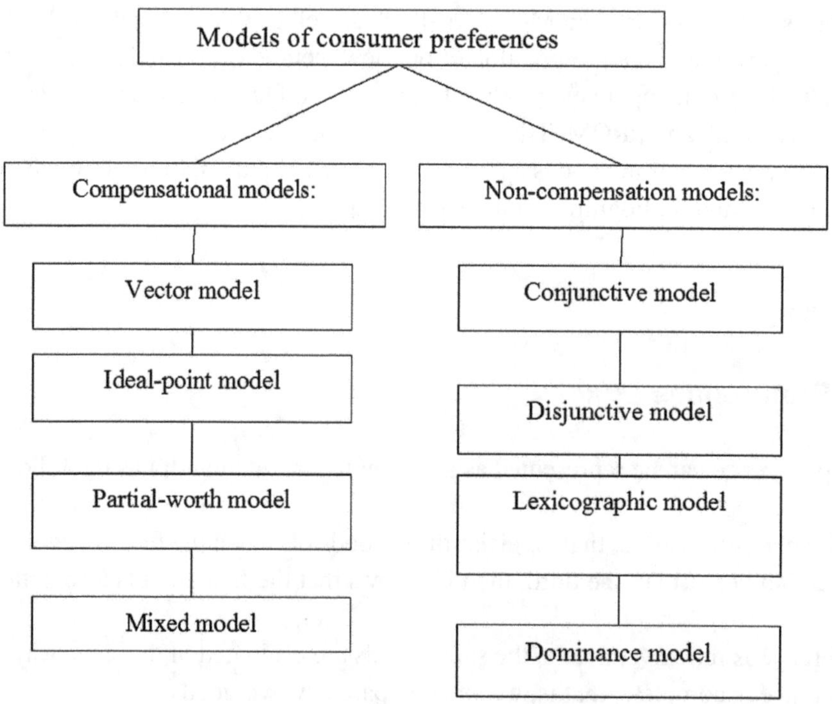

On the basis of the achievements of classical economics, supplemented by mathematical analysis, theories of marginal utility appeared, thus creating a new direction called neoclassical economics. In this theory, the following assumptions as to consumer decisions are made:

- The customer makes decisions which satisfy his/her needs (is not driven by the interest of other participants in the market);
- The customer's decisions are rational;
- The customer's preferences are consistent;
- The customer has complete information which applies to the decision making process;
- The customer can process the available information without limitations; and
- The customer's goal is to maximize the expected utility.

In the 20th century it was observed that customers do not always make decisions according to the assumptions of neoclassical economy. The main departure from these assumptions are limitations in the access to information necessary to make rational decisions, as well as an observed inconsistency of preferences. As a result, the same customer in the same situation can make different decisions related to the purchase of certain goods. Research on such behavior of the participants in the market led to a new direction, called behavioral economics. An important role in this direction falls to empirical utility and the theory of perspective (Tversky & Kahneman, 1979).

A problem that appears in the analysis of decision making by customers is measuring those factors which play a crucial role in this process. When purchasing a good, the customer tries to satisfy his/her needs. To take into account numerous limitations and expectations related to the fulfillment of customer needs, it becomes necessary to express his/her preferences numerically. One of the tools used to describe consumer preferences is the notion of utility. Utility is a measure which reflects the preferences of the customer. In the literature numerous utility theories have appeared, which attempt to explain consumer behavior.

- Ordinal utility theory,
- Cardinal utility theory:
  - Expected utility theory,
  - Axiomatic utility theory.
- Random utility theory, and
- Modern utility theory.

Each of these utility theories allows to read a value on a certain measurement scale. The first theory assumes that the goods being compared are elements of a discrete set. The only relation which can be defined is an ordering relation, hence this theory uses an ordinal scale.

The cardinal utility theory takes into account the possibility of measuring utility on an interval scale, on which not only the ordering of the goods analyzed can be determined, but it is also possible to give a meaning to the differences between the particular measurement values. Within this theory, two directions appeared: the expected utility theory and the axiomatic utility theory.

During the measurement certain factors can appear on which the customer has no influence or which she/he has not considered. In this situation, uncertainty and risk can occur in the decision making process, both of which can be related either to the measurement of the characteristics of the goods purchased or to the customer's preferences.

First, the customer may be unable to find out in detail all the characteristics of the goods he/she wants to purchase. This can be caused by a lack of information on the characteristics of the goods analyzed or else to the impossibility to find out all the values which characterize certain features of the product. Second, the customer is not always able to realize what his/her preferences are or else they can undergo a change due to certain factors. Because of this, a measurement-related uncertainty occurs.

If we know neither the character of the uncertainty nor the probability density function, such a situation is called measurement under uncertainty conditions. If the distribution of the quantity measured is given, we call this situation measurement under risk. This additional knowledge allows to apply certain methods of statistical data analysis. The above relationships are shown in Figure 2.

Measuring Consumer Preferences

We distinguish two kinds of measurement of consumer preferences. The first kind consist in researching historical data; it allows to decipher revealed preferences. The second kind allows to measure hypothetical consumer preferences, called stated preferences. It is useful in the introduction of a new product, when we do not have any historical data and have to estimate the necessary quantities.

When researching expressed preferences we can apply compositional, decompositional, and mixed methods. Measurement methods are illustrated in Figure 3.

In compositional methods vector models are used. The total score is the weighted sum of the attribute levels.

Decompositional methods use the conjoint analysis method and choice-based methods. Conjoint analysis methods are of the form:

- Metric and non-metric,
- Additive and with interactions,
- Linear and non-linear,
- With hidden classes.

Figure 2. Types of decision made under uncertainty and risk
Source: Bąk (2013, p. 17) based on Coombs,Dawes & Tversky (1970).

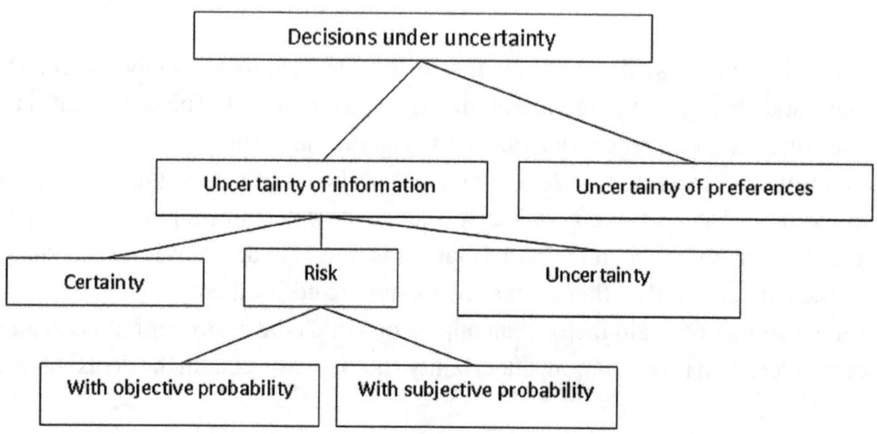

Figure 3. Measuring consumer preferences
Source: Bąk (2004, p. 42), Zwerina (1997, pp, 2-3).

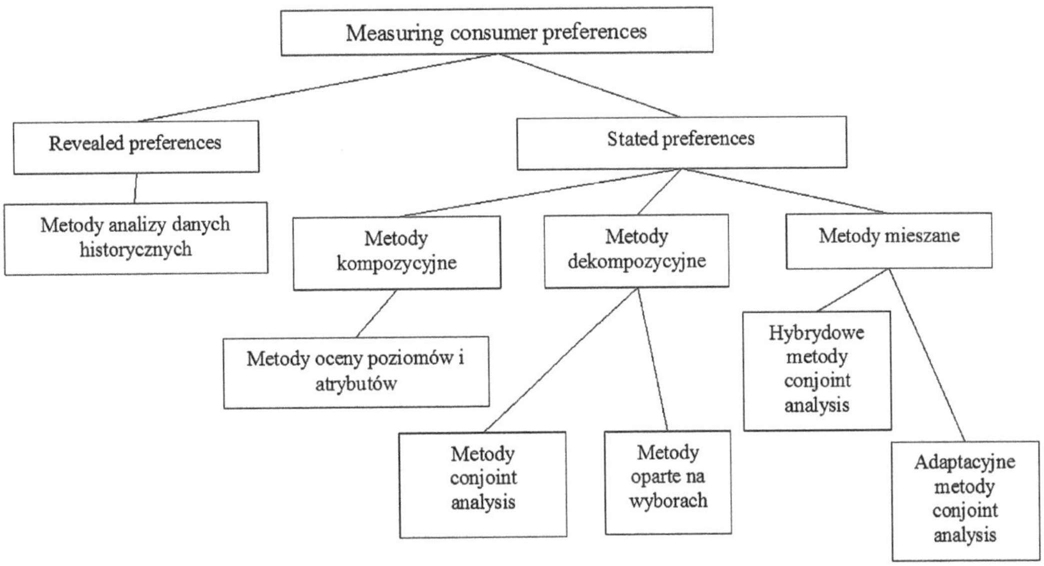

Methods based on choices uses the following models:

- Logit,
- Probit,
- With hidden classes, and
- With random parameters.

In decompositional methods, the analysis aims at the decomposition of the total scores into partial scores of the individual attributes and at estimating the weight coefficients which determine the influence of the given attribute on the total score.

In mixed models the compositional and decompositional approaches are combined. Two-stage procedures are applied. In the first stage, the values of the attributes and their weight coefficients are investigated; in the second one, the scores of the selected pairs or subsets of the goods under consideration.

Multiple Criteria Decision Making

In recent years, decision making processes in various disciplines are often extensively supported by multiple criteria models.

Consider the vector maximization problem, in which we want to maximize the values of all goals considered. These goals are usually conflicting, which means that improving the value of one criterion is done at the expense of decreasing the value of another one. It is therefore rare that a dominating solution exists, that is, one which is better than all the remaining solutions (with respect to all the goals considered simultaneously). If such a solution exists, we assume that it is a vector optimal solution.

If a dominating solution does not exist, then we regard it as sufficient to find non-dominating solutions, in which case we have to relinquish the requirement that all criteria functions occurring in the problem be simultaneously maximized. For such solutions no better solution exists, that is, it is not possible to improve the value of other criteria with having to decrease the value of at least one other criterion. Such solutions are called vector optimal solutions.

Solving a multiple criteria problem consist in finding the set of optimal solutions. While in single criterion problems very often only one optimal solution exists, in multiple criteria problems the set of optimal solutions is usually very large.

Thus an additional problem appears, that of selecting the solution which will be the basis for the final decision. When making the final choice, the decision maker takes into account his/her own preferences. Since the preferences of the individual decision makers often differ, one can expect that various decision makers will select various final solutions. However, to make the final decision it is usually not necessary to generate the set of all efficient solutions.

The final solution can be generated in many ways. We will discuss some of them when presenting multiple criteria models of consumer preferences.

The multiple criteria approach is used also when the decision maker has already determined a certain finite set of alternatives $Z = \{z^1, z^2, \ldots z^n\}$, from among which he/she wants to choose the alternative which best suits his/her preferences. The choice is based on the decision criteria $G = \{g_1(\bullet),\ldots,g_m(\bullet)\}$, indicated by the decision maker, and the methods applied are called discrete multiple criteria methods.

In the multiple criteria decision support process the analyst's task is to obtain from the decision maker the information which allows to determine how the decision maker evaluates the individual alternatives with respect to each criterion (partial utility functions $u_k(g_k(z^i))$). This information should also allow to define a synthetic measure which allows to aggregate these scores into a single function reflecting his/her preferences – that is, the corresponding global utility function. For this purpose, it is necessary to determine the relative importance for the decision maker of the individual criteria and the best form of the global utility function.

The importance of the individual criteria is typically determined by means of the weight vector $\boldsymbol{w} = [w_1,\ldots,w_k]$, which satisfies the following conditions:

$$\underset{k=1,\ldots,m}{\forall} w_k \geq 0, \sum_{i=1}^{m} w_k = 1$$

and the most frequently used form of the global utility function is the linear form:

$$u\left(z^i, \boldsymbol{w}\right) = \sum_{k=1}^{n} w_k u_k \left(g_k \left(z^i\right)\right)$$

In the remainder of the paper we present two multiple criteria methods: the classical PROMETHEE II method, and the SMAA method, which constitutes a basis for the proposed methodology of consumer preference research.

Multiple Criteria Models of Consumer Preferences

The multiple criteria approach is often applied to consumer preference modeling. Below we present the fundamental models used in practice, which are shown in Figure 1.

The Vector Model

For each good, we determine its total score. The consumer chooses the good with the highest total score. The total score O_{ik} of the ith good assigned by the kth customer can be expressed in the following form:

$$O_{ik} = \sum_{j=1}^{n} w_{jk} \cdot g_{ij}$$

Here n is the number of the criteria, w_{jk} is the weight reflecting the preferences of the kth customer with respect to the jth criterion of the good analyzed and g_{ij} is the value of the jth criterion for the ith good. To ensure the compatibility of the evaluations performed by various consumers, we assume that weights w_{jk} are normalized and their sum for the kth customer is 1:

$$\sum_{j=1}^{n} w_{jk} = 1$$

Moreover, since we do not want the total score to be dominated by the highest-valued criteria, the scores g_{ij}, can be normalized so that the lowest score for the ith good is 0, and the highest, 1.

The Ideal-Point Model

We assume that there exists a model good, described by model values of scores for the individual attributes. The customer chooses the good whose total score is closest to that of the model good. For this purpose we introduce a metric which allows to measure the distance of the score of the ith good from the ideal good:

$$O_{ik} = \left[\sum_{j=1}^{n} \left| g_{ij} - g_{kj}^{*} \right|^{p} \right]^{\frac{1}{p}}$$

In this formula $p \geq 1$ determines a particular form of the Minkowski distance. For $p = 1$ we obtain the taxicab distance, for $p = 2$ the Euclidean distance, and for $p \to \infty$ the Chebychev distance. The quantity g^*_{kj} is the value of the jth attribute of the ideal good for the kth customer.

The Partial-Worth Model

This model allows to determine the total score of the good analyzed on the basis of the utility functions of the individual attributes:

$$O_{ik} = \sum_{j=1}^{n} u_j \left(g_{ij}\right)$$

In this formula, u_j is the partial utility function of the jth attribute. To avoid the domination by the highest-valued attribute, the partial utility functions should be normalized to take values from the interval [0; 1].

Mixed Model

This model is a combination of the models described earlier. In particular, one can combine the vector model with the partial utility model to obtain the following form of the total score:

$$O_{ik} = \sum_{j=1}^{n} w_{jk} \cdot u_j \left(g_{ij}\right)$$

Conjunctive Model

Certain minimal values G_{kj} of the scores of the individual attributes are determined. The kth customer chooses the goods whose scores for all the attributes are at least at the threshold levels G_{kj}:

$$O_{ik} = \prod_{j=1}^{n} \delta_{ij}$$

In this formula, the coefficients δ_{ij} are defined as follows:

$$\delta_{ij} = \begin{cases} 1 & if\ g_{ij} \geq G_{kj} \\ 0 & otherwise \end{cases}$$

Disjunctive Model

This model differs from the conjunctive model in that the customer chooses the goods for which at least one attribute exceeds the threshold level G_{kj}:

$$O_{ik} = min\left\{\sum_{j=1}^{n} \delta_{ij}, 1\right\}$$

Lexicographic Model

Each consumer has a strict hierarchy of criteria. The good is chosen on the basis of the values of the highest-level criteria. If several goods have the same value of a higher-level criterion, the decision is made on the basis of the values of lower-level criteria.

Dominance Model

The consumer chooses a single most important criterion. The good chosen is that for which the score with respect to this attribute is highest.

MULTICRITERIA DECISION AID–SELECTED METHODS

Promethee II

The methods from the PROMETHEE family, created by J. P. Brans, are among the most frequently used multiple criteria decision aid methods, thanks to their simplicity and good mathematical properties. They have found applications in many fields, such as banking, water management, medicine, or chemistry, and have been described in many publications (Brans and Mareschal, 2005) (Bahzadian, Kazemzadeh, Albadvi i Aghdasi, 2010).

Next to the PROMETHEE I (partial ranking) and PROMETHEE II (complete ranking) methods, introduced in the early 1980s by J. P. Brans, methods such as PROMETHEE III (ranking based on intervals) and PROMETHEE IV (continuous case), PROMETHEE V (including segmentation constraints) and PROMETHEE VI (representation of the human brain) (Brans and Mareschal, 2005) have been created, as well and the EXPROM method, which allows to express preferences on a cardinal scale (Diakoulaki and Koumoutsos, 1991).

For the classical versions of PROMETHEE I and II solutions based on fuzzy numbers have been implemented (Goumas and Lygerou, 2000), as well as stochastic dominance (Nowak, 2005). A graphical module GAIA, supporting the analysis of the results of this method, has been also created (Mareschal and Brans, 1988).

The methods from this family use the idea of the outranking relation (Roy, 1974). To evaluate the individual alternatives, comparisons with respect to each criterion separately, mutual comparisons of all objects, and calculations of the differences r^k_{ij} are used.

$$r^k_{ij} = \begin{cases} g_k\left(z^i\right) - g_k\left(z^j\right) & when\ k^{th}\ criterion \to max \\ g_k\left(z^j\right) - g_k\left(z^i\right) & when\ k^{th}\ criterion \to min \end{cases}$$

The larger the difference in evaluation, the more preferred is one object over another. This does not have to be a linear relation. Moreover, small differences in the evaluation of the individual criteria may be of no importance for the decision maker. Additionally, it is important that the decision maker's preferences with respect to different criteria be comparable. For that reason, we assign an appropriate preference function $H^k(r^k_{ij})$ to each criterion.

The preference function has the following properties:

$$0 \leq H^k\left(r_{ij}^k\right) \leq 1$$

$$H^k\left(r_{ij}^k\right) > 0 \Rightarrow H^k\left(r_{ji}^k\right) = 0$$

We call the pair $\{g_k(\bullet),H^k(\bullet)\}$, consisting of a criterion and its corresponding preference function, a generalized criterion. In the PROMETHEE II method six types of preference functions are used, shown in Table 1.

Next, we calculate the multiple criteria preference indices π_{ij} from the formula:

$$\pi\left(z^i, z^j\right) = \sum_{k=1}^{n} w_k H^k\left(z^i, z^j\right)$$

The last step consists in the calculation of dominance flows for each alternative.

Positive (output) $\varphi^+(z^i)$:

$$\varphi^+\left(z^i\right) = \frac{1}{m-1}\sum_{x \in A} \pi\left(z^i, x\right)$$

negative (input) $\varphi^-(z^i)$:

$$\varphi^-\left(z^i\right) = \frac{1}{m-1}\sum_{x \in A} \pi\left(x, z^i\right)$$

and of net flows $\varphi(z^i)$:

$$\varphi\left(z^i\right) = \varphi^+\left(z^i\right) - \varphi^-\left(z^i\right)$$

The final ranking is obtained by sorting the objects in decreasing order by net dominance flow values. The object with the largest net dominance flow value best satisfies the decision maker's needs (Brans and Mareschal, 2005).

In 1988 B. Mareschal and J. P. Brans presented GAIA, a graphical module supporting the PROMETHEE method (Mareschal and Brans, 1988). Their approach was based on the decomposition of net flows according to the formula:

$$\varphi\left(z^i\right) = \sum_{k=1}^{n} w_k \varphi_k\left(z^i\right)$$

Table 1. Types of generalized criteria and their corresponding preference functions

Name of the Criterion	Preference Function	Parameters
Type I: Usual Criterion	$H^k\left(z^i,z^j\right)=\begin{cases}0 & if\ r_{ij}^k\le 0\\ 1 & if\ r_{ij}^k>0\end{cases}$	None
Type II: U-shape Criterion	$H^k\left(z^i,z^j\right)=\begin{cases}0 & if\ r_{ij}^k\le q_k\\ 1 & if\ r_{ij}^k>q_k\end{cases}$	q_k
Type III: V-shape Criterion	$H^k\left(z^i,z^j\right)=\begin{cases}0 & if\ r_{ij}^k\le 0\\ r_{ij}^k/p & if\ 0<r_{ij}^k\le p_k\\ 1 & if\ r_{ij}^k>p_k\end{cases}$	p_k
Type IV: Level Criterion	$H^k\left(z^i,z^j\right)=\begin{cases}0 & if\ r_{ij}^k\le q_k\\ 1/2 & if\ q_k<r_{ij}^k\le p_k\\ 1 & if\ r_{ij}^k>p_k\end{cases}$	q_k, p_k
Type V: V-shape with indifference Criterion	$H^k\left(z^i,z^j\right)=\begin{cases}0 & if\ r_{ij}^k\le q_k\\ \frac{\left(r_{ij}^k-q_k\right)}{\left(p_k-q_k\right)} & if\ q_k<r_{ij}^k\le p_k\\ 1 & if\ r_{ij}^k>p_k\end{cases}$	q_k, p_k
Type VI: Gaussian Criterion	$H^k\left(z^i,z^j\right)=\begin{cases}0 & r_{ij}^k\le 0\\ 1-exp\left(-\frac{\left(r_{ij}^k\right)^2}{2s^2}\right) & r_{ij}^k>0\end{cases}$	s_k

Source: Based on Brans & Mareschal (2005).

where $\varphi_k(z^i)$ are single criterion net flows calculated from the formula (Brans and Mareschal, 2005):

$$\varphi_k\left(z^i\right)=\frac{1}{m-1}\sum_{x\in A}\left[H^k\left(z^i,x\right)-H^k\left(x,z^i\right)\right]$$

This decomposition turns out to be very convenient for calculations under uncertainty, since the calculations are repeated many times, changing weights only or scores only for certain criteria. This is applied in the SMAA method, described below.

Stochastic Multiobjective Acceptability Analysis (SMAA)

One of the main disadvantages of the commonly used multiple criteria decision support methods is the necessity to determine the decision maker's preferences with respect to the criteria (the weight vector w) unambiguously. Often, the decision maker does not want or is not able to define his/her preferences precisely.

A good example of such a situation are social or community projects, in which the decision makers are a large group of scattered stakeholders. In such a case, it is not possible to reach each decision maker, and therefore to determine their preferences precisely. The situation does not improve if we can reach the politician who represents the interests of this group of stakeholders, because politicians are hardly ever willing to define their preferences precisely.

With such situations in view, the Stochastic Multiobjective Acceptability Analysis (SMAA) method has been worked out (Lahdelma, Hokkanen, & Salminen, 1998). This method allows to obtain additional information on the conditions under which the individual alternatives would be preferred, and this enables a single decision maker to choose a compromise solution. It also allows to take into account various types of uncertainty, related not only to the decision maker's preferences, but also to the scores $g_k(z^i)$ of the alternatives with respect to all the criteria. This method can be easily combined with other, classical multiple criteria methods of decision support, such as AHP, ELECTRE (Tervonen, Figueira, 2008) or the PROMETHEE method (Corrente, Figueira, & Greco, 2014), used in our paper.

The SMAA method is based on the idea of surveying the entire space W of admissible weights. In the case of a total lack of information on the decision maker's preferences regarding the importance of the criteria, we assume that the weight vector w comes from the multidimensional uniform distribution spanned over the space of admissible weights with the density function $f_W(w)$:

$$f_W(w) = 1/vol(W)$$

where

$$vol(W) = \int_W dw$$

The space W of admissible weights is defined in this case as:

$$w \in W, W = \left\{ w \in R^n : w_i \geq 0, \sum_{i=1}^{n} w_i = 1 \right\}$$

If we have additional information, the set of admissible weights is made smaller by the imposition of additional constraint conditions, such as the information that the kth criterion is more important than the jth one. In such a case, the set of admissible weights has the following form:

$$w \in W, W = \left\{ w \in R^n : w_i \geq 0, w_k \geq w_j, \sum_{i=1}^{n} w_i = 1 \right\}$$

An additional advantage of the SMAA method is that it can take into account a partial lack of information regarding the scores $g_k(z^i)$ of the alternatives. In such a situation deterministic scores are replaced by random variables ξ_{ik} with the joint multidimensional density function $f_\chi(\xi)$.

The goal of the SMAA method is to analyze the space W of admissible weights and to determine for which of its subsets the individual alternatives would be preferred. In other words, we have to find such a combination of weights w, for which the ith alternative has the largest value of the global utility function, as compared with all other alternatives. We call such a weight space a space of favorable weights W_i and we define:

$$W_i(\xi) = \left\{ w \in W : u(\xi_{i\bullet}, w) \geq u(\xi_{k\bullet}, w), \forall k = 1, \ldots, m \right\}$$

In the SMAA method we calculate three basic coefficients for each alternative: the acceptability index a_i, the central vector of favorable weights w_i^c and the certainty coefficient p_i^c.

The acceptability index a_i shows the size of the space W_i (the weights favoring the ith alternative) as the share of the weight space W. It is defined as a multidimensional integral of the form:

$$a_i = \frac{E\left(vol\left(W_i\right)\right)}{vol\left(W\right)} = \int_{\xi \in \chi} f_\chi(\xi) \int_{w \in W_i(\xi)} f_W(w)\, dw d\xi$$

The larger the value of this index, the larger the range of various weight combinations for which the given alternative is preferred. The value 0 means that the given alternative is dominated by the others. The value of the acceptability index can be therefore interpreted as the expected percentage of decision makers who prefer the given alternative.

To find out the weight combinations for which the ith alternative is preferred, we determine the central vector w_i^c of favorable weights as the expected center of the space of favorable weights:

$$w_i^c = \frac{1}{a_i} \int_{\xi \in \chi} f_\chi(\xi) \int_{w \in W_i(\xi)} f_W(w)\, w dw d\xi$$

This coefficient reflects the typical preferences of the decision maker which would select the ith alternative.

For numerical reasons all the coefficients of the SMAA method are calculated using Monte Carlo simulation. First, the weight vector w and random scores ξ of the alternatives are generated from the assumed distribution. On the basis of these values and the assumed global utility function a ranking of the alternatives is created.

This process is repeated K_w times, recording each time the weight vector and the highest-ranking alternative. On the basis of this information, the actual values of the central weight vectors w_i^c are calculated (as the mean of the weights) as well as the acceptability indices a_i (as the percentage of the wins of the given alternative among all the repetitions of the algorithm).

Given the central weight vector we can determine, in another simulation, the certainty coefficients p_i^c. To achieve this, first we generate random scores ξ of the alternatives. Next, for each alternative we check whether the ith alternative is still the winner in the ranking based on the randomly generated scores and the central weight vector for the ith alternative.

This procedure is repeated K_c times, and the certainty coefficient p_i^c is calculated as the percentage of the repetitions in which the winner of the ranking remains the same. A detailed description of the algorithms for both simulations can be found in (Tervonen, Lahdelma, 2007).

Since all the coefficients are calculated using simulation, the problem of accuracy of the results arises. In the case of the acceptability indices and the central weight vector the accuracy depends solely on the number K_w of repetitions of the first simulation. For the given acceptable measurement error d_b and the assumed confidence level a, the number K_w of necessary repetitions can be calculated from the formula:

$$K_w = \frac{u_\alpha^2}{4d_b^2}$$

where u_α is the distribution function of the standard normal distribution for the assumed confidence level.

Since in the calculation of the certainty coefficient we use the central vectors of favorable weights calculated previously, the number K_c of necessary repetitions is significantly greater and depends of the acceptability indices a_i (Tervonen, Lahdelma, 2007):

$$K_c = \frac{u_\alpha^2}{a_i 4d_b^2}$$

In the SMAA method, the form of the global utility function is not uniquely determined. Additionally, to calculate all the coefficients we need only to determine the ranking of the alternatives. Therefore, it is possible to combine the SMAA method with an arbitrary MCDA ranking method. So far, the following combinations of methods have been presented in the literature: with AHP (Durbach, Lahdelma & Salminen, 2014), with PROMETHEE (Corrente et al., 2014), with ELECTRE (Tervonen, Figueira, Lahdelma & Salminen 2004; Tervonen & Figueira 2008) and with TOPSIS (Okul, Gencer & Aydogan, 2014).

CONSUMER PREFERENCE STUDY

General Characteristics of the Problem

We consider a market of goods to be purchased and customers who approach the purchase rationally. Prior to each purchase, the customers gather detailed information on the products and rationally choose the product which best satisfies their needs. This is therefore a classical discrete multiple criteria problem, such as is handled by multiple criteria decision support methods.

In such a situation we can assume that the customers, prior to making their choices, will not only analyze thoroughly the available alternatives and will consider several criteria, but also that they will apply multiple criteria decision support methods, in particular PROMETHEE II. Their purchase decisions will then be based on the ranking of the products obtained from the multiple criteria method selected. Since there are many customers on the market with different preferences with respect to the criteria, they will select different products. In general, we will analyze a situation where the same decision problem will be solved many times by various decision makers.

The SMAA method is applied to problems which can be described as decision problems approached only once, jointly by many decision makers. It is, however, easy to find an analogy between this situation and the marketing situation presented above. In both cases there are many decision makers with various preferences who encounter an identical decision problem. The only difference consists in that in the classical MCDA problem the decision is made jointly, on the basis of an analysis, while in the marketing case the decisions are made many times by each decision maker individually.

In the former case the subject of the analysis is the set of stakeholders, while in the latter, the market under investigation. The calculations of the SMAA method are identical in both cases; the only difference would be in the interpretation of the coefficients obtained. In the marketing case, the central weight vector would not identify the typical preferences of the decision maker, but would constitute the profile of the customers who select the given product. The acceptability index would not refer to the expected percentage of customers who prefer the given alternative, but could be interpreted as the market share of the given product. To make this possible, however, the random choice of the weights in the SMAA calculations would have to be based on the actual distribution of customer market preferences.

The description of the algorithm for the application of the SMAA method in consumer preference research

Step 1: Determine a finite list of products or services to be selected and a list of criteria to be considered by the customers.

Step 2: Perform the SMAA analysis, assuming that the weight vector is chosen randomly from a multidimensional uniform distribution, and the set of decision alternatives is limited to the products present on the market.

Step 3: By comparing the actual market shares of the individual products with the acceptability indices obtained in Step 2, estimate the parameters of the actual weight distribution in the customer population.

Step 4: Perform the SMAA analysis, by randomly selecting weights from the actual weight distribution and extending the set of alternatives by the products analyzed.

To obtain appropriate results it is crucial to appropriately formulate the multiple criteria decision problem corresponding to the market segment under consideration. The number of products analyzed should be as large as possible. One should keep in mind, however, that it is exactly the selection of products that defines the analyzed market segment. If we select too many products for our analysis, we will have to determine an appropriately large set of criteria so as to reflect the actual diversity of the customers.

Too small a number of criteria brings much more adverse effects. If we do not take into account all the criteria considered by the consumers, the acceptability indices for some products will be 0. This would mean that these products are dominated and no rationally behaving customer would choose them. In this case we should expand the set of criteria and repeat the calculations.

For this reason, it is very important to perform a preliminary analysis in Step 2. This analysis will allow to identify potential errors in the specification of our multiple criteria decision problem. Second, in this step central weight vectors are calculated which should be interpreted as average profiles of the customers who select the given product. Third, the results obtained constitute a basis for further calculations in Step 3.

The estimation of the actual weight distribution is not simple. This problem is inverse to the problem of computing the acceptability indices, which are calculated from the formula:

$$a_i = \int_{\xi \in \chi} f_\chi(\xi) \int_{w \in W_i(\xi)} f_W(w)\, dw d\xi$$

Therefore, we have to find $f_\chi(\xi)$ and $f_W(w)$ which minimize the difference between a_i and the actual market shares. The situation is made more difficult by the fact that in the stochastic case – when the scores of the criteria are also regarded as random variables with an unknown distribution – these scores influence the form of the set of favorable weights. Therefore, some parameters being estimated are within the limits of the integral. In the simpler, deterministic case when we assume that all the scores of the alternatives are evaluated in the same way by the customers, according to the their technical parameters, the problem is much simpler, and the acceptability index can be calculated from the formula:

$$a_i = \int_{w \in W_i} f_W(w)\, dw$$

This is still a cumbersome approach, but solutions of this problem can be found in the literature. Berry, Levinsohn and Pakes (1995) estimate the parameters of a population distribution in an analogous problem of preference research. In their approach, however, it is necessary to supply detailed information about the individual transactions, while in the approach proposed here it is sufficient to know the market shares.

It turns out that it is not necessary to know exactly the actual weight distribution $f_w(w)$; it suffices to be able to map this distribution when randomly selecting the weights in Step 4. To do this, we modify the computational algorithm of SMAA used in Step 2. In the algorithm proposed by Tervonen and Lahdelma (2007), the central weight vector is calculated immediately by summing the weight vectors (when the given alternative won the ranking) and then by dividing this sum by the number of wins in the ranking of the given alternative. In the modification suggested the outcome of the algorithm is given not in the form of central weight vectors only, but as an entire table containing the values of the weight vector for the given repetition and the alternative which won in this repetition. With the computational capabilities of modern computers, an extension of the algorithm by recording the values of such a variable does not present any difficulty. For the case of 10,000 repetitions, the size of the variable storing the values of all randomly selected weights and the name of the alternative winning the given repetition is approx. 860 Kb.

The weight table thus obtained is the basis for the random selection of weights in Step 4. In this case, the weights are selected in two stages. First, one alternative is selected randomly, with the probability equal to its market share. Next, one vector, favoring this alternative, is selected randomly from the weight table obtained in Step 2. Each vector is selected with the same probability. Thus it is possible to map the actual weight distribution in the population; this distribution results in the acceptability indices equal to market shares.

Illustrative Example

We consider a market with goods to be purchased and customers approaching their purchases rationally. Prior to each purchase, the customers gather detailed information on the products and rationally select the product which satisfies their needs best. In such a situation many criteria are taken into account – sometimes a very large number.

To simplify the problem and to present the results graphically, we limited the number of criteria to three. Since the criteria used by the consumers can be divided into three categories: price, quality, and availability of the given good, we assumed in this example that these three criteria are taken into account by the consumers.

In our example we have a company that wants to obtain information on the expected future market shares of two new products to be introduced. The company has two new products, N1 and N2. Three variants of their introduction are considered: product N1 only, product N2 only, both products N1 and N2 at once.

Since the products are expensive, we can assume that the consumers will make carefully thought-out decisions, using the PROMETHEE II method.

Step 1: Define the multiple criteria problem describing the market investigated.

We consider the problem of the potential market position of the newly introduced products. Currently, five offers are already on the market: A, B, C, D, and E. Experience shows that products on this market are evaluated with respect to three criteria: price (in $), service completion time (in days), and product quality (on the scale 1-5, published by a trade magazine). The values of the criteria and the current market shares of each product are presented in Table 2.

Step 2: Preliminary analysis using SMAA.

Knowing the data from Table 2, we construct the discrete multiple criteria problem for the products already present on the market and calculate their SMAA coefficients. Since we assume that all the consumers have access to data from Table 2 and interpret them in the same way, all the scores of the alternatives should be regarded as deterministic values. Therefore, it is not necessary to calculate the certainty coefficients. The calculated values of the acceptability indices and the central weight vectors are shown in Table 3.

Table 2. Input data for the illustrative example

	Price	Time	Quality	Share
Product A	510	54	4.01	49.50%
Product B	1589	88	9.19	24.00%
Product C	1749	95	9.75	9.90%
Product D	459	95	4.54	8.90%
Product E	1789	140	10.9	7.70%
Product N1	909	65	6.2	
Product N2	1039	65	6.75	

Table 3. Values of the SMAA coefficients calculated in Step 2

	a_i	Central Weight Vector		
		Price	**Time**	**Quality**
Product A	0.660	0.391	0.407	0.201
Product B	0.087	0.163	0.355	0.482
Product C	0.133	0.139	0.211	0.650
Product D	0.035	0.707	0.018	0.275
Product E	0.086	0.217	0.048	0.735

Step 3: Estimation of the actual distribution of weights in the population.

According to the scheme proposed, the actual weight distribution is simulated by a two-stage random selection from the weight table obtained in Step 2. Figure 4 contain the randomly selected weights of each product.

Step 4: Calculating the forecast market shares.

In three separate simulations we have tested how the shares of the individual products (those already present on the market and the ones newly introduced) will change. In the first case, the set of products consisted of A through E and N1 (see Figure 5). In the second simulation, we replaced N1 by N2 (see Figure 6). In the last simulation we assumed that both N1 and N2 are introduced (see Figure 7), and therefore the calculations have been performed for seven products (A through E, N1 and N2). The weights were chosen at random according to the selection scheme from the actual

Figure 4. Weights favoring the consecutive alternatives
Source: Author's own elaboration.

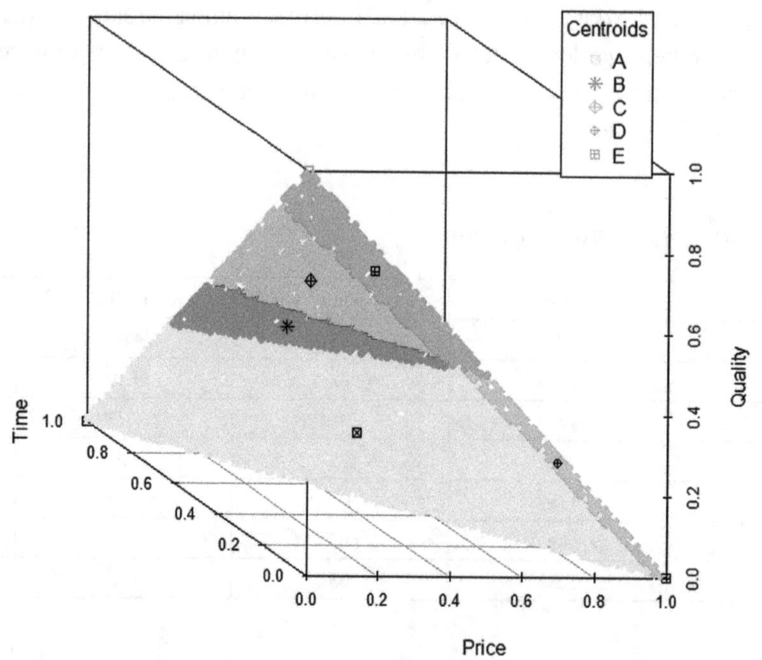

Figure 5. Weights favoring the consecutive alternatives
Source: Author's own elaboration.

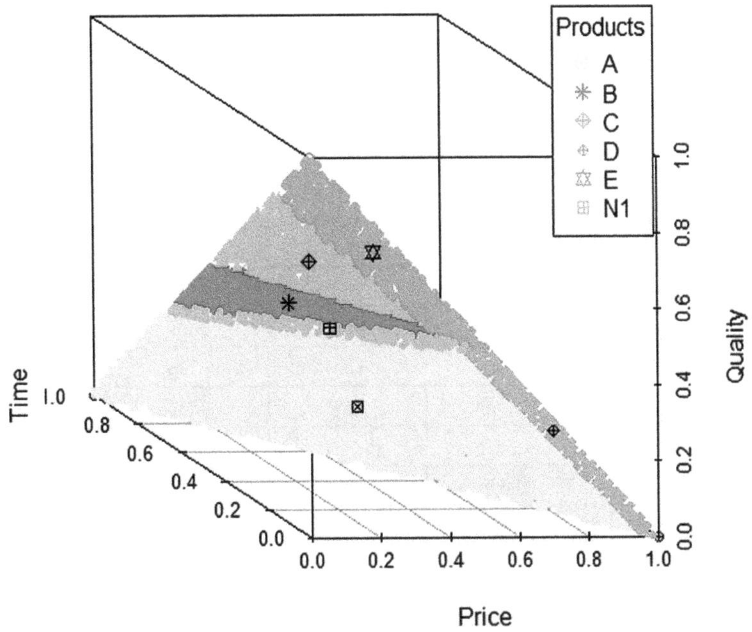

Figure 6. Weights favoring the consecutive alternatives
Source: Author's own elaboration.

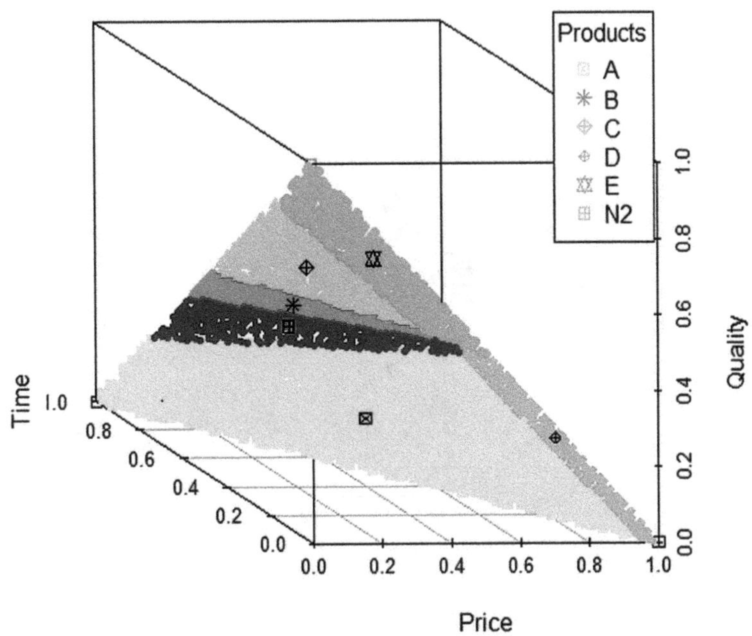

distribution. Table 4 presents the acceptability coefficients obtained, that is, the expected market shares (fms), and the change as compared with the actual market shares before the introduction of the new products (Δms).

Central weight vectors for the three variants of the introduction of the new products to the market are shown in Table 5.

Table 4. Forecast shares and the expected change in shares after the introduction of the new products

	N1		N2		N1&N2	
	fms	Δms	Fms	Δms	fms	Δms
Product A	46.26%	-3.24pp	43.33%	-6.17pp	41.19%	-8.31pp
Product B	22.01%	-1.99pp	15.57%	-8.43pp	17.91%	-6.09pp
Product C	8.45%	-1.45pp	8.67%	-1.23pp	7.70%	-2.20pp
Product D	9.84%	0.94pp	9.87%	0.97pp	10.38%	1.48pp
Product E	8.61%	0.91pp	9.45%	1.75pp	9.71%	2.01pp
Product N1	4.83%		-		0.61%	
Product N2	-		13.11%		12.50%	

Figure 7. Weights favoring the consecutive alternatives
Source: Author's own elaboration

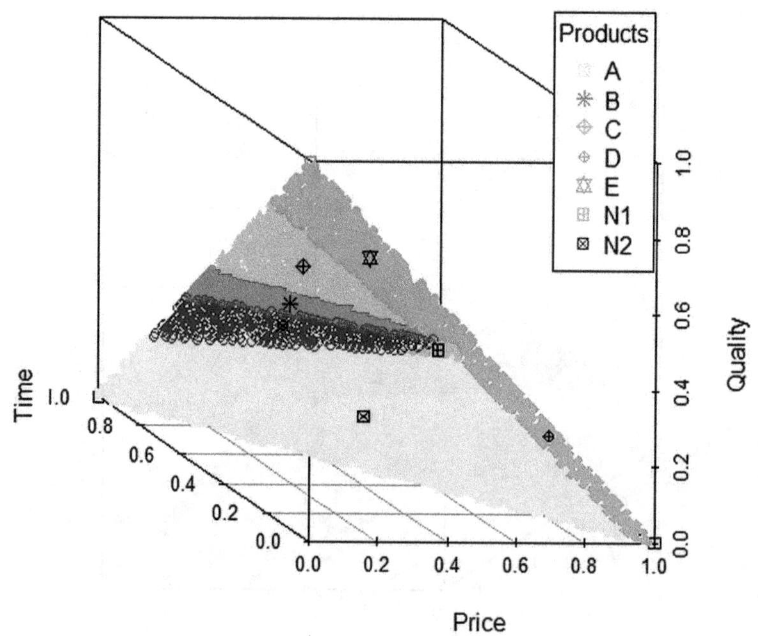

Table 5. Central weight vectors for the introduction of the new products to the market

	N1			N2			N1 & N2		
	Price	Time	Quality	Price	Time	Quality	Price	Time	Quality
Product A	0.393	0.421	0.186	0.410	0.413	0.177	0.405	0.420	0.175
Product B	0.156	0.360	0.484	0.157	0.343	0.500	0.155	0.349	0.496
Product C	0.133	0.221	0.646	0.123	0.236	0.641	0.123	0.240	0.638
Product D	0.710	0.019	0.271	0.705	0.020	0.275	0.708	0.021	0.271
Product E	0.213	0.056	0.731	0.210	0.059	0.731	0.205	0.065	0.731
Product N1	0.255	0.311	0.433				0.429	0.109	0.462
Product N2				0.172	0.408	0.420	0.173	0.415	0.412

DISCUSSION

Analysis clearly shows that the most cost-effective solution for our company is the introduction of product N2. If it is introduced on its own, its market share can be as much as 13.11%. If both products N1 and N2 are introduced simultaneously, the market share of our company will be also 13.11%, but it will be split between N1 and N2, with shares equal to 0.61% and 12.50%, respectively.

Introducing new products will harm products A and B most. If N2 is introduced, the two products will lose between 6% and more than 8% of the market. The losses of product C are small: at most 1.5% of the market. An interesting phenomenon can be observed in the case of products D and E: the introduction of new products increases their competitive power.

This phenomenon can be interpreted in many ways. The most likely cause is that the results are affected by the properties of the PROMETHEE method or by the method of random selection of the weight vectors. Such a situation can, however, occur in reality and is explained in behavioral economics as the effect of cognitive dissonance.

The average weight vector characterizing the average consumer on the market in question can be easily calculated by aggregating data from Step 2 and market shares. This vector is of the form $w^p = [0.246; 0.330; 0.424]$ when the criteria are: price, availability, quality. This means that the average consumer pays most attention to quality (as much as 42% of the score depends on this criterion), less to the fulfillment time (33% of the score), and least to price (only 25% of the score, that is, 8% less than if all three criteria were equally important).

Closest to such a customer profile is the buyer of product B, except that the average consumer choosing this product pays half as much attention to price as the average consumer at large. A similar criteria hierarchy is exhibited by the average buyer of product C. In this case, however, the difference in the criteria importance, quality, and fulfillment time is significantly greater. For this customer, quality constitutes as much as 65% of the total score of the product.

The most balanced as regards preferences is the average buyer of product A. For this customer, price and time are practically equally important, and they constitute 40% each of the total product score. Buyers of products D and E are least balanced as regards the importance of the individual criteria. In each case, one criterion contributes over 70% of the total product score. For the average buyer of product D this criterion is price; of product E, quality.

Analysis of central weight vectors obtained for the new products shows that the profile of the customer selecting product N1 is closest to the profile of the average customer at large. The low value of the acceptability index obtained for this product in the first experiment shows that this group of customers is very small. On the other hand, customers selecting product N2 are closest to the profile of the average buyer of product B. Therefore, N2 will compete mainly with B.

A comparison of the profiles of buyers of products N1 and N2 indicates that these two products are mutually very competitive, but the situation of N2 is much better. When both new products are available, the buyers of N1 are those customers who focus on price much more than on fulfillment time as compared with the situation where N2 is not available.

To compare the effectiveness of the procedure of random weight selection from the actual distribution proposed here, an additional SMAA analysis has been performed. When selecting the weights from the actual distribution, SMAA analysis was performed for products A through E only. The acceptability indices thus obtained were compared with the actual market shares. According to the assumptions, these values should be identical. To measure the calculation error, the forecast error has been calculated by means of MAPE:

$$MAPE = \sum \sqrt{\frac{\left(ms_i - a'_i\right)^2}{ms_i}} \cdot 100\%$$

where ms_i is the market share of the *i*th product, and a'_i is the acceptability index calculated for the problem which tests the accuracy of the method of generating weights from the actual distribution.

It turned out that the acceptability indices thus obtained were only slightly different from the actual market shares: MAPE was only 0.18%.

FUTURE RESEARCH DIRECTIONS

A serious difficulty in the method proposed is an appropriate formulation of the multiple criteria decision problem reflecting the market segment in question. The selection of criteria causes particularly many difficulties. Appropriate statistical tests which would allow to verify the statistical significance of each criterion would be a very useful tool. Another very useful tool would be an analytic method for determining the actual weight distribution in the customer population. The solution currently used allows to omit this difficulty by generating weights from the expected weight distribution in the population. Knowing the actual distribution would allow to select the weight in Step 4 more accurately, and therefore, to obtain more accurate forecast results. Finding an appropriate method of estimation would also allow to find methods of criteria selection for our problem. The BLP model, proposed by Berry, Levinsohn and Pakes (1995) seems the best tool for this purpose. The starting point in their model is the market share function, identical with the formula for the acceptability index in the SMAA method. Unfortunately, to estimate the parameters of the BLP model, it is necessary to use additional information on each consumer separately, which makes the application of this technique very difficult.

Extending the analysis by subjective criteria is an additional issue. An example of such a criterion is the importance of the brand or the aesthetics of the product. In such a situation the evaluation of the individual alternatives with respect to such a criterion would vary from consumer to consumer. The SMAA method handles such issues without problems; one would need to know, however, the distribution of these scores in the consumer population. The estimation of the parameters of such a distribution, let alone of its shape, would cause significant difficulties and it seems that only other external research would allow to obtain such information.

Further research should concentrate on these problems and on testing of possible solutions.

CONCLUSION

At the preliminary stage of work on a new product, when many possible ideas are considered, a preliminary analysis allows to select the most promising variants, which should be further investigated. At this stage of research we need a simple and inexpensive tool which would allow to estimate the possible future market shares, as well as the best directions of the development of new products. The SMAA method seems to satisfy these requirements very well, and, additionally, it allows to characterize the potential target group.

REFERENCES

Bahzadian, M., Kazemzadeh, R. B., Albadvi, A., & Aghdasi, M. (2010). PROMETHEE: A comprehensive literature review on methodologies and applications. European Journal of Operational Research, (200), 198-215. doi:10.1016/j.ejor.2009.01.021

Bąk A. (2004). *Dekompozycyjne metody pomiaru preferencji w badaniach marketingowych*. Wrocław, Poland: Wydawnictwo Akademii Ekonomicznej im. Oskara Langego we Wrocławiu.

Bąk, A. (2013). *Mikroekonometryczne metody badania preferencji konsumentów z wykorzytsaniem programu R*. Warszawa, Poland: Wydawnictwo C.H. Beck.

Berry, S., Levinsohn, J., & Pakes, A. (1995). Automobile prices in market equlibrium. *Econometrica*, *63*(4), 841–890. doi:10.2307/2171802

Brans, J. P., & Mareschal, B. (2005). PROMETHEE methods. In J. Figueira, S. Greco, & M. Ehrgott (Eds.), *Multiple Criteria Decision Analysis. State of Art Surveys* (pp. 163–196). Boston: Springer.

Coombs, C. H., Dawes, R. M., & Tversky, A. (1970). *An Elementary Introduction. Mathematical Psychology*. Englewood Cliffs, NJ: Prentice-Hall, Inc.

Diakoulaki, D., & Koumoutsos, N. (1991). Cardinal Ranking of Alternative Actions: Extension of the PROMETHEE Method. *European Journal of Operational Research,* (53).

Goumas, M., & Lygerou, V. (2000). An extension of the PROMETHEE method for decision making in fuzzy environment: Ranking of alternative energy exploitation projects. *European Journal of Operational Research*, *123*(3), 606–613. doi:10.1016/S0377-2217(99)00093-4

Lahdelma, R., Miettinen, K., & Salminen, P. (2003). Ordinal criteria in stochastic multicriteria acceptability analysis (SMAA). *European Journal of Operational Research, 147*(1), 117–127. doi:10.1016/S0377-2217(02)00267-9

Lahdelma, R., & Salminen, P. (2001). SMAA-2: Stochastic multicriteria acceptability analysis for group decision making. *Operations Research, 49*(3), 444–454. doi:10.1287/opre.49.3.444.11220

Lilien, G. L., Kotler, P., & Moorthy, S. K. (1992). *Marketing Models*. Englewood Cliffs, NJ: Prentice-Hall, Inc.

Mareschal, B., & Brans, J.-P. (1988). Geometrical representation for MCDA. The GAIA module. *European Journal of Operational Research*, (33), 54–64. doi:10.1016/0377-2217(88)90254-8

Nowak, M. (2005). Investment Project Evaluation by Simulation and Multiple Criteria Decision Aiding Procedure. *Journal of Civil Engineering and Management,* (11), 193-202.

Roy, B. (1990). *Wielokryterialne wspomaganie decyzji*. Warszawa: Wydawnictwo Naukowo-Techniczne.

Tervonen, T., & Lahdelma, R. (2007). Implementing stochastic multicriteria acceptability analysis. *European Journal of Operational Research, 178*(2), 500–513. doi:10.1016/j.ejor.2005.12.037

Tversky, A., & Kahneman, D. (1979). Prospect Theory: An Analysis of Decision under Risk. *Econometrica, 47*(2), 263–291. doi:10.2307/1914185

Zwerina, K. (1997). *Discrete Choice Experiments in Marketing*. Heidelberg, Germany: Physica-Verlag. doi:10.1007/978-3-642-50013-8

Chapter 10
Modeling Consumer Opinion Using RIDIT and Grey Relational Analysis

Rohit Vishal Kumar
Xavier Institute of Social Service, India

Subhajit Bhattacharyya
Xavier Institute of Social Service, India

ABSTRACT

In order to understand consumers, researchers are forced to gather primary data on Likert scale. Such data is usually considered as ordinal or at best interval scaled data. One key requirement in research is to identify components which have high individual contribution to understanding the research problem. Hence the concept of ranking of the components comes under consideration. Most of the ranking techniques are based on simplistic mean ranks or overtly complicated methods. In this chapter the authors highlight two techniques - Grey Relational Analysis (GRA) and RIDIT - for the purpose. In this chapter the authors explain the techniques of the two methods and then try to show the simplicity and efficiency of GRA and RIDIT algorithms in analyzing a commonly available dataset. The outcome of the GRA and RIDIT analysis is also compared with the commonly used techniques and the authors would examine if GRA and RIDIT does a better job at ranking data than the commonly used techniques.

INTRODUCTION

In order to understand consumers and consumer behavior, researchers are forced to gather primary data on the consumer assertiveness, interest perceptions, behavioral changes, intentions, and knowledge. These types of information are frequently measured by Likert scale (Fink, 1995; Fink & Kosecoff, 1998; Peterson, 2000). Likert scaling assumes the existence of latent or continuous variable whose value characterizes the respondents' attitudes and opinions (Clason & Dormody, 1994). Though there is some criticism of Likert scale being used because of its subjective nature, still it is one of the most popular and frequently used measurement scales in the field of consumer research and social sciences as well.

DOI: 10.4018/978-1-5225-0997-4.ch010

Data gathered from Likert scale survey is usually considered as ordinal or at best interval scaled data (Clason & Dormody, 1994; Green, Tull, & Albaum, 1997).

One key requirement in consumer research is to identify components which have high individual contribution to understanding the research problem. Here the concept of ranking of the components comes under consideration. Commonly used statistical methods for Likert scale data analysis in the domain of social science researches are frequency tabulations, means, standard deviations, t-tests, chi square tests, correlation coefficients, factor analysis, cluster analysis and multivariate techniques etc (Clason & Dormody, 1994; Neter, Wasserman, & Whitmore, 1992). However, these techniques or approaches are not appropriate for measuring or ordering scale items or components in an ascending or in a descending order on the basis of priority. Most of the statistical ranking or ordering techniques is based either on simple mean ranks which can be affected by presence of skewed data. In case of factor analysis the objective it to group the number of scales into a smaller (artificially created) subsets-which, more often than not-are hypothetical in nature. The reduced scales so created are difficult to implement in the real world and the artificiality makes it difficult to work with. More so, both factor analysis and cluster analysis are highly sensitive to variable selection and different choices of variables may produce different results. To counter the problem of ranking of items in ascending or descending order two other techniques – Grey Relational Analysis (GRA) and RIDIT can be used.

The chapter would be divided in to the following sections – *section II* would deal with brief review of literature; *section III* would deal with the steps of conducting the RIDIT analysis, *section IV* would deal with the steps of Grey Relational Analysis. *Section V* deals with analysis of a common dataset under RIDIT and Grey Relational Analysis. *Section VI* reports the results of a small simulation exercise and the *section VII* deals issues with conclusion and recommendations. It is hoped that this would provide our researchers a couple of a more techniques to get better insight into the minds of the consumers.

REVIEW OF LITERATURE

In 1958, Irwin D. J. Bross had propounded the use of RIDIT ("Relative to an Identified Distribution") analysis for dealing with ordinal variables. Ordinal variables can be subjective scales such as – severe, moderate, or minor – or may take a numerical form. The measurement system relies heavily on the skills of the researcher involved in the measurement of the variable. According to Bross, these variables may not be adequately analyzed by Chi Square and t-test as they may not be appropriate due to assumption of a parametric distribution used by the test. (Bross, 1958). RIDIT calculates the probability that a given observation is better than a visible observation from a reference distribution. The outcomes from the RIDIT analysis can be used to arrange Likert scale items either in an ascending or in a descending order based on importance. This can also examine the relations among scale items in terms of degrees of significance or agreement. RIDIT approach is "distribution free" in nature, because there is no need of assumption about the distribution of the population under the study (Bross, 1958; Fleiss, Levin, & Paik, 2003).

RIDIT analysis has been comparatively less used in literature because of the complexity of interpreting the results. There seems to be two distinctive trends in the development of RIDIT literature. On one hand there are papers which have tried to improve the RIDIT analysis and remove its inherent shortcomings; while on the other there are papers which directly use the technique in analysis. In 1974, Jairus D. Flora Jr (1974), working at University of Michigan, published a technical work circulated to the Motor Vehicle

Manufacturer Organization of USA in which she pointed out that the problem with RIDIT analysis. She showed that the choice of reference population can lead to rejection or selection of null hypothesis that the two populations (reference and comparison) are equivalent or not. This is because the choice of reference population impacts the calculation of standard deviation used in the denominator for testing of hypothesis. Similarly other researchers had compared RIDIT to quantile ranks (Kantor, Winkelstein, & Ibrahim, 1968; Selvin, 1977). WJ Conover (1973) noticed similarities between RIDIT analysis and the Wilcoxon Rank Sum Test. Some researchers compared Raw, RIDIT, Normal Median and Normal Mean scoring methods and found that RIDIT scoring methods perform better than the Normal Mean and Raw scoring system. He also showed that under assumption of a uniform distribution, RIDIT scoring became the optimal scoring system (Brockett, 1981). The work on RIDIT analysis continues with other researcher contributing to the development of RIDIT in recent times (Oyeka, 1992; Uwawunkonye & Anaene, 2013)

The initial use of RIDIT analysis was in the field of epidemiology where it received a lot of attention (Dhillon, Goldstein, & Schiffman, 1978; Forthofer & Koch, 1973; Williams & Grizzle, 1972). Subsequently there was a lull in the usage of the technique as other techniques were developed. But use of RIDIT has been seen sporadically in some places. It was used to study atmospheric visibility in Britain (Craig & Faulkenberry, 1979; Doyle & Dorling, 2002). Robert D Lieberthal (2008) used a modified form of RIDIT analysis to Hospital Quality. The modification was that in the first step the RIDIT scores were calculated and in the second step the principal component analysis approach was used on RIDIT scores to extract factors for analysis. This approach – termed as PRIDIT approach – is gaining currency amongst researchers. In the Indian context, a renewed interest in RIDIT seems to be developing since 2008 when it was used to measure service quality indicators in education (Pradhan, 2008). In another study, the RIDIT analysis along with Grey Relational Analysis was used to evaluate the factors which influenced the purchase of NANO cars in the Indian markets (Bikash, Pravat, & Sreekumar, 2010). RIDIT approach has also been used to prioritize agribusiness issues in the Indian scenario (Panda & Sreekumar, 2012). In another work, Mahapatra and Sreekumar (2012) have used RIDIT analysis to identify the importance of factors which influence online shopping behavior. Mohanty and Gahan (2012) have used RIDIT analysis to understand the Buyer Supplier Relationship in the manufacturing sector in India. Similarly RIDIT analysis along with Grey Relational Analysis has been used to understand the importance of attributes for apparel buying amongst teenaged buyers in Lucknow region of India (Kaushal, 2013).

Grey Relational Analysis (GRA) was introduced in 1982 and the term grey refers to "incomplete" or "hazy" information. It believes that a situation with *no information* is "black" where as a situation with *full information* is "white". However as none of these situation occurs in real world – situations between these two is described as "grey". The GRA does not attempt to find the best solution but provide techniques for determining a good solution. Grey Relational Analysis was first propounded by Julong Deng in 1982 in People Republic of China (Deng, 1982). It was quickly picked up by Chinese scientist and software scientist and by 1989 was being used in variety of disciplines viz. –agriculture, ecology, economy meteorology, medicine, history, geography, industry, earthquake, geology, hydrology irrigation, strategy, military affairs, sports, traffic, management, material science, environment, biological protection, judicial system etc. (Deng, 1989). A detailed review of Grey Analysis is not provided because of the plethora of literature available on the subject. Interested readers can see the papers by Deng (1989) and by (Liu & Forrest, 2007) for a comprehensive coverage of development and usage of Grey Systems Theory.

Given the growing popularity of Grey Relational Analysis and RIDIT analysis it is hoped that this write-up would provide an impetus to Indian research scholars to take up further work in the subject.

In the next section the techniques of the two methods are explained and then try to show the simplicity and efficiency of GRA and RIDIT algorithms in analyzing a publicly available dataset.

STEPS OF RIDIT ANALYSIS

The use of RIDIT analysis was suggested for the use of ordinal data - data which are ordered, but are not on an interval scale. The procedure is as follows; from a reference population with the same categories one determines a "RIDIT" or score for each category. This score for each category is the percentile rank of an item in the reference population and is equal to the number of items in all lower categories plus one-half the number of items in the subject category, divided by the population size. Once the RIDIT's for each category have been determined, they are taken as values of a dependent variable for the comparison groups and the normal distribution is applied (Flora Jr, 1974).

In simpler terms, suppose that there are *m* items and *n* ordered categories listed from the most favoured to the least favoured in the scale, then using the steps as outlined by Chien-Ho Wu (2007) RIDIT analysis goes as follows:

1. Select a population to serve as a reference data set. In case the population cannot be easily identified then the total response set for the survey could be considered as the reference data set.
2. Compute the frequency (f_j) for each category of response, where j = 1, 2, 3, …, *n*.
3. Compute mid-point of accumulated frequency F_j for each category of responses as follows:

$$F_1 = \frac{1}{2} f_1$$

and

$$F_j = \frac{1}{2} f_j + \sum_{k=1}^{j-1} f_k$$

where $j = 2, 3, \ldots, n$.

4. Compute the RIDIT value R_j for each category of responses in the reference dataset as follows:

$$R_j = \frac{F_j}{N}$$

where $j = 1, 2, \ldots, n$, and where N is the total number of responses from the survey of interest. By definition the expected value of R for the reference dataset is always 0.5 (Agresti, 1984; Bross, 1958).

5. Compute r_{ij} for each category of scale items as follows:

$$r_{ij} = \frac{R_j \times \pi_{ij}}{\sum_{k=1}^{n} \pi_{ik}}$$

where $i = 1, 2, 3, \ldots, n$.

In the equation above, π_{ij} is the frequency of the category j for the i_{th} scale item and denominator represents the sum of frequencies for scale items i across all categories.

6. Compute the mean RIDIT (ρ_i) for each scale item as follows:

$$\rho_i = \sum_{k=1}^{n} r_{ik}$$

7. Compute confidence interval for ρ_i. When the size of the reference data set is very large relative to that of the comparison dataset, the 95% confidence interval of ρ_i is given by:

$$\rho_i = \frac{1}{\sqrt{3\pi_i}}$$

8. Using the Kruskall-Wallis test statistic W the H_0 that the mean RIDIT score is equal to 0.5 is tested against the alternative hypothesis that the mean RIDIT scores are not equal to 0.5. The test statistic W is computed as follows:

$$W = 12\sum_{i=1}^{m} \pi_i \left(\rho_i - 0.5\right)^2$$

If N is not of a sufficiently large size then the W statistic is computed as follows:

$$W = \frac{12N}{\left(N+1\right)T} \sum_{i=1}^{m} \pi_i \left(\rho_i - 0.5\right)^2$$

and where

$$T = 1 - \frac{\sum_{i=1}^{m} \pi_i^3 - \pi_i}{N^3 - N}.$$

W follows a χ^2 distribution with *(m-1)* degrees of freedom. If the null hypothesis cannot be accepted then the relationships between the confidence interval of ρ_i are examined.

9. The general rule for interpreting the values of ρ_i are as follows:
   a. A scale item whose ρ_i value shows a high deviation from 0.5 implies a significant difference in the response patterns between the reference data set and the comparison data set for the particular scale item. If the confidence interval of ρ_i contains 0.5, then it is accepted that the ρ_i value is not significantly deviate from 0.5
   b. A low value of ρ_i is preferred over a high value of ρ_i because a low value of ρ_i indicates a low probability of being in a negative propensity.
   c. The response patterns of scale items with overlapped confidence intervals of ρ_i are considered, among the respondents, to be statistically indifferent from each other.

STEPS OF GREY RELATIONAL ANALYSIS

With the publication of Grey Systems Theory by Prof. Julong Deng in 1982 the interest in Grey Analysis started to grow especially in China from where it spread on to other nations. One of the reasons for its continuous growth was that it allowed social science researchers to bridge the gap between the practical aspect and the uncertainty prevalent in the results. For example, even when social or marketing research is conducted the researcher is not sure of how good the response results are? The presence of uncertainty in social sciences – and in other fields – leads to a faster adoption of Grey Systems Theory. Other theories dealing with uncertainly were also present – for example fuzzy mathematics, rough sets etc.– but because grey systems could be used on uncertain problems with less data (small sample) and poor information it became the theory of choice for researchers in China. Another reason for its growth was the simplicity of application as compared to other mathematical theories. Some even propound that the Grey Systems Theory came in at the time when China was starting to develop and as such a new theory developed in China found patriotic favor (Liu & Forrest, 2007). Whatever be the reason, Grey Systems in well established in uncertainty literature and here are the steps of conducting GRA for ranking purpose (Chien-Ho Wu, 2007).

1. Generate a reference data series $x_0 = (d_{01}, d_{02}, d_{03}, \ldots d_{0m})$. This data series consists of m values such that d_{0i} refers to the most preferred response on the ith item. This can be thought of as the ideal or the benchmark series.
2. Generate the comparison data series $x_1 = (d_{11}, d_{12}, d_{13}, \ldots d_{1m})$ where $i = 1, 2, \ldots. k$. k is the number of scale items.
3. Compute a new series called the "absolute difference series" as follows (*for all i*):

$$\delta_i = \left(\left|d_{01} - d_{i1}\right|, \left|d_{02} - d_{i2}\right|, \left|d_{03} - d_{i3}\right| \ldots \left|d_{0m} - d_{im}\right|\right)$$

4. Find the global maximum value ($\delta_{\max}$) and the global minimum value ($\delta_{\min}$) from the absolute difference series computed above as follows:

$$\delta_{\max} = \max(\max \delta_i)\forall_i$$
$$\delta_{\min} = \min(\min \delta_i)\forall_i$$

5. Transform each data point in each reference series to Grey Relational Coefficient as follows:

$$\gamma_{ij} = \frac{\delta_{\min} - \tau\delta_{\max}}{\delta_{ij} - \tau\delta_{\max}}$$

where γ_{ij} is the jth value in the δ_i difference data series. τ is a value between 0 and 1. In general the value of τ can be set at 0.50. The coefficient τ is used to compensate for the effect of $\delta_{\max}$; should $\delta_{\max}$ be an extreme value in the data series.

6. Compute Grey Relational Grade (Γ_i) for each difference data series as follows:

$$\Gamma_i = \frac{1}{m}\sum_{j=1}^{m}\gamma_{ij}$$

This is done under the assumption that the data points in the series are of the same weights. In case, the data points are of different weights, the computation differs as follows:

$$\Gamma_i = \sum_{j=1}^{m}\left(\gamma_{ij} \times \omega_j\right)$$

Such that $\sum \omega_j = 1$ where ω_j is the weight of the nth data point. The magnitude of Γ_i reflects the overall degree of standardized deviance of the ith original data series from the reference data series. In general, a scale item with a high value of Γ_i indicates that the respondents, as a whole, have a high degree of favor on the particular item.

7. Sort Γ_i values into either descending or ascending order to facilitate the managerial interpretation of the results.

ANALYSIS OF DATA-SET

For the purpose of analysis the authors used a real data file published by Julie Pallant (2013) in her authoritative book *"SPSS Survival Manual: A step by step guide to data analysis using IBM SPSS"*. The dataset, named as "Survey5ED.sav" is available for download from the publishers Allen & Unwin (2013). The data file – condensed from a study in Educational Psychology – was designed to explore the factors that impact on respondents' psychological adjustment and wellbeing. The survey contained a variety of validated scales measuring constructs that the extensive literature on stress and coping suggest influence people's experience of stress. The survey was conducted amongst the general public in Melbourne, Australia and surrounding districts. The final sample size was 439, consisting of 42 per cent males and 58 per cent females, with ages ranging from 18 to 82 years. In that survey, one of the measuring scale used was the Optimism scale (Scheier, Carver, & Bridges, 1994) – which had 6 statements to be rated on a five point scale ranging from 1 (strongly disagree) to 5 (strongly agree). The statements are provided in Table 1.

To explain the procedure the authors shall use a small subset of the data-set consisting of 20 responses. These are reproduced in table A1 in the annexure and the procedure explained in the following subsections.

Analysis Using RIDIT

First and foremost a population to serve as a reference data set is required. This can be easily accomplished by considering the total response set for the survey as the reference dataset. Next the frequency of the responses in the dataset is counted and tabulated. This is accomplished with a bit of programming or by using the SUMIF() function in Microsoft Excel. Next the sum of frequencies (f_i) for each response category is computed and the mid-point of the sum of frequencies is found out by multiplying them by ½. Although this step is not entirely needed; but for the sake of ease of explanation the authors have included it here. Now the midpoint of the accumulated frequencies (F_i) as shown in step-3 of the procedure is calculated. F_1 is calculated as 0.5 x f_1. F_2 is calculated as 0.5 x f_2 plus the sum of frequencies of the previous class i.e. f_1. Similarly F_3 is calculated as 0.5 x f_3 plus the sum of frequencies of the previous classes i.e. f_1 and f_2 and so on. Next the RIDIT value R_j for each category of responses in the reference dataset is computed. This is done by dividing the midpoint of F_i by N – the total number of responses in the reference dataset. In this example N is equal to 120. The calculations are shown in Table 2.

To compute the r_{ij} the individual frequencies are multiplied with the corresponding RIDIT score for the scale item. For example to get r_{ij} for "opinion 1 response category 1" the frequency (2) is multiplied with the computed RIDIT score of 0.092 and the resultant is divided by the row total (20). The results of the computations are shown in Table 3. The RIDIT score (ρ_i) is the sum of r_{ij} for across the response categories for a scale item.

Once the ρ_i are calculated, the 95% upper and lower bound for ρ_i are also calculated by using step 7 above. Now the null hypothesis that all ρ_i are equal to 0.5 versus the alternate hypothesis that at least one of the ρ_i is different is tested using the the Kruskal Wallis Test Statistics (W). The calculations are shown in Table 4.

Table 1. Statements on the optimism scale

1. In uncertain times I usually expect the best.
2. If something can go wrong for me it will.
3. I am always optimistic about my future.
4. I hardly ever expect things to go my way.
5. Overall I expect more good things to happen to me than bad.
6. I rarely count on good things happening to me.

Table 2. RIDIT calculations (Steps 1 to 4)

Response	SD (1)	D (2)	NAND (3)	A (4)	SA (5)	Total (π_i)
Opinion 1	2	3	7	7	1	20
Opinion 2	5	4	7	3	1	20
Opinion 3	3	2	7	4	4	20
Opinion 4	4	5	5	5	1	20
Opinion 5	4	3	3	5	5	20
Opinion 6	4	3	5	6	2	20
Sum of Frequency (f_i)	22	20	34	30	14	120 (N)
0.5 x f_i	11	10	17	15	7	—
Midpoint of F_i	11	32	59	91	113	—
Computed R_i	0.092	0.267	0.492	0.758	0.942	—

Table 3. RIDIT calculations (Steps 5 to 7)

Response	SD (1)	D (2)	NAND (3)	A (4)	SA (5)	Rho (ρ_i)	LB	UB
Opinion 1	0.009	0.040	0.172	0.265	0.047	0.534	0.405	0.663
Opinion 2	0.023	0.053	0.172	0.114	0.047	0.409	0.280	0.538
Opinion 3	0.014	0.027	0.172	0.152	0.188	0.553	0.423	0.682
Opinion 4	0.018	0.067	0.123	0.190	0.047	0.445	0.315	0.574
Opinion 5	0.018	0.040	0.074	0.190	0.235	0.557	0.428	0.686
Opinion 6	0.018	0.040	0.123	0.228	0.094	0.503	0.374	0.632

W follows the χ^2 distribution with *(m – 1)* degrees of freedom. In this case the value of χ^2 for (6-1) degrees of freedom is 11.07 and hence the null hypothesis cannot be rejected. This leads to the conclusion that the scale items are not statistically different. From the confidence interval shown in Table 3, it is seen that the confidence interval for each of the ρ_i contains the value of 0.5, thereby leading to the conclusion that there may not be much difference in response patterns between the response dataset and the reference dataset. Now to work out which of the opinions are different; the ρ_i values are checked and it is seen that *opinion 2* which has the lowest ρ_i value seems to be the statement on which most of the respondents tend to disagree; where as *opinion 5* would be the statement on which most respondents tend to agree. A direct sorting of the mean RIDIT scores would give us the following ordering:

Opinion (5) > Opinion (3) > Opinion (1) > Opinion (6) > Opinion (4) > Opinion (2)

Table 4. Calculation of W

	Rho (ρ_i)	(ρ_i -0.5)	(ρ_i -0.5)^2	$\pi_{i\,x}$ (ρ_i -0.5)^2
Opinion 1	0.534	0.034	0.001	0.023
Opinion 2	0.409	-0.091	0.008	0.165
Opinion 3	0.553	0.053	0.003	0.055
Opinion 4	0.445	-0.055	0.003	0.061
Opinion 5	0.557	0.057	0.003	0.065
Opinion 6	0.503	0.003	0.000	0.000
Sum	—	—	—	0.370
W = 12 x sum				4.436

For the full data of 435 responses the computed RIDIT scores gave the following ordering:

Opinion (5) > Opinion (3) > Opinion (1) > Opinion (2) > Opinion (6) > Opinion (4)

It can be seen that the ranking on the partial dataset and the full dataset does not differ much except for opinion 2 – which sees a significant jump in position. This is because RIDIT is based on the frequency of responses and as such a larger set would show a higher diversity of responses. The correlation coefficient between the partial and full dataset is +0.828 which is fairly high. However there seems to be a fair amount of stability in ranking of opinion.

Analysis Using Grey Relational Analysis

For conducting the Grey Relational Analysis first the reference data series is generated. For the sake of explanation it is assumed that the reference data series consist of 5 (strongly agree) only. However this kind of simplification may not be justified in all circumstances as there may be opinions which are negative in nature and may have 1 (strongly disagree) as the reference point. The researcher should be careful with the choice of the reference data series. After choosing the reference series, compute the difference series. For example $|d_{01} - d_{11}| = |5 - 3| = 2$ and so on. Once the difference series is generated, find the overall maximum value and the overall minimum value – which in this case are 4 and 0 respectively.

Now the Grey Relational Coefficient (γ_{ij}) is computed. The $\delta_{\max}$ and $\delta_{\min}$ values are already known and let τ be 0.50 so it becomes easier to compute γ_{ij}. An example calculation for (difference series one; opinion one) is shown here

$$\gamma_{ij} = \frac{0 + 0.50 \times 4}{2 + 0.50 \times 4} = 0.50$$

Once the Grey Relational Coefficients have been calculated, the next step is to find the total of all the columns and divide them by the number of observations. This gives the Grey Relational Grade. The difference series (named as DOPn), the Grey Relational Coefficients (named as G-n) and the calculations for Grey Relational Grade are shown in table A2 in the annexure. Sorting the Grey Relational Grade from highest to the lowest values gives us the following ordering

Opinion (5) > Opinion (3) > Opinion (1) = Opinion (6) > Opinion (4) > Opinion (2)

For the full data of 435 responses the Grey Relational Coefficients were computed and sorted. The following ordering was found:

Opinion (5) > Opinion (3) > Opinion (1) > Opinion (6) > Opinion (2) > Opinion (4)

It can be seen that the ranking on the partial dataset and the full dataset does not differ much except for a minor change in position of opinion 2 and opinion 4. The correlation coefficient between the partial and full dataset is +0.918 which is really high. The stability of ranking on Grey Relational Analysis seems to be even better than under RIDIT.

COMPARISION WITH OTHER TECHNIQUES

In a bid to compare the ranking systems, the ranks of the various opinions using average score ranking and by principal component analysis was calculated. The average ranking system is nothing but the average of responses on a particular opinion. As the highest opinion was strongly agree (5) the rank of 1 has been given to the highest average value. For Principal Component Analysis it was found that three (3) principal components were extracted with eignevalues greater than unity giving a cumulative variance explained value of 54.44%. The ranking was done based on the extracted communalities. The results obtained are shown in Table 5.

The ranking obtained by average ranking and the RIDIT system was perfectly associated with a correlation of +1.00 where as the ranking obtained by the Grey Relational Analysis was also found to be very high. The lowest conformance was found to be in terms of ranking based on PCA. This was expected as the PCA is not a ranking system – rather it is a data reduction system which tends to club the

Table 5. Importance of opinions ranked

Item	Average	PCA	RIDIT	Grey Systems
Opinion 1	3	6	3	3
Opinion 2	4	5	4	5
Opinion 3	2	1	2	2
Opinion 4	6	4	6	6
Opinion 5	1	2	1	1
Opinion 6	5	3	5	4

original variables into a smaller set of artificial variables. Increasing the number of extracted principal components to 4 led to reduction in the correlation coefficients. This should act as a caution to researchers who blindly use PCA as a ranking technique.

Simulation of Data-Set

In order to check the validity of RIDIT a small simulation exercise of 100 runs was conducted using Microsoft Excel. The opinions were randomly generated and the results tabulated. The original ranks as obtained from the full dataset were compared to the modal ranks obtained from the simulated dataset and the spearman's rank correlation computed. The average rank correlation value and the standard deviation were also calculated and the results are tabulated in Table 6.

The null hypothesis of rank correlation equal to zero was tested against the alternative hypothesis that it is not and it was found that the null hypothesis is not rejected *(t-critical at 1% level of significance, 2 tail, 98 d.f. = 2.6264)* in both RIDIT and grey relational analysis. A simulation run of 100 is fairly small and it is well known that a larger simulation would be given better insight but even then it provides some useful advice. The very high correlation of modal ranks with the overall ranks came as a surprise – but it confirms the belief that the choice of reference dataset (especially in case of RIDIT analysis) would play a pivotal role in deciding the RIDIT scores. In case of RIDIT Analysis, it seems that practitioners were aware of the problem (Bross, 1958; Flora Jr, 1974). The majority of the work quoted in the review of literature has been in trying to propose alternative methods of RIDIT scoring so that the dependencies on the distribution can be removed.

The high correlation of Grey Relational Analysis has not been satisfactorily explained in literature – but it is believed that this would occur because of the restricted values of δ_{max} and δ_{min} – which in case of Likert Scales would be restricted to maximal difference and zero. In our case the maximal difference would be 4 (maximum opinion strength of strongly agree 5 – minimum opinion strength of strongly disagree 1). Thus as the numerator becomes a constant ($0 + 0.5 \times 4 = 2$), the variation in the grey relational coefficient occurs only because of the presence of δ_i in the denominator. In one paper it has been suggested to standardize the responses before calculating the grey relational coefficients (Tsai Chih-Hung, Chang Ching-Liang, & Chen Lieh, 2003). Another paper has suggested that researchers should use Artificial Neural Networks (ANN) when the amount of information is huge and grey analysis should be used when there are less input data (Lim, Anthony, Mun, & Wai, 2008). Hence the choice of reference data series become again becomes important and researcher should take outmost care in generate the reference data series.

Table 6. Data from simulation

	RIDIT Simulation	Grey Simulation
Modal Rank Correlation	+0.427	+0.561
Maximum Positive Correlation	+0.829	+0.943
Minimum Positive Correlation	-0.943	-0.886
Average Rank Correlation	-0.001	+0.107
Sample SD	0.421	0.448
t-test for rank correlation	-0.010	1.065

CONCLUSION

After going over the above discussion, it is clear that both RIDIT and Grey Relational Analysis provide researchers a simplified means of ranking the items measured on Likert scale. However a few things need to be noted.

Both the RIDIT analysis and the Grey Relational Analysis do not have any distribution assumption regarding the population. This provides a major advantage in calculating the importance of items on the Likert scale – as the researcher need not be bothered in assuming a distribution (mostly normal) and trying to test whether the data points conform to the distribution assumption. Both the analysis require a reference data series which needs to be generated cautiously based on the type of items being provided in the Likert scale.

Grey Relational Analysis should be used when the researcher believes that the underlying trait being measured in interval in nature. The grey relational grades are the relative intensities and provide the importance, satisfaction or agreement of scale items to the reference dataset. It is less time intensive and the reference data series can be set to have the highest (lowest) value in each category. On the other hand RIDIT analysis should be used when the data series are known to be ordinal in nature. The RIDIT value represents the probabilities of the scale items being in better off or worse off conditions than the reference data series. Calculation is much more complex and there are issues in correctly interpreting the ridit values (because of the overlap of the confidence intervals). It requires a large representative reference dataset to calculate reliable values and is highly sensitive to the choice of the reference data set. In case of non availability of the reference dataset – the entire response set can be used as the reference dataset. An advantage of RIDIT analysis is that it allows testing of hypothesis using the Kruskall-Wallis test statistics.

In this chapter, it is seen that the rankings derived from the two methods are very much consistent with each other. This can help in managerial decision making. The choice of grey relational analysis or RIDIT analysis – or for that matter any other ranking technique – is dependent on the researcher. It is hoped that this paper has been able to throw some light on the techniques and provide guidelines for helping in choosing between the two methods.

REFERENCES

Agresti, A. (1984). *Analysis of Ordinal Categorical Data*. New York: John Wiley and Sons.

Allen & Unwin. (2013). Datafile & Other Resources. *SPSS Survival Manual* (5th ed.). Retrieved 1st February, 2016, from http://spss.allenandunwin.com.s3-website-ap-southeast-2.amazonaws.com/data_files.html

Bikash, R. D., & Pravat, S. K., & Sreekumar. (2010). Factors Influencing Purchase of 'NANO' the Innovative Car from India - An Empirical Study. *Asian Journal of Business Management*, *2*(3), 48–56.

Brockett, P. L. (1981). A note on Numerical Assignment of Scores to Ranked Categorical Data. *The Journal of Mathematical Sociology*, *8*(1), 91–101. doi:10.1080/0022250X.1981.9989917

Bross, I. D. J. (1958). How to use Ridit Analysis. *Biometrics*, *14*(1), 18–38. doi:10.2307/2527727

Chien-Ho Wu. (2007). On the Application of Grey Relational Analysis and RIDIT Analysis to Likert Scale Surveys. *International Mathematical Forum, 2*(14), 675-687.

Chih-Hung, T., Ching-Liang, C., & Lieh, C. (2003). Applying Grey Relational Analysis to the Vendor Evaluation Model. *International Journal of the Computer, the Internet and Management, 11*(3), 45–53.

Clason, D. L., & Dormody, T. J. (1994). Analyzing Data Measured by Individual Likert-Type Items. *Journal of Agricultural Education, 35*(4), 31–35. doi:10.5032/jae.1994.04031

Conover, W. (1973). Rank Tests for One Sample, Two Samples and K Samples Without the Assumptions of a Continuous Distribution Function. *Annals of Statistics, I*(6), 1105–1125. doi:10.1214/aos/1176342560

Craig, C. D., & Faulkenberry, G. D. (1979). The application of ridit analysis to detect trends in visibility. *Atmospheric Environment, 13*(12), 1617–1622. doi:10.1016/0004-6981(79)90319-6

Deng, J. (1982). Control problems of Grey Systems. *Systems & Control Letters, 5*, 288–294.

Deng, J. (1989). Introduction to Grey Systems Theory. *Journal of Grey System, 1*, 1–24.

Dhillon, W. R., Goldstein, M., & Schiffman, L. (1978). On the appropriateness of Linear Discriminant and Multinomial Classification Analyisis in Marketing Research. *JMR, Journal of Marketing Research, 15*(1), 103–112. doi:10.2307/3150405

Doyle, M., & Dorling, S. (2002). Visibility Trends in UK 1950-1007. *Atmospheric Environment, 36*(19), 3161–3172. doi:10.1016/S1352-2310(02)00248-0

Fink, A. (1995). *How to Analyze Survey Data*. London: Sage Publishers.

Fink, A., & Kosecoff, J. (1998). *How To Conduct Surveys: A Step-by-Step Guide*. London: Sage Publications.

Fleiss, J., Levin, B., & Paik, M. (2003). *Statistical Methods for Rates and Proportions*. New York: John Wiley and Sons. doi:10.1002/0471445428

Flora, J. D. Jr. (1974). *A note on Ridit Analysis*. Ann Arbor: University of Michigan.

Forthofer, R. N., & Koch, G. (1973). An analysis for compounded functions of categorical data. *Biometrics, 29*(1), 143–157. doi:10.2307/2529683 PMID:4691050

Green, P. E., Tull, D. S., & Albaum, G. (1997). *Research for Marketing Decisions*. New Delhi: Prentice Hall of India Private Limited.

Kantor, S., Winkelstein, W., & Ibrahim, M. A. (1968). A note on Interpretetion of the ridit as quantile ranks. *American Journal of Epidemiology, 87*, 609–615. PMID:5654949

Kaushal, S. K. (2013). The Importance of Apparel Product Attributes for Teenaged Buyers. *NMIMS Management Review, XXIII*, 45–64.

Lieberthal, R. D. (2008). Hospital Quality: A PRIDIT Approach. *Health Services Research, 43*(3), 18. doi:10.1111/j.1475-6773.2007.00821.x PMID:18454777

Lim, D., Anthony, P., Mun, H. C., & Wai, N. K. (2008). *Assessing the Accuracy of Grey System Theory against Artificial Neural Network in Predicting Online Auction Closing Price.* Paper presented at the International MultiConference of Engineers and Computer Scientists, Hong Kong.

Liu, S., & Forrest, J. (2007). The Current Developing Status on Grey System Theory. *Journal of Grey System*, *2*, 111–123.

Mahapatra, S., & Sreekumar, N. A. (2012). A RIDIT apprach to evaluate factors influencing online shopping behaviour. *International Journal of Internet Marketing and Advertising*, *7*(1), 83–98. doi:10.1504/IJIMA.2012.044936

Mohanty, M. K., & Gahan, P. (2012). Buyer Supplier Relationship In Manufacturing Industry - Findings From Indian Manufacturing Sector. *Business Intelligence Journal*, *5*(1), 319–333.

Neter, J., Wasserman, W., & Whitmore, G. A. (1992). *Applied Statistics*. Boston: Allyn & Bacon.

Oyeka, I. C. A. (1992). A Modified Ridit Analysis. *Journal of Nigerian Statistical Association*, *8*(1), 45–69.

Pallant, J. (2013). *SPSS Survival Manual: A step by step guide to data analysis using SPSS* (5th ed.). Melbourne: Allen & Unwin.

Panda, R. K., & Sreekumar. (2012). Prioritizing Issues in Agribusiness Using Ridit Analysis: An Indian Perspective. *World Journal of Agricultural Sciences*, *8*(1), 80–88.

Peterson, R. A. (2000). *Constructing Effective Questionnaires*. London: SAGE Publications. doi:10.4135/9781483349022

Pradhan, B. K. (2008). *Service Quality Indicators in Education Setting: Application of RIDIT Method to Likert Scale Surveys.* (B.Tech Graduation Dissertation). National Institute of Technology, Rourkela.

Scheier, M. F., Carver, C. S., & Bridges, M. W. (1994). Distinguishing optimism from neuroticism (and trait anxiety, self-mastery, and self-esteem): A reevaluation of the Life Orientation Test. *Journal of Personality and Social Psychology*, *67*(6), 1063–1078. doi:10.1037/0022-3514.67.6.1063 PMID:7815302

Selvin, S. (1977). A Further Note on the Interpretetion of ridit analysis. *American Journal of Epidemiology*, *105*, 16–20. PMID:831461

Uwawunkonye, E. G., & Anaene, O. I. C. (2013). A comparative study between ridit and modified ridit analysis. *American Journal of Theoretical and Applied Statistics*, *2*(6), 248–254. doi:10.11648/j.ajtas.20130206.23

Williams, P. D., & Grizzle, J. E. (1972). Analysis of Contingency Table having Ordered Response Categories. *American Statistical Association*, *67*(337), 55–63. doi:10.1080/01621459.1972.10481205

APPENDIX

Table 7. Partial dataset of 20 responses used to explain RIDIT calculations

Case No.	Opinion 1	Opinion 2	Opinion 3	Opinion 4	Opinion 5	Opinion 6
1	3	2	3	2	4	2
2	2	3	4	3	5	4
3	3	1	3	3	3	4
4	3	1	5	3	5	1
5	3	2	3	2	1	3
6	2	2	2	2	3	4
7	3	5	1	4	1	4
8	4	1	3	1	4	2
9	3	4	2	4	2	4
10	1	3	1	4	1	5
11	5	1	5	1	5	1
12	4	1	4	1	5	1
13	2	4	5	5	2	2
14	4	3	3	3	4	3
15	4	3	1	4	4	3
16	1	3	5	3	1	5
17	3	3	3	2	3	3
18	4	3	4	2	4	4
19	4	4	4	4	2	3
20	4	2	3	1	5	1

Table 8. Difference series and grey relational coefficient series

DOP1	DOP2	DOP3	DOP4	DOP5	DOP6	G-1	G-2	G-3	G-4	G-5	G-6
2	3	2	3	1	3	0.500	0.400	0.500	0.400	0.667	0.400
3	2	1	2	0	1	0.400	0.500	0.667	0.500	1.000	0.667
2	4	2	2	2	1	0.500	0.333	0.500	0.500	0.500	0.667
2	4	0	2	0	4	0.500	0.333	1.000	0.500	1.000	0.333
2	3	2	3	4	2	0.500	0.400	0.500	0.400	0.333	0.500
3	3	3	3	2	1	0.400	0.400	0.400	0.400	0.500	0.667
2	0	4	1	4	1	0.500	1.000	0.333	0.667	0.333	0.667
1	4	2	4	1	3	0.667	0.333	0.500	0.333	0.667	0.400
2	1	3	1	3	1	0.500	0.667	0.400	0.667	0.400	0.667
4	2	4	1	4	0	0.333	0.500	0.333	0.667	0.333	1.000
0	4	0	4	0	4	1.000	0.333	1.000	0.333	1.000	0.333
1	4	1	4	0	4	0.667	0.333	0.667	0.333	1.000	0.333
3	1	0	0	3	3	0.400	0.667	1.000	1.000	0.400	0.400
1	2	2	2	1	2	0.667	0.500	0.500	0.500	0.667	0.500
1	2	4	1	1	2	0.667	0.500	0.333	0.667	0.667	0.500
4	2	0	2	4	0	0.333	0.500	1.000	0.500	0.333	1.000
2	2	2	3	2	2	0.500	0.500	0.500	0.400	0.500	0.500
1	2	1	3	1	1	0.667	0.500	0.667	0.400	0.667	0.667
1	1	1	1	3	2	0.667	0.667	0.667	0.667	0.400	0.500
1	3	2	4	0	4	0.667	0.400	0.500	0.333	1.000	0.333
Sum:						11.033	9.767	11.967	10.167	12.367	11.033
N						20	20	20	20	20	20
Grey Relational Grade (“ $_i$) = sum / N						0.552	0.488	0.598	0.508	0.618	0.552

Maximum Difference Value = 4; Minimum Difference Value = 1 in Difference Series.

Chapter 11
Sentiment Analysis as a Tool to Understand the Cultural Relationship between Consumer and Brand

Nicola Capolupo
University of Kent, UK

Gianpaolo Basile
University of Salerno, Italy

Giancarlo Scozzese
University of Perugia, Italy

ABSTRACT

One of the most relevant issues that companies, offices and marketing experts, sociologists and scholars must address studying a new brand or product launch is without any doubt the impact - in terms of feedback - on the consumer sentiment. The study of users' opinions on a specific product or brand has changed with the advent of Web 2.0, which has overcome the old surveys model leading consumers in a too complex and not genuine area, reaching more sophisticated research or even better tracking their opinions directly "on the field", i.e. in the community where this exchange of views and information happens naturally and not artificially. The analysis of consumers' opinions on social media provides enormous opportunities for the public and the private spheres. Concerning the last on the reputation of a certain product/brand or firm is strongly influenced by the voices and negative opinions published and shared by users on social networks. Indeed, companies need to adapt their behaviour monitoring public opinion.

DOI: 10.4018/978-1-5225-0997-4.ch011

1. INTRODUCTION: THE ENTERPRISE ACCORDING TO SYSTEMIC APPROACH-CAS

A complex adaptive system is a system which fits, organizes and evolves over time depending on the dynamics of the context in which it is structured. Some examples of complex systems are living organisms such as cells, animals and people, or companies, organizations, policies, cultures, for instance. Everyone is able to survive if it fits and/or influence the dynamics of the environment in which it lives. In recent decades the line of studies of management that considers the enterprise as a whole system of life it has prevailed. Duality enterprise-system refers to a set of complex and varied elements which performs the acquisition and production of informations related to the context, goods and services, to be exchanged with stakeholders in order to achieve a certain purpose of survival, social legitimacy and/or competitive advantage, through the creation of social-symbolic identity expressed by the product/brand. (Beer, 1985).

The firm as a complex system, which is constantly in conditions of instability due to the dynamic environment in which it is structured, re-organizes its components in order to adapt skills and competences to the requirements of the interlocutor (De Toni, 2011). In other words, the company - in order to ensure its survival - participates and/or stimulates an exchange with relevant stakeholders, characterized by specific interactions bidirectional/cybernetic governed by the needs of individuals (Ashby, 1962). Indeed, the result, to ensure mutual survival, will be represented by products/services which express common elements of the language and characteristics values. In a complex adaptive system such as an enterprise, the stage of adaptation is usually underlined by the constant redefinition of the relationship between it and its environment, in which various actors and factors must be taken into account, first of all the role of individual consumers. (Cipresso, Foresti, Balgera & Villamira, 2010).

The company, seen as a social organization, due to the bi-directional relationships created with stakeholders, is able of receiving necessary information both for the achievement of its competitive aims and the needs of interlocutors. Furthemore, informations gathered in these communication processes are the natural basis to understand the stakeholders needs and the self-organization ability, to adapt behavior and content. As a matter of fact, once identified, those informations will be combined with the other existing ones for a total reworking of corporate conduct, whose final product will be the consistent/consonant behavior that the company will adopt in relation to the interlocutors which compose the frame we refer.

The perception process of this information, or to better explain the input part, is given by the process of '*enactment*' (activation) thanks to which is made a distinction on the basis of which is part of its specific context and that where will seek to establish relationships, and instead of what belongs to the environment unknown. This stage is conducted by organ of governance, in other words an observer of the environment - generally understood as a set of tangible assets and interlocutors -, with which the enterprise system aims to interact. The governing body of the company identifies and organizes the resources for the creation of relationships necessary to achieve the final aium of the company, namely its survival.

Once gained such informations, the enterprise system will enable a range of behaviors aimed at creating and maintaining interactions with members. These behaviors may be the expression of scheduled and/or spontaneous roles. According to that, marketing strategies and communication product/brand play a key role always considered unconventional and placed in universal standards (thus refusing to implement the best practices, or standard models applicable to multiple contexts) and better suited to the heterogeneous scenario to be observed in order to provide a better interpretation of reality.

These strategies, therefore, are shaped on the needs of the individual/potential consumer, the bearer of purposes other than those of the enterprise, in order to realize interactions, capable during their evolution, to create cooperative preconditions or equifinality, representingt hus the attitude of a given company to achieve the same goals, starting from different production or trading conditions. The stage just described is necessary to the brand to adapt itself, wherever possible, to environmental dynamics that influence the behavior of potential consumers, faced with strong competition, and "support constantly the research to improve the quality of production processes and related products/services" (Basile, 2013).

This is the approach used by the Starbucks Corp, which has adopted since 1987 (date of acquisition of the company by Howard Schultz) a policy of renewal of its services to offer to American coffee lovers a better experience. Firstly, it secured a new standard of quality coffee going to ensure the genuineness of the product, after which the enterprise has introduced new drinks at special prices, especially for loyal customers. It improved also the environment by offering consumers, starting with a relaxing atmosphere to create new spaces to offer customers the opportunity to enjoy their drink in peace or to use computers to connect to the network (Berry Shankar, Parish, Cadwallader, Dotzel 2006). The possibility to be online, lastly, is the fundamental aspect of the environmental and the historical/cultural context. Technological innovation led to a series of another potential and opportunities for businesses and individuals, but also led to the need, from business, to innovate its services to remain competitive.

In this view, the consumer expects a particular offer by the company, as in this case the possibility to use a computer or smartphone and connect to Internet, when he has access to power outlets in order to load or just have a space where communicate with other consumers.

Adaptive processes, so far treated, have their roots, as part of management studies, in the theory of dynamic capabilities, that represents an evolution of the structure-conduct-performance paradigm and the Resource Based Theory, focusing the 'attention on the company's ability to renew their organizational skills for sustainable competitive advantage'. These capabilities, constantly expressed in environments subject to rapid change, involving the redefinition of resources configuration of everyday organization - internal and external - of the company. (Siano, 2001).

Therefore, it emerges a tie - even better a value - for the pursuit of competitive survival in the case of the business system, and psycho-social in the case of the individual/consumer: the first actor on the one hand, imposes itself on the market (legitimized by the community), adapting to it and obtaining a gain in terms of economics and reputation. The second one, on the other hand, in addition to use of services and functions more and more advanced socially most identifies itself with the brand, creating an isomorphic process result of which the brand becomes an instrument of social communication of the individual and the individual, in turn, changing/expanding its cultural values, expressed in the context of social dynamics, implementing the values expressed by the brand.

1.1 Cultural Relationship with the Consumer: Consumer Culture Theory and Value Creation

The concept of 'culture' as part of the dynamics between the company/brand and individual/consumer identify itself in the study area of Consumer Culture. It refers to the dominant model of consumption which is structured by the collective action of businesses in their marketing activities, to those flows of market research that approach the theme of consumption as a social phenomenon for which a group constructs practices, identity and meaning, in order to guide the experiences and the lives of its members. Arnould and Thompson (2007) argue that studies on CCT identify four structures of theoretical interest:

1. Sociohistoric patterning of consumption,
2. Consumer identity projects,
3. Marketplace cultures,
4. Mass-mediated ideologies and consumers interpretive strategies.

In this chapter will be taken into consideration, particularly, the third factor, namely the networks market-oriented and consumption built. It is based on two important conceptual topics:

- A culture is better conceptualized as a dynamic network connectivity;
- Social actions are placed in institutional settings and therefore, rational calculations, actors social, emotional feedback, choices and preferences are essentially influenced by institutional conditions.

Applying the systems approach to Consumer Culture Theory, the duopoly enterprise/brand and individual/consumer stands itself to vital system integrated in a social-economic and cultural system. Therefore, the system of consumption may be considered as that moment of creation and maintenance of cultural and symbolic relationships between the company and the individual/consumer or consumer communities. These reports are designed to establish a common language in order to achieve a level of consonance, understood as the point of compatibility between systems and/or actors adapted to allow that they may be related linking up themselves (Golinelli G., Gatti M., 2000), allowing both the consumer and the brand to develop, maintain and improve their sustainability. As a result of the mutual exchange of information, the enterprise and the consumer create a continuous two-way relationship that mutually benefits themselves.

While, thanks to the active role of the consumer, the company increases its expertise in terms of harmony/resonance, brand value, reputation and competitive advantage, on the other, the individual/consumer looking to satisfy their needs through the achievement of social objectives. The firm, therefore, may be conceived as an emergent property which represents the result of interactions between systems which affect considerably the subsequent events (Belew & Mitchell, 1996). The emergence of the property "brand", as a result of the continuous relations and interactions between the company and individual/consumer, will affect future aims of both the individual/consumer, in terms of self esteem and social identification, and of the enterprise. Emerging brand, as a matter of fact, allow the individual/consumer to represent, through social and cultural symbol, the social groups to which he belongs or which would like to participate. The company, for its part, through the brand will create/maintain relationships necessary for its survival (Dominici, Palumbo & Basile, 2005) (Figure 1).

In this given epistemological context, culture refers to a family of theoretical perspectives which address the dynamic relationship between the actions of consumers, the market, and structural meanings related to the construction of a two-way relationship between consumption and culture. The CCT illuminates the contextual aspects, symbolic and experiential consumption just as they unfold around the consumption cycle, from acquisition to consumption itself (Annamma Joy & Eric P.H. Li, 2012).

The result is a collective melting pot of texts, identity and reputation which guide consumers towards a purchase/perception culturally aware, shared and co-created. It creates, therefore, harmony of language and cultural values which guarantee trust, confidence, by the individual/consumer towards the company/brand, that is does not necessarily translated in the purchase of the product but in the dialogue with other individuals, through feedback, perception and sentiment of the firm/product. Mutual value creation occurs when consumers and businesses are able to co-create common values that enable them to act and

Figure 1.

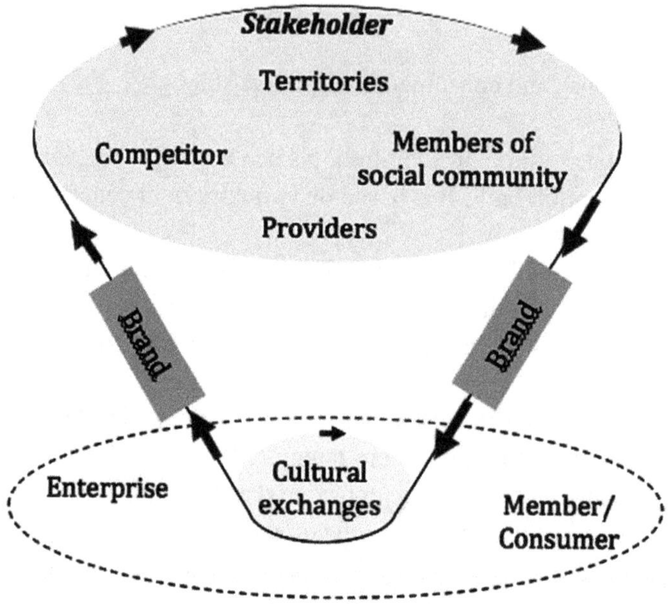

survive in the context in which they are pursuing a certain level of resonance (understood as achieving enterprise equifinality). The term refers to those elements which work for one purpose. In other words, the resonance can be defined as a harmonious interaction with the systemic context referenced in order to share cultural values and social practices (Barile, 2008).

1.2 VSM-CCT: New Perspectives of Analysis on the Relation Enterprise - Individual/Consumer

A fundamental approach to the co-creation of value of the product is given by the Viable Systems Model (VSM), which offers an heuristic vision which is fundamental in relation to the design of an advanced model which explains, in its complexity, in which way the exchange between the company/brand and individual/consumer takes place. This system of co-creation, according to Sandel, is based on offers of sale and consumer choice in the purchase moment. In a cybernetic/digital context, the more these relationships are dominated by impressive variety of values of one or the other, the more likely the cycle between them will create unsatisfactory markets and will push the consumer to a forced choice, led by the lack of a variety the supply of the product (Sandel, 2009).

Indeed, a too confused variety of products may affect the cognitive abilities of purchasers or potential ones, which are forced to choose between standardized products generated by an exceeded offer. The act of purchase becomes a forced process, detached from a logic based on considerations aware of the need for the product/brand, because the potential consumer, disoriented by so many copies of the same good, choose it superficially or too far from the quality - or purpose - of the product.

The cybernetics applied to study areas of marketing and management, in recent decades, has resulted in an exponential increase in online advertising: the reduction of costs for advertising promotions as a consequence, the emergence of social networks not just as a group of social aggregation but as tools of guerrilla marketing have made possible a so considerable presence in markets an infinite number of times than traditional media. The result is a saturated market which confuses the consumer: too much choice may paralyze the decision making process of individual consumers, which leads to a waste of resources and, if necessary, to psychological dissatisfaction (Krippendorf,....; Schwartz, 2009). People are constantly under pressure to decide and, consequently, they do not have the time to choose in an optimal manner.

The governing body of the company, therefore, should 'combine, dynamically, the set of capabilities embedded in the structure components (ie ability settled through the existing technical and technological knowledge and the progressive refinement achieved over time in function of their aims) with various information: various - mainly made up of innovations and possible solutions - which, coming from the outside context, must be precisely filtered and interpreted by the government itself ' (Barrel, 2012).

According to the cybernetic approach, for an informed purchase of a product will be necessary for consumers to be cognitively led to the sale, which is aware of his qualities and objectives that arises in obtaining it. It appears, therefore, the figure of the prosumer, a careful consumer who, while distancing itself from the classic role of a passive actor in the markets, takes a more active role in the process that involves the stages of creation, production, distribution and consumption of the product.

The real challenge for the enterprise therefore is to establish itself through markets and survive socially involving the user in the creation and product choice, evaluating their pleasure, satisfaction, perception, the 'sentiment' which it ensues. To obtain the co-creation of value with the individual consumer, a brand should meets certain attitudes which favor the creation and/or maintenance of relationships consolidating the created dynamic platform:

1. By increasing customer loyalty by developing satisfaction.
2. By creating a psycho-socio-economic significance specific to the product and create symbolic meanings related to it, which should meet the desires of the consumer both psychological and social oriented.
3. Developing products to the needs of consumers.

The guidelines listed above are essentially connected to each other: to enhance the consumer fidelity it is necessary that the products are created depending on the own needs, which may be of practical nature or psychological-social one. In this regard, it is necessary to build a culture around the product image and symbols which meet the desires of individuals/groups.

1.3 Effects of the Relationships for the Enterprise and for the Individual Consumer

The concept of network - or rather of the social group - dynamics is a key idea when we refer to the web, which, in turn, is an expression of the complexity, abundance and diversity of stakeholders/target enterprise system. The web is a complex system in which are many and various the factors that may influence the relationship between the actors of this double exchange, and it is also here that the dialogue takes place between them. In this context the enterprise has a better chance to acquire useful information to adapt and revise their strategies and behaviors and marketing, the individual/consumer is able to improve the ability to consciously choose a product/brand in order to achieve its goals of self esteem (individual/consumer) and social identification within the social groups to which they belong or to which they would like to belong (community).

The development and the creation of these communities, and more generally the web, has helped changing the concept of the creation of value of a particular product. The consumer, as part of these development, has a central role which is considered an actor participating in the creation of the product/brand and not just a passive target to which direct it. Individual consumers and producers give life, therefore, to a system-active consumption which consists of numerous and constant exchange of meaning. The product become the result of a meeting between the individual/consumer and corporate/brand. The community, understood as a social group, however, assumes institutional features. It was conceived as a place of expression of the needs and/or user informations about a specific product or brand; it develops and stabilizes itself thanks to the order created by the figures of opinion leaders, which confer legitimacy on the group main topics. Consumers are the main characters of the community: the act of discussion becomes the key moment in which one, two or more people share information, feedback, opinions and feelings about the brand or product.

1.4 From the Traditional "Consumer Analysis" to Sentiment Analysis

The main issue that companies, offices and marketing experts, sociologists and scholars must face when a new brand or product is launched is without any doubts which may be the response, feedback or consumer sentiment. The study of users on a specific product or brand has changed with the advent of Web 2.0, which has overcome the old pollster model leading consumers in an unknown territory, to arrive to a more sophisticated research or, to better say, 'on the field', ie in the community where this exchange of views and information occurs naturally and not artificially. In this regard, it felt the need to investigate the reasons why consumers search opinions about products online, but also those motivations which may have influenced the purchase. Researchers have reported a number of factors, including risk reduction, popularity, lower costs, the easy retrieval of information, accidents, perception, inspiration from other media such as TV and a preliminary step acquisition of information before the purchase (Jansen, Zhang, Sobel, & Chowdury, 2009).

In the nowadays scenario the web has made several changes to its own structure depending on the needs of its users. The most important modify was a redefinition of itself from 'read-only' to 'read - write' perspective. In other words, the Web has completely redefined its borders opened itself to the user, sharing with it the process of creating space. This definition has increased at the enthusiasm of the users, which actually tend to be suited to blackberries their interactions and sharing views and sentiment through social networks, communities, blogs, wikis, and other collaborative media. therefore, it has been witnesses of the development of collective knowledge spread across the Web, Particularly in the areas of daily life, such as trade, tourism, education and health. (Cambria, Schuller, Xia & Havasi, 2013).

Monitoring and analysis of opinions on social media provides enormous opportunities for both sectors, public and private. Regarding the last one, it was noted that the reputation of a certain product or company is strongly influenced by the voices and negative opinions published and shared between users on social networks. Including this observation, companies need to realize that the monitoring and detection of public opinion may lead to building better relationships with its customers, a better understanding of the needs of themselves and a better response to market changes. Saif, Yulan and Alani presented a research on the Apple case study, demonstrating that the products/entities "iPad", "iPod" and "Mac Book Pro" have appeared more often in tweets of positive polarity and are all related to the semantic concept " Product/Apple ". The example chosen for the demonstration of this process is to a user satisfied with the purchase of his iPhone: "Finally, I got my iPhone. Such a product!" (Saif, Yulan, & Alani, 2012).

Sentiment analysis, also called opinion mining, is the field of study which examines opinions, feelings, values, attitudes, and emotions of people to entities such as products, services, organizations, individuals, issues, events and their attributes (Bing Liu, 2012). The two-way relationship which occurs between producer and consumer, accomplices in a mutual exchange of co- creation of the product, born from the needs of developing new businesses and social organizations, the need for which is to draw the views of consumers or the public about their products and services, and those of individual consumers who also want to know the opinions of an existing product before buying it.

Bo Pang and Lillian Lee (....) propose a method of automatic learning of sentiment analysis which applies the techniques of categorization of parts of a given text to analyze the subjective portions of the document. It is composed of two moments:

1. Label the phrases in the document both subjective and objective, discarding the latter;
2. Apply a classifier machine learning standards for the part extracted.

Today social media are the perfect setting to extrapolate this type of informations and make an assessment about the relationship between product and consumer sentiment, thus creating a condition of sense-making (Weick,....). In this sense Twitter plays a fundamental role, because:

- Twitter has a huge number of text messages and growing every day. The corpus collected can be arbitrarily large.
- The audience varies from regular users of Twitter to celebrities, corporate representatives, politicians. Therefore, they can be collected text messages of users on different social groups and interests. (Pak & Paroubek, 2010)

In addition, the syntax of Twitter is much more streamlined, direct and easy to categorize and interpret than those of other social media. Facebook, for instance, tends to redundancy of the message because it still remains the same. The proposed analysis starts with the identification of keywords - called hashtag, composed of a word that identifies the product or brand preceded by the pound - the tweets of users on the network:

Maria serena somma ⌉@serenasom71 3 h3 ore fa

Lw mie inseparabili #Armani ♥♥♥

razoneh✿ ⌉@razanaliif 4 h4 ore fa

I can't wait for my #armani's

Dominik Bauer ⌉@DominikBauer11 1 h1 ora fa Schwieberdingen, Baden-Württemberg

the most awesome men's underwear on this planet ?? by ➡ @armani @ArmaniExchange #armani #GiorgioArmani #emporio

The first three tweets collected with the keyword #armani represent positive feedback on three different products of the brand Armani: the first girl shoes, glasses the second, the third intimate.

Carmelo Briguglio ⌉@c_briguglio 26 giu

Macché @ItaloTreno: ora d'improvviso ha annullato #Torino-#Roma delle 17, piantando in asso i viaggiatori. #Italo è peggio. Non prendetelo.

Marilena La Mura ⌉@la_marilena 25 giu

```
Perché nè #italo nè #frecciarossa hanno pensato ad un vagone dedicato a chi
viaggia con bambini? — stufa
Luca Dondoni ˥@lucadondoni 3 giu
Aggiungomi a chi soffre per caldazza proveniente dalla Spagna. In più se #Italo
va avanti così (30' tra Rogoredo e Garibaldi) lo mollo.
```

The #italo examples are all negative. However, they can be considered as a starting point for improving its services in terms of punctuality, comfort and racing: in the second case the user suggests 'a product Italo' different than the current one. In other words it would participate, if Italo's administration considers the possibility to include in their wagon trains special for families based on one or more reports of this kind, to the co-creation of a new Italo.

2. PRACTICAL APPLICATIONS

2.1 Symbolism in Marketing between Environment and Meaning

Markets and, in particular, marketing practices, falling in a non-conventional - however widely understood and shared - scenario of symbols and meanings global. The consumer, therefore, constitutes a primary process, understood as a moment when a transaction takes place between two fundamental actors driven by interests and purposes, while the production is seen as a means of creating commodities and real standards, taking then the values depending on the context of use. In other words, goods and services do not have meanings ready for consumption as such, but rather take them during the process of consumption. The context, better to say the environment, in this regard is a key aspect for the understanding of the meaning, but to be able to explain itself it has to define the self as different from the system. In other words, the system represented by the consumers - and psychological and social implications - is considered different from the environment of the market, only to emerge when the common environment adopts those social characteristics of its users which are inside: the consumer who buys an Apple smartphone rather than a competing product expresses a sense of self esteem, in the sense that the membership of a particular social group - rather a community - leads to purchase and discuss of it with other members. This product/brand is represented as a facilitator for social effect of customization for both aesthetic content. In this regard, the theorists of the Consumer Culture Theory focus their attention on the interpretation of social sites, such as communities, tribes consumer, microcultures and value systems. This research tends to deal with micro-cultural meanings from the point of view of an individual and places less emphasis on the macro-market implications. Understanding the meaning of fundamental importance because it is a complex social phenomenon that pushes individuals to assume certain behaviors and to take certain decisions in one direction rather than in another (D. Kadirov, Varey RJ, 2010). This suggests, then, that the marketing operations in this regard should take into account not only 'physical' trade between consumer and enterprise (ie the act of purchase), but also the interactions and symbolic processes which reside within.

2.2 Goals and Objectives

The epistemological premise of this research sets the stage to show how the web is an extremely varied and unpredictable scenario, the dynamics of which are the result of complex relationships between individuals and reality different from each other, the purpose of which, sometimes, can differ. Because of that, explaining why a particular choice using a deterministic approach based on the principle of cause and effect is, roughly, impossible.

The aim of this paper is not to "discover" the reason why the consumer purchases a product or brand, instead is aimed at understanding the perception of users of one or more certain community towards a product-brand, their 'sentiment' in relation to certain dynamics carried out in the same community; identify the social dynamics of the community that lead to the co-creation of value of a product; explain the processes that revolve around the sharing of a product culture in a digital environment.

2.3 Identification of Tools

The social network's main sentiment analysis based on practical case studies is Twitter. The use of Twitter is composed for 59% by a male audience, with an average age of 35 years and its geographic distribution now reflects the user profile web, with a primary focus in large urban centers. The Twitter user is a major user of social networks: almost all, 93%, is also member of Facebook, Linkedin and 31% of the 12% of options and the average online user makes more use of e- commerce (65% compared to 60%). Generally, it uses more of all media, in particular of satellite TV (+11 percentage points) and the press both daily magazine. Communication initiatives of brands and bloggers/opinion leaders are activities that are generally barycentric the average user. In particular:

- The hashtag is the main driver of navigation on Twitter and webusers use the hashtag in contexts external to Twitter as well (owned media, advertising).
- Twitter has become the thermometer of a media event: exploiting trends and bind to large media events to gain audience.
- High competitiveness issue raises the risk of poor visibility in Twitter: Adv invest in Twitter to gain visibility and reach the target.
- Twitter is mostly used with logic and dynamics of real time: react quickly to prevent cases of crisis management and opportunities.
- The trending topics on Twitter are often initiated and influenced by power users: engage influencers in discussions and create a Twitter ecosystem (Connecto.it).

2.4 Applying Sentiment Analysis to Microsoft Italia

In this paragraph will be taken into account and analyzed the case of Microsoft Italy to point out structural differences with the other mentioned reality. The first one, for example is related to the fact that the Microsoft Italy brand concerns different physical products which can be purchased in different contexts, both online and offline - such as a Nokia Lumia Smartphone or Windows 10 OS - unlike other mentioned reality concerning places, services and tourism. Nevertheless, the most relevant aspect, for which Microsoft Italia differs from the others, is that for an effective sentiment analysis should not be considered the brand as such, because there are brand products but not specifically Microsoft Italy branded, and especially since the expression of the brand online is given by the quality of its products that are not under the Microsoft name. For example, to search for the sentiment of a user relative to the Microsoft brand Italy is no need to use text strings that do not include directly #MicrosoftItalia but the products for which it provides its own brand. In this analysis will be taken into account the opinion mining of a specific Microsoft product belonging to one of the first and most important Microsoft services, that of the operative systems.#Windows10 is a pc operating system released by Microsoft which extends its range to different devices such as tablet, computers and smarthphone. On Twitter, we have collected a series of tweets related to the period of time of January 2016.

2.4.1 Negative Sentiment

Antonio Scarano ˥@antonyscarano 10 gen Siamo quasi a metà gennaio, e dell'aggiornamento a #Windows10 sugli smartphone, manco l'ombra! #echecazz #muovetevi #Lumia930 #Microsoft
∞Luckshots~ ˥@EdoardoGrimaldi 10 gen #Windows10 però eri bello.Come al solito i più belli nascondono le peggiori insidie. #Crepi
LUDOVICO TODINI ˥@LUDOVICOTODINI 6 gen #Windows8 e #Windows10 fanno schifo! #XP e #Windows7 i migliori. Abbandonerò #Microsoft
Chiara ˥@higheyeofheaven 4 gen Grande #delusione da un PC che ha meno di un anno. Aggiornando #windows10 non funziona più nulla

Tweets with negative sentiment are the most relevant ones in this analysis because they show different critical and constructive difficulties which users have when they approach to that specific product. In other words they participate in the process of co-creation of value of the product entrusting or not quality values. The first user complains for a delay of operating system updates, criticizing not specifically the product itself but the company services; the second one invites to be wary of Windows 10 because such beauty does not match with quality: using the word 'insidie' (difficulties) he gives to the product a feedback made of hidden and unspoken meanings, but quite negative and to be avoided, as the final hashtag #Crepi - which means 'die'- suggests. The third is is an absolutely negative feedback, a disastrous result for the brand because the user, having voiced his dissatisfaction with the products Windows 8 and 10 ('they suck') and praising the oldest product Microsoft XP and 7, announces that he is leaving Microsoft as a brand. Lastly, the user is disappointed because updating Windows 10 her PC purchased for less than year no longer works as before.

2.4.2 Positive Sentiment

Matteo Roselli ˥@_MatteoRoselli 6 gen Matteo Roselli ha Ritwittao OM_ ZeroMag#SamsungGalaxyTabProS finalmente anche l'azienda coreana ha capito che il futuro del settore è #Windows10

The most worrying aspect that Microsoft Italia must take into account is that in the selected period of time (1 to 15 January 2016) only one positive feedback regarding # Windows10 has been produced and a tracked. The users, involving the brand company Samsung, is satisfied of the fact that for the tablet

Samsung Galaxy Tab Pro S has been chosen a Windows 10 operating system rather than an Android OS, defining it "il futuro del settore" (the future of the industry).

2.4.3 Null Sentiment

```
WindowsBlogItalia ‏@WindowsBlogIta 2 gen Iniziate il 2016 con la raccolta di
guide e trucchi più completa per #Windows10 I migliori… http://ift.tt/1hlzE8F
Cor.Com ‏@Cor_Com 5 gen #Windows10, semestre sprint: sbarca su oltre 200 mil-
ioni di dispositivi http://bit.ly/1SwOPuC#Micorsoft
Daniele Moretti ‏@danieleneiposti 4 genintertweetters: Mercato sistemi opera-
tivi: #Windows10 ha quasi raggiunto #Windows 8.1http://goo.gl/ABcmpA  #inter-
twine #technology 0 Retweet 0 Mi piace
```

The most numerous group of tweets concern neutral feedback, which contain support services for use of the product as in the case of the first tweet:

```
Start 2016 with the collection of more comprehensive guides and tricks for
#Windows10. The best one http://ift.tt/1hlzE8F
```

In addition, as well as the first issue, are also relevant newspapers industry news on the operating system as in the case of the second ("Windows10, sprint: arrives on over 200 million devices") and third (Market operating systems: #Windows10 has almost reached #WINDOWS 8) tweets, because these news contribute to the product online virality and to spread the reputation of the company.

3. CONCLUSION

The idea of social environment in a specific context such as that of the enterprise should be explained both in economic and in social terms, as 'social and economic context within which the company is required to perform its functions' (Basile, Kaufmann, Czinkota, 2014). The above context is regulated by a series of political, legislative, cultural, social and economic conditions which define the behavior of the enterprise. Sciarelli S. (2008) proposes zoning of the four sub-systems general:

- The system or the political and institutional environment;
- The cultural system technology;
- Population and social system;
- The economic system.

In conclusion, this research takes into account the cultural environment-technology which can be understood as the context in which the traditional manifestations of material life, social and spiritual life of a people may be tracked. Culture is made up of a number of elements - the traditions and habits of users, art and technology - which influence the system of values of an individual or society as a whole. Culture, indeed, shapes human behavior and affects both consumers and those who work within the company, both external groups. Science and technology are a product of culture, even if they have a particular type of values and range of applications to which they refer.

Looking for applying a practical distinction, technology 'especially influence the use of resources, while culture is also reflected in their consumption in the form of goods and services produced'. The first, in this regard, can be considered as a subsystem of the cultural environment, as close to the company than to the wider socio-economic environment (Sciarelli S., 2008).

This chapter aimed to figured out how the relationship between the consumer and the enterprise/brand is nowadays increasingly and dynamically changed and shared. The issue considered is that the concept of network - or rather of the social group - is a key idea when we refer to the web, expression of the complexity and diversity of stakeholders/target enterprise system, because it represents complex dynamics and variables between the individual/consumer and the firm/brand. In this context the role of sentiment analysis have a relevant importance because, as established from the case study #Windows10 of Microsoft Italia, it may be seen as the ideal tool for the analysis of the cultural relationship between individual and brand/company: on the one hand, trace the feelings of the users on products/brands and help the firm and the individual/consumer to improve them or to co-create new ones; on the other, it allows users to find opinions on those specific products, giving feedback, create networks and communities of consumers to exchange views on brands and, most important, to create the product with the company helping to give it an added value.

REFERENCES

Arnould, E. J., & Thompson, C. J. (2007). Consumer Culture Theory (and We Really Mean Theoretics): Dilemmas and Opportunities Posed by an Academic Branding Strategy. In Consumer Culture Theory. Oxford, UK: Elsevier.

Ashby, W. (1962), Principles Self-Organization.*Transaction of the University of Illinois Symposium*. Pergamon Press.

Barile, S. (2012). *L'approccio sistemico vitale per lo sviluppo del territorio*. Sinergie Italian Journal of Management.

Basile, G. (2013). *Relazioni tra impresa e individuo-consumatore*. Franco Angeli.

Beer, S. (1985). *Diagnosing the system for organizations*. London: Wiley.

Belew, M. (1996). *Adaptive individuals in evolving populations*. Boston: Addison-Wesley Longman Publishing Co., Inc.

Berry, S., & Parish, T. (2006). Cadwallader, & Dotzel, (2006) *Creating New Markets Through Service Innovation,* MIT. *Sloan Management Review*.

Pang Bo, & Lee, L. (2008). Opinion Mining and Sentiment Analysis. *Journal Foundations and Trends in Information Retrieval, 2*(1-2).

Buchanan, M. (2003). *Nexus. Perché la natura, la società, l'economia e la comunicazione funzionano allo stesso modo*. Oscar Mondadori.

Calcagno, M., & Casarin, F. (2014). *Mercati reali vs mercati virtuali? Uscire dalla crisi ripensando gli spazi della relazione con il consumatore, Mercati e competitività, Rivista della Società Italiana di Marketing, N.3.* Franco Angeli.

Cambria, S., & Xia, H. (2013). New Avenues in Opinion Mining and Sentiment Analysis. *IEEE Intelligent Systems, 28*(2), 15–21. doi:10.1109/MIS.2013.30

Cipresso, P., Foresti, R., Balgera, A., & Villamira, M. (2010). *E-learning, gestione e condivisione della conoscenza: Moodlemootitalia 2007 Modena.* Artestampa.

Codeluppi, V. (2005). *Manuale di Sociologia dei consumi.* Carocci editore.

Czinkota, M., Kaufmann, H. R., & Basile, G. (2014). The relationship between legitimacy, reputation, sustainability and branding for companies and their supply chains. *Industrial Marketing Management, 43*(1), 91–101. doi:10.1016/j.indmarman.2013.10.005

De Toni, A. F. (2011). *Teoria della complessità e implicazioni manageriali: verso l'auto-organizzazione.* Sinergie Italian Journal of Management.

Dominici, G., Palumbo, F., & Basile, G. (2013). *Consumer Culture Theory: A conceptual Framework.* Organizational Transformation and Social Change.

Golinelli, G. S., & Gatti, S. (2000). *L'impresa sistema vitale. Il governo dei rapporti inter-sistemici.* Symphonya. Emerging Issues in Management.

Hassan, S., Yulan, H., & Harith, A. (2012). Alleviating data sparsity for Twitter sentiment anal- ysis. In: 2nd Workshop on Making Sense of Microposts (#MSM2012): Big things come in small packages at the 21st International Conference on theWorld Wide Web (WWW'12). *CEUR Workshop Proceedings* (CEUR-WS.org)

Hatch, M. J., & Schultz, M. (2008). *Taking Brand Initiative. How companies Can Align Strategy, Culture, and Identity Through Corporate Branding.* Jossey-Bass.

Holt, D. B. (2002). Why Do Brands Cause Trouble? A Dialectical Theory of Consumer Culture and Branding. *The Journal of Consumer Research, 29*(1), 70–90. doi:10.1086/339922

Jansen, B. J., Zhang, M., Sobel, K., & Chowdury, A. (2009). Twitter Power: Tweets as Electronic Word of Mouth. *Journal of the American Society for Information Science and Technology, 60*(11), 2169–2188. doi:10.1002/asi.21149

Joy, A., & Li, E. P. H. (2012). Studying Consumption Behaviour through Multiple Lenses: An Overview of Consumer Culture Theory. *Journal of Business Anthropology, 1*(1).

Kadirov, D., & Varey, R. J. (2010). Symbolism in Marketing Systems. *Journal of Macromarketing, 31*(2), 160–171. doi:10.1177/0276146710393519

Liu, B. (2012). Sentiment Analysis and Opinion Mining. *Synthesis Lectures on Human Language Technologies, 5*(1).

Maffesoli, M. (2004). *Il tempo delle tribù. Il declino dell'individualismo nelle società postmoderne.* Edizioni Angelo Guerini e Associati SpA.

Chapter 12
Improving Customer Experience Using Sentiment Analysis in E-Commerce

Vinay Kumar Jain
Jaypee University of Engineering and Technology, India

Shishir Kumar
Jaypee University of Engineering and Technology, India

ABSTRACT

In today's world, millions of online users post their opinions on product features, services, quality, benefits and other values of the products. These opinions or sentiment data generated via different communication mediums often include vital data points that can be fruitful for businesses in understanding customer experiences, products quality and services. The E-commerce companies considered social media platform for new product launch, promotion of products and features or establishing a successful business to customer relationship which produces great results. Analytics on this Social media data helps in identifying the customers in the right demographic, psychographic and lifestyle group. This chapter identifying important characteristics of customer reviews which help businesses houses to improve their marketing strategies.

INTRODUCTION

E-commerce is a new platform for shopping and marketing medium for products and services. It can help to realize sustainable progress for humans and the environment. Due to the increase of Internet access and usage in households and companies, E-commerce has grown rapidly in recent years. People use the web for many reasons like online shopping, entertainment, personal communication, and so on.

E-commerce, which includes business to business (B2B) which means cutting costs in transactions between businesses and, business to consumer (B2C) which reflects sales of goods and services. E-Commerce is carried out on the Internet and has become the lifeline for the phenomenal growth of the Internet industry.

DOI: 10.4018/978-1-5225-0997-4.ch012

It brings a new platform for a new product launch with huge information that is not possible in a physical store in front of a massive audience which participates and provides reliable feedbacks which can be used in the improvement of marketing strategy.

To increase the efficiency and reliability towards sales, most E-commerce providers encourage users to comment on their products and services. People are now expressing their opinions, attitudes and feelings in these E-commerce websites in the form of customer reviews or online reviews. Through these reviews, users express their opinions on whatever they feel and these reviews provided by e-commerce companies are widely read are others. Hence, for the decision, making it becomes difficult for the customers as well as retailers to read all the reviews. In business, a long-term relationship strategy is to keep customers satisfied by considering customer reviews (feedbacks) and experiences. These reviews help in improving product quality and usability for potential customers.

The rise of the Internet technology has resulted in a variety of new information which helps online retailers improve their marketing efforts and distinguish themselves from competitors to gain customers' business. Various technologies such as Natural Language Processing, Recommendation system, and Text mining techniques are used to shape the shopping experience, according to consumers' personal preferences (Jain & Kumar, 2015a).

The explosion of these customer reviews presents a challenge for retailers and manufacturers of analysis and discovers useful information which helps in improving customer experience is explained by Mattosinho (2010). On the other side, mining and summarizing opinions from the text about specific entities and their aspects can help consumers decide what to purchase.

According to Liu (2012), Sentiment analysis is the process to extract the opinions or sentiments from customer reviews placed on blogs, forums, shopping websites etc. It is used to identify and extract subjective information contains in the text, such as opinions and feelings. The work of Gowtamreddy (2014) explained that an opinion expressed by customers helped manufacturers to improve their products or services. Potential customers also used these opinions for purchase decisions making. According to Alghamdi (2013), accurate understanding of these sentiments or opinions expressed in social media websites could bring tremendous business opportunities and help in decision making.

One of the importance's of these sentiments is to identify important aspects of your products or services by tracking regularly or for a particular time period about your brand or product across any channel. Social media such as Tweets, blog posts, YouTube videos, News stories, Facebook posts also help in knowing, how people feel about your brand. A typical sentiment analysis model is given in Figure 1.

IMPORTANCE OF CUSTOMERS' REVIEWS

The amount of unstructured data produced by customers in E-commerce websites increased dramatically during the phase known as Web 2.0. Customers' opinions represent a valuable and important type of information which should not be neglected or ignored by the e-commerce industry. From the customer perspective, considering others users' opinions before purchasing a product is a common behavior long on the Internet. According to Liu(2010), various survey agencies claimed that 70-90% customers buying decisions are influenced by online reviews through this E-commerce websites customer has access to thousands of opinions, which significantly improves decision making. This feature shows that customer reviews are the proven sales drivers.

Figure 1. A typical sentiment analysis model

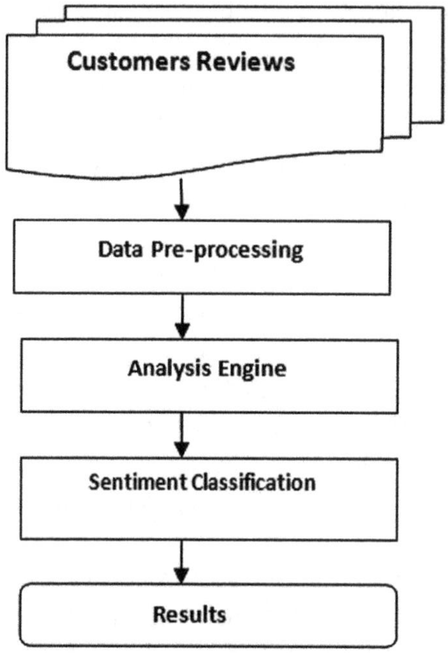

The basic intention of customers is to find the best for the lowest price or purchase that products which fulfill their needs inside a price range by analyzing other opinions come from their neutral nature, which will definitely benefit them.These opinions are usually not linked to an organization or company. These opinions represent the voice of ordinary consumers, and that differs greatly from advertisements. From these opinions, customers can easily understand the positives and negative aspects of the product.

From the e-commerce perspective, receiving consumer reviews/feedbacks can significantly improve its business action plan in order to increase profits. These reviews help in gaining business intelligence and improving customer satisfaction. It is common to find products with millions of opinions, thus, it could be a hard task for a customer to analyze all of them. Sentiment analysis tool and social media analyst's platform help the customer in decision making.

Social Media Analytics and E-Commerce

Social media provides a platform where companies can distribute their high-value content to the audience using hyperlinks, blogs, facebook profiles, Twitter hashtags etc. This marketplace used by E-commerce industries in two ways.Firstly it provides a virtual marketing platform such as Twitter and facebook, that are used by E-commerce industry to build online communities and market their products. Secondly by provide a huge amount of unstructured data in the forms of tweets, blogs etc. Millions of internet users post their opinion on features, benefits and the value of products or the company itself in forums, blogs and social media channels such as facebook or Twitter.

Social media helps in increasing sales, promotion of products or establishing a successful business to customer relationship which produces great results. One of the best and inexpensive activities that can be successfully organized on this platform by launching or promote a new product. Schneider (2015) gives some ways to launch a product using social media platform are:

1. **Create a Teaser:** In order to make attention towards the new product, create various creative images or videos of your product and share it.
2. **Online Promotion:** Conducts various contests and sweepstakes to increase interest and engagement of public.
3. **Introduce a Hashtag:** Share all activities using a common hashtag and regularly publish a post related to your new product and features which help audience for a better understanding of your product.
4. **Share the Impressions:** After the official date for launching has passed, share valuable comments in the form of images and videos about the impressions of your product.

Discovery of important facts and knowledge from social media data are very important and valuable for various departments in industries such as Public relations & marketing, Corporate management, Product management and Customer management. E-commerce vendors are adopting social media analytics for the following reasons:

- To gain competitive advantage and business values,
- Drive customer traffic,
- Boost customer loyalty and retention,
- Improve sales and revenues,
- Improving customer satisfaction, and
- Create brand awareness and build reputation.

SENTIMENT ANALYSIS AND OPINION MINING

Sentiment analysis is the computational study of people's opinions, sentiments, emotions, and attitudes. It focuses on developing automatic systems that can analyze natural language texts to determine the sentiment expressed in them. The word "sentiment" is often used in a wide sense to refer to expressions of subjectivity, opinion, affect, attitude, orientation, feelings, emotions, and tone in the text (Jain & Kumar, 2015b). Much of the current work in sentiment analysis has focused on the task of determining the presence of sentiment in the given text, and on determining its valence, that is, the classification of sentiment according to positive or negative orientation.

The sentiment classification task is quite often contrasted with that of topic-based categorization (Pang et al.(2002). Whitelaw et al.(2005) have empirically investigated that if sentiment classification can be regarded as a special case of topic-based categorization, with the positive and negative sentiment being taken as the two topics. They found that accuracy achieved in the sentiment classification problems is not as high as achieved in the conventional topic-based categorization, despite the different types of features tried for representing text. The results indicate that sentiment classification is comparably more challenging, because while topics are frequently expressed by relevant keywords, sentiment information is often embedded in the text in more subtle ways.

The automatic recognition of sentiment, particularly in large volumes of documents, can have a variety of applications, notably in summarizing popular sentiment about any product or issue. Such information may particularly be of interest to policy-makers, economists and market researchers, political analysts, and social scientists (Jain & Kumar, 2015b).

One of the earliest areas to attract the attention of researchers in sentiment analysis is that of movie reviews. There are many popular movie review sites on the web which have a tremendous amount of user opinions data. The addition of sentiment information to movie reviews can provide additional information to the readers and increase the popularity of the reviews. It can also help in the automatic analysis of movie reviews to determine the viewers' opinions.

One particular area of sentiment analysis, which focuses on identifying expression of opinion in the text as well as of their orientation, is called Opinion Mining or Opinion Analysis. Hurst and Nigam (2004) combine shallow NLP techniques and statistical machine learning to find the opinion sentences about the given topics from a corpus of data containing both relevant and irrelevant sentences.

Pang and Lee (2004) demonstrate the effectiveness of extracting subjective portions of text before performing polarity classification of movie reviews. Chesley et al. (2006) have also investigated the problem of subjectivity and polarity classification of blog posts. This fascinating problem is increasingly important in business and society. Sentiments of customers are used in three different ways:

1. **For Manufacturers:** It helps you track down which products are generating positive/negative sentiments and consumer trends.
2. **For Retailers:** It helps in Analyzing customer sentiments on what people are saying about their products being sold and the services being delivered.
3. **For Customers:** Customers sentiments towards products and services help in decision making for purchase.

Figure 2 shows a general architecture for sentiment analysis. Customer's reviews or social media reviews are feed to sentiment analysis engine and get sentiments of the customers

Figure 2. General architecture for sentiment analysis

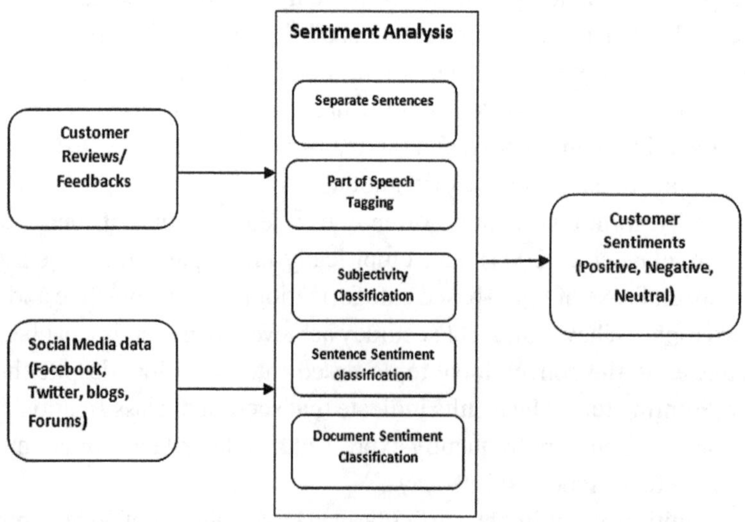

SENTIMENT ANALYSIS METHODS

The existing work on sentiment analysis can be classified as the problem of text classification in different forms such as Document-level sentiment analysis, Sentence-level sentiment analysis, Aspect-based sentiment analysis, Comparative sentiment analysis and Sentiment lexicon acquisition.

1. **Document-Level Sentiment Analysis:** This technique assumed that every document contains an opinion or opinion related words. Classification of these documents is carried out using two approaches: supervised learning and unsupervised learning.
2. **Sentence-Level Sentiment Analysis:** This technique is based on specialization of documents which contains various sentences and every sentence contains an opinion behind it.
3. **Aspect-Based Sentiment Analysis:** Attribute(aspect) based classification is performed such as in customer reviews of a mobile phone which have different attributes like battery, camera, screen size or resolutions, processor, memory etc. Every attribute opinion of the product is considered for better understanding sentiments.
4. **Comparative Sentiment Analysis:** In this technique identification of sentences which contain comparative opinions are filter out and opinions are extracted by considering sequential patterns as features.
5. **Sentiment Lexicon Acquisition:** This is most popular and crucial resource for most of the sentiment analysis algorithms. In this technique, acquisition of the sentiment lexicon is performed by manually, dictionary-based approaches and corpus-based approaches.

IMPORTANCE OF SENTIMENT ANALYSIS

Sentiment analysis is important for businesses because it identifies ways for them to improve their operations and the products they offer. This is done by measuring the public's perception of different products, services, and even advertisements. Business owners and advertising companies will often use sentiment analysis to discover unique strategies for their advertising campaigns, whether it's for direct mail postcards or online banner advertisements. According to various business analyst, customer reviews is the new battleground for brands.

The overall purpose is to build loyalty with consumers, which helps the business to grow and expand. It is much easier in this day and age to find out how the public feels about certain items because there are so many different social networking websites and other techniques for measurement. Business owners can use websites, such as Facebook and Twitter, to find out what the public likes and do not like so that they can prevent negativity and encourage the public to purchase their products or services.

ADVANTAGES OF SENTIMENT ANALYSIS

E-commerce industries should raise their social media footprint because their success truly depends on the effectiveness of their social engagement action plans. It is very important to get information about what your customers' likes, dislikes, wants and their needs. Sentiment plays important role to gain advantages over other techniques or policies and helps in improving market strategy. Following are the key benefits provided by sentiment analysis:

1. **Accessibility:** It can Accessible 24/7 and provide real-time sentiments.
2. **Gain Business Intelligence:** It provides you insightful business intelligence using which you can take impactful decisions that would leverage your business.
3. **Quickly Identify the Tonality:** Easy to identify key conversations, trends and issues along with positive and negative spikes in the conversation.
4. **Identification of Topics:** Easy to find a relevant topic regarding brands/products.
5. **Easily Built Engagement Platform:** You can participate in the negative or positive conversation and improve your marketing strategy.
6. **Beat Competition:** Track competitor sentiments improve action plan over time.
7. **Alerts Service:** Alerts can be set up for the brands to be notified of specific key positive or negative conversations and issues affected that brand.
8. **Improve Customer Service:** Improve customer service and engagement strategies by building on the positive sentiments and formulating methods to combat negative sentiments.

TOOLS FOR SENTIMENT ANALYSIS

Sentiment tools provide sentiment analysis of all types of unstructured data present in social media across different languages. The core functionality of the system depends on various techniques used in Natural Language Processing, Text Mining, Machine learning and rules-based system to assign either a positive, negative or neutral sentiment.

Considering the various benefits discussed in the chapter, companies uses sentiment analysis as a major aid in measuring sales and improving their marketing strategies as well. To accomplish this, some companies develop their own tools and others rely on outsourcing companies that specialize in sentiment analysis. Some are the popular tools are:

1. **Datumbox Machine Learning Framework:** It is an open-source framework which used for rapid development of Statistical and Machine Learning applications. It includes a large number of machine learning algorithms & statistical tests and be able to handle large-sized datasets. Datumbox API offers a large number of Classifiers and Natural Language Processing services which can be used in a broad spectrum of applications including Sentiment Analysis, Topic Classification, Language Detection, Subjectivity Analysis, Spam Detection, Reading Assessment, Keyword and Text Extraction and more (Datumbox, 2015).
2. **The Clarabridge CX Suite:** The Clarabridge CX Suite used customer feedback so you can use it to drive strategy, improve operations and empower the enterprise (Clarabridge, 2015).
3. **IBM Watson Analytics:** This software provides various sets of powerful analytics capabilities. It has automated data preparation, predictive analytics, reporting, dashboards, visualization and collaboration capabilities, enable you to take control of your own analysis (IBM, 2015).

4. **SAS Text Miner:** It employs text analysis framework to predict the overall and feature-based ratings for online application reviews. The entire major task for sentiment analysis can be easily performed (SAS Institute Inc., 2015).
5. **SentiPort:** This software used for brand reputation, design targeted campaigns, uncover opportunities and spot threats on social media channels are easily done using SentiOPort (CIGNEX Datamatics, 2015).

CONCLUSION

This chapter describes the potential of Sentiment analysis in solving a various problem related to businesses. Methods and tools are presented in this chapter can be used for analysis of social media data or customers reviews which give important and valuable knowledge towards improvement in various departments such as public relations & marketing, corporate management, product management and customer management

REFERENCES

Alghamdi, E. (2013). *The Influence of Social Media on E-Commerce Sites.* (Master Thesis). Dalhousie University, Halifax, Nova Scotia.

Chesley, P., Vincent, B., Xu, L., & Srihari, R. (2006). Using Verbs and Adjectives to Automatically Classify Blog Sentiment. In *Proceedings of the AAAI-2006 Spring Symposium on Computational Approaches to Analyzing Weblogs.*

Clarabridge. (2015). *The Clarabridge CX Suite.* Retrieved October 13, 2015, from http://www.clarabridge.com/product/

Datumbox. (2015). *Datumbox Machine Learning Framework.* Retrieved October 26, 2015, from http://www.datumbox.com/machine-learning-framework

Gowtamreddy, P. (2014). *Opinion Mining of Online Customer Reviews.* (Master Thesis). National Institute of Technology Rourkela.

Hurst, M., & Nigam, K. (2004). Retrieving Topical Sentiments from Online Document Collections. In *Proceedings of SPIE, Document Recognition and Retrieval XI* (pages 27-34).

IBM. (2015). *IBM Watson Analytics.* Retrieved October 16, 2015, from http://www-03.ibm.com/software/products/en/watson-analytics

Jain, V. K., & Kumar, S. (2015a). Big Data Analytic Using Cloud Computing. In *Proceeding of 2015 Second International Conference on Advances in Computing and Communication Engineering* (pp. 667-672).

Jain, V. K., & Kumar, S. (2015b). An Effective Approach to Track Levels of Influenza-A (H1N1) Pandemic in India Using Twitter. *Procedia Computer Science., 70*(1), 801–807. doi:10.1016/j.procs.2015.10.120

Liu, B. (2012). *Sentiment Analysis and Opinion Mining*. Morgan & Claypool Publishers.

Mattosinho, F. J. A. P. (2010). *Mining Product Opinions and Reviews on the Web*. (Master Thesis). Technische University Dresden.

Pang, B., Lee, L., & Vaithyanathan, S. (2002). Thumbs up? Sentiment Classification using Machine Learning Techniques. In *Proceedings of the 2002 Conference on Empirical Methods in Natural Language Processing* (pp. 79-86).

SAS Institute Inc. (2015). *SAS Text Miner*. Retrieved October 29, 2015, from http://support.sas.com/software/products/txtminer/

Schneider, J. (2015). Tactics for Launching a Product Using Social Media. *Harvard Business Review*. Retrieved October 13, 2015, from https://hbr.org/2015/04/10-tactics-for-launching-a-product-using-social-media

Wallace, L. (2015). *Improving the Consumer E-commerce Experience through Text Mining Industry View*. Retrieved November 23, 2015, from http://www.softwareadvice.com/bi/industryview/text-mining-report-2015

Whitelaw, C., Garg, N., & Argamon, S. (2005). Using Appraisal Taxonomies for Sentiment Analysis. In *Proceedings of MCLC-05, the Second Midwest Computational Linguistic Colloquium* (pp. 625-631).

KEY TERMS AND DEFINITIONS

Machine Learning: A science of getting computers to act without being explicitly programmed.

Natural Language Processing: Uses methods of computer science, artificial intelligence, and computational linguistics to understand interactions between computers and human languages.

Opinion Mining: Categorization of opinions.

Social Media: Group of Internet-based applications or platforms used for create, share, or exchange information in the form of text, images and videos.

Text Classification: Classification of documents into a fixed number of predefined categories.

Text Mining: Process of deriving high-quality information from text.

Section 4

Marketing Analytics:
Digital Market Place

Chapter 13
Adoption of Online Marketing for Service SMEs with Multi-Criteria Decision-Making Approach

Lanndon Ocampo
University the Philippines Cebu, Philippines

Dennis Anthony Kilongkilong
University of San Jose-Recoletos, Philippines

Rosalin Merry Berdin Alarde
University of San Jose-Recoletos, Philippines

Antonio Esmero
University of San Jose-Recoletos, Philippines

ABSTRACT

This chapter attempts to fill in the gap of evaluating the viability of adopting online marketing for small and medium enterprises (SMEs) in service industries. As SMEs are generally characterized by shortage of resources, the use of online marketing strategies is apparently difficult. However, the current landscape of competition among SMEs in a global market economy prompts the necessity of adopting online marketing. With these, the decision-making process of SMEs in this area becomes complex and the decisions must integrate complex and interrelating criteria and constructs in order to provide a more holistic solution. Thus, this work adopts a multi-criteria decision-making (MCDM) method particularly the analytic network process (ANP) in order to evaluate the practicability of using online marketing for service SMEs. It becomes highly relevant as it provides significant insights to decision-makers in SMEs regarding the use of online marketing strategy. The contribution of this chapter lies in the application of MCDM in evaluating viability of online marketing in service SMEs.

INTRODUCTION

On a global scale, small and medium enterprises (SMEs) are growing and are expected to compete strategically. In the U.S., SMEs are categorized according to the number of employees and asset size; particularly with less than 250 employees and annual sales of not more than US$ 50 million (Barad and Gien, 2001; Gonzalez et al., 2012). In the Philippines, SMEs are those enterprises that have 10-199

DOI: 10.4018/978-1-5225-0997-4.ch013

employees with Php 3 million to Php 100 million asset size (Jumamil-Mercado, 2013). SMEs have been a significant sector in economic development and are essential in generating employment (Harvie and Lee, 2005). A decade ago, Harvie and Lee (2005) estimated that 70% of new jobs creation in Southeast Asia came from SMEs. Across domain literature, SMEs are considered crucial in employment generation, output and export growth, poverty alleviation and better distribution of wealth (Asasen et al., 2003; Harvie, 2008). In the Philippines, SMEs play a vital role in "rural industrialization, development and decentralization of industries, creation of employment opportunities and more equitable income distribution, use of indigenous resources, earning of foreign exchange (forex) resources, creation of backward and forward linkages with existing industries, and entrepreneurial development" (Jumamil-Mercado, 2013). They are considered vital in dispersing new industries to the countryside and stimulating gainful employment (Jumamil-Mercado, 2013). Around 70% of non-agricultural employment was contributed by SMEs in the Philippines (Harvie and Lee, 2003). SMEs are known to be labor-intensive such that they generate jobs in the locality where they are situated (Jumamil-Mercado, 2013). This setup gains relevance in developing countries such as the Philippines. SMEs are quick in assimilating new design trends, developing contemporary products, and bringing them to the marketplace ahead of the competition (Jumamil-Mercado, 2013). This promotes SMEs as the seedbed for the development of entrepreneurial skills and innovation can make an important contribution to regional development programs (Department of Trade and Industry, 2008).

The trend of present economic progress demands businesses to compete more strategically, especially that various firms struggle to think of viable solutions in addressing customer needs. Implications of these requirements brought firms to gauge more on how to maintain and increase a good standing relationship with other businesses. This triggers fundamental questions to businesses the location, the time, and the components of the target market. The key to answer these questions relies largely by the appropriateness of the marketing tool carried out by SMEs. Coming up with a good marketing strategy attracts more customers and introduces the market with the products that firms can offer. For instance, firms seek to gauge into marketing program in order to promote their product and services through various strategic marketing implementation. This could be pursued with the use of traditional marketing and online marketing.

The widespread use of the internet across the globe highlights communication and mobility between buyers and suppliers. In this regard, online marketing has gained increasing attention over the past decade or so and has helped overcome the barriers of several business-related communications. As internet users carry out more active roles as expected, online marketing increases visibility of firm's profiles and products, and thus, it becomes an arguably good avenue for marketing and advertising. However, with the cost of pursuing online marketing which is a relevant issue in SMEs and the conditions that govern a geographical area, the decision of pursuing online marketing is certainly nontrivial that requires attention and focus. This decision of whether or not to implement online marketing strategy becomes complex due to the presence of several factors which oftentimes constitute inherent relationships. This decision domain exposes a multi-criteria decision-making (MCDM) problem.

The use of MCDM methods is widely accepted in current literature. Coulter and Sarkis (2005) adopted the ANP evaluating web or internet media advertising strategies. Wu et al. (2010) utilized an integrated ANP-TOPSIS in evaluating a marketing strategy for the hotel industry. Wang and Tzeng (2012) applied the combination of DEMATEL, ANP and VIKOR methods in evaluating customers' satisfaction through brand marketing in electronic manufacturing firms in Taiwan and concluded that value pricing yields as the most important factor in brand marketing strategies. Furthermore, Tsai et al. (2011) applied similar approach with DEMATEL, ANP and VIKOR methods in evaluating web-based marketing for air transportation industry. Similarly, Chiu et al. (2013) proposed a hybrid MCDM method involving DEMATEL, ANP and VIKOR to improve e-store business. Yang and Chang (2012) combined means-end chain and fuzzy ANP to explore customers' decision processes in choosing product bundles.

In this chapter, a decision model that depicts the intricacies of real-life decision-making assessing the viability of online marketing in SMEs is developed. An Analytic Network Process (ANP), developed by Saaty (2001), is used to handle the decision-making problem. ANP is used due to the multi-criteria nature of the problem where criteria exhibit overarching dependence relations. The goal is to come up with a decision of implementing online marketing strategy in SMEs from complex relations of several factors which include online marketing, traditional marketing, technology, and criteria. A case study in the province of Cebu which is located in central Philippines is carried out in this work. The contribution of this chapter is the development of a decision model that assesses the viability of implementing online marketing in SMEs.

BACKGROUND

The trend of current modernization underlines the use of technology and promotes intensified but positive rivalry of business sectors on which strategy formulation must be of high regard. There are factors to consider in obtaining the advantage of using online marketing and knowledge of these factors becomes increasingly important. In addition, the motivation behind departing from the traditional marketing to online marketing must be made clear and plausible. The role of the decision-maker is to ensure the viability of the marketing strategy. Current competitive scenarios require strong foundation in product promotion and implementation. In order to gain an understanding and perception of both traditional and online marketing strategies, this section provides the benefits and challenges of each strategy.

Traditional marketing utilizes strategies such as direct sales, TV, radio, mail, print advertising and promotional materials. The advantage of this approach is that traditional methods may be the only means of reaching a particular group of the market. For instance, if the firm is interested in targeting a group of farmers in a remote area, online marketing may not be appropriate. Furthermore, a person-to-person selling strategy of traditional marketing may be the most effective way for a particular time and place. In addition, there is something to be said about handling a customer some tangible printed material they can read at their convenience. However, challenges of traditional marketing include: expensive and cost prohibitive, difficulty in tacking results, requires technical help from outside the firm and is forced upon the customer.

Online marketing promotes and advertises the products and services through the use of the internet. Through instant leverage of wide marketing spectrum, organizations can build qualified potential customers and take business development to a much higher opportunities than the traditional one by utilizing such strategies like website creation, search engine optimization (SEO), banner ads, social media, pay-per-click advertising and email marketing. Some of the advantages of online marketing include: results are more measureable, decisions can be based on using real data and qualitative results, ability to drill down into demographics to accurately reach its target market, social media as essentially the word-of-mouth marketing based on personal experiences, inexpensive data and results are available immediately, accessible to any size business, and the ability to build direct relationships with the customers using social media and communities. However, the main downfall of online marketing is that it relies heavily on customers being highly interactive on the internet. Online marketing often demands time to continuously create, edit, approve and publish contents. Comments in several platforms must be responded to and sites and pages must be well maintained.

Thus, the challenge for businesses is in assessing the viability of adopting online marketing strategy. The assessment is highly nontrivial due to several factors that must be considered in the decision-making process. This complexity is further enhanced by taking SMEs into consideration with meager resources and lack of economies of scale. The assessment process becomes a multi-criteria decision-making (MCDM) problem and requires the adoption of MCDM methods. In this area, several previous studies reported the adoption of MCDM approaches in online marketing domains. Coulter and Sarkis (2005) developed a media selection model using ANP with internet/media advertising as one of its alternatives. Yang and Chang (2012) combined means-end chain and fuzzy ANP to explore customers' decision processes in choosing product bundles. Wu et al. (2010) provided an integration of ANP and technique order preference similar to an ideal solution (TOPSIS) as a five-step decision support to assess marketing strategies. Wang and Tzeng (2012) combined DEMATEL with ANP and VIKOR method to verify the interrelationships of brand marketing and then to identify the best strategy. Tsai et al. (2011) proposed an effectiveness evaluation model for web-based marketing of the airline industry which is an integration of marketing mix, i.e. the 4Ps, and website quality. Chiu et al. (2013) proposed a hybrid multi-attribute decision-making (MADM) model which combines linking the DEMATEL, DEMATEL-based Analytic Network Process (DANP), and VIKOR in the creation of marketing strategies of e-store business. Ocampo and Promentilla (2016) utilized the ANP in developing a sustainable manufacturing strategy which is an integration of both manufacturing strategy and sustainability. A review of literature shows that ANP was used in related studies; however, there were no studies which dealt with ANP in determining the viability of online marketing for service SMEs. One of the major issues that must be addressed is the interrelationships between traditional marketing, digital marketing, technologies, audience, and cost which are critical factors in adopting an online marketing strategy.

ANALYTIC NETWORK PROCESS (ANP)

ANP is the general theory of analyzing complex decision problems wherein analytic hierarchy process (AHP) is a special case (Saaty, 1980). AHP considers a decision problem with linear hierarchical structure while ANP extends this into a network of interdependent components. AHP/ANP is grounded on its three basic features: modeling system's complexity, measuring on a ratio scale and synthesizing as presented by Promentilla et al. (2008). See Table 1 as described by Promentilla et al. (2008).

Using pairwise comparisons and judgments, local priorities in ANP are computed in similar to how local priorities in AHP are generated. Unlike other MCDM methods, ANP captures both qualitative and quantitative criteria in an analytical decision model with components that are interrelating. Figure 1 represents an example of the form of the network structure used in a particular decision-making process.

Figure 1 shows a hierarchical network or a hiernet which is a digraph. The goal is composed of a single element and it controls the criteria and the alternatives components as represented by arcs 6 and 7, respectively. These arcs allow the network to be a strongly connected digraph in order to form an irreducible supermatrix (Saaty, 2001). Arcs 1 and 2 are unilateral hierarchical dependence. Arc 4 represents a feedback loop which means that the alternatives also depend on the elements of the criteria component. Arc 5 represents an interdependence loop which means that each element of the criteria

Table 1. The main basic characteristics of AHP/ANP

Functions/Features	AHP	ANP
(1) Structuring system's complexity	One-directional hierarchical structure with the assumption of mutual dependence of elements	A non-linear network structure of interdependence and feedback. Hierarchy, a linear structure, is a special case
(2) Measuring on a ratio scale	Local priorities derived from pairwise comparison matrices	Local (or initial) priorities derived from pairwise comparison matrices
(3) Synthesizing	Global or overall priorities from hierarchic composition or additive synthesis	Overall (or final) priorities from supermatrix calculations

Adopted from Promentilla et al., 2008.

Figure 1. A sample network structure and its corresponding supermatrix
Promentilla et al., 2006.

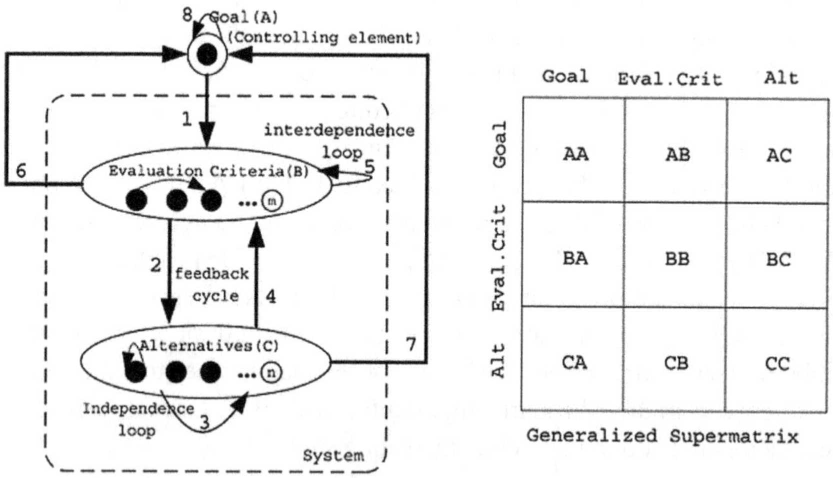

component is interrelated with some or all of the elements in the component. Arc 3 is an independence loop which means that the alternative depends only on itself. In this digraph, the direction of the arrow or arc determines the dominance of the elements of the component to other elements of another component or being dominated by other elements of another component. When an arc is pointing to a component (Arc 1 and 2), it means that the elements of that component influence the elements of the component from which the arc is emanating. The construction of the supermatrix is detailed in the reference books of the ANP, e.g. Saaty (2001).

CASE STUDY: VIABILITY OF ONLINE MARKETING IN SMALL AND MEDIUM ENTERPRISES – CENTRAL PHILIPPINE SCENARIO

A case study was conducted in Cebu City where majority of the business firms in central Philippines is located. The economic stability of Cebu City is known to be the next of the busiest enterprises in the Philippines. Cebu is less than 2% of the entire Philippines in terms of surface area. Despite of its size, it accounts for 4.9% of the total population and 10% of the exports. It also has more than one million tourists, which means that about half of the visitors of the country choose to come to Cebu.

Cebu has a large population which means that it could support a good number of small and medium enterprises (SMEs). In fact, long before the last population count in 2007, Cebu had already close to 3,000 SMEs with estimated assets of about Php 5.5 billion (around US$ 122 million), sales of Php 12 billion (around US$ 266 million) and total employment of about 180,000 workers (Fajardo, 2010). The Department of Trade and Industry of the Philippine government Cebu provincial office established the Small and Medium Enterprises Development Council – Cebu (SMEDC-Cebu) and was formally organized in February 21, 1996 by virtue of a law otherwise known as the Magna Carta for Small Enterprises. It was created to effectively spur the growth and development of SMEs throughout the country by way of facilitating and closely coordinating national and local efforts to promote the viability of SMEs.

These service industries were selected as they are still emerging industries on the use of online marketing. Although a handful companies on these industries are currently engaging on online marketing, in general, their orientation is still primitive. Target firms range from small to medium enterprises. Out of ten respondents, two of them belong to medium enterprise and the rest were from small enterprises. In this approach, specific category of firm is irrelevant as long as these firms have not fully engaged in online marketing. Respondents had to be owners or marketing managers of these SMEs who have adequate information and experience in making critical business decisions. Based from previous works, these respondents were sufficient to draw relevant findings. This had to be taken from a point of analytic generalization described by Yin (1994) as opposed to widely adopted statistical generalization. Unlike statistical generalization where the selected sample describes the population, analytic generalization aims to develop, strengthen, or contest a theory. Thus, this study did not intend to describe all service SMEs but to provide findings related to the use of online marketing. Table 2 shows the profile of case respondents.

Thorough literature review has been conducted to identify literature gaps. Literature review was divided into two parts. The first part focused on the review of online and traditional marketing literature. The second one highlighted the review on several MCDM methodologies that attempted to address a complex decision problem. Further on the study, it noticed that current literature lacks assessment of the viability of online marketing for SMEs. This is a significant issue as it provided guidelines for SMEs on choos-

Table 2. The profile of SMEs under consideration

Respondents	Type of Industry	Workforce Size	Asset Size (Million Php)	Classification
Coffee Dream	food and beverage services	100 - 120 crews	40-60	medium
Gilnaks Food Industries	accommodation and food service activities / food manufacturing	13 workers	8	small
Prime Nurselink Review Center	training services	11 staffs	7	small
Claire's Bakeshop	accommodation and food services activities	10 workers	4	small
88DB Phils., Inc.	advertising services	90 employees	100	medium
iRepublique	wholesale and retail trade	10 workers	3	small
Masaji Oriental Spa	spa services	12 therapists	5	small
Verlan Lending Inc.	lending investor services	10 staffs	7	small
Berdin's Firecrackers	pyrotechnics services	12 workers	8	small
Sofia Store	mini groceries services	10 crews	3	small

ing whether or not online marketing is appropriate for them taking into account several components in decision-making. It also found out that ANP is the most appropriate tool in handling complex decisions. Thus, this work focused on applying ANP to assess the viability in using online marketing for SMEs.

A survey questionnaire was formulated to collect adequate data from respondents involved in the study such as SMEs and decision-makers. The questions in the questionnaire were based from the operational model developed in Figure 2. Ten sets of questionnaires were disseminated to respondents in an administered manner. The survey questionnaire enables the respondents to perform pairwise comparisons in the context of the ANP.

The objective of this work in general is to guide SMEs in their attempt to implement online marketing strategy. There are five components or cluster in the digraph. These are the goal, criteria, non-online marketing promotion, technology, and viability of online marketing. Figure 2 shows the goal as a main controlling element with interdependencies with the rest of the components. This model was verified by the case respondents. To facilitate easy recall and ease of presentation, a coding system was provided in this study. Table 3 presents the codes of each element in the decision model.

Table 3 presents identified clusters or decision components with their corresponding codes. Goal, technology, criteria, and non-online marketing promotions are coded with G, T, C and N, respectively. The sub-criteria are coded in a way that shows reference from their parent criterion. For instance, the elements under component criteria are coded as C1 and C2. Likewise, other decision components and elements were coded similarly.

Figure 2. Decision model on the viability of online marketing for SMEs

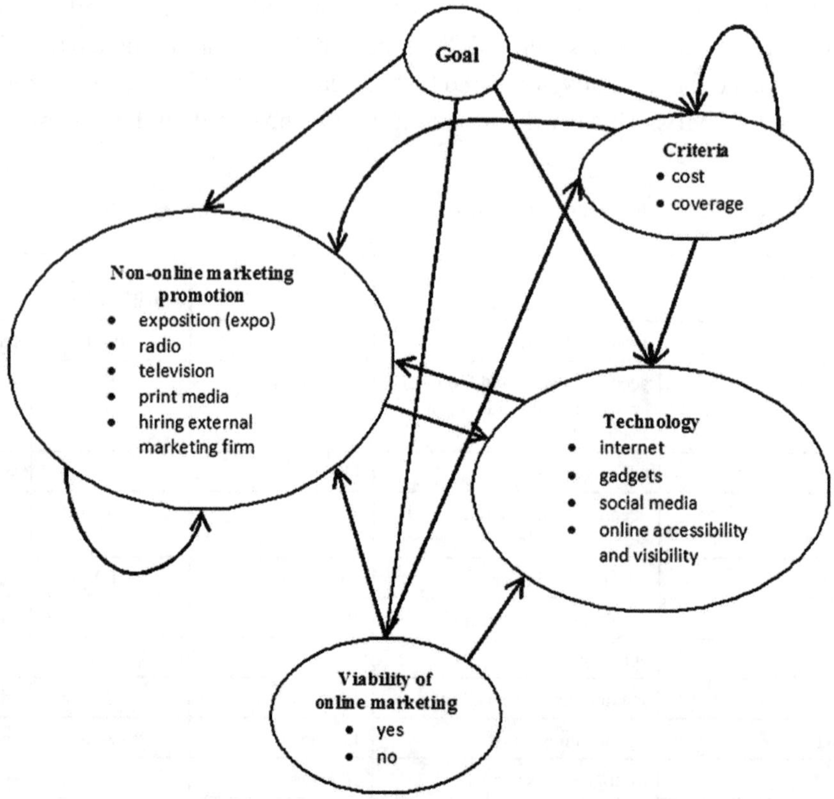

Table 3. Codes used in the study

Code	Decision Components and Elements
G	Goal (component)
O	Online marketing (component)
O1	yes to online marketing
O2	no to online marketing
T	Technology (component)
T1	internet
T2	gadgets
T3	social media
T4	website
C	Criteria (component)
C1	cost
C2	coverage
N	Non-online marketing promotions (component)
N1	expo
N2	radio
N3	television
N4	print media
N5	external marketing firm

METHODOLOGY

In general, the proposed method in determining the viability of online marketing for SMEs can be described in the following steps:

1. *Decompose the decision problem into a network.* This has been made in a form of wide-ranging review of literature with identification of gaps. It has been established from the review that previous studies failed to identify the viability of online marketing for SMEs. It was also found realized that the problem requires an MCDM approach, particularly ANP, because of the interdependencies and the number of factors that must be present in the decision model. From this, five decision components were recognized which are the goal, criteria, non-online marketing promotions, technology and alternatives. The interdependencies of these components were structured as shown in Figure 2.
2. *Elicit pairwise comparisons based from the network model developed in step 1.* A questionnaire was developed and distributed purposively to all identified respondents. The questionnaire in itself was prepared to allow pairwise comparisons among elements of the decision network. A supervised survey was implemented so that questions raised by the decision-makers (respondents) would be clearly and promptly assisted. This approach enabled the decision-maker to re-examine the pairwise comparisons matrices if in case the decisions are inconsistent. In eliciting pairwise comparisons, generally the question being asked is: "Given a control element, a component (element) of a given

network, and given a pair of components (or elements), how much more does a given member of the pair dominate the other member of the pair with respect to the control element?" (Promentilla et al., 2006). The Saaty's Fundamental Scale (Saaty, 1980), shown in Table 4, was utilized to compare the elements pairwise. Pairwise comparisons matrices were generated with a reciprocal characteristic. For instance, comparing C1 and C2 with respect to G has a ratio scale of 5, then comparing C2 and C1 must have a ratio scale of 1/5 as the reciprocal of 5. Local priority vectors were computed using equation (1); consistency ratios are checked using equations (5) and (6).

3. *Compute the local relative weights obtained from the pairwise comparisons processes in step 2.* The input to the supermatrix of a hierarchical network depends on the presence and type of dependencies described in the digraph. The eigenvector method is one of the popular methods used to quantify the relative dominance of the elements from pairwise comparison matrices. Saaty (1980) proposed the following eigenvalue formulation to obtain the desired ratio-scale priority vector (or weights) w of n elements:

$$Aw = \lambda_{max} w \quad (1)$$

where A is the positive reciprocal pairwise comparisons matrix, λ_{max} is the maximum (or principle) eigenvalue of the matrix A. λ_{max} can be computed using the following formulations:

$$Aw - \lambda_{max} w = 0 \quad (2)$$

$$\left(A - \lambda_{max} I\right) w = 0 \quad (3)$$

$$A - \lambda_{max} I = 0 \quad (4)$$

Table 4. Saaty's fundamental scale

Rating	Definition	Explanation
1	Equal importance	Two elements contribute equally to the objective
2	Weak	between equal and moderate
3	Moderate importance	Experience and judgment slightly favor one element over another
4	Moderate plus	between moderate and strong
5	Strong importance	Experience and judgment strongly favor one element over another
6	Strong plus	between strong and very strong
7	Very strong or demonstrated importance	An element is favored very strongly over another; its dominance demonstrated in practice
8	Very, very strong	between very strong and extreme
9	Extreme importance	The evidence favoring one element over another is one of the highest possible order or affirmation

Equation 4 yields a polynomial of λ to the degree n and the largest root of the polynomial is the λ_{max}. For consistent judgment, $\lambda_{max} = n$, otherwise, $\lambda_{max} > n$. The measure of consistency of judgment is measured through the Consistency Index (CI) and Consistency Ratio (CR). The Consistency Index (CI), as a measure of degree of consistency, was calculated using the formula

$$CI = \left(\lambda_{max} - n\right) / \left(n - 1\right) \tag{5}$$

The consistency ratio (CR) is computed as

$$CR = CI \;/\; RI \tag{6}$$

where RI is the mean random consistency index (see Alonso and Lamata (2006) for values of RI). Acceptable CR values must be less than 0.1. Decision-makers were asked to repeat the pairwise comparisons for CR values greater than 0.1.

4. *Aggregate expert judgments.* Corresponding pairwise comparisons from SMEs decision-makers were then aggregated into a matrix where each element consists of aggregated judgment elicited by all decision-makers. The aggregation process requires determining the geometric mean of all elicited judgments. To compute the aggregated value, it is said that for each pairwise comparison matrix, a total of k number of samples was taken which corresponds to k number of decision-makers. To aggregate judgment of these decision makers, a geometric mean method is used as prescribed by Saaty (2001). Aggregation using geometric is described as follows,

$$X_{ij} = \left(\prod_{k} x_{ij}^{k}\right)^{1/k} \tag{7}$$

where X_{ij} is the aggregate score of comparing row element i and column element j in any pairwise comparison matrix, k is the number of decision-makers or assessors and x_{ij}^{k} is the score of the kth decision-maker of comparing row element i and column element j in a given pairwise comparisons matrix.

5. *Populate the initial supermatrix with the relative weights from step 3.* Global priority ratio scales or priorities can be obtained based on the synthesizing concept of the supermatrix. By raising the matrix to large powers, the transmission of influence along all possible paths defined in the decision structure is captured in the process (Saaty, 2001). The convergence of initial priorities (stochastic matrix) to an equilibrium value in the limit supermatrix provides a set of meaningful synthesized priorities from the underlying decision structure (Promentilla et al., 2008). Saaty (2001) assured that as long as the supermatrix representation is a primitive irreducible matrix derived a strongly connected digraph, the initial supermatrix will converge to a limit supermatrix. Each column of the limit supermatrix is a unique positive column eigenvector which corresponds to the stable priorities from the limit supermatrix and can be used to measure the overall relative dominance of one element over another in a network structure (Promentilla et al., 2006).

RESULTS

An illustrative decision model, presented in Figure 2, is carried out in the case study. The decision problem consists of goal component, non-online marketing component with five elements, the technology component with four elements, criteria component with two elements and lastly, the alternative viability of online marketing with two elements. Note that the given framework is not only limited to the number of factors but could extend to sufficiently large number of components and elements. The structure of the decision problem must agree with reliable information obtained from related studies and from practical experience of field experts.

There are seven types of pairwise comparisons carried out in the study. First, pairwise comparisons are done on the outer dependence of the elements of non-online marketing promotions, criteria, technology, and viability of online marketing with respect to the goal. Second, pairwise comparisons are done on the dependence among the elements of the criteria component. Third, pairwise comparisons are done on the dependence relationships of non-online marketing promotion component towards criteria elements. Fourth, pairwise comparisons are done on the independence of non-online marketing promotions elements. This is due to the interrelationships on the factors influence by the component. Fifth, pairwise comparisons are done on the dependence relationships of the elements of the technology component towards criteria component. Sixth, pairwise comparisons are done on the feedback loop between non-online marketing promotion and technology components. Lastly, pairwise comparisons are done on the dependence relationships of the elements of non-online marketing promotion, criteria and technology components towards the elements of the viability of online marketing component. Note that only upper triangle of the matrix is filled out as the lower triangle represents the straightforward reciprocal of the upper triangle. For succinctness, all pairwise comparisons in all types and in all experts could not be presented in this chapter due to the large amount of space requirement. Nonetheless, aggregated pairwise comparisons matrix of each type is shown here for discussion. The decision model in Figure 2 served as the basis for pairwise comparisons among components and elements.

An aggregated pairwise comparison of the first type is shown in Table 5. The question being asked in Table 5 is like this: "From non-online marketing promotions component, comparing expo (N1), radio (N2), television (N3), print media (N4), and external marketing firm (N5), which one more dominates the goal (G) and by how much?". The resulting eigenvector or priority vector together with the maximum eigenvalue and consistency ratio CR are shown in Table 5.

Table 5. Aggregated pairwise comparisons comparing non-online marketing elements with respect to the goal

G	N1	N2	N3	N4	N5	e-Vector
N1	1	0.8272	0.7410	1.2821	1.8015	0.1983
N2	1.2089	1	1.4140	1.1962	2.1689	0.2534
N3	1.3493	0.7071	1	2.3246	2.1946	0.2642
N4	0.7800	0.8360	0.4300	1	2.8772	0.1849
N5	0.5551	0.4611	0.4560	0.3476	1	0.0993

$\lambda_{max} = 5.143$, CR = 0.032

Table 6 shows an aggregated pairwise comparisons matrix of the relative importance of the elements in the criteria component with respect to the goal. The question being asked in Table 6 is like this: "Comparing cost (C1) and coverage (C2), which one more dominates the goal (G), and by how much?". The resulting eigenvector as well as the maximum eigenvalue and the consistency ratio CR value are reported in Table 6.

Table 7 shows the aggregated pairwise comparisons of the third type. The question being asked in Table 7 goes this way: "Comparing expo (N1), radio (N2), television (N3), print media (N4), and external marketing firm (N5), which one more dominates cost (C1), and by how much?" The resulting eigenvector or priority vector with consistency ratio CR are shown in Table 7.

Table 8 shows another type of aggregated pairwise comparisons of the elements in the non-online marketing promotions component. The question being asked in Table 8 goes this way: "From non-online marketing promotions component, comparing expo (N1), radio (N2), television (N3), print media (N4), and external marketing firm (N5) elements, which one more dominates the goal (G), and by how much? The resulting eigenvector with the maximum eigenvalue and consistency ratio CR are shown in Table 8.

Table 9 shows another pairwise comparisons of the fifth type. The question being asked in Table 9 is like this: "Comparing internet (T1), gadgets (T2), social media (T3), online accessibility or otherwise known as website (T4), which one more dominates coverage (C2), and by how much?" The resulting priority vector with the maximum eigenvalue and consistency ratio CR are reported in Table 9.

Table 10 and 11 show another type of pairwise comparisons in a form of feed-backing from non-online marketing promotions (N) component to the technology (T) component. The question being asked in Table 10 is like this: "Comparing expo (N1), radio (N2), television (N3), print media (N4), hiring external firm (N5), which one more dominates the element internet (T1) of the technology (T) component, and by how much?" In respond to the feedback of the element internet (T1) to elements of non-online marketing promotions (N), the question being asked in Table 11 is like this: "Comparing internet (T1),

Table 6. Aggregated pairwise comparisons comparing elements of the criteria with respect to the goal

G	C1	C2	e-Vector
C1	1	1.5337	0.6053
C2	0.652	1	0.3947

λ_{max} = 2.000, CR = 0.000

Table 7. Aggregated pairwise comparisons of comparing non-online marketing promotions with respect to criteria

C1	N1	N2	N3	N4	N5	e-Vector
N1	1	0.7042	0.8424	0.7499	1	0.1545
N2	1.4200	1	1.7731	1.8684	2.2442	0.2912
N3	1.1871	0.5640	1	3.1867	3.1867	0.2807
N4	1.3335	0.5352	0.3138	1	3.1533	0.1751
N5	1	0.4456	0.3138	0.3171	1	0.0985

λ_{max} = 5.345, CR = 0.078

Table 8. Aggregated pairwise comparisons of comparing non-online marketing elements with respect to the goal

G	N1	N2	N3	N4	N5	e-Vector
N1	1	0.5493	0.5887	0.6335	0.9390	0.1275
N2	1.8206	1	1.5060	3.1366	2.2180	0.3230
N3	1.6986	0.6640	1	3.4418	3.0840	0.2965
N4	1.5784	0.3188	0.2905	1	2.4210	0.1500
N5	1.0649	0.4509	0.3243	0.4131	1	0.1030

λ_{max} = 5.266, CR = 0.060

Table 9. Aggregated pairwise comparisons of comparing the elements of technology component with respect to the criteria

C2	T1	T2	T3	T4	e-Vector
T1	1	2.0998	1.0481	1.1487	0.3052
T2	0.4762	1	0.5863	0.5863	0.1540
T3	0.9541	1.7056	1	1.1233	0.2815
T4	0.8706	1.7056	0.8902	1	0.2594

λ_{max} = 4.003, C.R. = 0.001

gadgets (T2), social media (T3), online accessibility and visibility (T4), which one more dominates the element expo (N1) of the non-online marketing promotions component, and by how much?" Again, the eigenvector is computed together with the maximum eigenvalue and consistency ratio CR are shown in Tables 10 and 11.

Table 12 shows another aggregated pairwise comparisons of the last type on the dependence of technology (T) with respect to the element yes to online marketing (O1). The question asked in Table 12 is like this: "Comparing internet (T1), gadgets (T2), social media (T3), and online accessibility and visibility (T4), which one more dominates the element yes to online marketing (O1), and by how much?" The resulting eigenvector or priority local vector with maximum eigenvalue and CR are likewise presented in Table 12.

Table 10. Aggregated pairwise comparisons of non-online marketing with respect to technology

T1	N1	N2	N3	N4	N5	e-Vector
N1	1	0.5065	0.5065	0.4427	1.1962	0.1230
N2	1.9744	1	0.933	1.6719	2.6531	0.2774
N3	1.9744	1.0718	1	1.9512	2.3771	0.2911
N4	2.2587	0.5981	0.5125	1	2.4464	0.2067
N5	0.8360	0.3769	0.4207	0.4088	1	0.1017

λ_{max} = 5.073, C.R. = 0.016

Table 11. Aggregated pairwise comparisons of technology with respect to non-online marketing

N1	T1	T2	T3	T4	e-Vector
T1	1	2.3618	1.2821	1.1487	0.3235
T2	0.4234	1	0.4023	0.572	0.1328
T3	0.78	2.4856	1	0.9936	0.2800
T4	0.8706	1.7482	1.0065	1	0.2638

$\lambda_{max} = 4.016$, CR = 0.006

Table 12. Aggregated pairwise comparisons of technology with respect to online marketing

O1	T1	T2	T3	T4	e-Vector
T1	1	2.7305	1.6438	2.2036	0.4138
T2	0.3662	1	1.6141	2.2505	0.2474
T3	0.6084	0.6196	1	2.0560	0.2116
T4	0.4538	0.4443	0.4864	1	0.1272

$\lambda_{max} = 4.150$, CR = 0.056

These local eigenvectors were plugged into their respective locations in the supermatrix. By assigning G, C, T, N, A of goal, criteria, technology, non-online marketing promotions and viability of online marketing components, respectively, a generalized supermatrix of the decision-making as shown in Figure 2 can be drawn. Local priority vectors obtained from the pairwise comparisons are populated in the generalized supermatrix. The initial supermatrix (unweighted) is presented in Table 13. After populating the supermatrix with the local priority vectors, a column stochastic supermatrix is obtained which is dome by obtaining column sums and dividing each element with its column sum. Table 14 provides the column stochastic supermatrix.

The column stochastic matrix in Table 14 is raised to large powers in order to obtain limiting supermatrix. When the supermatrix converges to its Cesaro sum (Saaty, 2001), column values become identical. Each column represents the principal right eigenvector or the global eigenvector of the supermatrix. Table 15 shows the limiting supermatrix with the global eigenvector.

Table 13. Initial (unweighted) supermatrix

	G	O1	O2	T1	T2	T3	T4	C1	C2	N1	N2	N3	N4	N5
G	1	1	1	1	1	1	1	1	1	1	1	1	1	1
O1	0.688	1	0	0	0	0	0	0	0	0	0	0	0	0
O2	0.312	0	1	0	0	0	0	0	0	0	0	0	0	0
T1	0.399	0.414	0.294	1	0	0	0	0.377	0.305	0.324	0.277	0.383	0.312	0.422
T2	0.256	0.247	0.244	0	1	0	0	0.118	0.154	0.133	0.128	0.160	0.170	0.157
T3	0.183	0.212	0.247	0	0	1	0	0.244	0.282	0.280	0.318	0.264	0.305	0.253
T4	0.163	0.127	0.216	0	0	0	1	0.261	0.259	0.264	0.278	0.192	0.214	0.169
C1	0.567	0.668	0.514	0.596	0.561	0.515	0.526	1	0	0	0	0	0	0
C2	0.433	0.332	0.486	0.404	0.439	0.485	0.474	0	1	0	0	0	0	0
N1	0.198	0.161	0.085	0.123	0.175	0.116	0.117	0.155	0.110	0	0	0	0	0
N2	0.253	0.328	0.259	0.277	0.252	0.295	0.251	0.291	0.251	0	0	0	0	0
N3	0.264	0.259	0.373	0.291	0.265	0.243	0.261	0.281	0.346	0	0	0	0	0
N4	0.185	0.154	0.166	0.207	0.189	0.200	0.228	0.175	0.188	0	0	0	0	0
N5	0.099	0.099	0.117	0.102	0.119	0.146	0.143	0.099	0.106	0	0	0	0	0

Table 14. Column supermatrix

	G	O1	O2	T1	T2	T3	T4	C1	C2	N1	N2	N3	N4	N5
G	0.200	0.200	0.200	0.250	0.250	0.250	0.250	0.250	0.250	0.500	0.500	0.500	0.500	0.500
O1	0.138	0.200	0	0	0	0	0	0	0	0	0	0	0	0
O2	0.062	0	0.200	0	0	0	0	0	0	0	0	0	0	0
T1	0.080	0.083	0.059	0.250	0	0	0	0.094	0.076	0.162	0.138	0.192	0.156	0.211
T2	0.051	0.049	0.049	0	0.250	0	0	0.030	0.038	0.066	0.064	0.080	0.085	0.079
T3	0.036	0.042	0.049	0	0	0.250	0	0.061	0.070	0.140	0.159	0.132	0.152	0.126
T4	0.033	0.025	0.043	0	0	0	0.250	0.065	0.065	0.132	0.139	0.096	0.107	0.084
C1	0.113	0.134	0.103	0.149	0.140	0.129	0.132	0.25	0	0	0	0	0	0
C2	0.087	0.066	0.097	0.101	0.110	0.121	0.118	0	0.250	0	0	0	0	0
N1	0.040	0.032	0.017	0.031	0.044	0.029	0.029	0.039	0.027	0	0	0	0	0
N2	0.051	0.066	0.052	0.069	0.063	0.074	0.063	0.073	0.063	0	0	0	0	0
N3	0.053	0.052	0.075	0.073	0.066	0.061	0.065	0.070	0.086	0	0	0	0	0
N4	0.037	0.031	0.033	0.052	0.047	0.050	0.057	0.044	0.047	0	0	0	0	0
N5	0.020	0.020	0.023	0.025	0.030	0.037	0.036	0.025	0.027	0	0	0	0	0

Table 15. Limiting supermatrix

	G	O1	O2	T1	T2	T3	T4	C1	C2	N1	N2	N3	N4	N5
G	0.279	0.279	0.279	0.279	0.279	0.279	0.279	0.279	0.279	0.279	0.279	0.279	0.279	0.279
O1	0.048	0.048	0.048	0.048	0.048	0.048	0.048	0.048	0.048	0.048	0.048	0.048	0.048	0.048
O2	0.022	0.022	0.022	0.022	0.022	0.022	0.022	0.022	0.022	0.022	0.022	0.022	0.022	0.022
T1	0.100	0.100	0.100	0.100	0.100	0.100	0.100	0.100	0.100	0.100	0.100	0.100	0.100	0.100
T2	0.050	0.050	0.050	0.050	0.050	0.050	0.050	0.050	0.050	0.050	0.050	0.050	0.050	0.050
T3	0.070	0.070	0.070	0.070	0.070	0.070	0.070	0.070	0.070	0.070	0.070	0.070	0.070	0.070
T4	0.059	0.059	0.059	0.059	0.059	0.059	0.059	0.059	0.059	0.059	0.059	0.059	0.059	0.059
C1	0.105	0.105	0.105	0.105	0.105	0.105	0.105	0.105	0.105	0.105	0.105	0.105	0.105	0.105
C2	0.081	0.081	0.081	0.081	0.081	0.081	0.081	0.081	0.081	0.081	0.081	0.081	0.081	0.081
N1	0.028	0.028	0.028	0.028	0.028	0.028	0.028	0.028	0.028	0.028	0.028	0.028	0.028	0.028
N2	0.050	0.050	0.050	0.050	0.050	0.050	0.050	0.050	0.050	0.050	0.050	0.050	0.050	0.050
N3	0.052	0.052	0.052	0.052	0.052	0.052	0.052	0.052	0.052	0.052	0.052	0.052	0.052	0.052
N4	0.035	0.035	0.035	0.035	0.035	0.035	0.035	0.035	0.035	0.035	0.035	0.035	0.035	0.035
N5	0.020	0.020	0.020	0.020	0.020	0.020	0.020	0.020	0.020	0.020	0.020	0.020	0.020	0.020

The global priority vector was analysed on a component basis. Table 16 provides the ranking of elements per decision component. Note that each element in the supermatrix determines the influence or dependence of row component on column component. Shown in Table 16 are the raw global priority vector, and the distributive, ideal, ranking of elements according to their components. The raw column indicates the column values obtained from the limiting supermatrix found in Table 15. Distributive column is computed by normalizing each element in the raw column with the component sum. Thus, each component in the distributive column has sum equal to 1. Ideal column is also computed by dividing each element in the distributive column with the maximum value in that column. Ideal column provides decision-makers pertinent information on the distance of a particular element to the ideal element, on a normal scale. Rank column which provides the rank of the element relative to the component is computed by assigning a rank order of the elements in a component in a descending fashion. Thus, large values in the distributive or ideal column are assigned with higher ranks.

DISCUSSION AND CONCLUSION

Ranking shows that with the given decision model, online marketing is viable in service SMEs. This implies that SMEs decision-makers must consider adopting online marketing strategies to promote their products and services. The magnitude of this priority as shown in the ideal rank is twice compared to its contrast of not adopting online marketing. In the technology component, internet is the most prioritized technology followed by social media, online accessibility, and gadgets with the least priority. In this context, this can be explained as follows. Decision-makers perceived internet as an enabling resource in promoting online marketing. Inaccessibility of firms and markets with the internet fails any online marketing program and initiatives. Thus, appropriate policies regarding internet accessibility and use must be in placed by the government, firms and other sectors in order to promote online marketing. Secondly, social media is considered as second from the top priority in supporting online marketing. This can be easily understood from the point of view of community's desire for greater communication and socialization. In this respect, SMEs and markets can divulge on feedback mechanisms towards better

Table 16. Global priority vector

Elements	Global Priority Vector			Rank
	Raw	Distributive	Ideal	
G	0.279	1	1	1
O1	0.048	0.688	1	1
O2	0.022	0.312	0.454	2
T1	0.100	0.358	1	1
T2	0.050	0.180	0.504	4
T3	0.070	0.249	0.696	2
T4	0.059	0.213	0.595	3
C1	0.105	0.566	1	1
C2	0.081	0.434	0.766	2
N1	0.028	0.152	0.545	4
N2	0.050	0.269	0.965	2
N3	0.052	0.279	1	1
N4	0.035	0.190	0.680	3
N5	0.020	0.110	0.394	5

products and services. This can be observed as a growing number of firms, both small and large, which promote their products and services through social media. Online visibility, e.g. websites, is considered third in the list as it highlights the details of firms' profile, structure, programs, products and services. With respect to service SMEs, this approach seems to have been outperformed by internet and social media because these firms have not yet established their name and brand in the market and internet and social media are faster approaches to catch the attention of the market. While gadgets support mobility, these are heavily dependent on internet and social media in the context of online marketing. Thus, this is considered as the least priority.

In the criteria component, cost is more prioritized compared to coverage. This is relevant because SMEs have tighter financial constraints. They are also likely considering short term benefits over long term goals. Thus, any initiatives which entail considerable costs are usually brought to long discussion tables with firm's decision-makers. Thus, SMEs must optimize the use of online marketing by drawing out strategies that could possibly lower down associated costs. Lastly, considering the non-online marketing component, television, and radio are highlighted as relevant supports to online marketing as well as its relevant alternatives. These are relevant because these media cover wider coverage at a modest cost and maintenance. Hiring an external marketing firm is an unlikely strategy for SMEs as it entails additional investment which is a major constraint to most SMEs. As support media, carefully integrating this with online marketing could be a possible route for SMEs.

REFERENCES

Alonso, J. A., & Lamata, M. T. (2006). Consistency in the Analytic Hierarchy Process: A new approach. *International Journal of Uncertainty, Fuzziness and Knowledge-based Systems*, *14*(4), 445–459. doi:10.1142/S0218488506004114

Asasen, C., Asasen, K., & Chuangcham, N. (2003). A proposed ASEAN Policy Blueprint for SME development 2004–2014. *REPSF Project*, *02/005*(33), 145.

Barad, M., & Gien, D. (2001). Linking improvement models to manufacturing strategies – a methodology for SMEs and other enterprises. *International Journal of Production Research*, *39*(12), 2675–2695. doi:10.1080/002075400110051824

Chiu, W. Y., Tzeng, G. H., & Li, H. L. (2013). A new hybrid MCDM model combining DANP with VIKOR to improve e-store business. *Knowledge-Based Systems*, *37*, 48–61. doi:10.1016/j.knosys.2012.06.017

Coulter, K., & Sarkis, J. (2005). Development of a media selection model using the analytic network process. *International Journal of Advertising: The Review of Marketing Communications*, *24*(2), 193–215.

Department of Trade & Industry (Philippines). (2008). *Micro, Small and Medium Enterprises (MSMES)*. Retrieved January 28, 2016, from http://www.dti.gov.ph/dti/index.php?p=532

Gonzalez, M. E., Quesada, G., & Mora-Monge, C. (2012). An international study on manufacturing competitive priorities. *Journal of Management Policy and Practice*, *13*(3), 116–128.

Harvie, C. (2008). SMEs in regional trade and investment development. In T. Van Hoa & C. Harvie (Eds.), *Regional Trade Agreements in East Asia* (pp. 149–186). Cheltenham, UK: Edward Elgar.

Harvie, C., & Lee, B. C. (2003). *Public policy and SME development*. Working Paper 03-18. Department of Economics, University of Wollongong.

Jumamil-Mercado, G. (2013). Philippines. In S. Sato (Ed.), Impact of the global financial crisis on SMEs: What happens on SMEs through the global financial crisis? (pp. 61-78). Asian Productivity Organization (APO).

Ocampo, L. A., & Promentilla, M. A. B. (2016). Development of a sustainable manufacturing strategy using analytic network process. *International Journal of Business and Systems Research*, *10*(2-4), 262–290. doi:10.1504/IJBSR.2016.075744

Promentilla, M. A. B., Furuichi, T., Ishii, K., & Tanikawa, N. (2006b). Evaluation of remedial countermeasures using the analytic network process. *Waste Management (New York, N.Y.)*, *26*(12), 1410–1421. doi:10.1016/j.wasman.2005.11.020 PMID:16412627

Promentilla, M. A. B., Furuichi, T., Ishii, K., & Tanikawa, N. (2008). A fuzzy analytic network process for multi-criteria evaluation of contaminated site remedial countermeasures. *Journal of Environmental Management*, *88*(3), 479–495. doi:10.1016/j.jenvman.2007.03.013 PMID:17467879

Saaty, T. L. (1980). *The Analytic Hierarchy Process*. New York: McGraw-Hill.

Saaty, T. L. (2001). *Decision making with dependence and feedback: The Analytic Network Process* (2nd ed.). Pittsburgh, PA: RWS Publications.

Tsai, W. H., Chou, W. C., & Leu, J. D. (2011). An effectiveness evaluation model for the web-based marketing of the airline industry. *Expert Systems with Applications*, *38*(12), 15499–15516.

Wang, Y. L., & Tzeng, G. H. (2012). Brand marketing for creating brand value based on a MCDM model combining DEMATEL with ANP and VIKOR methods. *Expert Systems with Applications*, *39*(5), 5600–5615. doi:10.1016/j.eswa.2011.11.057

Wu, C. S., Lin, C. T., & Lee, C. (2010). Optimal marketing strategy: A decision-making with ANP and TOPSIS. *International Journal of Production Economics*, *127*(1), 190–196. doi:10.1016/j.ijpe.2010.05.013

Yang, H. W., & Chang, K. F. (2012). Combining means-end chain and fuzzy ANP to explore customers' decision process in selecting bundles. *International Journal of Information Management*, *32*(4), 381–395. doi:10.1016/j.ijinfomgt.2011.11.005

Yin, R. (1994). Case study research: Design and methods. Thousand Oaks, CA: Sage Publications.

Chapter 14
E-Retailing from Past to Future:
Definitions, Analysis, Problems, and Perspectives

Zehra Kamisli Ozturk
Anadolu University, Turkey

Mehmet Alegoz
Anadolu University, Turkey

ABSTRACT

In this chapter, first, the definition, the advantages and disadvantages of e-retailing are given and the related literature about e-retailing is briefly explained in order to give a background to unfamiliar readers. Then, the qualitative and quantitative criteria which affect the e-retailer selection are determined and some e-retailers are evaluated by using a multi-phase, integrated Multi Criteria Decision Making (MCDM) approach. In first phase of proposed MCDM approach, the weight of each criterion is determined. In second phase, a pre-evaluation is made and some of the e-retailers are eliminated. In last phase, the remaining retailers are evaluated and the best one is determined. Finally, the study is concluded by discussions, inferences and recommendations for future work.

INTRODUCTION

From past to present, human habits have changed as a result of technological improvements and globalization. Internet is one of the most important actors in this change. According to Internet world stats, in 2016, more than 3.3 billion of people use Internet. This is more than 46.4 percent of the whole world population. In North America 87.9 percent of people use Internet which is the highest rate. However, only 28.6 percent of people in Africa use Internet. Although, the Internet use in developing countries is low compared to developed countries, it still continues to increase. For example, only 420 millions of people were using Internet in 2000 and this number increased to one billion in 2005. From 2005 to today, it increased to 3.3 billion as it is mentioned (Internet World Stats).

DOI: 10.4018/978-1-5225-0997-4.ch014

Since the Internet allows people to access easily everything they need with only a few click, it became an integral part of life. Unlike traditional habits, people begin do almost everything on the Internet. This change in habits increased the potential on the Internet and make the investors focus on it. Today, there is no doubt that Internet channel is one of the fundamental channels for marketing.

Nowadays, there are lots of Internet retailers. For instances, one of the largest Internet retailers, Amazon is founded by Jeff Bezos in 1994. It provides a worldwide service and it has announced a revenue of US$ 88.988 billion for 2014. This amount shows the potential of the Internet retailing. In addition to Amazon, there are numerous national and international retailers in almost all the countries. The number of Internet retailers increases every day. As a result, the competition in Internet channel also increases every day.

Even if it seems easy at first, in fact Internet retailing may be more difficult than traditional retailing. It needs a real time information system, cooperation and a well-designed supply chain network. Some Internet retailers use a minimum cost oriented supply chain network while some others use a supply chain network which minimizes the delivery time. In addition, a few of the Internet retailers like Amazon, use a flexible supply chain network which gives the opportunity of minimizing either the cost or delivery time according to customer request. Of course, this flexibility increases the preference of customers.

The chapter is organized as follows: Section 2 introduces the literature review of Internet retailing from both customers and retailers view. The models developed to obtain the criteria and Internet retailer alternatives' weights are discussed in Section 3. Section 4 provides suggestions to customers and Internet retailers based on the multi criteria evolutions. The chapter ends with future research directions and conclusion.

BACKGROUND

In this part of study, we have given some definitions and concepts to the readers. We have briefly explained the definition of retailing, Internet retailing (e-retailing), advantages and disadvantages of Internet retailing and the potential of it. By this way, in this part we have aimed to give the necessary background to the unfamiliar readers.

Retailing includes all the activities involved in selling goods or services to the final consumers for personal, non-business use. Selling to the final consumers whether it is by a manufacturer, a wholesaler or a retailer-is retailing irrespective of the fact that the goods or services are sold (by person, mail, telephone, vending machine or Internet or where they are sold – in a store, on the street or in the consumer's home (Kotler, 2007).

- Internet retailing (also known as e-retailing, e-tailing, online retailing, e-commerce) refers to retailing over the internet (Francis and White, 2004).
- There are lots of different definitions about internet retailing which are made by different researchers. It is a new retail channel which can be used for various activities (Chaffey et al., 2000).
- Internet retail sites are not those which provide free downloads, product reviews etc. They are web sites where in fact visitors purchase products (Pastore, 1999).
- Web retailing includes transactions of products/services by using the internet (Sinha and Gvili, 2001).
- E-Retailing is the sale of products/services over the internet (Kolesar and Galbraith, 2000). Consumers purchase over the internet and this is called as e-tailing.

According to Subramanian et al. (2014), the population of online consumers worldwide is growing at a tremendous rate i.e. 15–20% per annum. Moreover, the growth rate is highly exponential in some countries like China and at 75% per annum. They also indicates that as Internet use grows dramatically, e-commerce also increases. Today, many people use online shopping for their various needs from vegetable for their dinner to seats for their home. E-retailers should not only provide superior products, but also offer ''a better purchasing environment, better personalization choice, and greater customer control'' and make sure that the online purchase process is convenient and efficient for customers.

Unimportance of location, size flexibility, saves on the costs, reachability to larger people, time flexibility and opportunities about CRM are some of the advantages of e-retailing. In addition to these advantages, Dennis et al., (2004) indicates substantial costs (set-up, investment etc.) complex logistics, legal problems, pressure on margins and prices in store as disadvantages of e-retailing.

There are various kind of studies in the literature about this subject. We will mention a few of them as follows. Lee and Tan (2003) proposed an approach which integrates extant literature on retailing and consumer choice to develop an economic model of consumer choice in which a consumer self-selects between on-line and in-store shopping. They identified the retail context utility and the consumers' perceived product and service risks as the two important factors impacting consumer choice between on-line versus in store shopping. Kim et al. (2012) empirically examine the effect of various Internet shopping site qualities on the utilitarian and hedonic values of Internet shopping. They also focused on the influence of the perceived level of Internet shopping value on customer satisfaction and repurchase intention. They perform structural equation analysis with a sample of 293 observations consisting of two different income groups (workforce and student). The results show that while system and service qualities are critical factors affecting utilitarian shopping value, information and service qualities are the factors most closely associated with hedonic shopping value. These findings suggest that service quality plays a significant role in increasing both utilitarian and hedonic shopping values.

Cho (2015) examines customers' experience with a retailer's web site and order fulfillment experiences' interactive effects on repurchase intention. In this research, it's mentioned that the type of product can likewise affect a customer's experience with the retailer's web site and order fulfillment. Results of multiple-group structural equation modeling (SEM) from customer reviews of 306 Internet retailers demonstrate that the interactive effects of a web site experience and order fulfillment are significant. In the interactive mechanism, order fulfillment experience is proven to serve as a proximal cause of repurchase intention. The moderating role of product type is significant as well. Cho (2015a) is the first survey-based study on the relationship between resources and market coverage for small Internet retailing. The study examines the practices of Internet retailing and the resources required, based on insights on marketing, operations management, and management information systems. This survey-based study collects data from 147 North American florists who use web sites as e-channels. The data are analyzed through a set of multi-nominal logistic regressions, and multiple analysis of covariance. Measurement validation is conducted before data analysis. Considering two resources, e-IT competence and e-service agility – both critical for providing e-services – this study finds that e-service agility is significantly associated with market coverage. Wu et al. (2014) demonstrate that web technologies, which are used to develop retail stores' web design and virtual atmosphere, are critical to customer purchase intention. In their study, web layout design creates a positive customer attitude towards the web site; the positive atmosphere increases emotional arousal, which in combination, create purchase intention. Essentially, achieving a satisfactory customer experience requires sophisticated web technologies that produce positive psychological signals within the customer (Cho, 2015a).

There are lots of issues in Internet retailing to consider. Researchers try to focus on these issues in their studies and proposed some approaches. Ethics is also one of the fundamental issues in customer satisfaction. However, less attention is given to this important issue. Elbeltagi and Agag (2016) are two of those researchers who focused on this subject. They developed and tested a comprehensive model of online retailing ethics. Subramanian et al. (2014) focused on customer satisfaction and proposed an approach for this issue. They handle the Chinese e-retailing on both customer and e-retailer perspectives. They suggest two structural equation models to capture the role of service quality, e-service quality and selection of logistics providers on customer satisfaction and e-retailers' competitiveness. They also indicate that product recovery is another issue in e-retailing. Zhang et al. (2015) investigated service recovery in the context of e-retailing industry from the perspective of operations management and aimed more fully understanding of potential factors affecting market performance. In another study, Zhang et al. (2015a) focused on E-Service quality in the context of the Chinese e-retailing industry.

AN INTEGRATED MULTI CRITERIA DECISION MAKING (MCDM) APPROACH TO EVALUATE INTERNET RETAILERS

In this section, we propose an integrated MCDM approach to evaluate Internet retailers. First of all the qualitative and quantitative criteria which affect the e-retailer selection are determined. In first phase of proposed MCDM approach the weight of each criterion is determined. In second phase, a pre-evaluation is made and some of the e-retailers are eliminated. In last phase, the remaining retailers are evaluated and the best one is determined. All of these steps are given below, respectively.

Determination of Criteria

In first step, we determined all the criteria which are important for Internet retailing. During this determination process, we have used two main resources. One of them is the literature and the second one is surveys which are applied to randomly selected customers and retailers. After collecting the data from both the literature review and surveys, we brought them together and determined the criteria as given in Table 1.

A Fuzzy AHP Approach to Evaluate the Criteria

It can be easily seen that there are both qualitative and quantitative criteria which affect the e-retailing process and all of them must be put into consideration in order to make a reliable analysis and obtain accurate results. For this reason, we have used type-2 fuzzy sets and Buckley's fuzzy AHP algorithm which works with type-2 fuzzy sets. We will not mention the properties of type-2 fuzzy sets due to the limited space, the reader may refer to Chen and Lee (2010) for detailed information about it.

Buckley's fuzzy AHP algorithm mainly consists of seven important steps. These steps are summarized as follows. (Buckley, 1985 and Celik et al., 2014)

Step 1: Consult expert for pairwise comparison of the critical success factors using linguistic variables given in Table 2.

Table 1. Criteria for Internet retailing evaluation

Criteria	Sub-Criteria	Performance Indicator
Web Site	User Interface	Is the web site compact, simple, well designed and attractive?
	Ease of purchase	Is it easy to purchase a product from that website or is it include complex, time-consuming steps?
	Accessibility	Is it always possible to access the website or is there some disconnections in some days?
	Information Accuracy	Is the information in the website correct or is there wrong information about the product or service?
Service	On Time Delivery	After the purchase, is the delivery made on time or are there delays?
	Online Customer Support	Is there someone to help before during or after purchase?
	Payment Security	Is the payment system secure enough to make the payment without any concern?
	Order Track	Is there a real time system to track the orders?
	Promotions	Time by time, are there promotions?
Product	Guaranty	In addition to manufacturer guaranty, is there e-retailer guaranty for the products?
	Cost	How are the cost of products compared to other retailers?
	Quality	How are the quality of products compared to other retailers?
	Number of Product Types	Are there a wide-range of options for a product (i.e. wallet)?
	Availability	Generally, are the products available to purchase or is the e-retailer need some time to bring it?
E-Retailer	Innovation	Is the e-retailer give importance to innovation, research and development and technology?
	Reputation	Is the e-retailer reputable?
	Experience	Is the e-retailer experienced?

Table 2. Linguistic terms

Absolutely strong (AS)	((8;9;9;10;1;1),(8,5;9;9;9,5;0,9;0,9))
Very strong (VS)	((6;7;7;8;1;1),(6,5;7;7;7,5;0,9;0,9))
Fairly strong (FS)	((4;5;5;6;1;1),(4,5;5;5;5,5;0,9;0,9))
Slightly strong (SS)	((2;3;3;4;1;1),(2,5;3;3;4,5;0,9;0,9))
Equal (E)	((1;1;1;1;1;1),(1;1;1;1;0,9;0,9))
Slightly weak (SW)	((0,25;0,33;0,33;0,5;1;1),(0,22;0,33;0,33;0,4;0,9;0,9))
Fairly weak (FW)	((0,17;0,2;0,2;0,25;1;1),(0,18;0,2;0,2;0,22;0,9;0,9))
Very weak (VW)	((0,13;0,14;0,14;0,17;1;1),(0,13;0,14;0,14;0,15;0,9;0,9))
Absolutely weak (AW)	((0,1;0,11;0,11;0,13;1;1),(0,11;0,11;0,11;0,12;0,9;0,9))

Step 2: Examine the consistency of the pairwise comparison using crisp values proposed by by Saaty (1990).

Step 3: Construct type-2 fuzzy pair wise comparison matrix among all the criteria in the hierarchical structure as shown in equation (1).

$$\begin{bmatrix} 1 & \tilde{\alpha}_{12} & \cdots & \tilde{\alpha}_{1n} \\ \tilde{\alpha}_{21} & 1 & \cdots & \tilde{\alpha}_{2n} \\ \cdots & \cdots & \ddots & \cdots \\ \tilde{\alpha}_{n1} & \tilde{\alpha}_{n2} & \cdots & 1 \end{bmatrix} \tag{1}$$

Step 4: Define the fuzzy geometric mean as given in Equation (2).

$$\tilde{r}_i = \left(\tilde{\alpha}_{i1} \otimes \tilde{\alpha}_{i2} \otimes \ldots \otimes \tilde{\alpha}_{in}\right)^{1/n} \tag{2}$$

Step 5: Calculate the fuzzy weights of each criterion by using Equation (3).

$$\tilde{w}_i = \tilde{r}_1 \otimes \left(\tilde{r}_1 \oplus \tilde{r}_2 \oplus \ldots \oplus \tilde{r}_n\right)^{-1} \tag{3}$$

Step 6: Defuzzify the fuzzy number in order to calculate the weights of the criteria by using Equation (4).

$$w_i' = \frac{1}{2}\left(\frac{1}{2}\sum_{i=1}^{4}\left(a_i^L + a_i^L\right)\right) \otimes \frac{1}{4}\left(\sum_{i=1}^{2}\left(H_i\left(A^L\right) + H_i\left(A^U\right)\right)\right) \tag{4}$$

Step 7: Normalize the crisp weights by using the following equation.

$$w_i = w_i' / \sum_{i=1}^{n} w_i' \text{, } i = 1, \ldots, \text{t} \tag{5}$$

We applied this algorithm to our problem. The fuzzy geometric means and fuzzy weights of main criteria are given below in Table 3 and Table 4, respectively.

After fuzzy evaluation process, the weights of criteria and sub-criteria of Internet retailing are obtained as in Table 5.

Evolution of Internet Retailers with VIKOR

The VIKOR method which focuses on ranking and selecting from a set of alternatives, and determines compromise solution for a problem with conflicting criteria, developed as a multi attribute decision making method to solve a discrete decision making problem with non-commensurable (different units) and conflicting criteria (Opricovic and Tzeng, 2007; Opricovic and Tzeng, 2008; Sayadi et al., 2009).

Assuming that we have *n* criteria and each alternative (A_1, A_2,..., A_m) is evaluated according to each criterion function, the compromise ranking could be performed by comparing the measure of closeness to the ideal alternative. For alternative A_i, the rating of the jth aspect is denoted by the value of jth criterion function for the alternative A_i (f_{ij}). Sayadi et al. (2009) give the steps of the algorithm as follows:

Table 3. Fuzzy geometric means for main criteria

C_1	0,45	0,51	0,51	0,59	1,00	1,00	0,45	0,51	0,51	0,54	0,90	0,90
C_2	1,00	1,31	1,31	1,68	1,00	1,00	1,08	1,31	1,31	1,69	0,90	0,90
C_3	0,50	0,57	0,57	0,71	1,00	1,00	0,47	0,57	0,57	0,63	0,90	0,90
C_4	2,21	2,82	2,82	3,36	1,00	1,00	2,52	2,82	2,82	3,51	0,90	0,90

Table 4. Fuzzy weights for main criteria

C_1	0,07	0,10	0,10	0,14	1,00	1,00	0,07	0,10	0,10	0,12	0,90	0,90
C_2	0,16	0,25	0,25	0,40	1,00	1,00	0,17	0,25	0,25	0,37	0,90	0,90
C_3	0,08	0,11	0,11	0,17	1,00	1,00	0,07	0,11	0,11	0,14	0,90	0,90
C_4	0,35	0,54	0,54	0,81	1,00	1,00	0,40	0,54	0,54	0,78	0,90	0,90

Table 5. Weights of criteria and sub-criteria of Internet retailing

#	Criteria	Weight	Sub-Criteria	Local Weight	Global Weight
C1	Product	0,413	Cost	0,276	0,114
C2	Product	0,413	Guaranty	0,274	0,113
C3	Service	0,277	Payment Security	0,406	0,112
C4	Product	0,413	Quality	0,241	0,099
C5	Web Site	0,176	Information Accuracy	0,487	0,086
C6	E-Retailer	0,134	Experience	0,551	0,074
C7	Service	0,277	On Time Delivery	0,201	0,056
C8	Service	0,277	Online Customer Support	0,168	0,047
C9	Product	0,413	Number of Product Types	0,112	0,046
C10	Web Site	0,176	Ease of Purchase	0,254	0,045
C11	Product	0,413	Availability	0,098	0,040
C12	E-Retailer	0,134	Reputation	0,287	0,038
C13	Service	0,277	Order Track	0,116	0,032
C14	Service	0,277	Promotions	0,109	0,030
C15	Web Site	0,176	Accessibility	0,135	0,024
C16	Web Site	0,176	User Interface	0,124	0,022
C17	E-Retailer	0,134	Innovation	0,162	0,022

1. Determine the best f_j^* and the worst f_j^- values of all criterion functions, $j = \overline{1,n}$. If the jth function represents a benefit then:

$$f_j^* = \max_i f_{ij},\ f_j^- = \min_i f_{ij}. \tag{6}$$

2. Compute the values S_i and R_i, $i = \overline{1,m}$.

$$S_i = \sum_{j=1}^{n} w_j \left(f_j^* - f_{ij}\right) / \left(f_j^* - f_j^-\right), \tag{7}$$

$$R_i = \max_j w_j \left(f_j^* - f_{ij}\right) / \left(f_j^* - f_j^-\right) \tag{8}$$

where w_j are the weights of criteria, expressing their relative importance.

3. Compute the values $Q_i \left(i = \overline{1,m}\right)$, by equation (9):

$$Q_i = \frac{v\left(S_i - S^*\right)}{\left(S^- - S^*\right)} + \left(1 - v\right)\frac{\left(R_i - R^*\right)}{\left(R^- - R^*\right)} \tag{9}$$

where

$S^* = \min_i S_i$,
$S^- = \max_i S_i$,
$R^* = \min_i R_i$,
$R^- = \max_i R_i$,
v is introduced as weight of the strategy of the majority of criteria.

4. Sort *S*, *R* and *Q* values in decreasing order to determine the rank of alternatives. The results are three ranking lists.
5. Propose as a compromise solution the alternative A', which is ranked the best by the measure Q (minimum).

The best alternative, is the one with the minimum value of *Q*.

We applied the VIKOR algorithm to our problem. We evaluated nine e-retailers according to five most important criteria. These are cost, guaranty, payment security, quality and information accuracy respectively. The S, Q and R values are given below in Table 6. According to that table A2, A9, A8, A3 and A7 are the five Internet retailers which pass to evaluation phase.

Determination of the Best Internet Retailer with TOPSIS

In this last phase of the integrated MCDM method, the five Internet retailers are evaluated with TOPSIS method based on all criteria that were determined in the first phase.

Table 6. VIKOR evaluation results

	S	R	Q
A1	0,483	0,216	0,658
A2	0,416	0,163	**0,137**
A3	0,479	0,216	**0,648**
A4	0,616	0,214	0,980
A5	0,603	0,189	0,782
A6	0,479	0,217	0,657
A7	0,483	0,214	**0,648**
A8	0,469	0,216	**0,623**
A9	0,472	0,143	**0,141**

TOPSIS (technique for order preference by similarity to an ideal solution) method is presented in Chen and Hwang (1992), with reference to Hwang and Yoon (1981). The basic principle is that the chosen alternative should have the shortest distance from the ideal solution and the farthest distance from the negative-ideal solution (Opricovic and Tzeng, 2004). The steps of the method are as follows:

1. Calculate the normalized decision matrix. Use equation (10) to normalize r_{ij}.

$$r_{ij} = f_{ij} \Big/ \sqrt{\sum_{j=1}^{J} f_{ij}^2}, j = 1,\ldots,J; i = 1,\ldots,n \tag{10}$$

2. Calculate the weighted normalized decision matrix. Calculate the weighted normalized value (v_{ij}) by equation (11).

$$v_{ij} = w_i r_{ij}, j = 1,\ldots,J; i = 1,\ldots,n \tag{11}$$

where w_i is the weight of the ith criterion, and $\sum_{i=1}^{n} w_i = 1$

3. Determine the ideal (A^*) and negative-ideal (A^-) solution.

$$A^* = \left\{v_1^*,\ldots,v_n^*\right\} = \left\{\left(\max_j v_{ij} \middle| i \in I'\right),\left(\min_j v_{ij} \middle| i \in I''\right)\right\}, \tag{12}$$

$$A^- = \left\{v_1^-,\ldots,v_n^-\right\} \tag{13}$$

where I' is associated with benefit criteria, and I'' is associated with cost criteria.

4. Calculate the separation measures, using the n-dimensional Euclidean distance. The separation of each alternative from the ideal solution (D_j^*) is given as

$$D_j^* = \sqrt{\sum_{i=1}^{n} \left(v_{ij} - v_i^*\right)^2}, j = 1, \ldots, J \tag{14}$$

Similarly, the separation from the negative ideal solution (D_j^-) is given as

$$D_j^- = \sqrt{\sum_{i=1}^{n} \left(v_{ij} - v_i^-\right)^2}, j = 1, \ldots, J \tag{15}$$

5. Calculate the relative closeness to the ideal solution. The relative closeness of the alternative a_j with respect to A^* is defined as

$$C_j^* = D_j^- / \left(D_j^* + D_j^-\right), j = 1, \ldots, J. \tag{16}$$

6. Rank the preference order. The alternative with the highest C_j^* value is the best one.

In this last phase of this study, the best five e-retailers are evaluated according to all criteria by using TOPSIS method. The weighted normalized decision matrix and D_j^*, D_j^-, and C_j^* values are given in Table 7 and Table 8. Our analysis shows that the best e-retailer with the highest C_j^* value is A9, then the second one is A3 and the third one is A2.

SUGGESTIONS TO CUSTOMERS AND RETAILERS

In this part of study, we will give some suggestions both to customers and to retailers. Our suggestions will be according to criteria weights we obtained in previous phase.

It is certain that the *security* issue is one of the fundamental issues in e-retailing. Customers want to be sure about that their personal information and payment information (information about their credit card

Table 7. Weighted normalized decision matrix

	C1	C2	C3	C4	C5	C6	C7	C8	C9	C10	C11	C12	C13	C14	C15	C16	C17
A2	0,045	0,052	0,063	0,056	0,020	0,018	0,037	0,012	0,006	0,017	0,027	0,014	0,017	0,010	0,008	0,008	0,015
A9	0,045	0,039	0,051	0,045	0,051	0,035	0,022	0,024	0,028	0,029	0,022	0,007	0,017	0,016	0,011	0,013	0,009
A8	0,059	0,065	0,025	0,022	0,041	0,035	0,015	0,031	0,028	0,006	0,011	0,014	0,004	0,016	0,004	0,003	0,003
A3	0,045	0,039	0,063	0,056	0,031	0,026	0,029	0,018	0,022	0,029	0,005	0,014	0,013	0,016	0,015	0,011	0,009
A7	0,059	0,052	0,038	0,034	0,041	0,044	0,015	0,012	0,006	0,006	0,016	0,029	0,017	0,006	0,011	0,011	0,009

Table 8. D_j^*, D_j^-, and C_j^* values for Internet retailer alternatives

	D_j^*	D_j^-	C_j^*
A2	0,058	0,065	0,5296
A9	0,045	0,066	**0,5926**
A8	0,069	0,051	0,4268
A3	0,051	0,065	0,5608
A7	0,059	0,052	0,4663

etc.) will be strongly protected. If there is a little doubt about that, they decide not to buy anything from that website even if the product quality is really high and cost is really low compared to others. For this reason, e-retailers should firstly focus on security issue. They must clearly emphasize that the website is secure enough and the payment information will strongly be protected. When a customer enters the website, (s)he should directly be sure about the information and payment security.

Information accuracy is another important issue in e-retailing. When a customer looks at a product (s)he wants to know all the details about that product. For example, if it is a smartphone, all the technical properties of that must be written. Some e-retailers write only the camera, display size and memory. However, anyone may want to know about the technical specifications of its chip or its battery. If all the information about the product is not provided, customers may decide not to buy that product from that e-retailer or they may be disappointed after purchase because of unwritten specifications of a product. Even then, they may want to return that product to e-retailer. This may bring extra cost in addition to customer dissatisfaction. For this reason, e-retailers must provide all possible information accurately. A customer should see all possible details about the product and make the decision in this context. This is also an ethical responsibility of e-retailers. By this way, the customers begin to trust that e-retailer and the customer satisfaction begin to increase.

The third issue is customer support before, during and after sales. Time by time, customers may face with problems. For example, they may not be able to register to buy a product, they may not complete the payment process, they may have problems about the product after the sale. All these problems must be solved by the customer support services of e-retailers as soon as possible. Unsolved problems before and during the sale may make the customer change his/her decision and not to buy anything from that e-retailer. Unsolved problems after the sale may make the customer return the product and since a dissatisfied customer will explain the problems to his friends/colleagues etc. the reputation of that e-retailer may be damaged. For this reason, e-retailers must give special attention to customer service. They must support the customers via all possible channels like e-mail, phone etc. By this way, the customer satisfaction will increase and the loyalty may begin.

One last important issue is ease of use. In some websites, the registration and/or the purchasing process is really difficult. E-retailers must keep the system as easy as possible. A customer should be able to buy anything within a few time without dealing with complex forms etc. This ease of use definitely increase the customer satisfaction and bring the loyalty together. The e-retailers which require filling complex, time consuming forms will possibly face with customer dissatisfaction and profit losses.

We have mentioned some important issues in this part of study. However, it is beneficial to emphasize that all the criteria mentioned in the previous part of study are important. An e-retailer must focus on all the mentioned criteria to be successful in competition.

FUTURE RESEARCH DIRECTIONS

No doubt that Internet use will increase in the next years as a result of continuous technological improvements. By this way, people will try to do more things via the Internet. This will not only increase the role of Internet in our life but also bring new habits together.

For example, as mobile phones and tablet PC's begin to grow up, mobile Internet usage is begin to increase dramatically and traditional desktop PC and laptop usage is decreased. In order to adapt this situation, all the webmasters try to adapt their website to mobile use. Mobile responsive themes are created by web designers, mobile applications are created by developers and people begin to use mostly their mobile devices for their needs. In addition, the social media begin to be an integral part of life. In fact, technological improvements do not only change the life styles of people but also bring a more competitive environment for retailers. Companies must definitely take action to survive in this competitive environment. From another perspective, technological developments bring lots of new things to focus on for researchers. We will mention a few of them as follows.

- Retailing via mobile devices,
- Retailing via social media,
- Optimum web design and product layout for e-retailing,
- Effect of promotions and advertisements on e-retailing success,
- Effect of payment methods (payment at the door, via credit card or with PayPal etc.) and flexible payment plans on e-retailing success,
- Strategies to increase the loyalty on e-retailing (customer clubs, retailer cards etc.).

Please note that there are few studies about some of the topics mentioned above. However, it is not possible to say that this issues are totally understood and solved.

CONCLUSION

In this chapter, first, the definition, the advantages and disadvantages of e-retailing are given and the related literature about e-retailing is briefly explained. Then, the qualitative and quantitative criteria which affect the e-retailer selection are determined and some e-retailers are evaluated by using a multi-phase, integrated Multi Criteria Decision Making (MCDM) approach. In first phase of proposed MCDM approach the weight of each criterion is determined. In second phase, a pre-evaluation is made and some of the e-retailers are eliminated by Fuzzy AHP method. In last phase, the remaining retailers are evaluated and the best one is determined with VIKOR and TOPSIS methods. In VIKOR linear normalization and in TOPSIS vector normalization is used to eliminate the units of criterion functions.

Beside the criteria dealt with in this chapter, there are also various other criteria that can be considered in the Internet retailing process. Based on the literature review and surveys we considered 17 criteria.

According to MCDM approach that we proposed here, security, information accuracy, customer support and ease of use criteria are determined as the most important ones.

All e-retail companies are in competition with the other companies. According to the company specific considerations and constraints, the judgments may change from one company to another. Even so, the integrated model proposed here can provide a general framework to obtain the weights/priorities of criteria. Therefore, this study will support the e-retailers in regard to policy development and so compete with each other.

REFERENCES

Beal, T. (2010). *Small and Medium Enterprises in Asian Pacific Countries* (M. A. Abdullah & M. I. Baker, Eds.). New York: Nova Science Publishers Inc.

Buckley, J. (1985). Fuzzy hierarchical analysis. *Fuzzy Sets and Systems*, *17*(3), 233–247. doi:10.1016/0165-0114(85)90090-9

Celik, E., Gumus, A. T., & Alegoz, M. (2014). A Trapezoidal Type-2 Fuzzy MCDM method to identify and evaluate critical success factors for humanitarian relief logistics management. *Journal of Intelligent & Fuzzy Systems*, *27*(6), 2847–2855.

Chaffey, D., Mayer, R., Johnston, K., & Ellis-Chadwick, F. (2000). *Internet Marketing*. London: Prentice Hall.

Chen, S., & Lee, L. (2010). Fuzzy multiple attributes group decision-making based on the interval type-2 TOPSIS method. *Expert Systems with Applications*, *37*(4), 2790–2798. doi:10.1016/j.eswa.2009.09.012

Cho, Y. K. (2015). Creating customer repurchase intention in Internet retailing: The effects of multiple service events and product type. *Journal of Retailing and Consumer Services*, *22*, 213–222. doi:10.1016/j.jretconser.2014.11.002

Cho, Y. K. (2015a). The relationship between resources and market coverage in small local internet retailing. *International Journal of Retail & Distribution Management*, *43*(7), 597–616. doi:10.1108/IJRDM-12-2013-0220

Dennis, C., Fenech, T., & Merrilees, B. (2004). *e-Retailing*. Routledge. Taylor & Francis Group.

Elbeltagi, I., & Agag, G. (2016). E-retailing ethics and its impact on customer satisfaction and repurchase intention. *Internet Research*, *26*(1), 288–310. doi:10.1108/IntR-10-2014-0244

Francis, J. E., & White, L. (2004). Internet retailing: Back to the Future. In *Proceedings of the Australian and New Zealand Marketing Academy Conference*. Wellington, New Zealand: Australian and New Zealand Marketing Academy.

Kim, C., Galliers, R. D., Shin, N., Ryoo, J., & Kim, J. (2012). Factors influencing internet shopping value and customer repurchase intention. *Electronic Commerce Research and Applications*, *11*(4), 374–387. doi:10.1016/j.elerap.2012.04.002

Kolesar, M. B., & Galbraith, R. W. (2000). A services-marketing perspective on e-retailing: Implications for e-retailers and directions for further research. *Internet Research: Electronic Networking Applications and Policy*, *10*(5), 424–438. doi:10.1108/10662240010349444

Kotler, P., Keller, K. L., Koshi, A., & Jha, M. (2007). *Marketing Management*. New Delhi: Pearson Education.

Lee, K. S., & Tan, S. J. (2003). E-retailing versus physical retailing A theoretical model and empirical test of consumer choice. *Journal of Business Research*, *56*(11), 877–885. doi:10.1016/S0148-2963(01)00274-0

Opricovic, S., & Tzeng, G. H. (2004). Compromise solution by MCDM methods: A comparative analysis of VIKOR and TOPSIS. *European Journal of Operational Research*, *156*(2), 445–455. doi:10.1016/S0377-2217(03)00020-1

Opricovic, S., & Tzeng, G. H. (2007). Extended VIKOR method in comparison with outranking method. *European Journal of Operational Research*, *178*(2), 514–529. doi:10.1016/j.ejor.2006.01.020

Pastor, M. (1999, Aug 18). *July's E-Tailing Stats*. Retrieved from https://www.clickz.com/clickz/news/1698171/julys-e-tailing-stats

Saaty, T. (1990). How to make a decision: The analytic hierarchy process. *European Journal of Operational Research*, *48*(1), 9–26. doi:10.1016/0377-2217(90)90057-I

Sayadi, M. K., Heydari, M., & Shahanaghi, K. (2009). Extension of VIKOR method for decision making problem with interval numbers. *Applied Mathematical Modelling*, *33*(5), 2257–2262. doi:10.1016/j.apm.2008.06.002

Sinha, I., & Gvili, Y. (2001). *A Cross-Regional Study of Consumer Perceptions of Shopping on the Internet*. EBI Working paper (number EBI-2001-03). Temple University, Fox School.

Subramanian, N., Gunasekaran, A., Yu, J., Cheng, J., & Ning, K. (2014). Customer satisfaction and competitiveness in the Chinese E-retailing: Structural equation modeling (SEM) approach to identify the role of quality factors. *Expert Systems with Applications*, *41*(1), 69–80. doi:10.1016/j.eswa.2013.07.012

Wu, W.-Y., Lee, C.-L., Fu, C.-S., & Wang, H.-C. (2014). How can online store layout design and atmosphere influence consumer shopping intention on a website? *International Journal of Retail & Distribution Management*, *42*(1), 4–24. doi:10.1108/IJRDM-01-2013-0035

Zhang, M., Dai, X., & He, Z. (2015). An empirical investigation of service recovery in e-retailing. *Journal of Service Theory and Practice*, *25*(3), 348–367. doi:10.1108/JSTP-03-2014-0046

Zhang, M., Huang, L., He, Z., & Wang, A. G. (2015a). E-service quality perceptions: An empirical analysis of the Chinese e-retailing industry. *Total Quality Management & Business Excellence*, *26*(11-12), 1357–1372. doi:10.1080/14783363.2014.933555

Chapter 15
Fuzzy Time Series:
An Application in E-Commerce

Ali Karasan
Yıldız Technical University, Turkey

İsmail Sevim
Yıldız Technical University, Turkey

Melih Çinar
Yıldız Technical University, Turkey

ABSTRACT

In this chapter, we are planning to make a comparison between conventional Time Series Models and Fuzzy Time Series Models by an application in an e-commerce company. Future sales of furniture will be predicted. The performance of different models and forecasting periods are going to be analyzed to discuss advantages and disadvantages of each method. MAE is chosen as performance indicators of each model and forecasting period combination. As a conclusion to this chapter, generic strategies for prediction in an e-commerce company will be formulated in consideration of these indicators.

1. INTRODUCTION

"Forecasting is about predicting the future as accurately as possible, given all of the information available, including historical data and knowledge of any future events that might impact the forecasts" (Hyndman & Athanasopoulos, 2014). On the other hand, "digital marketing is the marketing which aims to promote brands and reach customers by using all advertisement segments in an electronic medium" (Kahraman et. al, 2015).

This chapter introduces an application of fuzzy time series for a furniture company which makes sells via online. Time series is a part of forecasting methods and such a vague environment like we have, using time series with fuzzy methods is the most appropriate way for forecasting. So in this framework, we search the Scopus database for forecasting, fuzzy time series and e-commerce, then give the obtained review results in tabular and graphical forms.

DOI: 10.4018/978-1-5225-0997-4.ch015

Our chapter is organized as follows. We would like to introduce a mixed way of forecasting and digital marketing, an application of e-commerce for possible solutions with fuzzy time series. Section 2 presents digital marketing. Section 3 presents forecasting and its characteristics. Section 4 presents fuzzy logic. Section 5 presents fuzzy time series and includes a brief literature review about it. Rest of the chapter starts with the Singh's method, follow as Hwang-Chen- Lee's method, regression analysis, and double exponential smoothing using Holt's Method then ends with a conclusion.

2. DIGITAL MARKETING

The Digital Marketing Institution's (DMI) definition for digital marketing is "The use of digital technologies to create an integrated, targeted and measurable communication which helps to acquire and retain customers while building deeper relationships with them".

Digital Marketing's definition for digital marketing is "Digital Marketing is a sub-branch of traditional Marketing and uses modern digital channels for the placement of products e.g. downloadable music, and primarily for communicating with stakeholders e.g. customers and investors about the brand, products, and business progress" (Royle & Laing, 2014).

The concepts "digital marketing" and "e-commerce" are often misused interchangeably. The synonyms to digital marketing are e-marketing, online marketing, or web-marketing and it is related to e-commerce in that manner digital marketing is the tool supporting e-commerce process with supplementary ways such as email marketing, search engine marketing, and social media marketing. Section 6 introduces methods that what we are going to use and includes Singh's method.

Some areas of digital marketing can be sorted as below:

- Advanced Search Engine Optimization (SEO),
- Advertising Support,
- Brand Management,
- Campaign Management,
- Competition Tracking,
- Digital Public Relations,
- E-Commerce,
- Event Management,
- Export Marketing,
- Impact Analysis,
- Mobile Marketing,
- Social Media Management,
- Training,
- Web Analytics, and
- Web Content.

3. FORECASTING

Before we start an extent properties and components of time series and fuzzy time series, we mention forecasting briefly with a list of characteristics' that a decision maker must understand the plan and manage his or her decisions on it effectively for the company's future. Forecasts are made to guide decisions in a variety of fields. This list is given for where forecasts are used and in return diversity of decisions aided by forecasts.

1. Operations planning and control,
2. Economics,
3. Marketing,
4. Financial asset management,
5. Financial risk management,
6. Business and government budgeting,
7. Risk management,
8. Elections,
9. Accidents, and
10. Traffics.

3.1 Characteristics of Forecasts

Companies and managers should take into consideration the some characteristics of forecasts while taking some actions for the future strategies. For being explanatory and more understandable, we use Chopra's and Nahmias' books as a reference explaining of them. Characteristics of the forecast are taken from Nahmias' (2009) book is given with explanations in Table 1.

As in Nahmias' book refers, Chopra and Meindl (2007) determine the same things as properties. It can be shown in Table 2.

Mary Ann Anderson et al (2013) also indicate that in addition to those characteristics:

Table 1. Characteristics of forecasts that were taken from Nahmias' book

1. Forecasts are usually wrong.	Inflexible and sensitive planning system, unexpectable conditions, not included criteria while forecasting may lead too far from results which are anticipated from managers.
2. A good forecast is usually more than a single number.	As Nahmias says a good forecast has not only results but also some measure of expected forecast error.
3. For a good forecasting, aggregation is usually more correct.	"On a percentage basis, the error made in forecasting sales for an entire product line is generally less than the error made in forecasting sales for an individual item."
4. "The longer the forecast horizon, the less accurate the forecast will be."	This one is quite vague. In a high fuzziness environment, one can predict tomorrow's value of the stock market value more accurately than next year's value.
5. "Forecasts should not be used to the exclusion of known information."	If the company is planning a special promotional sale, so that the demand will probably be higher than normal. This information must be annually factored into the forecast.

Table 2. Characteristics of forecasts that were taken from Nahmias' book

1. "Forecasts are always wrong and should thus include both the expected value of the forecast and a measure of forecast error."
2. "Long-term forecasts are usually less accurate than short-term forecasts; that is, long-term forecasts have a larger standard deviation of error relative to the mean than short-term forecasts."
3. "Aggregate forecasts are usually more accurate than disaggregate forecasts, as they tend to have a smaller standard deviation of error relative to the mean."
4. "In general, the farther up the supply chain a company is (or the farther it is from the consumer), the greater is the distortion of information it receives. One classic example of this is the bullwhip effect, in which order variation is amplified as orders move farther from the end customer. As a result, the farther up the supply chain, an enterprise is, the larger is the forecast error. Collaborative forecasting based on sales to the end customer helps upstream enterprises reduce forecast error."

- "If a simple technique yields acceptable accuracy, don't use a more advanced technique",
- Select a forecasting technique that makes good use of the available data,
- There is no single best forecasting technique.

3.2 Elements of a Forecast and Forecasting Methods

A company must be enlightened about numerous factors that are related to forecasting of the future strategies. Some of these factors are listed below:

- Past demand and sales,
- State of the economy,
- Planned price discounts and raises,
- Actions against to competitors,
- Interest rates,
- Inflation rates, and
- Country's environmental conditions.

Francis X. Diebold (1998) clarify six considerations basis for successful forecasting;

- Decision Environment and Loss Function,
- Forecast Aim,
- Forecast Expression,
- Forecast Horizon,
- Information Data Set, and
- Method and Its Complexity.

In light of the foregoing, we must choose the way we will study. There are four types of forecasting where are listed below as Chopra and Meindl (2007) refers;

- **Qualitative:** "Qualitative forecasting methods are primarily subjective and depend on human judgment. They are most appropriate when little historical data is available or when experts have market intelligence that may affect the forecast." This method can be useful and right to accurate when a company joins a new market or develop a new strategy that has no historical data.

- **Causal:** Causal forecasting methods pretend to something that the decision maker wants to find out is highly correlated with certain environmental factors (the state of the economy, interest rates, stock marketing, accidents, etc.). "Causal forecasting methods find this correlation between demand and environmental factors and use estimates of what environmental factors will be to forecast future demand." For example, current account deficit is strongly correlated value of the import. Current account deficit of a country can be reduced by raising the volume of its exports relative to the volume of imports.
- **Simulation:** "Simulation forecasting methods imitate the consumer choices that give rise to demand to arrive at a forecast." Using simulation, a government can combine time-series and causal methods to answer such questions as What will be the impact of local services on vote increases? What will be the impact of a skyscraper construction on urban environment? In a different field with simulation, many facilities' layout plans are imitated to find most productive one. In a conclusion, simulation is distinctly from the other methods and gives us to see results with a way of imitating real word processes.
- **Time Series:** "In these forecasting methods, historical demand is used to make a forecast. They are supported by the hypothesis which event of past demand is a good index of future demand. When the elementary demand motive doesn't differ considerably from one year to the next, these methods are most proper. These are the most easiest approaches to implementing and can serve as a good starting point for a demand forecast." We will use this information as a starting point and build on it with a way of fuzziness.

3.3 Time Series

Therewithal we will go with Time Series and its properties after on. Time series methods are often called naive methods, as they require no information other than the past values of the variable being predicted. Time series is a collection of observations of some economic or physical phenomenon drawn at a discrete point in time. The idea is that information can be inferred from the pattern of past observations and can be used to forecast future values of the series. (Nahmias, 2009)

In time series analysis the goal is to isolate the patterns that arise most often. These include the following as Nahmias (2009) refers;

Trend: *Trend refers to the disposition of a time series to exhibit a stable pattern of rises or decreases. Distinguishing between linear trend (the pattern described by a straight line) and nonlinear trend (the pattern described by a nonlinear function, such as a quadratic or exponential curve). When the pattern of the trend is not specified, it is generally understood to be linear.*

Seasonality: *A seasonal pattern is one that repeats at fixed intervals. In time series, generally thinking of the pattern repeating every year, although daily, weekly, and monthly seasonal patterns are common as well. Fashion wear, ice cream, sunglasses, tanning cream, and heating oil exhibit a yearly seasonal pattern. Consumption of electricity exhibits a strong daily seasonal pattern.*

Cycles: *Cyclic variation is similar to seasonality, except that the length and the magnitude of the cycle may vary. One associates cycles with long-term economic variations (that is, business cycles) that may be present in addition to seasonal fluctuations.*

Randomness: *A pure random series is one in which there is no recognizable pattern to the data. One can generate patterns purely at random that often appear to have structure. An example of this the methodology of stock market chartists who impose forms on random patterns of stock market price data. On the other side of the coin, data that appear to be random could have a very definite structure. Truly random data that fluctuate around a fixed mean form what is called a horizontal pattern.*

4. FUZZY LOGIC

Fuzzy Logic was firstly presented in 1965 by Lotfi A. Zadeh who is a professor of computer science.

While in Boolean logic, there are only two possibilities about the truth values of variables (They might only be '0' or '1'), in Fuzzy logic, a form of many-valued logic, the truth values of variables might be any real number between '0' and '1'. We can say that concept of partial truth, in which the truth value might range between thoroughly true and thoroughly false is solved by means of Fuzzy logic.

There are numerous fields used Fuzzy logic such as robotics, artificial intelligence, optimization, image processing, control theory and thousands of researchers has published a lot of scientific publications (articles, papers, research papers etc.) about Fuzzy logic and Fuzzy Sets. When viewed from this aspect, Fuzzy logic is very useful and fruitful topic for researchers and presents important contributions. Some of these significant contributions of Fuzzy logic was expressed by Lotfi A. Zadeh as the following: (Zadeh, 2008)

1. *FL-generalization. Any bivalent-logic-based theory, T, may be FL-generalized, and hence upgraded, through addition to T of concepts and techniques drawn from fuzzy logic. Examples: fuzzy control, fuzzy linear programming, fuzzy probability theory and fuzzy topology.*
2. *Linguistic variables and fuzzy if–then rules. The formalism of linguistic variables and fuzzy if–then rules is, in effect, a powerful modeling language which is widely used in applications of fuzzy logic. Basically, the formalism serves as a means of summarization and information compression through the use of granulation.*
3. *Cointensive precisiation. Fuzzy logic has a high power of cointensive precisiation. This power is needed for a formulation of cointensive definitions of scientific concepts and cointensive formalization of human-centric fields such as economics, linguistics, law, conflict resolution, psychology, and medicine.*
4. *NL-Computation (computing with words). Fuzzy logic serves as a basis for NL-Computation, that is, computation with information described in natural language. NL-Computation is of direct relevance to mechanization of natural language understanding and computation with imprecise probabilities. More generally, NL-Computation is needed for dealing with second-order uncertainty, that is, uncertainty about uncertainty, or uncertainty for short.*

In summary, progression from bivalent logic to fuzzy logic is a significant positive step in the evolution of science. In large measure, the real-world is a fuzzy world. To deal with fuzzy reality what is needed is fuzzy logic. In coming years, fuzzy logic is likely to grow in visibility, importance, and acceptance.

5. FUZZY TIME SERIES

Fuzzy Time Series (FTS) is a quite new approximation and it is used for finding a solution linguistic time series data problems.

5.1 Definition

Let $Y(t)$ $(t=0,1,2,...)$, a subset of real numbers, be the universe of discourse on which fuzzy sets $f_i(t)$ $(i=1,2,...)$ are defined and $F(t)$ is a collection of $f_i(t)$ $(i=1,2,...)$. Then $F(t)$ is called a Fuzzy Time Series defined on $Y(t)$ $(t=0,1,2,...)$. (Song & Chissom, 1993)

Fuzzy time series methods comprise of three steps, respectively, as the following:

- Fuzzification,
- Identification of fuzzified relations,
- Defuzzification.

A search in the SCOPUS database for the concept "fuzzy time series" gives 4409 papers, it in their titles, abstract and keywords. We analysis 49 of them in detail and only give 33 in below table as a literature review. We will give this review as fuzzy time series and its application area in Table 3. Contextually, Table 3 shows a brief literature review to introduce our framework.

Figure 1 shows the publications that we are examining with respect to subject area, and the distribution is in that way: 24 of the papers are related to computer science (24 papers); engineering (22 papers); mathematics (13 papers); environmental sciences (7 papers); decision sciences (5 papers); social science (5 papers); business, management and accounting (3 papers); other areas (11 papers).

Table 3 illustrates the countries that published the furthest number of fuzzy time series papers. The distribution is given in Table 4.

6. FORECASTING FURNITURE SALES USING SINGH'S METHOD (SINGH, 2008)

6.1 Forecasting Method

It is hard to find a trend or a cycle component in most of the time series data of real world problems and this fact makes conventional time series methods unsuitable for forecasting. Thus, using fuzzy time series is necessary for many real life situations. (Singh, 2008) proposes a fuzzy time series forecasting method to forecast enrollments of Alabama University. Steps of the algorithm of the method are given as:

Table 3. A brief literature reviews about fuzzy time series

Researchers	Problem Definition	Analysis Method	Disadvantages of the Proposed Method	Advantages of the Proposed Method
Wong et. al (2010)	Forecasting the amount of Taiwan export	Comparison of traditional forecasting methods (ARIMA and Vector ARMA) with fuzzy time series models (Two-factor time-variant model, Heuristic model, and Multivariate fuzzy time series Markov model).	Larger forecasting errors in longer experiment time period.	More accurate in the limited information and urgent decision-making circumstances.
Reuter & Möller (2010)	Necessity of predetermining process model to simulate and forecast time series possessing fuzzy random characteristics	Artificial neural networks	Deciding the parameters of artificial neural network is a challenging process.	"Neural networks for fuzzy time series neither need a predetermined process model nor any prior knowledge of the random characteristics to simulate and forecast time series with fuzzy data."
Hwang & Oh (2010)	Predicting the daily and weekly open, high, low, and close prices of the Korea Composite Stock Price Index.	The information used in traditional candlestick chart analysis was newly employed as input variables. A multi-input-multi-output model is decomposed into many multi-input single output models.	Decomposition strategy may cause a loss of valuable information.	The stock market trend can be forecasted based on the predicted open, high, low, and close values. The daily predicted KOSPI information will be useful in trading future prices.
Hadavandi et. al (2010)	Stock price prediction	"Integrated approach based on genetic fuzzy systems (GFS), artificial neural networks (ANN), a hybrid artificial intelligence method called clustering-genetic fuzzy system (CGFS)"	It incurred high computational complexity and lacked stability.	The results of the proposed method showed that forecasting accuracy of CGFS outperforms the rest of approaches regarding MAPE evaluation, and CGFS can be used as a suitable forecasting tool to deal with stock price forecasting problems.
Huang et. al (2011)	To improve forecasting models under fuzzy fluctuations	Fuzzy time series and particle swarm optimization	Comparison with the other models is insufficient due to the low number of selected models and their types.	"Proposed AFPSO model gets higher forecasting accuracy than any existing models at all. It also performs best for fuzzy time series with various orders in training and testing phases, respectively."
Bahrepour et. al (2011)	FOREX forecasting	Self-organizing map method and fuzzy time series	"This hybrid algorithm also requires more computation. While this limitation is not severely hampering for the considered example, since decisions are made only on a daily basis here, it can become a limiting factor when the fast decision and adaptation are required."	"Results indicate that the proposed method surpasses the two earlier studies by providing more accurate prediction."
Oztaysi & Bolturk (2012)	Performance analysis of fuzzy methods on demand forecasting.	Comparison of fuzzy time series, fuzzy regression, adaptive network-based fuzzy inference system and fuzzy rule based system.	"The temporal patterns were defined by rigid regions that were hard to adjust when there is noise in phase space."	Hwang, Chen, Lee's Method outperforms Singh's Method.

continued on next page

Table 3. Continued

Researchers	Problem Definition	Analysis Method	Disadvantages of the Proposed Method	Advantages of the Proposed Method
Ge et. al (2013)	Forecast university enrollments	Integrated fuzzy time series with the exponential smoothing method	"The temporal patterns were defined by rigid regions that were hard to adjust when there is noise in phase space."	"The empirical analysis shows that the proposed model reflects the fluctuations in fuzzy time series better and provides better overall forecasting results."
Singh & Borah (2013)	An efficient time series forecasting model	Mean-Based Discretization(MBD) approach	1. "Apply the proposed model in different regions of temperature data set and check its accuracy and performance with different sizes of intervals and orders." 2. "To test the performance of the model for different types of financial, stocks and marketing data set." 3. This study determines a weight for each FLRs based on the "IBWT". However, Artificial Neuron Networks and Genetic Algorithm may be the feasible alternatives for determining the weight. 4. This study performs defuzzification operation based on the "IBDT". However, researchers can employ Artificial Neuron Networks as an alternative for defuzzification operation, and compare the forecasted results with the presented ones in this paper.	Empirical analyzes signify that the proposed model have the robustness to handle one-factor time series data set very efficiently than the conventional fuzzy time series models.
Petr Dostal (2013)	Companies don't share all the details of their applications. Therefore, information about companies is vague.	Use of fuzzy logic for forecasting purposes.	The temporal patterns were defined by rigid regions that were hard to adjust when there is noise in phase space.	Fuzzy approaches can be used as a support for a decision making on the stock market.
Pandey et. al (2013)	Forecasting for diffusion of innovation by analyzing Tata Nano Car sales in India	Comparison of four fuzzy time series forecasting models and Bass model.	Methods have computational complexity.	All of the four fuzzy time series forecasting models give more accurate results than Bass model where Singh's Algorithm is the most accurate model.
Wang & Xiong (2014)	Forecast the daily wind speed in Hainan province	The first part, "the hybrid model has three steps: an initial ARMA model, outlier detection, and cubic spline interpolation. The second part, a hybrid forecasting model is used to estimate the forecasting model, and the hybrid model is composed of an ARMA model and a bivariate fuzzy time-series model."	Despite the number of observation sites that can useable, they only use at four observation sites in Hainan for daily wind speed forecasting. Due to the a low number of data they have been lacked stability.	"Numerous studies have been conducted to improve the accuracy of wind speed forecasting, but few studies have attempted to improve the forecasting accuracy by removing the outliers in the original wind speed data set that seriously affect the construction and forecasting ability of the models." "Across the population will lead to the greatest preventive impact on fatal traffic injuries among young people and fatal non-traffic injuries among older people."
Ramli et. al (2014)	Early warning system for predicting currency crisis	"AHP to get weights of indicators and ARIMA to forecast the individual indicator and finally by using fuzzy optimization theory to compute the general risk-based relative membership grade."	Founded results show that from a combination of ARIMA and fuzzy optimization models are quite poor especially in predicting future crises.	Proposed method constructed an early warning system by using fuzzy optimization for assessing various currency crisis risks and ARIMA models to forecast individual EWS indicators.

continued on next page

Table 3. Continued

Researchers	Problem Definition	Analysis Method	Disadvantages of the Proposed Method	Advantages of the Proposed Method
Sadaei et. al (2014)	Multilayer stock forecasting	Fuzzy time series	The method is used for stock market forecasting purposes. In short, although presenting a new model is not a definite proposition because not everyone will agree on the principles followed.	The results show that the proposed model can be considered as a standard systematic model whereby it is possible to develop stock predictions by using FTS.
Marszałek et. al (2014)	To predict movement direction of futures contract on WIG20	Fuzzy time series model	It often generated a false-positive prediction.	Proposed method's representation of financial data using the concept of the ordered fuzzy candlestick can be very useful and allows the construction the forecasting models with more relevant information about the modeled process.
Jiang et. al (2015)	Alcohol consumption and fatal injuries in Australia before and after major traffic safety initiatives	ARIMA model	The traditional method needs a large amount of sample data and long-term historical data and also, this study has no certain solutions that can be used in the subject area.	"Study has presented analyzes of what the magnitude and distribution of the reduction in injury mortality might be per liter less of per capita alcohol consumption, suggesting that reducing alcohol consumption."
Wang et. al (2015)	Water quality prediction	Cloud model and fuzzy forecasting	In the proposed method, there are still limitations needed to improve such as the efficient method of employing the approximate periodicity of the water quality parameters.	A fuzzy time series prediction model was applied to generate the computation rule and calculate the predicted value. Compared with the traditional models, it represented the historical numerical data as linguistic value and predicted the water quality parameter based on the fuzzy logical relationship groups, which can better handle the uncertain dataset.
Ismail et. Al (2015)	Electric Load Forecasting	Fuzzy Time Series (FTS) model	More options in selecting the appropriate model to be developed for analyzing future time series data.	A straightforward approach is introduced that is easier to follow. In this forecasting model, authors also make use of the differencing approach to smoothen and to achieve better forecast results.
Prema & Rao (2015)	Necessity of finding an appropriate model for short-term prediction of solar irradiance	Moving Average, Exponential Smoothing, and Decomposition Models are compared.	When the beginning date of past data gets earlier, forecasting error increases.	Decomposition model is more accurate with limited information.
Yi & Chan (2015)	Assess the nonlinear and delayed effects of temperatures on cause-specific and age-specific mortality	A Quasi-Poisson model combined with a distributed lag non-linear model	It incurred high computational complexity and lacked stability.	Allows simultaneous estimation of the non-linear effects across lags.
Kuo et. al (2015)	Fuzzy time series forecasting models usually do not use a learning mechanism to extract valuable information from historical data.	"Evolutionary fuzzy forecasting model in which a learning technique for a fuzzy relation matrix is designed to fit the historical data."	Evolutionary models may not work well for some instances.	"The method can naturally smooth the defuzzification process, thus obtaining better results than many other fuzzy time series forecasting models."
Kocak (2015)	Lack of usage of Moving Averages variables in fuzzy time series models	Autoregressive Moving Averages (ARMAs) models that are based not only on the lagged values of the time series (AR variables) but also on the lagged values of the error series (MA variables).	Identification and estimation can be badly distorted by outlier effects.	Since ARMA models are based on AR and MA variables, they are more realistic than AR models.

continued on next page

Table 3. Continued

Researchers	Problem Definition	Analysis Method	Disadvantages of the Proposed Method	Advantages of the Proposed Method
Chan et. al (2015)	Test the effectiveness of fuzzy time series forecasting system in a supply chain experiencing disruptions	Discrete event simulation based on the popular beer game model is used.	If tiers are higher, fuzzy time series forecasting gets inferior.	If tiers are not high, fuzzy time series forecasting outperforms classic time series models such as ARIMA.
Baş et. al (2015)	To propose a new hybrid method	Fuzzy time series and a new hybrid forecasting method	"Confidence intervals for the forecasts can not be obtained because the proposed method does not include a stochastic approach. Second, inputs of the network cannot be determined by taking advantage of statistical hypothesis tests. Having the input choice made by the stochastic method rather than by trial and error and obtaining confidence intervals for forecasts is an important step and will constitute the main objective of our future work."	"The application of the proposed method reveals that the proposed method has good forecasting performance. In addition, the proposed method is the first hybrid approach of a fuzzy-time-series method and an autoregressive method. With this hybrid method, a network approach that can model both linear and nonlinear structures in time series was proposed. Applying a fuzzy-time-series method within a network structure allows a connection between ANNs and fuzzy-time-series methods to be established."
Telfer et. al (2015)	To obtain relative search engine traffic for terms relating to foot and ankle pain and common treatments	A time series analysis of internet search terms	The proposed method has not enough stability and robustness.	The proposed method may provide insights into some conditions at population levels.
Moosa et. al (2015)	In food insecure countries	A structural time series approach	"A question was raised by an anonymous referee about the possibility of multicollinearity arising from the correlation between the trend and the explanatory variable. This is unlikely to be the case because the trend is not a variable but rather a time series component that is equivalent to the intercept term and a deterministic time trend in a conventional regression equation. In any case, when the correlation coefficient between the trend and the explanatory variable is calculated, it turns out to be statistically insignificant."	"The model does exceptionally well in out-of-sample forecasting."
Lee et. al (2015)	To examine effects of particulate matter	A multicity time-series	They used PM 2.5 concentrations from a single monitoring station for several cities, which may have created a larger exposure measurement error.	Results indicate that stringent air quality regulations are necessary for the East Asia region, as the region continues to produce large amounts of PM emissions with minimal regulation.
D'Urso et. al (2015)	Classifying time series	Autoregressive model, Robust fuzzy C-medoids clustering	The disadvantage of the method is that optimum model order is not known a priori.	Their robust fuzzy clustering model is more appropriate than standard procedures to analyze air quality data properly, inheriting the features of the theoretical and methodological approaches adopted in the clustering process. In particular: It does not depend on the order in which the time series are presented, except when equivalent solutions exist, which very rarely occurs in practice (this is not the case for many other algorithms present in literature).
Davenport et. al (2015)	To analyze grain prices	Time series	A major disadvantage of CBC is that the distance matrices can change quickly. Changes in dissimilarity values should only be interpreted substantively if they persist through time.	The method allows identifying markets where price behavior is either different from other markets in a country or region

continued on next page

Table 3. Continued

Researchers	Problem Definition	Analysis Method	Disadvantages of the Proposed Method	Advantages of the Proposed Method
Bessec et. al (2016)	Forecasting electricity spot prices in France	Comparison of linear regressions, Markov-switching models, threshold models with a smooth transition and also different combinations of these models.	"The temporal patterns were defined by rigid regions that were hard to adjust when there is noise in phase space."	Markov-switching models give most accurate results but the pooling forecasts.
Cheng et. al (2016)	Forecasting the Taiwan stock exchange capitalization weighted stock index (TAIEX)	The method contains fuzzy time series, fuzzy logical relationships, the particle swarm optimization techniques, the K-means clustering algorithm, and similarity measures.	Metaheuristic nature of the method may deteriorate the performance of forecasting for some instances.	Forecasts of TAIEX predicted by the proposed method are more accurate than the predictions of existing models.

Figure 1. Fuzzy time series publications with respect to subject area

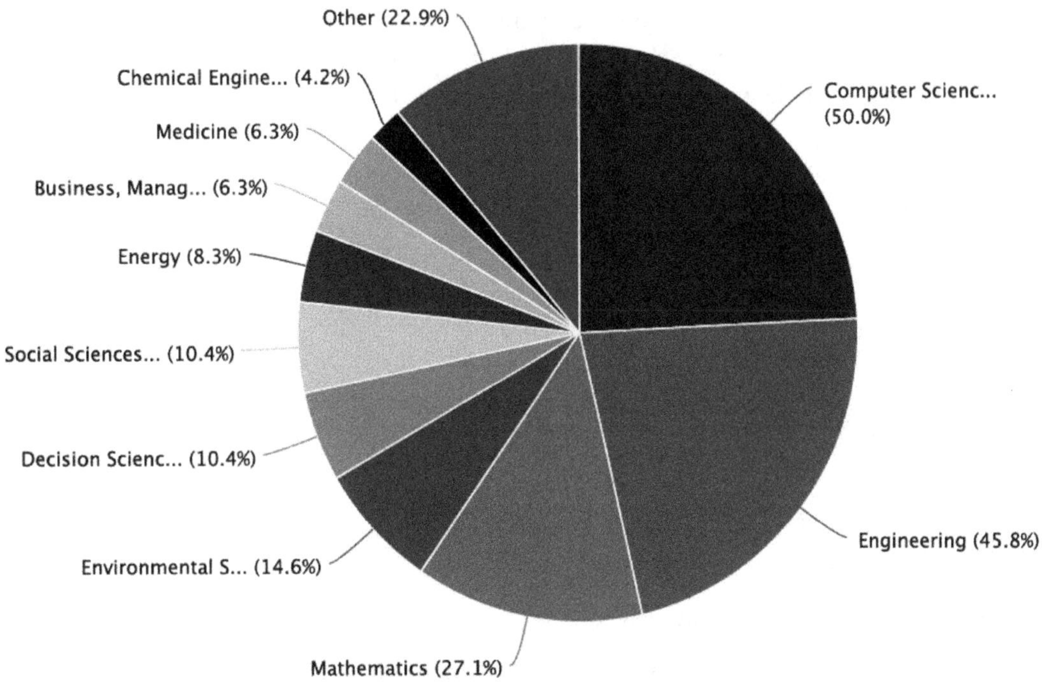

1. Let D be a time series data, D_{min} be the minimum value of D, and, D_{max} be the maximum value of D. Then define the universe of discourse (U),

$$U = \left[D_{\min} - D_1, D_{\max} + D_2\right]$$

Table 4. Furthest number of fuzzy time series papers with respect to the countries

Country/Territory	Documents
China	11
Malaysia	6
Taiwan	6
India	5
Turkey	4
Iran	4
United States	3
Australia	2
Germany	2
Indonesia	2

where D_1 and D_2 are two suitable nonnegative numbers.

2. Partition U into equal length of intervals: $u_1, u_2, u_3, \ldots, u_m$. A number of intervals must be equal to the numbers of linguistic variables: A_1, A_2, $A_3, \ldots, A_m$.
3. Construct the fuzzy sets A_i in accordance with the intervals in the previous step and apply the triangular membership rule to each interval i=1,2,…,m in each A_i.
4. Fuzzify the historical data and establish the fuzzy logical relationships by the rule:

Let A_i be the fuzzified figure of period n, and let A_j be the fuzzified figure of period n+1, then the fuzzy logical relation is shown as $A_i \rightarrow A_j$. Note that A_i is the current state and A_j is the next state.

5. Forecast.

6.1.1 Rules for Forecasting

Notation will be used in the algorithm are defined as

- $\left[*A_j\right]$: Corresponding interval u_j for which membership in A_j is Supremum. (i.e. 1)
- $L\left[*A_j\right]$: The lower bound of interval u_j.
- $U\left[*A_j\right]$: The upper bound of interval u_j.
- $l\left[*A_j\right]$: The length of interval u_j whose membership in A_j is Supremum. (i.e. 1)
- $M\left[*A_j\right]$: The midvalue of interval u_j having Supremum value in A_j.

For $A_i \rightarrow A_j$:

Let A_i be the fuzzified figure of period n,

Let A_j be the fuzzified figure of period $n+1$,

Let E_i be the crisp figure of period n,

Let E_{i-1} be the crisp figure of period $n-1$,

Let E_{i-2} be the crisp figure of period $n-2$, and

Let F_j be the crisp forecasted figure of period $n+1$.

This order of three model uses figures of periods $n-2$, $n-1$ and n for framing rules to implement on fuzzy logical relation, $A_i \rightarrow A_j$. The method forecasts the figures of period $n+1$ by utilizing actual figures of $n-2$, $n-1$ and n.

6.1.2 Computational Algorithm

Let K be the number of elements in a time series data. Forecasting algorithm of Singh's Method:

```
for k=3:K
R=0;
S=0;
D(k)=||(E(k)-E(k-1))|-|(E(k-1)-E(k-2))||;
X(k)=E(k)+D(k)/2;
XX(k)=E(k)-D(k)/2;
Y(k)=E(k)+D(k);
YY(k)=E(k)-D(k);
P(k)=E(k)+D(k)/4;
PP(k)=E(k)-D(k)/4;
Q(k)=E(k)+2*D(k);
QQ(k)=E(k)-2*D(k);
G(k)=E(k)+D(k)/6;
GG(k)=E(k)-D(k)/6;
H(k)=E(k)+3*D(k);
HH(k)=E(k)-3*D(k);
if X(k)>=L[*A(k+1)] & X(k)<=U[*A(k+1)] then
        R=R+X(k);
        S=S+1;
endif
if XX(k)>=L[*A(k+1)] & XX(k)<=U[*A(k+1)] then
        R=R+XX(k);
        S=S+1;
endif
if Y(k)>=L[*A(k+1)] & Y(k)<=U[*A(k+1)] then
        R=R+Y(k);
        S=S+1;
endif
if YY(k)>=L[*A(k+1)] & YY(k)<=U[*A(k+1)] then
        R=R+YY(k);
```

```
        S=S+1;
endif
if P(k)>=L[*A(k+1)] & P(k)<=U[*A(k+1)] then
        R=R+P(k);
        S=S+1;
endif
if PP(k)>=L[*A(k+1)] & PP(k)<=U[*A(k+1)] then
        R=R+PP(k);
        S=S+1;
endif
if Q(k)>=L[*A(k+1)] & Q(k)<=U[*A(k+1)] then
        R=R+Q(k);
        S=S+1;
endif
if QQ(k)>=L[*A(k+1)] & QQ(k)<=U[*A(k+1)] then
        R=R+QQ(k);
        S=S+1;
endif
if G(k)>=L[*A(k+1)] & G(k)<=U[*A(k+1)] then
        R=R+G(k);
        S=S+1;
endif
if GG(k)>=L[*A(k+1)] & GG(k)<=U[*A(k+1)] then
        R=R+GG(k);
        S=S+1;
endif
if H(k)>=L[*A(k+1)] & H(k)<=U[*A(k+1)] then
        R=R+H(k);
        S=S+1;
endif
if HH(k)>=L[*A(k+1)] & HH(k)<=U[*A(k+1)] then
        R=R+HH(k);
        S=S+1;
endif
F(k+1)=(R+M(*A(k+1)))/(S+1);
endfor
```

6.2 Application

Sales figures of an online furniture company are analyzed to show the forecasting ability of Singh's Method. Monthly sales of Product-ES3 belongs to the period 01/01/2014-04/30/2015 are given in Table 5.

Steps of the forecasting process:

Table 5. Monthly sales of Product-ES3

#	Period	#Sold
1	01/01/2014-01/31/2014	1
2	02/01/2014-02/28/2014	2
3	03/01/2014-03/31/2014	3
4	04/01/2014-04/30/2014	3
5	05/01/2014-05/31/2014	8
6	06/01/2014-06/30/2014	6
7	07/01/2014-07/31/2014	10
8	08/01/2014-08/31/2014	22
9	09/01/2014-09/30/2014	32
10	10/01/2014-10/31/2014	29
11	11/01/2014-11/30/2014	33
12	12/01/2014-12/31/2014	36
13	01/01/2015-01/31/2015	59
14	02/01/2015-02/28/2015	49
15	03/01/2015-03/31/2015	61
16	04/01/2015-04/30/2015	68

1. $D_{min} = 1$ and $D_{max} = 68$. Let $D_1 = 0$ and $D_2 = 2$. Then $U = [1,70]$.
2. Let us decide that there are 7 intervals have equal length. Then intervals are given in Table 6.

   Fuzzy sets (Linguistic Variables) and corresponding definitions are given in Table 7.

3. Membership grades to fuzzy sets defined in the previous step are

$$A_1 = 1/\mu_1 + 0.5/\mu_2 + 0/\mu_3 + 0/\mu_4 + 0/\mu_5 + 0/\mu_6 + 0/\mu_7,$$
$$A_2 = 0.5/\mu_1 + 1/\mu_2 + 0.5/\mu_3 + 0/\mu_4 + 0/\mu_5 + 0/\mu_6 + 0/\mu_7,$$
$$A_3 = 0/\mu_1 + 0.5/\mu_2 + 1/\mu_3 + 0.5/\mu_4 + 0/\mu_5 + 0/\mu_6 + 0/\mu_7,$$
$$A_4 = 0/\mu_1 + 0/\mu_2 + 0.5/\mu_3 + 1/\mu_4 + 0.5/\mu_5 + 0/\mu_6 + 0/\mu_7,$$
$$A_5 = 0/\mu_1 + 0/\mu_2 + 0/\mu_3 + 0.5/\mu_4 + 1/\mu_5 + 0.5/\mu_6 + 0/\mu_7,$$
$$A_6 = 0/\mu_1 + 0/\mu_2 + 0/\mu_3 + 0/\mu_4 + 0.5/\mu_5 + 1/\mu_6 + 0.5/\mu_7,$$
$$A_7 = 0/\mu_1 + 0/\mu_2 + 0/\mu_3 + 0/\mu_4 + 0/\mu_5 + 0.5/\mu_6 + 1./\mu_7.$$

4. Fuzzified sales figures of Product-ES3 is given in Table 8.
5. For forecast the 15th period, variable values can be seen in Table 9 - note that $k = 14$, $L[*A(15)] = 61$, $U[*A(15)] = 70$, and $M[*A(15)] = 65$.

Table 6. Intervals

	Interval
u_1	1-10
u_2	11-20
u_3	21-30
u_4	31-40
u_5	41-50
u_6	51-60
u_7	61-70

Table 7. Fuzzy sets and definitions

Fuzzy Sets	Definition
A_1	
A_2	
A_3	Average Sales
A_4	
A_5	
A_6	Excellent Sales
A_7	Extraordinary Sales

By using values in Table 5, $R = 62$, and $S = 1$. Thus,

$$F(15) = (62 + 65) / (1 + 1) = 63.5.$$

Actual and forecasted monthly sales of Product-ES3 are given in Table 10. A comparison of actual and forecasted sales can be seen in Figure 2.

7. FORECASTING FURNITURE SALES USING HWANG, CHEN, LEE'S METHOD (HWANG, CHEN, & LEE, 1998)

7.1 Forecasting Method

Let x be an element of a time series data corresponding to period t, and y be the element corresponding to period $t-1$. Then difference $x-y$ is the variation between period t and $t-1$. (Hwang, Chen, & Lee, 1998) proposes a fuzzy time series forecasting method based on fuzzified variations of a time series data. The fuzzified variation of the historical data between period t and period $t-1$ is as follows:

$$F(t) = u_1 / A_1 + u_2 / A_2 + \cdots + u_m / A_m$$

where $F(t)$ denotes fuzzified variation between periods t and $t-1$, u_i is the grade of membership to linguistic variable A_i, m is the number of intervals in universe of discourse - note that $1 \le i \le m$.

Table 8. Linguistic variables of Product-ES3 sales

#	Period	#Sold	Sales in Linguistic Variables
1	01/01/2014-01/31/2014	1	A_1
2	02/01/2014-02/28/2014	2	A_1
3	03/01/2014-03/31/2014	3	A_1
4	04/01/2014-04/30/2014	3	A_1
5	05/01/2014-05/31/2014	8	A_1
6	06/01/2014-06/30/2014	6	A_1
7	07/01/2014-07/31/2014	10	A_1
8	08/01/2014-08/31/2014	22	A_3
9	09/01/2014-09/30/2014	32	A_4
10	10/01/2014-10/31/2014	29	A_3
11	11/01/2014-11/30/2014	33	A_4
12	12/01/2014-12/31/2014	36	A_4
13	01/01/2015-01/31/2015	59	A_6
14	02/01/2015-02/28/2015	49	A_5
15	03/01/2015-03/31/2015	61	A_7
16	04/01/2015-04/30/2015	68	A_7

Order of proposed model is chosen as a parameter called $windowbasis$. Let w be the window basis. Then the variation of last year is constitutes the criterion matrix and other w past years are used to construct the operation matrix. Assume that it is intended to forecast the value of period t. Then criterion matrix $C\left(t\right)$ and operation matrix $O^{w}\left(t\right)$ are built as follows:

$$C(t) = F(t-1) = [C_1 \quad C_2 \quad \cdots \quad C_m],$$

Table 9. Variable values for forecast of 15th period

Variable	Value	Is Value ∈ [61, 70] ?
D(14)	13.00	-
X(14)	55.50	No
XX(14)	42.50	No
Y(14)	62.00	Yes
YY(14)	36.00	No
P(14)	52.25	No
PP(14)	45.75	No
Q(14)	75.00	No
QQ(14)	23.00	No
G(14)	51.17	No
GG(14)	46.83	No
H(14)	88.00	No
HH(14)	10.00	No

Table 10. Actual and forecasted sales of Product-ES3 using Singh's Method

#	Period	Actual Sales	Forecasted Sales
1	01/01/2014-01/31/2014	1	-
2	02/01/2014-02/28/2014	2	-
3	03/01/2014-03/31/2014	3	-
4	04/01/2014-04/30/2014	3	3.15
5	05/01/2014-05/31/2014	8	3.15
6	06/01/2014-06/30/2014	6	6.50
7	07/01/2014-07/31/2014	10	14.00
8	08/01/2014-08/31/2014	22	25.00
9	09/01/2014-09/30/2014	32	34.33
10	10/01/2014-10/31/2014	29	27.25
11	11/01/2014-11/30/2014	33	32.88
12	12/01/2014-12/31/2014	36	33.15
13	01/01/2015-01/31/2015	59	55.00
14	02/01/2015-02/28/2015	49	47.00
15	03/01/2015-03/31/2015	61	63.50
16	04/01/2015-04/30/2015	68	62.60

Figure 2. Comparison of actual and forecasted sales of Product-ES3 by period using Singh's Method

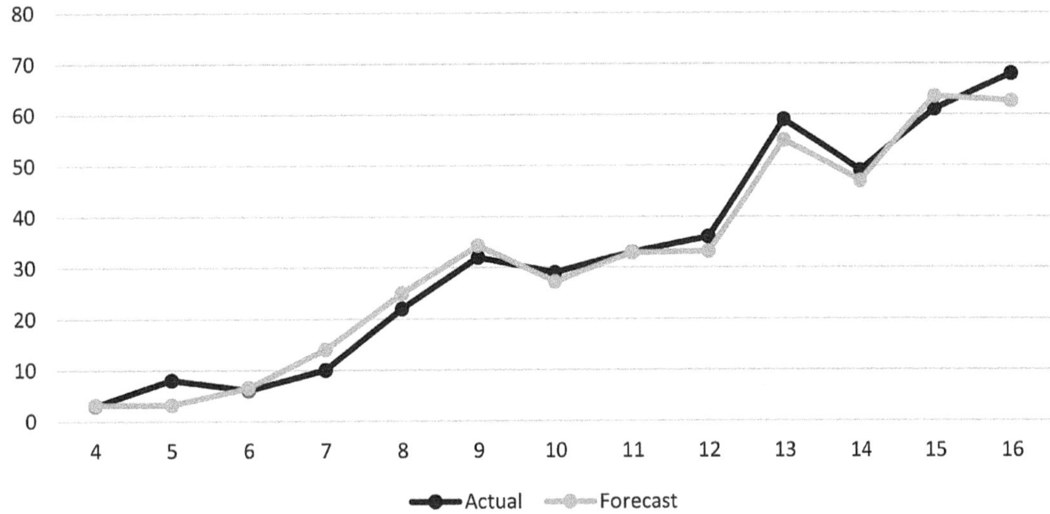

$$O^w(t) = \begin{bmatrix} F(t-2) \\ F(t-3) \\ \vdots \\ F(t-w-1) \end{bmatrix} = \begin{bmatrix} O_{11} & O_{12} & \cdots & O_{1m} \\ O_{21} & O_{22} & \cdots & O_{2m} \\ \vdots & \vdots & \vdots & \vdots \\ O_{w1} & O_{w2} & \cdots & O_{wm} \end{bmatrix}$$

A relation matrix $R(t)$ is built to calculate the relation between $C(t)$ and $O^w(t)$ and

$$R(t) = O^w(t) \otimes C(t)$$

where

$$R(t) = \begin{bmatrix} O_{11} \times C_1 & O_{12} \times C_2 & \cdots & O_{1m} \times C_m \\ O_{21} \times C_1 & O_{22} \times C_2 & \cdots & O_{2m} \times C_m \\ \vdots & \vdots & \vdots & \vdots \\ O_{w1} \times C_1 & O_{w2} \times C_2 & \cdots & O_{wm} \times C_m \end{bmatrix} = \begin{bmatrix} R_{11} & R_{12} & \cdots & R_{1m} \\ R_{21} & R_{22} & \cdots & R_{2m} \\ R_{31} & R_{32} & \cdots & R_{3m} \\ R_{w1} & R_{w2} & \cdots & R_{wm} \end{bmatrix}$$

where

$$R_{ij} = O_{ij} \times C_j, 1 \le i \le w, 1 \le j \le m$$

and x is the multiplication operator. Then we get fuzzified forecasted variation between period t and $t-1$ where

$$F(t) = \left[\max\left(R_{11}, R_{21}, \cdots, R_{w1}\right) \cdots \max\left(R_{w1}, R_{22}, \cdots, R_{w2}\right) \cdots \max\left(R_{1m}, R_{2m}, \cdots, R_{wm}\right)\right]$$

7.2 Application

Step by step calculations of forecasted monthly sales of Product-ES3 belongs to the period 01/01/2014-04/30/2015 are given as follows:

1. Monthly sales of Product-ES3 and variations between consecutive periods are given in Table 11. Assume that variation between 6th and 7th period is needed. Then $variation = 10 - 6 = 4$. Minimum increase D_{min} and maximum increase D_{max} in Product-ES3 sales, and two suitable nonnegative numbers D_1 and D_2 must be determined to define the universe of discourse. $D_{min} = -10$ and $D_{max} = 23$. Let $D_1 = 0$ and $D_2 = 2$. Then the universe of discourse

$$U = \left[D_{\min} - D_1, D_{\max} + D_2\right] = [-10, 25].$$

2. The universe of discourse U must be partitioned into some number of intervals have even length. Let interval length be equal to 5. Then number of intervals is equal to 7. Intervals are given in Table 12.
3. Fuzzy sets and linguistic variables on the universe of discourse U must be defined. Linguistic variables represented by fuzzy sets are described in Table 13.

Fuzzy sets on the universe of discourse U is as follows:

$$A_1 = 1/u_1 + 0.5/u_2 + 0/u_3 + 0/u_4 + 0/u_5 + 0/u_6 + 0/u_7,$$

$$A_2 = 0.5/u_1 + 1/u_2 + 0.5/u_3 + 0/u_4 + 0/u_5 + 0/u_6 + 0/u_7,$$

$$A_3 = 0/u_1 + 0.5/u_2 + 1/u_3 + 0.5/u_4 + 0/u_5 + 0/u_6 + 0/u_7,$$

$$A_4 = 0/u_1 + 0/u_2 + 0.5/u_3 + 1/u_4 + 0.5/u_5 + 0/u_6 + 0/u_7,$$

$$A_5 = 0/u_1 + 0/u_2 + 0/u_3 + 0.5/u_4 + 1/u_5 + 0.5/u_6 + 0/u_7,$$

$$A_6 = 0/u_1 + 0/u_2 + 0/u_3 + 0/u_4 + 0.5/u_5 + 1/u_6 + 0.5/u_7,$$

$$A_7 = 0/u_1 + 0/u_2 + 0/u_3 + 0/u_4 + 0/u_5 + 0.5/u_6 + 1/u_7.$$

Table 11. Actual and forecasted sales of Product-ES3 using Singh's method

#	Period	Actual Sales	Variations
1	01/01/2014-01/31/2014	1	-
2	02/01/2014-02/28/2014	2	1
3	03/01/2014-03/31/2014	3	1
4	04/01/2014-04/30/2014	3	0
5	05/01/2014-05/31/2014	8	5
6	06/01/2014-06/30/2014	6	-2
7	07/01/2014-07/31/2014	10	4
8	08/01/2014-08/31/2014	22	12
9	09/01/2014-09/30/2014	32	10
10	10/01/2014-10/31/2014	29	-3
11	11/01/2014-11/30/2014	33	4
12	12/01/2014-12/31/2014	36	3
13	01/01/2015-01/31/2015	59	23
14	02/01/2015-02/28/2015	49	-10
15	03/01/2015-03/31/2015	61	12
16	04/01/2015-04/30/2015	68	7

Table 12. Intervals

	Interval
u_1	(-10)-(-5)
u_2	(-5)-0
u_3	0-5
u_4	5-10
u_5	10-15
u_6	15-20
u_7	20-25

Table 13. Linguistic variables represented by fuzzy sets

Fuzzy Sets	Definition
A_1	Too Big Decrease
A_2	Big Decrease
A_3	Decrease
A_4	No Change
A_5	Increase
A_6	Big Increase
A_7	Too Big Increase

4. Sales of Product-ES3 must be fuzzified. If the variation between period t and $t-1$ is p where $p \in u_j$, and if there is a value represented by A_k in which the maximum membership value occurs at u_j, then p is translated to A_k. The fuzzified variations of sales of Product-ES3 is given in Table 14.

Table 14. Fuzzified variations of sales of Product-ES3

#	Period	Actual Sales	Variations	Fuzzified Variations
1	01/01/2014-01/31/2014	1	-	-
2	02/01/2014-02/28/2014	2	1	A_3
3	03/01/2014-03/31/2014	3	1	A_3
4	04/01/2014-04/30/2014	3	0	A_3
5	05/01/2014-05/31/2014	8	5	A_4
6	06/01/2014-06/30/2014	6	-2	A_2
7	07/01/2014-07/31/2014	10	4	A_3
8	08/01/2014-08/31/2014	22	12	A_5
9	09/01/2014-09/30/2014	32	10	A_5
10	10/01/2014-10/31/2014	29	-3	A_2
11	11/01/2014-11/30/2014	33	4	A_3
12	12/01/2014-12/31/2014	36	3	A_3
13	01/01/2015-01/31/2015	59	23	A_7
14	02/01/2015-02/28/2015	49	-10	A_1
15	03/01/2015-03/31/2015	61	12	A_5
16	04/01/2015-04/30/2015	68	7	A_4

5. A suitable window basis w must be chosen. Let $w = 2$, and $t = 7$. Then the criterion matrix $C(7)$ is fuzzy variation of 6th period. Thus

$$C(7) = \begin{bmatrix} 0.5 & 1 & 0.5 & 0 & 0 & 0 & 0 \end{bmatrix}.$$

The operation matrix

$$O^2(7) = \begin{bmatrix} Fuzzy\ variation\ of\ period\ 5 \\ Fuzzy\ variaton\ of\ period\ 4 \end{bmatrix} = \begin{bmatrix} A_4 \\ A_3 \end{bmatrix}$$

$$O^2(4) = \begin{bmatrix} 0 & 0 & 0.5 & 1 & 0.5 & 0 & 0 \\ 0 & 0.5 & 1 & 0.5 & 0 & 0 & 0 \end{bmatrix}.$$

Then the relation matrix

$$R(7) = O^2(7) \otimes C(7) = \begin{bmatrix} 0 & 0 & 0.5 & 1 & 0.5 & 0 & 0 \\ 0 & 0.5 & 1 & 0.5 & 0 & 0 & 0 \end{bmatrix} \otimes \begin{bmatrix} 0.5 & 1 & 0.5 & 0 & 0 & 0 & 0 \end{bmatrix}$$

$$R(7) = \begin{bmatrix} 0 & 0 & 0.25 & 0 & 0 & 0 & 0 \\ 0 & 0.5 & 0.5 & 0 & 0 & 0 & 0 \end{bmatrix}.$$

Then fuzzified forecasted variation of 7th period

$$F(7) = \begin{bmatrix} 0 & 0.5 & 0.5 & 0 & 0 & 0 & 0 \end{bmatrix}.$$

6. Fuzzified forecasted variations must be defuzzified. If the grades of membership of the fuzzified forecasted variation have only one maximum u_i, then the forecasted variation is equal to midpoint of u_i, m_i. If there are more than one maximum in the grades of membership of the fuzzified forecasted variation, then the forecasted variation is equal to the average of the midpoints of intervals have maximum grade. For example, forecasted variation of 7th period is equal to $\left[(-2.5) + 2.5\right] / 2 = 0$. Note that if all membership grades are equal to 0, then forecasted variation is equal to 0.
7. Forecasted sales must be calculated. The forecasted sales of a period t is equal to forecasted variation of period t plus sales of period $t-1$. For instance forecasted sales of 7th period is equal to 6, sales of 6th period, plus 0, forecasted variation of 7th period. Then forecasted sales of 7th period is 6.

Actual and forecasted sales of Product-ES3 for all periods are given in Table 15 (Window basis $w = 2$). Also a curve compares actual and forecasted sales can be found in Figure 3.

Table 15. Actual and forecasted sales of Product-ES3 using Hwang, Chen, Lee's Method

#	Period	Actual Sales	Forecasted Sales
1	01/01/2014-01/31/2014	1	-
2	02/01/2014-02/28/2014	2	-
3	03/01/2014-03/31/2014	3	-
4	04/01/2014-04/30/2014	3	-
5	05/01/2014-05/31/2014	8	5.50
6	06/01/2014-06/30/2014	6	13.00
7	07/01/2014-07/31/2014	10	6.00
8	08/01/2014-08/31/2014	22	12.50
9	09/01/2014-09/30/2014	32	29.50
10	10/01/2014-10/31/2014	29	44.50
11	11/01/2014-11/30/2014	33	36.50
12	12/01/2014-12/31/2014	36	33.00
13	01/01/2015-01/31/2015	59	38.50
14	02/01/2015-02/28/2015	49	66.50
15	03/01/2015-03/31/2015	61	46.50
16	04/01/2015-04/30/2015	68	78.50

Figure 3. Comparison of actual and forecasted sales of Product-ES3 by period using Hwang, Chen, Lee's Method

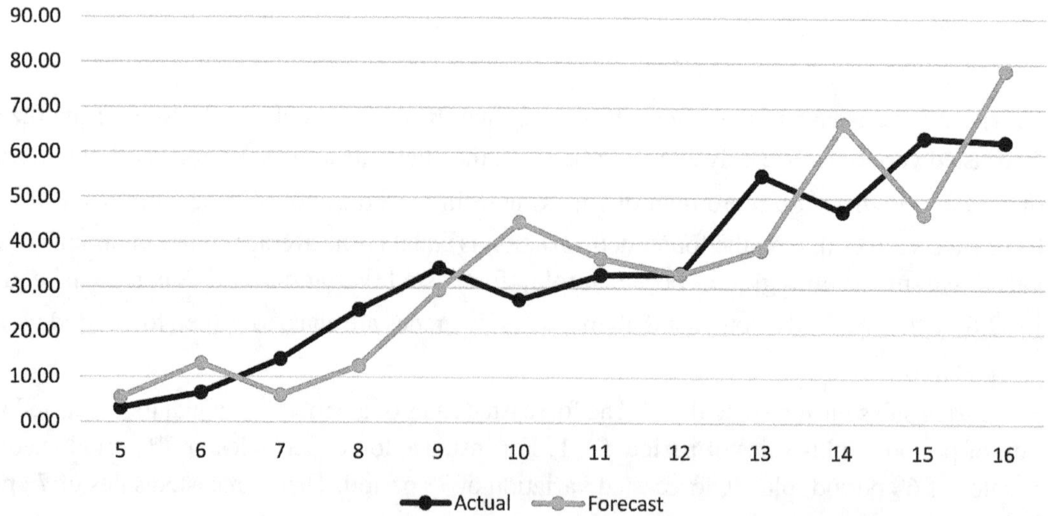

8. FORECASTING FURNITURE SALES USING LINEAR REGRESSION ANALYSIS

8.1 Linear Regression Analysis (Taylor III, 2010)

Linear regression is a forecasting method measures the relationship between two variables. One of these variables is called dependent where the other one is called independent. Relationship is shown in the form of a linear equation:

$$y = a + bx.$$

where y is dependent variable, a is intercept, b is slope, and x is independent variable. The slope and the intercept must be calculated to develop the linear equation given below. By using the following least squares formulas:

$$b = \frac{\sum xy - n\overline{x}\overline{y}}{\sum x^2 - n\overline{x}^2},$$

$$a = \overline{y} - b\overline{x}.$$

where $\overline{x}$ is the mean of the x data and $\overline{y}$ is the mean of the y data. Once linear equation is developed, forecasts of periods can be calculated by using the equation.

8.2 Application

Monthly sales of Product-ES3 is given in Table 1. For sales data, an independent variable is a period number and the dependent variable is actual sales of Product-ES3. Thus, the data to be used in linear regression analysis can be given as Table 16.

By using least squares formulas, an intercept a and slope b is found -13.375 and 4.6765, respectively. Thus linear equation is

$$y = 4.6765x - 13.375.$$

Assume that forecasted sales of 12th period is needed. If $F(t)$ is the forecasted sales of period t, then $F(12)$ is equal to y where $x = 12$. Therefore

$$F(12) = 4.6765 \times 12 - 13.375 = 42.743.$$

Table 16. Sales data in terms of dependent and independent variables for linear regression analysis

x	1	2	3	4	5	6	7	8	9	10	11	12	13	14	15	16
y	1	2	3	3	8	6	10	22	32	29	33	36	59	49	61	68

Actual and forecasted sales of Product-ES3 for all periods are given in Table 17. Also, a curve compares actual and forecasted sales can be found in Figure 4.

Table 17. Actual and forecasted sales of Product-ES3 using linear regression analysis

#	Period	Actual Sales	Forecasted Sales
1	01/01/2014-01/31/2014	1	-8.70
2	02/01/2014-02/28/2014	2	-4.02
3	03/01/2014-03/31/2014	3	0.65
4	04/01/2014-04/30/2014	3	5.33
5	05/01/2014-05/31/2014	8	10.01
6	06/01/2014-06/30/2014	6	14.68
7	07/01/2014-07/31/2014	10	19.36
8	08/01/2014-08/31/2014	22	24.04
9	09/01/2014-09/30/2014	32	28.71
10	10/01/2014-10/31/2014	29	33.39
11	11/01/2014-11/30/2014	33	38.07
12	12/01/2014-12/31/2014	36	42.74
13	01/01/2015-01/31/2015	59	47.42
14	02/01/2015-02/28/2015	49	52.10
15	03/01/2015-03/31/2015	61	56.77
16	04/01/2015-04/30/2015	68	61.45

Figure 4. Comparison of actual and forecasted sales of Product-ES3 by period using linear regression analysis

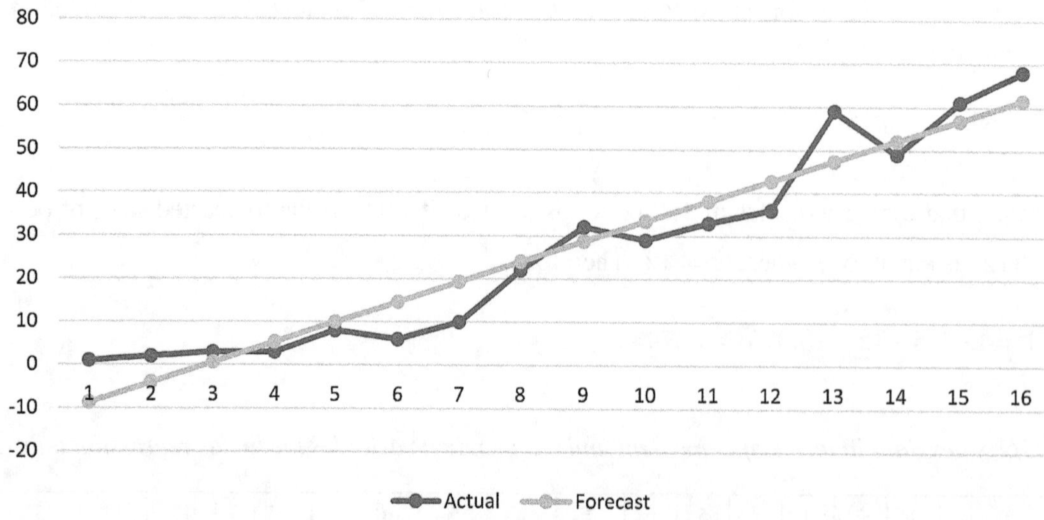

9. FORECASTING FURNITURE SALES USING DOUBLE EXPONENTIAL SMOOTHING USING HOLT'S METHOD

9.1 Double Exponential Smoothing Using Holt's Method (Nahmias, 2009)

Holt's method is a version of double exponential smoothing developed to forecast time series follow a linear trend. Two smoothing constants α and β must be determined for forecasting, α is for the value of time series (intercept) and β is for the trend (slope). Method uses two equations to calculate S_t as the value of intercept at period t and G_t as the value of the slope at period t. These two equations are as follows where D_t is the actual figure of period t:

$$S_t = \alpha D_t + (1-\alpha)(S_{t-1} + G_{t-1}),$$

$$G_t = \beta(S_t - S_{t-1}) + (1-\beta)G_{t-1}.$$

If the current period is t and figures of τ periods after from period t is needed to be forecasted, then following formula is used for forecasting:

$$F_{t,t+\tau} = S_t + \tau G_t.$$

Four parameters must be defined before applying Holt's method formulas: α, β, S_0 and G_0.There are two rules for α and β:

1. $\alpha, \beta \in [0,1]$,
2. $\beta \leq \alpha$.

The first rule is obligatory. However latter one is not an obligation but recommended for stability. There is no certain rule for choosing S_0 and G_0 One option can be choosing intercept and slope of a linear regression equation as S_0 and G_0, respectively. This strategy is used in application of this method in this study.

9.2 Application

Monthly sales of Product-ES3 may be found in Table 5. Assume that for sales data $\alpha = \beta = 0.8$, $S_0 = -13.375$, $G_0 = 4.6765$, and $\tau = 1$ (Note that S_0 is equal to interception value of linear regression analysis and G_0 is equal to slope value of linear regression analysis).

For forecasting sales of 1st period:

$$S_1 = 0.8 \times 1 + (1-0.8) \times (-13.375 + 4.6765) = -0.9397,$$

$$G_1 = 0.8 \times \left(-0.9397 + 13.375\right) + \left(1 - 0.8\right) \times 4.6765 = 10.88354\,,$$

$$F_{1,1} = -0.9397 + 1 \times 10.88354 = 9.94384\,.$$

Actual and forecasted sales of Product-ES3 for all periods are given in Table 18. Also, a curve compares actual and forecasted sales can be found in Figure 5.

10. CONCLUSION

It is well-known that main advantage of e-commerce companies over traditional "brick-and-mortar" retailers is a substantial reduction in infrastructure related costs. The number of e-commerce companies has been increased since the 1990s. Developments in internet technologies and electronic payment methods enable e-commerce companies to reach many customers around the world. Therefore, these companies serve more people than traditional companies. However, this constitutes a problem: Forecasting demand accurately. Selling different types of products, serving customers from all around the world and different cultures, and possibility to gain new customers day by day make forecasting the customer demand a challenging problem. Thus, forecasting methods work properly for traditional retailers may not forecast demands of e-commerce companies accurately.

Table 18. Actual and forecasted sales of Product-ES3 using Double Exponential Smoothing Using Holt's Method

#	Period	Actual Sales	Forecasted Sales
1	01/01/2014-01/31/2014	1	9.94
2	02/01/2014-02/28/2014	2	9.39
3	03/01/2014-03/31/2014	3	5.99
4	04/01/2014-04/30/2014	3	3.40
5	05/01/2014-05/31/2014	8	9.82
6	06/01/2014-06/30/2014	6	7.06
7	07/01/2014-07/31/2014	10	11.59
8	08/01/2014-08/31/2014	22	28.76
9	09/01/2014-09/30/2014	32	42.27
10	10/01/2014-10/31/2014	29	34.08
11	11/01/2014-11/30/2014	33	34.95
12	12/01/2014-12/31/2014	36	38.20
13	01/01/2015-01/31/2015	59	70.56
14	02/01/2015-02/28/2015	49	55.23
15	03/01/2015-03/31/2015	61	65.46
16	04/01/2015-04/30/2015	68	74.73

Figure 5. Comparison of actual and forecasted sales of Product-ES3 by period using double exponential smoothing using Holt's method

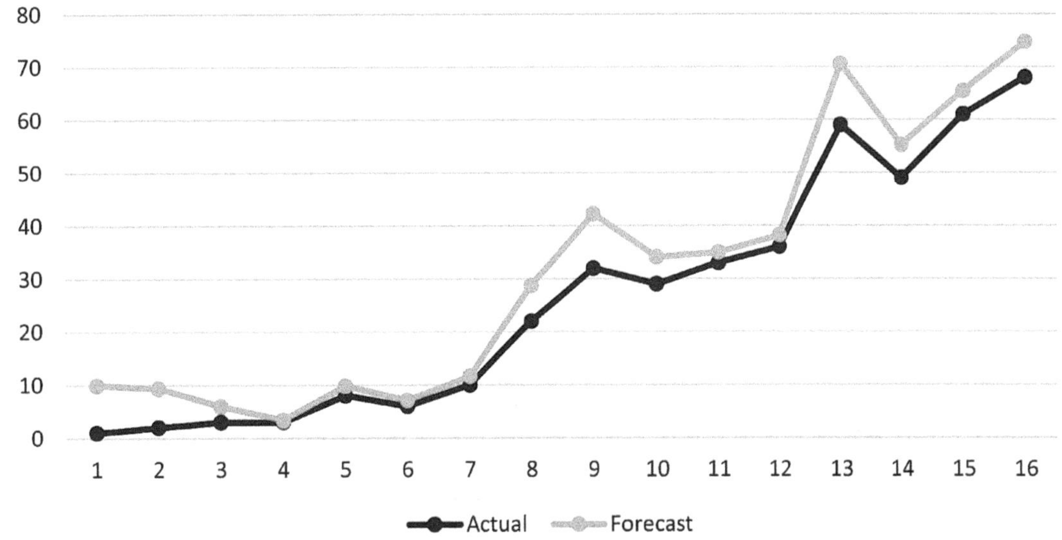

Different kinds of techniques are used for forecasting. Forecasting methods can be grouped into four categories as qualitative, casual, simulation, and time series. Each group has its own pros-and-cos and it is said that there is not a method works best for all situations. Qualitative methods are preferred when no historical data exists where causal methods are used when two or more variables are thought to be correlated. Simulation methods incorporate time series and causal relations into models to imitate consumer choices. Fuzzy set theory can help forecasters to incorporate human intuition and experience into forecasting models while handling uncertainty.

In this study, a brief literature review about fuzzy time series is given in discussions about the relation between digital marketing and e-commerce, fuzzy set theory and fuzzy time series forecasting methods. One causal model, one-time series method, and two different fuzzy time series forecasting methods are compared for a product sold by an e-commerce company of furniture sales. Mean absolute error (MAE) is used as performance measure where $MAE = \frac{1}{n}\sum_{i=1}^{n}\left|f_i - y_i\right|$ where n is the number of elements in a dataset, y_i is the value of ith element of the dataset, and f_i is the forecasted value of ith element of the dataset. Singh's method has a MAE value of 2.61 where Hwang, Chen, Lee's method, Linear Regression Analysis, and double exponential smoothing using Holt's method have MAE values 13.01, 9.17, and 6.28 respectively. Note that lower MAE values are preferred among others.

As future study given Product-ES3 sales data may be analyzed by other fuzzy time series forecasting methods to compare the accuracy of each method. Also superiority of fuzzy time series forecasting models over conventional time series methods may be studied by comparison of fuzzy and conventional methods.

REFERENCES

Bahrepour, M., Akbarzadeh-T, M. R., Yaghoobi, M., & Naghibi-S, M. B. (2011). An adaptive ordered fuzzy time series with application to FOREX. *Expert Systems with Applications*, *38*(1), 475–485. doi:10.1016/j.eswa.2010.06.087

Bas, E., Egrioglu, E., Aladag, C. H., & Yolcu, U. (2015). Fuzzy-time-series network used to forecast linear and nonlinear time series. *Applied Intelligence*, *43*(2), 343–355. doi:10.1007/s10489-015-0647-0

Bessec, M., Fouquau, J., & Meritet, S. (2016). Forecasting electricity spot prices using time-series models with a double temporal segmentation. *Applied Economics*, *48*(5), 361–378. doi:10.1080/00036846.2015.1080801

Bolturk, E., Oztaysi, B., & Sari, I. U. (2012, November). Electricity consumption forecasting using fuzzy time series. In *Computational Intelligence and Informatics (CINTI), 2012 IEEE 13th International Symposium on* (pp. 245-249). IEEE. doi:10.1109/CINTI.2012.6496768

Chan, F. T., Samvedi, A., & Chung, S. H. (2015). Fuzzy time series forecasting for supply chain disruptions. *Industrial Management & Data Systems*, *115*(3), 419–435. doi:10.1108/IMDS-07-2014-0199

Cheng, S. H., Chen, S. M., & Jian, W. S. (2016). Fuzzy time series forecasting based on fuzzy logical relationships and similarity measures. *Information Sciences*, *327*, 272–287. doi:10.1016/j.ins.2015.08.024

Chopra, S., & Meindl, P. (2007). Supply chain management. In *Strategy, planning & operation* (pp. 265-275). Gabler.

D'Urso, P., De Giovanni, L., & Massari, R. (2015). Time series clustering by a robust autoregressive metric with application to air pollution. *Chemometrics and Intelligent Laboratory Systems*, *141*, 107–124. doi:10.1016/j.chemolab.2014.11.003

Davenport, F., & Funk, C. (2015). Using time series structural characteristics to analyze grain prices in food insecure countries. *Food Security*, *7*(5), 1055–1070. doi:10.1007/s12571-015-0490-5

Deng, W., Wang, G., & Zhang, X. (2015). A novel hybrid water quality time series prediction method based on cloud model and fuzzy forecasting. *Chemometrics and Intelligent Laboratory Systems*, *149*, 39–49. doi:10.1016/j.chemolab.2015.09.017

Diebold, F. X. (1998). *Elements of forecasting*. South-Western College Publ.

Dostál, P. (2013). Forecasting of Time Series with Fuzzy Logic. In Nostradamus 2013: Prediction, Modeling, and Analysis of Complex Systems (pp. 155-161). Springer International Publishing. doi:10.1007/978-3-319-00542-3_16

Efendi, R., Ismail, Z., & Deris, M. M. (2015). A new linguistic out-sample approach of fuzzy time series for daily forecasting of Malaysian electricity load demand. *Applied Soft Computing*, *28*, 422–430. doi:10.1016/j.asoc.2014.11.043

Ge, P., Wang, J., Ren, P., Gao, H., & Luo, Y. (2013). A new improved forecasting method integrated fuzzy time series with the exponential smoothing method. *International Journal of Environment and Pollution*, *51*(3-4), 206–221. doi:10.1504/IJEP.2013.054030

Hadavandi, E., Shavandi, H., & Ghanbari, A. (2010). Integration of genetic fuzzy systems and artificial neural networks for stock price forecasting. *Knowledge-Based Systems*, *23*(8), 800–808. doi:10.1016/j.knosys.2010.05.004

Huang, Y. L., Horng, S. J., He, M., Fan, P., Kao, T. W., Khan, M. K., & Kuo, I. H. et al. (2011). A hybrid forecasting model for enrollments based on aggregated fuzzy time series and particle swarm optimization. *Expert Systems with Applications*, *38*(7), 8014–8023. doi:10.1016/j.eswa.2010.12.127

Huarng, K. (2001). Heuristic models of fuzzy time series for forecasting. *Fuzzy Sets and Systems*, *123*(3), 369–386. doi:10.1016/S0165-0114(00)00093-2

Hwang, H., & Oh, J. (2010). Fuzzy models for predicting time series stock price index. *International Journal of Control, Automation, and Systems*, *8*(3), 702–706. doi:10.1007/s12555-010-0325-2

Hwang, J. R., Chen, S. M., & Lee, C. H. (1998). Handling forecasting problems using fuzzy time series. *Fuzzy Sets and Systems*, *100*(1), 217–228. doi:10.1016/S0165-0114(97)00121-8

Hyndman, R. J., & Athanasopoulos, G. (2014). *Forecasting: principles and practice*. OTexts.

Ismail, Z., Efendi, R., & Deris, M. M. (2015). Application of Fuzzy Time Series Approach in Electric Load Forecasting. *New Mathematics and Natural Computation*, *11*(3), 229–248. doi:10.1142/S1793005715500076

Javedani Sadaei, H., & Lee, M. H. (2014). Multilayer stock forecasting model using fuzzy time series. *The Scientific World Journal*. PMID:24605058

Jiang, H., Livingston, M., & Room, R. (2015). Alcohol consumption and fatal injuries in Australia before and after major traffic safety initiatives: A time series analysis. *Alcoholism, Clinical and Experimental Research*, *39*(1), 175–183. doi:10.1111/acer.12609 PMID:25623416

Kahraman, C., Yazıcı, I. & Karaşan, A. (2015). *A Literature Survey on the Usage of Fuzzy MCDM Methods for Digital Marketing*. doi: 10.4018/978-1-4666-8808-7.ch001

Kocak, C. (2013). First-order ARMA type fuzzy time series method based on fuzzy logic relation tables. *Mathematical Problems in Engineering*.

Kuo, I. H., Horng, S. J., Kao, T. W., Lin, T. L., Lee, C. L., & Pan, Y. (2009). An improved method for forecasting enrollments based on fuzzy time series and particle swarm optimization. *Expert Systems with Applications*, *36*(3), 6108–6117. doi:10.1016/j.eswa.2008.07.043

Marszałek, A., & Burczyński, T. (2014). Modeling and forecasting financial time series with ordered fuzzy candlesticks. *Information Sciences*, *273*, 144–155. doi:10.1016/j.ins.2014.03.026

Mary Ann Anderson, M. S. E., Anderson, E. J., & Parker, G. (2013). *Operations Management for Dummies*. John Wiley & Sons.

Moosa, I. (2015). The effect of oil prices on stock prices: A structural time series approach. *International Journal of Global Energy Issues*, *38*(4-6), 232–241. doi:10.1504/IJGEI.2015.070261

Nahmias, S. (2009). *Production and operations analysis* (International Edition). McGraw-Hill.

Pandey, P., Kumar, S., & Shrivastav, S. (2013). Forecasting using Fuzzy Time Series for Diffusion of Innovation: Case of Tata Nano Car in India. *National Academy Science Letters*, *36*(3), 299–309. doi:10.1007/s40009-013-0140-4

Prema, V., & Rao, K. U. (2015). Development of statistical time series models for solar power prediction. *Renewable Energy*, *83*, 100–109. doi:10.1016/j.renene.2015.03.038

Ramli, N. A., & Ismail, T. (n.d.). *Application of Fuzzy Optimization and Time Series for Early Warning System in Predicting Currency Crisis*. Academic Press.

Reuter, U., & Möller, B. (2010). Artificial neural networks for forecasting of fuzzy time series. *Computer-Aided Civil and Infrastructure Engineering*, *25*(5), 363–374. doi:10.1111/j.1467-8667.2009.00646.x

Singh, P., & Borah, B. (2013). An efficient time series forecasting model based on fuzzy time series. *Engineering Applications of Artificial Intelligence*, *26*(10), 2443–2457. doi:10.1016/j.engappai.2013.07.012

Song, Q & Chissom, B. S. (1993). Forecasting enrollments with fuzzy time series-Part I. *Fuzzy Sets and Systems, 54*, 1–9. doi:0165-0114/93/$06.001

Song, Q & Chissom, B. S. (1993). Forecasting enrollments with fuzzy time series-Part II. *Fuzzy Sets, and Systems, 62*, 1–8. doi:0165-0114/94/$07.00

Song, Q., & Chissom, B. S. (1993). Forecasting enrollments with fuzzy time series-Part I. *Fuzzy Sets and Systems*, *54*(1), 1–9. doi:10.1016/0165-0114(93)90355-L

Taylor, B. W. III. (2010). *Introduction to Management Science* (10th ed.). Upper Saddle River, NJ: Prentice Hall.

Telfer, S., & Woodburn, J. (2015). Let me Google that for you: a time series analysis of seasonality in internet search trends for terms related to foot and ankle pain. *Journal of Foot and Ankle Research*, *8*(1), 1-10.

Wang, J., & Xiong, S. (2014). A hybrid forecasting model based on outlier detection and fuzzy time series–A case study on Hainan wind farm of China. *Energy*, *76*, 526–541. doi:10.1016/j.energy.2014.08.064

Wong, W. K., Bai, E., & Chu, A. W. C. (2010). Adaptive time-variant models for fuzzy-time-series forecasting. Systems, Man, and Cybernetics, Part B: Cybernetics. *IEEE Transactions on*, *40*(6), 1531–1542.

Yi, W., & Chan, A. P. (2015). Effects of temperature on mortality in Hong Kong: A time series analysis. *International Journal of Biometeorology*, *59*(7), 927–936. doi:10.1007/s00484-014-0895-4 PMID:25179530

Zadeh, L. A. (1965). Fuzzy Sets. *Information and Control*, *8*(3), 338–353. doi:10.1016/S0019-9958(65)90241-X

Zadeh, L. A. (1968). Fuzzy algorithms. *Information and Control*, *12*(2), 94–102. doi:10.1016/S0019-9958(68)90211-8

Zadeh, L. A. (1973). Outline of A New Approach to the Analysis of-of Complex Systems and Decision Processes. *IEEE Transactions on Cybernetics*, *3*(1), 28–44. doi:10.1109/TSMC.1973.5408575

Zadeh, L. A. (2002). Is there a need for fuzzy logic. *Information Sciences*, *178*(13), 2751–2779. doi:10.1016/j.ins.2008.02.012

Chapter 16
Understand the Frequency of Application Usage by Smartphone Users:
Door Is Open, but Closes Quickly

Geetika Jain
UP Technical University, India

Sapna Rakesh
IMS Ghaziabad, India

ABSTRACT

Smartphone users download the apps after the enormous popularity in this mobile world and then eventually delete those apps. There are various factors like frequency, relevance and space it consumes in the phone, which decide a user's preference for an app. All the app provider companies are trying hard to fit into right place, so that they can increase the engagement with the users. Companies are upgrading their technology to make an app convenient and relevant based on user's requirement. This study is trying to understand the frequency of application usage and the importance of various factors like time to complete transaction, relevance, space it consumes, features, User Index, and ease of use for a user which leads to purchase intention. The study has found that UX/UI is the most important factor followed by other factors. The output of the study has the practical implication for online retailer.

1. INTRODUCTION

In India, the mobile user's base is increasing day by day. Indian Telecom sector announced that the penetration rate of mobile service subscribers in India was 197.5 percent in May 2011. In other words, every person has almost 2 mobile phones on an average. This data also makes India as the world highest region of mobile service in terms of penetration level. The mobile market in developed countries is estimated to reach an average of 116 subscriptions per 100 inhabitants at the end of 2010 (Sun et al 2010). A study by Verhagen, M., Sauri, R., Caselli, T., and Pustejovsky, J. (2010) give insights that over

DOI: 10.4018/978-1-5225-0997-4.ch016

24,000 consumers in 35 markets and concluded that India was also at the forefront of global smart phone usage. "Almost half (48%) of respondents in India own a smart phone, more than double the global rate of 23%". The internet usage over the mobile phone has come out as the primary one. Mobile apps are coming as new platform of doing business in both local and international regions.

In 2013, more than one billion smartphone units were shipped worldwide in a single year for the first time. This was a 38.4 percent increase from 2012 and the volume has doubled in just two years (International Data Corporation, 2014). Meanwhile, mobile app marketplaces are also booming. In 2012, worldwide annual downloads in mobile app stores reached 64 billion and generated $18 billion in revenue (Gartner, 2013). The forecast predicts that by 2017 worldwide annual downloads in mobile app stores will reach $268.7 billion (Gartner, 2013). By offering great opportunities in marketing and branding in mobile apps, the app market is now attracting more and more big companies with well-known brand names (Banham, 2010). Bellman et al. (2011) studied the effect of apps use on brand attitude and purchase intention and found that using popular apps increased participants' interest in the brand and product category, since when the company's brand name is attached to the app, the company's loyal customers would continually appreciate their relationship with the brand and therefore value and adopt the app.

1.1 Research Objectives

This paper is an attempt to understand the importance of various factors like time to complete transaction, relevance, space it consumes, features, User Index, and ease of use related to a mobile application for a user. My paper will help marketers and researchers to understand the consumer's preference towards the mobile application usage. Specifically, the objective of the paper is to understand the followings:

The purpose of this research is, first, to understand the importance of various factors like time to complete transaction, relevance, space it consumes, features, User Index, and ease of use for a user towards a mobile application. Secondly, to study these factors, which has an impact on consumer buying behavior?

2. BACKGROUND AND LITERATURE REVIEW

2.1 Theoretical Literature Review

The current study uses the TAM (Technology Acceptance Model), a well-accepted and well known theory to define the individual's behavior towards technology (Davis, 1989), work as a theoretical concept to understand the various factors that may influence the consumer buying behavior based upon the technology usage. TAM is a very popular model that will help the researcher to understand the consumer's adoption towards a technology and its use also for various purposes. The current study will also use TRA (Theory of Reasoned Action Model), a well-defined model to investigate the consumer attitude towards online shopping (Fishbein & Ajzen's, 1980). According to (Fishbein & Ajzen, 1980) theory of reasoned action suggests that, a person's intention is a function of two basic determinants i.e. attitude towards behavior and subjective norm. The theory is based on the assumption that human beings are rational and they use information available to them, systematically. The determinant attitude towards behavior is personal in nature. It describes the individual's positive and negative evaluation of performing the behavior. Subjective norm reflects the social influence of an individual while performing his/her behavior. According to this theory, an individual's attitude toward performing a behavior was a function of two components:

1. Beliefs (bi) that performing a behavior has certain attributes; and
2. The individual's evaluation (ei) of those beliefs.

The attitude was estimated using the following formula:

$$Ab = \sum biei$$

Basically it is the person's perception of the social pressures put on him/her to show a particular behavior at a particular time. It depends on situation, whether attitude towards behavior dominates or social norm dominates. Also the relative weights of attitudinal and normative factors differ from person to person. While TRA is a base model, numbers of other factors are also considered by researchers which have an impact on behavioral intention. Subjective norms are influenced by perception which has been created through friends, relatives, colleagues, partner etc. The relationship between students' attitudes and their intentions of shopping online for apparel products was explored, with comparison made between students living in rural and urban areas. The theory is based on the assumption that human beings are rational and they use information available to them, systematically. The determinant attitude towards behavior is personal in nature. It describes the individual's positive and negative evaluation of performing the behavior. Subjective norm reflects the social influence of an individual while performing his/her behavior. Basically it is the person's perception of the social pressures put on him/her to show a particular behavior at a particular time. It depends on situation, whether attitude towards behavior dominates or social norm dominates. Also the relative weights of attitudinal and normative factors differ from person to person. While TRA is a base model, numbers of other factors are also considered by researchers which have an impact on behavioral intention.

As, it has been found already, that, there is a healthy relationship between technology acceptance of a consumer to its personal characteristics. So, this study will try to understand the relationship of demographics variables such as age, education, lifestyle, gender and income with the frequency of application usage while using the mobile phone.

2.2 Overview of the Mobile Apps

Due to change in environment and culture, Mobile applications have come up as a new platform of doing shopping playing, and even in improving sales for firms in this field (Brousell, 2012), each an estimated $46 billion (Beccue, 2012). Due to shift in usage, millions of organizations have pitched into a new way of doing business through mobile applications.

Lin (2007) mentioned in the study that the switching cost is almost negligible for customers while using mobile application as a platform to do shopping. The rate of failure is very high in case of mobile applications. Flurry (2011) has mentioned in the study that the probability of continuous usage of mobile applications over one year is very less. The study says that approximately 33% users will continue to use the mobile application after one month period and rest will drop the facility. Savitz, (2012), in his article offers insight and ideas for technology leaders about mobile commerce (m-commerce) via apps which is broken into the categories of mobile e-commerce, mobile payment, and mobile commerce (in-store). M-commerce is considered a tool that can help transform the way retailers engage their customers.

Consumers preference towards online shopping have increased over the time due to two major reasons, one is delivery services convenience, time saving and require less efforts also (Seiders et al., 2000, 2005, 2007). Seiders et al. (2000) also mentioned in the study that customer convenience by providing various services like one-stop shopping, home delivery and sale service is there, but retailer needs to understand the importance of other factors like ease of use, feature and functionalities, ease of selection of a specific product, product information and transaction quality. Berry et al., 2002 ; Seiders et al., 2007, mentioned in the study that the researcher needs to identify two major important elements which leads to selection of a specific retailer like time-saving and effort-saving, both go hand-in-hand.

Minimization of efforts leads to reduce the efforts in various activities like cognitive, physical, and emotional that decides customer preference to purchase a specific product good and service (Berry et al, 2002). Despite various studies have spoken about the customer convenience as the top most factor, earlier research has given emphasis more on human effort element (Brown, 1990; Hui et al., 1998; Seiders et al., 2000).

Larivière et al. (2013), found for major benefits through mobile apps like instrumental, experiential, identity, and social benefits. Instrumental benefits refer to better task performance or enhanced productivity. Mobile applications face lot of challenges also like low speed while searching and loading because of low bandwidth, less number of features and display buttons comparatively to the website version (Hsi & Yu, 2009). Davis et al. (1992) explained the factors that motivate to adapt new technology, which leads to use new technology like mobile apps for shopping purpose.

3. RESEARCH METHODOLOGY

3.1 Data Collection Methodology

A predominantly descriptive research method has been used for this paper. This study has included primary source of information and respondents were selected Delhi/ NCR region. The random sampling method was used in the research and the sample size of 200 respondents of 18 – 75 year age located in Delhi/NCR region. The online shopper have asked questions based upon their experience while selecting a product during shopping and the experience of using the mobile application based on various factors. The primary data as collected by conducting a survey.

Although there are so many complex formulas to formulate the ideal number of sample size, the thumb rule is no less than 8 participants per predictor variable for a regression and correlation test (Wilson Van Voorhis & Morgan, 2007). The formula is:

$$N > 50+8m$$

where m is the number of IVs.

3.2 Data Analysis Methodology

To do the data analysis, the statistical analysis methods have been used like reliability test, regression and multiple regression analysis. The study has been analyzed the influence of various factors like UI/UX (User interface and User Experience), functionality and feature, privacy and security for a users' towards purchase intention using mobile application. SPSS 17.0 has been used to analyze the relationship with the help of various statistical analysis tools.

The hypotheses that have been developed from the research questions of this study are as follow:

H1: There is a positive influence of factors like UI/UX (User Interface & User Experience) for a user towards purchasing intention using mobile intention.
H2: There is a positive influence of factors like functionality and features and ease of use for a user towards purchasing intention using mobile application.
H3: There is a positive influence of factors like privacy and security for a user towards purchasing intention using mobile application.

Table 1. Descriptive statistics

	N	Minimum	Maximum	Mean	Std. Deviation
Gender	198	1.00	2.00	1.5303	.50035
Age	198	1.00	3.00	1.6212	.71457
Marital Status	198	1.00	3.00	1.4848	.53056
Place	198	1.00	3.00	1.0606	.34371
Education	198	1.00	4.00	3.3182	.85779
Occupation Status	198	1.00	5.00	3.3636	1.15283
Personal Income	177	.00	5.00	1.9492	1.36211
Current Occupation	192	.00	3.00	2.2188	.84013
Own a smartphone	198	1.00	1.00	1.0000	.00000
Time spent on smartphone on daily basis (in hrs)	198	1.00	3.00	1.7727	.71522
Preference Internet access on smartphone	198	.00	2.00	1.0455	.27215
Time spent on smartphone while accessing internet	198	0	3	1.41	.872
Frequency of using mobile application	123	.00	2.00	1.1951	.70894
Functionality of website	198	1.00	5.00	3.7576	1.15842
Features of app	195	1.00	5.00	3.7077	.95879
Design of app	195	1.00	5.00	3.5538	1.11268
App loading time	198	1.00	5.00	3.4848	1.24927
Information about the product on app	198	1.00	5.00	3.4697	1.13397
GPS tracker of app	198	1.00	5.00	3.4091	.98688
Valid N (listwise)	114				

4. RESULTS AND INTERPRETATION

4.1 Descriptive Statistics

See Table 1.

4.2 Regression Analysis

The result indicates in the Table 1 shows that functionality, features, design, loading speed of web page and searching product on website, looking for information about the product, locates the device in least time as accurately as possible, which is associated to frequently using mobile application for shopping purpose. Mobile application functionality and features considered to be the top most factors for customers with high loading compare to other factors while doing shopping using an app. Regression analysis is done for various factors having effect with frequency of using mobile application for shopping purpose. The frequency of using mobile application work as dependent variable and other factors consider as an independent variables as mentioned in the descriptive statistics. The findings of the study clearly shows that a significant relation between these major factors (R square = 0.239 and the significance=0.000, $p<0.01$), Hence, the model is found to be significant.

The result for the preliminary test shows that null hypothesis will be accepted.

A Shapiro-Wilk's test ($p>0.05$) (Shapiro & Wilk, 1965, Razali & Wah, 2011) has a significant relationship for using mobile application for shopping purpose. A visual inspection of histograms for using mobile application for shopping shows about to normal picture, there is hardly one peak which shows out of the normal distribution.

The normal P-P plot & box plots showed that the exam scores were approximately normally distributed for using mobile application for shopping purpose frequently, with a skewness of -0.102 (SE= 0.221) and a kurtosis of 0.018 (SE=0.438). The P-P plot shows that the data is near to normal and almost fits into the scree plot region. The BOX plot also has the same observation which shows that the data is about to normal apart for few data entries which shows out of the normal region like entries no 192, 126 and 80.

Histrogram shape shows that the data is near to normal for using mobile application for shopping purpose frequently as dependent variable. Table 4 determine that various factors like functionality, features, design, loading speed of web page and searching product on website, looking for information about the product, locates the device in least time as accurately as possible accept null hypothesis because p-value is above 0.05.

Table 2. Regression analysis

Model Summary[b]				
Model	**R**	**R Square**	**Adjusted R Square**	**Std. Error of the Estimate**
1	.489[a]	.239	.177	.64055

a. Predictors: (Constant), Time spent on smartphone on daily basis (in hrs), Preference Internet access on smartphone, Time spent on smartphone while accessing internet, Frequency of using mobile application, Functionality of website, Features of app, Design of app, App loading time, Information about the product on app, GPS tracker of app.

b. Dependent Variable: Frequency of using mobile app for shopping purpose.

Table 3. Multiple regression analysis

Coefficients[a]								
Model		Unstandardized Coefficients		Standardized Coefficients	t	Sig.	Collinearity Statistics	
		B	Std. Error	Beta			Tolerance	VIF
1	(Constant)	.802	.383		2.096	.038		
	Time spent on smartphone on daily basis (in hrs)	.239	.137	.238	1.748	.083	.375	2.669
	Preference of Internet access on smartphone	.058	.213	.026	.272	.786	.771	1.297
	Time spent on smartphone while accessing internet	-.331	.109	-.430	-3.047	.003	.348	2.874
	Functionality of website	.199	.105	.335	1.904	.060	.223	4.477
	Features of app	-.076	.118	-.113	-.647	.519	.228	4.384
	Design of app	.061	.083	.095	.742	.460	.425	2.354
	App loading time	.063	.080	.109	.788	.432	.361	2.774
	Information about the product on app	-.153	.087	-.256	-1.751	.083	.323	3.093
	GPS tracker of app	-.005	.115	-.007	-.045	.964	.262	3.812

a. Dependent Variable: Frequency of using mobile app for shopping purpose

Table 4. Tests of between-subjects effects

Dependent Variable: Frequency of Using Mobile App for Shopping Purpose					
Source	Type III Sum of Squares	df	Mean Square	F	Sig.
Corrected Model	46.481[a]	28	1.660	11.761	.000
Intercept	6.307	1	6.307	44.684	.000
Time spent on smartphone on daily basis (in hrs)	2.676	2	1.338	9.479	.000
Preference Internet access on smartphone	3.237	2	1.619	11.469	.000
Time spent on smartphone while accessing internet	8.980	3	2.993	21.209	.000
Functionality of website	3.259	3	1.086	7.698	.000
Features of app	1.377	3	.459	3.251	.025
Design of app	2.569	3	.856	6.067	.001
App loading time	2.034	4	.508	3.602	.009
Information about the product on app	2.831	3	.944	6.685	.000
GPS tracker of app	9.083	3	3.028	21.450	.000
Error	12.844	91	.141		
Total	225.000	120			
Corrected Total	59.325	119			

a. R Squared =.783 (Adjusted R Squared =.717)

The result of normality test proves that the data is normal. As per table no – 7, collinearity statistics has VIF (variance inflation factor) value is low than 5 which proves that the predictors are not correlated to each other. Some variables like respondent give preference to mobile while accessing internet, time spent on internet and website design have VIF near to 1 which is very low as per the limit standard and proves that the predictors are not correlated to each other.

The reliability of the questionnaire found to be very high with Cronbach Alpha value of 0.813 showing the good internal consistency of the scale.

So, null hypothesis will be accepted for factors like UI/UX (User Interface & User Experience, functionality and features and ease of use, privacy and security for a user towards purchasing intention using mobile application frequently basis.

5. DISCUSSION AND CONCLUSION

The purpose of the present study was to examine the linkage between various factors like UI/UX (User Interface & User Experience, functionality and features and ease of use, privacy and security for a user towards purchasing intention using mobile application frequently basis. Our findings suggest respondents consider features and functionalities as the top priorities factors which respondents considered as the main factors to lead mobile application shopping on frequent basis

We have attempted to formulate Consumer Choice dimensions to capture perceptions for mobile application for shopping purpose only for consumers of developed countries but also for consumers of developing countries (basically cultural variations).

Figure 1. Histogram; dependent variable: frequency of using mobile app for shopping purpose

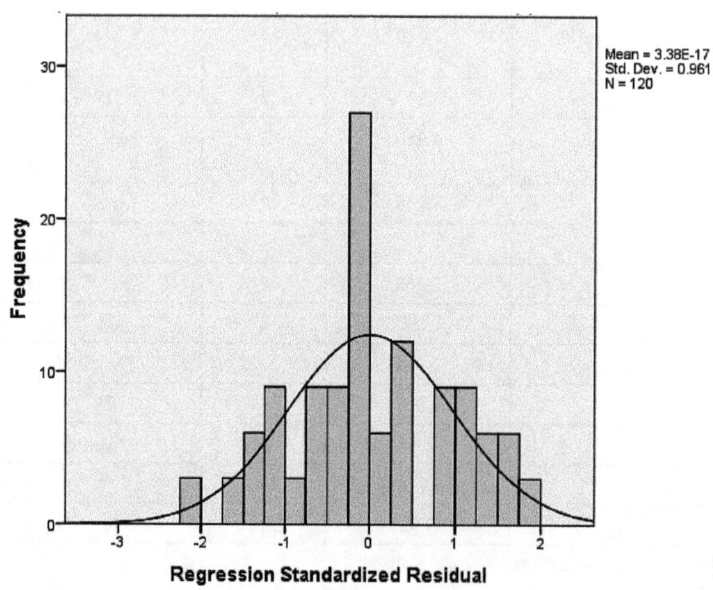

Figure 2. Normal P-P plot of regression standardized residual; dependent variable: frequency of using mobile app for shopping purpose

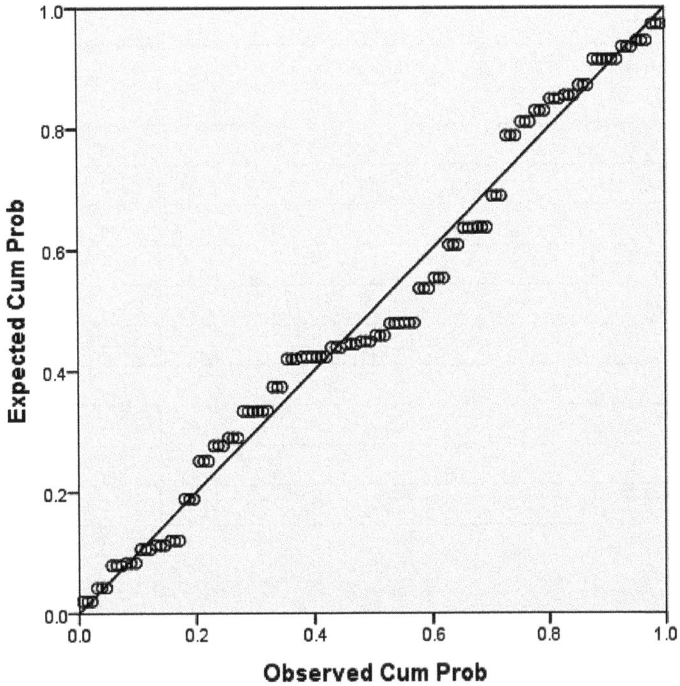

Figure 3. Standardized residual for frequency of using mobile app for shopping purpose

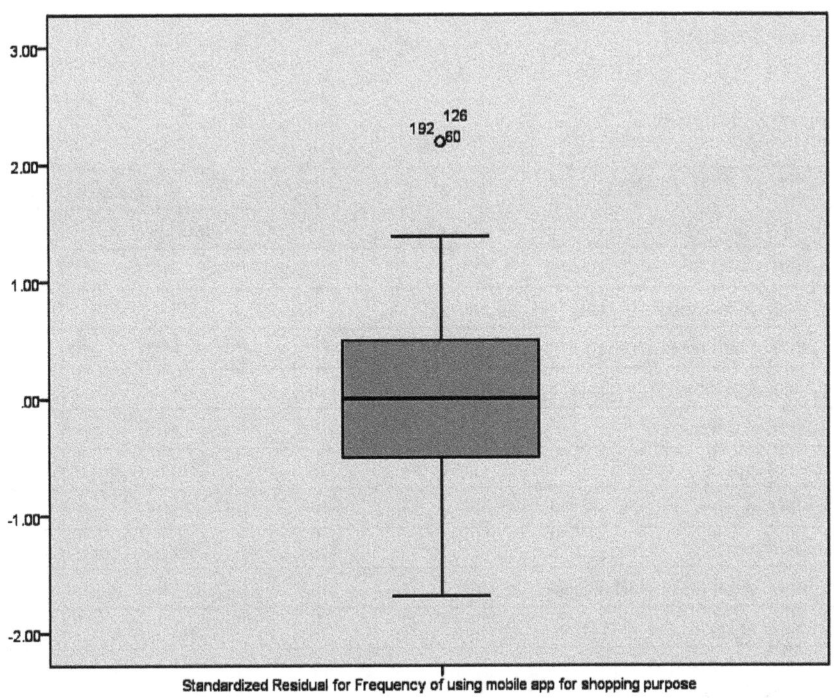

Table 5. Standardized residual test

Standardized Residual for Frequency of Using Mobile App for Shopping Purpose		Statistic	Std. Error
Mean		.0000	.07983
95% Confidence Interval for Mean	Lower Bound	-.1581	
	Upper Bound	.1581	
5% Trimmed Mean		-.0089	
Median		.0000	
Variance		.765	
Std. Deviation		.87447	
Minimum		-1.69	
Maximum		2.19	
Range		3.88	
Interquartile Range		1.02	
Skewness		.102	.221
Kurtosis		.018	.438

Table 6. Normality test

	Kolmogorov-Smirnov[a]			Shapiro-Wilk		
	Statistic	df	Sig.	Statistic	df	Sig.
Standardized Residual for Frequency of using mobile app for shopping purpose	.132	120	.000	.954	120	.000

a. Lilliefors Significance Correction

Table 7. Collinearity statistics

Model		Collinearity Statistics	
		Tolerance	VIF
1	(Constant)		
	Time spent on smartphone on daily basis (in hrs)	.375	2.669
	Preference of Internet access on smartphone	.771	1.297
	Time spent on smartphone while accessing internet	.348	2.874
	Functionality of website	.223	4.477
	Features of app	.228	4.384
	Design of app	.425	2.354
	App loading time	.361	2.774
	Information about the product on app	.323	3.093
	GPS tracker of app	.262	3.812

Table 8. Reliability statistics for questionnaire

Cronbach's Alpha	Cronbach's Alpha Based on Standardized Items	N of Items
.813	.764	9

6. MANAGERIAL IMPLICATIONS

The implications of this research could provide interest to both practitioners and researchers. If the results of this study hold across other samples, managers could be encouraged to know that Cause related marketing approach may simultaneously enhance their Brand equity. Researchers should be encouraged at the possibility of exploring other individual and organizational peculiarities that might explain the mechanism through which using mobile application as a only platform for customers to do shopping online. The results of the study will help managers to understand the emergence of this phenomenon in the area of electronic commerce where large number of customer base show positive influence on their purchase intention towards using mobile application for shopping purpose on frequent basis if it fulfills all the basic factors of customer expectations towards the hygiene factors related to aesthetic factors of a particular mobile application.

7. LIMITATIONS

1. The numbers of companies practicing mobile application for shopping in India are coming up and this a altogether a industry to look forward hence other variables have not been considered in the study.
2. An industry wise study needs to be considered which may also provide deep insight into the common motivators for using mobile application for shopping purpose and the customer preference it.

8. FUTURE RESEARCH PROSPECTS

Since the study is conducted in Delhi/NCR it is difficult to predict the complex buying behaviour of India consumers as a whole especially due to the cross-sectional nature of the data, drawing causal inferences among the variables explored may not be appropriate therefore the current study need to be replicated using longitudinal study designs in order to establish more certain causality of the relationship between the key constructs. In this study, few parameters have been considered to understand the consumer intention towards mobile application usage for shopping purpose on frequent basis approach. After taking a holistic view of the study, researcher may look for further innovative and game changing business model related to mobile application and may look forward to do a comparison study to fulfill some of the gaps

REFERENCES

Bomhold, C. R. (2013). Educational use of smart phone technology. *Program - electronic library and information systems, 47*(4), 424-436.

Broadbridge, A., & Calderwood, E. (2002). Rural grocery shoppers: Do their attitudes reflect their actions? *International Journal of Retail & Distribution Management, 30*(8), 394–406. doi:10.1108/09590550210435282

Carmo, R. M. (2001). Mobile agents applications. *Internet Research, 11*(1), 49–54. doi:10.1108/10662240110365715

Chai, Y. D. (2015). Emotions and continued usage of mobile applications. *Industrial Management & Data Systems, 115*(5), 833–852. doi:10.1108/IMDS-11-2014-0338

Chung, S. (2014). An empirical analysis of usage dynamics in a mobile music app: Evidence from large-scale data. *Internet Research, 24*(4), 436–456. doi:10.1108/IntR-05-2013-0088

Davis, G. (1995). Bringing stores to shoppers - not shoppers to stores. *International Journal of Retail & Distribution Management, 23*(1), 18–23. doi:10.1108/09590559510078089

Farris, A. B. (2014). Mobile Shopper Marketing: Assessing the Impact of Mobile Technology on Consumer Path to Purchase. *Shopper Marketing and the Role of In store Marketing, 11*, 1-25.

Funk, J. L. (2004). Key technological trajectories and the expansion of mobile Internet applications. *Info, 6*(3), 208–215. doi:10.1108/14636690410549543

Groß, M. (2015). Mobile shopping: A classification framework and literature review. *International Journal of Retail & Distribution Management, 43*(3), 221–241. doi:10.1108/IJRDM-06-2013-0119

Hsi, P., & Lu Philip, Y. J. (2015). Factors affecting purchase intention on mobile shopping web sites. *Internet Research, 19*(4), 442–458.

Jiang, L. A., Yang, Z., & Jun, M. (2013). Measuring consumer perceptions of online shopping. *Journal of Service Management, 24*(2), 191–214. doi:10.1108/09564231311323962

Joaquin Aldas Manzano, C. R. (2008, December). Exploring individual personality factors as drivers of M-shopping acceptance. *Industrial Management & Data Systems, 109*(6), 739–757. doi:10.1108/02635570910968018

Kim, K. Y.-Y. (2012). Mobile shopping motivation: An application of multiple discriminant analysis. *International Journal of Retail & Distribution Management, 40*(10), 778–789. doi:10.1108/09590551211263182

Kuo Fang Peng, Y. C. (2014, July). Brand relationship, consumption values and branded app adoption. *Industrial Management & Data Systems, 114*(8), 1131–1143. doi:10.1108/IMDS-05-2014-0132

Lembke, J. (2002). Mobile Commerce and the creation of a marketplace. *Info, 4*(3), 50–56. doi:10.1108/14636690210440013

Levin, D. G. (2014). Predicting mobile app usage for purchasing and information sharing. *International Journal of Retail & Distribution Management, 42*(8), 759–774. doi:10.1108/IJRDM-11-2012-0108

Min Li, Z. Y. (2012). Factors Influencing consumption experience of mobile commerce. *Internet Research, 22*(2), 120–141. doi:10.1108/10662241211214539

Moore, M. (2012). Interactive media usage among millennial consumers. *Journal of Consumer Marketing, 29*(6), 436–444. doi:10.1108/07363761211259241

Park, S. B. (2014). The impact of mobile tablet devices on human information behaviour. *The Journal of Documentation, 70*(4), 622–639. doi:10.1108/JD-09-2012-0123

Rowley, A. H. (2013). Mobile shopping behaviour: Insights into attitudes, shopping process involvement and location. *International Journal of Retail & Distribution Management, 42*(1), 25–39. doi:10.1108/IJRDM-10-2012-0096

Shen, M. K. (2008). Explaining the adoption of transactional B2C mobile commerce. *Journal of Enterprise Information Management, 21*(2), 110–124. doi:10.1108/17410390810851372

Sonia San Martín Blanca López-Catalán María, A. (2012). Factors determining firms perceived performance of mobile commerce. *Industrial Management & Data Systems, 112*(6), 946–963. doi:10.1108/02635571211238536

Tang, F. L. (2015). Roles of perceived value and individual differences in the acceptance of mobile coupon applications. *Internet Research, 25*(3), 471–495. doi:10.1108/IntR-02-2014-0053

2012 Women Ethnic Wear Market in India Outlook. (2015). Dublin: Research and Market.

Section 5

Advanced Modelling Applications:

Business Analytics

Chapter 17
Car Safety:
A Statistical Analysis for Marketing Management

António Carrizo Moreira
University of Aveiro, Portugal

Monica Gouveia
University of Aveiro, Portugal

Pedro Macedo
University of Aveiro, Portugal

ABSTRACT

Car safety is an essential feature of marketing strategies for automobile companies. In this work, a statistical analysis on crash tests is conducted based on data available from European New Car Assessment Programme (Euro NCAP). The research work developed in this chapter presents a statistical analysis of the information produced by Euro NCAP, using the SPSS and MATLAB software, and seeks to answer the following research questions: - are there statistically significant differences on adult occupant safety in the six years under study? - are there statistically significant differences among the best-selling car classes regarding safety in frontal collisions? - are electric and hybrid automobiles less secure than their traditional counterparts with respect to frontal collisions?

INTRODUCTION

Car marketers know that car buyers need far more than the basic transportation needs. Marketing cars is a kind of art: from the necessity to by a new car because the previous one broke down, or new needs arise for everyday activity, one realizes that hedonic considerations like excitement (power sliding a sports car through a rain-slick city) or emotional attachment (freedom sensation driving thought beautiful landscapes) among advertising themes used by car marketers are well more familiar to car buyers than utilitarian considerations like gas mileage, airbags, safety rating, and number of seats.

DOI: 10.4018/978-1-5225-0997-4.ch017

Although hedonic aspects are very important to position vehicles characteristics as speed, price, shape, handling, and prestige in the consumer minds, most people shopping a brand new car resorts to utilitarian aspects, such as gas mileage, and airbags.

When advertising cars, marketers take the consumer needs into account placing high emphasis on complementing utilitarian with hedonic considerations in order to create new needs among consumers. Moreover, car marketers know they can develop attitudes and associations toward specific brands based on aggressive marketing campaigns that include excitement and emotional attachment when developing their brands. However, one thing is clear: most people have difficulties analyzing how different cars and brands perform on safety performance.

Institutional marketing seeks to work the identity, the formation and the image consolidation of an organization. As such, public recognition and exerting a strong influence on decision-making of the public are essential for institutions that seek to promote a solid reputation of their activities. Institutional marketing seeks to develop methodologies that can be developed to facilitate communication with the general population, with the aim of clarifying and involving the public in its decision making.

The chapter is structured in four sections. The first section presents the introduction of the chapter. The second section presents the importance of safety tests, a description of the Euro NCAP safety tests and the way they are performed. While the third section presents the methodology, the results of the study and its discussion, the fourth section presents the conclusions and suggestions for future work.

THE IMPORTANCE OF CAR SAFETY

Safety has an increasingly important role in vehicle research because of its economic and social importance. Car safety needs have been disclosed quite long time ago (Seidel, Loch, & Chahil, 2005). For example, Marin and Lenguerrand (2008) show that the risk of a driver being killed in two-car crashes is larger than in single-car crashes. Moreover, the study also shows that when a recent car collides with an older car the driver of the former is more protected than the driver of the latter, which clearly indicates that there has been an improvement of safety and production systems among carmakers. Gronostajski, Bandola, and Karbowski (2006) analyzed the effect of crashworthiness parameters on the behavior of car-body elements, which might have important consequences for passive safety and a threat to life of passengers and persons involved in car accidents. Modelling techniques have also been used to predict the effect on passengers (Orsi, Marchetti, Montomolli, & Morandi, 2013; Pawlus, Karimi, & Robbersmyr, 2013), which is a clear indication of how important car safety has become.

Although research on car accidents has been increasing, papers on how major car brands differ in terms of performance are still scarce (Huang, Li, & Zeng, 2016; Huang, Hu, & Abdel-Aty, 2014). While Huang et al. (2014) analyzed crash worthiness and crash aggressivity involving 34,356 cars of 23 major brands, concluding that European cars have relatively good self-protection when compared with Japanese cars, South-Korean cars being associated with the lowest crash worthiness, Huang et al. (2016) investigated vehicle's crash protectiveness on occupant injury and vehicle damage using Bayesian bivariate hierarchical ordered logistic model for 23 major brands in total of 7,335 two-vehicle-crash. Huang et al. (2016) found that occupant protectiveness index is relatively coherent with the crash worthiness index found by Huang et al. (2014).

The Euro NCAP

The European New Car Assessment Programme (Euro NCAP) was founded in 1997. It performs safety tests and evaluates accident prevention systems in passenger light and business cars that are available in the European market. It is composed by ten members from European government institutions and motoring organizations, with testing facilities in six countries.

The Euro NCAP provides information for anyone wishing to purchase a new car, aiming to draw attention to the importance of vehicle safety and convey the message that "safety is not a luxury" (Euro NCAP, 2014). In addition, Euro NCAP aims to encourage improvements in safety and security issues in the design of new cars and to increase the safety requirements the law provides. Road fatalities decreased by 17% in the European Union between 2010 and 2013 (Campos, 2014), and it was estimated that about nine thousand lives have been saved, as stated by Siim Kallas, Commission Vice-President and European Commissioner for mobility and transport, quoted by Campos (2014). However, Campos (2014) recalls that around 70 people die every day on Europe's roads. As such, there is plenty to be done to stop those numbers.

Since it is not possible for the Euro NCAP test neither all cars nor all variants/models of each car, each year a selection of the best-selling models to the general public is made. In most cases, the Euro NCAP tests cars that are not yet on the market, as it is important to publish the results as soon as possible so that more consumers can make an informed choice. However, occasionally, cars that are already on sale can also be tested.

In order to evaluate a model of a car, the Euro NCAP requires at least four cars. If they are already in the market, automobiles are anonymously purchased from car dealers, in the same way that consumers do. Before being tested, it is asked the manufacturer to check (through the vehicle identification number) if any change was introduced during production. If it was introduced, for example, a new security equipment, it will also be installed in the vehicle being tested in order to ensure that the results are representative of the current car production. If the vehicle is not yet in the market, cars are randomly selected in factories or from a list provided by the manufacturer. In such a way, it is assured the randomness of the sample.

The rating is sponsored by the Euro NCAP member organizations (each member organization sponsors the evaluation of at least one car per year) and sometimes by the car manufacturers themselves.

The Euro NCAP rating involves a five-star classification for three different areas for cars tested until 2009, and four areas for cars tested from 2010 onwards. For vehicles tested before 2009 the three areas are: adult protection (for the driver and passenger), child protection, and pedestrian protection. From 2010 onwards, the overall score, besides being more demanding involves the following new area: safety assist technologies, that includes the alert speed assistance system, the electronic stability control, the seat belt reminders control (that formerly was part of the adult protection test), among others.

Generally, the number of stars mirrors the car performance in Euro NCAP tests, although it is also influenced by the safety equipment the manufacturer incorporates. So the higher the number of stars, the better the result, and the more safety equipment in the tested model is readily available to all European consumers. According to the Euro NCAP (2016), the meaning of the number of stars is the following:

- **5 Stars Safety:** Overall good performance in crash protection. Well equipped with robust crash avoidance technology;
- **4 Stars Safety:** Overall good performance in crash protection; additional crash avoidance technology may be present;

- **3 Stars Safety:** Average to good occupant protection but lacking crash avoidance technology;
- **2 Stars Safety:** Nominal crash protection but lacking crash avoidance technology;
- **1 Star Safety:** Marginal crash protection.

To carry out safety tests, the Euro NCAP uses steel and rubber dummies that simulate the adult and child passengers. In all tests, it is used a dummy from which the intensities of the injuries that a human could possibly suffer are measured. Each dummy may have a cost of 100,000 euros.

The head is made of aluminum and covered with rubber. Inside the dummy there are three accelerometers, each providing information on the forces that the brain is subjected in an accident. A device is placed in the neck in order to measure the forces to which it is subject during an impact. The steel ribs dummy is a device that records the forces applied to the chest in a frontal impact. Since the dummy used to simulate side impacts is equipped with three different ribs that record the compression of the thorax and the velocity of this compression. Similar equipment (measuring forces and impact velocity) are placed in the abdomen, pelvis, thighs, legs, ankles, and feet (Euro NCAP, 2016).

Thanks to its stringent crash tests, Euro NCAP has rapidly become a booster of the greatest advances in the safety of new vehicles. Success during the Euro NCAP tests may contribute to the increase of the brand reliability, as well as to clarifying the public opinion.

Adult Occupant Protection

The Adult Occupant Protection score is determined from frontal impact (Offset-Deformable Barrier (ODB) test, and frontal full width rigid barrier test), side impact (side mobile barrier and side pole tests), whiplash tests, and Autonomous Emergency Breaking (AEB), which are carried out to evaluate the protection of adult driver and passengers offered by the vehicle.

In the ODB crash test the crash forces needed to be safely and efficiently absorbed when the vehicle structure is put to the test. As the front end of the vehicle collapses, the passenger compartment needs to remain as undeformed as possible. Moreover, in order to avoid serious injuries to the passenger, the steering wheel and the pedals rear movement must be limited as much as possible.

The frontal full width rigid barrier, which was introduced in 2015, is another frontal crash test that simulates a head-on collision between two oncoming cars at moderately high speeds. This test has placed stricter limits, namely on the degree of chest deflection. With stiffer car structures and higher compartment decelerations, this test has also contributed to the reduction of lower leg and head injuries.

The side mobile barrier test seeks to ensure that critical body regions are adequately protected. This test has led vehicle manufacturers to strengthen the structures of vehicles around the between the doors pillar, the fitment of side impact as well as the development of less obvious energy-absorbing structures in seats and door panels.

The side pole test involves simulating a car travelling sideways into rigid roadside objects such as a tree, which might have lethal consequences for drivers or passengers. This test seeks to test the vehicle's ability to protect the driver's head. This test has led to the introduction of head protection airbags.

Whiplash is a trauma caused by sudden movements of the neck, associated with rapid and excessive distortion of the spine. Although whiplash injuries can occur in all kind of accidents, they are very common in rear-end collisions (Ratingen et al., 2009). It is the most common injury in road accidents with about two million records per year in Europe (cases where the problem does not manifest immediately and cases where one does not need police or toeing assistance are not included in the statistics)

(Ratingen et al., 2009). It is a serious problem with enormous implications for the individual and for society because, in addition to personal suffering, implies high economic costs (Watanabe et al., 2000).

According to Carmen Rodarius, a research scientist in the vehicle safety area, a good seat can protect the occupant to jointly support the back and neck, reducing the "S" curve between the head and the back and hence the risk of injury. If the car seat is poorly designed, it just supports the back leaving the head and neck unrestrained (Euro NCAP, 2014).

Euro NCAP's whiplash tests are designed to test excessive head movement, i.e. to approve those designs that provide the most effective protection. The dynamic sled tests indicate how effectively the seat and head restraint operate to provide whiplash protection in typical crash scenarios.

The Euro NCAP integrated neck protection tests on the rear-end collision testing program in 2009. This procedure aims to promote improvements in seat design, headrest and ease of adjustment (Euro NCAP, 2014).

The AEB City systems intervene by applying the brakes to try to avoid a collision at low speed. It simulates a rear-end collision in which the driver of the striking car is distracted and does not notice that the car ahead has stopped (Euro NCAP, 2016). Such accidents can cause neck injuries to the occupants of both cars. This AEB function allows the driver to brake detecting when there is an eminent danger or when an accident is likely to occur. In this case the systems intervene by applying the brakes in order to avoid a collision. The AEB test was introduced in 2014.

When the collision is avoided maximum points are awarded during tests. However, some points are granted if the speed of collision has been reduced, as even small speed reductions can mitigate the likelihood of collision.

Child Occupant Protection

The assessment of Child Occupant Protection (COP) covers three aspects: the protection offered by the Child Restraint Systems (CRSs) in the frontal and side impact tests, the accommodation of child restraints of various sizes and designs, and the availability of CRSs installation checks for safe transport of children in the car. The results of these tests are a contribution to reduce the misuse of child restrain installation conditions and to improve the safety of children (Euro NCAP, 2016).

Euro NCAP CRS performance test checks how well different child restraints fit and verifies the protection offered by the recommended child restraints in the event of a front or side crash.

To assess this COP parameter, some of the most used chairs that have shown to provide good protection in independent tests are installed. The Euro NCAP also evaluates how children's chairs are accommodated in the vehicle, its stability, the seat length, seat belt length and the belt buckle location. It is also checked whether the child seat can be installed properly in all appropriate places of the vehicle and if it is possible to place the child seat facing backwards. The vehicle handbook should clearly mention the seating positions where a CRS cannot be installed.

In another part of the assessment, child dummies are placed in the car seat, properly installed according to the safety recommendations. The vehicle is subject to bumps and head movement, neck loads and chest accelerations are the main child dummy criteria in the allocation of classification. The lower the head movement, neck loads and chest accelerations, the larger the score of the vehicle. They are also awarded points if the dummy is maintained inside the vehicle during the accident. The score also takes into account whether the child chairs are adequate to the various child ages and weights.

The Euro NCAP rewards extra points if the vehicle supplies other resources that provide important features that facilitate safe transport of children, as front seat airbag-disabling switch with clear user instructions, integrated child seats, among others.

Pedestrian Protection

According to Euro NCAP (2014), the deaths of pedestrians account for 14% of deaths recorded in road accidents in Europe. As such it is essential to encourage the improvement of security systems to halt the numerous human losses and the emotional and psychological trauma that drivers that injured pedestrians endure. The inclusion of the score obtained in the pedestrian safety tests aims to contribute to improving performance in this area.

In the pedestrian protection tests, the potential risk at injuries to pedestrian head, pelvis, upper and lower leg are assessed. The score is determined from tests to the most important vehicle front-end structures such as the bonnet and windshield, the bonnet leading edge, and the bumper.

In order to score the vehicles, accidents involving adults and children pedestrians are simulated. As it is difficult to simulate the accident with a complete dummy – it is difficult to predict the point of impact on the head – the Euro NCAP carries out the tests separately, i.e. one test simulates and evaluates the impact of the lower leg with the bumper, another evaluates the impact of hip with the hood, and another test evaluates the impact of the head with the hood. The score in this pedestrian protection tests results from the performance of the vehicle in the various tests. From tests performed one can conclude that the impact is not as severe when it reaches the leg away from the knee and when the impact force is spread over an area of the leg. Unnecessary rigid structures in front of the automobile should be avoided.

The AEB pedestrian test, introduced in 2016, is meant to reduce the risk of pedestrian accidents in real world driving as AEB pedestrian technology is able to bring the car to a safe halt before a pedestrian is struck or which can at least reduce the speed of the collision.

One major factor that influences pedestrian injury outcome during a collision is the vehicle speed at the point of impact. An increasing number of vehicle manufacturers are offering systems which are able to bring the car to a safe halt before a pedestrian is struck or which can at least reduce the speed of the collision. For this reason, Euro NCAP only rewards the technology if the pedestrian impact tests show that the car has a forgiving front design (Euro NCAP, 2016).

Safety Assist Score

The safety assist score is determined from tests to the most important driver assist technologies that support safe driving to avoid accidents and mitigate injuries. The safety assist score is meant to prize the functionality and the performance of the safety system during normal driving and in typical accident scenarios.

The Electronic Stability Control (ESC) system varies among European Union countries and among brands. In its development car manufacturers perform various tests in order to verify its response under different circumstances: different speeds, different road conditions, different maneuvers and different responses of the driver. Studies of real accidents have shown that vehicles with electronic stability control system are involved in fewer and less severe accidents than vehicles that do not have this system available. However, it was not possible to differentiate the security offered among the different types of electronic stability control systems.

To evaluate this system, the Euro NCAP tests are carried out at speeds of 80 km/h with sudden steering wheel rotations up to 270 degrees. The sideway displacement, the stability and the vehicle's ability to follow a straight path are evaluated. The ESC was introduced in Euro NCAP's tests in 2009. In 2014, the fitment of ESC systems has become mandatory for all new vehicles and therefore Euro NCAP has stopped testing the system (Euro NCAP, 2016).

The seat belt is a key component in any vehicle and the statistics confirm that the majority of accidents where the vehicle occupants were driving without wearing their seatbelts end in serious and fatal injuries. Studies also show that occupants are more likely to travel without a seat belt when the car is not equipped with a seatbelt warning signal (Euro NCAP, 2014).

The Euro NCAP evaluates the intensity and duration of the beep, the position and clarity of visual warning, in how many places is the Seatbelt Reminder (SBR), and if the belt responds properly and attempts to recreate all possible scenarios that occupants can be subjected when not wearing their seatbelts. The position and clarity of any visual warning is checked to ensure that it is visible to occupants of different sizes, rewarding manufacturers who fit intelligent SBR systems on all seating positions (Euro NCAP, 2016).

As is well known, speeding, voluntary or involuntary, is a factor that has strongly contributed to car accidents. Driving within the expected speed limits, not only can prevent accidents, but also contributes to ensuring the safety of motorists and other road users. In this sense, the Euro NCAP evaluates and encourages the installation Speed Assistance Systems (SAS) that support drivers to control their speed. The main function of SASs are: (1) to inform the driver of the current speed; (2) to warn the driver when the speed limit is exceeded; (3) to prevent the car from exceeding a threshold limit (Euro NCAP tests if the threshold limit set is not exceeded) (Euro NCAP, 2014). The functionality of the system is considered to make sure that the system can be used without undue distraction to the driver.

According to Euro NCAP (2016), car-to-car rear impacts are one of the most frequent accidents. The AEB Interurban systems tests, introduced in 2014, are meant to support drivers in avoiding a rear-end crash by warning and supporting adequate braking or ultimately stopping the vehicle by itself. High scores are awarded to AEB systems that are able to avoid a collision in all test conditions, or to significantly reduce the severity of the crash.

Lane Support Systems (LSS) can assist and warn drivers when they unintentionally leave the road lane or when they change lane without indication. The LSS are important to avoid any unintentional lane departure, which can lead the vehicle to run off from the road, or to impact an obstacle or collide with another vehicle (Euro NCAP, 2016). This test was introduced in 2014.

Literature Support

There are several studies comparing the results of tests conducted by Euro NCAP with the real accident consequences. For example, taking into account the police data, Lie et al. (2001) conducted a comparative study of the results of the Euro NCAP tests with data from accidents and injuries in the real world and concluded that there is, overall, a relationship between the Euro NCAP classification in stars and police data.

Similar conclusions were drawn by Fails and Minton (2001), where a comparative analysis showed a good correlation between the results of the Euro NCAP and the actual data. The protection of collision identified during the tests is often visible in real life and the damage caused is realistic when compared to accidents.

In another comparative study by Lie and Tingvall (2002), in which children and pedestrian scores were not considered, it was concluded that the vehicles classified with three or four stars were approximately 30% more secure compared with two-star or unrated vehicles.

Taking into account police and insurance injury data, Kullgren et al. (2010) concluded that the Euro NCAP five-star vehicles occupants have a lower risk of injury compared to two-star vehicle occupants. This difference in risk is about $10 \pm 2.5\%$. For serious and fatal injury the difference was $23 \pm 8\%$ and for fatal injuries alone the difference was $68 \pm 32\%$, i.e. the most significant one.

In short, the literature shows a good relationship between the results published by Euro NCAP and what actually happens in real life. In addition, there is also a good agreement between the state of the vehicles after the simulated crash tests by Euro NCAP and the damage observed in real accidents.

RESEARCH MEHODOLOGY AND MAIN RESULTS

The statistical analysis performed in this work is based on some well-known descriptive statistics techniques and hypothesis testing theory, namely normality tests (Kolmogorov-Smirnov and Shapiro-Wilk) and nonparametric tests (Mann-Whitney U and Kruskal-Wallis). For an overview on these methodologies see Wilcox (2003) and Mittelhammer (2013).

Data for analyzing the number of stars, adult occupant protection score, child occupant protection scores, pedestrian scores, and safety assist score were withdrawn from Euro NCAP website, for the 2010-2015 period. After an initial presentation of descriptive statistics regarding the main car brands and the main car classes, the rating of number of stars is analyzed taking into account its evolution per year and per vehicle class. The adult protection score is also analyzed per year and per class. The child protection score is analyzed taking into account its evolution over the six-year period. The pedestrian protection score is analyzed per class for every year. Finally, the safety assist score is analyzed over the six-year period.

In what pertains to the three research questions raised, we used inferential statistics to draw our conclusions.

Main Car Brand and Car Classes Analyzed

Forty-one different car brands were tested during the six-year term of this study, as well as several different classes, namely Supermini, Small Family Car, Large Family Car, Executive, Small MPV, Large MPV, Small off-road 4x4, Large off-road 4x4, Pick-up, Roadster Sport, and Business and Family Vans. The frequency table describing the vehicle brands tested throughout the six-year study period is presented in Table 1.

According to Table 1, Ford was the brand with more models tested by Euro NCAP – to be more precise, 14 vehicles – which corresponds do 5.9% of the automobiles tested during the analysis period. The brands with the least reviewed models are Alfa Romeo, Landwind, Geely Emgrand, Qorus, Maserati, Porsche and Tesla, with a single tested model.

During this six-year period Euro NCAP reviewed 236 automobile models, belonging to 11 classes. It is possible to check from the frequency table (Table 2), that the Small Family Car was the class which had more tested models, followed by the Supermini class. Among the vehicles with fewer reviews are the Roadster Sport class, with three tested models, and the Pick-up class, with five tested models, which corresponds to a percentage of 1.3% and 2.1%, respectively.

Table 1. Main car brands

	Frequency	Percent	Cumulative Percent
Audi	8	3.4	3.4
Citroen	13	5.5	8.9
Nissan	11	4.7	13.6
Suzuki	4	1.7	15.3
Alfa Romeo	1	0.4	15.7
Honda	5	2.1	17.8
Seat	5	2.1	19.9
VW	13	5.5	25.4
BMW	9	3.8	29.2
Jaguar	4	1.7	30.9
Mercedes Benz	13	5.5	36.4
Ford	14	5.9	42.4
Kia	12	5.1	47.5
Landwind	1	0.4	47.9
Mini	3	1.3	49.2
Opel	10	4.2	53.4
Toyota	9	3.8	57.2
Hyundai	10	4.2	61.4
Mazda	7	3.0	64.4
Chevrolet	6	2.5	66.9
Fiat	6	2.5	69.5
Mitsubishi	6	2.5	72.0
Lexus	4	1.7	73.7
MG	2	0.8	74.6
Renault	12	5.1	79.7
Subaru	3	1.3	80.9
Geely Emgrand	1	0.4	81.4
Peugeot	11	4.7	86.0
Volvo	4	1.7	87.7
Lancia	3	1.3	89.0
Dacia	4	1.7	90.7
Land Rover	3	1.3	91.9
Jeep	4	1.7	93.6
Skoda	5	2.1	95.8
Isuzu	2	0.8	96.6
Qorus	1	0.4	97.0
Infiniti	2	0.8	97.9
Maserati	1	0.4	98.3
Smart	2	0.8	99.2
Tesla	1	0.4	99.6
Porsche	1	0.4	100.0
Total	**236**	**100.0**	

Table 2. Main car classes

	Frequency	Percent	Cumulative Percent
Supermini	50	21.2	21.2
Small Family Car	54	22.9	44.1
Large Family Car	22	9.3	53.4
Executive	10	4.2	57.6
Small MPV	31	13.1	70.8
Large MPV	8	3.4	74.2
Small off - road 4x4	32	13.6	87.7
Large off-road 4x4	8	3.4	91.1
Pick-up	5	2.1	93.2
Business and Family Vans	13	5.5	98.7
Roadster Sport	3	1.3	100.0
Total	**236**	**100.0**	

Distribution of the Classification According to the Number of Stars

The star rating is a discrete quantitative variable, which awards each tested automobile a rating using a scale from 1 to 5. The statistical information about the star ratings regarding each of the tested automobiles is presented in Table 3 and in Figure 1.

From all the information gathered, one can witness that the most frequent rating during the six year period of this analysis was the five star rating, and that the average rating was approximately 4.5 stars. Due to the fact that the levels of requirement and rigor were changed, the collected data is not directly comparable from year to year. However, it is important to mention that despite the fact that the rating in 2015 having been the most demanding of all the six years analyzed, only one vehicle, the Lancia Ypsilon 1.2 Gold, obtained the minimum rating of two stars out of the 44 evaluated vehicles; 28 (63.6%) obtained the maximum five star rating, with special focus on the Volvo XC90 D5 Momentum, which achieved a score of 100% in what concerns safety equipment and 97% in adult occupant score.

Table 3. Rating of number of stars

Year	N	Minimum	Maximum	Mean	Std. Deviation
2010	27	2	5	4.52	0.753
2011	46	4	5	4.74	0.444
2012	44	2	5	4.48	0.952
2013	33	3	5	4.64	0.603
2014	42	3	5	4.24	0.790
2015	44	2	5	4.50	0.762

Figure 1. Star rating, per car class
Source: Own preparation.

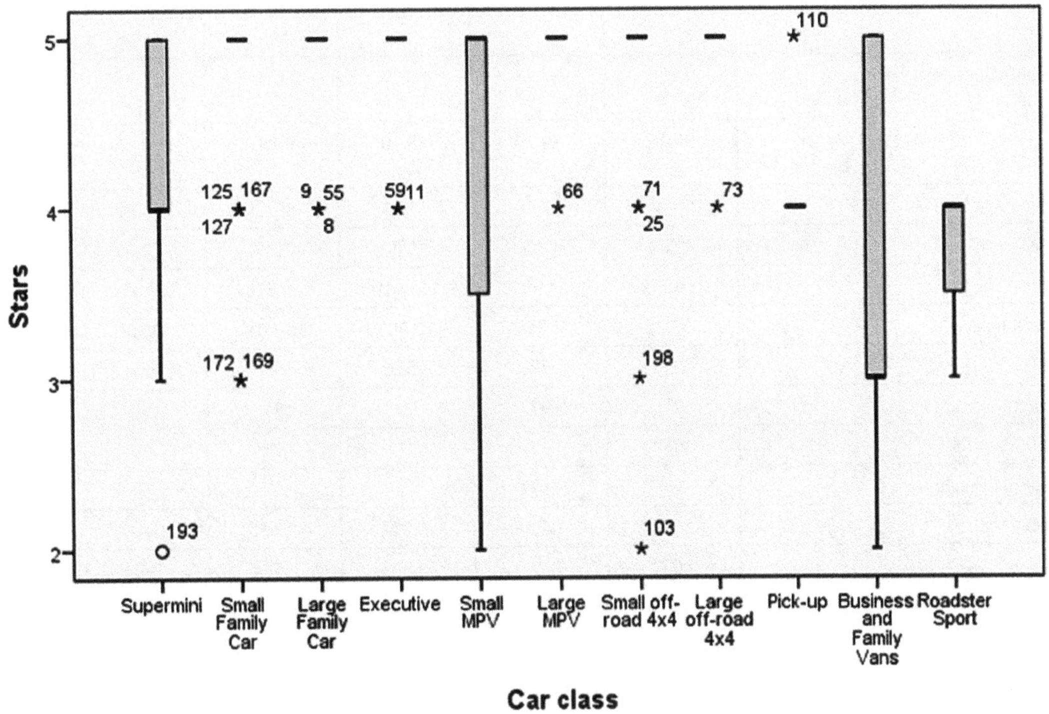

Adult Occupant Protection Scores per Year and per Class

The score referring to adult safety (%) is a continuous quantitative variable. Between 2010 and 2013 its calculation accounted for the scores obtained from frontal, rear and side impact poles. In 2014 the AEB city score was introduced, and in 2015 the ratings for the frontal impact pole was split in frontal offset deformable barrier and frontal full width rigid barrier. Table 4 presents the comparative study on the achieved ratings for these parameters throughout the six-year period and for all the considered classes. They include results for some of the central location measures (mean, median and 5% trimmed mean), relative location (minimum and maximum), dispersion (range, inter-quartile range, standard deviation and variance), asymmetry and kurtosis. All these measures allow for a description of the scores relating to adult safety, through numerical characteristics that summarize the available information. For instance, there is the presence of a negative skewness in all the studied years, which means a concentration of frequencies for higher sample values. This analysis is supported by the skewness value, since it holds a negative value in every year.

Figure 2 presents the comparative boxplots from the scores obtained in regards to adult occupant protection within the six-year study. They provide indications in what concerns central location, quartiles, extremes, dispersion, symmetry and the existence of outliers. The use of the same scale for all the boxplots allows for a global idea of the differences between all six years of study.

Through the observation of the boxplots one observes that the medians in the first four years are almost identical, whereas the medians of the last two years are lower, particularly in 2014. It was in 2010 that a wider range of the data was registered. This is the result of the presence of an outlier – Landwind

Table 4. Adult occupation protection score (%), per year

		2010	2011	2012	2013	2014	2015
Mean		85.11	86.91	84.75	88.58	80.31	89.93
95% Confidence Interval for Mean	Lower Bound	79.96	84.73	80.80	86.34	77.36	80.57
	Upper Bound	90.26	89.10	88.70	90.81	83.26	87.30
5% Trimmed Mean		86.94	87.18	85.68	89.23	80.87	85.25
Median		89.00	89.00	91.00	91.00	82.00	86.50
Variance		169.718	53.992	168.610	39.814	89.536	122.577
Std. Deviation		13.028	7.348	12.985	6.310	9.462	11.071
Minimum		34	72	55	68	56	44
Maximum		97	97	96	95	96	97
Range		63	25	41	27	40	53
Interquartile Range		10	10	17	7	8	6
Skewness		-2.734	-0.738	-1.212	-1.658	-1.184	-2.277
Kurtosis		9.032	-0.490	-0.043	2.784	1.419	5.334

Figure 2. Adult occupant protection score (%), per year
Source: Own preparation.

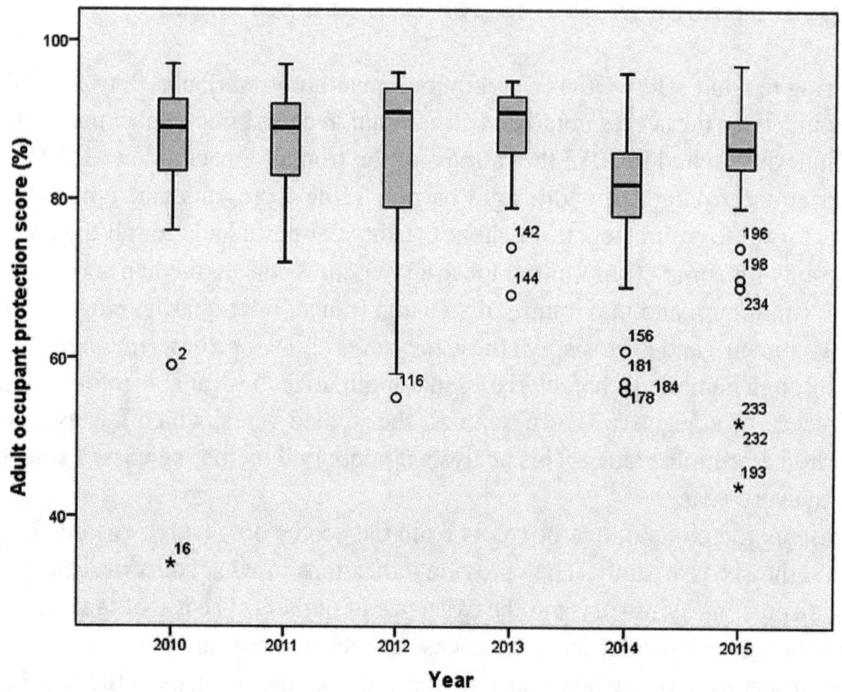

CV9 – the first Chinese brand to be commercialized in Europe. This is a severe outlier as its score (34) is below the second inferior barrier for outliers

$$1^{st}Q - 3\times(3^{rd}Q - 1^{st}Q) = 83 - 3\times(93 - 83) = 53)$$

2011 is the year that presents the narrowest range and lowest negative skewness (Table 4).

Another relevant analysis is the comparison of the adult safety scores from all analyzed vehicles classes. Table 5 summarizes some statistical measures of interest.

Analyzing Table 5, one can conclude that the highest mean regarding adult safety belongs to the Large off-road 4x4 class, whereas the Business and Family Vans class presents the lowest mean value. It is also shown that Small MPV, Small Family Car and Large off-road 4x4 classes obtain the highest scores. It is interesting to note that the lowest score belongs to a Small MPV class (Landwind CV9), thus making it the class with the widest range in the collected data.

Figure 3 illustrates a comparative analysis of the adult occupant protection scores for the various classes under study. It should be noted that it is positive that the values are concentrated near the highest scores, despite some exceptions.

Child Occupant Protection Scores

The child occupant protection score is also a continuous quantitative variable. The weighting for this classification includes the evaluation of the supplied instructions, the ease and safety of the installation of child car seats of various sizes and designs, and the evaluation based on the vehicle (seatbelt length, seat depth, among others).

In the six years of study, one can witness a strong concentration in the upper values (Table 6), which accounts for the existence of negative skewness of the frequency distribution. This is, undoubtedly, good news in what pertains to child occupant protection, although it would be desirable that the score could have been larger.

Table 5. Adult occupant protection score (%), per class

Class	N	Minimum	Maximum	Mean	Std. Deviation
Supermini	50	44	95	81.58	10.014
Small Family Car	54	71	97	88.50	6.598
Large Family Car	22	75	95	89.05	5.232
Executive	10	78	95	86.70	6.290
Small MPV	31	34	97	81.32	14.531
Large MPV	8	79	96	87.63	6.323
Small off-road 4x4	32	61	96	87.56	7.641
Large off-road 4x4	8	81	97	92.00	5.182
Pick-up	5	79	96	85.00	6.671
Business and Family Vans	13	52	93	70.08	19.950
Roadster Sport	3	69	84	78.00	7.937

Figure 3. Adult occupant protection score (%), per class
Source: Own preparation.

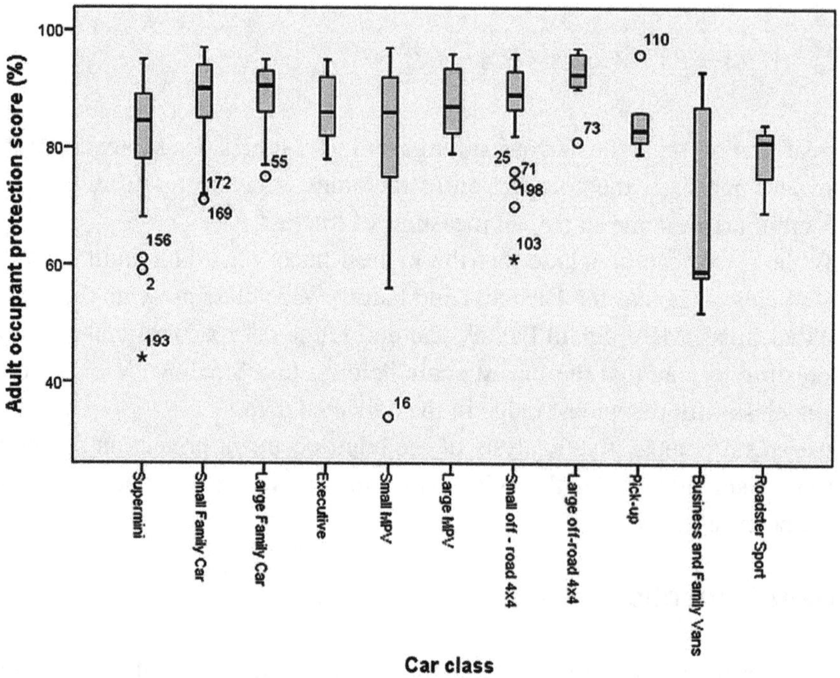

Table 6. Child occupant protection score (%), per year

Year	N	Minimum	Maximum	Mean	Median	Skewness	Std. Error Skewness
2010	27	45	88	77.00	79.00	-1.866	0.448
2011	46	63	90	80.54	81.00	-0.983	0.350
2012	44	67	92	82.84	83.50	-0.613	0.357
2013	33	69	88	80.06	80.00	-0.386	0.409
2014	42	71	88	80.40	80.50	-0.192	0.365
2015	44	61	91	82.93	85.00	-1.323	0.357

Pedestrian Protection Scores

The score relating to pedestrian protection is a continuous quantitative variable. Scores regarding the protection of the head, pelvis and legs are taken into consideration for its calculation. This is a variable that is only directly comparable in 2010 and 2011.

Some statistics regarding this variable are gathered in Table 7, and Figure 4 shows the boxplots for each class and year.

The scores of Business and Family Vans class stand out negatively from the observation of Figure 4. The highest mean value (approximately 89%) belongs to Roadster Sport in 2015, followed by Executive (80%) in the same year, and Large MPV (80%) in 2013. In 2010, 2011, 2012 and 2014, the mean scores are inferior to 70% in any of the classes.

Table 7. Pedestrian protection score (%), per year and per class

Car Class	N	Range	Minimum	Maximum	Mean
Year: 2010					
Supermini	4	13	49	62	56.00
Small Family Car	3	28	43	71	59.00
Large Family Car	2	4	50	54	52.00
Executive	3	35	43	78	60.00
Small MPV	8	38	31	69	54.75
Large MPV	1	0	46	46	46.00
Small off-road 4x4	5	21	43	64	51.40
Pick-up	1	0	47	47	47.00
Year: 2011					
Supermini	12	19	41	60	48.25
Small Family Car	13	23	37	60	49.00
Large Family Car	5	17	40	57	44.60
Executive	3	21	41	62	54.00
Small MPV	4	15	49	64	55.50
Large MPV	3	4	46	50	47.67
Small off-road 4x4	5	25	28	53	44.40
Large off-road 4x4	1	0	45	45	45.00
Year: 2012					
Supermini	6	13	53	66	58.50
Small Family Car	15	31	57	88	68.00
Large Family Car	3	14	64	78	69.00
Small MPV	3	23	44	67	58.67
Small off-road 4x4	6	50	23	73	59.67
Large off-road 4x4	3	11	60	71	64.67
Pick-up	2	30	51	81	66.00
Business and Family Vans	6	22	26	48	31.33
Year: 2013					
Supermini	7	15	57	72	64.29
Small Family Car	10	28	57	85	68.60
Large Family Car	2	0	66	66	66.00
Executive	2	7	67	74	70.50
Small MPV	6	12	56	68	62.17
Large MPV	1	0	80	80	80.00
Small off-road 4x4	4	4	64	68	66.25
Business and Family Vans	1	0	32	32	32.00

continued on next page

Table 7. Continued

Car Class	N	Range	Minimum	Maximum	Mean
Year: 2014					
Supermini	13	18	56	74	65.62
Small Family Car	9	35	54	89	64.22
Large Family Car	4	11	66	77	69.75
Executive	1	0	66	66	66.00
Small MPV	7	8	55	63	60.14
Small off-road 4x4	6	15	60	75	67.50
Business and Family Vans	1	0	67	67	67.00
Year: 2015					
Supermini	8	20	64	84	74.50
Small Family Car	4	20	71	91	79.25
Large Family Car	6	14	67	81	73.33
Executive	1	0	80	80	80.00
Small MPV	3	16	58	74	67.67
Large MPV	3	9	70	79	76.00
Small off-road 4x4	6	32	50	82	69.50
Large off-road 4x4	3	9	70	79	73.67
Pick-up	2	2	76	78	77.00
Business and Family Vans	5	11	53	64	59.60
Roadster Sport	3	11	82	93	88.67

Safety Assist Score

Just like the adult, children, and pedestrians protection scores, the safety assist score is also a continuous quantitative variable. Its measure is expressed in percentage values. Driver and passenger seatbelt reminders, electronic stability control, speed assistance (taken into consideration since 2013), AEB interurban and lane support (introduced in 2014) are included in weighting this score. In 2013, the speed assistance score became differentiated depending on the type of assistance (standard, speed limit information system, and speed assistance system).

Figure 5 presents the comparative boxplots of all the six years of study. Table 8 presents some descriptive statistics.

The analysis of this information must be carefully done, as it is only possible to establish a direct comparison between the data from 2010 and 2012, and 2014 and 2015. Although the obtained scores present a decreasing tendency, this may be due to the fact that the exigency level of this parameter has been increasing.

Figure 4. Pedestrian occupant protection score (%), per class, per year
Source: Own preparation.

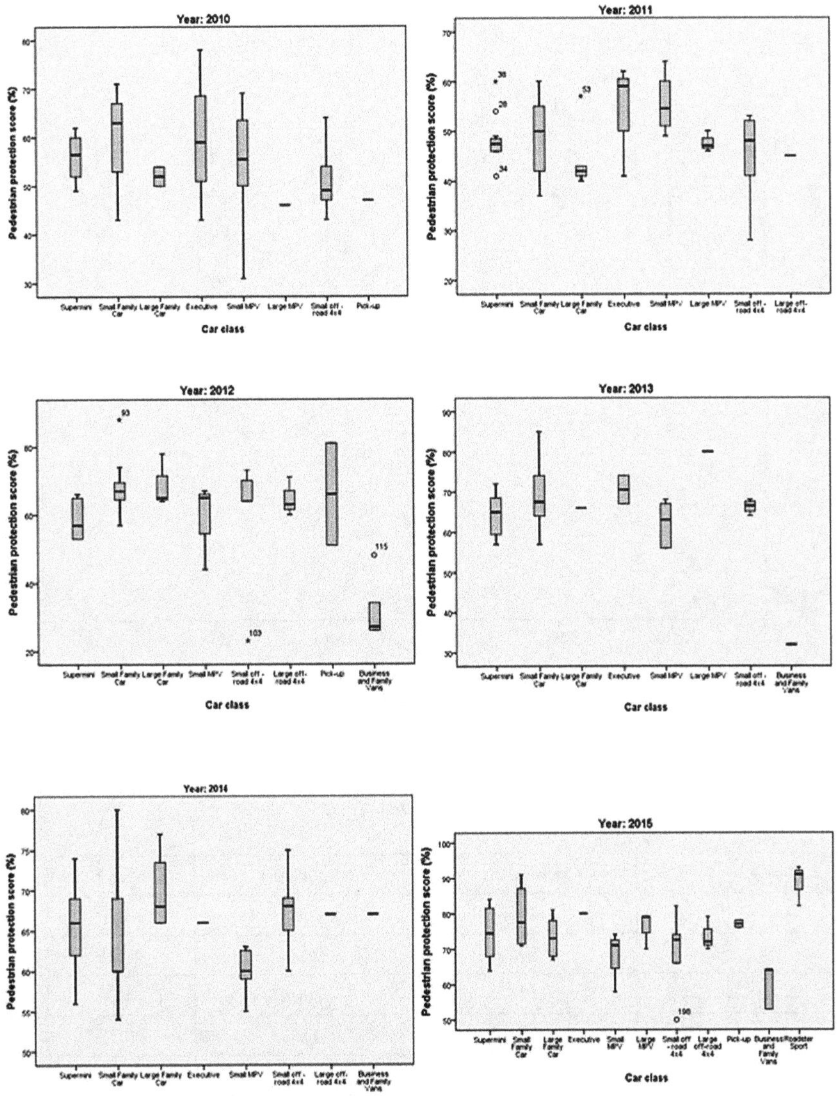

Inferential Analysis

Are electric and hybrid automobiles less safe than their traditional counterparts in what concerns frontal collision?

Considering that electric and hybrid automobiles are relatively recent in the market, it is relevant to verify if there are differences in terms of safety, comparing them to classic fuel automobiles. Since some changes were introduced in the last few years, which make the comparison more difficult, the following analysis merely contemplates the period between 2010 and 2013. To that end, and with the purpose of choosing the appropriate statistical method, this analysis is initiated by conducting normality tests, according to Table 9.

Figure 5. Safety assist score (%), per year
Source: Own preparation.

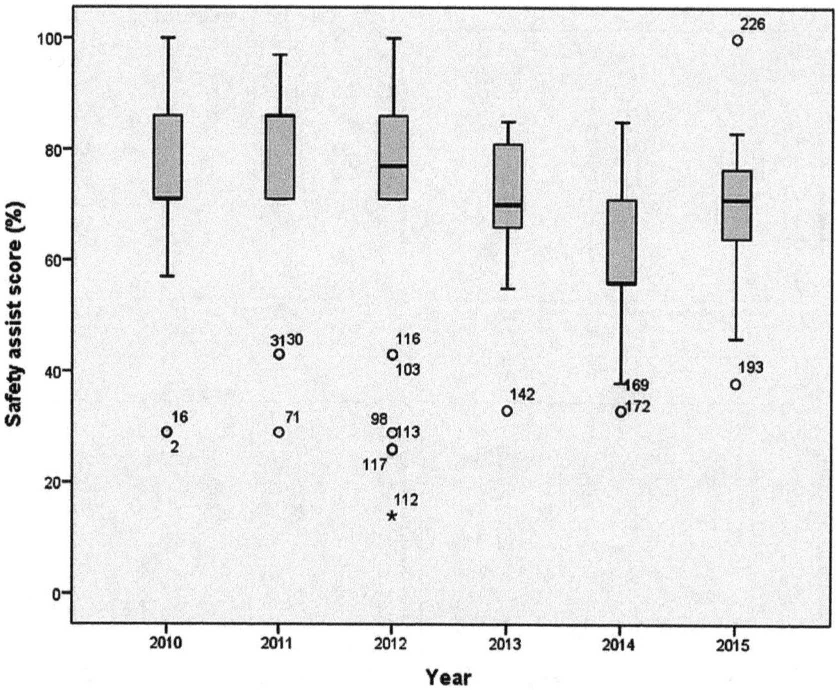

Table 8. Score statistics on safety assist equipment, per year

Year	N	Minimum	Maximum	Mean	Std. Deviation
2010	27	29	100	73.30	16.938
2011	46	29	97	77.85	13.627
2012	44	14	100	74.00	22.271
2013	33	33	85	70.73	12.089
2014	42	33	85	60.07	13.506
2015	44	38	100	70.30	10.663

Table 9. Normality tests for frontal impact score

Fuel	Kolmogorov-Smirnov[a]			Shapiro-Wilk		
	Statistic	df	Sig.	Statistic	df	Sig.
Classic	0.175	137	0.000	0.849	137	0.000
Electric and hybrid	0.210	13	0.122	0.868	13	0.049

a. Lilliefors Significance Correction.

From the p-value obtained from Table 9 regarding the Kolmogorov-Smirnov test (appropriate for large samples), there is a clear rejection of the null hypothesis of normality for the scores of frontal impact in classic fuel automobiles and for any level of usual significance, since the p-value is approximately zero. As the electric and hybrid automobiles sample is very small (13 vehicles), the recommended test is Shapiro-Wilk's, which also leads to the rejection of the null hypothesis of normality for levels of significance greater than or equal to 4.9%, in which the usual 5% and 10% are included. The potential absence of normality is also identified by the comparison of the sample quartiles and the normal distribution quartiles (Normal Q-Q plots of frontal impact score, which are not shown). Therefore, since normality is not validated for both types of fuel, the comparison of central tendency between the scores obtained from frontal impacts on classic fuel automobiles and on electric and hybrid automobiles should be conducted in a non-parametric context, being Mann-Whitney's U test the most appropriate for this case.

In a non-parametric context, the median becomes the location parameter in evaluation, which means that, while the t-Student test compares the population means based on two random independent samples, the Mann-Whitney U test compares the medians (location centers) of both populations.

The initial question is reflected in the following hypothesis test:

$$H_0 : \mu_{classic} = \mu_{electric+hybrid} \ vs. \ H_1 : \mu_{classic} \neq \mu_{electric+hybrid}$$

where μ represents the population median of the frontal impact score.

Through the analysis of Tables 10 and 11, the null hypothesis of equal population medians for the usual 1% level of significance is not rejected, since the obtained asymptotic p-value (0.019) is greater than 0.010. On the other hand, in what concerns the usual levels of significance of 5% and 10%, there is a clear rejection of the null hypothesis of equal population medians, since the asymptotic p-value is inferior to 0.05 and 0.10. The obtained conclusion is different for different levels of significance, which is not unusual (briefly summarizing, the null hypothesis is rejected for levels of significance that are greater than or equal to 1.9%).

From Table 10, it appears that there is a trend towards higher scores regarding frontal impact in classic fuel automobiles, since the mean rank is higher for that type of vehicle. It should be noted that since the electric and hybrid vehicle sample is fairly small, it is not advisable to compare the sum of the ranks. Figure 6 presents the comparative boxplot for the results regarding the frontal impact (in %) in classic fuel and in electric and hybrid automobiles.

Table 10. Mann-Whitney U test for frontal impact score (mean rank and sum of ranks)

Fuel	N	Mean Rank	Sum of Ranks
Classic	137	78.07	10695.00
Electric and hybrid	13	48.46	630.00
Total	150		

Table 11. Mann-Whitney U test for frontal impact score

	Frontal Impact Score
Mann-Whitney U	539.000
Wilcoxon W	630.000
Z	-2.350
Asymp. Sig. (2-tailed)	0.019

Figure 6. Frontal impact score for different types of fuel
Source: Own preparation.

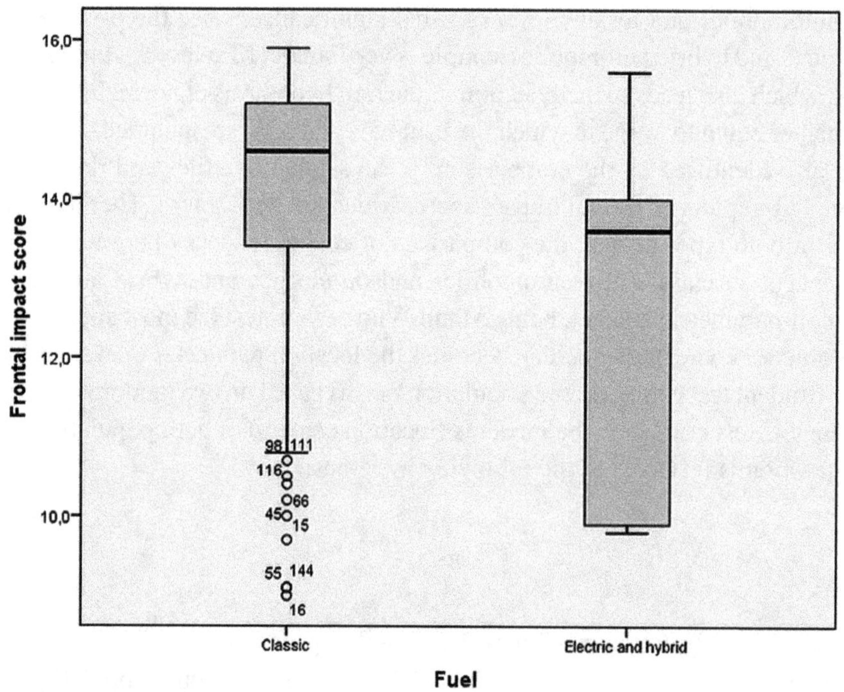

As Table 10, Figure 6 illustrates the unfavorable scores for electric and hybrid automobiles when compared with the classic fuel cars. For this reason, it would be convenient to test

$$H_0 : \mu_{classic} - \mu_{electric+hybrid} = 0 \ vs. \ H_1 : \mu_{classic} - \mu_{electric+hybrid} > 0$$

Since the samples point towards the alternative hypothesis, the p-value is half of the value obtained in the bilateral test, which, being inferior to the usual levels of significance, leads to the rejection of the null hypothesis, and allows to conclude that there is statistical evidence that the median score concerning frontal impact is higher in the population of classic fuel automobiles.

It should be noted that 137 classic fuel automobiles and only 13 electric and hybrid automobiles were tested, therefore the present conclusions should be taken into consideration with due caution.

After the first question, another relevant question arises: are there statistically significant differences concerning the adult occupants' safety during the six years of study?

Although there have been some updates on this parameter (see the Euro NCAP website for additional details), it is pertinent and relevant to establish a comparison betwen the scores gathered from the models evaluated during the six-year period. This question originates the following hypothesis test:

$$H_0 : \mu_{2010} = \mu_{2011} = \mu_{2012} = \mu_{2013} = \mu_{2014} = \mu_{2015} = \mu \ vs. \ H_1 : \mu_i \neq \mu,$$

at least for one value of $i\left(i = 2010, 2011, \ldots, 2015\right)$, where μ represents a location parameter for the adult occupants safety scores.

Once more, the process begins by testing the normality of the population from where these samples have been extracted, which allows for the selection of the methodology to employ.

Considering that the size of the sample from 2010 is small (less than 30 observations), one needs to interpret the p-value retrieved from the Shapiro-Wilk test, which leads to the rejection of the null hypothesis for normality for any of the usual levels of significance (Table 12). As for the remaining years, the Kolmogorov-Smirnov's test was deemed as the most appropriate, which also leads to the rejection of the null hypothesis for normality. These assumptions are supported by the histograms with their respective normal distribution curves, and Q-Q Plots, which are not shown here due to space limitations.

As the conditions for the application of parametric tests are not fulfilled since the data strongly contradicts the normality hypothesis, it is necessary to fall back to non-parametric tests as an alternative. The test chosen for this analysis is the Kruskal-Wallis' as there are six years to be compared (six independent samples). Presented in Tables 13 and 14 is the application of Kruskal-Wallis' test, which was used to test if there are statistically significant differences in the population medians for the adult occupant safety score (in the six years of study).

Table 12. Normality tests for adult occupant protection score

Year	Kolmogorov-Smirnov[a]			Shapiro-Wilk		
	Statistic	Df	Sig.	Statistic	df	Sig.
2010	0.213	27	0.003	0.707	27	0.000
2011	0.155	46	0.007	0.905	46	0.001
2012	0.258	44	0.000	0.764	44	0.000
2013	0.190	33	0.004	0.824	33	0.000
2014	0.189	42	0.001	0.887	42	0.001
2015	0.275	44	0.000	0.727	44	0.000

a. Lilliefors Significance Correction.

Table 13. Kruskal-Wallis test for adult occupant protection score (mean rank)

Years	N	Mean Rank
2010	27	127.28
2011	46	128.61
2012	44	135.02
2013	33	143.33
2014	42	75.11
2015	44	108.82
Total	236	

Table 14. Kruskal-Wallis test for adult occupant protection score

	Adult Occupant Protection Score (%)
Chi-Square	26.320
df	5
Asymp. Sig.	0.000

Based on the analysis of Kruskal-Wallis test one can conclude that the population medians of the adult occupant protection scores, for the car models launched between 2010 and 2015, are considered significantly different, since the asymptotic p-value from the test presented in Table 13 is approximately zero. The reason for this difference may reside in the change of the evaluation criteria of Euro NCAP in the last two years, and not necessarily in real differences in adult safety. For example, it is interesting to note that performing the same test on car models launched in Europe between 2010 and 2013, the score medians retrieved from adult safety are not considered significantly different in those four years, since the asymptotic p-value from the test becomes much greater than the usual levels of significance.

The final research question is: are there statistically significant differences between the most sold automobile classes in what concerns frontal impact protection?

Frontal collision is a frequent scenario in accidents, and it often carries serious consequences. Comparing the scores retrieved from frontal impact protection among different automobile classes is certainly of interest to many drivers. Once there were modifications introduced in the last few years, which make establishing a comparison more difficult, the following analysis only includes the period between 2010 and 2013. However, in these four years of study, there are classes with few tested models, such as the Pick-up class, with only three models tested. Therefore, the option was to develop this study considering the classes in which 20 or more models were tested. For this purpose, the following hypotheses were considered:

$$H_0 : \mu_1 = \mu_2 = \mu_3 = \mu_4 = \mu \ vs. \ H_1 : \mu_i \neq \mu,$$

for at least one value of $i\left(i = 1, 2, 3, and\ 4\right)$, in which μ represents a location parameter for the score relative to frontal impact, and i identifies the class to be considered, being that 1 is for Supermini, 2 is for Small Family Car, 3 is for Small MPV and 4 is for Small off-road 4×4.

To define the proper methodology to perform the previous hypothesis test, it is required to evaluate the normality of the studied populations by using the usual normality tests (Kolmogorov-Smirnov, with Lilliefors significance correction, and Shapiro-Wilk) and, for example, by inspecting the boxplots, as shown in Table 15 and Figure 7.

The inexistence of symmetry in the comparative boxplots in Figure 7 suggests the absence of normality in the respective studied populations; however, this conjecture requires a more rigorous statistical analysis through the use of normality tests. Based on the information from Table 15 and the usual levels

Table 15. Normality tests for frontal impact score

Car Class		Kolmogorov-Smirnov[a]			Shapiro-Wilk		
		Statistic	df	Sig.	Statistic	df	Sig.
Frontal impact score	Supermini	0.202	29	0.004	0.869	29	0.002
	Small Family Car	0.245	41	0.000	0.709	41	0.000
	Small MPV	0.175	21	0.091	0.880	21	0.015
	Small off-road 4x4	0.173	20	0.118	0.860	20	0.008

a. Lilliefors Significance Correction

Figure 7. Frontal impact score by class
Source: Own preparation.

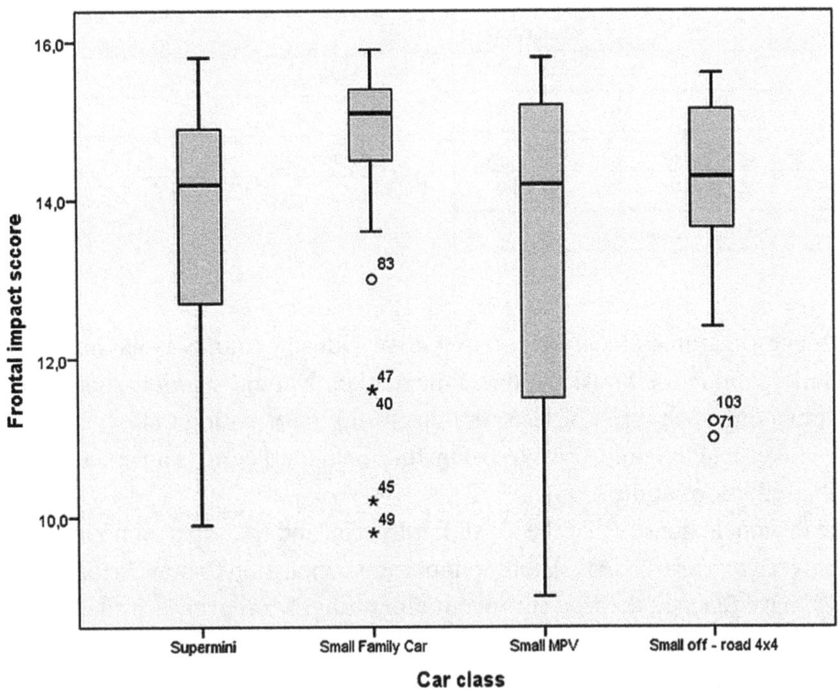

of significance, it is seen that the tests lead to the rejection of the null hypothesis of normality in each of the studied populations (except Small MPV class for $\alpha = 1\%$), which supports the initial suspicion.

Since the normality hypothesis is unsupported by the previous analysis, a test is made to compare the central locations in a non-parametric context, choosing the Kruskal-Wallis test for that purpose (Table 16).

Referring to Table 17 and given the asymptotic p-value from Kruskal-Wallis test (0.016), there are two conclusions to be drawn: one for the levels of significance that are greater than or equal to 1.6% (including the usual 5% and 10%), and one for the levels of significance that are inferior to 1.6% (including the usual 1%). In regards to the first case, one rejects the null hypothesis for the equality of the population medians for the frontal impact score in all four classes. In the second case, there is no rejection of the null hypothesis and, therefore, there is no reason to believe in statistically significant differences in the population medians for the frontal impact scores among the different classes. This two-sided conclusion in terms of the accepted level of significance is an indication that there should be precaution regarding the observation of the corresponding conclusion to consider.

CONCLUSION

Despite the fact that hedonic concerns are on the agenda of most of the automotive industry manufacturers, who present hedonic and emotional artefacts in the exploitation of the market needs, there is a clear concern regarding the utility aspects, such as passive or active safety.

Table 16. Kruskal-Wallis test in frontal impact score (mean rank)

Car Brand	N	Mean Rank
Supermini	29	46.43
Small Family Car	41	68.62
Small MPV	21	48.57
Small off-road 4x4	20	51.80
Total	111	

Table 17. Kruskal-Wallis test in frontal impact score

	Frontal Impact Score
Chi-Square	10.349
df	3
Asymp. Sig.	0.016

One of the biggest features of the main automotive industry brands is having on marketing a key success factor underpinning their positioning on the market. Notwithstanding, institutions such as Euro NCAP, by implementing such types of tests, are disclosing information that would be difficult for the general audience to reach. Certainly, this type of institutional marketing is an asset to all those interested in obtaining unbiased information.

One of the main conclusions is that the small family cars and the supermini are the two classes with more models analyzed by Euro NCAP. Another important conclusion to draw is that most of the vehicles (63.6%), in 2015, have reached the five star maximum rating. Moreover, it is also worth noting that in 2013 Mercedes-Benz CITAN Kombi got only three stars, which would not be expected from such a reputable brand that is Mercedes-Benz. This reveals that disclosing the information from Euro NCAP is important for the general public to be aware of the market's realities, which are well beyond the images based on hedonic aspects and emotions provided by most of the main car brands.

In what concerns adult occupant protection, the main conclusion is that brands display a big concern in what regards to their image. However, in 2015 there are six brands whose scores are much lower than the other brands in what concerns adult occupant protection, which means that there is an urgent need to pressure some brands towards the improvement of their safety performance. In regards to adult protection per class, Business and Family Vans present the lowest scores (70.08%), as well as the highest standard deviation (19.95), which indicates a concern for the market, and that it should be more widespread.

Child occupant protection shows a positive evolution, which means that most brands are investing in this type of safety.

It is possible to conclude that classic vehicles are safer than hybrid and electric vehicles in what pertains to frontal impact score in the period between 2010 and 2013. These results should be analyzed cautiously as the sample size was quite different for both. Moreover, although there is a strong concentration on the two upper quartiles in classic vehicles, this type of vehicles shows a larger range than in electric and hybrid vehicles.

It was confirmed that there are statistically significant differences in adult occupant protection for the car models launched between 2010 and 2015, although this difference may be due to changes in the evaluation criteria of Euro NCAP in the last two years and not necessarily in real differences in adult safety. Ultimately, one cannot conclude that there are significant differences among the most important classes (in which 20 or more models were tested between 2010 and 2013) in what concerns the frontal impact protection.

From the marketing point of view, it is possible to state that it is important to disclose information to the general public so that they are aware of the safety intricacies that hardly get revealed to them. On the other hand, disclosing this information is one way of pressuring manufactures to improve the safety innovation trend, so that new car launches are safer for the public.

If electric and hybrid cars are to catch up with new safety market trends, new efforts need to be implemented so that their safety performance may increase. This is an important issue that deserves new studies as the numbers for electric and hybrid cars are expected to grow in the near future.

It is important to realize that using intelligent techniques allows for the understanding of how important safety is for car manufacturers. Moreover, one can witness how brands perform in the market. On the other hand, it is possible to conclude that although the disclosure of information about safety regarding different brands might be important, institutional marketing is not enough to change the customers' awareness about the different brand images and brand equity.

FUTURE RESEARCH DIRECTIONS

In order to complement this study, future research needs to address how the number of stars, for instance, (a) is correlated with child occupant real fatal injuries; (b) is connected with fatal injuries in single-car or two-car crashes. Future studies might also address how brand equity and future repurchase intention are affected when customers are shown how certain brands underperform in safety tests.

ACKNOWLEDGMENT

This work was supported in part by the Portuguese Foundation for Science and Technology (FCT – Fundação para a Ciência e a Tecnologia), through CIDMA – Center for Research and Development in Mathematics and Applications, within project UID/MAT/04106/2013.

REFERENCES

Fails, A., & Minton, R. (2001). *Comparison of Euro NCAP assessments with injury causation in accidents*. Retrieved September 1, 2014 from http://www-nrd.nhtsa.dot.gov/pdf/esv/esv17/Proceed/00034.pdf

Gronostajski, Z., Bandola, P., & Karbowski, P. (2006). The effect of crashworthiness parameters on the behaviour of car-body elements. *Archives of Civil and Mechanical Engineering*, *6*(1), 31–46. doi:10.1016/S1644-9665(12)60075-2

Huang, H., Hu, S., & Abdel-Aty, M. (2014). Indexing crash worthiness and crash aggressivity by major car brands. *Safety Science*, *62*, 339–347. doi:10.1016/j.ssci.2013.09.002

Huang, H., Li, C., & Zeng, Q. (2016). Crash protectiveness to occupant injury and vehicle damage: An investigation on major car brands. *Accident; Analysis and Prevention*, *86*, 129–136. doi:10.1016/j.aap.2015.10.008 PMID:26551733

Kullgren, A., Lie, A., & Tingvall, C. (2010). Comparison between Euro NCAP test results and real-world crash data. *Traffic Injury Prevention*, *11*(6), 587–593. doi:10.1080/15389588.2010.508804 PMID:21128188

Lie, A., Kullgren, A., & Tingvall, C. (2001). *Comparison of Euro NCAP test results with Folksam car model safety ratings.* Retrieved September 2, 2014 from http://www.euroncap.com/files/ESV_paper_2001---57a2e10b-23a9-4ffb-88e5-a17b21f8923c.pdf

Lie, A., & Tingvall, C. (2002). How do Euro NCAP results correlate with real-life injury risks? A paired comparison study of car-to-car crashes. *Traffic Injury Prevention*, *3*(4), 288–293. doi:10.1080/15389580214632

Martin, J.-L., & Lenguerrand, E. (2008). A population based estimation of the driver protection provided by passenger cars: France 1996–2005. *Accident; Analysis and Prevention*, *40*(6), 1811–1821. doi:10.1016/j.aap.2008.07.001 PMID:19068281

Mittelhammer, R. C. (2013). *Mathematical statistics for economics and business.* New York, NY: Springer. doi:10.1007/978-1-4614-5022-1

Orsi, C., Marchetti, P., Montomoli, C., & Morandi, A. (2013). Car crashes: The effect of passenger presence and other factors on driver outcome. *Safety Science*, *57*, 35–43. doi:10.1016/j.ssci.2013.01.017

Pawlus, W., Karimi, H., & Robbersmyr, K. (2013). Data-based modeling of vehicle collisions by nonlinear autoregressive model and feedforward neural network. *Information Sciences*, *235*(20), 65–79. doi:10.1016/j.ins.2012.03.013

Ratingen, M., Ellway, J., Avery, M., Gloyns, P., Sandner, V., & Versmissen, T. (2009). *The Euro NCAP Whiplash test.* Retrieved September 2, 2014 from http://www.euroncap.com/files/Paper_09-0231---0-155567f6-80a9-4d6d-91b6-e1ca2656b132.pdf

Seidel, M., Loch, C., & Chahil, S. (2005). Quo vadis, automotive industry? A vision of possible industry transformations. *European Management Journal*, *23*(4), 439–449. doi:10.1016/j.emj.2005.06.005

Watanabe, Y., Ichikawa, H., Kayama, O., Ono, K., Keneoka, K., & Inami, S. (2000). Influence of seat characteristics on occupant motion in low rear-end impacts. *Accident; Analysis and Prevention*, *32*(2), 243–250. doi:10.1016/S0001-4575(99)00082-2 PMID:10688480

Wilcox, R. R. (2003). *Applying contemporary statistical techniques.* San Diego, CA: Elsevier.

KEY TERMS AND DEFINITIONS

AEB City Test: Autonomous Emergency Braking (AEB) systems are expected to detect when a low-speed, rear-end collision in which the driver of the striking car is distracted and does not notice that the car ahead has stopped. AEB test when such an accident is likely to occur and the AEB system is expected to intervene by applying the brakes to try to avoid the collision. The test vehicle is driven towards the back of a ‘dummy’ target vehicle at speeds between 10 and 50km/h.

Child Occupant Protection Test: It covers the protection offered by the child restraint systems in the frontal and side impact tests, the accommodation of child restraints of various sizes and designs, and the availability of child restraint systems installation checks for safe transport of children in the car.

Frontal Full Width Rigid Barrier Test: Introduced in 2015, it tests cars against a rigid barrier with full overlap at a test speed of 50km/h. It simulates a head-on collision between two oncoming cars at moderately high speeds.

Frontal Impact Score: This test simulates frontal impact between two cars with a speed of about 55km/h. Tests prove that airbags are of added value to support the occupant's head and that seat belts prevent the occupant's chest to be projected against the wheel.

Frontal Offset-Deformable Barrier Test: A test carried out in which two frontal impact dummies, representing the average male and child, are placed in the car compartment. This test replicates a crash between two cars of the same weight, both travelling at a speed of 50km/h. Thus, the vehicle structure is evaluated.

Pedestrian Protection Tests: These tests involve the simulation of accidents involving adult and child pedestrians. They assess the potential risk at injuries to pedestrian head, pelvis, and upper and lower leg. The score is determined from tests to the most important vehicle front-end structures such as the bonnet and windshield, the bonnet leading edge, and the bumper.

Safety Assist Score: It is determined from tests to the most important driver assist technologies that support safe driving, and are meant to avoid accidents and mitigate injuries. The tests involve: electronic stability control, seatbelt reminders, speed assistance, AEB interurban, and lane support systems. The aim is to test the functionality of the system, and the performance during normal driving or in typical accident scenarios.

Side Mobile Barrier Test: In this test a deformable barrier is mounted on a trolley and is driven at 50km/h into the side of the stationary test vehicle at right angles. A side impact dummy representing an average male is put in the driver's seat and child dummies are placed in child restraint systems in the rear seat.

Side Pole Test: A single average male side impact dummy is placed in the driver's seat and a car is propelled sideways at 32km/h against a rigid, narrow pole. This is a very severe test of a car's ability to protect the driver's head.

Whiplash Test: This test is designed to test excessive head movement. It was introduced in 2009 as an integrated neck protection tests on the rear-end collision testing program. The dynamic sled tests indicate how effectively the seat and head restraint operate to provide whiplash protection in typical crash scenarios.

Chapter 18
Banking Credit Scoring Assessment Using Predictive K-Nearest Neighbour (PKNN) Classifier

Saroj Kanta Jena
BML Munjal University, India

Anil Kumar
BML Munjal University, India

Maheshwar Dwivedy
BML Munjal University, India

ABSTRACT

Credit scoring models is a scientific methodology adopted by credit providers to assess the credit worthiness of applicants. The primary objective of such models has been to predict the potentiality of the loan applicant. A proper evaluation of the credit can help the service provider to determine whether to grant or to reject credit. Therefore, the objective of the study is to predict banking credit scoring assessment using Predictive K-Nearest Neighbour (PKNN) classifier. For the purpose of analysis two different credit approval datasets: Australian credit and German credit have been used. The results from the study show that the proposed model used for classification works better on credit dataset. Here, the study firstly attempted to find the optimal 'K' value of the neighbourhood so that the classifier is tuned to forecast the credit worthiness and secondly, validated our proposed model on two credit approval datasets by checking the performance of the proposed models on the basis of classification accuracy.

DOI: 10.4018/978-1-5225-0997-4.ch018

1. INTRODUCTION

The business of financial institutions depends largely on the growth in the demand for credit and other financial services (Kim, 2004). The business community today pays more attention towards credit scoring assessment methods to better understand their customers and their purchasing capacity and the academic world is also interested in indulging in newer methods to develop and evaluate credit risk models. In this scenario, credit scoring plays an important role towards comprehending if it is feasible or not to grant loan to the applicant. Typically, all such scoring models are designed to predict the probability whether a loan applicant is a good credit or a bad credit through a systematic method to evaluate and assess credit. The primary objective remains to quantify and manage the financial risks associated with credit decisions. The most important takeaway of such an iterative process enables financial firms to increase the processing speed of loan applications. Financial institutions through such assessment models can take advantage through the systematic automation of the lending. The credit limit of the customer can also be determined by considering their credit scores.

The key focus amongst academicians lately has been to utilize credit scoring models so as to prescribe the right customer segment of a product for the marketer. Reduction of the cost of analysing the credit in order to enable the manager to take faster credit decisions in return ensures higher credit collections which is the key to better performance. Therefore, financial institutions are using different classification models to find the credit scoring of the customer. The central idea behind such classification schemes has been to determine and identify good loan applicant groups from bad loan applicant groups.

The nature of decision making towards identifying the right application for disbursing loan remains a complex task. Here, the study has attempted to categorize loan applicants broadly into either good credit or bad credit applications. The model considers the different features of an applicant like age of the applicant, income sources and marital status to categorize them into the specified classes. Financial institutions could then accept the application for loan for those identified good credit members who could in probability honour the repayment of their financial obligations. The classification rules could be individually designed by the creditors based on the features from previously accepted and rejected applications received for all previous loans. In doing so, it is vitally essential to find the accuracy of the proposed models especially designed for credit scoring and improvement in order to reduce the potential of risk associated with the credit system.

In previous literatures, many predictive models have been proposed by different authors. Though Linear Discriminant Analysis (LDA) methods have traditionally been used for credit scoring, it cannot distinguish the applicants owing to the type of the data which is mostly categorical in nature. It has been observed that the covariance matrices are not the same for both the classes. The method of K-Nearest Neighbours (KNN) for predicting credit risk assessment has also been studied by several researchers. Therefore to predict the classification of a new sample point the K-Nearest Neighbours (KNN) algorithm can be applied to databases where the data points are separated into several separate classes. But very limited studies are available in the literature where the researchers used K-Nearest Neighbours (KNN) on the Australian and German credit datasets for credit approval. Therefore, the objective of the study is to use Predictive K-Nearest Neighbours (PKNN) classifier for Australian and German banking credit assessment analysis so that they predict and segment the customers properly.

2. LITERATURE REVIEW

Corporate bankruptcies and their prediction remains an important and widely investigated topic even today. Such studies are found to have substantial impact on the entire process of loan approval decisions and profitability. Atiya (2001) after reviewing several Neural Network (NN) models proposed a NN bankruptcy forecast model for bankruptcy prediction. MERTON (1974) is reported to have considered several traditional models for credit risk to propose innovative indicators for the NN system. Similarly, Carling et al. (2001) reported on the different hazard (risk) associated with the loan approval process of the bank. The authors in their study considered the risk of non-payment and the risk of early recovery of loans.

Nearest neighbour algorithms has lately been the most common and extremely competitive technique which is widely adopted in pattern recognition studies. Holmes & Adams (2002) presented a probabilistic construction for the K-nearest neighbourhood algorithm to overcome some of the challenges. Hoffmann et al. (2002) compared and evaluated two different types of fuzzy classifiers for credit assessment. The first method involved Fuzzy classification rules that could be optimized and boosted by the new classifier and the second approach involved a neural network based fuzzy classifier with fuzzy back-propagation method. It was reported by the authors that the new classifier scheme achieved better performance than the others.

Given that KNN models are very sensitive to both noise and outliers that are enclosed in the training data set, several methods have since been proposed by different researchers that help in editing the training data for better performance of the classifier. Jiang and Zhou (2004) proposed an ANN based ensemble method to manipulate the training dataset for classifying KNN. The accuracy of the KNN based classifier could be improved by combining multiple classifiers. Approaches like Error Correcting Output Coding, Bagging, and Boosting are available to overcome such challenges of neural networks and decision trees classifiers. However, these techniques do not address the challenges of nearest neighbour classifiers. Bao et al. (2004) reported a new method for classifying KNN based on distance functions to overcome the challenges of KNN performance.

There have been very few studies involving the KNN method, which addresses the concern of identifying the optimal K-value. Cross-validation method is used for such problems. Ghosh et al. (2005) proposed a Bayesian measure of strength by exploring a measure of evidence for the given classes. Simple weighted averaging technique can also be used to aggregate the results of various nearest neighbour methods to reach the final decision. Atiya (2005) proposed a new posterior probability estimator that considers the K-nearest neighbours with a specific weight to each neighbour for estimating posterior probabilities. In their approach weights were projected using a maximum likelihood method. Models that help the decision maker in classifying credit and enable the managers to correctly estimate the credit score of each applicant. In this direction, the SVM (Support Vector Machine) classification scheme remains a dynamic research area that could solve classification problems in different fields. Compared to decision tree (DT) classifiers, NN, and genetic programming (GP), the SVM classifier reportedly assures a higher classificatory accuracy with moderately few input features. Huang et al. (2007) reported a hybrid genetic algorithm (GA) and SVM classifier scheme that not only performs feature selection job but also optimizes the model parameters. KNN has been extensively used as an active classification model. Jiang et al. (2007) have identified three key limitations that threaten the usage of KNN for classifying purposes while outlining three main approaches for overcoming such limitations. The most popular statistical and neural network based methods are used to evaluate credit risk through classification.

Yeh et al. (2009) investigated several data of customers defaulting on payments in Taiwan and made a comparative study on the accuracy of prediction of different variants of data mining by taking the probability of default. They presented the novel "Sorting Smoothing Method" to estimate the actual probability of default. Here, the authors reported that out of the 6 models they compared the artificial neural network models proved to be the most accurate estimate of the actual defaulting probability. Ngai et al. (2009) investigated the significance of data mining methods to CRM (Customer Relationship Management). The study reportedly considered 900 articles from 24 journals from 2000 to 2006 and proposed a classification pattern to classify the articles. Li et al. (2009) studied the rapid growth of the credit industry using several classifiers. The authors report that primitive classifiers failed to accomplish reasonable classification results.

Paleologo et al. (2010) reportedly used the logistic regression statistical structure for credit risk assessment. In all the studies previously reported, identifying a better classifier that predicts the real world data remains a vital yet challenging research topic. Soft computing techniques can also be considered to be a worthy alternative method to statistical methods. Lahsasna et al. (2010) summarized the advantages and shortcomings of soft computing techniques that were applied towards constructing credit scoring models. They suggested further investigation on different soft computing techniques for credit scoring models. Govindarajan and Chandrasekaran (2010) applied the KNN classifier for classification and prediction while researching on direct marketing. The authors observed that the model works better in prediction over classification. Further, while using the KNN technique for comparative cross-validation of the classifier, the authors found that performance of KNN classifier is less owing to the inherent bias of the model.

Yu (2011) reported that AI techniques performed better with increased accuracy in comparison to Multi Criteria Decision Making (MCDM) models. Of all the methods, the author found that SVM technique classifies better than other techniques. The study also reported that AI-based techniques could be utilized for implementing enterprise resource planning (ERP) systems. Keramati and Yousefi (2011) summarized the advantages and limitations of data mining methods as a tool for credit assessment. The authors carried out a broad literature survey on several data mining techniques suited for credit scoring setting. Singh and Aggarwal (2011) investigated several tools like LDA (Linear Discriminant Analysis), GP, SVM, KNN and Kernel density estimation technique in credit risk assessment. The authors observed that SVM and GP outperformed others in classifying credit risk applications. Zareapoor et al. (2012) investigated the increase in financial fraud through advanced technology and communication systems. Several financial houses have lost substantial money through such fraudulent activities. Therefore, it becomes more imperative for all the financial houses to develop a fraud detection system in the credit card issue system to minimize their loss. Methods like SVM, NN, Artificial Immune System (AIS), fuzzy system, GA, rule-induction techniques, and KNN algorithms have been frequently reported in the literature that addresses this issue. Wu et al. (2012) investigated several upgraded algorithms of KNN to propose an enriched algorithm DKNDAW (Dynamic KNN with Distance and Attribute Weighted).

Recently, credit scoring assessment studies have also been investigated for the microfinance sector as well. Blanco et al. (2013) in their latest research, report that neural network models squarely beat other methods like quadratic discriminant analysis (QDA), LDA, and logistic regression techniques. Yet another researcher, Khashei et al. (2013) investigated credit risk evaluation using data mining classification techniques. The authors used a hybrid model FMLP (fuzzy MLP) for credit scoring assessment based on ANN and fuzzy logic. The article utilized fuzzy numbers to update the weight and bias of the MLPs so as to achieve better results when both uncertain and complex data exist. This FMLP model outperforms other models such as SVM, KNN, QDA and LDA. They concluded that FMLP model can be an appropriate substitute for credit classification in uncertainty conditions.

Loan default prediction models are commonly used in credit risk management of financial institutions. The selection and evaluation of default classification models is a challenging task in prediction process. Kou et al. (2014) recommends an evaluation approach for default classification models constructed on MCDM methods. They also considered feature selection and sampling techniques for data pre-processing to handle imbalance and high dimensionality class of bank loan default data. They suggested that KNN model works better in bank loan default prediction. SVM remains a dominant method used for the prediction of credit risk; however, the presentation of SVM is delicate in features selection, parameter setting to form a model. Zhou et al. (2014) proposed a novel approach constructed on direct search together with attribute ranking to optimize parameter setting and features selection process. They also compared the proposed model with the GA technique and found better performance with the proposed model. Koh (2015) worked on the utility of data mining methods for building credit scoring models to propose a superior final model from the combination of credit scoring models. Yu et al. (2015) considered government agencies, corporations, and individual credit variations in online markets. They suggested that credit scoring theory could be categorized into two broad directions, namely the traditional theory and new evolving theory. The authors recommend that credit scoring approaches should typically include econometric models, AI techniques, expert systems, and their hybrid forms. They also recommend that mutual credit databases should be established having high consistency in data standards.

Recently, ensemble classification methodology has become prevalent in credit risk assessment. However, random sampling is also used to generate training subsets for building the base classifiers. The overall classification performance may be degraded for this reason. Xiao (2016) proposed an ensemble classification method constructed on supervised clustering for credit scoring. Supervised clustering is engaged to partition the data samples of each class into a number of clusters and clusters from diverse classes are then shared pairwise to form a number of training subsets. A base classifier is constructed for each training subset. The proposed model increases the credit scoring precision than the other ensemble classification methods. From the aforementioned literature, though several authors have investigated the KNN method to predict credit risk, not a single framework exists that could help the decision maker to find the size (K) of the neighbourhood. Therefore, an attempt is made here to study credit risk assessment through a new approach called as PKNN, wherein there is scope for identifying the optimal K-value (size) of the neighbourhood.

3. METHODOLOGY

3.1 Dataset Information

Two types of credit card applications have been considered in this study. The attributes names have been arbitrarily changed to random symbols so as to ensure confidentiality. The dataset used in our analysis consists of a combination of several attributes, like small number of values in continuous, nominal form, and larger numbers of values in continuous form. In this study, two types of data set have been used for credit classification: 1) German Credit Approval Dataset which classifies persons distinguished by a set of behavioural characteristics as bad credit risks or good credit risks to lenders. This is accomplished by using two different formats- numeric form and cost matrix form 2) Australian Credit Approval Dataset

Table 1. Credit approval dataset Australian and German

Characteristics	Australian	German
Characteristics of Dataset	Multivariate	Multivariate
Characteristics of Attributes	Categorical, Integer, Real	Categorical, Integer
Purpose	Classification	Classification
Number of Records	690	1000
Number of Attributes	14	20
Missing Value	Yes	N/A
Discipline	Financial	Financial
Date Donated	N/A	N/A
Number of Web Hits	70829	182499

which is a file that concerns credit card applications providing the basis for credit card approval process. This database exists elsewhere in the data repository in a non-identical form.

3.2 Predictive K-Nearest Neighbours (PKNN) Classifier

By the help of PKNN method the design set can be updated very easily. The new (recently) accepted customers passed through the process of selection for bad credit or good credit, which then become part of the design dataset to form a new database replacing the past surviving observations.

Causes for Credit Rejection

The KNN technique with the adjusted Euclidian distance metrics considers the regression weights to provide a cause for rejecting applications through information developed from class separation. The distance between the average of all bad applications and the new application can be calculated for each of the individual features of the model. The calculation of the above distance will help the decision maker to find the cause for rejection of credit. The approximated contribution of individual characteristic could be approximated by measuring the Euclidian distance metrics. The low values of this distance with respect to the previous bad applicants can be identified as the bad applicant and can be rejected.

3.3 Screening of Applicants

The methods of screening applicants and putting them in a separate class as red line people are always considered as controversial decisions taken by the credit granter. The proposed model performed better than linear or logistic regression model for the random variation in distance metric. However, with the increase in the value of database X, the response of the proposed model becomes increasingly dependent on the specific characteristic with large weight. This problem can be reduced by putting limits on the ratio of the regression weight. The accuracy of classification together with the regression score card is reduced for the above constraint. In order to solve the challenges of KNN classification, the use of distance weighted KNN classification algorithm is important. The KNN model considered the nearest neighbours of the new data point to classify the data point. The K-nearest neighbour of the new data point in a distributed system could be circulated among the 'n' nodes of the data set. We identify data from the database which are part of the K-nearest neighbours of the intended query to get the local grouping of the node of the intended query point. The classification of the new data point can be calculated by considering the new point itself in the calculation. The combination of the local classification of all the nodes will calculate the query point's global classification over the database. The KNN classification problem can now split into two sub-problems.

Nearest neighbour selection: To classify the new query instance 'x', it is essential to recognise all the K-nearest neighbours of 'x'.

- **Classification:** The local classification of 'x' for each node is calculated first and then the global classification of 'x' can be calculated.

3.4 Confusion Matrix

The knowledge discovery process of the available data is an important process of determining valid and useful patterns of data. Data mining is the most vital step for KDD (Knowledge Discovery in Database). An exhaustive system of classification is a requirement to distinguish the variety of the systems generated by KDD and to identify the most useful system for the user. To identify a dataset wherein a small number of rules are applicable is the major hurdle of rule mining. The classifier for predicting the class of any recent instance will be these rules. It is important that the classification algorithm is accurate, elegant and efficient. The algorithm will perform poorly on real world datasets as it is designed for a predefined distribution. To overcome this problem we need to divide the dataset into two parts 1) Training Dataset: It is the subset of the original dataset used to create the model, 2) Test Dataset: It is the whole dataset which is then applied on the model tested through the training data set.

A confusion matrix is a known tool used to measure the accuracy of the classifier in data mining. Accuracy of a classifier on a given test set can be measured as the % of test tuples that are accurately classified by the classifier.

The initial node programs a global distance vector (U_i) of length 'K' where each node is automatically made to be the largest possible distance between a given query and any data point, which is then conveyed to its successor.

A confusion matrix is generally of the form as shown in Table 2 and:

Table 2.

		Actual Class	
		1	**0**
Predicted Class	**1**	TP	FN
	0	FP	TN

T_P: True-Positive
T_N: True-Negative
F_P: False-Positive
F_N: False-Negative

$$Accuracy = \frac{Number\ of\ tuples\ classified\ correctly}{Total\ number\ of\ tuples}$$

$$Accuracy = \frac{T\_P + T\_N}{T\_P + T\_N + F\_P + F\_N} = \frac{T\_P + T\_N}{P + N}$$

where,

$$P = T\_P + F\_N \ and \ N = F\_P + T\_N$$

It is also important to find the error rate or misclassification rate of the classifier M.

Error rate (M) = 1- Accuracy (M), where Accuracy (M) is the accuracy of the classifier M. Error rate can be computed as

$$Error\ rate = \frac{F\_P + F\_N}{P + N}$$

The sensitivity & specificity measures can be computed and utilized to find the precise-ness of the model. Sensitivity is also referred to as the recognition rate, while specificity is the true negative rate.

$$Sensitivity = \frac{T\_P}{P},$$

$$Specificity = \frac{T\_N}{N}$$

The Algorithm

The dataset's nodes are mapped on a ring in a random fashion in the protocol. Though the nodes are in a ring, it has a predecessor and a successor node also. In the initial stage, starting node is selected by a specially designed initial module from the n-participating nodes and a set of parameters are programmed for the localized calculation of the algorithm. A multi-round protocol is designed to engage the node in the process of local algorithm which is then conveyed to its successor.

Nearest Neighbour Selection

For each node of the database which is part of the K-nearest neighbours of 'x', calculate 'K' least distances between 'x' and the data values in the database. Here, a privacy protecting algorithm is used to determine the 'K' least distances between the union of the global 'K' nearest distance of the complete dataset and 'x'. As the nodes of the database are not aware of the exact location by distance, the algorithm is designed to find the 'K^{th}' neighbourhood for the purpose. Algorithm-1, the nearest distance selection algorithm is a multi-round protocol. In this procedure the design of the algorithm that puts in a certain quantity of randomization is the key of the procedure. Each node determines its point in the database i.e., in the K-neighbourhood of 'x' and then a local classification vector is formed by each node of the database for the query instance. The amount of support received by the 'ith' class from the K-nearest neighbours of 'x' can be taken as the 'ith' element. In this way, in order to achieve global classification, the nodes identify the global classification vector.

Algorithm 1: Selecting K-Nearest Distances

Input: The inputs are S_i, which is the local K-proximate distance vector considered between each node of the dataset and the query instance 'x'

Output: U_i, is the global K-proximate distance vector considered amongst all nodes and query record 'x'.

The initial node of the dataset programmes a global distance vector U_i of length K where every part of the set is assumed to be highest likely distance between any query record and a particular data value, which is conveyed to the successor. Each node '*i*', on receiving a vector U_{i-1} from its predecessor, the node '*i*' will compute U_i using a randomized algorithm which shall be transmitted to the successor. These steps are repeated for the next r-rounds. On receiving a vector from its predecessor, the starting node of the dataset transmits the same to all the nodes of the set.

Algorithm 2: Adding the Local Classification Vectors

Input: The input is the local classification vector of each node, S_i

Output: Compute *U* which is the global classification vector, $U = \sum_{i=1}^{n} S_i$

The starting node of the dataset computes a global classification vector (*U*) to a random vector '*rv*' and the node then refers the same to its successor. After getting a vector v_i from its predecessor, every node of the dataset will transmit $S_i + v_i$ to its successor. On receiving a vector v_i from its predecessor, the starting node transmits the vector $v_i - rv + S$ to all the nodes of the same set.

Once each node of the set recognizes the global classification vector U, the nodes from the set can identify the class having the majority global vote by computing the maximum index value in the global classification vector.

Algorithm 3: Classification of PKNN

Input: The input x, which is a record that is to be classified.

Output: Find classification (x), which refers to classification of x.

Each node of the dataset calculates from their respective databases, the distance *d* (x, y) between each data point 'y' and the query instance 'x', thereby selecting 'K' least distances which are stored in vector *S*. With *S* as input, algorithm-1 is executed by each node to select K-nearest distances for *U*.

The k-nearest distance $\Delta : \Delta = U(K)$ is used by each node. Given *v* classes are there, and *S* can be calculated by each node of the set for all *y* points in the database using the expression:

$$S(i) = \sum_y w\left(d\left(x, y\right)\right) * \left[f\left(y\right) = i\right] * \left[d\left(x, y\right) \leq \Delta\right], \forall 1 \leq i \leq v$$

Here *d*(x, y) is the distance considered between x and y, *f* (*y*) is the classification output of the point y, and [*p*] =1, if *p* is true, else 0 otherwise. Taking *S* as input, the nodes of the set utilizes the classification algorithm to calculate the *U*. Classification (x) can be identified as

$$classification\left(x\right) \leftarrow \arg\max_i \in V_{U(i)}$$

K-Nearest Neighbour Classification Algorithm

The Rote classifier is a simple and trivial classifier; where the classifier learns the entire training dataset and classifies the object of the test dataset only if there is an exact match with the training tuple. The only disadvantage of this approach is the matching of test data with the training data is found to be very poor because exact match with the training tuples cannot be found. To overcome this problem of Rote classifier, a more refined approach i.e., KNN classification is used, where a cluster of 'K' objects taken from the training dataset that are close to the tested object, and on this basis the principal class label of the neighbourhood is considered as the class of the tested object. Three important points considered while using this approach are a set of records with its class label, a distance metric, and, the number of elements in the cluster (K).

To classify an unlabelled object, it is necessary to compute the distance of the given object from the labelled objects, the cluster of the object with respect to distance are found, and the class labels of the elements of the cluster can be considered as the class label of the object.

Input: The set of 'K' training objects *T* and test object $R = \left(X', y'\right)$
Process: Compute $d\left(X', X\right)$, the distance between *R* and every object, $\left(X, y\right) \in T$.

Select, $T_r \subseteq T$ the set of 'K' closest training objects to *R*.

Output: The output is $y' = \arg\max \sum \left(x_i, y_i\right) \in T_r \, I\left(v = y_i\right)$

Given a training set *T* and a test object $x = \left(X', y'\right)$, we need to determine T_r (the nearest neighbour list) for the given object. For this we employ the distance algorithm to calculate distance between *R* and $\left(X, y\right) \in T$, where *X* is the training data, while *y* is its class. Here X' is the test data and y' is its class. The objective is to identify the list of elements of the cluster, identify the class of the test object using the principal class label of its nearest neighbours of the cluster.

Majority Voting: $y' = \arg\max_v \sum_{(x_i, y_i) \in T_r} I(v = y_i)$ (1)

Here v refers to label of the class, y_i refers to the class label for the ith nearest neighbours of the object, and I (.) refer to indicator function which would return a value 1 when its argument is true else it is 0 otherwise. The performance of KNN model is also affected by other vital issues that need to be resolved. Of which, the selection of the 'K' value is the most significant one. The result of the model can be controlled from noise data points if the assumed value taken for 'K' is too small. For larger 'K' values, other class data points could be included to the neighbourhood. Combining the class labels is the strength of our approach. One can consider the majority vote for the object, but it might create new problems due to the variation of nearest neighbours. The best way to address this is by considering the voted distance weight, where the weight taken for the object is the inverse of the squared distance: $w_i = 1/d(x', x_i)^2$

The KNN algorithm can now be modified as:

Voted Distance Weight:

$$y' = \arg\max_v \sum_{(x_i, y_i) \in T_r} w_i I(v = y_i) \quad (2)$$

It is very crucial to select a best distance measure for identifying the cluster. Although several methods can be used to work out the distance among two points, we need to find the best one for the purpose of this study. To find the greater likelihood of the similar class, it required to select a desirable distance measure which will compute a lesser distance amongst two objects. It is better to use *cosine* measure instead of Euclidean distance in the KNN model for classification. We also find that some distance measures suffer from the issues of high dimensionality of the data set where Euclidean distance will work better in such cases.

4. ANALYSIS

PKNN method as discussed above is a very simple technique that could be implemented easily for the purpose of predicting the class. The proposed model in this study is found to perform better in many circumstances. Our model works better for multi-modal and it is well suited for studying applications involving multi class label objects. The results shown in Table 3 to Table 9 are the performance accuracy of the model on different values of neighbourhood size 'K' and S1 to S10 represents the 10 simulations taken to compute the performance of the model for each 'K' value.

Table 3. Classification performance for K=3

Data Set	S1	S2	S3	S4	S5	S6	S7	S8	S9	S10
Ger-Credit	72	68.6	71	70.2	71.2	67.6	68	71.8	68	69.8
Aus-Credit	64.92	66.95	66.66	70.72	66.37	65.79	68.98	69.27	67.53	67.24

Table 4. Classification performance for K=5

Data Set	S1	S2	S3	S4	S5	S6	S7	S8	S9	S10
Ger-Credit	74	72.4	68	71.8	67.8	70	71.2	68.4	68.8	68.4
Aus-Credit	69.56	66.08	64.34	67.82	67.53	66.37	66.95	70.14	70.72	67.82

Table 5. Classification performance for K=7

Data Set	S1	S2	S3	S4	S5	S6	S7	S8	S9	S10
Ger-Credit	69	72.4	73	70.8	68.6	71	71.8	70.2	71.4	69.4
Aus-Credit	71.01	68.69	66.08	70.14	68.40	68.69	65.79	69.27	67.82	65.21

Table 6. Classification performance for K=9

Data Set	S1	S2	S3	S4	S5	S6	S7	S8	S9	S10
Ger-Credit	72.6	75.6	71.2	70.2	74	72.8	71.8	68.4	69.4	70.8
Aus-Credit	71.30	68.40	68.40	66.37	66.66	66.66	72.17	70.14	68.98	68.11

Table 7. Classification performance for K=11

Data Set	S1	S2	S3	S4	S5	S6	S7	S8	S9	S10
Ger-Credit	68	71.6	72	70.4	71.4	72.2	70.8	69.4	69.6	70.4
Aus-Credit	71.30	66.08	68.11	68.40	69.56	69.85	68.40	70.72	69.27	65.21

Table 8. Classification performance for K=13

Data Set	S1	S2	S3	S4	S5	S6	S7	S8	S9	S10
Ger-Credit	74.2	70.6	70.6	69	71.6	72.6	70.6	0.4	68.8	68.6
Aus-Credit	70.14	67.53	69.27	65.50	66.95	68.69	70.14	64.34	64.92	72.17

Table 9. Classification performance for K=15

Data Set	S1	S2	S3	S4	S5	S6	S7	S8	S9	S10
Ger-Credit	67	71	70.6	71.2	70	69.6	70.2	70.8	71.6	71.2
Aus-Credit	68.98	68.11	71.01	69.56	68.98	69.56	67.24	68.40	64.92	66.08

Table 10. Comparison of average classification performance for different value of k

Data Set	K=3	K=5	K=7	K=9	K=11	K=13	K=15
German Credit	69.92	70.08	70.78	71.68	70.58	70.7	70.32
Australian Credit	67.44	67.73	68.11	68.71	68.69	67.96	68.384

Ten (10) simulations for both the datasets have been considered and the average performance accuracy of the model for each of the K values have been computed and mentioned in Table 10. In this study, we considered different 'K' value as 3, 5, 7, 9, 11, 13, and 15.The graph (Figure 1) shows that in the Australian credit data set, the average performance accuracy is high when the value of K=9. It is concluded that for the given data set, 9-NN is an appropriate neighbourhood size and can be considered for classifying the Australian Credit dataset with the proposed PKNN model. As for the German credit data set, the average performance accuracy of the model is also high for K=9. Therefore, we conclude that 9-NN is an appropriate neighbourhood size and can be considered for classifying the German credit dataset with the proposed PKNN model.

Table 11 and Table 12 consists the output values of the different measures of the confusion matrix designed for the test and training datasets of the German credit dataset for the 10 different simulations.

The various performance measures sensitivity, specificity, precision and accuracy have been computed by considering the values from Table 11 and Table 12 for test and training datasets respectively. The average performance of the different measures has been calculated for both test and training datasets

Figure 1. Performance of PKNN for different K values
Australian & German Credit Dataset.

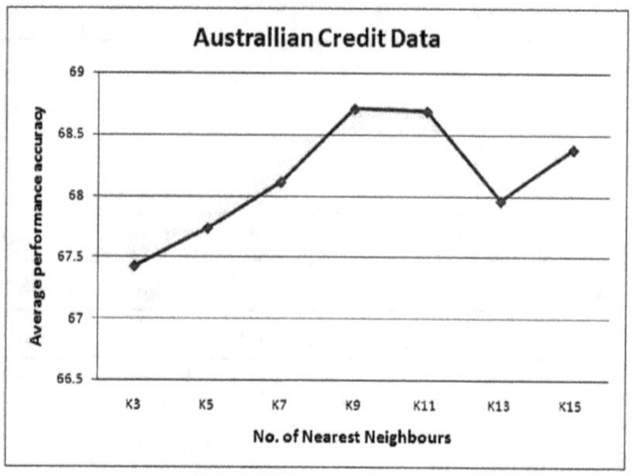

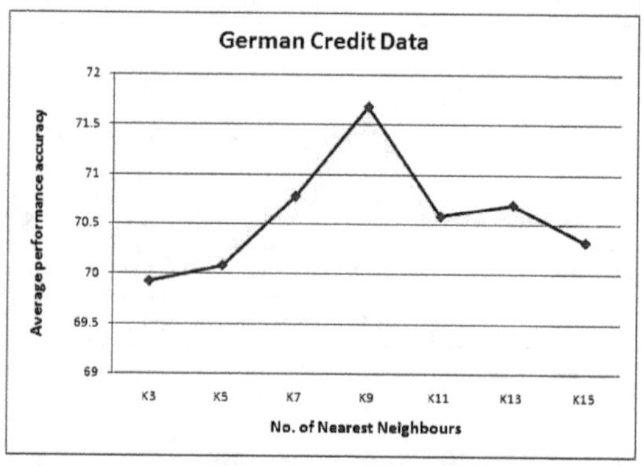

Table 11. Confusion matrix result for German credit test dataset for KNN model

Simulation	S1	S2	S3	S4	S5	S6	S7	S8	S9	S10
True Positive	326	316	316	324	324	325	316	316	314	321
False Negative	9	31	31	29	30	27	32	31	31	28
False Positive	146	120	123	103	114	119	127	118	126	118
True Negative	19	33	30	44	32	29	25	35	29	33

Table 12. Confusion matrix result for German credit training dataset for KNN model

Simulation	S1	S2	S3	S4	S5	S6	S7	S8	S9	S10
True Positive	359	343	333	322	323	328	339	338	341	331
False Negative	6	10	20	25	23	20	13	15	14	20
False Positive	109	97	108	99	103	100	100	104	100	108
True Negative	26	50	39	54	51	52	48	43	45	41

Figure 2. Performance of KNN model for German credit data

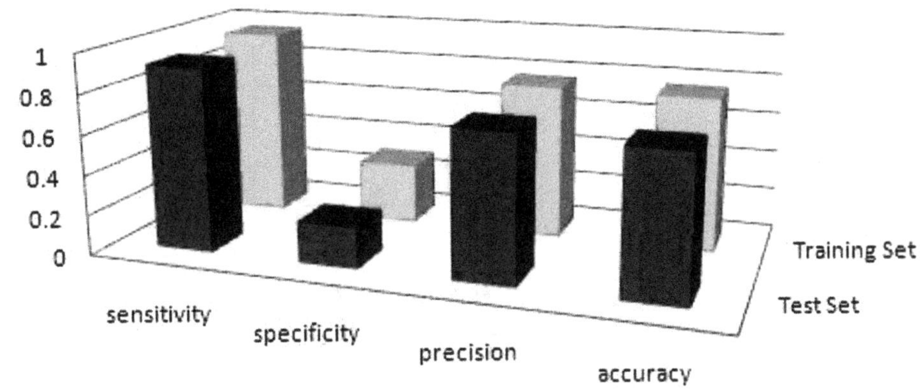

	sensitivity	specificity	precision	accuracy
■ Test Set	0.9199	0.204	0.7252	0.7014
■ Training Set	0.9526	0.3026	0.7655	0.7612

of the German credit dataset. The graph (Figure 2) shows that the sensitivity is 95% from the training set of the German credit dataset. The accuracy label of the model is 76% with the training dataset. The model classifies "good credit" applicant as a "good credit" for the loan approval process. The potential customer is accepted by the model for the credit with 95% probability. The proposed model was found to be a better classification model with substantial percentage of accuracy.

Table 13 and Table 14 consists the output values of the of the confusion matrix designed for the test and training datasets of the Australian credit dataset for the 10 different simulations. The average performance of the different measures has been calculated for both test and training datasets of the Australian credit dataset in a similar fashion.

The graph (Figure 3) shows that the average specificity is more than 82% from the training set of the Australian credit dataset. The accuracy label of the model is 74% with the training dataset. The model classifies "bad credit" applicant as a "bad credit" for the loan approval process. The non-potential customer is rejected by the model for the credit with 82% probability. Here, for the Australian credit dataset the model is able to successfully classify better with high percentage of accuracy in the results obtained.

Table 13. Confusion matrix for Australian credit test dataset for KNN model

Simulation	S1	S2	S3	S4	S5	S6	S7	S8	S9	S10
True Positive	85	87	93	85	100	81	86	81	92	89
False Negative	69	68	57	69	56	75	65	60	75	64
False Positive	41	46	61	46	66	34	43	52	39	49
True Negative	150	144	134	145	123	155	151	152	139	143

Table 14. Confusion matrix for Australian credit training dataset for KNN model

Simulation	S1	S2	S3	S4	S5	S6	S7	S8	S9	S10
True Positive	100	99	101	107	107	89	102	106	89	98
False Negative	53	53	56	46	44	62	54	60	51	56
False Positive	31	35	36	29	38	25	31	38	37	32
True Negative	161	158	152	163	156	169	158	141	168	159

Figure 3. Performance of KNN model for Australian credit data

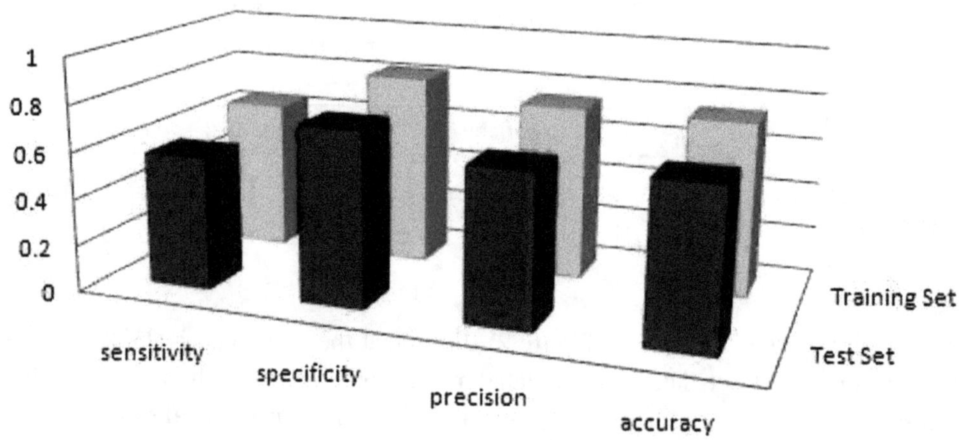

	sensitivity	specificity	precision	accuracy
■ Test Set	0.5722	0.7509	0.6511	0.671
■ Training Set	0.651	0.8265	0.7508	0.7486

5. MANAGERIAL APPLICATIONS AND CONCLUSION

Previously, credit scoring was used by the financial houses to make credit decisions. Currently, the application of credit scoring is broad based and used in the decision making process in areas like insurance, housing, basic utility services etc. The financial institutions commonly use credit scoring for loan applications. Setting credit limits, managing existing customers, and profit forecasting are the vital functions of the financial institutions. The application of credit scoring is more useful for these functions. Nowadays, even landlords are considering these scores to select potential tenants. Utility suppliers are using credit scoring to determine the potential consumers for their services. In some special cases like where the employee needs to handle big amount of money, the employers make use of this scoring and credit history of the applicants for the said post.

This study presents a work that demonstrates the advantages of PKNN model credit analysis. PKNN has shown to be a promising and a significant technique for classification. There is a substantial number of research works in KNN classification and it is found that it works better than the traditional statistical methods. In this research work, we have used PKNN, the KNN based model has been modified to properly classify the credit applications as either bad credit or good credit in the process of credit assessment. The need identified has been that the financial houses require credit scoring models to minimize the risk associated in the lending process.

Rigorous simulations were conducted to calculate the average accuracy level for each of the K values considered to form the neighbourhood. Overall, the simulation predicts that 9-NN gives better result for classification in both the datasets with the neighbourhood approach. The performance matrices, such as sensitivity, specificity, precision and accuracy have been considered to compare the relative performance of the model. The model has been evaluated ten (10) times for each dataset. For each evaluation, the dataset is randomly divided into two datasets called training dataset and test dataset. The model is built using the training dataset, and then the model so developed is evaluated for both the training dataset and test dataset. During each evaluation, the confusion matrix is generated and from this confusion matrix the four performance matrices were evaluated.

The simulation results calculated from confusion matrix clearly vindicate that PKNN is more flexible than other approaches discussed in the literature. In summary, our model has the potential to accurately perform credit scoring assessment in real time.

AKNOWLEDGMENT

The authors want to extend their gratitude towards Prof. Tapan Kumar Panda (Dean, School of Management, BML Munjal University) and Dr. Nandita Chaudhary for their indispensable suggestions and comments that improved the quality of the paper significantly.

REFERENCES

Atiya, A. F. (2001). Bankruptcy prediction for credit risk using neural networks: A survey and new results. *Neural Networks. IEEE Transactions on*, *12*(4), 929–935. PMID:18249923

Atiya, A. F. (2005). Estimating the posterior probabilities using the k-nearest neighbor rule. *Neural Computation*, *17*(3), 731–740. doi:10.1162/0899766053019971 PMID:15802013

Baesens, B., Van Gestel, T., Viaene, S., Stepanova, M., Suykens, J., & Vanthienen, J. (2003). Benchmarking state-of-the-art classification algorithms for credit scoring. *The Journal of the Operational Research Society*, *54*(6), 627–635. doi:10.1057/palgrave.jors.2601545

Bao, Y., Ishii, N., & Du, X. (2004). Combining multiple k-nearest neighbor classifiers using different distance functions. In *Intelligent Data Engineering and Automated Learning–IDEAL 2004* (pp. 634–641). Springer Berlin Heidelberg; doi:10.1007/978-3-540-28647-9_60

Blanco, A., Pino-Mejías, R., Lara, J., & Rayo, S. (2013). Credit scoring models for the microfinance industry using neural networks: Evidence from Peru. *Expert Systems with Applications*, *40*(1), 356–364. doi:10.1016/j.eswa.2012.07.051

Carling, K., Jacobson, T., & Roszbach, K. (2001). Dormancy risk and expected profits of consumer loans. *Journal of Banking & Finance*, *25*(4), 717–739. doi:10.1016/S0378-4266(00)00093-5

Chen, M. C., & Huang, S. H. (2003). Credit scoring and rejected instances reassigning through evolutionary computation techniques. *Expert Systems with Applications*, *24*(4), 433–441. doi:10.1016/S0957-4174(02)00191-4

Chouhan, S., Singh, D., & Singh, A. (2016). A Survey and Analysis of Various Agricultural Crops Classification Techniques. *International Journal of Computers and Applications*, *136*(11).

Data set. (n.d.). Retrieved from https://archive.ics.uci.edu/ml/datasets/Statlog+%28German+Credit+Data%29

Demyanyk, Y., & Hasan, I. (2010). Financial crises and bank failures: A review of prediction methods. *Omega*, *38*(5), 315–324. doi:10.1016/j.omega.2009.09.007

Ghosh, A. K., Chaudhuri, P., & Murthy, C. A. (2005). On visualization and aggregation of nearest neighbor classifiers. *Pattern Analysis and Machine Intelligence. IEEE Transactions on*, *27*(10), 1592–1602.

Govindarajan, M., & Chandrasekaran, R. M. (2010). Evaluation of k-nearest neighbor classifier performance for direct marketing. *Expert Systems with Applications*, *37*(1), 253–258. doi:10.1016/j.eswa.2009.04.055

Hoffmann, F., Baesens, B., Martens, J., Put, F., & Vanthienen, J. (2002). Comparing a genetic fuzzy and a neurofuzzy classifier for credit scoring. *International Journal of Intelligent Systems*, *17*(11), 1067–1083. doi:10.1002/int.10052

Holmes, C. C., & Adams, N. M. (2002). A probabilistic nearest neighbour method for statistical pattern recognition. *Journal of the Royal Statistical Society. Series B, Statistical Methodology*, *64*(2), 295–306. doi:10.1111/1467-9868.00338

Huang, C. L., Chen, M. C., & Wang, C. J. (2007). Credit scoring with a data mining approach based on support vector machines. *Expert Systems with Applications*, *33*(4), 847–856. doi:10.1016/j.eswa.2006.07.007

Jiang, L., Cai, Z., Wang, D., & Jiang, S. (2007, August). Survey of improving k-nearest-neighbor for classification. In FSKD (pp. 679-683). IEEE. doi:10.1109/FSKD.2007.552

Jiang, Y., & Zhou, Z. H. (2004). Editing training data for kNN classifiers with neural network ensemble. In *Advances in Neural Networks–ISNN 2004* (pp. 356–361). Springer Berlin Heidelberg.

Keramati, A., & Yousefi, N. (2011, January). A proposed classification of data mining techniques in credit scoring. In *Proceeding of 2011 International Conference of Industrial Engineering and Operations Management* (pp. 22-4).

Khashei, M., Rezvan, M. T., Hamadani, A. Z., & Bijari, M. (2013). A bi-level neural-based fuzzy classification approach for credit scoring problems. *Complexity*, *18*(6), 46–57. doi:10.1002/cplx.21458

Kim, K. J. (2004). Artificial neural networks with feature transformation based on domain knowledge for the prediction of stock index futures. *International Journal of Intelligent Systems in Accounting Finance & Management*, *12*(3), 167–176. doi:10.1002/isaf.252

Koh, H. C. (2015). A two-step method to construct credit scoring models with data mining techniques. *International Journal of Business and Information*, *1*(1).

Kou, G., Peng, Y., & Lu, C. (2014). MCDM approach to evaluating bank loan default models. *Technological and Economic Development of Economy*, *20*(2), 292–311. doi:10.3846/20294913.2014.913275

Laha, A. (2007). Building contextual classifiers by integrating fuzzy rule based classification technique and k-nn method for credit scoring. *Advanced Engineering Informatics*, *21*(3), 281–291. doi:10.1016/j.aei.2006.12.004

Lahsasna, A., Ainon, R. N., & Teh, Y. W. (2010). Credit Scoring Models Using Soft Computing Methods: A Survey. *Int. Arab J. Inf. Technol.*, *7*(2), 115–123.

Lai, K. K., Yu, L., Wang, S., & Zhou, L. (2006). Credit risk analysis using a reliability-based neural network ensemble model. In *Artificial Neural Networks–ICANN 2006* (pp. 682–690). Springer Berlin Heidelberg. doi:10.1007/11840930_71

Leung, K., Cheong, F., & Cheong, C. (2007, September). Consumer credit scoring using an artificial immune system algorithm. In *Evolutionary Computation, 2007. CEC 2007. IEEE Congress on* (pp. 3377-3384). IEEE. doi:10.1109/CEC.2007.4424908

Li, F. C., Wang, P. K., & Wang, G. E. (2009, December). Comparison of the primitive classifiers with extreme learning machine in credit scoring. In *Industrial Engineering and Engineering Management, 2009. IEEM 2009. IEEE International Conference on* (pp. 685-688). IEEE. doi:10.1109/IEEM.2009.5373241

Ngai, E. W., Xiu, L., & Chau, D. C. (2009). Application of data mining techniques in customer relationship management: A literature review and classification. *Expert Systems with Applications*, *36*(2), 2592–2602. doi:10.1016/j.eswa.2008.02.021

Ong, C. S., Huang, J. J., & Tzeng, G. H. (2005). Building credit scoring models using genetic programming. *Expert Systems with Applications*, *29*(1), 41–47. doi:10.1016/j.eswa.2005.01.003

Paleologo, G., Elisseeff, A., & Antonini, G. (2010). Subagging for credit scoring models. *European Journal of Operational Research*, *201*(2), 490–499. doi:10.1016/j.ejor.2009.03.008

Raman, B., & Ioerger, T. R. (2003). *Enhancing learning using feature and example selection*. College Station, TX, USA: Texas A&M University.

Roszbach, K. (2004). Bank lending policy, credit scoring, and the survival of loans. *The Review of Economics and Statistics*, *86*(4), 946–958. doi:10.1162/0034653043125248

Singh, R., & Aggarwal, R. R. (2011). Comparative Evaluation of Predictive Modeling Techniques on Credit Card Data. *International Journal of Computer Theory and Engineering*, *3*(5), 598–603. doi:10.7763/IJCTE.2011.V3.377

Tantithamthavorn, C., McIntosh, S., Hassan, A. E., & Matsumoto, K. (2016). Automated Parameter Optimization of Classification Techniques for Defect Prediction Models. In *Proceedings ofthe International Conference on Software Engineering (ICSE)*. doi:10.1145/2884781.2884857

Tsai, C. F., & Wu, J. W. (2008). Using neural network ensembles for bankruptcy prediction and credit scoring. *Expert Systems with Applications*, *34*(4), 2639–2649. doi:10.1016/j.eswa.2007.05.019

Wu, J., Cai, Z. H., & Ao, S. (2012). Hybrid dynamic k–nearest–neighbour and distance and attribute weighted method for classification. *International Journal of Computer Applications in Technology*, *43*(4), 378–384. doi:10.1504/IJCAT.2012.047164

Xiao, H., Xiao, Z., & Wang, Y. (2016). Ensemble classification based on supervised clustering for credit scoring. *Applied Soft Computing*, *43*, 73–86. doi:10.1016/j.asoc.2016.02.022

Xiao, W., Zhao, Q., & Fei, Q. (2006). A comparative study of data mining methods in consumer loans credit scoring management. *Journal of Systems Science and Systems Engineering*, *15*(4), 419–435. doi:10.1007/s11518-006-5023-5

Yeh, I. C., & Lien, C. H. (2009). The comparisons of data mining techniques for the predictive accuracy of probability of default of credit card clients. *Expert Systems with Applications*, *36*(2), 2473–2480. doi:10.1016/j.eswa.2007.12.020

Yu, L., Li, X., Tang, L., Zhang, Z., & Kou, G. (2015). Social credit: A comprehensive literature review. *Financial Innovation*, *1*(1), 1–18. doi:10.1186/s40854-015-0005-6

Yu, L., Wang, S., & Lai, K. K. (2008). Credit risk assessment with a multistage neural network ensemble learning approach. *Expert Systems with Applications*, *34*(2), 1434–1444. doi:10.1016/j.eswa.2007.01.009

Yu, M. C. (2011). Multi-criteria ABC analysis using artificial-intelligence-based classification techniques. *Expert Systems with Applications*, *38*(4), 3416–3421. doi:10.1016/j.eswa.2010.08.127

Zareapoor, M., Seeja, K. R., & Alam, M. A. (2012). Analysis on Credit Card Fraud Detection Techniques: Based on Certain Design Criteria. *International Journal of Computers and Applications*, *52*(3).

Zhou, L., Lai, K. K., & Yen, J. (2014). Bankruptcy prediction using SVM models with a new approach to combine features selection and parameter optimisation. *International Journal of Systems Science*, *45*(3), 241–253. doi:10.1080/00207721.2012.720293

Chapter 19
Prediction of the Quality of Fresh Water in a Basin

Sira M. Allende
Universidad de La Habana, Cuba

Carlos N. Bouza
Universidad de La Habana, Cuba

Daniel C. Chen
Smith and King College, UK

Agustin Santiago
Universidad Autónoma de Guerrero, Mexico

Jose Maclovio Sautto
Universidad Autónoma de Guerrero, Mexico

ABSTRACT

Derivatives play an important role in social and economic studies. They describe the behavior of conditional expectations. Once a phenomena is characterized by parametric specifications, the conditional expectation m(x) may be modeled by a regression function. Then, derivatives may be computed by fitting the regression function. In applications, parametric estimators are commonly used, because of the unknowledge of other more effective methods. The validity of a regression fitting approach depends on the knowledge of certain aspects related with the true functional form. In this paper, we develop a study on the usage of soft computing methods for providing an alternative to the use of non-parametric regression. We develop our modeling including neural networks and rough sets approaches. The studied problem is the eutrophication due to the growth of the population of algae. Real life data is provided by a study on a fresh water basin. They are used for developing a comparison of different approaches. A methodology is recommended for implementing a monitoring system of the water quality.

INTRODUCTION

Commonly, environment the studies of the quality of fresh water consider the level of eutrophication of a source. It is well-known that eutrophication plays a key role in evaluating water quality, nutrition status, organic pollution extent etc. The need of monitoring Chl-a leads to sampling field water, which is costly and time-consuming. Modernly, reliable data are obtained by using remote sensing. They should allow obtaining the necessary information on variables close related with Chl-a. Mathematically, this information permits to model the relationship of variables with Chl-a. Obtaining a mathematically based method will reduce costs and maintaining an adequate level of accuracy of the prediction on Chl-a.

DOI: 10.4018/978-1-5225-0997-4.ch019

The objectives of this study are accomplished by comparing the behavior of various classification techniques for establishing the quality of the water in the sample sites. A derivative model is used for predicting Chl-a. The data used for fixing an equation are derived by Allende et al. (2016) are used for prediction. The data were divided into a training sample and a validation sample. The true values of Chl-a allowed classifying the records as satisfying “is a source of potable water”, “is a source usable only for agriculture and similar proposes” and “is source of highly contaminated water”.

We derived a procedure based on the statistical ideas of classifying using the minimum distance of the variables to the mean vector of the class or to the nearest neighbor. A Neuronal Network was used with the same purposes. Bayesian principles supported establishing when the network was well trained. The validation sample was analyzed and the misclassification probabilities were computed for each method. Section 2 is concerned with the aspects of classification using statistical methods or Neural Networks. Section 2 and 3 presents issues on Rough Sets. In section 4 an evaluation of the behavior of the methods was made using a large set of data on contamination in a basin.

CLASSIFICATION

Classification is one of the most used techniques of the multivariate static tool-box. It may be described roughly as a technique concerned with assigning data cases (i.e. observations) to one of a fixed number of possible classes, see Sharma (1996). Classifing is present when dealing with the needs grouping. It has been developed firstly by statisticians. Machine learning researchers have given new insights both from the theoretical and computation issues of classification. They consider that classification is a process that permits learning the existence of patterns. It ends fixing how cases must be classified different predetermined classes of data. See discussion on this problem in Brooks (2010), Hastie-Tibshirani-Friedman (2001). Once the model is built, it can be used to classify new data. Hence, the goal of Classification is sorting observations into two or more labeled classes. The emphasis of it is on deriving a rule that can be used to optimally assign new objects to the classes.

When classifying we assign a membership to each data item (case). Each record is related to a variable of interest (Y), which allows classifying, and a set of covariates $\left(\underline{X}\right)$. Statisticians denominate the covariables “independent variables” and computer scientists “input variables”. A functional relationship between Y and $\underline{X}$ should be described. Take a case (observation) k. We evaluate, where $\underline{x}_k$, is the vector of attributes measured in case k and $\vec{w}$ represents a vector of parameters which $y_k = y_k\left(\underline{x}_k, \vec{w}\right)$ weights the importance of each coordinate of $\underline{x}_k$.

Let us consider that we have two classes c_1 and c_2. The outcome of the classification may be modeled the dichotomous variable

$$y_k = \begin{cases} 1 & if\ case\ k \in c_1 \\ 0 & if\ case\ k \in c_2 \end{cases}$$

The statistical community uses a decision theory framework for establishing the normative that leads to decide looking for the optimal class membership. An approach is considering as objective deriving a method for obtaining $Max\left\{P\left(Y \mid \underline{X}\right)\right\}$. Another approach is deriving an accurate model for describing $P\left(Y \mid \underline{X}\right)$. The expected result is not only to assign each data item to a class using y_k but to determine the probability of belonging to a certain class.

The modeling of this problem may be developed using different approaches such as Logistic Regression (LR), Artificial Neural Networks (ANN) or some particular clustering procedure. Their supporting theory are considerably different but the models look for providing a functional form and parameter vector and to express adequately (estimate, predict) the conditional probability $P\left(Y \mid \underline{X}\right) = \frac{P\left(Y, \underline{X}\right)}{P\left(\underline{X}\right)}$.

Statistical Motivated Methods

From a statistical point of view, the models lead to the development of clustering algorithms. They try determining groups of components or data, by considering the existence of a certain similarity in terms of their features. These ideas are in the kernel of the methods presented standardly, see Morrison (2004) and Sharma (1996) for example. The determination of a classification may be obtained by using different models. Each one determines the derivation of computing algorithms. The most commonly used procedures are classification rules, decision trees, or some mathematical formulae.

Is possible that the decision maker determines clusters by fixing some classification issues. One of them is fixing for each cluster *j* a point $\vec{q}_j = \left(q_{1j},..,q_{pj}\right)^T$, centroid. The centroid is a point that represents an equilibrium of the set of data

Another one is establishing a similarity criterion and grouping the most similar cases into a cluster. Once the clusters are formed we may determine the centroid of each group of data sets (cluster), $\hat{q}_j = \left(\hat{q}_{1j},..,\hat{q}_{pj}\right)^T$. Generally, it is the vector of the means of the parameter values of all the cases classified each clusters.

A popular approach for obtaining the clusters is to classify evaluating the distance between a point and the cluster centroid: $d\left(y_k, \theta_j\right)$, $\theta_j = q_{j,}\ \hat{q}_j$. The final output of a computer algorithm provides the membership of each case and a statistical description of the cluster centroids, together with the number of components in each of them.

A popularly used method is the so called K-means clustering. The decision maker fixes the number of clusters in advance. The cases are allocated to the clusters by using the decision rule

$$k \in c_j \ if \ d\left(y_k, \theta_j\right) = \min_t \left\{d\left(y_k, \theta_t\right)\right\}$$

The basic ideas in for implementing the existing software is using as cluster centroids the means. Their objective is minimizing intra-cluster dissimilarity. The distance measure are available in the modules of the packages.

The performance of the clustering is evaluated by partitioning, previously, the data set into training and test sets. Usually we select a sample from the original data set (training set). The records in the training set are used for determining the clusters. To each one is assigned a label identifying the belonging of record k to a certain class $c_j, j = 1,\ldots,J$. It is a function of the values of the attributes and identifies the class to which it is assigned. A good model assigns to the unseen records a correct class with a high frequency. Therefore, the accuracy of the classification model is measured by its ability to correctly classifying, the records of the validation set, once the analysis of the training set determines the clusters. Say, when the model performs well, its usage for classifying future or unknown objects provides adequate outputs.

Many reasons may be pointed out for suggesting that the testing set must be independent of the training set. The most important one is the over-fitting that occurs otherwise. Sometimes the data set is small and training set and testing set coincides. In these cases the estimation of the generalization error is often low. However estimating the bias is possible but provides an optimistic view of the model performance.

The evaluation of the behavior of a classification procedure is made by comparing the true classification of the records of the test sample with those derived by the model. The performance is measured by the accuracy rate. It is the percentage of the records in the test set that are correctly classified by the model.

A classification procedure yields for each record that $i \in c_j$ if $\underline{x}_i$ is close to a certain predetermined point $\underline{x}_j$. As mentioned, the closeness is measured by a certain distance or similarity measure. In our case we deal with continuous variables, then will use a distance measure.

Firstly consider using the Mahalanobis distance of the multivariate vector of covariables $\underline{x}_i = \left(x_{i1},\ldots,x_{iR}\right)^T$, from a class c_j. It is determined as a function of the mean vector $\underline{\mu}_j = \left(\mu_{j1},\ldots,\mu_{jR}\right)^T$ and the estimated covariance matrix S:

$$D_M\left(i,c_j\right) = \sqrt{\left(\underline{x}_i - \underline{\mu}_j\right)^T S^{-1}\left(\underline{x}_i - \underline{\mu}_j\right)}$$

The training sample is classified using the following classification rule:

$$y_{ic_j} = \begin{cases} 1 & if\ D_M\left(i,c_j\right) < \gamma \\ 2 & if\ \gamma \le D_M\left(i,c_j\right) < \vartheta \\ 3 & if\ D_M\left(i,c_j\right) \ge \vartheta \end{cases}$$

Then the validation set is studied and this rule is used for classifying the records. The number of misclassification is measured.

Another criteria for classifying the records is using the Nearest Neighbor Analysis (NN). It examines the distances between each record $\underline{x}_i$ to its closest point in the class c_j. A criteria is using Mahalanobis distance (generalized squared inter-point distance). Considering that we deal with two random vectors $\underline{x}_i$ and $\underline{x}_{C_j}$ with the same distribution and covariance matrix S we use

$$D_M\left(i,C_j\right) = \sqrt{\left(\underline{x}_i - \underline{x}_{C_j}\right)^T S^{-1}\left(\underline{x}_i - \underline{x}_{C_j}\right)}$$

The new classification rule is:

$$y_{iNN} = j \ if \ D_M\left(i, C_j\right) = Min_{t=1,..,J} D_M\left(i, C_t\right)$$

Take m as the size of the validation sample and

$$m_{ij} = \begin{cases} 1 & if \ is \ uncorrectly \ classified \ in \ C_j \\ 0 & otherwise \end{cases}$$

We compute the observed proportion

$$f_j = \frac{\sum_{i=1}^{m} m_{ij}}{m}$$

Then we may estimate the probability of misclassification by:

$$f = \sum_{j=1}^{J} f_j$$

The smaller is f the better is the clustering.

Artificial Neural Networks Motivated Methods (ANN)

Artificial Neural Networks (ANN) appears as a competitive procedure to statistical classification methods. This fact is pointed out in many books and papers, see for example Duda, Hart and Stork (2001), Han and Kambe (2006) and Ripley (1996. The growing popularity of this approach is due to its proved advantages for dealing with the representation of non-linear mappings for describing the behavior of multivariate data. That is commonly present when, the form of the mapping, is governed by several adjustable parameters. ANN predicts categorical class labels (discrete or nominal) and also classifies data (constructs a model). It uses a training set and the values (class labels) for classifying the attribute and uses the resulting model for classifying new input data.

ANN is used frequently by different professional in their practical research. ANN is preferred by computer scientists for classifying. They usually deal with finding out properties of non-symbolic information and in learning systems. Statisticians use ANN when is needed some flexibility, as is the case in nonlinear regression and classification models. Engineers use ANN because of the behaviour of its models performs well when studying signal processing and automatic control, for example. Advanced scientists of the Social Sciences and neuro-physiologists consider that ANN allows designing theoretical models for characterizing the complexity of the fact that thinking and consciousness are generated by multivariate variables that describe the High-level brain function. Physicists use this point of view for describing phenomena in statistical mechanics. There are a lot of areas where ANN is being introduced for describing and modelling. See Russel- Norvig (1995), Vapnik. (2000).

The fact that neural computing requires a number of interconnected neurons leads to the use of neural networks. The network is designed by considering that the neurons are arranged in layers. Each neuron within the network is usually a simple processing unit. Each neuron is feed on by one or more input variables and produces an output. A weight is assigned to each input. The weights modify the strength of each input. The work of the neuron is adding all the inputs and make the needed calculations for determining an output. Commonly the activation function is non-linear. The nature of our problem suggests using supervised training principles, as both the inputs and the outputs are provided. The input data x enters into the network by feeding the input layer. The ANN processes the input data with the resultant values steadily "percolating" through the network. The output of a layer is the input of the next layer. The outputs of the network are compared with the expected outputs. The ANN outputs are known in our case. The behaviour of the process is evaluated by computing an error. This value and the connection weights, assigned to the variables, are gradually adjusted. It works by working backwards, from the output layer, by feeding-back the previous hidden layers. The adjustment performed, when arriving to the input layer, determines the learning on the problem. The process is repeated again and again, until adequately correct outputs are obtained. Hence through this process that the network learns.

Another approach is based on using a Bayesian point of view. Let us consider that each attribute and class label are random variables and denote the attributes by $\left(A_1, A_2, \ldots, A_R\right)$. We aim predicting the class where each record should be classified. That is, we want to find the value that maximizes $\left(C_j \mid A_1, A_2, \ldots, A_R\right)$. With the results we may estimate the probability directly from the data by using the well-known Bayes theorem formula

$$P\left(C_j \mid A_1 A_2 \cdots A_R\right) = \frac{P\left(A_1 A_2 \cdots A_R \mid C_j\right) P\left(C_j\right)}{P\left(A_1 A_2 \cdots A_R\right)}$$

The independence assumption may not hold for some attributes but commonly practitioners assume that it holds for simplifying the analysis.

For discrete attributes, under the assumed independence among attributes we have that for a generic class C

$$P\left(A_1, A_2, \ldots, A_R \mid C\right) = P\left(A_1 \mid C\right) P\left(A_2 \mid C\right) \ldots P\left(A_R \mid C\right)$$

Each factor may be estimated using the observed n results by using, for the class c_j

$$\hat{P}\left(A_t \mid c_j\right) = \frac{\textit{number of observations of } A_t \textit{ when belonging to } c_j \textit{ is true}}{\textit{number of observations of } c_j} = \frac{n\left(tn_j\right)}{n\left(C_j\right)},$$

$$\hat{P}\left(C_j\right) = \frac{n\left(C_j\right)}{n}$$

For continuous attributes is needed to discretize the range of each one. Then the attributes are partitioned into bins and are counted the number of observation within each of them. Hence we use the estimator

$$P\left(C_j \mid A_1, A_2, \ldots, A_R\right) = \frac{number\ of\ observations\ of \left(A_1 A_2 \ldots A_R C_j\right)}{number\ of\ observations\ of\ P\left(A_1 A_2 \ldots A_R\right)}$$

Take $n\left(t\right)$ = number of observations of $A_t, t = 1, \ldots, R$. Due to the independence

$P\left(A_1 A_2 \ldots A_R\right) = \Pi_{t-1}^{R} n\left(t\right) / n$.

We will compare the Naïve Bayes Classifiers (NBC):
Original:

$$\hat{P}\left(A_t \mid C_j\right) = \frac{n\left(tC_j\right)}{n\left(C_j\right)}$$

then

$$\hat{P}_0\left(C_J \mid A_1, \ldots, A_R\right) = \hat{P}_{oc}\left(C_j\right) \frac{n\left(C_j\right)}{n} \Pi_{t-1}^{R} \frac{n\left(tC_j\right)}{n\left(C_j\right) \Pi_{t-1}^{R} n\left(t\right) / n}$$

Laplace:

$$\hat{P}\left(A_t \mid C_j\right) = \frac{n\left(tC_j\right) + 1}{n\left(C_j\right) + J}$$

then

$$\hat{P}_L\left(C_J \mid A_1, \ldots, A_R\right) = \hat{P}_{LC}\left(C_j\right) \frac{n\left(C_j\right)}{n} \Pi_{t-1}^{R} \frac{n\left(tC_j\right) + 1}{n\left(C_j\right) \Pi_{t-1}^{R} n\left(t\right) / n}$$

ξ – estimate:

$$\hat{P}\left(A_t \mid C_j\right) = \frac{n\left(i \int C_j\right) + \xi p}{n\left(C_j\right) + \xi}$$

then

$$\hat{P}_{\xi e}\left(C_J \mid A_1,\ldots,A_R\right)=\hat{P}_{\xi eC}\left(C_j\right)\frac{n\left(C_j\right)}{n}\Pi_{t-1}^{R}\frac{n\left(tC_j\right)+\xi p}{\left(n\left(C_j\right)+\xi\right)\Pi_{t-1}^{R}n\left(t\right)/n}$$

where p is a prior probability and ξ a known parameter.

The advantages of this methodology is that it is easy to implement and that it usually provides good results. The disadvantages are that the assuming class conditional independence generates a loss of accuracy (this is important as practically, dependencies exist among variables)

We designed a two-layer, feed-forward network. The initial weights were the parameters of the adjusted regression equation. Each record in the validation sample was an input. The prediction of the belonging to a class was the output. The regression parameters were adjusted looking for obtaining a sufficiently small value of the posterior probabilities for each class.

The learning ended when the NBC supported that the estimated posterior probabilities satisfied that

$$\hat{P}_{HC}\left(C_j\right)<n\left(j\right),\ H=O,L,\xi e;j=1,\ldots,J$$

Once the NNN was trained classify a record i of the validation sample and compute

$$z_{iHj}=\begin{cases}1 & if\ i\in C_j\ and\ is\ classified\ incorrectly\\ 0 & otherwise\end{cases},H=O,L,\xi e,j=1,..,J$$

The frequency of units in C_j incorrectly classified is given by:

$$f_{Hj}=\sum_{i\in C_j}\frac{z_{iHj}}{m\left(j\right)},H=O,L,\xi e,j=1,\ldots,J$$

$$m\left(j\right)=number\ of\ units\ of\ the\ validation\ sample\ in\ C_j.$$

ROUGH SETS DECISION RULES

RS theory is coming to the stock of intelligent data of more intelligence analysts. It has been pointed out that it overcomes, frequently, other intelligent methods as those based on fuzzy sets and statistical methods. This fact follows because it does not require of external parameters as it uses only the information provided by the data. Seminal ideas appear in Ning et al. (1995); Slowinski (1995) and Ziarko (1999).

Rough sets (RS) theory provides a new method for classifying. The mathematics tools, supporting it, allow extracting accurate knowledge from the available information. It is particularly useful when we deal with uncertainty and incomplete data. It assumes the existence of the needed information (knowledge) on the objects. Additionally in the theory is considered that both the universe and the objects may be divided into different groups. Objects are characterized by the same information and is indiscernible (similar). The indiscernibility Basic for mathematizing RS. Indiscernibility establishes the validity of considering that, if we have exactly the same information of two objects, it will be impossible distinguishing between them by using the available knowledge. In a learning system RS tries discovering the existence of redundancies and/or dependencies between the given features in the data to be classified.

The theory of RS can be used to find:

- Dependence relationships among data,
- The importance of attributes,
- Discover the patterns of data,
- Obtain knowledge on common decision-making rules,
- How to reduce all redundant objects and attributes, and
- The minimum subset of attributes that allows classifying correctly.

Moreover, RS has motivated the development of reduction algorithms enabling to approximate the decision classes. A discussion of particularities of RS is available in books as Kent (1994); Ning et al. (1995); Lin-Cercone (1997); Polkowski-Skowron (1998a and 1998b); Grzymala-Busse et al.(1999); Zhong-Skowron (2000).

In an information system there often exists some condition on the attributes that does not provide any additional information about the objects in U. So, we should remove those attributes, since the complexity and cost of decision process can be reduced, if those condition attributes are eliminated.

In many application we deal with attribute domains and classes where a preference-ordered is established. Our study is one of these cases. The class of potable water sources is preferred to that of being only usable for agriculture and it to sources with highly contaminated water. The domains of the attributes in our case are not ordered by a simple preference order. Some contaminants are more important than others, as greater values of them describes higher risks, when the water is consumed. Neglecting the importance may lead to wrong conclusions.

RS deals with inconsistencies that are not detectable by other knowledge discovery procedures. The discovery of inconsistencies in the frame work of RS relies on the so called dominance principle. Qualifying an object as better than another one, say "not being worse", is derived by the evaluation of analyzed attributes. Then it cannot be assigned to a worse class. The Dominance-based Rough Set Approach (DRSA) was first proposed in the papers of Greco- Matarazzo-Slowinski, (1998, 1999).

Denote U as a finite set of objects (universe), Q as a finite set of attributes, V_q as the domain of the q-*th* attribute and

$$f\left(\underline{x}, q\right): U \times Q \rightarrow V_q,$$

as a function that assigns an object to the q-*th* class.

Take a partition of the set Q into a set C of condition attributes when considering a decision attribute d. Note that the data information about the objects determine a matrix. Its rows are labelled by the objects. They represent the values of the attributes for each object. The columns are vectors of attributes. They represent the values of each attribute for the objects. We have that the decision attribute d induces a partition

$$U = \cup_{L=1}^{L^*} CL = \cup_{t\in T}\{CL_t, t \in T\}, T = \{1,\dots,n\}$$

The preference for the classes that formed CL is obtained by using the decision rule

$$\{\forall r,s \in T \textit{ the objects in } CL_r \textit{ are preferred to those in } CL_s \textit{ if } r > s\}$$

We are interested in approximating the sets defined by upward unions $CL_t^{\geq} = \cup_{s\geq t} CL_s$ and by downward unions $CL_t^{\leq} = \cup_{s\leq t} CL_s$ of classes. Note that:

- $CL_t^{\geq}$ contains objects $u \in CL_t$ or belonging to a more preferred class.
- $CL_t^{\leq}$ contains objects $u \in CL_t$ or belonging to a less preferred class.

Let us consider the weak preference relation on U given by the relationship $x \succsim_q y$ ("x is at least as good as y with respect to the criterion q"). That is "x dominates y with respect to P⊆ C, ($xD_P y$), when $x \succsim_q y$ holds for all q∈P". That may be modeled by fixing a function "f" such that

$$\forall q \in P : x \succsim_q y f(x,q) f(y,q).$$

A common criteria, coming from Decision Theory, leads to establish as a thumb-rule denominating as "P-dominating set" a set of objects dominating x such that

$$D_P^+(x) = \{y \in U | yD_P x\}.$$

Its counterpart is the set of objects dominated by x, called "P-dominated set" determined by:

$$D_P^-(x) = \{y \in U | xD_P y\}.$$

Fix P⊆C and consider the inclusion of a x∈U into $CL_t^{\geq}$, t=2, …, n. We deal then with a dominance principle inconsistency, whenever is observed that $x \in CL_t^{\geq}$ but $D_P^+(x) \cap CL_t^{\leq} \neq \varnothing$ or $xCL_t^{\geq}$, but $D_P^-(x) \cap CL_t^{\geq} \neq \varnothing$. When P⊆C, the inclusion creates an inconsistency in the sense of the dominance principle (DP). Hence, establishing $x \in CL_t^{\geq}$ has some ambiguity. It makes sense considering $x \in CL_t^{\geq}$, with respect to P⊆C, if the decision attribute d, assigns x to CL_t or, according to d, $\lambda_1, \lambda_2, \lambda_3$ and λ_4. There is inconsistency in the sense of the DP with another object $y \in CL_t^{\geq}$. For P⊆C, P-lower approximation (PLA) of $CL_t^{\geq}$ and P-upper approximation (PUA) are defined, respectively, by

$$\underline{P}\left(CL_t^{\geq}\right)=\left\{x\in U\left|D_P^{+}\left(x\right)CL_t^{\geq}\right.\right\}$$

and

$$\overline{P}\left(CL_t^{\geq}\right)=\left\{x\in U\left|D_P^{-}\left(x\right)\cap CL_t^{\geq}\neq\varnothing\right.\right\},t\in T\,.$$

Taking $CL_t^{\leq}$ we may define alternatively the PUA and PLA as

$$\overline{P}\left(CL_t^{\leq}\right)=\left\{x\in U\left|D_P^{+}\left(x\right)\cap CL_t^{\leq}\neq\varnothing\right.\right\}$$

and

$$\underline{P}\left\{x\in U\left|D_P^{-}\left(x\right)CL_t^{\leq}\right.\right\}.$$

If and $u\in CL_t^{\geq}$ clearly we have an ambiguity. This fact determines the existence of a boundary. They are given by the so called P-boundaries of

$$CL_t^{\geq},B_{nP}\left(CL_t^{\geq}\right)=\overline{P}\left(CL_t^{\geq}\right)-\underline{P}\left(CL_t^{\geq}\right)$$

and of

$$CL_t^{\leq},B_{nP}\left(CL_t^{\leq}\right)=\overline{P}\left(CL_t^{\leq}\right)-\underline{P}\left(CL_t^{\leq}\right).$$

Note that PLA´s of unions of classes model the existence of knowledge provided by the criteria coming from P⊆C, while the PUA´s similarly represent the existence of information. On the other hand the P-boundaries contain doubtful knowledge.

The measurement of the classification quality of a certain set of attributes P and the criteria CL is made by the ratio

$$\gamma_P\left(CL\right)=\frac{Card\left\{U-\cup_{t\in T}B_{nP}\left(CL_t^{\geq}\right)\right\}}{Card\ U}=\frac{Card\left\{U-\cup_{t\in T}B_{nP}\left(CL_t^{\leq}\right)\right\}}{Card\ U}$$

Note that this expression is a proportion. Then once a sample is selected, we may compute an estimate of the true value of the quality measure of the classification. Following the appeal to the Moivre-Laplace´s Theorem is sustained that using a sample s.

$$\widehat{\gamma_P}\left(CL\right) = \frac{Card\left\{s - \cup_{t\in T} B_{nP}\left(CL_t^{\geq}\left|s\right.\right)\right\}}{Card\ s} \sim> N\left(\gamma_P\left(CL\right), \frac{\gamma_P\left(CL\right)\left(1-\gamma_P\left(CL\right)\right)}{Card\ s}\right)$$

This approximation allows considering the construction of confidence intervals and performing normal based testing.

As discussed previously the true values of Chl-a allowed classifying the records in the classes:

Pot = A source of potable water.
Ag = A source usable only for agriculture and similar proposes.
HC = A source of highly contaminated water.

The partition is denoted by:

$$CL = \left\{CL_{Pot}, CL_{AG}, CL_{HC}\right\}$$

is obviously ordered in terms of preference (usefulness).

THE STUDY OF THE BASIN

The study of the quality of the water in basins is of importance in environmental studies of water pollution. A key factor is the concentration of chlorophyll. It is considered as the most important parameter as it allows determining the water quality, the nutrition status as well as the organic pollution extent.

The biologists commonly use the hyper spectral reflectance, as it is provides measurements of different variables on the water components. Among them is chlorophyll-a. An emerging approach to laboratory spectroscopic analysis is using derivatives, due to the similarity of its research objectives with those coped in economy and financial. The growing use of this mathematical method is due to the fact that the first-order derivative (FOD) seems to remove pure water effects and the second-order derivative (SOD) has proved abilities for removing suspended sediment effects. For serious discussions see, Han (2005) for example. Additionally, advanced researchers has established the existence of an evident capability, of the FOD spectrum, for overcoming the traditional band ratio model. Some examples are the papers of Chen et al. (2007): Duan et al. [2010], Han (2005) and Le et al (2009). They made different comparisons of semi-empirical algorithms, founding that the FOD-model described the real data more accurately than the usual band ratio and three-band model. The derived empirical results also supported that the FOD-model also was better than the single-band and band ratio model.

We will consider as variables the reflectance at the wavelengths $\lambda_1, \lambda_2, \lambda_3$ and λ_4 denoted

$$B_{nP}\left(CL_t^{\leq}\right) = \overline{P}\left(CL_t^{\leq}\right) - \underline{P}\left(CL_t^{\leq}\right).$$

The relation among the variables is described by Clorophyll concentration at measurement:

$$t = CC_t = c + m\left(\vec{X}_t\right) + \varepsilon_t = c + \sum_{b=1}^{4} f_b\left(X_b\right).$$

The regression function is:

$$\widehat{m_H}\left(\vec{x}\right) = \begin{cases} \sum_{t=1}^{T} \frac{CC_t K_H\left(\frac{\vec{x}_t - \vec{x}}{h}\right)}{\sum_{t=1}^{T} K_H\left(\frac{\vec{x}_t - \vec{x}}{h}\right)}, & K_H\left(\frac{\vec{x}_t - \vec{x}}{h}\right) \neq 0 \\ 0, & otherwise \end{cases}$$

Bouza et al. (2016) analyzed the behavior of the kernels

$K_{NW}\left(u\right) = I\left(\left|u\right|\right) \leq 1$, Nadaraya-Watson

$K_E\left(u\right) = \frac{3}{4}\left(1 - u^2\right) I\left(\left|u\right|\right) \leq 1$, Epanechnikov

$K_G\left(u\right) = \exp\left(-\frac{u^2}{2}\right) / \sqrt{2\pi}$, Gaussian

Following the experiments of Cheng et al. (2013), Bouza et al. (2016) generated randomly the ´s using the existing data and the model tuning method of Zimba and Gitelson [2006]. The four-band model was built according to the method of Le et al. [2009].

The studied population consisted of 12 035 measurements obtained from an environmental satellite used for monitoring (see Table 1).

The procedure of Yang et al. (2003) with Härdle-Stoker (1989) method were compared with these data set by Bouza et al. (2016). The main result was determining that the kernel of Epanechnikov had the best performance and the method the derived by Yang et al. (2003) the best method. A training sample of 6 000 records was selected randomly from the population. The data were classified in C_1, C_2 or C_3 using the real values of CC_t. We use both Epanechikovkenel and Yang et al.´s method for predicting CC_t in the validation sample.

The training sample was classified using the following classification rule

$$C_1 = \left\{t \middle| CC_t < 40mg.m^3\right\}$$

$$C_2 = \left\{t \middle| 40mg.m^3 \leq CC_t < 67{,}5\,mg.m^3\right\}$$

Table 1. Statistical results of the population

	Chl-a mg-m^{-3}	X_1	X_2	X_3	X_4
Minimum	3,8	647,6	698,4	660,4	643,1
Maximum	160,3	689,2	718,3	849.2	747,7
Mean	34,2	674,3	700,3	750,8	695,6
Median	28,8	652,9	707,9	753,1	683,6
Standard deviation	40,7	1,4	6,67	33,6	44,7

$$C_3 = \left\{ t \middle| CC_t \geq 67{,}5 mg.m^3 \right\}$$

The validation sample was classified with respect to the mean vectors of the classes using the rule:

$$y_{iC} = \begin{cases} 1 & if\ D_M\left(i, C_1\right) < 4,50 \\ 2 & if\ 4,50 \leq D_M\left(i, C_1\right) < 15,50 \\ 3 & if\ D_M\left(i, C_1\right) \geq 15,50 \end{cases}$$

When using the nearest neighbor the classification rule used was:

$$y_{iNN} = j\ if\ D_M\left(i, C_j\right) = Min_{t=1,..,J} D_M\left(i, C_t\right)$$

For the NNN classifying using NCB criteria we fixed $\eta\left(j\right) = 0,2$. The prior was the less informative and ζ was the population mean.

The first criteria are continuous and the data matrix analyzed for using the Dominance-based Rough Set Approach yielded that:

- The consistency of data matrix for every water quality criteria (the C-lower approximation and C-upper approximation of coincide).
- With 5 reducts of the criteria we ensured an adequate quality level of the classification when compared with the set of the 4 criteria (Hence some subsets of criteria are equally good and sufficient for deriving an accurate approximation of the classification). They are:
  - REDCl ={A1, A4 }, REDCl ={A2, A4}, REDCl ={A3, A4},
  - REDCl ={A1, A4}, REDCl ={A2, A3, A4},
- Are usable the minimal sets of decision rules:

M1: $if\ X_1 \geq 650\ and\ X_4 > 700\ then\ HC$

M2: $if\ X_2 < 700\ and\ X_4 \leq 610\ then\ AG$

M3: $if\ X_3 > 700\ and\ X_4 > 660\ or\ X_1 > 660\ and\ X_2 \geq 700\ then\ HC$

M4: $if\ X_3 < 700, X_4 \left\langle 600\ and\ X_1 \right\rangle 650\ then\ Pot$

We computed the proportion of wrong classification provided by each minimal set

$$f\left(M\left(t,j\right)\right) = \frac{number\ of\ missclassifictaions\ of\ records\ using\ Mt\ in\ the\ class\ j}{number\ of\ record\ in\ the\ sample},$$

$t = 1,\ldots,4, j = 1,2,3$

The estimation of the probabilities of misclassification are given in Table 2.

Table 2. Estimated misclassification probabilities

	Classes (j)			Total Misclassification Probability
	1	2	3	
Distance to the mean	0,119	0,136	0,043	0,259
Nearest Neighbor Distance	0,040	0,113	0,097	0,250
Artificial Neural Networks Motivated Methods				
f_{Oj}	0,120	0,148	0,127	0,395
f_{Lj}	0,146	0,094	0,177	0,417
f_{mej}	0,031	0,185	0,091	0,307
Rough Sets Decision Rules				
$f\left(M\left(1,j\right)\right)$	0,130	0,117	0,069	0,318
$f\left(M\left(2,j\right)\right)$	0,207	0,116	0,077	0,400
$f\left(M\left(3,j\right)\right)$	0,134	0,095	0.054	0,283
$f\left(M\left(4,j\right)\right)$	0,096	0,127	0,106	0,329

CONCLUSION

The best overall classification method is using the "Nearest Neighbor Distance". If the most important issue is classifying correctly the potable water, the best method is the ANNMM with the m-estimate; while the behavior of f_{Lj} provides the smaller misclassification probability when classifying the water for agricultural use. The "Distance to the mean" appeared as the best procedure for classifying as highly contaminated. The performance of the decision rule M3 was the best when applying Rough Sets and for ANNMM the same qualification is obtained by f_{mej}.

REFERENCES

Allende, S. M., Chen, D. C., Bouza, C. N., Sautto, J. M., & Santiago, A. (2016): Estimation of derivatives, from economy to environment: a study of the management of eutrophication of a fresh water basin's data. In Models and Methods for Supporting Decision Making in Human Health and Environment Protection. Nova Science Publishers.

Brooks, R. (2010). *Advanced Derivatives and Strategies. Introduction to Derivatives and Risk Management* (8th ed.,). Mason, OH: Cengage Learning.

Chen, C. Q., Tang, S. L., Xing, Q. G., Yang, J. K., Zhan, H. G., & Shi, H. Y. (2007): A Derivative Spectrum Algorithm for Determination of Chlorophyll-a Concentration in the Pearl River Estuary. In *Proceedings of Geoscience and Remote Sensing Symposium*. doi:10.1109/IGARSS.2007.4422949

Cheng, C., Wei, Y., Sun, X., & Zhou, Y. (2013). Estimation of Chlorophyll-a Concentration in Turbid Lake Using Spectral Smoothing and Derivative Analysis. *International Journal of Environmental Research and Public Health, 10*(7), 2979–2994. doi:10.3390/ijerph10072979 PMID:23880727

Duan, H. T., Ma, R. H., Xu, J. P., Zhang, B., & Zhang, B. (2010). Comparison of different semi-empirical algorithms to estimate chlorophyll-a concentration in inland lake water. *Environmental Monitoring and Assessment, 170*(1-4), 231–244. doi:10.1007/s10661-009-1228-7 PMID:19908152

Duda, R. O., Hart, P. E., & Stork, D. G. (2001). *Pattern Classification* (2nd ed.). John Wiley & Sons.

Greco, S., Matarazzo, B., & Slowinski, R. (1998). A new rough set approach to evaluation of bankruptcy risk. In Operational Tools in the Management of Financial Risk. Boston: Kluwer Academic Publishers.

Greco, S., Matarazzo, B., & Slowinski, R. (1999). In T. Gal, T. Hanne, & T. Stewart (Eds.), *The use of rough sets and fuzzy sets in MCDM. In Advances in Multiple Criteria Decision Making* (pp. 14.1–14.59). Boston: Kluwer Academic Publishers.

Grzymala-Busse, J., Pawlak, Z., Slowinski, R., & Ziarko, W. (1999). Rough sets. *Communications of the ACM, 38*(11).

Han, J., & Kamber, M. (2006). *Data Mining: Concepts and Techniques* (2nd ed.). Morgan Kaufmann Publishers.

Han, L. H. (2005). Estimating chlorophyll-a concentration using first-derivative spectra in coastal water. *International Journal of Remote Sensing, 26*(23), 5235–5244. doi:10.1080/01431160500219133

Härdle, W., & Stoker, T. M. (1989). Investigating Smooth Multiple Regression by the Method of Average Derivatives. *Journal of the American Statistical Association, 84*(408), 986–995.

Hastie, T., Tibshirani, R., & Friedman, J. (2001). *The elements of statistic all earning: data mining, inference, and prediction*. New York: Springer.

Kent, R. E. (1994). Rough concept analysis, rough sets, fuzzy sets knowledge discovery. *Proceedings of the International Workshop on Rough, Sets, Knowledge, Discovery*. Springer-Verlag Berlin. doi:10.1007/978-1-4471-3238-7_30

Le, C. F., Li, Y. M., Zha, Y., Sun, D. Y., Huang, C. H., & Lu, H. (2009). A four-band semi-analytical model for estimating chlorophyll a in highly turbid lakes: The case of Taihu Lake, China. *Remote Sensing of Environment, 113*(6), 1175–1182. doi:10.1016/j.rse.2009.02.005

Lin, T. Y., & Cercone, N. (1997). *Rough Sets and Data Mining*. Kluwer Academic Publishers.

Morrison, D. F. (2004). Multivariate Statistical Methods (4th ed.). Duxbury Press.

Pal, S. K. (2004). Soft data mining, computational theory of perceptions, and rough-fuzzy approach. *Information Science, 163*(1-3), 5–12. doi:10.1016/j.ins.2003.03.014

Pitois, S., Jackson, M. H., & Wood, B. J. (2001). Sources of the eutrophication problems associated with toxic algae: An overview. *Journal of Environmental Health, 64*, 25–32. PMID:11764678

Polkowski, L., & Skowron, A. (1998). Rough Sets in Knowledge Discovery: Vol. 1. *2. Studies in Fuzziness and Soft Computing series*. Berlin: Physica–Verlag.

Ripley, B. D. (1996). *Pattern Recognition and Neural Networks*. Cambridge, UK: Cambridge University Press. doi:10.1017/CBO9780511812651

Russel, S., & Norvig, P. (1995). *Artificial Intelligence - A Modern Approach*. Upper Saddle River, NJ: Prentice Hall.

Sharma, S. (1996). Applied Multivariate Techniques. John Wiley & Sons.

Slowinski, R. (1995). Rough set approach to decision analysis. *AI Expert*, (March), 19–25.

Vapnik, V. (2000): The nature of of statistical learning theory (2nd ed.). New York: Springer. doi:10.1007/978-1-4757-3264-1

Yang, L., Sperlichb, S., & Härdle, W. (2003). Derivative estimation and testing in generalized additive models. *Journal of Statistical Planning and Inference, 115*, 521 – 542.

Zhang, Y. L., & Qin, B. Q. (2001). Study prospect and evolution of eutrophication in lakeTaihu. *Shanghai Environ. Sci., 20*, 263–265.

Ziarko, W. (1999). Discovery through rough set theory. Knowledge Discovery: Viewing wisdom from all perspectives. *Communications of the ACM, 42*(11), 54–57. doi:10.1145/319382.319393

Zimba, P. V., & Gitelson, A. A. (2006). Remote estimation of chlorophyll concentration inhypereutrophic aquatic systems: Model tuning and accuracy optimization. *Aquaculture (Amsterdam, Netherlands), 256*(1-4), 272–286. doi:10.1016/j.aquaculture.2006.02.038

Chapter 20
Operating Commodities Market by Automated Traders

Fodil Laib
CEVITAL Group, Algeria

Mohammed Said Radjef
Unit Research LaMOS, Algeria

ABSTRACT

This is an introductory work to the field of automatizing futures markets, related to commodities, so far operated by human traders. First, we build a mathematical framework for a futures market with many producers and consumers represented by automated traders in the market platform. Then we suggest an automatic trading strategy for the automatons. This strategy takes into account the forecasts of supply and demand streams as well as the evolution of nominal price. Later, we recall a set of analytical criteria used to measure the performance of a trading strategy. Next, we illustrate our approach by showing a price pattern generated by the automatic strategy and calculate its performances. Finally, we exhibit a heuristic based on simulation allowing to compute a quasi-optimal parameters matrix for this automatic trading system.

INTRODUCTION

Since their inception in mid-1850 in the US, initially intended for corn and wheat trading, futures markets had expanded and diversified in the community of merchants, producers, farmers, consumers, speculators, thanks to the flexibility brought in hedging prices of crops, metals, crude oil, etc (CBOT, 1998 ; Hull, 2002). The basic instrument traded in this market is a *futures contract* which is a binding agreement between a seller and a buyer, it is related to a specific commodity (the underlying), with specific delivery time and location. The main feature of a futures transaction is that the price of the commodity is fixed at the present time, whereas the effective delivery of the merchandize, from the seller to the buyer, will occur in a future date, which could be several months or years ahead (Teweles & Jones, 1999).

Automation in futures markets had partially started in the last two decades by replacing pit brokers by central computers receiving orders from outside human traders. The computer saves the orders, sort

DOI: 10.4018/978-1-5225-0997-4.ch020

them depending on their types and price values, performs transactions and updates traders' positions (Barcley et al., 2003; Weber, 2006). A detailed mathematical description of the futures market's platform was provided in (Laib & Radjef, 2011a), the market mechanism was explained as well as the evolution of traders' positions. Nowadays, another step in the automation process is necessary. We suggest herein to replace the human traders, so far operating futures market, by automated traders sufficiently intelligent to react to the supply and demand (S&D) forecasts and make price projections, then issue sale and buy orders which are channeled to market platform where they are executed. We consider a market where two groups of automated traders are involved. The first group is representing the interests of producers looking to hedge their selling price and the second group of automatons are working on behalf of consumers looking to hedge their buying price. This new practice may bring more rationality to the futures market and avoid major financial crashes and speculative bubbles due to irrational behavior of human traders (Ohara, 1998; Roll, 1988).

Several studies in the literature suggested approaches based on technical analysis (Murphy, 1999) to automate the process of trading in futures markets. These approaches assesses the price history and other indicators, like exchanged daily volumes and open interest, in order to establish the relevant order to put in the market platform. Shelton (Shelton, 1997) suggested an original approach of trading futures formulated as a theoretical 2-person game against nature between a trader and the market; the market was assumed to have different moods (risky, less risky, etc.), and the trader has several strategies (takes an aggressive position, less aggressive, exiting the market). The price formation process and its link with investors' behavior has inspired many authors like Levy (Levy, 2008) who applied the principle of phase transition known in statistical mechanics to interpret price patterns. Preist (Preist, 1999) has suggested an agent-based technic for trading commodities via the Internet; a set of agents, representing the participants, enter into negotiation in a series of double auctions in order to determine the market price. A genetic approach developed in (Arthur et al., 1996) helped to clarify the link between fundamental trading and technical trading and showed how bubbles occur.

The next section outlines the mathematical formulation of the futures market's mechanism designed for many producers and consumers, it shows how transactions occur and how traders' positions are updated. The third section introduces the automatic trading strategy used by automatons to issue their selling and buying orders. This strategy takes into account the stream of S&D forecasts as well as the evolution of nominal price. The strategy was parameterized in order to facilitate its tuning later in conjunction with the stochastic profiles of the producers and consumers' S&D forecasts profiles. A set of seven analytical criteria measuring the performance of a trading strategy are provided in the fourth section. When aggregated, these criteria provide the average performance of the strategy measured on one set of S&D forecasts time-series; over a sample of time-series, we compute the global performance. The fifth section illustrates our study by the mean of two computational examples, in both cases we consider a market with 3 producers and 4 consumers having specific S&D forecasts profiles. In the first example, we assume a fixed trading parameters matrix, then a Matlab code plots the price pattern resulting from our automatic trading strategy and displays the obtained average and global performances. The second example is a simulation-based heuristic allowing to compute the quasi-optimal parameters matrix for our trading strategy.

THE FUTURES MARKET SETUP

Consider a raw commodity which is produced by n_1 producers and purchased by n_2 consumers or users. The producers and consumers are going to use the futures market (Teweles & Jones, 1999) to hedge their prices for a future delivery. Each producer is represented in the futures market platform by an automated seller designed to hedge the selling price of the forthcoming crop of this producer. Similarly, each consumer is represented by an automated buyer conceived to fix the purchasing price of the commodity ahead of it actual reception by this consumer. Herein, $n = n_1 + n_2$ automated traders are allowed to trade. Let's $\mathcal{N}_1$ be the set of sellers, $\mathcal{N}_2$ the set of buyers and $\mathcal{N}$ the set of all players, given by

$$N_1 = \left\{f_1;\ldots;n1\right\}g; N2 = fn1+1;::::;ng; N = N1 \setminus N2 :$$

$$\mathcal{N}_1 = \left\{1,\ldots,n_1\right\}, \mathcal{N}_2 = \left\{n_1+1,\ldots,n\right\}, \mathcal{N} = \mathcal{N}_1 \cap \mathcal{N}_2$$

The trading process evolves over discrete periods t_j, $j=1,\ldots,m$; an initial period t_0 is added to the game, though no transaction takes place at this instant, t_0 serves only to initiate some variables. Each producer $i \in \mathcal{N}_1$ will deliver his crop at the final instant t_m, and only at this time, he will have a precise value of the exact quantity he will be able to deliver; at a prior instant t_j, $j=0,\ldots,m-1$, the supplier has only a forecasted value $S_i(t_j)$ of his crop, $S_i \in \mathrm{R}^+$. In parallel, consumer $i \in \mathcal{N}_2$ will know the exact amount of his needs at the final time t_m; before this instant, he has only forecasted values $D_i(t_j)$, $j=0,\ldots, m-1$, of his demand, $D_i \in \mathrm{R}^+$.

As illustrated by Figure 1, the setup of the futures market proposed herein is inspired partially from the setup of a real futures market where sale and buy orders are directed respectively to the list of selling orders LSO and buying orders LBO (Laib & Radjef, 2011a).

Figure 1. Futures market with many producers and consumers

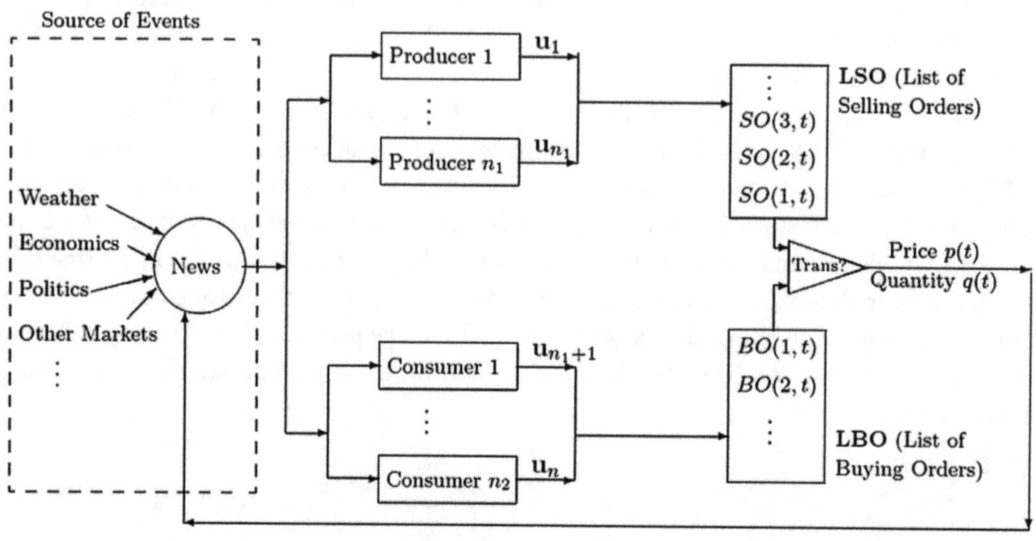

Let's $SD(t_j) = [S_1(t_j), \ldots, S_{n1}(t_j), D_1(t_j), \ldots, D_{n2}(t_j)]^T$. At instant t_j, total forecasted supply and demand are respectively

$$S(t_j) = \sum_{i=1}^{n_1} SD_i(t_j), D(t_j) = \sum_{i=n_1+1}^{n} SD_i(t_j)$$

The order of an automated seller has the following form

$$\boldsymbol{u}_i(t_j) = \left[u_{i1}(t_j), u_{i2}(t_j)\right] \equiv [selling\text{ - }price, selling\text{ - }quantity], i \in \mathcal{N}_1,$$

$u_{i1} \in R^+$, $u_{i2} \in Z^-$, meaning that seller i would like to sell a maximum quantity of $u_{i2}(t_j)$ units with a minimum unit price of $u_{i1}(t_j)$. Similarly, the order of an automated buyer is

$$\boldsymbol{u}_i(t_j) = \left[u_{i1}(t_j), u_{i2}(t_j)\right] \equiv [buying\text{ - }price, buying\text{ - }quantity], i \in \mathcal{N}_2,$$

$u_{i1} \in R^+$, $u_{i2} \in Z^+$, where $u_{i2}(t_j)$ is the maximum quantity buyer i would like to buy and $u_{i1}(t_j)$ is the maximum unit price he would like to pay for this quantity.

Assuming that at instant t_j, the best sale order is

$$LSO(t_j, 1) = \left[i_s, j_s, u_{i_s1}, u_{i_s2}\right]$$

and the best buy order is

$$LBO(t_j, 1) = \left[i_b, j_b, u_{i_b1}, u_{i_b2}\right],$$

a transaction will occur at this instant, between the seller i_s and buyer i_b, if selling-quantity and buying-quantity verify

$$u_{i_s2} > 0 \text{ and } u_{i_b2} > 0$$

and the selling-price and buying-price satisfy

$$u_{i_s1} \leq u_{i_b1}.$$

In this case, the transactional price and quantity will be

$$p(t_j) = u_{i_s1} 1_{[j_s \leq j_b]} + u_{i_b1} 1_{[j_s > j_b]}, q(t_j) = \min\left\{\mid u_{i_s2} \mid, u_{i_b2}\right\}$$

where j_s and j_b are respectively the issuing times of the seller order LSO(t_j, 1) and buyer order LBO(t_j, 1); and the condition-function $1_{[C]}=1$ if condition C is satisfied, otherwise $1_{[C]}=0$.

Positions $y_i(t_j)$ of traders are initiated as $y_i(t_0)=0, \forall i \in \mathcal{N}$, then updated as follows

$$y_{i_s}(t_j)=y_{i_s}(t_{j-1})-q(t_j),$$

$$y_{i_b}(t_j)=y_{i_b}(t_{j-1})+q(t_j),$$

$$y_i(t_j)=y_i(t_{j-1}), \forall i \in \mathcal{N} \setminus \{i_s, i_b\}$$

for j=1,…,m. If no transaction takes place at instant t_j, then we set conventionally $p(t_j)=p(t_{j-1})$, $q(t_j)=0$ and

$$y_i(t_j)=y_i(t_{j-1}), \forall i \in \mathcal{N}.$$

We assume that at any instant t_j, a maximum of three elementary events can occur in a prescribed sequence: At most one new forecast, either supply or demand, can be received by an automated trader, then at most one new selling or buying order can be issued by a trader, then at most one transaction can be executed; Figure 2 illustrates different scenarios.

AUTOMATIC TRADING STRATEGY

Herein we suggest a trading strategy allowing to the automated traders to operate the futures market by issuing sale and buy orders based on the stream of S&D forecasts and the moves in the underlying nominal price, p_N. As a measure of S&D balance, we use the gap function defined by

$$G(t_j)=S(t_j)-D(t_j).$$

Figure 2. Unfolding of events at instant t_j

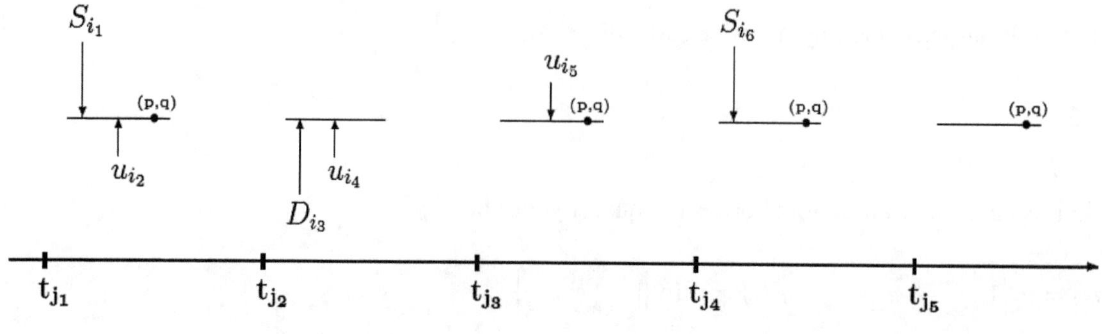

Then, we define the relative change in the gap by

$$\delta G\left(t_j\right) = \frac{G\left(t_j\right) - G\left(t_{j-1}\right)}{\left|G\left(t_{j-1}\right)\right| + \int},$$

where ε is a small positive number guaranteeing the fact that the above denominator is always positive. The relative change $\delta G(t_j)$ compares the state of S&D balance of the current instant with that of the prior instant. The sign and value of this function is the catalyst of the next price move.

Firstly, according to this strategy, the selling-price of an automated seller $i \in \mathcal{N}_1$ and/or the buying-price of an automated buyer $i \in \mathcal{N}_2$, are established by the following formula

$$u_{i1}(t_j) = \left[\alpha_{i1} p_{_N}(t_j) - (1 - \alpha_{i1}) p(t_{j-1})\right] \times \left[1 - \alpha_{i2} \delta G(t_j)\right].$$

This relation works for both sellers and buyers, the only difference from one trader to another is the value of parameters $\alpha_{i1}, \alpha_{i2} \in [0,1]$, $i \in \mathcal{N}$. In relation (11), the purpose of the first parameter α_{i1} is to find a good equilibrium between the current nominal price $p_N\left(t_j\right)$ and the price of the prior transaction, $p\left(t_{j-1}\right)$. The second parameter α_{i2} attempts to assign the right weight for S&D balance, via the relative change function $\delta G\left(t_j\right)$, in the construction of command $u_{i1}\left(t_j\right)$ of trader i. As we will see later, in order to maximize the global performance of this trading strategy, the choice of these parameters should be carried out in an optimal way.

Secondly, our trading strategy suggests to compute the selling-quantity of seller i by the following relation

$$u_{i2}(t_j) = -\frac{SD_i(t_j) + y_i\left(t_{j-1}\right)}{\alpha_{i_3}(m - j + 1)}, i \in \mathcal{N}_1.$$

Namely, this strategy considers the current position $y_i\left(t_{j-1}\right)$ of seller *i* and the remaining quantity he needs to sell $SD_i\left(t_j\right)$, then dividing the difference by the number of periods remaining in the trading process. Parameter $\alpha_{i_3} \in [0,1]$ offers the ability to adjust in an optimal way the offered quantities by the seller. Applying the same reasoning on the buying side, the buying-quantity requested by buyer *i* is calculated by

$$u_{i2} t_j = \frac{SD_i(t_j) - y_i(t_{j-1})}{\alpha_{i_3}(m - j + 1)}, i \in \mathcal{N}_2.$$

Summarizing, this strategy assigns to each trader *i*, three parameters $\alpha_{11}, \alpha_{12}, \alpha_{13}$ which need to be calculated by an optimization method to guarantee a maximum performance of the trading strategy. The parameters of all automated traders are arranged in the following $\left(n_1 + n_2\right) \times 3$ *parameters-matrix* $\underline{\alpha}$ where the upper part is the sellers' parameters and the lower part is buyers' parameters

$$\underline{\alpha} = \begin{bmatrix} \alpha_{11} & \alpha_{12} & \alpha_{13} \\ \vdots & \vdots & \vdots \\ \alpha_{n_1,1} & \alpha_{n_1,2} & \alpha_{n_1,3} \\ \alpha_{n_1+1,1} & \alpha_{n_1+1,2} & \alpha_{n_1+1,3} \\ \vdots & \vdots & \vdots \\ \alpha_{n,1} & \alpha_{n,2} & \alpha_{n,3} \end{bmatrix}.$$

MEASURING PERFORMANCE OF A TRADING STRATEGY

Let's $\boldsymbol{S} = [S(t_0), \ldots, S(t_m)]$ and $\boldsymbol{D} = [D(t_0), \ldots, D(t_m)]$ be two time-series of S&D forecasts respectively. In order to measure the efficiency (Laib & Radjef, 2011b) of a trading strategy γ, we use the below criteria,

$$z_1(\gamma, \mathbf{S}, \mathbf{D}) = \frac{1}{m} \sum_{j=1}^{m} 1_{\left[sign\left(G(t_j) - G(t_{j-1})\right) = -sign\left(p(t_j) - p(t_{j-1})\right)\right]},$$

$$z_2(\gamma, \mathbf{S}, \mathbf{D}) = \frac{1}{m-1} \sum_{j=1}^{m-1} 1_{\left[sign\left(G(t_{j+1}) - G(t_j)\right) = sign\left(p(t_j) - p(t_{j-1})\right)\right]},$$

$$z_3(\gamma, \mathbf{S}, \mathbf{D}) = \frac{1}{m} \sum_{j=1}^{m} 1_{\left[sign\left(G(t_j)\right) = -sign\left(p(t_j) - p_N(t_j)\right)\right]},$$

$$z_4(\gamma, \mathbf{S}, \mathbf{D}) = \frac{1}{m-h} \sum_{k=1}^{m-h} 1_{\left[\left|\sigma_G(t_k, t_{k+h}) - \sigma_p(t_k, t_{k+h})\right| \le \epsilon\right]},$$

$$z_5(\gamma, \mathbf{S}, \mathbf{D}) = \frac{1}{m} 1_{\left[q(t_j) > 0\right]},$$

$$z_6(\gamma, \mathbf{S}, \mathbf{D}) = \frac{1}{m-h} \sum_{k=1}^{m-h} 1_{\left[\sigma_q(t_k, t_{k+h}) \le \epsilon\right]},$$

$$z_7(\gamma, \mathbf{S}, \mathbf{D}) = \frac{1}{n} \sum_{i \in \mathcal{N}} \frac{\min\left\{ | y_i(t_m) |; SD_i(t_m) \right\}}{\max\left\{ | y_i(t_m) |; SD_i(t_m) \right\}}.$$

where ϵ is a small positive number; σ_G, σ_p and σ_q are respectively standard deviations of the variables relative change *G*, transactional price *p* and exchanged quantities *q*; and h is a fixed integer. z_i is a ratio taking its values in the range [0, 1], it measures the efficiency of the trading strategy relatively to hypotheses *i*: if z_i is close to 0 then the strategy has a very weak performance relatively to this hypothesis; inversely, if z_i is close to 1 then this strategy fully respects this hypothesis.

Criterion z_1 measures the effects of S&D over actual or transactional price *p*. Criterion z_2 assesses the influence of price *p* over the S&D balance. Criterion z_3 quantifies the relationship between nominal price p_N, transactional price *p* and S&D. Criteria z_4 compares the volatility of price to that of S&D. Regarding the transactional or exchanged quantities *q*, criteria z_5 and z_6 respectively measure the stability and volatility of this variable. Finally, z_7 indicates the satisfaction degree of traders' objectives in terms of overall sold and purchased quantities (Laib & Radjef, 2011b).

We may favor one criterion over another, this is done by associating different weights $w_1, \ldots, w_7$ to these criteria, with $0 \leq w_k \leq 1$, $k = 1, \ldots, 7$ and $\sum_{k=1}^{7} w_k = 1$. The *average performance* of a trading strategy γ, over the forecasts times-series $\mathbf{S}$ and $\mathbf{D}$, is

$$\bar{z}(\gamma, \mathbf{S}, \mathbf{D}) = \sum_{k=1}^{7} w_k z_k.$$

Now, assuming that two sets of representative samples of S&D time-series, $\mathbb{S} = \left\{ \mathbf{S}^{(1)}, \ldots, \mathbf{S}^{(K)} \right\}$ and $\mathbb{D} = \left\{ \mathbf{D}^{(1)}, \ldots, \mathbf{D}^{(K)} \right\}$ are available, and the strategy γ was parameterized by a parameters-matrix $\underline{\alpha} \in \mathbb{A}^{(n_1 + n_2) \times 3}$, then for a specific $\underline{\alpha}^{(0)} \in \mathbb{A}$, the *global performance* of strategy γ over the sets of samples $\mathbb{S}$ and $\mathbb{D}$, is

$$\bar{\bar{z}}\left(\gamma\left(\underline{\alpha}^{(0)}\right), \mathbb{S}, \mathbb{D}\right) = \frac{1}{K} \sum_{k=1}^{K} \bar{z}\left(\gamma\left(\underline{\alpha}^{(0)}\right), \mathbf{S}^{(k)}, \mathbf{D}^{(k)}\right).$$

Therefore, the optimal parameters-matrix for this strategy over $\mathbb{S}$ and $\mathbb{D}$, is

$$\underline{\alpha}^{*} = \arg\max_{\underline{\alpha} \in \mathbb{A}} \bar{\bar{z}}\left(\gamma(\underline{\alpha}), \mathbb{S}, \mathbb{D}\right).$$

NUMERICAL EXAMPLES

Computing Average and Global Performances

In case of a trading game with n_1=3 producers and n_2=4 consumers, and a specified parameters-matrix $\underline{\alpha}^{(0)}$, a dedicated Matlab code has generated the set of S&D forecasts time-series shown in Figure 3 for the corresponding agents: On the left column are shown the supply forecasts of the three producers and on the right are the demand forecasts of the four consumers. The trading process evolves over m=100 periods. We will use this kind of data as inputs to the automatons in order to test the functioning of our trading strategy and compute its performance.

Feeding the data shown on Figure 3 as inputs to the above trading strategy, described by relations (11), (12) and (13), has generated the price pattern on Figure 4d.

Figure 3. Samples of supply and demand (S\&D) forecasts time-series

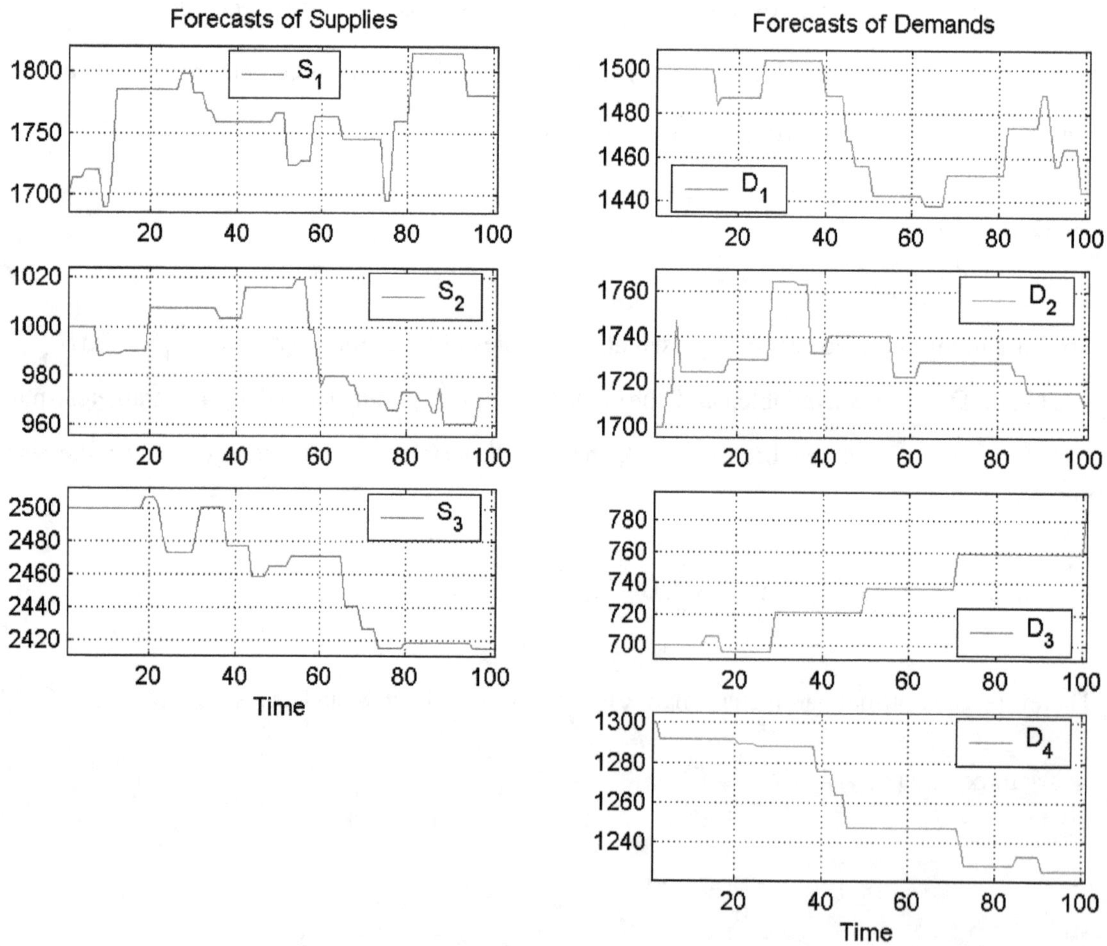

Figure 4. Pricing obtained by the automatic trading strategy

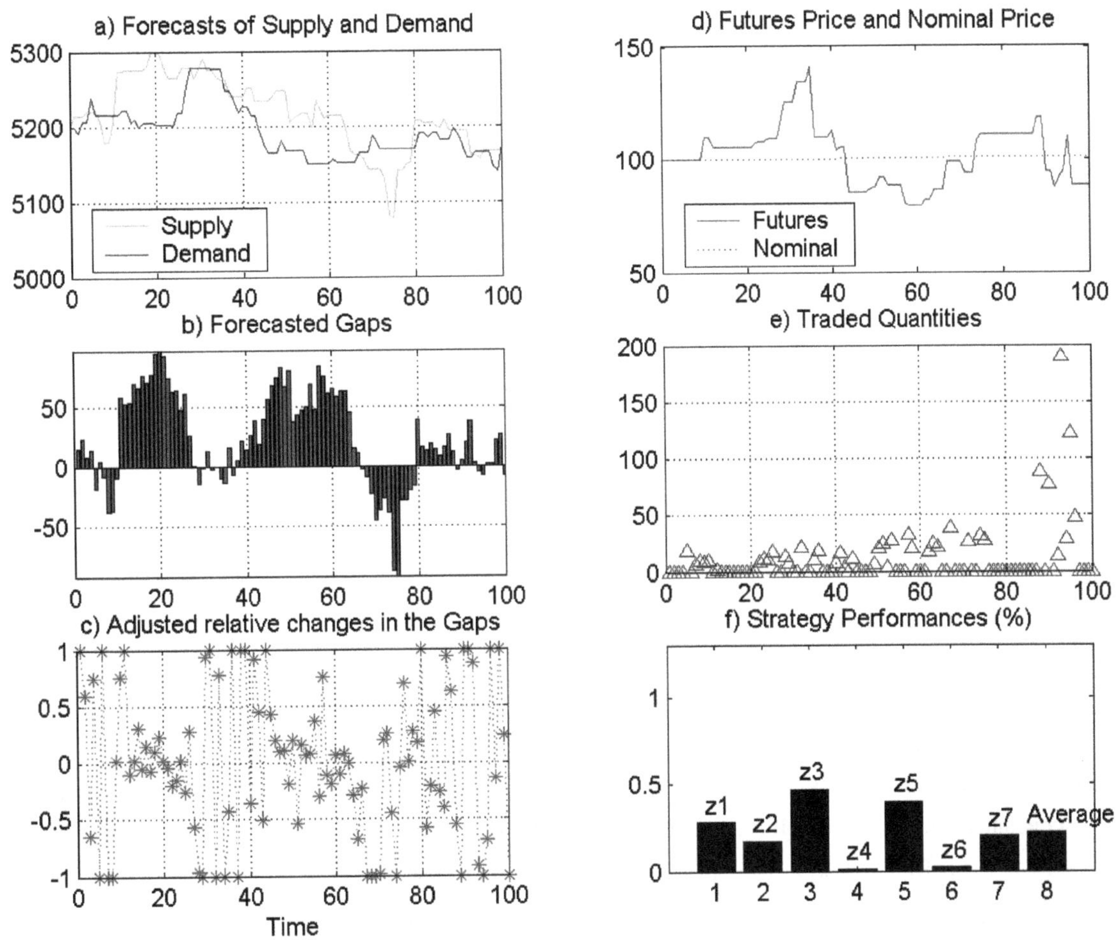

Figure 4a shows time-series of total supply S and total demand D. Figure 4b represents the evolution of the gap function G. The obtained performances in respect to each criterion are

$z_1 = 0.2800$

$z_2 = 0.1717$

$z_3 = 0.4700$

$z_4 = 0.0111$

$z_5 = 0.4000$

$z_6 = 0.0222$

$z_7 = 0.3712$

with an average performance $\overline{z} = 0.2226$. Running the Matlab code over a large set of forecasts time-series, K=30, the calculated global performance was $\overline{\overline{z}} = 0.3203$.

Parameters Optimization by Simulation Heuristic

We know that each parameter $\alpha_{ik}, i \in \mathcal{N}$ and $k = 1,2,3$, can take an infinity of feasible values. However, in order to obtain a quasi-optimal solution in a short time, we simplify the problem by considering that the set of feasible solutions is limited. Since parameters α_{ik} are weighing factors, then their values are generally belonging to the interval [0, 1]. Let's take three representative values in this interval, for instance,

$$\alpha_{ik} \in \mathbb{A} = \{0.1, 0.5, 0.9\}$$

Even in this restrictive case, it will be hard to deal with all possible combinations of parameters-matrices $\underline{\alpha}$. Indeed, for instance in the case of the above mentioned game with n_1=3 producers and n_2=4 consumers, the number of possible parameters-matrices is

$$card(\mathbb{A})^{(n_1+n_2)\times 3} = 3^{21} = 10,460,353,203.$$

This huge number will render running time on computer very prohibitive. In addition, even if we obtain the optimal solution, say $\underline{\alpha}^*$, maximizing the global performance of our trading system, then $\underline{\alpha}^*$ is not necessarily the optimal solution. This is due to the fact that the choice of α_{ik} was carried out only in the set $\{0.1, 0.5, 0.9\}$ whereas the optimal value of a given parameter α_{ik} may not belong to this set.

In order to obtain rapidly a solution, the current heuristic simplifies further the problem by assuming that a) all the producers have the same parameters and b) all the consumers have the same parameters equally. In other words, the first n_1 lines of parameters-matrix $\underline{\alpha}$ are all the same and the last n_2 lines of this matrix are also identical. A parameters-matrix $\underline{\alpha}$ satisfying the requirements of this heuristic could be written into a new (reduced) matrix $\underline{\alpha}'$, with 2×3 dimension. Consequently, the number of different matrices that we can build in this manner with the elements of the set $\mathbb{A}$ is $card(\mathbb{A})^{2\times 3} = 3^6 = 729$.

This heuristic was written into a Matlab code testing all the 729 different parameters-matrices gathered into groups of 50 matrices. The code computes the individual performances of each matrice and its global performance. The best solution in each group is displayed in Table 1.

Over the set of 729 tested matrices, the best global performance was 0.3735 corresponding to the following quasi-optimal reduced parameters-matrix

$$\underline{\alpha}^{*\prime} = \begin{bmatrix} 0.1 & 0.1 & 0.1 \\ \%0.1 & 0.1 & 0.1 \end{bmatrix}.$$

Comparing global performance $\overline{\overline{z}} = 0.3203$ obtained in the previous section and the current one, $\overline{\overline{z}} = 0.3735$, we conclude that this heuristic based on simulation, even restrictive, has nevertheless improved the solution by almost 17%.

Table 1. Results obtained by the simulation heuristic

Group	z_1	z_2	z_3	z_4	z_5	z_6	z_7	$\bar{\bar{z}}$
001-050	0.3210	0.2226	0.7527	0	0.4353	0.0100	0.8728	**0.3735**
051-100	0.3170	0.2209	0.7317	0.0011	0.4320	0.0104	0.8732	0.3695
101-150	0.2510	0.1751	0.6957	0.0037	0.3493	0.1437	0.7662	0.3407
151-200	0.3160	0.2232	0.7027	0.0033	0.4333	0.0100	0.8743	0.3661
201-250	0.3303	0.2451	0.5673	0.0022	0.4833	0.0067	0.8876	0.3604
251-300	0.3187	0.2195	0.6683	0	0.4367	0.0081	0.8721	0.3605
301-350	0.3367	0.2327	0.6823	0.0037	0.4557	0.0196	0.8765	0.3725
351-400	0.3407	0.2404	0.6780	0.0033	0.4690	0.0185	0.4843	0.3192
401-450	0.3220	0.2209	0.6703	0.0033	0.4373	0.0081	0.8701	0.3617
451-500	0.3303	0.2391	0.5863	0.0026	0.4800	0.0089	0.8897	0.3624
501-550	0.3100	0.2199	0.5883	0	0.4323	0.0100	0.8741	0.3478
551-600	0.2997	0.2098	0.6877	0.0026	0.4153	0.0678	0.8349	0.3597
601-650	0.3187	0.2222	0.5893	0.0015	0.4440	0.0115	0.6438	0.3187
651-700	0.3007	0.2088	0.6533	0.0033	0.4113	0.0267	0.8583	0.3518
701-729	0.3220	0.2266	0.5953	0.0048	0.4490	0.0074	0.4861	0.2988

CONCLUSION AND PERSPECTIVES

The current work has proved that it is possible to automate thoroughly a futures market and replace human decision-makers by computer-based programs. The suggested strategy for trading takes into account the main ingredients of the futures market, namely the evolution of S&D forecasts as well as nominal price, positions of traders and the remaining time for trading at each stage. The mathematical criteria suggested for measuring performance of a trading strategy proved to be a practical and efficient tool for classifying strategies and selecting optimal parameters' values.

The framework of the suggested market was large enough to take into account the major actors of a real futures market, though we can enlarge it by considering the intervention of speculators who bring a lot of market liquidity. On the other hand, we need to increase the global strategy performance by improving the efficiency of the trading strategy. This can be carried out by several means, for instance introducing a new parameterization system, or imbedding several terms in the trading strategy each terme related to a specific criterion, or building price bands around the nominal price line, if price frequency in a specific band has exceeded a typical threshold value then it will trigger a particular behavior from the automated traders side. Establishing optimal trading strategies could also be considered from an optimal control perspective where it will be necessary to find an optimal command pattern for each automated trader in reaction to the stream of S&D forecasts. Finally, optimization of parameters could be done via other technics like genetic algorithms and training neural nets.

REFERENCES

Arthur, W. B., Holland, J. H., LeBaron, B., Palmer, R., & Tayler, P. (1997). Asset pricing under expectations in an artificial stock market. *Economic Notes*, *26*, 297–330.

Barcley, M. J., Hendershott, T., & McCormick, D. T. (2003). Competition among trading venues: Information and trading on electronic communications networks. *The Journal of Finance*, *58*(6), 2637–2665. doi:10.1046/j.1540-6261.2003.00618.x

CBOT. (Ed.). (1998). *Commodity trading manual*. Chicago: Chicago Board of Trade of the city of Chicago.

Hull, J. C. (2002). Fundamentals of futures and options markets (4th ed.). Upper Saddle River, NJ: Pearson Education Inc.

Laib, F., & Radjef, M. S. (2011a). Commodity futures market mechanism: Mathematical formulation and some analytical properties. *Journal of Engineering and Computer Innovations.*, *2*, 106–124.

Laib, F., & Radjef, M. S. (2011b). Automated traders in commodities markets: Case of producer-consumer institution. *Expert Systems with Applications*, *38*(12), 15134–15142. doi:10.1016/j.eswa.2011.05.091

Levy, M. (2008). Stock market crashes as social phase transitions. *Journal of Economic Dynamics & Control*, *32*(1), 137–155. doi:10.1016/j.jedc.2007.01.023

Murphy, J. J. (1999). *Technical analysis of the financial markets*. New York: New York Institute of Finance.

O'Hara, M. (1998). *Market microstructure theory*. New York: Willey.

Preist, C. (1999). Commodity trading using an agent-based iterated double auction. In *Proceedings of the ACM conference on autonomous agents*. New York: ACM. doi:10.1145/301136.301179

Roll, R. (1988). The international crash of October 1987. *Financial Analysts Journal*, *44*(5), 19–35. doi:10.2469/faj.v44.n5.19

Shelton, R. B. (1997). *Gaming the market: applying game theory to generate winning trading strategies*. New York: John Wiley & Sons Inc.

Teweles, R. J., & Jones, F. J. (1999). *The futures game: who wins? who loses? and why?* New York: McGraw-Hill.

Weber, B. W. (2006). Adoption of electronic trading at the International Securities Exchange. *Decision Support Systems*, *41*(4), 728–746. doi:10.1016/j.dss.2004.10.006

Compilation of References

2012 Women Ethnic Wear Market in India Outlook. (2015). Dublin: Research and Market.

Abdella, M., & Marwala, T. (2005). The use of genetic algorithms and neural networks to approximate missing data in database. In *Proceedings of the IEEE 3rd international conference on computational cybernetics*. doi:10.1109/ICCCYB.2005.1511574

Acharjya, D. P. (2013). Rough computing based Information Retrieval in Knowledge Discovery Databases. In Information and Knowledge Management-Tools, Techniques and Practices (pp. 123 - 153). New Delhi: New India Publishing Company.

Acharjya, D. P. (2009). Comparative study of rough sets on fuzzy approximation spaces and intuitionistic fuzzy approximation spaces. *International Journal of Computational and Applied Mathematics*, *4*(2), 95–106.

Acharjya, D. P., & Tripathy, B. K. (2012). Intuitionistic fuzzy rough set on two universal sets and knowledge representation. *Mathematical Sciences International Research Journal*, *1*(2), 584–598.

Aghdaie, M. H., Zolfani, S. H., & Zavadskas, E. K. (2013). Market segment evaluation and selection based on application of fuzzy AHP and COPRAS-G methods. *Journal of Business Economics and Management*, *14*(1), 213–233. doi:10.3846/16111699.2012.721392

Aghdaie, M. H., Zolfani, S. H., & Zavadskas, E. K. (2014). Synergies of data mining and multiple attribute decision making. *Procedia: Social and Behavioral Sciences*, *110*, 767–776. doi:10.1016/j.sbspro.2013.12.921

Agostinho, F. (2013). *Humanitarian Logistics: How to Help Even More?*. doi:10.3182/20130911-3-BR-3021.00075

Agrawal, R., Imielinski, T., & Swami, A. (1993). Mining association rules between sets of items in large databases. In *Proceedings of the 1993 ACM SIGMOD Conference on Management of Data*(pp. 207-216). Washington, DC:ACM Press. doi:10.1145/170035.170072

Agrawal, R., & Srikant, R. (1994). Fast algorithms for mining association rules. In *Proceedings of the 20th International Conference on VLDB Conference*(pp. 487-499).

Agresti, A. (1984). *Analysis of Ordinal Categorical Data*. New York: John Wiley and Sons.

Alatas, B., Akim, E., & Akim, E. (2008). MODENAR: Multi-objective differential evolution algorithm for mining numeric association rules. *Applied Soft Computing*, *8*(1), 646–656. doi:10.1016/j.asoc.2007.05.003

Alghamdi, E. (2013). *The Influence of Social Media on E-Commerce Sites*. (Master Thesis). Dalhousie University, Halifax, Nova Scotia.

Allen & Unwin. (2013). Datafile & Other Resources. *SPSS Survival Manual* (5th ed.). Retrieved 1st February, 2016, from http://spss.allenandunwin.com.s3-website-ap-southeast-2.amazonaws.com/data_files.html

Allende, S. M., Chen, D. C., Bouza, C. N., Sautto, J. M., & Santiago, A. (2016): Estimation of derivatives, from economy to environment: a study of the management of eutrophication of a fresh water basin's data. In Models and Methods for Supporting Decision Making in Human Health and Environment Protection. Nova Science Publishers.

Alonso, J. A., & Lamata, M. T. (2006). Consistency in the Analytic Hierarchy Process: A new approach. *International Journal of Uncertainty, Fuzziness and Knowledge-based Systems*, *14*(4), 445–459. doi:10.1142/S0218488506004114

Anandhavalli, M., Kumar, S.S., Kumar, A., & Ghose, M. K. (2009). Optimized association rule mining using genetic algorithm. *Advances in Information Mining*, 1-4.

Anderberg, M. (2014). *Cluster analysis for applications: Probability and Mathematical Statistics: A Series of Monographs and Textbooks. 19*. London: Academic press.

Anderson, E., Fornell, C., & Lehmann, D. (1994). Customer satisfaction, market share, and profitability: Findings from Sweden. *Journal of Marketing*, *58*(3), 53–66. doi:10.2307/1252310

Andrews, R., & Beynon, M. (2010). Organizational form and strategic alignment in a local authority: A preliminary exploration using fuzzy clustering. *Public Organization Review*, *11*(3), 201–218. doi:10.1007/s11115-010-0117-4

Ankaiah, N., & Ravi, V. (2011). A novel soft computing hybrid for data imputation. In *Proceedings of the 7th international conference on data mining (DMIN)*.

Arnould, E. J., & Thompson, C. J. (2007). Consumer Culture Theory (and We Really Mean Theoretics): Dilemmas and Opportunities Posed by an Academic Branding Strategy. In Consumer Culture Theory. Oxford, UK: Elsevier.

Arthur, W. B., Holland, J. H., LeBaron, B., Palmer, R., & Tayler, P. (1997). Asset pricing under expectations in an artificial stock market. *Economic Notes*, *26*, 297–330.

Asadi, A., Afzali, M., Shojaei, A., & Sulaimani, S. (2012). New binary PSO based method for finding best thresholds in association rule mining. *Applied Soft Computing*, 260–264.

Asasen, C., Asasen, K., & Chuangcham, N. (2003). A proposed ASEAN Policy Blueprint for SME development 2004–2014. *REPSF Project*, *02/005*(33), 145.

Ashby, W. (1962), Principles Self-Organization.*Transaction of the University of Illinois Symposium*. Pergamon Press.

Atanasov, K. T. (1986). Intuitionistic fuzzy sets. *Fuzzy Sets and Systems*, *20*(1), 87–96. doi:10.1016/S0165-0114(86)80034-3

Atiya, A. F. (2001). Bankruptcy prediction for credit risk using neural networks: A survey and new results. *Neural Networks. IEEE Transactions on*, *12*(4), 929–935. PMID:18249923

Atiya, A. F. (2005). Estimating the posterior probabilities using the k-nearest neighbor rule. *Neural Computation*, *17*(3), 731–740. doi:10.1162/0899766053019971 PMID:15802013

Austin, P. C., & Escobar, M. D. (2005). Bayesian modeling of missing data in clinical research. *Computational Statistics & Data Analysis*, *49*(3), 821–836. doi:10.1016/j.csda.2004.06.006

Aydilek, I. B., & Arslan, A. (2013). A hybrid method for imputation of missing vlaues using optimized fuzzy c-means with support vector regression and a genetic algorithm. *Information Sciences*, *233*, 25–35. doi:10.1016/j.ins.2013.01.021

Babuska, R. (2009). *Fuzzy And Neural Control Disc Course Lecture Notes*. Retrieved 5 October 2012 from http://www.dcsc.tudelft.nl/~disc_fnc/transp/fncontrol.pdf

Baesens, B., Van Gestel, T., Viaene, S., Stepanova, M., Suykens, J., & Vanthienen, J. (2003). Benchmarking state-of-the-art classification algorithms for credit scoring. *The Journal of the Operational Research Society*, *54*(6), 627–635. doi:10.1057/palgrave.jors.2601545

Bahrepour, M., Akbarzadeh-T, M. R., Yaghoobi, M., & Naghibi-S, M. B. (2011). An adaptive ordered fuzzy time series with application to FOREX. *Expert Systems with Applications*, *38*(1), 475–485. doi:10.1016/j.eswa.2010.06.087

Bahzadian, M., Kazemzadeh, R. B., Albadvi, A., & Aghdasi, M. (2010). PROMETHEE: A comprehensive literature review on methodologies and applications. European Journal of Operational Research, (200), 198-215. doi:10.1016/j.ejor.2009.01.021

Bąk A. (2004). *Dekompozycyjne metody pomiaru preferencji w badaniach marketingowych*. Wrocław, Poland: Wydawnictwo Akademii Ekonomicznej im. Oskara Langego we Wrocławiu.

Bąk, A. (2013). *Mikroekonometryczne metody badania preferencji konsumentów z wykorzytsaniem programu R*. Warszawa, Poland: Wydawnictwo C.H. Beck.

Balcik, B., Beamon, B. M., Krejci, C. C., Muramatsu, K. M., & Ramirez, M. (2010). Coordination in humanitarian relief chains: Practices, challenges and opportunities. *International Journal of Production Economics*, *126*(1), 22–34. doi:10.1016/j.ijpe.2009.09.008

Ballings, M., & Poel, D. V. D. (2013). Kernel Factory: An ensemble of kernel machines. *Expert Systems with Applications*, *40*(8), 2904–2913. doi:10.1016/j.eswa.2012.12.007

Bao, Y., Ishii, N., & Du, X. (2004). Combining multiple k-nearest neighbor classifiers using different distance functions. In *Intelligent Data Engineering and Automated Learning–IDEAL 2004* (pp. 634–641). Springer Berlin Heidelberg; doi:10.1007/978-3-540-28647-9_60

Barad, M., & Gien, D. (2001). Linking improvement models to manufacturing strategies – a methodology for SMEs and other enterprises. *International Journal of Production Research*, *39*(12), 2675–2695. doi:10.1080/00207540110051824

Barcley, M. J., Hendershott, T., & McCormick, D. T. (2003). Competition among trading venues: Information and trading on electronic communications networks. *The Journal of Finance*, *58*(6), 2637–2665. doi:10.1046/j.1540-6261.2003.00618.x

Barile, S. (2012). *L'approccio sistemico vitale per lo sviluppo del territorio*. Sinergie Italian Journal of Management.

Bas, E., Egrioglu, E., Aladag, C. H., & Yolcu, U. (2015). Fuzzy-time-series network used to forecast linear and nonlinear time series. *Applied Intelligence*, *43*(2), 343–355. doi:10.1007/s10489-015-0647-0

Basile, G. (2013). *Relazioni tra impresa e individuo-consumatore*. Franco Angeli.

Batista, G., & Monard, M. C. (2002). A study of K-nearest neighbor as an imputation method. Hybrid intelligent systems, ser front artificial intelligence applications. IOS Press.

Batista, G., & Monard, M. C. (2003). *Experimental comparison of K-nearest neighbor and mean or mode imputation methods with the internal strategies used by C4.5 and CN2 to treat missing data. Technical Report*. University of Sao Paulo.

Beales, H. (2010). *The Value of Behavioral Targeting*. Retrieved from www.networkadvertising.org/pdfs/Beales_NAI_Study.pdf

Beal, T. (2010). *Small and Medium Enterprises in Asian Pacific Countries* (M. A. Abdullah & M. I. Baker, Eds.). New York: Nova Science Publishers Inc.

Beer, S. (1985). *Diagnosing the system for organizations*. London: Wiley.

Behavioral Ads Offer a Windfall for Marketers, Publishers. (n.d.). Retrieved from http://www.forbes.com/2010/03/24/behavioral-targeted-ads-advertising-ftc-privacy-cmo-network-ads.html

Beiranvand, V., Kashani, M. M., & Bakar, A. (2014). Multi-objective PSO algorithm for mining numerical association rules without a priori discretization. *Expert Systems with Applications*, *41*(9), 4259–4273. doi:10.1016/j.eswa.2013.12.043

Belacel, N., Hansen, P., & Mladenovic, N. (2002). Fuzzy J-means: A new heuristic for fuzzy clustering. *Pattern Recognition*, *35*(10), 2193–2200. doi:10.1016/S0031-3203(01)00193-5

Belew, M. (1996). *Adaptive individuals in evolving populations*. Boston: Addison-Wesley Longman Publishing Co., Inc.

Bellman, R. E., & Zadeh, L. A. (1970). Decision-making in a fuzzy environment. *Management Science*, *17*(4), B-141–B-164. doi:10.1287/mnsc.17.4.B141

Belobaba, P. (1987). *Air travel demand and airline seat inventory management*. Cambridge, MA: Flight Transportation Laboratory, Massachusetts Institute of Technology.

Belobaba, P. P. (1989). OR Practice-Application of a Probabilistic Decision Model to Airline Seat Inventory Control. *Operations Research*, *37*(2), 183–197. doi:10.1287/opre.37.2.183

Berry, S., Levinsohn, J., & Pakes, A. (1995). Automobile prices in market equlibrium. *Econometrica*, *63*(4), 841–890. doi:10.2307/2171802

Berry, S., & Parish, T. (2006). Cadwallader, & Dotzel, (2006) *Creating New Markets Through Service Innovation,* MIT. *Sloan Management Review*.

Bessec, M., Fouquau, J., & Meritet, S. (2016). Forecasting electricity spot prices using time-series models with a double temporal segmentation. *Applied Economics*, *48*(5), 361–378. doi:10.1080/00036846.2015.1080801

Beynon-Davis, P. (2009). *Business Information Systems*. Palgrave Macmillan.

Beynon, M. J., & Peel, M. J. (2001). Variable precision rough set theory and data discretisation: An application to corporate failure prediction. *Omega*, *29*(6), 561–576. doi:10.1016/S0305-0483(01)00045-7

Beynon, M., McDermott, A., & Heffernan, M. (2012). Psychological Contracts and Job Satisfaction: Clustering Analysis using Evidential C-Means and Comparison with other Techniques. *Intelligent Systems in Accounting, Finance & Management*, *19*(4), 247–273. doi:10.1002/isaf.1334

Bezdek, C. (1980). A convergence theorem for the fuzzy ISODATA clustering algorithms. *IEEE Transactions on Pattern Analysis and Machine Intelligence*, *2*(1), 1–8. doi:10.1109/TPAMI.1980.4766964 PMID:22499617

Bezdek, J. C. (1981). *Pattern Recognition with Fuzzy Objective Function Algorithms*. Kluwer Academic Publishers. doi:10.1007/978-1-4757-0450-1

Bikash, R. D., & Pravat, S. K., & Sreekumar. (2010). Factors Influencing Purchase of 'NANO' the Innovative Car from India - An Empirical Study. *Asian Journal of Business Management*, *2*(3), 48–56.

Blanco, A., Pino-Mejías, R., Lara, J., & Rayo, S. (2013). Credit scoring models for the microfinance industry using neural networks: Evidence from Peru. *Expert Systems with Applications*, *40*(1), 356–364. doi:10.1016/j.eswa.2012.07.051

Blut, M., Beatty, S. E., Evanschitzky, H., & Brock, C. (2014). The impact of service characteristics on the switching costs-customer loyalty link. *Journal of Retailing*, *90*(2), 275–290. doi:10.1016/j.jretai.2014.04.003

Bodea, T., & Ferguson, M. (2014). *Segmentation, Revenue Management and Pricing Analytics*. Routledge.

Bolturk, E., Oztaysi, B., & Sari, I. U. (2012, November). Electricity consumption forecasting using fuzzy time series. In *Computational Intelligence and Informatics (CINTI), 2012 IEEE 13th International Symposium on* (pp. 245-249). IEEE. doi:10.1109/CINTI.2012.6496768

Bomhold, C. R. (2013). Educational use of smart phone technology. *Program - electronic library and information systems, 47*(4), 424-436.

Bonarini, A., Bonacina, C., & Matteucci, M. (2000). Fuzzy and crisp representations of real-valued input for learning classifier systems. In Learning Classifier Systems (pp. 107-124). Springer Berlin Heidelberg. doi:10.1007/3-540-45027-0_5

Brans, J. P., & Mareschal, B. (2005). PROMETHEE methods. In J. Figueira, S. Greco, & M. Ehrgott (Eds.), *Multiple Criteria Decision Analysis. State of Art Surveys* (pp. 163–196). Boston: Springer.

Breese, J., Hackerman, D., & Kadie, C. (1998). *Anonymous Microsoft Web Dataset.* Retrieved August 13, 2013, from http://archive.ics.uci.edu/ml/datasets/Anonymous+Microsoft+Web+Data

Broadbridge, A., & Calderwood, E. (2002). Rural grocery shoppers: Do their attitudes reflect their actions? *International Journal of Retail & Distribution Management, 30*(8), 394–406. doi:10.1108/09590550210435282

Brockett, P. L. (1981). A note on Numerical Assignment of Scores to Ranked Categorical Data. *The Journal of Mathematical Sociology, 8*(1), 91–101. doi:10.1080/0022250X.1981.9989917

Brooks, R. (2010). *Advanced Derivatives and Strategies. Introduction to Derivatives and Risk Management* (8th ed.,). Mason, OH: Cengage Learning.

Bross, I. D. J. (1958). How to use Ridit Analysis. *Biometrics, 14*(1), 18–38. doi:10.2307/2527727

Brown, S., & Swartz, T. (1989). A gap analysis of professional service quality. *Journal of Marketing, 53*(2), 92–98. doi:10.2307/1251416

Buchanan, M. (2003). *Nexus. Perché la natura, la società, l'economia e la comunicazione funzionano allo stesso modo.* Oscar Mondadori.

Buckinx, W., & Van den Poel, D. (2005). Customer base analysis: Partial defection of behaviourally loyal clients in a non-contractual FMCG retail setting. *European Journal of Operational Research, 164*(1), 252–268. doi:10.1016/j.ejor.2003.12.010

Buckley, J. J. (1985). Fuzzy hierarchical analysis. *Fuzzy Sets and Systems, 17*(3), 233–247. doi:10.1016/0165-0114(85)90090-9

Bult, J. R., & Wansbeek, T. (1995). Optimal selection for direct mail. *Marketing Science, 14*(4), 378–394. doi:10.1287/mksc.14.4.378

Büyüközkan, G. (2004). Multi-criteria decision making for e-marketplace selection. *Internet Research, 14*(2), 139–154. doi:10.1108/10662240410530853

Calcagno, M., & Casarin, F. (2014). *Mercati reali vs mercati virtuali? Uscire dalla crisi ripensando gli spazi della relazione con il consumatore, Mercati e competitività, Rivista della Società Italiana di Marketing, N.3.* Franco Angeli.

Cambria, S., & Xia, H. (2013). New Avenues in Opinion Mining and Sentiment Analysis. *IEEE Intelligent Systems, 28*(2), 15–21. doi:10.1109/MIS.2013.30

Canbas, S. C., & Kilic, S. B. (n.d.). *Spanish dataset.* Retrieved from http://www.tbb.org.tr/english/bulten/yillik/2000/ratios.xls

Canbas, S., Caubak, A., & Kilic, S. B. (2005). Prediction of commercial bank failure via multivariate statistical analysis of financial structures: The Turkish case. *European Journal of Operational Research*, *166*(2), 528–546. doi:10.1016/j.ejor.2004.03.023

Carling, K., Jacobson, T., & Roszbach, K. (2001). Dormancy risk and expected profits of consumer loans. *Journal of Banking & Finance*, *25*(4), 717–739. doi:10.1016/S0378-4266(00)00093-5

Carmo, R. M. (2001). Mobile agents applications. *Internet Research*, *11*(1), 49–54. doi:10.1108/10662240110365715

Caruana, A. (2002). Service loyalty: The effects of service quality and the mediating role of customer satisfaction. *European Journal of Marketing*, *36*(7/8), 811–828. doi:10.1108/03090560210430818

Castaño, A., Fernández-Navarro, F., & Hervás-Martínez, C. (2013). PCA-ELM -A Robust and Pruned ELM Approach Based on PCA. *Neural Processing Letter, 37*, 377–392. doi:10.1007/s11063-012-9253-x

CBOT. (Ed.). (1998). *Commodity trading manual*. Chicago: Chicago Board of Trade of the city of Chicago.

Celik, E., Gumus, A. T., & Alegoz, M. (2014). A Trapezoidal Type-2 Fuzzy MCDM method to identify and evaluate critical success factors for humanitarian relief logistics management. *Journal of Intelligent & Fuzzy Systems*, *27*(6), 2847–2855.

Chaffey, D., Mayer, R., Johnston, K., & Ellis-Chadwick, F. (2000). *Internet Marketing*. London: Prentice Hall.

Chai, Y. D. (2015). Emotions and continued usage of mobile applications. *Industrial Management & Data Systems*, *115*(5), 833–852. doi:10.1108/IMDS-11-2014-0338

Chan, C. C. H. (2008). Intelligent value-based customer segmentation method for campaign management: A case study of automobile retailer. *Expert Systems with Applications*, *34*(4), 2754–2762. doi:10.1016/j.eswa.2007.05.043

Chan, F. T., Samvedi, A., & Chung, S. H. (2015). Fuzzy time series forecasting for supply chain disruptions. *Industrial Management & Data Systems*, *115*(3), 419–435. doi:10.1108/IMDS-07-2014-0199

Chang, H. C., & Tsai, H. P. (2011). Group RFM analysis as a novel framework to discover better customer consumption behavior. *Expert Systems with Applications*, *38*(12), 14499–14513. doi:10.1016/j.eswa.2011.05.034

Chan, T. C., Killeen, J., Griswold, W., & Lenert, L. (2004). Information technology and emergency medical care during disasters. *Academic Emergency Medicine : Official Journal of the Society for Academic Emergency Medicine*, *11*(11), 1229–1236. doi:10.1111/j.1553-2712.2004.tb00709.x PMID:15528589

Chen, C. Q., Tang, S. L., Xing, Q. G., Yang, J. K., Zhan, H. G., & Shi, H. Y. (2007): A Derivative Spectrum Algorithm for Determination of Chlorophyll-a Concentration in the Pearl River Estuary. In *Proceedings of Geoscience and Remote Sensing Symposium*. doi:10.1109/IGARSS.2007.4422949

Cheng, C. H., & Chen, Y. S. (2009). Classifying the segmentation of customer value via RFM model and RS theory. *Expert Systems with Applications*, *36*(3), 4176–4184. doi:10.1016/j.eswa.2008.04.003

Cheng, C., Wei, Y., Sun, X., & Zhou, Y. (2013). Estimation of Chlorophyll-a Concentration in Turbid Lake Using Spectral Smoothing and Derivative Analysis. *International Journal of Environmental Research and Public Health*, *10*(7), 2979–2994. doi:10.3390/ijerph10072979 PMID:23880727

Cheng, H. D., Chen, J. R., & Li, J. (1998). Threshold selection based on fuzzy c-partition entropy approach. *Pattern Recognition*, *31*(7), 857–870. doi:10.1016/S0031-3203(97)00113-1

Cheng, S. H., Chen, S. M., & Jian, W. S. (2016). Fuzzy time series forecasting based on fuzzy logical relationships and similarity measures. *Information Sciences*, *327*, 272–287. doi:10.1016/j.ins.2015.08.024

Chen, J., Huang, H., Tian, F., & Tian, S. (2008). A selective Bayes Classifier for classifying incomplete data based on gain ratio. *Knowledge-Based Systems*, *21*(7), 530–534. doi:10.1016/j.knosys.2008.03.013

Chen, M. C., & Huang, S. H. (2003). Credit scoring and rejected instances reassigning through evolutionary computation techniques. *Expert Systems with Applications*, *24*(4), 433–441. doi:10.1016/S0957-4174(02)00191-4

Chen, S., & Lee, L. (2010). Fuzzy multiple attributes group decision-making based on the interval type-2 TOPSIS method. *Expert Systems with Applications*, *37*(4), 2790–2798. doi:10.1016/j.eswa.2009.09.012

Chen, Y. L., Kuo, M. H., Wu, S. Y., & Tang, K. (2009). Discovering recency, frequency, and monetary (RFM) sequential patterns from customers' purchasing data. *Electronic Commerce Research and Applications*, *8*(5), 241–251. doi:10.1016/j.elerap.2009.03.002

Chesley, P., Vincent, B., Xu, L., & Srihari, R. (2006). Using Verbs and Adjectives to Automatically Classify Blog Sentiment. In *Proceedings of the AAAI-2006 Spring Symposium on Computational Approaches to Analyzing Weblogs.*

Chiang, W. Y. (2011). To mine association rules of customer values via a data mining procedure with improved model: An empirical case study. *Expert Systems with Applications*, *38*(3), 1716–1722. doi:10.1016/j.eswa.2010.07.097

Chien-Ho Wu. (2007). On the Application of Grey Relational Analysis and RIDIT Analysis to Likert Scale Surveys. *International Mathematical Forum, 2*(14), 675-687.

Chih-Hung, T., Ching-Liang, C., & Lieh, C. (2003). Applying Grey Relational Analysis to the Vendor Evaluation Model. *International Journal of the Computer, the Internet and Management*, *11*(3), 45–53.

Chiu, C. Y., Chen, Y. F., Kuo, I. T., & Ku, H. C. (2009). An intelligent market segmentation system using k-means and particle swarm optimization. *Expert Systems with Applications*, *36*(3), 4558–4565. doi:10.1016/j.eswa.2008.05.029

Chiu, W. Y., Tzeng, G. H., & Li, H. L. (2013). A new hybrid MCDM model combining DANP with VIKOR to improve e-store business. *Knowledge-Based Systems*, *37*, 48–61. doi:10.1016/j.knosys.2012.06.017

Choi, C., Jeong, M., & Mattila, A. S. (2015). Revenue management in the context of movie theaters: Is it fair&quest. *Journal of Revenue & Pricing Management*, *14*(2), 72–83. doi:10.1057/rpm.2014.30

Chopra, S., & Meindl, P. (2007). Supply chain management. In *Strategy, planning & operation* (pp. 265-275). Gabler.

Chou, D. C., Tan, X., & Yen, D. C. (2004). Web technology and supply chain management. *Information Management & Computer Security*, *12*(4), 338–349. doi:10.1108/09685220410553550

Chouhan, S., Singh, D., & Singh, A. (2016). A Survey and Analysis of Various Agricultural Crops Classification Techniques. *International Journal of Computers and Applications*, *136*(11).

Cho, Y. K. (2015). Creating customer repurchase intention in Internet retailing: The effects of multiple service events and product type. *Journal of Retailing and Consumer Services*, *22*, 213–222. doi:10.1016/j.jretconser.2014.11.002

Cho, Y. K. (2015a). The relationship between resources and market coverage in small local internet retailing. *International Journal of Retail & Distribution Management*, *43*(7), 597–616. doi:10.1108/IJRDM-12-2013-0220

Christopher, M., & Peck, H. (2004). Building the resilient supply chain. *The International Journal of Logistics Management*, *15*(2), 1–14. doi:10.1108/09574090410700275

Chung, S. (2014). An empirical analysis of usage dynamics in a mobile music app: Evidence from large-scale data. *Internet Research*, *24*(4), 436–456. doi:10.1108/IntR-05-2013-0088

Cios, K. J., Kurgan, L. A., & Goodenday, L. S. (n.d.). *Spectf Heart dataset.* Retrieved from http://archive.ics.uci.edu/ml/machine-learning-databases/spect

Cipresso, P., Foresti, R., Balgera, A., & Villamira, M. (2010). *E-learning, gestione e condivisione della conoscenza: Moodlemootitalia 2007 Modena.* Artestampa.

Clarabridge. (2015). *The Clarabridge CX Suite.* Retrieved October 13, 2015, from http://www.clarabridge.com/product/

Clason, D. L., & Dormody, T. J. (1994). Analyzing Data Measured by Individual Likert-Type Items. *Journal of Agricultural Education, 35*(4), 31–35. doi:10.5032/jae.1994.04031

Codeluppi, V. (2005). *Manuale di Sociologia dei consumi.* Carocci editore.

Colombo, R., & Jiang, W. (1999). A stochastic RFM model. *Journal of Interactive Marketing, 13*(3), 2–12. doi:10.1002/(SICI)1520-6653(199922)13:3<2::AID-DIR1>3.0.CO;2-H

Conover, W. (1973). Rank Tests for One Sample, Two Samples and K Samples Without the Assumptions of a Continuous Distribution Function. *Annals of Statistics, 1*(6), 1105–1125. doi:10.1214/aos/1176342560

Coombs, C. H., Dawes, R. M., & Tversky, A. (1970). *An Elementary Introduction. Mathematical Psychology.* Englewood Cliffs, NJ: Prentice-Hall, Inc.

Cortez, P., & Morais, A. (n.d.). *Forest Fire dataset.* Retrieved from http://archive.ics.uci.edu/ml/machine-learning-databases/forest-fires/forestfires.csv

Coulter, K., & Sarkis, J. (2005). Development of a media selection model using the analytic network process. *International Journal of Advertising: The Review of Marketing Communications, 24*(2), 193–215.

Cozzolino, A. (2012). *Humanitarian {Logistics}: {Cross}-{Sector} {Cooperation} in {Disaster} {Relief} {Management}.* Springer Science & Business Media. doi:10.1007/978-3-642-30186-5

Craig, C. D., & Faulkenberry, G. D. (1979). The application of ridit analysis to detect trends in visibility. *Atmospheric Environment, 13*(12), 1617–1622. doi:10.1016/0004-6981(79)90319-6

Cravens, W. D., & Piercy, N. F. (2012). *Strategic Marketing.* McGraw-Hill Higher Education.

Cronin, J., & Taylor, S. (1992). Measuring service quality: A re-examination and extension. *Journal of Marketing, 56*(3), 55–68. doi:10.2307/1252296

Czinkota, M., Kaufmann, H. R., & Basile, G. (2014). The relationship between legitimacy, reputation, sustainability and branding for companies and their supply chains. *Industrial Marketing Management, 43*(1), 91–101. doi:10.1016/j.indmarman.2013.10.005

D'Urso, P., De Giovanni, L., & Massari, R. (2015). Time series clustering by a robust autoregressive metric with application to air pollution. *Chemometrics and Intelligent Laboratory Systems, 141*, 107–124. doi:10.1016/j.chemolab.2014.11.003

Dao, T. H., Jeong, S. R., & Ahn, H. (2012). A novel recommendation model of location-based advertising: Context-Aware Collaborative Filtering using GA approach. *Expert Systems with Applications, 39*(3), 3731–3739. doi:10.1016/j.eswa.2011.09.070

Das, T. K., & Acharjya, D. P. (2014). A decision making model using soft set and rough set on fuzzy approximation spaces, Int. J. *Intelligent Systems Technologies and Applications, 13*(3), 170–186. doi:10.1504/IJISTA.2014.065172

Das, T. K., Acharjya, D. P., & Patra, M. R. (2015). General Characterization of Classifications in Rough Set on Two Universal Sets. *Information Resources Management Journal*, *28*(2), 1–19. doi:10.4018/IRMJ.2015040101

Das, T. K., Acharjya, D. P., & Patra, M. R. (2015). Multi- Criterion Decision Making using Intuitionistic Fuzzy Rough Set on Two Universal Sets, I.J. *Intelligent Systems and Applications*, *7*(4), 26–33. doi:10.5815/ijisa.2015.04.04

Das, T. K., Mohapatro, A., & Abburu, S. (2015). A Decision Making Mechanism During Disaster Event Monitoring and Control. *Middle-East Journal of Scientific Research*, *23*(9), 2251–2255.

Data Mining in Dynamic Social Networks and Fuzzy Systems. (2014). User Segmentation Based on Twitter Data Using Fuzzy Clustering: the Case of Sports News. IGI Global.

Data set. (n.d.). Retrieved from https://archive.ics.uci.edu/ml/datasets/Statlog+%28German+Credit+Data%29

Datumbox. (2015). *Datumbox Machine Learning Framework*. Retrieved October 26, 2015, from http://www.datumbox.com/machine-learning-framework

Davenport, F., & Funk, C. (2015). Using time series structural characteristics to analyze grain prices in food insecure countries. *Food Security*, *7*(5), 1055–1070. doi:10.1007/s12571-015-0490-5

Davidson, A. L. (2006). *Key performance indicators in humanitarian logistics* (Thesis). Massachusetts Institute of Technology.

Davies, M. A. P. (1994). A Multicriteria Decision Model Application for Managing Group Decisions. *The Journal of the Operational Research Society*, *45*(1), 47–58. doi:10.1057/jors.1994.6

Davis, G. (1995). Bringing stores to shoppers - not shoppers to stores. *International Journal of Retail & Distribution Management*, *23*(1), 18–23. doi:10.1108/09590559510078089

De Toni, A. F. (2011). *Teoria della complessità e implicazioni manageriali: verso l'auto-organizzazione*. Sinergie Italian Journal of Management.

De, S. K. (1999). *Some aspects of fuzzy sets, rough sets and intuitionistic fuzzy sets*. (Ph.D. Thesis). Kharagpur: IIT.

Dekhtyar, A., & Verburg, J. (2009). *Extended Bakery Dataset*. Retrieved August 13, 2013, fromhttps://wiki.csc.calpoly.edu/datasets/wiki/ExtendedBakery

Dempster, A. P., Laird, N. M., & Rubin, D. B. (1977). Maximum-likelihood from incomplete data via the EM algorithm. *Journal of the Royal Statistical Society. Series A (General)*, *39*, 1–38.

Demyanyk, Y., & Hasan, I. (2010). Financial crises and bank failures: A review of prediction methods. *Omega*, *38*(5), 315–324. doi:10.1016/j.omega.2009.09.007

Deng, J. (1982). Control problems of Grey Systems. *Systems & Control Letters*, *5*, 288–294.

Deng, J. (1989). Introduction to Grey Systems Theory. *Journal of Grey System*, *1*, 1–24.

Deng, J. L. (1982). Control problems of grey system. *Systems & Control Letters*, *1*(5), 288–294. doi:10.1016/S0167-6911(82)80025-X

Deng, W., Wang, G., & Zhang, X. (2015). A novel hybrid water quality time series prediction method based on cloud model and fuzzy forecasting. *Chemometrics and Intelligent Laboratory Systems*, *149*, 39–49. doi:10.1016/j.chemolab.2015.09.017

Dennis, C., Fenech, T., & Merrilees, B. (2004). *e-Retailing*. Routledge. Taylor & Francis Group.

Department of Trade & Industry (Philippines). (2008). *Micro, Small and Medium Enterprises (MSMES)*. Retrieved January 28, 2016, from http://www.dti.gov.ph/dti/index.php?p=532

der Laan, E. A., De Brito, M. P., & Vergunst, D. A. (2009). Performance measurement in humanitarian supply chains. *International Journal of Risk Assessment and Management*, *13*(1), 22–45. doi:10.1504/IJRAM.2009.026388

Dhandayudam, P., & Krishnamurthi, I. (2014). A rough set approach for customer segmentation. *Data Science Journal*, *13*(0), 1–11. doi:10.2481/dsj.13-019

Dhillon, W. R., Goldstein, M., & Schiffman, L. (1978). On the appropriateness of Linear Discriminant and Multinomial Classification Analyisis in Marketing Research. *JMR, Journal of Marketing Research*, *15*(1), 103–112. doi:10.2307/3150405

Diakoulaki, D., & Koumoutsos, N. (1991). Cardinal Ranking of Alternative Actions: Extension of the PROMETHEE Method. *European Journal of Operational Research*, (53).

Diebold, F. X. (1998). *Elements of forecasting*. South-Western College Publ.

Dominici, G., Palumbo, F., & Basile, G. (2013). *Consumer Culture Theory: A conceptual Framework*. Organizational Transformation and Social Change.

Donkers, B., Verhoef, P. C., & de Jong, M. G. (2007). Modeling CLV: A test of competing models in the insurance industry. *Quantitative Marketing and Economics*, *5*(2), 163–190. doi:10.1007/s11129-006-9016-y

Doove, L. L., Buuren, S. V., & Dusseldorp, E. (2013). Recursive partitioning for missing data imputation in the presence of interaction effects. *Computational Statistics & Data Analysis*, *27*, 92–104.

Dorasamy, M., Raman, M., & Kaliannan, M. (2013). Knowledge management systems in support of disasters management: A two decade review. *Technological Forecasting and Social Change*, *80*(9), 1834–1853. doi:10.1016/j.techfore.2012.12.008

Dostál, P. (2013). Forecasting of Time Series with Fuzzy Logic. In Nostradamus 2013: Prediction, Modeling, and Analysis of Complex Systems (pp. 155-161). Springer International Publishing. doi:10.1007/978-3-319-00542-3_16

Doyle, M., & Dorling, S. (2002). Visibility Trends in UK 1950-1007. *Atmospheric Environment*, *36*(19), 3161–3172. doi:10.1016/S1352-2310(02)00248-0

Duan, H. T., Ma, R. H., Xu, J. P., Zhang, B., & Zhang, B. (2010). Comparison of different semi-empirical algorithms to estimate chlorophyll-a concentration in inland lake water. *Environmental Monitoring and Assessment*, *170*(1-4), 231–244. doi:10.1007/s10661-009-1228-7 PMID:19908152

Dubois, D., & Prade, H. (1990). Rough fuzzy sets and fuzzy rough sets. *International Journal of General Systems*, *17*(2-3), 191–208. doi:10.1080/03081079008935107

Duda, R. O., Hart, P. E., & Stork, D. G. (2001). *Pattern Classification* (2nd ed.). John Wiley & Sons.

Dueck, G., & Scheuer, T. (1990). Threshold Accepting: A general purpose optimization algorithm appearing superior to simulated annealing. *Journal of Computational Physics*, *90*(1), 161–175. doi:10.1016/0021-9991(90)90201-B

Duma, M., Marwala, T., Twala, B., & Nelwamondo, F. (2013). Partial imputation of unseen records to improve classification using a hybrid multi-layered artificial immune system and genetic algorithm. *Applied Soft Computing*, *13*(12), 4461–4480. doi:10.1016/j.asoc.2013.08.005

Duncan, E., & Elliott, G. (2002). Customer service quality and financial performance among Australian retail financial institutions. *Journal of Financial Services Marketing*, *7*(1), 25–41. doi:10.1057/palgrave.fsm.4770070

Dunn, J. C. (1973). A Fuzzy Relative of the ISODATA Process and Its Use in Detecting Compact Well-Separated Clusters. *Journal of Cybernetics*, *3*(3), 32–57. doi:10.1080/01969727308546046

Eberhart, R. C., & Kennedy, J. (1995). A new optimizer using particle swarm theory. In *Proceedings of Sixth International Symposium on Micro Machine and Human Science*(pp. 39-43). Nagoya, Japan: IEEE Press. doi:10.1109/MHS.1995.494215

Eberhart, R. C., & Kennedy, J. (1995). Particle swarm optimization. *Proceedings of Neural Networks*, *4*, 1942–1948.

Eberhart, R. C., & Kennedy, J. (1997). A discrete binary version of the particle swarm algorithm. In *Proceedings of the Conference on Systems, Man, and Cybernetics*(pp. 4104-4109). Orlando, FL: IEEE Press.

Efendi, R., Ismail, Z., & Deris, M. M. (2015). A new linguistic out-sample approach of fuzzy time series for daily forecasting of Malaysian electricity load demand. *Applied Soft Computing*, *28*, 422–430. doi:10.1016/j.asoc.2014.11.043

El Assady, M., Hafner, D., Hund, M., Jäger, A., Jentner, W., Rohrdantz, C., . . . Keim, D. A. (2013). Visual Analytics for the Prediction of Movie Rating and Box Office Performance. *IEEE VAST Challenge USB Proceedings*.

Elbeltagi, I., & Agag, G. (2016). E-retailing ethics and its impact on customer satisfaction and repurchase intention. *Internet Research*, *26*(1), 288–310. doi:10.1108/IntR-10-2014-0244

Elshorbagy, A., Simonovic, S. P., & Panu, U. S. (2002). Estimation of missing stream flow data using the principles of chaos theory. *Journal of Hydrology (Amsterdam)*, *255*(1-4), 123–133. doi:10.1016/S0022-1694(01)00513-3

EPC RFID. (2013). *What is RFID?* Retrieved March 24, 2015, from http://www.epc-rfid.info/rfid

Estrada, A., Real, R., & Vargas, J. (2008). Using crisp and fuzzy modelling to identify favourability hotspots useful to perform gap analysis. *Biodiversity and Conservation*, *17*(4), 857–871. doi:10.1007/s10531-008-9328-1

Fader, P. S., Hardie, B. G., & Lee, K. L. (2005). RFM and CLV: Using iso-value curves for customer base analysis. *JMR, Journal of Marketing Research*, *42*(4), 415–430. doi:10.1509/jmkr.2005.42.4.415

Fails, A., & Minton, R. (2001). *Comparison of Euro NCAP assessments with injury causation in accidents*. Retrieved September 1, 2014 from http://www-nrd.nhtsa.dot.gov/pdf/esv/esv17/Proceed/00034.pdf

Farris, A. B. (2014). Mobile Shopper Marketing: Assessing the Impact of Mobile Technology on Consumer Path to Purchase. *Shopper Marketing and the Role of In store Marketing*, *11*, 1-25.

Fetscherin, M. (2010). The main determinants of Bollywood movie box office sales. *Journal of Global Marketing*, *23*(5), 461–476. doi:10.1080/08911762.2010.521117

Fink, A. (1995). *How to Analyze Survey Data*. London: Sage Publishers.

Fink, A., & Kosecoff, J. (1998). *How To Conduct Surveys: A Step-by-Step Guide*. London: Sage Publications.

Fisher, R. A. (n.d.). *Iris dataset*. Retrieved from http://archive.ics.uci.edu/ml/machine-learning-databases/iris/iris.data

Fleiss, J., Levin, B., & Paik, M. (2003). *Statistical Methods for Rates and Proportions*. New York: John Wiley and Sons. doi:10.1002/0471445428

Flora, J. D. Jr. (1974). *A note on Ridit Analysis*. Ann Arbor: University of Michigan.

Flores, B. E. (1986). A pragmatic view of accuracy measurement in forecasting. *Omega*, *14*(2), 93–98. doi:10.1016/0305-0483(86)90013-7

Forina, M. (n.d.). *Wine dataset*. Retrieved from http://archive.ics.uci.edu/ml/machine-learning-databases/wine/wine.data

Fornell, C., Johnson, M., Anderson, E., Cha, J., & Bryant, B. (1996). The American customer satisfaction index: Nature, purpose, and findings. *Journal of Marketing*, *60*(4), 7–18. doi:10.2307/1251898

Forthofer, R. N., & Koch, G. (1973). An analysis for compounded functions of categorical data. *Biometrics*, *29*(1), 143–157. doi:10.2307/2529683 PMID:4691050

Fournier, S., & Mick, D. (1999). Rediscovering satisfaction. *Journal of Marketing*, *63*(4), 5–23. doi:10.2307/1251971

Francis, J. E., & White, L. (2004). Internet retailing: Back to the Future. In *Proceedings of the Australian and New Zealand Marketing Academy Conference*. Wellington, New Zealand: Australian and New Zealand Marketing Academy.

Frayley, C., & Raftery, E. (1998). How many clusters? Which clustering method? Answers via model-based cluster analysis. *The Computer Journal*, *41*(8), 578–588. doi:10.1093/comjnl/41.8.578

Fugate, B., Sahin, F., & Mentzer, J. T. (2006). Supply Chain Management Coordination Mechanisms. *Journal of Business Logistics*, *27*(2), 129–161. doi:10.1002/j.2158-1592.2006.tb00220.x

Funk, J. L. (2004). Key technological trajectories and the expansion of mobile Internet applications. *Info*, *6*(3), 208–215. doi:10.1108/14636690410549543

Gabrys, B. (2002). Neuro-fuzzy approach to processing inputs with missing values in pattern recognition problems. *International Journal of Approximate Reasoning*, *30*(3), 149–179. doi:10.1016/S0888-613X(02)00070-1

Gader, P., Mohamed, M., & Chiang, J. (1995). Comparison of crisp and fuzzy character neural networks in handwritten word recognition. *Fuzzy Systems. IEEE Transactions on*, *3*(3), 357–363.

García, J. C. F., Kalenatic, D., & Bello, C. A. L. (2011). Missing data imputation in multivariate data by evolutionary algorithms. *Computers in Human Behavior*, *27*(5), 1468–1474. doi:10.1016/j.chb.2010.06.026

Garcia-Laencina, P. J., Sancho-gomez, J., & Figueiras-vidal, A. R. (2013). Classifying patterns with missing values using Multi-Task Learning perceptrons. *Expert Systems with Applications*, *40*(4), 1333–1341. doi:10.1016/j.eswa.2012.08.057

Gath, I., & Geva, A. B. (1989). Unsupervised optimal fuzzy clustering. *IEEE Transactions on Pattern Analysis and Machine Intelligence*, *11*(7), 773–781. doi:10.1109/34.192473

Gaudet, A. (2004). *Customer relationship marketing and effects of demographics and technology on customer satisfaction and loyalty in financial services*. Old Dominion University.

Gautam, C., & Ravi, V. (2014). Evolving clustering based data imputation. In *Proceedings of the 3rd international conference on Circuits, Power and Computing Technologies (ICCPCT)*, (pp. 1763-1769). doi:10.1109/ICCPCT.2014.7054988

Gautam, C., & Ravi, V. (2015). Counter Propagation Auto Associative Neural Network based Data Imputation.Information Sciences, 325, 288-299.

Gautam, C., & Ravi, V. (2015). Data Imputation via Evolutionary Computation. *Clustering and a Neural Network, Neurocomputing, Elsevier*, *153*, 134–142.

Ge, P., Wang, J., Ren, P., Gao, H., & Luo, Y. (2013). A new improved forecasting method integrated fuzzy time series with the exponential smoothing method. *International Journal of Environment and Pollution*, *51*(3-4), 206–221. doi:10.1504/IJEP.2013.054030

Geraghty, S., & Torres, A. M. (2009). The Irish wine market: A market segmentation study. *International Journal of Wine Business Research*, *21*(2), 143–154. doi:10.1108/17511060910967980

Ghiassi, M., Lio, D., & Moon, B. (2015). Pre-production forecasting of movie revenues with a dynamic artificial neural network. *Expert Systems with Applications*, *42*(6), 3176–3193. doi:10.1016/j.eswa.2014.11.022

Ghosh, A. K., Chaudhuri, P., & Murthy, C. A. (2005). On visualization and aggregation of nearest neighbor classifiers. *Pattern Analysis and Machine Intelligence. IEEE Transactions on*, *27*(10), 1592–1602.

Ghosh, A., & Nath, B. (2004). Multi-Objective rule mining using genetic algorithms. *Information Sciences*, *163*(1-3), 123–133. doi:10.1016/j.ins.2003.03.021

Glorot, X., Bordes, A., & Bengio, Y. (2011). Deep Sparse Rectifier Neural Networks.*International Conference on Artificial Intelligence and Statistics*.

Golinelli, G. S., & Gatti, S. (2000). *L'impresa sistema vitale. Il governo dei rapporti inter-sistemici*. Symphonya. Emerging Issues in Management.

Gomes, G. S. S., Ludermir, T. B., & Lima, L. M. M. R. (2011). Comparison of new activation functions in neural network for forecasting financial time series. *Neural Computing and Applications, Springer*, *20*, 417–439. doi:10.1007/s00521-010-0407-3

Gonzalez, M. E., Quesada, G., & Mora-Monge, C. (2012). An international study on manufacturing competitive priorities. *Journal of Management Policy and Practice*, *13*(3), 116–128.

Gorane, S. J., & Kant, R. (2013). Modelling the SCM enablers: An integrated ISM-fuzzy MICMAC approach. *Asia Pacific Journal of Marketing and Logistics*, *25*(2), 263–286. doi:10.1108/13555851311314059

Gorane, S. J., & Kant, R. (2013). Supply chain management: Modelling the enablers using {ISM} and fuzzy {MICMAC} approach. *International Journal of Logistics Systems and Management*, *16*(2), 147–166. doi:10.1504/IJLSM.2013.056158

Goumas, M., & Lygerou, V. (2000). An extension of the PROMETHEE method for decision making in fuzzy environment: Ranking of alternative energy exploitation projects. *European Journal of Operational Research*, *123*(3), 606–613. doi:10.1016/S0377-2217(99)00093-4

Govindarajan, M., & Chandrasekaran, R. M. (2010). Evaluation of k-nearest neighbor classifier performance for direct marketing. *Expert Systems with Applications*, *37*(1), 253–258. doi:10.1016/j.eswa.2009.04.055

Gowtamreddy, P. (2014). *Opinion Mining of Online Customer Reviews*. (Master Thesis). National Institute of Technology Rourkela.

Greco, S., Matarazzo, B., & Slowinski, R. (1998). A new rough set approach to evaluation of bankruptcy risk. In Operational Tools in the Management of Financial Risk. Boston: Kluwer Academic Publishers.

Greco, S., Matarazzo, B., & Slowinski, R. (1999). In T. Gal, T. Hanne, & T. Stewart (Eds.), *The use of rough sets and fuzzy sets in MCDM. In Advances in Multiple Criteria Decision Making* (pp. 14.1–14.59). Boston: Kluwer Academic Publishers.

Greco, S., Matarazzo, B., & Slowinski, R. (2001). Rough sets theory for multicriteria decision analysis. *European Journal of Operational Research*, *129*(1), 129–147. doi:10.1016/S0377-2217(00)00167-3

Green, P. E., Tull, D. S., & Albaum, G. (1997). *Research for Marketing Decisions*. New Delhi: Prentice Hall of India Private Limited.

Gremler, D., & Brown, S. (1996). Service loyalty: its nature, importance and implications. In Caruana, A. (2002). Service loyalty: the effects of service quality and the mediating role of customer satisfaction. *European Journal of Marketing*, *36*(7/8), 811–828.

Gronostajski, Z., Bandola, P., & Karbowski, P. (2006). The effect of crashworthiness parameters on the behaviour of car-body elements. *Archives of Civil and Mechanical Engineering*, *6*(1), 31–46. doi:10.1016/S1644-9665(12)60075-2

Groß, M. (2015). Mobile shopping: A classification framework and literature review. *International Journal of Retail & Distribution Management*, *43*(3), 221–241. doi:10.1108/IJRDM-06-2013-0119

Grzymala-Busse, J., Pawlak, Z., Slowinski, R., & Ziarko, W. (1999). Rough sets. *Communications of the ACM*, *38*(11).

Gupta, A., & Lam, M. S. (1996). Estimating missing values using neural networks. *The Journal of the Operational Research Society*, *47*(2), 229–238. doi:10.1057/jors.1996.21

Gupta, M. (2012). Application of weighted particle swarm optimization in association rule mining. *International Journal of Computer Science and Informatics*, *1*, 2231–5292.

Gustavsson, L. (2003). *Humanitarian logistics: Context and challenges*. Academic Press.

Gwo-Guang, L., & Lin, H.-F. (2005). Customer perceptions of e-service quality in online shopping. *International Journal of Retail & Distribution Management*, *33*(2), 161–176. doi:10.1108/09590550510581485

Hadavandi, E., Shavandi, H., & Ghanbari, A. (2010). Integration of genetic fuzzy systems and artificial neural networks for stock price forecasting. *Knowledge-Based Systems*, *23*(8), 800–808. doi:10.1016/j.knosys.2010.05.004

Hadian, A., Nasiri, M., & Bidgoli, B. M. (2010). Clustering based multi-objective rule mining using genetic algorithm. *International Journal of Digital Content Technology and its Applications, 4*, 37-42.

Hair, J. F., Anderson, R. E., Tatham, R. L., & Black, W. C. (1995). *Multivariate data analysis*. Upper Saddle River, NJ: Prentice Hall.

Han, F., Yao, H. F., & Ling, Q. H. (2012). An Improved Extreme Learning Machine Based on Particle Swarm Optimization, Bio-Inspired Computing and Applications.*7th International Conference on Intelligent Computing.*

Han, J., & Kamber, M. (2006). *Data Mining: Concepts and Techniques* (2nd ed.). Morgan Kaufmann Publishers.

Han, J., Pei, H., & Yin, Y. (2000). Mining frequent patterns without candidate generation. In *Proceedings of Conference on the Management of Data, SIGMOD 2000* (pp. 1–12). Dallas, TX: ACM Press. doi:10.1145/342009.335372

Han, L. H. (2005). Estimating chlorophyll-a concentration using first-derivative spectra in coastal water. *International Journal of Remote Sensing*, *26*(23), 5235–5244. doi:10.1080/01431160500219133

Härdle, W., & Stoker, T. M. (1989). Investigating Smooth Multiple Regression by the Method of Average Derivatives. *Journal of the American Statistical Association*, *84*(408), 986–995.

Harrison, D., & Rubinfeld, D. L. (n.d.). *Boston Housing dataset*. Retrieved from http://archive.ics.uci.edu/ml/machine-learning-databases/housing/housing.data

Harvie, C., & Lee, B. C. (2003). *Public policy and SME development*. Working Paper 03-18. Department of Economics, University of Wollongong.

Harvie, C. (2008). SMEs in regional trade and investment development. In T. Van Hoa & C. Harvie (Eds.), *Regional Trade Agreements in East Asia* (pp. 149–186). Cheltenham, UK: Edward Elgar.

Hassan, S., Yulan, H., & Harith, A. (2012). Alleviating data sparsity for Twitter sentiment anal- ysis. In: 2nd Workshop on Making Sense of Microposts (#MSM2012): Big things come in small packages at the 21st International Conference on theWorld Wide Web (WWW'12). *CEUR Workshop Proceedings* (CEUR-WS.org)

Hastie, T., Tibshirani, R., & Friedman, J. (2001). *The elements of statistic all earning: data mining, inference, and prediction*. New York: Springer.

Hatch, M. J., & Schultz, M. (2008). *Taking Brand Initiative. How companies Can Align Strategy, Culture, and Identity Through Corporate Branding*. Jossey-Bass.

Haughton, D., McLaughlin, M. D., Mentzer, K., & Zhang, C. (2015). *Movie Analytics: A Hollywood Introduction to Big Data*. Academic Press.

Hauser, W. J. (2007). Marketing analytics: The evolution of marketing research in the twenty-first century. *Direct Marketing: An International Journal*, *1*(1), 38–54. doi:10.1108/17505930710734125

Hoffmann, F., Baesens, B., Martens, J., Put, F., & Vanthienen, J. (2002). Comparing a genetic fuzzy and a neurofuzzy classifier for credit scoring. *International Journal of Intelligent Systems*, *17*(11), 1067–1083. doi:10.1002/int.10052

Hole, G. (n.d.). Retrieved from www.sussex.ac.uk/Users/grahamh/RM1web/WilcoxonTable2005.pdf

Holmes, C. C., & Adams, N. M. (2002). A probabilistic nearest neighbour method for statistical pattern recognition. *Journal of the Royal Statistical Society. Series B, Statistical Methodology*, *64*(2), 295–306. doi:10.1111/1467-9868.00338

Holt, D. B. (2002). Why Do Brands Cause Trouble? A Dialectical Theory of Consumer Culture and Branding. *The Journal of Consumer Research*, *29*(1), 70–90. doi:10.1086/339922

Hong, D. H., & Choi, C. H. (2000). Multi-criteria fuzzy decision making problems based on vague set theory. *Fuzzy Sets and Systems, Vol*, *114*(1), 103–113. doi:10.1016/S0165-0114(98)00271-1

Houtsma, M., & Swami, A. (1995). Set-oriented data mining in relational databases. *Data & Knowledge Engineering*, *17*(3), 245–263. doi:10.1016/0169-023X(95)00024-M

Hsi, P., & Lu Philip, Y. J. (2015). Factors affecting purchase intention on mobile shopping web sites. *Internet Research*, *19*(4), 442–458.

Huang, C. L., Chen, M. C., & Wang, C. J. (2007). Credit scoring with a data mining approach based on support vector machines. *Expert Systems with Applications*, *33*(4), 847–856. doi:10.1016/j.eswa.2006.07.007

Huang, G. B., Zhu, Q., & Siew, C. (2004). Extreme Learning Machine: A New Learning Scheme of Feedforward Neural Networks.*International Joint Conference on Neural Networks*, 2, 985-990.

Huang, G. B., Zhu, Q., & Siew, C. (2006). Extreme Learning Machine: Theory and Applications. *Neurocomputing*, *70*(1-3), 489–501. doi:10.1016/j.neucom.2005.12.126

Huang, H., Hu, S., & Abdel-Aty, M. (2014). Indexing crash worthiness and crash aggressivity by major car brands. *Safety Science*, *62*, 339–347. doi:10.1016/j.ssci.2013.09.002

Huang, H., Li, C., & Zeng, Q. (2016). Crash protectiveness to occupant injury and vehicle damage: An investigation on major car brands. *Accident; Analysis and Prevention*, *86*, 129–136. doi:10.1016/j.aap.2015.10.008 PMID:26551733

Huang, Y. L., Horng, S. J., He, M., Fan, P., Kao, T. W., Khan, M. K., & Kuo, I. H. et al. (2011). A hybrid forecasting model for enrollments based on aggregated fuzzy time series and particle swarm optimization. *Expert Systems with Applications*, *38*(7), 8014–8023. doi:10.1016/j.eswa.2010.12.127

Huarng, K. (2001). Heuristic models of fuzzy time series for forecasting. *Fuzzy Sets and Systems*, *123*(3), 369–386. doi:10.1016/S0165-0114(00)00093-2

Hughes, A. M. (1994). *Strategic database marketing*. Chicago, IL: Probus Publishing.

Hull, J. C. (2002). Fundamentals of futures and options markets (4th ed.). Upper Saddle River, NJ: Pearson Education Inc.

Hurst, M., & Nigam, K. (2004). Retrieving Topical Sentiments from Online Document Collections. In *Proceedings of SPIE, Document Recognition and Retrieval XI* (pages 27-34).

Hu, Y. H., & Yeh, T. W. (2014). Discovering valuable frequent patterns based on RFM analysis without customer identification information. *Knowledge-Based Systems, 61*, 76–88. doi:10.1016/j.knosys.2014.02.009

Hwang, H., & Oh, J. (2010). Fuzzy models for predicting time series stock price index. *International Journal of Control, Automation, and Systems, 8*(3), 702–706. doi:10.1007/s12555-010-0325-2

Hwang, J. R., Chen, S. M., & Lee, C. H. (1998). Handling forecasting problems using fuzzy time series. *Fuzzy Sets and Systems, 100*(1), 217–228. doi:10.1016/S0165-0114(97)00121-8

Hyndman, R. J., & Athanasopoulos, G. (2014). *Forecasting: principles and practice*. OTexts.

Iacobucci, D., Ostrom, A., & Grayson, K. (1995). Distinguishing service quality and customer satisfaction: The voice of the consumer. *Journal of Consumer Psychology, 4*(3), 277–303. doi:10.1207/s15327663jcp0403_04

Iakovou, E., & Douligeris, C. (2001). An information management system for the emergency management of hurricane disasters. *International Journal of Risk Assessment and Management*. Retrieved from http://www.inderscienceonline.com/doi/abs/10.1504/IJRAM.2001.001508

iBeacon - Creative iBeacon Solutions. (n.d.). Available from: http://www.ibeacon.com.tr/#news

iBeacon Wars- A guide to the major iBeacon solutions, iBeacon.com Insider. (n.d.). Available from: http://www.ibeacon.com/ibeacon-wars-a-guide-to-the-major-ibeacon-companies/

IBM. (2015). *IBM Watson Analytics*. Retrieved October 16, 2015, from http://www-03.ibm.com/software/products/en/watson-analytics

Ismail, Z., Efendi, R., & Deris, M. M. (2015). Application of Fuzzy Time Series Approach in Electric Load Forecasting. *New Mathematics and Natural Computation, 11*(3), 229–248. doi:10.1142/S1793005715500076

Jaeger, P. T., Shneiderman, B., Fleischmann, K. R., Preece, J., Qu, Y., & Fei Wu, P. (2007). Community response grids: E-government, social networks, and effective emergency management. *Telecommunications Policy, 31*(10–11), 592–604. doi:10.1016/j.telpol.2007.07.008

Jain, V. K., & Kumar, S. (2015a). Big Data Analytic Using Cloud Computing. In *Proceeding of 2015 Second International Conference on Advances in Computing and Communication Engineering* (pp. 667-672).

Jain, D., & Singh, S. S. (2002). Customer lifetime value research in marketing: A review and future directions. *Journal of Interactive Marketing, 16*(2), 34–46. doi:10.1002/dir.10032

Jain, V. K., & Kumar, S. (2015b). An Effective Approach to Track Levels of Influenza-A (H1N1) Pandemic in India Using Twitter. *Procedia Computer Science., 70*(1), 801–807. doi:10.1016/j.procs.2015.10.120

Jansen, B. J., Zhang, M., Sobel, K., & Chowdury, A. (2009). Twitter Power: Tweets as Electronic Word of Mouth. *Journal of the American Society for Information Science and Technology, 60*(11), 2169–2188. doi:10.1002/asi.21149

Javedani Sadaei, H., & Lee, M. H. (2014). Multilayer stock forecasting model using fuzzy time series. *The Scientific World Journal*. PMID:24605058

Jefferson, T. L. (2006). Evaluating the role of information technology in crisis and emergency management. *Vine*, *36*(3), 261–264. doi:10.1108/03055720610703542

Jeong, N., Yoo, Y., & Heo, T.-Y. (2009). Moderating effect of personal innovativeness on mobile-RFID services: Based on Warshaw's purchase intention model. *Technological Forecasting and Social Change*, *76*(1), 154–164. doi:10.1016/j.techfore.2008.08.007

Jerez, J., Molina, I., Subirates, J., & Franco, L. (2006). Missing data imputation in breast cancer prognosis. In *Proceedings of the 24th IASTED international conference on biomedical engineering (BioMed'06).*

Jiang, L., Cai, Z., Wang, D., & Jiang, S. (2007, August). Survey of improving k-nearest-neighbor for classification. In FSKD (pp. 679-683). IEEE. doi:10.1109/FSKD.2007.552

Jiang, H., Livingston, M., & Room, R. (2015). Alcohol consumption and fatal injuries in Australia before and after major traffic safety initiatives: A time series analysis. *Alcoholism, Clinical and Experimental Research*, *39*(1), 175–183. doi:10.1111/acer.12609 PMID:25623416

Jiang, L. A., Yang, Z., & Jun, M. (2013). Measuring consumer perceptions of online shopping. *Journal of Service Management*, *24*(2), 191–214. doi:10.1108/09564231311323962

Jiang, Y., & Zhou, Z. H. (2004). Editing training data for kNN classifiers with neural network ensemble. In *Advances in Neural Networks–ISNN 2004* (pp. 356–361). Springer Berlin Heidelberg.

Joaquin Aldas Manzano, C. R. (2008, December). Exploring individual personality factors as drivers of M-shopping acceptance. *Industrial Management & Data Systems*, *109*(6), 739–757. doi:10.1108/02635570910968018

Johns, N., Avci, T., & Karatepe, O. (2004). Measuring service quality of travel agents: Evidence from Northern Cyprus. *Service Industries Journal*, *24*(3), 82–100. doi:10.1080/0264206042000247777

Johnson, R. W. (n.d.). *Bodyfat dataset*. Retrieved from http://lib.stat.cmu.edu/datasets/bodyfat

Johnson, R., & Wichern, D. (2002). *Applied Multivariate Statistical Analysis* (5th ed.). Upper Saddle River, NJ: Prentice Hall.

Jones, M., & Suh, J. (2000). Transaction-specific satisfaction and overall satisfaction: An empirical analysis. *Journal of Services Marketing*, *14*(2), 147–159. doi:10.1108/08876040010371555

Jonker, J. J., Piersma, N., & Van den Poel, D. (2004). Joint optimization of customer segmentation and marketing policy to maximize long-term profitability. *Expert Systems with Applications*, *27*(2), 159–168. doi:10.1016/j.eswa.2004.01.010

Joshi, A. (2015). Movie Stars and the Volatility of Movie Revenues. *Journal of Media Economics*, *28*(4), 246–267. doi:10.1080/08997764.2015.1094079

Joy, A., & Li, E. P. H. (2012). Studying Consumption Behaviour through Multiple Lenses: An Overview of Consumer Culture Theory. *Journal of Business Anthropology*, *1*(1).

Jumamil-Mercado, G. (2013). Philippines. In S. Sato (Ed.), Impact of the global financial crisis on SMEs: What happens on SMEs through the global financial crisis? (pp. 61-78). Asian Productivity Organization (APO).

Kabra, G., & Ramesh, A. (2015b). Analyzing ICT Issues in Humanitarian Supply Chain Management: A SAP-LAP Linkages Framework. *Global Journal of Flexible Systems Management*, 1–15. doi:10.1007/s40171-014-0088-3

Kabra, G., Ramesh, A., & Arshinder, K. (2015). Identification and prioritization of coordination barriers in humanitarian supply chain management. *International Journal of Disaster Risk Reduction*.

Kabra, G., & Ramesh, A. (2015a). An emprical investigation of enablers in {Humanitarain} {Supply} {Chain} {Management} in {India}: {A} {Case} {Study}. *Journal of Advances Research in Management, 11*(1).

Kadirov, D., & Varey, R. J. (2010). Symbolism in Marketing Systems. *Journal of Macromarketing, 31*(2), 160–171. doi:10.1177/0276146710393519

Kahan, R. (1998). Using database marketing techniques to enhance your one-to-one marketing initiatives. *Journal of Consumer Marketing, 15*(5), 491–493. doi:10.1108/07363769810235965

Kahraman, C., Yazıcı, I. & Karaşan, A. (2015). *A Literature Survey on the Usage of Fuzzy MCDM Methods for Digital Marketing*. doi: 10.4018/978-1-4666-8808-7.ch001

Kahraman, C. (2008). *Fuzzy multi-criteria decision making: theory and applications with recent developments.* New York: Springer. doi:10.1007/978-0-387-76813-7

Kahraman, C., Cebeci, U., & Ulukan, Z. (2003). Multi-criteria supplier selection using fuzzy AHP. *Logistics Information Management, 16*(6), 382–394. doi:10.1108/09576050310503367

Kandasamy, W. B. V., Smarandache, F., & Ilanthenral, K. (2007). *Elementary fuzzy matrix theory and fuzzy models for social scientists*. Academic Press.

Kang, P. (2013). Locally linear reconstruction based missing value imputation for supervised learning. *Neurocomputing, 118*, 65–78. doi:10.1016/j.neucom.2013.02.016

Kantor, S., Winkelstein, W., & Ibrahim, M. A. (1968). A note on Interpretetion of the ridit as quantile ranks. *American Journal of Epidemiology, 87*, 609–615. PMID:5654949

Kapucu, N. (2006). Interagency Communication Networks During Emergencies Boundary Spanners in Multiagency Coordination. *American Review of Public Administration, 36*(2), 207–225. doi:10.1177/0275074005280605

Karlik, B., & Olgac, A. V. (2010). Performance Analysis of Various Activation Functions in Generalized MLP Architectures of Neural Networks. *International Journal of Artificial Intelligence and Expert Systems, 1*, 111–122.

Kaushal, S. K. (2013). The Importance of Apparel Product Attributes for Teenaged Buyers. *NMIMS Management Review, XXIII*, 45–64.

Kaya, M., & Alhajj, R. (2004). Mining optimized fuzzy association rules using multi-objective genetic algorithm. In *Proceedings of8th IEEE International Conference on Intelligent Engineering Systems* (pp.38-43). Cluj-Napoca, Romania: IEEE Press.

Kehler, N. (2004). *Coordinating Humanitarian Assistance: A Comparative Analysis of Three Cases*. Virginia Polytechnic Institute and State University.

Keiningham, T., Goddard, M., Vavra, T., & Source, A. (1999). Customer delight and the bottom line. *Marketing Management, 8*(3), 57–63.

Kent, R. E. (1994). Rough concept analysis, rough sets, fuzzy sets knowledge discovery. *Proceedings of the International Workshop on Rough, Sets, Knowledge, Discovery*. Springer-Verlag Berlin. doi:10.1007/978-1-4471-3238-7_30

Keramati, A., & Yousefi, N. (2011, January). A proposed classification of data mining techniques in credit scoring. In *Proceeding of 2011 International Conference of Industrial Engineering and Operations Management* (pp. 22-4).

Kersuliene, V., & Turskis, Z. (2011). Integrated fuzzy multiple criteria decision making model for architect selection. *Technological and Economic Development of Economy, 17*(4), 645–666. doi:10.3846/20294913.2011.635718

Kersuliene, V., Zavadskas, E. K., & Turskis, Z. (2010). Selection of Rational Dispute Resolution Method by Applying New Step-Wise Weight Assessment Ratio Analysis (SWARA). *Journal of Business Economics and Management*, *11*(2), 243–258. doi:10.3846/jbem.2010.12

Keskin, G. A. (2015). Using integrated fuzzy DEMATEL and fuzzy C: Means algorithm for supplier evaluation and selection. *International Journal of Production Research*, *53*(12), 3586–3602. doi:10.1080/00207543.2014.980461

Ketchen, D. Jr, & Shook, C. (1996). The application of cluster analysis in strategic management research: An analysis and critique. *Strategic Management Journal*, *17*(6), 441–458. doi:10.1002/(SICI)1097-0266(199606)17:6<441::AID-SMJ819>3.0.CO;2-G

Khajvand, M., & Tarokh, M. J. (2011). Estimating customer future value of different customer segments based on adapted RFM model in retail banking context. *Procedia Computer Science*, *3*, 1327–1332. doi:10.1016/j.procs.2011.01.011

Khajvand, M., Zolfaghar, K., Ashoori, S., & Alizadeh, S. (2011). Estimating customer lifetime value based on RFM analysis of customer purchase behavior: Case study. *Procedia Computer Science*, *3*, 57–63. doi:10.1016/j.procs.2010.12.011

Khashei, M., Rezvan, M. T., Hamadani, A. Z., & Bijari, M. (2013). A bi-level neural-based fuzzy classification approach for credit scoring problems. *Complexity*, *18*(6), 46–57. doi:10.1002/cplx.21458

Kim, C., Galliers, R. D., Shin, N., Ryoo, J., & Kim, J. (2012). Factors influencing internet shopping value and customer repurchase intention. *Electronic Commerce Research and Applications*, *11*(4), 374–387. doi:10.1016/j.elerap.2012.04.002

Kimes, S. E., & Chase, R. B. (1998). The strategic levers of yield management. *Journal of Service Research*, *1*(2), 156–166. doi:10.1177/109467059800100205

Kimes, S. E., Chase, R. B., Choi, S., Lee, P. Y., & Ngonzi, E. N. (1998). Restaurant revenue management applying yield management to the restaurant industry. *The Cornell Hotel and Restaurant Administration Quarterly*, *39*(3), 32–39. doi:10.1177/001088049803900308

Kim, H., & Yoon, C. (2004). Determinants of subscriber churn and customer loyalty in the Korean mobile telephony market. *Telecommunications Policy*, *28*(9), 751–765. doi:10.1016/j.telpol.2004.05.013

Kim, K. J. (2004). Artificial neural networks with feature transformation based on domain knowledge for the prediction of stock index futures. *International Journal of Intelligent Systems in Accounting Finance & Management*, *12*(3), 167–176. doi:10.1002/isaf.252

Kim, K. Y.-Y. (2012). Mobile shopping motivation: An application of multiple discriminant analysis. *International Journal of Retail & Distribution Management*, *40*(10), 778–789. doi:10.1108/09590551211263182

Kim, T., Hong, J., & Kang, P. (2015). Box office forecasting using machine learning algorithms based on SNS data. *International Journal of Forecasting*, *31*(2), 364–390. doi:10.1016/j.ijforecast.2014.05.006

Kim, T., Hong, J., & Koo, H. (2013). Forecasting box-office revenue by considering social network services in the Korean market. *Sains Humanika*, *64*(2), 97–101.

Kline, R. B. (1998). *Principles and Practice of Structural Equation Modeling*. New York: Guliford Press.

Klumpp, M., Abidi, H., de Leeuw, S., & Klumpp, M. (2014). Humanitarian supply chain performance management: A systematic literature review. *Supply Chain Management: An International Journal*, *19*(5/6), 592–608. doi:10.1108/SCM-09-2013-0349

Kocak, C. (2013). First-order ARMA type fuzzy time series method based on fuzzy logic relation tables. *Mathematical Problems in Engineering*.

Koh, H. C. (2015). A two-step method to construct credit scoring models with data mining techniques. *International Journal of Business and Information, 1*(1).

Kolesar, M. B., & Galbraith, R. W. (2000). A services-marketing perspective on e-retailing: Implications for e-retailers and directions for further research. *Internet Research: Electronic Networking Applications and Policy, 10*(5), 424–438. doi:10.1108/10662240010349444

Kotler, P., & Armstrong, G. (2012). Principles of Marketing. Studia Universitatis Babes-Bolyai, 58(3), 3-19.

Kotler, P., Keller, K. L., Koshi, A., & Jha, M. (2007). *Marketing Management.* New Delhi: Pearson Education.

Kou, G., Peng, Y., & Lu, C. (2014). MCDM approach to evaluating bank loan default models. *Technological and Economic Development of Economy, 20*(2), 292–311. doi:10.3846/20294913.2014.913275

Kovacs, G., & Spens, K. M. (2007). Humanitarian logistics in disaster relief operations. *International Journal of Physical Distribution & Logistics Management, 37*(2), 99–114. doi:10.1108/09600030710734820

Krishna, M., & Ravi, V. (2013). Particle swarm optimization and covariance matrix based data imputation.*IEEE International Conference on Computational Intelligence and Computing Research (ICCIC)*. doi:10.1109/ICCIC.2013.6724232

Kullgren, A., Lie, A., & Tingvall, C. (2010). Comparison between Euro NCAP test results and real-world crash data. *Traffic Injury Prevention, 11*(6), 587–593. doi:10.1080/15389588.2010.508804 PMID:21128188

Kumar, V., & Rajan, B. (2009). Profitable customer management: Measuring and maximizing customer lifetime value. *Management Accounting Quarterly, 10*(3), 1.

Kuo Fang Peng, Y. C. (2014, July). Brand relationship, consumption values and branded app adoption. *Industrial Management & Data Systems, 114*(8), 1131–1143. doi:10.1108/IMDS-05-2014-0132

Kuo, I. H., Horng, S. J., Kao, T. W., Lin, T. L., Lee, C. L., & Pan, Y. (2009). An improved method for forecasting enrollments based on fuzzy time series and particle swarm optimization. *Expert Systems with Applications, 36*(3), 6108–6117. doi:10.1016/j.eswa.2008.07.043

Kuo, R. J., & Tapia, A. (2011). Application of particle swarm optimization to association rule mining. *Applied Soft Computing, 11*(1), 326–336. doi:10.1016/j.asoc.2009.11.023

Laha, A. (2007). Building contextual classifiers by integrating fuzzy rule based classification technique and k-nn method for credit scoring. *Advanced Engineering Informatics, 21*(3), 281–291. doi:10.1016/j.aei.2006.12.004

Lahdelma, R., Miettinen, K., & Salminen, P. (2003). Ordinal criteria in stochastic multicriteria acceptability analysis (SMAA). *European Journal of Operational Research, 147*(1), 117–127. doi:10.1016/S0377-2217(02)00267-9

Lahdelma, R., & Salminen, P. (2001). SMAA-2: Stochastic multicriteria acceptability analysis for group decision making. *Operations Research, 49*(3), 444–454. doi:10.1287/opre.49.3.444.11220

Lahsasna, A., Ainon, R. N., & Teh, Y. W. (2010). Credit Scoring Models Using Soft Computing Methods: A Survey. *Int. Arab J. Inf. Technol., 7*(2), 115–123.

Laib, F., & Radjef, M. S. (2011a). Commodity futures market mechanism: Mathematical formulation and some analytical properties. *Journal of Engineering and Computer Innovations., 2*, 106–124.

Laib, F., & Radjef, M. S. (2011b). Automated traders in commodities markets: Case of producer-consumer institution. *Expert Systems with Applications, 38*(12), 15134–15142. doi:10.1016/j.eswa.2011.05.091

Lai, K. K., Yu, L., Wang, S., & Zhou, L. (2006). Credit risk analysis using a reliability-based neural network ensemble model. In *Artificial Neural Networks–ICANN 2006* (pp. 682–690). Springer Berlin Heidelberg. doi:10.1007/11840930_71

Le, C. F., Li, Y. M., Zha, Y., Sun, D. Y., Huang, C. H., & Lu, H. (2009). A four-band semi-analytical model for estimating chlorophyll a in highly turbid lakes: The case of Taihu Lake, China. *Remote Sensing of Environment*, *113*(6), 1175–1182. doi:10.1016/j.rse.2009.02.005

Lee, H., Lee, Y., & Yoo, D. (2000). The determinants of perceived service quality and its relationship with satisfaction. *Journal of Services Marketing*, *14*(3), 217–231. doi:10.1108/08876040010327220

Lee, K. S., & Tan, S. J. (2003). E-retailing versus physical retailing A theoretical model and empirical test of consumer choice. *Journal of Business Research*, *56*(11), 877–885. doi:10.1016/S0148-2963(01)00274-0

Lembke, J. (2002). Mobile Commerce and the creation of a marketplace. *Info*, *4*(3), 50–56. doi:10.1108/14636690210440013

Leung, K., Cheong, F., & Cheong, C. (2007, September). Consumer credit scoring using an artificial immune system algorithm. In *Evolutionary Computation, 2007. CEC 2007. IEEE Congress on* (pp. 3377-3384). IEEE. doi:10.1109/CEC.2007.4424908

Levin, D. G. (2014). Predicting mobile app usage for purchasing and information sharing. *International Journal of Retail & Distribution Management*, *42*(8), 759–774. doi:10.1108/IJRDM-11-2012-0108

Levy, M. (2008). Stock market crashes as social phase transitions. *Journal of Economic Dynamics & Control*, *32*(1), 137–155. doi:10.1016/j.jedc.2007.01.023

Li, F. C., Wang, P. K., & Wang, G. E. (2009, December). Comparison of the primitive classifiers with extreme learning machine in credit scoring. In *Industrial Engineering and Engineering Management, 2009. IEEM 2009. IEEE International Conference on* (pp. 685-688). IEEE. doi:10.1109/IEEM.2009.5373241

Li, D. C., Dai, W. L., & Tseng, W. T. (2011). A two-stage clustering method to analyze customer characteristics to build discriminative customer management: A case of textile manufacturing business. *Expert Systems with Applications*, *38*(6), 7186–7191. doi:10.1016/j.eswa.2010.12.041

Lie, A., Kullgren, A., & Tingvall, C. (2001). *Comparison of Euro NCAP test results with Folksam car model safety ratings.* Retrieved September 2, 2014 from http://www.euroncap.com/files/ESV_paper_2001---57a2e10b-23a9-4ffb-88e5-a17b21f8923c.pdf

Lie, A., & Tingvall, C. (2002). How do Euro NCAP results correlate with real-life injury risks? A paired comparison study of car-to-car crashes. *Traffic Injury Prevention*, *3*(4), 288–293. doi:10.1080/15389580214632

Lieberthal, R. D. (2008). Hospital Quality: A PRIDIT Approach. *Health Services Research*, *43*(3), 18. doi:10.1111/j.1475-6773.2007.00821.x PMID:18454777

Li, J., & Li, L. (2014). A Location Recommender Based on a Hidden Markov Model: Mobile Social Networks. *Journal of Organizational Computing and Electronic Commerce*, *24*(2-3), 2–3, 257–270. doi:10.1080/10919392.2014.896730

Li, K., & Du, T. C. (2012). Building a targeted mobile advertising system for location-based services. *Decision Support Systems*, *54*(1), 1–8. doi:10.1016/j.dss.2012.02.002

Lilien, G. L., Kotler, P., & Moorthy, S. K. (1992). *Marketing Models.* Englewood Cliffs, NJ: Prentice-Hall, Inc.

Lim, D., Anthony, P., Mun, H. C., & Wai, N. K. (2008). *Assessing the Accuracy of Grey System Theory against Artificial Neural Network in Predicting Online Auction Closing Price.* Paper presented at the International MultiConference of Engineers and Computer Scientists, Hong Kong.

Lin, T. Y., & Cercone, N. (1997). *Rough Sets and Data Mining*. Kluwer Academic Publishers.

Liu, B. (2012). Sentiment Analysis and Opinion Mining. *Synthesis Lectures on Human Language Technologies, 5*(1).

Liu, B. (2012). *Sentiment Analysis and Opinion Mining*. Morgan & Claypool Publishers.

Liu, D. R., & Shih, Y. Y. (2005a). Hybrid approaches to product recommendation based on customer lifetime value and purchase preferences. *Journal of Systems and Software, 77*(2), 181–191. doi:10.1016/j.jss.2004.08.031

Liu, D. R., & Shih, Y. Y. (2005b). Integrating AHP and data mining for product recommendation based on customer lifetime value. *Information & Management, 42*(3), 387–400. doi:10.1016/j.im.2004.01.008

Liu, G. L. (2010). Rough set theory based on two universal sets and its applications. *Knowledge-Based Systems, 23*(2), 110–115. doi:10.1016/j.knosys.2009.06.011

Liu, H., Darabi, H., Banerjee, P., & Liu, J. (2007). Survey of Wireless Indoor Positioning Techniques and Systems. *IEEE Transactions on Systems, Man and Cybernetics. Part C, Applications and Reviews, 37*(6), 1067–1080. doi:10.1109/TSMCC.2007.905750

Liu, H., & Zhang, S. (2012). Noisy data elimination using mutual k-nearest neighbor for classification mining. *Journal of Systems and Software, 85*(5), 1067–1074. doi:10.1016/j.jss.2011.12.019

Liu, S., & Forrest, J. (2007). The Current Developing Status on Grey System Theory. *Journal of Grey System, 2*, 111–123.

Li, Y., Ning, P., Wang, X. S., & Jajodia, S. (2003). Discovering calendar-based temporal association rules. *Data & Knowledge Engineering, 44*(2), 193–218. doi:10.1016/S0169-023X(02)00135-0

Long, D. C., & Wood, D. F. (1995). The logistics of famine relief. *Journal of Business Logistics, 16*, 213–213.

Lowry, R. (2008). *Concepts & Applications of Inferential Statistics*. Academic Press.

Luna, J. M., Romero, J. R., & Ventura, S. (2013). Grammar-Based Multi-Objective Algorithms for Mining Association Rules. *Data & Knowledge Engineering, 86*, 19–37. doi:10.1016/j.datak.2013.01.002

MacQueen, J. (1967). Some methods for classification and analysis of multivariate observations. In *Proceedings of the 5th Berkeley Symposium on Mathematical Statistics and Probability*. University of California Press.

Maffesoli, M. (2004). *Il tempo delle tribù. Il declino dell'individualismo nelle società postmoderne*. Edizioni Angelo Guerini e Associati SpA.

Mahapatra, S., & Sreekumar, N. A. (2012). A RIDIT apprach to evaluate factors influencing online shopping behaviour. *International Journal of Internet Marketing and Advertising, 7*(1), 83–98. doi:10.1504/IJIMA.2012.044936

Maheshkumar, Y., Ravi, V., & Abraham, A. (2013). A particle swarm optimization-threshold accepting hybrid algorithm for unconstrained optimization. *Neural Network World*, 191-221.

Mahmoud, Q. H., & Yu, L. (2006). Havana agents for comparison shopping and location-aware advertising in wireless mobile environments. *Electronic Commerce Research and Applications, 5*(3), 220–228. doi:10.1016/j.elerap.2005.09.005

Maiers, C., Reynolds, M., & Haselkorn, M. (2005). Challenges to effective information and communication systems in humanitarian relief organizations. *IEEE Proceedings*.

Maji, P. K., Roy, A. R., & Biswas, R. (2002). An Application of Soft Sets in A Decision Making Problem. *Computers & Mathematics with Applications (Oxford, England), 44*(8-9), 1077–1083. doi:10.1016/S0898-1221(02)00216-X

Malone, D. W. (1975). An introduction to the application of interpretive structural modeling. *Proceedings of the IEEE, 63*(3), 397–404. doi:10.1109/PROC.1975.9765

Marcus, C. (1998). A practical yet meaningful approach to customer segmentation. *Journal of Consumer Marketing, 15*(5), 494–504. doi:10.1108/07363769810235974

Mareschal, B., & Brans, J.-P. (1988). Geometrical representation for MCDA. The GAIA module. *European Journal of Operational Research*, (33), 54–64. doi:10.1016/0377-2217(88)90254-8

Marseguerra, M., & Zoia, A. (2002). The auto-associative neural network in signal analysis II. Application to on-line monitoring of a simulated BWR component. *Annals of Nuclear Energy, 32*(11), 1207–1223. doi:10.1016/j.anucene.2005.03.005

Marszałek, A., & Burczyński, T. (2014). Modeling and forecasting financial time series with ordered fuzzy candlesticks. *Information Sciences, 273*, 144–155. doi:10.1016/j.ins.2014.03.026

Martínez-Ballesteros, M., Martínez-Álvarez, F., Lora, A. T., & Riquelme, J. C. (2014). Selecting the best measures to discover quantitative association rule. *Neurocomputing, 126*, 3–14. doi:10.1016/j.neucom.2013.01.056

Martínez-Ballesteros, M., Nepomuceno-Chamorro, I. A., & Riquelme, J. C. (2014). Discovering gene association networks by multi-objective evolutionary quantitative association rule. *Journal of Computer and System Sciences, 80*(1), 118–136. doi:10.1016/j.jcss.2013.03.010

Martin, J.-L., & Lenguerrand, E. (2008). A population based estimation of the driver protection provided by passenger cars: France 1996–2005. *Accident; Analysis and Prevention, 40*(6), 1811–1821. doi:10.1016/j.aap.2008.07.001 PMID:19068281

Marwala, T., & Chakraverty, S. (2006). Fault classification in structures with incomplete measured data using auto associative neural networks and genetic algorithm. *Current Science India, 90*, 542–548.

Mary Ann Anderson, M. S. E., Anderson, E. J., & Parker, G. (2013). *Operations Management for Dummies*. John Wiley & Sons.

MATLAB version 7.10.0. (2010). Natick, MA: The MathWorks Inc.

Mattosinho, F. J. A. P. (2010). *Mining Product Opinions and Reviews on the Web*. (Master Thesis). Technische University Dresden.

McDonald, M., & Dunbar, I. (2004). *Market segmentation: How to do it, how to profit from it*. Butterworth-Heinemann.

McDonald, M., & Wilson, H. (2011). *Marketing plans: How to prepare them, how to use them*. John Wiley & Sons.

McEntire, D. A. (2002). Coordinating multiorganisational responses to disaster: Lessons from the {March} 28, 2000, {Fort} {Worth} tornado. *Disaster Prevention and Management: An International Journal, 11*(5), 369–379. doi:10.1108/09653560210453416

McGill, R., Tukey, J. W., & Larsen, W. A. (1978). Variations of box plots. *The American Statistician, 32*(1), 12–16.

Merlin, P., Sorjamaa, A., Maillet, B., & Lendasse, A. (2010). X-SOM and L-SOM: A double classification approach for missing value imputation. *Neurocomputing, 73*(7-9), 1103–1108. doi:10.1016/j.neucom.2009.11.019

Michael, K., & Michael, M. G. (2011). The social and behavioral implications of location-based services. *Journal of Location Based Services, 5*(3-4), 3–4, 121–137. doi:10.1080/17489725.2011.642820

Miglautsch, J. R. (2000). Thoughts on RFM scoring. *The Journal of Database Marketing, 8*(1), 67–72.

Miguéis, V. L., Camanho, A. S., & Cunha, J. F. (2012, August). Customer data mining for lifestyle segmentation. *Expert Systems with Applications*, *39*(10), 9359–9366. doi:10.1016/j.eswa.2012.02.133

Milligan, G., & Cooper, M. (1980). An examination of the effect of six types of error perturbation on fifteen clustering algorithms. *Psychometrika*, *45*(3), 159–179. doi:10.1007/BF02293907

Millonig, A., & Gartner, G. (2011). Identifying motion and interest patterns of shoppers for developing personalised way finding tools. *Journal of Location Based Services*, *5*(1), 1, 3–21. doi:10.1080/17489725.2010.535029

Min Li, Z. Y. (2012). Factors Influencing consumption experience of mobile commerce. *Internet Research*, *22*(2), 120–141. doi:10.1108/10662241211214539

Minaei-Bidgoli, B., Barmaki, R., & Nasir, M. (2013). Mining numerical association rules via multi-objective genetic algorithms. *Information Sciences*, *233*, 15–24. doi:10.1016/j.ins.2013.01.028

Mittelhammer, R. C. (2013). *Mathematical statistics for economics and business*. New York, NY: Springer. doi:10.1007/978-1-4614-5022-1

Mohanty, M. K., & Gahan, P. (2012). Buyer Supplier Relationship In Manufacturing Industry - Findings From Indian Manufacturing Sector. *Business Intelligence Journal*, *5*(1), 319–333.

Molodtsov, D. (1999). Soft Set Theory-First Results. *Computers & Mathematics with Applications (Oxford, England)*, *37*(4-5), 19–31. doi:10.1016/S0898-1221(99)00056-5

Mooi, E., & Sarstedt, M. (2011). *Cluster analysis*. Heidelberg, Germany: Springer Berlin.

Moore, M. (2012). Interactive media usage among millennial consumers. *Journal of Consumer Marketing*, *29*(6), 436–444. doi:10.1108/07363761211259241

Moosa, I. (2015). The effect of oil prices on stock prices: A structural time series approach. *International Journal of Global Energy Issues*, *38*(4-6), 232–241. doi:10.1504/IJGEI.2015.070261

Morrison, D. F. (2004). Multivariate Statistical Methods (4th ed.). Duxbury Press.

Murphy, J. J. (1999). *Technical analysis of the financial markets*. New York: New York Institute of Finance.

Murphy, T., & Jennex, M. E. (2006). Knowledge Management and Hurricane Katrina Response. *International Journal of Knowledge Management*, *2*(4), 52–66. doi:10.4018/jkm.2006100104

Nahmias, S. (2009). *Production and operations analysis* (International Edition). McGraw-Hill.

Najjar, L., & Bishu, R. (2006). Service quality: A case study of a bank. *The Quality Management Journal*, *13*(3), 35–44.

Nandhini, M., Janani, M., & Sivanandham, S. N. (2012).Association rule mining using swarm intelligence and domain ontology. In *Proceedings ofIEEE International Conference on Recent Trends in Information Technology(ICRTIT)* (pp. 537-541). Coimbatore, Tamilnadu: IEEE Press. doi:10.1109/ICRTIT.2012.6206763

Narayanan, M., & Cherukuri, A. K. (2016). A study and analysis of recommendation systems for location-based social network (LBSN) with big data. *IIMB Management Review*, 1–6.

National Research Council. (1999). *Reducing Disaster Losses Through Better Information*. Washington, DC: National Academy Press.

Naveen, N., Ravi, V., Rao, C. R., & Sarath, K. N. V. D. (2012). Rule extraction using firefly optimization: application to banking. In *Proceedings of IEEE International Conference on Industrial Engineering and Engineering Management*(vol. 38, pp. 237-288). Hong Kong, China: IEEE Press.

Nelson, O. N. (2007). Relationship marketing and customer loyalty. *Marketing Intelligence & Planning*, *25*(1), 98–105. doi:10.1108/02634500710722425

Nelwamondo, F. V., Golding, D., & Marala, T. (2013). A dynamic programing approach to missing data estimation using Neural Networks. *Information Sciences*, *237*, 49–58. doi:10.1016/j.ins.2009.10.008

Neter, J., Wasserman, W., & Whitmore, G. A. (1992). *Applied Statistics*. Boston: Allyn & Bacon.

Newell, F. (1997). *The new rules of marketing: How to use one-to-one relationship marketing to be the leader in your industry*. New York: McGraw-Hills Companies Inc.

Ngai, E. W., Xiu, L., & Chau, D. C. (2009). Application of data mining techniques in customer relationship management: A literature review and classification. *Expert Systems with Applications*, *36*(2), 2592–2602. doi:10.1016/j.eswa.2008.02.021

Nishanth, K. J., & Ravi, V. (2013). A Computational Intelligence Based Online Data Imputation Method: An Application For Banking. *Journal of Information Processing Systems*, *9*(4), 633–650. doi:10.3745/JIPS.2013.9.4.633

Nishanth, K. J., Ravi, V., Ankaiah, N., & Bose, I. (2012). Soft computing based imputation and hybrid data and text mining: The case of predicting the severity of phishing alerts. *Expert Systems with Applications*, *39*(12), 10583–10589. doi:10.1016/j.eswa.2012.02.138

Nkuna, T. R., & Odiyo, J. O. (2011). Filling of missing rainfall data in Luvuvhu River Catchment using artificial neural networks. *Physics and Chemistry of the Earth Parts A/B/C*, *36*(14-15), 830–835. doi:10.1016/j.pce.2011.07.041

Nordbotten, S. (1996). Neural network imputation applied to the Norwegian 1990 population census data. *Journal of Official Statistics*, *12*, 385–401.

Nowak, M. (2005). Investment Project Evaluation by Simulation and Multiple Criteria Decision Aiding Procedure. *Journal of Civil Engineering and Management*, (11), 193-202.

Nuovo, A. G. D. (2011). Missing data analysis with fuzzy C-Means: A study of its application in a psychological scenario. *Expert Systems with Applications*, *38*(6), 6793–6797. doi:10.1016/j.eswa.2010.12.067

O'Hara, M. (1998). *Market microstructure theory*. New York: Willey.

Ocampo, L. A., & Promentilla, M. A. B. (2016). Development of a sustainable manufacturing strategy using analytic network process. *International Journal of Business and Systems Research*, *10*(2-4), 262–290. doi:10.1504/IJBSR.2016.075744

Oliver, R. (1997). Satisfaction: A behavioral perspective on the customer. New York: Academic Press.

Oliver, R. (1980). A cognitive model of the antecedents and consequences of satisfaction decisions. *JMR, Journal of Marketing Research*, *17*(4), 460–469. doi:10.2307/3150499

Oliver, R. (1999). Whence consumer loyalty? *Journal of Marketing*, *63*, 33–44. doi:10.2307/1252099

Olmeda, I., & Fernandez, E. (1997). Hybrid classifiers for financial multicriteria decision making: The case of bankruptcy prediction. *Computational Economics*, *10*(4), 317–335. doi:10.1023/A:1008668718837

Olorunniwo, F., Hsu, M., & Udo, G. (2006). Service quality, customer satisfaction, and behavioral intentions in the service factory. *Journal of Services Marketing*, *20*(1), 59–72. doi:10.1108/08876040610646581

Olsen, S. (2002). Comparative evaluation and the relationship between quality, satisfaction, and repurchase loyalty. *Journal of the Academy of Marketing Science*, *30*(3), 240–249. doi:10.1177/0092070302303005

Ong, C. S., Huang, J. J., & Tzeng, G. H. (2005). Building credit scoring models using genetic programming. *Expert Systems with Applications*, *29*(1), 41–47. doi:10.1016/j.eswa.2005.01.003

Opricovic, S., & Tzeng, G. H. (2004). Compromise solution by MCDM methods: A comparative analysis of VIKOR and TOPSIS. *European Journal of Operational Research*, *156*(2), 445–455. doi:10.1016/S0377-2217(03)00020-1

Opricovic, S., & Tzeng, G. H. (2007). Extended VIKOR method in comparison with outranking method. *European Journal of Operational Research*, *178*(2), 514–529. doi:10.1016/j.ejor.2006.01.020

Orsi, C., Marchetti, P., Montomoli, C., & Morandi, A. (2013). Car crashes: The effect of passenger presence and other factors on driver outcome. *Safety Science*, *57*, 35–43. doi:10.1016/j.ssci.2013.01.017

Overstreet, R. E., Hall, D., Hanna, J. B., & Kelly Rainer, R. Jr. (2011). Research in humanitarian logistics. *Journal of Humanitarian Logistics and Supply Chain Management*, *1*(2), 114–131. doi:10.1108/20426741111158421

Oyeka, I. C. A. (1992). A Modified Ridit Analysis. *Journal of Nigerian Statistical Association*, *8*(1), 45–69.

Oztaysi, B., & Isik, M. (2014). Supplier Evaluation Using Fuzzy clustering. In *Supply Chain Management Under Fuzziness: Recent Developments and Techniques*. Springer.

Paleologo, G., Elisseeff, A., & Antonini, G. (2010). Subagging for credit scoring models. *European Journal of Operational Research*, *201*(2), 490–499. doi:10.1016/j.ejor.2009.03.008

Pallant, J. (2013). *SPSS Survival Manual: A step by step guide to data analysis using SPSS* (5th ed.). Melbourne: Allen & Unwin.

Pal, N. R., & Bezdek, J. C. (1995). On cluster validity for the fuzzy c-means model. *IEEE Transactions on Fuzzy Systems*, *3*(3), 370–379. doi:10.1109/91.413225

Pal, S. K. (2004). Soft data mining, computational theory of perceptions, and rough-fuzzy approach. *Information Science*, *163*(1-3), 5–12. doi:10.1016/j.ins.2003.03.014

Panda, R. K., & Sreekumar. (2012). Prioritizing Issues in Agribusiness Using Ridit Analysis: An Indian Perspective. *World Journal of Agricultural Sciences*, *8*(1), 80–88.

Pandey, P., Kumar, S., & Shrivastav, S. (2013). Forecasting using Fuzzy Time Series for Diffusion of Innovation: Case of Tata Nano Car in India. *National Academy Science Letters*, *36*(3), 299–309. doi:10.1007/s40009-013-0140-4

Pang Bo, & Lee, L. (2008). Opinion Mining and Sentiment Analysis. *Journal Foundations and Trends in Information Retrieval*, *2*(1-2).

Pang, B., Lee, L., & Vaithyanathan, S. (2002). Thumbs up? Sentiment Classification using Machine Learning Techniques. In *Proceedings of the 2002 Conference on Empirical Methods in Natural Language Processing* (pp. 79-86).

Parasuraman, A., Zeithaml, V., & Berry, L. (1985). A conceptual model of service quality and its implications for future research. *Journal of Marketing*, *49*(4), 41–50. doi:10.2307/1251430

Parasuraman, A., Zeithaml, V., & Berry, L. (1988). SERQUAL. *Journal of Retailing*, *64*(1), 12–40.

Parasuraman, A., Zeithaml, V., & Berry, L. (1991). Refinement and reassessment of the SERVQUAL scale. *Journal of Retailing*, *67*(4), 420–450.

Parasuraman, A., Zeithaml, V., & Berry, L. (1994). Alternative scales for measuring service quality: A comparative assessment based on psychometric and diagnostic criteria. *Journal of Retailing*, *70*(3), 201–230. doi:10.1016/0022-4359(94)90033-7

Park, D. H., Kim, H. K., Choi, Y., & Kim, J. K. (2012). A literature review and classification of recommender systems research. *Expert Systems with Applications*, *39*(11), 10059–10072. doi:10.1016/j.eswa.2012.02.038

Park, J. S., Chen, M. S., Jeffrey, D., & Yu, P. S. (1995). An Effective Hash Based Algorithm For Mining Association Rules. In *Proceedings of the 1995 ACM SIGMOD International Conference on Management of Data*(pp. 175-186). New York, NY: ACM Press. doi:10.1145/223784.223813

Park, S. B. (2014). The impact of mobile tablet devices on human information behaviour. *The Journal of Documentation*, *70*(4), 622–639. doi:10.1108/JD-09-2012-0123

Pastor, M. (1999, Aug 18). *July's E-Tailing Stats*. Retrieved from https://www.clickz.com/clickz/news/1698171/julys-e-tailing-stats

Pasupuleti, R. S. (2013). Designing culturally responsive built environments in post disaster contexts: Tsunami affected fishing settlements in Tamilnadu, India. *International Journal of Disaster Risk Reduction*, *6*, 28–39. doi:10.1016/j.ijdrr.2013.03.008

Pawlak, Z. (1982). Rough Sets. *International Journal of Computer and Information Sciences*, *11*(5), 341–356. doi:10.1007/BF01001956

Pawlak, Z. (1983). Rough Classification. *International Journal of Man-Machine Studies*, *20*(5), 469–483. doi:10.1016/S0020-7373(84)80022-X

Pawlak, Z. (2004). Decision rules and flow networks. *European Journal of Operational Research*, *154*(1), 184–190. doi:10.1016/S0377-2217(03)00004-3

Pawlak, Z., & Sowinski, R. (1991). *Rough Sets, Theoretical aspect of Reasoning about Data*, Kluwer Academic Publishers, Pawlak, Z. and Slowinski, R. (1994). Rough set approach to multi attribute decision analysis. *European Journal of Operational Research*, *72*(3), 443–459. doi:10.1016/0377-2217(94)90415-4

Pawlus, W., Karimi, H., & Robbersmyr, K. (2013). Data-based modeling of vehicle collisions by nonlinear autoregressive model and feedforward neural network. *Information Sciences*, *235*(20), 65–79. doi:10.1016/j.ins.2012.03.013

Perry, M. (2007). Natural disaster management planning. *International Journal of Physical Distribution & Logistics Management*, *37*(5), 409–433. doi:10.1108/09600030710758455

Peterson, R. A. (2000). *Constructing Effective Questionnaires*. London: SAGE Publications. doi:10.4135/9781483349022

Pettit, S., & Beresford, A. (2009). Critical success factors in the context of humanitarian aid supply chains. *International Journal of Physical Distribution & Logistics Management*, *39*(6), 450–468. doi:10.1108/09600030910985811

Pfeifer, P. E., & Carraway, R. L. (2000). Modeling Customer Relationships as Markov Chains. *Journal of Interactive Marketing*, *14*(2), 43–55. doi:10.1002/(SICI)1520-6653(200021)14:2<43::AID-DIR4>3.0.CO;2-H

Phillips, R. (2005). *Pricing and revenue optimization*. Stanford University Press.

Pitois, S., Jackson, M. H., & Wood, B. J. (2001). Sources of the eutrophication problems associated with toxic algae: An overview. *Journal of Environmental Health*, *64*, 25–32. PMID:11764678

Polkowski, L., & Skowron, A. (1998). Rough Sets in Knowledge Discovery: Vol. 1. *2*. *Studies in Fuzziness and Soft Computing series*. Berlin: Physica–Verlag.

Powell, T. (1995). Total quality management as competitive advantage: A review and empirical study. *Strategic Management Journal, 16*(1), 15–37. doi:10.1002/smj.4250160105

Pradeep, G., & Ravi, V. (2014). *Association Rule Mining via Evolutionary Multi-objective Optimization* (pp. 35–46). Bangalore: MIWAI.

Pradhan, B. K. (2008). *Service Quality Indicators in Education Setting: Application of RIDIT Method to Likert Scale Surveys.* (B.Tech Graduation Dissertation). National Institute of Technology, Rourkela.

Prasanna, R., & Huggins, T. J. (2016). Factors affecting the acceptance of information systems supporting emergency operations centres. *Computers in Human Behavior, 57*, 168–181. doi:10.1016/j.chb.2015.12.013

Preist, C. (1999). Commodity trading using an agent-based iterated double auction. In *Proceedings of the ACM conference on autonomous agents.* New York: ACM. doi:10.1145/301136.301179

Prema, V., & Rao, K. U. (2015). Development of statistical time series models for solar power prediction. *Renewable Energy, 83*, 100–109. doi:10.1016/j.renene.2015.03.038

Promentilla, M. A. B., Furuichi, T., Ishii, K., & Tanikawa, N. (2006b). Evaluation of remedial countermeasures using the analytic network process. *Waste Management (New York, N.Y.), 26*(12), 1410–1421. doi:10.1016/j.wasman.2005.11.020 PMID:16412627

Promentilla, M. A. B., Furuichi, T., Ishii, K., & Tanikawa, N. (2008). A fuzzy analytic network process for multi-criteria evaluation of contaminated site remedial countermeasures. *Journal of Environmental Management, 88*(3), 479–495. doi:10.1016/j.jenvman.2007.03.013 PMID:17467879

Punj, G., & Stewart, D. (1983). Cluster analysis in marketing research: Review and suggestions for application. *JMR, Journal of Marketing Research, 20*(2), 134–148. doi:10.2307/3151680

Ragel, A., & Cremilleux, B. (1999). MVC—a preprocessing method to deal with missing values. *Knowledge-Based Systems, 12*(5-6), 285–291. doi:10.1016/S0950-7051(99)00022-2

Rahman, M., & Islam, M. Z. (2013). Missing value imputation using decision trees and decision forests by splitting and merging records: Two novel techniques. *Knowledge-Based Systems, 53*, 51–65. doi:10.1016/j.knosys.2013.08.023

Ramachandran, A., & Chidambaram, V. (2012). A review of customer satisfaction towards service quality of banking sector. *Periodica Polytechnica Social and Management Sciences, 20*(2), 71–79. doi:10.3311/pp.so.2012-2.02

Ramanathan, U., & Ramanathan, R. (2013). Investigating the impact of resource capabilities on customer loyalty: A structural equation approach for the UK hotels using online ratings. *Journal of Services Marketing, 27*(5), 404–415. doi:10.1108/JSM-12-2011-0186

Raman, B., & Ioerger, T. R. (2003). *Enhancing learning using feature and example selection.* College Station, TX, USA: Texas A&M University.

Ramli, N. A., & Ismail, T. (n.d.). *Application of Fuzzy Optimization and Time Series for Early Warning System in Predicting Currency Crisis.* Academic Press.

Ramos, E., & Donoho, D. (n.d.). *Auto MPG dataset.* Retrieved from http://archive.ics.uci.edu/ml/machine-learning-databases/auto-mpg/auto-mpg.data

Rao, X. R. (2007). *Issues and Challenges of Humanitarian Logistics in china.* University of Nottingham.

Ratingen, M., Ellway, J., Avery, M., Gloyns, P., Sandner, V., & Versmissen, T. (2009). *The Euro NCAP Whiplash test.* Retrieved September 2, 2014 from http://www.euroncap.com/files/Paper_09-0231---0-155567f6-80a9-4d6d-91b6-e1ca2656b132.pdf

Ravi, V., & Krishna, M. (2014). A new online data imputation method based on general re-gression auto associative neural network. *Neurocomputing, Elsevier, 138*, 207–212.

Ravi, V., Reddy, P. J., & Zimmermann, H.-J. (2000). Fuzzy global optimization of complex system reliability. *IEEE Transactions on Fuzzy Systems, 8*(3), 241–248. doi:10.1109/91.855914

Reinartz, W. J., & Kumar, V. (2003). The impact of customer relationship characteristics on profitable lifetime duration. *Journal of Marketing, 67*(1), 77–99. doi:10.1509/jmkg.67.1.77.18589

Reuter, U., & Möller, B. (2010). Artificial neural networks for forecasting of fuzzy time series. *Computer-Aided Civil and Infrastructure Engineering, 25*(5), 363–374. doi:10.1111/j.1467-8667.2009.00646.x

Rezaei, J. (2015). Best-worst multi-criteria decision-making method. *Omega, 53*, 49–57. doi:10.1016/j.omega.2014.11.009

Ripley, B. D. (1996). *Pattern Recognition and Neural Networks.* Cambridge, UK: Cambridge University Press. doi:10.1017/CBO9780511812651

Robinson, J. (1938). *The Economics of Imperfect Competition.* London: McMillan.

Robledo, M. (2001). Measuring and managing service quality: Integrating customer expectations. Managing Service Quality. *International Journal (Toronto, Ont.), 11*(1), 22–31.

Rodríguez, D., Busco, C., & Flores, R. (2014). Technology in Society Information technology within society ' s evolution. *Technology in Society*, 1–9. doi:10.1016/j.techsoc.2014.08.006

Roll, R. (1988). The international crash of October 1987. *Financial Analysts Journal, 44*(5), 19–35. doi:10.2469/faj.v44.n5.19

Romesburg, C. (2004). *Cluster Analysis for Researchers.* Lulu Press.

Roszbach, K. (2004). Bank lending policy, credit scoring, and the survival of loans. *The Review of Economics and Statistics, 86*(4), 946–958. doi:10.1162/0034653043125248

Rowley, A. H. (2013). Mobile shopping behaviour: Insights into attitudes, shopping process involvement and location. *International Journal of Retail & Distribution Management, 42*(1), 25–39. doi:10.1108/IJRDM-10-2012-0096

Roy, B. (1990). *Wielokryterialne wspomaganie decyzji.* Warszawa: Wydawnictwo Naukowo-Techniczne.

Ruspini, E. H. (1970). Numerical methods for fuzzy clustering. *Information Sciences, 2*(3), 319–350. doi:10.1016/S0020-0255(70)80056-1

Russel, S., & Norvig, P. (1995). *Artificial Intelligence - A Modern Approach.* Upper Saddle River, NJ: Prentice Hall.

Rust, R. T., Lemon, K. N., & Zeithaml, V. A. (2004). Return on marketing: Using customer equity to focus marketing strategy. *Journal of Marketing, 68*(1), 109–127. doi:10.1509/jmkg.68.1.109.24030

Saaty, T. (1990). How to make a decision: The analytic hierarchy process. *European Journal of Operational Research, 48*(1), 9–26. doi:10.1016/0377-2217(90)90057-I

Saaty, T. L. (1977). A scaling method for priorities in hierarchical structures. *Journal of Mathematical Psychology, 15*(3), 234–281. doi:10.1016/0022-2496(77)90033-5

Saaty, T. L. (1980). *The Analytic Hierarchy Process*. New York: McGraw-Hill.

Saaty, T. L. (2001). *Decision making with dependence and feedback: The Analytic Network Process* (2nd ed.). Pittsburgh, PA: RWS Publications.

Saggar, M., & Agrawal, A. K. (2004).Optimization of association rule mining using improved genetic algorithms. In *Proceedings of the IEEE International Conference on Systems Man and Cybernetics*(vol. 4, pp. 3725-3729). IEEE Press. doi:10.1109/ICSMC.2004.1400923

Sahu, H. B., Mahapatra, S. S., & Panigrahi, D. C. (2012). Fuzzy C-means Clustering Approach for Classification of Indian Coal Seams with Respect to Their Spontaneous Combustion Susceptibility. *Fuel Processing Technology*, *104*, 115–120. doi:10.1016/j.fuproc.2012.03.017

Samad, T., & Harp, S. A. (1992). Self-organization with partial data network. *Computation in Neural Systems*, *3*(2), 205–212. doi:10.1088/0954-898X_3_2_008

Sarath, K. N. V. D., & Ravi, V. (2013). Association rule mining using binary particle swarm optimization. *Engineering Applications of Artificial Intelligence*, *26*(8), 1832–1840. doi:10.1016/j.engappai.2013.06.003

SAS Institute Inc. (2015). *SAS Text Miner*. Retrieved October 29, 2015, from http://support.sas.com/software/products/txtminer/

Saunders, M., Lewis, P., & Thornhill, A. (2012). *Research Methods for Business Students* (6th ed.). Harlow: Person.

Sayadi, M. K., Heydari, M., & Shahanaghi, K. (2009). Extension of VIKOR method for decision making problem with interval numbers. *Applied Mathematical Modelling*, *33*(5), 2257–2262. doi:10.1016/j.apm.2008.06.002

Schafer, J. L. (1997). *Analysis of incomplete multivariate data*. Chapman & Hall. doi:10.1201/9781439821862

Scheier, M. F., Carver, C. S., & Bridges, M. W. (1994). Distinguishing optimism from neuroticism (and trait anxiety, self-mastery, and self-esteem): A reevaluation of the Life Orientation Test. *Journal of Personality and Social Psychology*, *67*(6), 1063–1078. doi:10.1037/0022-3514.67.6.1063 PMID:7815302

Schneider, J. (2015). Tactics for Launching a Product Using Social Media. *Harvard Business Review*. Retrieved October 13, 2015, from https://hbr.org/2015/04/10-tactics-for-launching-a-product-using-social-media

Seidel, M., Loch, C., & Chahil, S. (2005). Quo vadis, automotive industry? A vision of possible industry transformations. *European Management Journal*, *23*(4), 439–449. doi:10.1016/j.emj.2005.06.005

Selvin, S. (1977). A Further Note on the Interpretetion of ridit analysis. *American Journal of Epidemiology*, *105*, 16–20. PMID:831461

Sergey, B., Rajeev, M., Jeffrey, D., & Shalom, T. (1997). Dynamic itemset counting and implication rules for market basket data. In *Proceedings of the 1997 ACM SIGMOD international conference on Management of data*(vol. 26-2, pp. 255-264). New York, NY: ACM Press.

Sharma, S. (1996). Applied Multivariate Techniques. John Wiley & Sons.

Sharma, S., & Kumar, A. (2006). Cluster Analysis and Factor Analysis. In *Grover, R., and Vriens, M. (2006). The handbook of marketing research: uses, misuses, and future advances* (pp. 365–393). Sage Publications. doi:10.4135/9781412973380.n18

Sharpe, P. K., & Solly, R. J. (1995). Dealing with missing values in neural network based diagnostic systems. *Neural Computing & Applications*, *3*(2), 73–77. doi:10.1007/BF01421959

Sheffi, Y., & Rice, J. B. (2005). A Supply Chain View of the Resilient Enterprise. *MIT Sloan Management Review*, *47*(1).

Shelton, R. B. (1997). *Gaming the market: applying game theory to generate winning trading strategies*. New York: John Wiley & Sons Inc.

Shen, M. K. (2008). Explaining the adoption of transactional B2C mobile commerce. *Journal of Enterprise Information Management*, *21*(2), 110–124. doi:10.1108/17410390810851372

Shih, Y. Y., & Liu, D. R. (2008). Product recommendation approaches: Collaborative filtering via customer lifetime value and customer demands. *Expert Systems with Applications*, *35*(1), 350–360. doi:10.1016/j.eswa.2007.07.055

Shin, H. W., & Sohn, S. Y. (2004). Segmentation of stock trading customers according to potential value. *Expert Systems with Applications*, *27*(1), 27–33. doi:10.1016/j.eswa.2003.12.002

Shiou Yang, W., Chi Cheng, H., & Ben Dia, J. (2008). A location-aware recommender system for mobile shopping environments. *Expert Systems with Applications*, *34*(1), 437–445. doi:10.1016/j.eswa.2006.09.033

Shneiderman, B., & Preece, J. (2007). *911.Gov: Community Response Grids*. Academic Press.

Siegel, S. (1956). *Non-parametric statistics for the behavioral sciences*. New York: McGraw-Hill.

Sigillito, V. (n.d.). *Owner of dataset: National Institute of Diabetes and Digestive and Kidney Diseases, Pima Indian Diabetes dataset*. Retrieved from http://archive.ics.uci.edu/ml/datasets/Pima+Indians+Diabetes

Silva-Ramírez, E. L., Pino-Mejías, R., López-Coello, M., & Cubiles-de-la-Vega, M. D. (2011). Missing value imputation on missing completely at random data using multilayer perceptrons. *Neural Networks*, *24*(1), 121–129. doi:10.1016/j.neunet.2010.09.008 PMID:20875726

Simchi-Levi, D., Kaminsky, P., & Simchi-Levi, E. (2003). *Designing and Managing the Supply Chain: Concepts, Strategies, and Case Studies*. McGraw Hill Professional.

Singh, P., & Borah, B. (2013). An efficient time series forecasting model based on fuzzy time series. *Engineering Applications of Artificial Intelligence*, *26*(10), 2443–2457. doi:10.1016/j.engappai.2013.07.012

Singh, R., & Aggarwal, R. R. (2011). Comparative Evaluation of Predictive Modeling Techniques on Credit Card Data. *International Journal of Computer Theory and Engineering*, *3*(5), 598–603. doi:10.7763/IJCTE.2011.V3.377

Sinha, I., & Gvili, Y. (2001). *A Cross-Regional Study of Consumer Perceptions of Shopping on the Internet*. EBI Working paper (number EBI-2001-03). Temple University, Fox School.

Slowinski, R. (1995). Rough set approach to decision analysis. *AI Expert*, (March), 19–25.

Smith, W. R. (1956). Product differentiation and market segmentation as alternative marketing strategies. *Journal of Marketing*, *21*(1), 3–8. doi:10.2307/1247695

Song, Q & Chissom, B. S. (1993). Forecasting enrollments with fuzzy time series-Part I. *Fuzzy Sets and Systems, 54*, 1–9. doi:0165-0114/93/$06.001

Song, Q & Chissom, B. S. (1993). Forecasting enrollments with fuzzy time series-Part II. *Fuzzy Sets, and Systems, 62*, 1–8. doi:0165-0114/94/$07.00

Song, Q., & Chissom, B. S. (1993). Forecasting enrollments with fuzzy time series-Part I. *Fuzzy Sets and Systems*, *54*(1), 1–9. doi:10.1016/0165-0114(93)90355-L

Song, Q., & Kasasbov, N. (2000). Dynamic Evolving Neural-Fuzzy Inference System (DENFIS): On-line Learning and Application for Time-series Prediction. In *Proc. 6th International Conference on Soft Computing*.

Song, Q., & Kasasbov, N. (2001). ECM — A Novel On-line, Evolving Clustering Method and Its Applications. In *Proceedings of the Fifth Biannual Conference on Artificial Neural Networks and Expert Systems.*

Song, Q., & Shepperd, M. (2007). A new imputation method for small software project data sets. *Journal of Systems and Software*, *80*(1), 51–62. doi:10.1016/j.jss.2006.05.003

Sonia San Martín Blanca López-Catalán María, A. (2012). Factors determining firms perceived performance of mobile commerce. *Industrial Management & Data Systems*, *112*(6), 946–963. doi:10.1108/02635571211238536

Stephenson, R., & Anderson, P. S. (1997). Disasters and the information technology revolution. *Disasters*, *21*(4), 305–334. doi:10.1111/1467-7717.00065 PMID:9455005

Stone, B. (1995). *Successful direct marketing methods*. Lincolnwood, IL: NTC Business Books.

Subramanian, N., Gunasekaran, A., Yu, J., Cheng, J., & Ning, K. (2014). Customer satisfaction and competitiveness in the Chinese E-retailing: Structural equation modeling (SEM) approach to identify the role of quality factors. *Expert Systems with Applications*, *41*(1), 69–80. doi:10.1016/j.eswa.2013.07.012

Suh, E., Lim, S., Hwang, H., & Kim, S. (2004). A prediction model for the purchase probability of anonymous customers to support real time web marketing: A case study. *Expert Systems with Applications*, *27*(2), 245–255. doi:10.1016/j.eswa.2004.01.008

Tafreshi, P. F., Aghdaie, M. H., Behzadian, M., & Abadi, M. G. (2016). Developing a Group Decision Support System for Advertising Media Evaluation:A Case in the Middle East. *Group Decision and Negotiation*, *25*(1), 1021–1048. doi:10.1007/s10726-015-9464-4

Talluri, K. T., & Van Ryzin, G. J. (2006). *The theory and practice of revenue management* (Vol. 68). Springer Science & Business Media.

Tang, F. L. (2015). Roles of perceived value and individual differences in the acceptance of mobile coupon applications. *Internet Research*, *25*(3), 471–495. doi:10.1108/IntR-02-2014-0053

Tang, H., Liao, S. S., & Sun, S. X. (2013). A prediction framework based on contextual data to support Mobile Personalized Marketing. *Decision Support Systems*, *56*, 234–246. doi:10.1016/j.dss.2013.06.004

Tantithamthavorn, C., McIntosh, S., Hassan, A. E., & Matsumoto, K. (2016). Automated Parameter Optimization of Classification Techniques for Defect Prediction Models. In *Proceedings ofthe International Conference on Software Engineering (ICSE)*. doi:10.1145/2884781.2884857

Taylor, B. W. III. (2010). *Introduction to Management Science* (10th ed.). Upper Saddle River, NJ: Prentice Hall.

Telfer, S., & Woodburn, J. (2015). Let me Google that for you: a time series analysis of seasonality in internet search trends for terms related to foot and ankle pain. *Journal of Foot and Ankle Research, 8*(1), 1-10.

Telleen, S., & Martin, E. (2002). Improving information access for public health professionals. *Journal of Medical Systems*, *26*(6), 529–543. doi:10.1023/A:1020244726109 PMID:12385535

Tervonen, T., & Lahdelma, R. (2007). Implementing stochastic multicriteria acceptability analysis. *European Journal of Operational Research*, *178*(2), 500–513. doi:10.1016/j.ejor.2005.12.037

Teweles, R. J., & Jones, F. J. (1999). *The futures game: who wins? who loses? and why?* New York: McGraw-Hill.

Thakkar, J., Kanda, A., & Deshmukh, S. G. (2008). Interpretive structural modeling (ISM) of IT-enablers for Indian manufacturing SMEs. *Information Management & Computer Security*, *16*(2), 113–136. doi:10.1108/09685220810879609

Theodoridis, S., & Koutroumbas, K. (2008). *Pattern Recognition* (4th ed.). Elsevier.

Thomas, L. C., Edelman, D. B., & Crook, J. N. (2002). *Credit scoring and its applications*. Philadelphia: SIAM. doi:10.1137/1.9780898718317

Thomas, S. (2013). Linking customer loyalty to customer satisfaction and store image: A structural model for retail stores. *Indian Institute of Management Calcutta*, *40*(1), 15–25.

Thompson, D. (2013). *Introduction To Ibeacon: Taking Bluetooth Le For A Test Drive*. Retrieved March 27, 2015 from http://nerdery.com/mentions/346

Tian, J., Yu, B., Yu, D., & Ma, S. (2013). Missing data analyses: A hybrid multiple imputation algorithm using Gray System Theory and entropy based on clustering. *Applied Intelligence*, *40*(2), 376–388. doi:10.1007/s10489-013-0469-x

Toivonen, H. (1996). Sampling Large Databases for Association Rules. In *Proceedings of VLDB '96 Proceedings of the 22th International Conference on Very Large Data Bases*(pp. 134-145). Mumbai, India: Morgan Kaufmann Publishers.

Tokushige, S., Yadohisa, H., & Inada, K. (2007). Crisp and fuzzy k-means clustering algorithms for multivariate functional data. *Computational Statistics*, *22*(1), 1–16. doi:10.1007/s00180-006-0013-0

Tomasini, R. M., & Van Wassenhove, L. N. (2009). From preparedness to partnerships: Case study research on humanitarian logistics. *International Transactions in Operational Research*, *16*(5), 549–559. doi:10.1111/j.1475-3995.2009.00697.x

Tripathy, B. K., & Acharjya, D. P. (2012). Approximation of Classification and Measures of Uncertainty in Rough Set on Two Universal Sets. *International Journal of Advanced Science and Technology*, *40*, 77–90.

Tsai, C. F., & Wu, J. W. (2008). Using neural network ensembles for bankruptcy prediction and credit scoring. *Expert Systems with Applications*, *34*(4), 2639–2649. doi:10.1016/j.eswa.2007.05.019

Tsai, C. Y., & Chiu, C. C. (2004). A purchase-based market segmentation methodology. *Expert Systems with Applications*, *27*(2), 265–276. doi:10.1016/j.eswa.2004.02.005

Tsai, W. H., Chou, W. C., & Leu, J. D. (2011). An effectiveness evaluation model for the web-based marketing of the airline industry. *Expert Systems with Applications*, *38*(12), 15499–15516.

Tsay, Y. J., & Chiang, J. Y. (2005). CBAR: An efficient method for mining association rules. *Knowledge-Based Systems*, *18*(2-3), 99–105. doi:10.1016/j.knosys.2004.04.010

Tsiptsis, K. K., & Chorianopoulos, A. (2011). *Data mining techniques in CRM: inside customer segmentation*. John Wiley & Sons.

Tsiptsis, K., & Chorianopoulos, A. (2009). *Data Mining Techniques in CRM: Inside customer segmentation*. John Wiley and Sons, Ltd.

Tussyadiah, I. P. (2012). A Concept of Location-Based Social Network Marketing. *Journal of Travel & Tourism Marketing*, *29*(3), 205–220. doi:10.1080/10548408.2012.666168

Tversky, A., & Kahneman, D. (1979). Prospect Theory: An Analysis of Decision under Risk. *Econometrica*, *47*(2), 263–291. doi:10.2307/1914185

Uwawunkonye, E. G., & Anaene, O. I. C. (2013). A comparative study between ridit and modified ridit analysis. *American Journal of Theoretical and Applied Statistics*, *2*(6), 248–254. doi:10.11648/j.ajtas.20130206.23

Van Dongen, S. (2000). *Graph clustering by flow simulation.* (Unpublished PhD Thesis). Centre for Mathematics and Computer Science (CWI) in Amsterdam. Available at: http://dspace.library.uu.nl/bitstream/handle/1874/848/full.pdf?sequence=1

Van Wassenhove, L. N. (2006). Humanitarian aid logistics: Supply chain management in high gear†. *The Journal of the Operational Research Society*, *57*(5), 475–489. doi:10.1057/palgrave.jors.2602125

Vapnik, V. (2000): The nature of of statistical learning theory (2nd ed.). New York: Springer. doi:10.1007/978-1-4757-3264-1

Vogt, M., Hertweck, D., & Hales, K. (2011). Strategic ICT Alignment in Uncertain Environments: An Empirical Study in Emergency Management Organizations. *2011 44th Hawaii International Conference on System Sciences*. doi:10.1109/HICSS.2011.387

Waiswa, P. P. W., & Baryamureeba, V. (2008). Extraction of interesting association Rules using genetic algorithms. *International Journal of Computing and ICT Research*, *2*(1), 26–33.

Wallace, L. (2015). *Improving the Consumer E-commerce Experience through Text Mining Industry View*. Retrieved November 23, 2015, from http://www.softwareadvice.com/bi/industryview/text-mining-report-2015

Wang, J., & Xiong, S. (2014). A hybrid forecasting model based on outlier detection and fuzzy time series–A case study on Hainan wind farm of China. *Energy*, *76*, 526–541. doi:10.1016/j.energy.2014.08.064

Wang, Y. L., & Tzeng, G. H. (2012). Brand marketing for creating brand value based on a MCDM model combining DEMATEL with ANP and VIKOR methods. *Expert Systems with Applications*, *39*(5), 5600–5615. doi:10.1016/j.eswa.2011.11.057

Ward, J. Jr. (1963). Hierachical Grouping to Optimize an Objective Function. *Journal of the American Statistical Association*, *58*(301), 236–244. doi:10.1080/01621459.1963.10500845

Watanabe, Y., Ichikawa, H., Kayama, O., Ono, K., Keneoka, K., & Inami, S. (2000). Influence of seat characteristics on occupant motion in low rear-end impacts. *Accident; Analysis and Prevention*, *32*(2), 243–250. doi:10.1016/S0001-4575(99)00082-2 PMID:10688480

Weber, B. W. (2006). Adoption of electronic trading at the International Securities Exchange. *Decision Support Systems*, *41*(4), 728–746. doi:10.1016/j.dss.2004.10.006

Wei, J. T., Lee, M. C., Chen, H. K., & Wu, H. H. (2013). Customer relationship management in the hairdressing industry: An application of data mining techniques. *Expert Systems with Applications*, *40*(18), 7513–7518. doi:10.1016/j.eswa.2013.07.053

Wei, J. T., Lin, S. Y., Weng, C. C., & Wu, H. H. (2012). A case study of applying LRFM model in market segmentation of a children's dental clinic. *Expert Systems with Applications*, *39*(5), 5529–5533. doi:10.1016/j.eswa.2011.11.066

Weinstein, A. (1994). *Market segmentation: Using demographics, psychographics, and other niche marketing techniques to predict and model customer behavior*. Probus Publishing Company.

Werners, B. (1988). Aggregation models in mathematical programming. In G. Mitra (Ed.), *Mathematical Models for Decision Support* (pp. 295–319). Berlin: Springer. doi:10.1007/978-3-642-83555-1_19

Whitelaw, C., Garg, N., & Argamon, S. (2005). Using Appraisal Taxonomies for Sentiment Analysis. In *Proceedings of MCLC-05, the Second Midwest Computational Linguistic Colloquium* (pp. 625-631).

Whiting, M. C., & Ayala-Öström, B. E. (2009). Advocacy to promote logistics in humanitarian aid. *Management Research News*, *32*(11), 1081–1089. doi:10.1108/01409170910998309

Wilcoxon, F. (1945). *Individual comparisons by ranking methods*. Academic Press.

Wilcox, R. R. (2003). *Applying contemporary statistical techniques*. San Diego, CA: Elsevier.

Williams, P. D., & Grizzle, J. E. (1972). Analysis of Contingency Table having Ordered Response Categories. *American Statistical Association*, *67*(337), 55–63. doi:10.1080/01621459.1972.10481205

Wind, Y. J., & Bell, D. R. (2007). Market segmentation. In M. Baker & S. Hart (Eds.), *The Marketing Book*. Butterworth Heinemann.

Wong, W. K., Bai, E., & Chu, A. W. C. (2010). Adaptive time-variant models for fuzzy-time-series forecasting. Systems, Man, and Cybernetics, Part B: Cybernetics. *IEEE Transactions on*, *40*(6), 1531–1542.

Wu, C. S., Lin, C. T., & Lee, C. (2010). Optimal marketing strategy: A decision-making with ANP and TOPSIS. *International Journal of Production Economics*, *127*(1), 190–196. doi:10.1016/j.ijpe.2010.05.013

Wu, J., Cai, Z. H., & Ao, S. (2012). Hybrid dynamic k–nearest–neighbour and distance and attribute weighted method for classification. *International Journal of Computer Applications in Technology*, *43*(4), 378–384. doi:10.1504/IJCAT.2012.047164

Wur, S. Y., & Leu, Y. (1998).An effective Boolean algorithm for mining association rules in large databases. In *Proceedings of the 6th International Conference on Database Systems for Advanced Applications*(pp. 179-186). Hsinchu, Taiwan: IEEE Press.

Wu, W.-Y., Lee, C.-L., Fu, C.-S., & Wang, H.-C. (2014). How can online store layout design and atmosphere influence consumer shopping intention on a website? *International Journal of Retail & Distribution Management*, *42*(1), 4–24. doi:10.1108/IJRDM-01-2013-0035

Xiao, H., Xiao, Z., & Wang, Y. (2016). Ensemble classification based on supervised clustering for credit scoring. *Applied Soft Computing*, *43*, 73–86. doi:10.1016/j.asoc.2016.02.022

Xiao, W., Zhao, Q., & Fei, Q. (2006). A comparative study of data mining methods in consumer loans credit scoring management. *Journal of Systems Science and Systems Engineering*, *15*(4), 419–435. doi:10.1007/s11518-006-5023-5

Xie, X. L., & Beni, G. (1991). A validity measure for fuzzy clustering. *IEEE Transactions on Pattern Analysis and Machine Intelligence, Volume*, *13*(8), 841–847. doi:10.1109/34.85677

Yadav, D. K., & Barve, A. (2015). Analysis of critical success factors of humanitarian supply chain: An application of Interpretive Structural Modeling. *International Journal of Disaster Risk Reduction*, 1–13. doi:10.1016/j.ijdrr.2015.01.008

Yang, L., Sperlichb, S., & Härdle, W. (2003). Derivative estimation and testing in generalized additive models. *Journal of Statistical Planning and Inference, 115*, 521 – 542.

Yang, H. W., & Chang, K. F. (2012). Combining means-end chain and fuzzy ANP to explore customers' decision process in selecting bundles. *International Journal of Information Management*, *32*(4), 381–395. doi:10.1016/j.ijinfomgt.2011.11.005

Yang, X. S. (2012). Firefly Algorithm, Stochastic test functions and design optimization. *International Journal of Bio-inspired Computation*, *2*(2), 78–84. doi:10.1504/IJBIC.2010.032124

Yeh, I. C., & Lien, C. H. (2009). The comparisons of data mining techniques for the predictive accuracy of probability of default of credit card clients. *Expert Systems with Applications*, *36*(2), 2473–2480. doi:10.1016/j.eswa.2007.12.020

Yeh, I. C., Yang, K. J., & Ting, T. M. (2009). Knowledge discovery on RFM model using Bernoulli sequence. *Expert Systems with Applications*, *36*(3), 5866–5871. doi:10.1016/j.eswa.2008.07.018

Yeoman, I., & McMahon-Beattie, U. (2004). *Revenue management and pricing: Case studies and applications*. Cengage Learning EMEA.

Yim, J. (2008). Introducing a decision tree-based indoor positioning technique. *Expert Systems with Applications*, *34*(1), 1296–1302. doi:10.1016/j.eswa.2006.12.028

Yin, R. (1994). Case study research: Design and methods. Thousand Oaks, CA: Sage Publications.

Yi-Ting, Y., & Dean, A. (2001). The contribution of emotional satisfaction to consumer loyalty. *International Journal of Service Industry Management*, *12*(3), 234–250. doi:10.1108/09564230110393239

Yi, W., & Chan, A. P. (2015). Effects of temperature on mortality in Hong Kong: A time series analysis. *International Journal of Biometeorology*, *59*(7), 927–936. doi:10.1007/s00484-014-0895-4 PMID:25179530

Yoon, S. Y., & Lee, S. Y. (1999). Training algorithm with incomplete data for feed-forward neural networks. *Neural Processing Letters*, *10*(3), 171–179. doi:10.1023/A:1018772122605

Yu, L., Li, X., Tang, L., Zhang, Z., & Kou, G. (2015). Social credit: A comprehensive literature review. *Financial Innovation*, *1*(1), 1–18. doi:10.1186/s40854-015-0005-6

Yu, L., Wang, S., & Lai, K. K. (2008). Credit risk assessment with a multistage neural network ensemble learning approach. *Expert Systems with Applications*, *34*(2), 1434–1444. doi:10.1016/j.eswa.2007.01.009

Yu, M. C. (2011). Multi-criteria ABC analysis using artificial-intelligence-based classification techniques. *Expert Systems with Applications*, *38*(4), 3416–3421. doi:10.1016/j.eswa.2010.08.127

Zadeh, L. A. (1965). Fuzzy sets. *Information and Control*, *8*(3), 338–353. doi:10.1016/S0019-9958(65)90241-X

Zadeh, L. A. (1968). Fuzzy algorithms. *Information and Control*, *12*(2), 94–102. doi:10.1016/S0019-9958(68)90211-8

Zadeh, L. A. (1973). Outline of A New Approach to the Analysis of-of Complex Systems and Decision Processes. *IEEE Transactions on Cybernetics*, *3*(1), 28–44. doi:10.1109/TSMC.1973.5408575

Zadeh, L. A. (2002). Is there a need for fuzzy logic. *Information Sciences*, *178*(13), 2751–2779. doi:10.1016/j.ins.2008.02.012

Zarandi, M., Turksen, I., & Saghiri, S. (2002). Supply chain: Crisp and fuzzy aspects. *International Journal of Applied Mathematics and Computer Science*, *12*(3), 423–435.

Zareapoor, M., Seeja, K. R., & Alam, M. A. (2012). Analysis on Credit Card Fraud Detection Techniques: Based on Certain Design Criteria. *International Journal of Computers and Applications*, *52*(3).

Zeithaml, V. (2000). Service quality, profitability, and the economic worth of customers: What we know and what we need to learn. *Journal of the Academy of Marketing Science*, *28*(1), 67–85. doi:10.1177/0092070300281007

Zeithaml, V., Berry, L., & Parasuraman, A. (1996). The behavioural consequences of service quality. *Journal of Marketing*, *60*(2), 31–46. doi:10.2307/1251929

Zhang, L., Luo, J., & Yang, S. (2009). Forecasting box office revenue of movies with BP neural network. *Expert Systems with Applications*, *36*(3), 6580–6587. doi:10.1016/j.eswa.2008.07.064

Zhang, M., Dai, X., & He, Z. (2015). An empirical investigation of service recovery in e-retailing. *Journal of Service Theory and Practice*, *25*(3), 348–367. doi:10.1108/JSTP-03-2014-0046

Zhang, M., Huang, L., He, Z., & Wang, A. G. (2015a). E-service quality perceptions: An empirical analysis of the Chinese e-retailing industry. *Total Quality Management & Business Excellence*, *26*(11-12), 1357–1372. doi:10.1080/14783363.2014.933555

Zhang, S. (2012). Nearest neighbor selection for iteratively kNN imputation. *Journal of Systems and Software*, *85*(11), 2541–2552. doi:10.1016/j.jss.2012.05.073

Zhang, X., Edwards, J., & Harding, J. (2007). Personalized online sales using web usage data mining. *Computers in Industry*, *58*(8-9), 772–782. doi:10.1016/j.compind.2007.02.004

Zhang, Y. L., & Qin, B. Q. (2001). Study prospect and evolution of eutrophication in lakeTaihu. *Shanghai Environ. Sci.*, *20*, 263–265.

Zhou, L., Lai, K. K., & Yen, J. (2014). Bankruptcy prediction using SVM models with a new approach to combine features selection and parameter optimisation. *International Journal of Systems Science*, *45*(3), 241–253. doi:10.1080/00207721.2012.720293

Ziarko, W. (1999). Discovery through rough set theory. Knowledge Discovery: Viewing wisdom from all perspectives. *Communications of the ACM*, *42*(11), 54–57. doi:10.1145/319382.319393

Zimba, P. V., & Gitelson, A. A. (2006). Remote estimation of chlorophyll concentration inhypereutrophic aquatic systems: Model tuning and accuracy optimization. *Aquaculture (Amsterdam, Netherlands)*, *256*(1-4), 272–286. doi:10.1016/j.aquaculture.2006.02.038

Zimmermann, H.-J. (1991). *Fuzzy Set Theory and Applications* (2nd ed.). Boston, MA: Kluwer. doi:10.1007/978-94-015-7949-0

Zimmermann, H.-J., & Zysno, P. (1980). Latent connectives in human decision making. *Fuzzy Sets and Systems*, *4*(1), 37–51. doi:10.1016/0165-0114(80)90062-7

Zwerina, K. (1997). *Discrete Choice Experiments in Marketing*. Heidelberg, Germany: Physica-Verlag. doi:10.1007/978-3-642-50013-8

About the Contributors

Anil Kumar is a faculty of Operation and Quantitative Techniques in the School of Management at BML Munjal University, Gurgaon India. He completed his Ph.D in Management from Indian Institute of Information Technology and Management, Gwalior. He earned his MBA, MSc (Mathematics) from Department of Mathematics (Kurukshetra University, Kurukshetra) and Graduation in Mathematics-Hons from the same University. He also qualified UGC-NET. He published more than 27 research papers/book chapters and also two books in his credit. His research interest includes marketing analytics, multi-criteria decision making, fuzzy multi-criteria decision making, fuzzy optimisation, application of soft-computing and econometrics modelling in marketing, multi-criteria decision making and fuzzy applications in e-commerce and M-commerce.

* * *

Mohammad Hasan Aghdaie received his Bachelor's and Master's degrees in Industrial Engineering from Shomal University, in Amol. He is the author of more than 21 scientific papers in international conferences and international journals which were published, accepted or under reviewing. His current research interests include operations research, decision analysis, multiple criteria decision analysis, system dynamics, business analytics, data mining, data science and big data, application of fuzzy sets and systems, and water resource management. He has published in journals such as Journal of Business Economics and Management, International Journal of Business Innovation and Research, The Baltic Journal of Road and Bridge Engineering, Quarterly Journal of Research and Planning in Higher Education, Engineering Economics, Expert systems with Applications, Technological and Economic Development of Economy, Group Decision and Negotiation, and several others.

Mehmet Alegoz, after graduating from Yildiz Technical University Department of Industrial Engineering in 2013, joined Anadolu University, Department of Industrial Engineering as a research and teaching assistant. He completed his master degree education in 2015 and nowadays, he has been continuing his Ph.D. education. Closed loop supply chains (particularly collection, remanufacturing, redistribution processes), supplier relationship management and multiple-criteria decision making are a few of his research interests. He is the co-author or some SCI articles, book chapters, conference proceedings and he is currently researcher in a few scientific projects which are supported by university.

Mashhour H. Baeshen is a Lecturer in Marketing at College of Business, University of Jeddah. Ph.D Researcher at Cardiff Business School.

Andrzej Bajdak is an Associate Professor (dr hab.) at University of Economics in Katowice. Head of Marketing Research Department. Main interest: marketing, marketing research, marketing communication, customer behavior on the B2C and B2B market.

Gianpaolo Basile is an Adjunct Professor in Place Marketing, Department of Political, Social and Media Sciences, University of Salerno; Visiting Professor in International Business, Vitez University (Bosnia and Herzegovina); Business Systems Laboratory President (www.bslaboratory.net).

Malcolm J. Beynon is Professor of Uncertain Reasoning at Cardiff Business School, Cardiff University. His main research areas includes the development and application of 'uncertain reasoning' techniques (including Fuzzy Set Theory and Dempster Shafer Theory) in business oriented areas. Malcolm's work has been published in multiple journals including the European Journal of Operational Research, OMEGA, Environment and Planning (A and C), European Journal of Marketing and Journal of Business Research, amongst others.

Subhajit Bhattacharya received his PhD degree in Business Administration from the University of Burdwan. Dr. Bhattacharya's has more than eight years' experience in academics and teaches different courses in marketing area. His areas of experience and expertise include teaching Marketing Management, Consumer Behaviour, Services Marketing and Managing Retail Business. Dr. Bhattacharya has published articles in quite a few national and international journals and has also presented papers in several national and international conferences. Currently he is working in the areas of Brand Chemistry, Consumer Insight and Consumer Psychology.

Nicola Capolupo has an MA Political Strategy and Communication and is CEO Nadir Global Media Communication.

Melih Çinar is a Ph.D. student and research assistant at Yıldız Technical University. His department is Mathematical Engineering and his research interests are optimal control, fuzzy logic, multi-criteria decision making.

T. K. Das received his Ph.D from VIT University,India in the year 2015 and M. Tech. in computer science from Utkal university, India in the year 2003. He is currently working as Associate Professor in VIT University, India. He has authored many international journal and conference papers to his credit. His research interests include Artificial Intelligence, Data Analysis and Data Mining, Databases. He is associated with many professional bodies CSI, and ISCA.

Kate L. Daunt (PhD) is a Reader in Marketing at Cardiff Business School, Cardiff University, where she also currently serves as the Deputy Director of the PhD programme. Kate's main research areas include services marketing, customer misbehaviour, service dysfunction and servicescape design. Kate's work has been published in multiple journals including the Journal of Retailing, the Journal of Service Research, the European Journal of Marketing and the Journal of Business Research.

Maheshwar Dwivedy received his B.Tech in mechanical engineering from CET-Bhubaneswar in 1999, MTech in production engineering from NIT-Rourkela in 2005 and a PhD in industrial engineering from BITS-Pilani in 2014. He has been teaching as a lecturer at BITS, Pilani for over nine years. His research focuses on sustainability studies through systems approaches such as life-cycle assessment to model technological progress and product diffusion. Dr. Dwivedy is interested in the life-cycle of electronic goods and, ultimately the waste generated with special focus on the environmental benefits and economic potential of a circular and green economy.

Chandan Gautam holds an M.Tech (IT) degree from University of Hyderabad and IDRBT, Hyderabad. He is currently a research scholar at IIT Indore.

Uğur Gökdere has a wealth of experience having worked in telecommunications and payment systems for several years with several payment schemes and mobile operators. The holder of a degree in Industrial Engineering, Mr. Gokdere began his professional career with the Dogus Group in Garanti Technology in 2007. From then he had participated several projects such as customer risk management models, customer attrition and retention programs and mainly Near Field Communication(NFC) projects 2008. Also participated and took part as a project manager in Europe's first commercial Trusted Service Manager(TSM) project, Turkcell Cuzdan project, P2P money send project, Remote Payment and Service Booster architecture. He also played a technical analyst role of the export of Garanti TSM module and managed to build technical infrastructure of wallet manager for eSE based on Samsung. He has worked as a team member in Turkcell as Mobile Finance Business as well. During Mobile Payment Gateway (MPG) project he has successfully migrated over 50 e-commerce companies to Remote Payments scheme with a collaborative effort of MasterCard and Garanti. For a couple of months he was the lead analyst for the Turkcell Cuzdan project. He has been studying MA in Marketing Communications in Istanbul Bilgi University and MBA in Okan University since at the same time with a curiosity to new projects and new technologies.

Mónica Gouveia obtained a Master's degree in Applied Mathematics (statistics and operational research) and a licentiate degree in Teaching Math, both from the University of Aveiro. She worked as a teacher in several public schools and is currently a maths tutor at Espaço Nota+ tutorial center.

Geetika Jain is working as an Assistant Professor in the Amity School of Business, Amity University, Noida. Her areas of interest are Online Consumer Buying Behavior, Social Media Marketing, Retail Management, Public Relation.

Vinay Kumar Jain is a PhD scholar in Department of Computer Science and Engineering, Jaypee University of Engineering and Technology, Guna.

Slawomir Jarek graduated in 1994 from University of Silesia in Katowice, Poland, with the degree of Master of Information Science. He obtained a PhD in economics from the University of Lodz, Poland in 2004 in the field of operational research. Since 2014 he has been employed at the University of Economics in Katowice, Poland. He is a member of the Polish Chapter of INFORMS. The main focus of his research is the field of soft computing and multicriteria decision making.

Saroj K. Jena is a faculty of Information Systems in the School of Management at BML Munjal University. He has over seventeen years of experience in teaching various Computer Sciences and Engineering courses, particularly in the fields of Data Structures, Database Management Systems, and Data Mining, Software Engineering and Operating Systems in both the undergraduate and post graduate levels. He has also teaching experience in Business Mathematics, Quantitative Techniques for Managers, Business Analytics, Operation Research and Management Information Systems for under graduate and post graduate courses of management studies. His teaching interests also include Advertising Management and Consumer Buying Behavior. He did his MCA from Utkal University, Odisha and MTech (CSE) from BPUT, Odisha. He did his MBA from BPUT, Odisha. He secured second position both for MBA and MTech in the University. Mr. Jena's research interests focus on Credit analysis using data mining techniques, Consumer buying behavior using econometrics as well as using data mining techniques. He has presented papers in both National and International conferences and published in an International Journal.

Kedar P. Joshi is currently working with operations management group at T A Pai Management Institute, Manipal. He has successfully completed a Fellow (Ph.D) degree from Indian Institute of Management, Lucknow. Further, he holds an M.E. degree in Production Engineering from VJTI, Mumbai University and a B.E degree in Mechanical Engineering from Shivaji University. In the past He has a total 7 years of experience in academia. His research interests are multi-criteria decision making in management, supply chain management, pricing & revenue optimization.

Gaurav Kabra is a research scholar in the Department of Management Studies in Indian Institute of Technology Roorkee. He did 5 year integrated (B.Tech (Information Technology) and MBA) from Indian Institute of Information Technology and Management, Gwalior, India. He has published various research paper in Journals of National and International repute such as International Journal of Disaster Risk Reduction, Benchmarking: An International Journal, etc. His areas of interest are Supply Chain Management, humanitarian logistics, coordination in humanitarian supply chain management and application of IT in Business.

Ali Karasan is a research assistant at the Technical University of Yıldız, Department of Industrial Engineering. Interesting at Decision-Making under Fuzziness. Multi-Attribute Decision Making. Supply Chain system particularly Location Selection of Freight Village.

Rohit Vishal Kumar is currently working as Associate Professor in the Department of Marketing at Xavier Institute of Social Service, Ranchi. He did his schooling from Ram Krishna Mission Ashram Vidyalaya, Narendrapur (WB) and his plus two (+2) from Ram Krishna Mission Residential College, Narendrapur (WB) in the stream of Humanities. Subsequently he did his graduation from St. Xavier's College Kolkata and then he went on to do his MA in Economics from Centre for Economic Studies and Planning (CESP) Jawaharlal Nehru University, New Delhi. In 1996 he joined Indian Institute of Social Welfare and Business Management (IISWBM) Kolkata to do his MBA in the area of Marketing. He was picked up by Indica Research Private Limited from campus and for the next three years he worked in the Marketing Research sector with various clients and organisations. He worked in ORG-MARG Research Limited, New Delhi and TNS-MODE, Kolkata and has handled clients like ITC Limited, TATA Steel, Bengal Ambuja Realty, ABP Group, Eveready Industries, Smithkline Beecham and Maruti

Udyog Limited. Given his Economics, Marketing and Research combination and his love for reading, he joined academics when his alma mater came calling. In 2001 he joined IISWBM Kolkata as Research Associate and within one year he was promoted to Lecturer. In 2003 he registered for his Doctorate with the University of Calcutta and was awarded the degree in 2007. His topic of doctoral research work was "Lifestyle and Psychographic Segmentation & Classification of Metropolitan Consumers in India for Effective Marketing". In 2006 he joined Xavier Institute of Social Service (XISS) Ranchi as Reader in the Department of Marketing. He was promoted to the post of Associate Professor in 2009. As on date he has a total of 16 journal publications out of which 08 are in international journals of repute. He is also empanelled as a doctoral guide with West Bengal University of Technology, Indian School of Mines (Dhanbad) and ICFAI University Jharkhand. He has successfully co-guided one doctoral level student from ISM Dhanbad. Few other scholars are also pursuing doctorate under his guidance. In his free time Dr. Kumar loves to play with computers and read novels. He is well versed in statistical softwares like R, SPSS, Systat, & Statistica; Data Mining Softwares like WEKA and typesetting languages like LaTeX. His technical document "Making Friends with LaTeX (MFwL)" is available at CTAN Repositories worldwide.

Shishir Kumar is working as Professor of Computer Science at Jaypee University of Engineering & Technology, Guna (MP) India.

Nikhil Lohiya is a final year PGDM student at T A Pai Management Institute. His areas of interests are Operations and Finance.

Pedro Macedo obtained his PhD in Mathematics from the University of Aveiro and a MSc in Economics from the University of Porto, Portugal. He worked as a statistician in EDP Gas Distribution, a natural gas supply company from EDP Group, and is currently Assistant Professor at the Department of Mathematics, University of Aveiro. He is a researcher at CIDMA – Center for Research & Development in Mathematics and Applications.

António C. Moreira obtained a Bachelor's degree in Electrical Engineering and a Master's degree in Management, both from the University of Porto, Portugal. He received his PhD in Management from UMIST-University of Manchester Institute of Science and Technology, England. He has a solid international background in industry leveraged working for a multinational company in Germany as well as in Portugal. He has also been involved in consultancy projects and in research activities. He is an Assistant Professor at the Department of Economics, Management, Industrial Engineering, and Tourism, University of Aveiro, Portugal, where he headed the Bachelor and Master Degrees in Management for five years. He is member of GOVCOPP research unit.

Piotr Namiecinski graduated in 2010 from University of Lodz Poland, with the degree of Master of Econometrics. Since 2010 he is working in Operational Reaserch Chear of University of Lodz as research assistant.

Lanndon A. Ocampo is an Assistant Professor in the Business Management Cluster, University of the Philippines Cebu. He received his Ph.D. in Industrial Engineering from De La Salle University (DLSU), Manila, Philippines and his M.Eng. and B.Sc. (cum laude) degrees in Industrial Engineering from the University of San Carlos (USC), Philippines. He has currently over 30 journal articles with over 15 Scopus-indexed articles and is a regular reviewer of international peer-reviewed, indexed journals in industrial and production engineering, decision science, management science and manufacturing research. He is currently the Editor-in-Chief of the International Journal of Applied Industrial Engineering, IGI-Global. Dr. Ocampo is a member of the International Society of Multiple Criteria Decision Making, Industrial Engineering & Operations Management Society, International Association of Engineers and the Mathematical Society of the Philippines.

Ceren Öner received her MS degree in Industrial Engineering Department from Çukurova University in 2011. In 2011, she was hired as a research assistant in Istanbul Technical University and is currently a PhD candidate in the same university. She writes and presents widely on issues of location based systems, data mining and fuzzy logic.

Başar Öztayşi is a full time Associate Professor at Industrial Engineering Department of Istanbul Technical University, where he teaches courses on data management, information systems and customer relationship management. His research interests include business analytics, decision making, data mining and intelligent systems.

Zehra Kamisli Ozturk was born in Turkey in 1979. She received the B.E. degree in industrial engineering, and the M.E., and PhD. degrees in operations research from the Eskisehir Osmangazi University, Turkey, in 2001, 2004 and 2010 respectively. In 2002, she joined the Open Education Faculty, Anadolu University as a Research Assistant. Since 2012, she has been with the Department of Industrial Engineering, Anadolu University as an Assistant Professor. Her current research interests include multi criteria decision making, multi objective decision making, vehicle routing, scheduling and big data.

G. Pradeep holds an M.Tech (IT) from University of Hyderabad. His research interests include data mining, machine learning and evolutionary computing. He currently works for Teradata India.

Mohammed Said Radjef is a full Professor in Operational Research at University of Bejaia, where he leads: the research team "Cybernetic Methods and Optimization" in the Unit Research LaMOS and the doctoral training "Operational Research and Decision Support" in Department of Operational Research. His research interests include Game theory, Multicriteria programming, Generalized convexity and Applications.

A. Ramesh is working as Assistant Professor in the Department of Management Studies at Indian Institute of Technology Roorkee and completed his doctoral research in the area of Supply Chain Management from Indian Institute of Technology Delhi, India in 2011. He has received best paper award in many international conference and Journal. His research interests include Humanitarian Supply Chain Management, Humanitarian Logistics, Sustainable Supply Chain Management, Six Sigma and Data Mining. He has presented and published his research work in many reputed national and international journals of repute.

Vadlamani Ravi is a Professor in the Institute for Development and Research in Banking Technology (IDRBT), Hyderabad. He holds a PhD in Soft Computing from Osmania University, Hyderabad and RWTH Aachen, Germany (2001). Earlier, he worked as a Faculty at National University of Singapore from 2002-2005. He visited RWTH Aachen under DAAD Long Term Fellowship from 1997–1999. In the last 27 years, he worked in soft computing, data/text mining, global/multi-criteria optimization, Big Data. He published 170 papers in refereed international/national journals/conferences and invited chapters. He also edited a Book published by IGI Global, USA, 2007. He is a referee and Editorial Board Member for several International Journals of repute.

Agustin Santiago-Moreno is a Professor at the Autonomous University of Guerrero. Department of Statistics and Probability and has a PhD in Statistics and Operations Research from the University of Granada, Spain.

Giancarlo Scozzese is an Assistant Professor in Marketing, University for Foreigners, Perugia (Italy).

İsmail Sevim is an MSc student in Industrial and Systems Engineering Program of Istanbul Sehir University and RA at Yıldız Technical University.

Esra Nur Şimşek is analyst and data scientist at Blesh, a company working on beacons and sensor technologies located in İstanbul. Esra is a graduate of Boğaziçi University, where she received a BS degree on Computer Engineering. After graduation, Esra launched her career in Blesh, and involved in two R&D projects with bluetooth sensors, one is about customer segmentation using location data, the other is about analysing of queue and passenger flow in airports using beacon data.

Tadeusz Trzaskalik graduated in 1973 from University of Silesia in Katowice, Poland, with the Master degree of Mathematics. Since 1975 he has been employed at the University of Economics in Katowice, Poland. He obtained his Ph.D. (1980), habilitation (1991) and professorship (1999) in the field of operational research. In 1996-1999 he served as Vice-Rector in charge of international relations. In 1999-2006 he was Director of Ph.D. studies. Since 1999 he has been Head of the Department of Operations Research. Since 2007 he has been also Director of International Postgraduate Studies in Project Management. At the same time, in 1991-2004 he was employed at the University of Łódź and in 1991-1996 he was Head of Department of Operational Research. The focus of his research is the field of multicriteria decision making and dynamic programming. He is a author of many articles published in such periodicals and series as: ASAC, CEJORE, EJOR, Engineering Costs and Economics, Foundation on Computing and Decision Science, INFOR, Journal of Global Optimization, Mathematics Today, Operations Research and Decision, Research on Finance, Springer Lecture Notes in Economics and Mathematical Systems, and Statistical Review. He is the author and editor of many books, including: "Multicriteria Dynamic Programming. Theory and Economic Applications" (1990)," Multiobjective Analysis in Dynamic Environment" (1998), "Multiobjective Programming and Goal Programming. Recent Developments" (2002), "Computer-assisted Introduction to Operational Research" (2003, 2008), "Multicriteria Methods on Polish Financial Market" (2006), "Multicriteria Decision Aid. Methods and Applications" (2014), and the series "Preference Modeling versus Risk" and "Multiple Criteria Decision Making". He organized and chaired "The Fourth International Conference on Multiobjective Programming and Goal Programming. Theory and Applications" (2000). He has been Chair of the national conference "Preference Modeling versus Risk" and the Chair of "International Workshop on Multiple Criteria Decision Making". He is a member of the Polish Mathematical Society (President of the Commission of Mathematical Education in Economy, 1999-2006; Vice President of the Upper-Silesia chapter of the Society since 2004), INFORMS (President of the Polish Chapter since 2015) and the International Society on Multiple Criteria Decision Making. He was a member of the scientific committee of many scientific conferences as well as an editor in chief of the scientific journal Multiple Criteria Decision Making, and a member of the editorial board of other scientific journals.

Index

I

L

M

N

O

P

R

S

T

V

W

www.ingramcontent.com/pod-product-compliance
Lightning Source LLC
LaVergne TN
LVHW060358300926
849162LV00006B/1295